MY GLASSES, MY GLASSES...

M y *Black Cat* week goes like this: I spend four days writing the story and two days drawing. (The remaining day is spent sleeping!) When you work in manga, you tend to lose track of the calendar. My editor and I are always saying to each other, "What?! Today is a holiday in the rest of the world?!"

—Kentaro Yabuki, 2002

Kentaro Yabuki made his manga debut with *Yamato Gensoki*, a short series about a young empress destined to unite the warring states of ancient Japan and the boy sworn to protect her. His next series, *Black Cat*, commenced serialization in the pages of *Weekly Shonen Jump* in 2000 and quickly developed a loyal fan following. *Black Cat* has also become an animated TV series, first hitting Japan's airwaves in the fall of 2005.

BLACK CAT VOL. 9
The SHONEN JUMP Manga Edition

STORY AND ART BY
KENTARO YABUKI

English Adaptation/Kelly Sue DeConnick
Translation/JN Productions
Touch-up Art & Lettering/Gia Cam Luc
Design/Courtney Utt
Editor/Jonathan Tarbox

Managing Editor/Frances E. Wall
Editorial Director/Elizabeth Kawasaki
Editor in Chief, Books/Alvin Lu
Editor in Chief, Magazines/Marc Weidenbaum
Sr. Director of Acquisitions/Rika Inouye
Sr. VP of Marketing/Liza Coppola
Exec. VP of Sales & Marketing/John Easum
Publisher/Hyoe Narita

Printed in the U.S.A.

Published by VIZ Media, LLC
P.O. Box 77010
San Francisco, CA 94107

SHONEN JUMP Manga Edition
10 9 8 7 6 5 4 3 2 1
First printing, July 2007

THE WORLD'S
MOST POPULAR MANGA

www.viz.com

www.shonenjump.com

BLACK CAT

VOLUME 9

SHOWDOWN AT THE OLD CASTLE

STORY & ART BY **KENTARO YABUKI**

characters

BLACK CAT

SVEN VOLLFIED

EVE

RINSLET WALKER

SAYA MINATSUKI

TRAIN HEARTNET

CHRONO NUMBERS

No. X SHAOLEE

No. II BELZE

No. I SEPHIRIA

No. XI BELUGA

No. V NIZER

No. VII JENOS

SHIKI

DOCTOR

KYOKO

LEON

CHARDEN

CREED DISKENTH

ECHIDNA

MARO

A fearless "eraser" responsible for the deaths of countless powerful men, Train "Black Cat" Heartnet carries an ornate pistol called "Hades." The gun is engraved with the Roman numeral XIII, Train's agent number as an assassin for the crime syndicate Chronos, a mysterious organization that quietly controls one-third of the world's economy. Two years after his departure from Chronos, Train lives a carefree wanderer's life, working with his partner Sven as a bounty hunter ("sweeper") and pursuing Creed Diskenth, the man who murdered Train's beloved friend Saya. The two sweepers are allied with sexy thief-for-hire Rinslet Walker and Eve, a young girl (and experimental living weapon) whom they rescued from a nanotech lab.

When Creed appears and asks Train to join his "Apostles of the Stars" in their revolution against Chronos and the world, Train refuses and fights him to a vicious stalemate. The Apostles emerge from hiding to make an attack on a summit of world leaders, resulting in multiple assassinations. Chronos scrambles to respond, sending their top agent, Sephiria Arks, to Train ask for assistance, but she receives no response. Soon thereafter, an Apostle named Durham gets impatient and challenges Train directly. That move raises Creed's ire and he executes Durham for his impertinence. Meanwhile, Chrono Number VII hires Rinslet to locate the Apostles' safe house as Cerberus (the Chronos commando unit comprised of Numbers V, VII and XI) springs into action. At the same time, Sephiria lures Train, Sven and Eve to Creed's hideout. It seems another battle is about to begin.

BLACK CAT

VOLUME 9 SHOWDOWN AT THE OLD CASTLE

CONTENTS

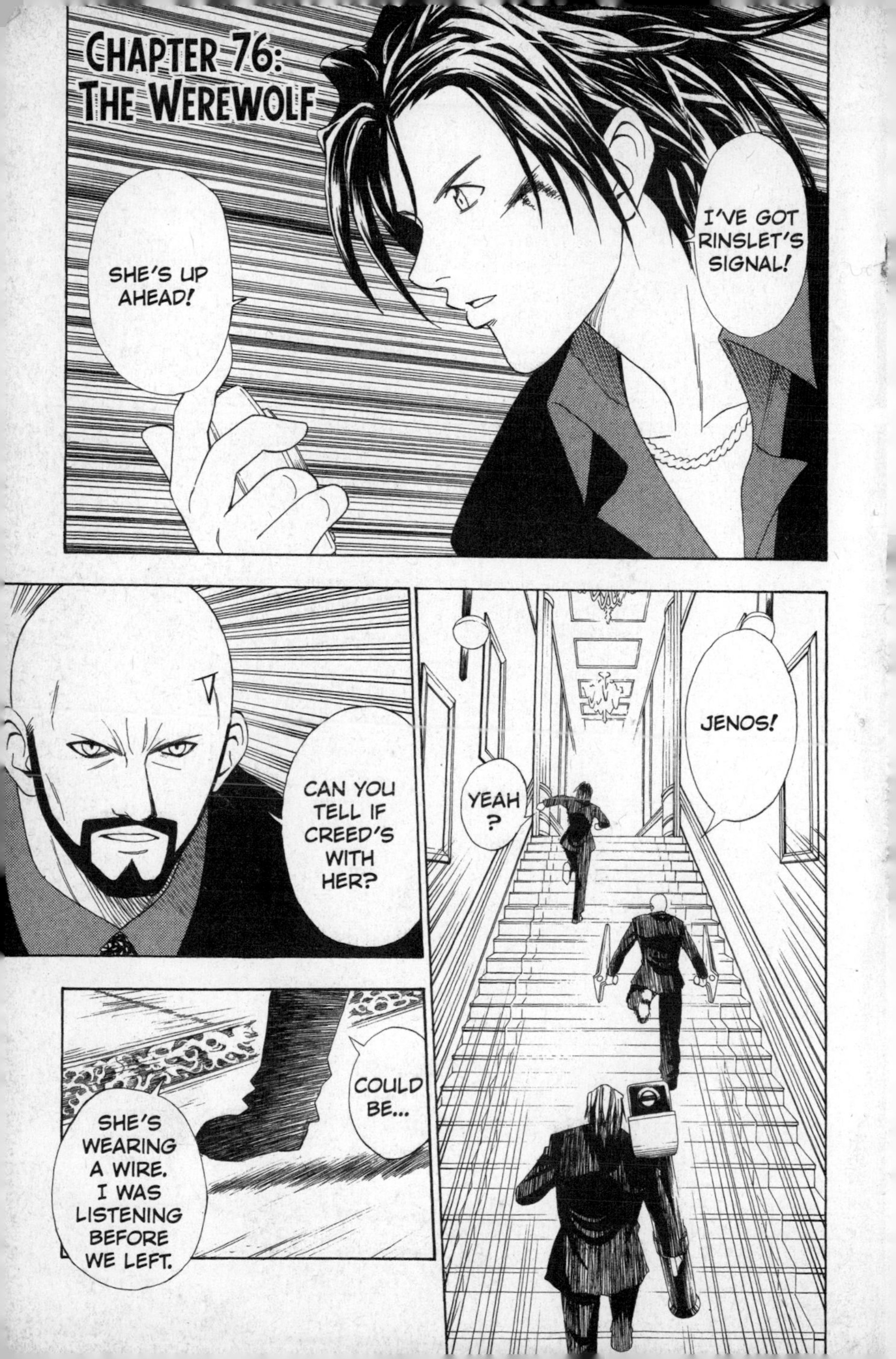
CHAPTER 76: THE WEREWOLF
I'VE GOT RINSLET'S SIGNAL!
SHE'S UP AHEAD!
JENOS!
YEAH?
CAN YOU TELL IF CREED'S WITH HER?
COULD BE...
SHE'S WEARING A WIRE. I WAS LISTENING BEFORE WE LEFT.

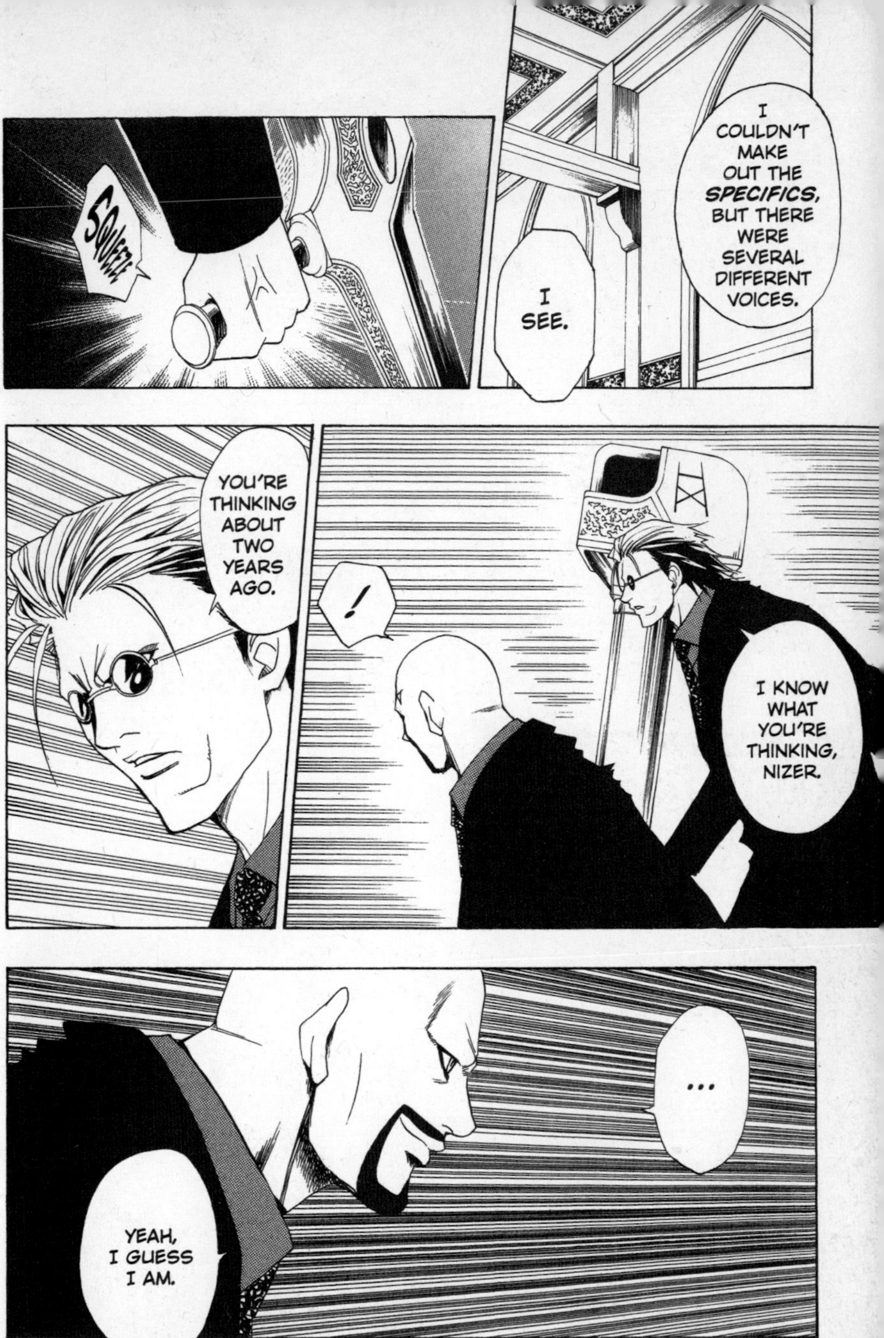
I COULDN'T MAKE OUT THE *SPECIFICS*, BUT THERE WERE SEVERAL DIFFERENT VOICES.
I SEE.
SQUEEZE
I KNOW WHAT YOU'RE THINKING, NIZER.
!
YOU'RE THINKING ABOUT TWO YEARS AGO.
...
YEAH, I GUESS I AM.

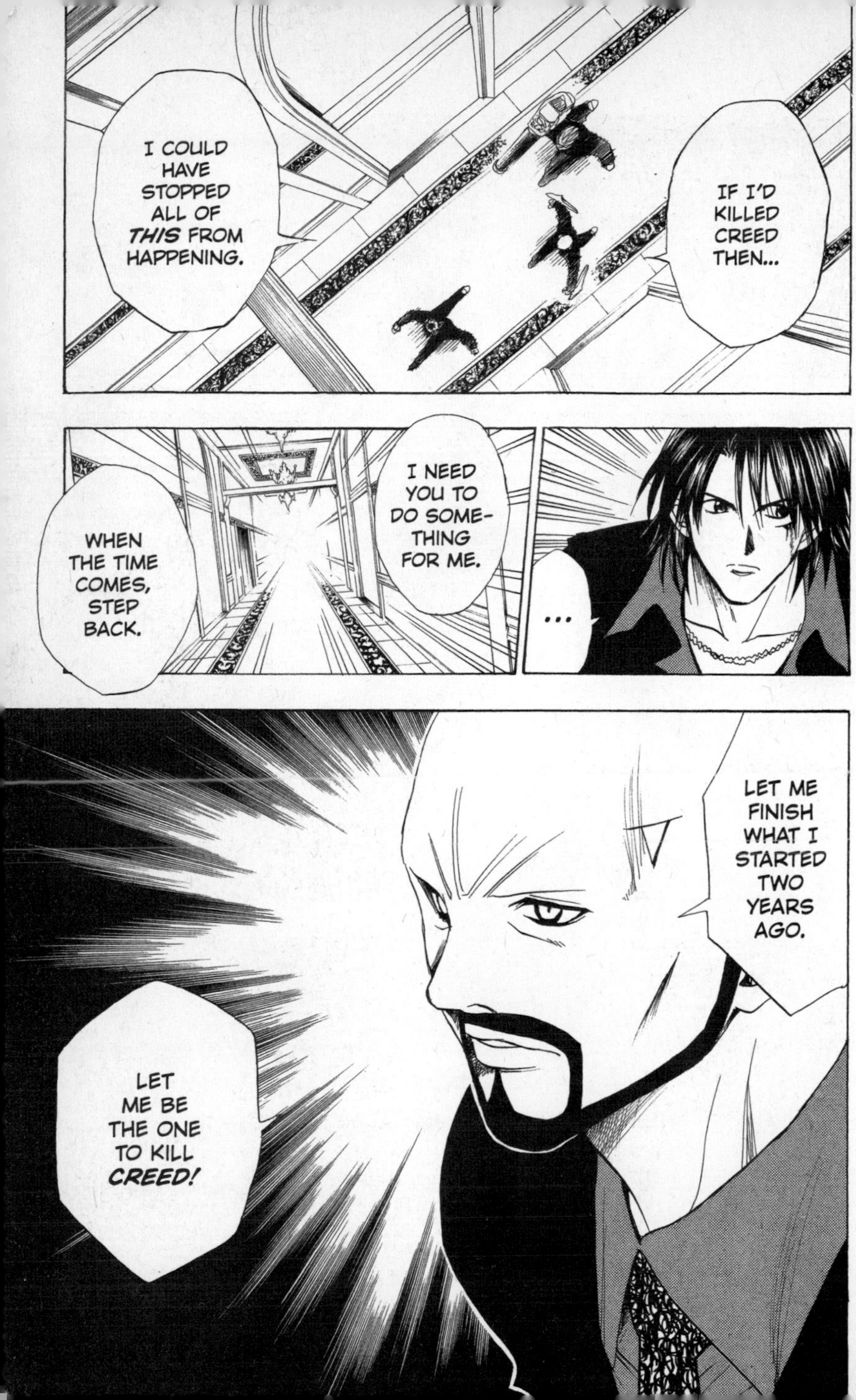

IF I'D KILLED CREED THEN...
I COULD HAVE STOPPED ALL OF *THIS* FROM HAPPENING.
...
I NEED YOU TO DO SOME-THING FOR ME.
WHEN THE TIME COMES, STEP BACK.
LET ME FINISH WHAT I STARTED TWO YEARS AGO.
LET ME BE THE ONE TO KILL *CREED!*

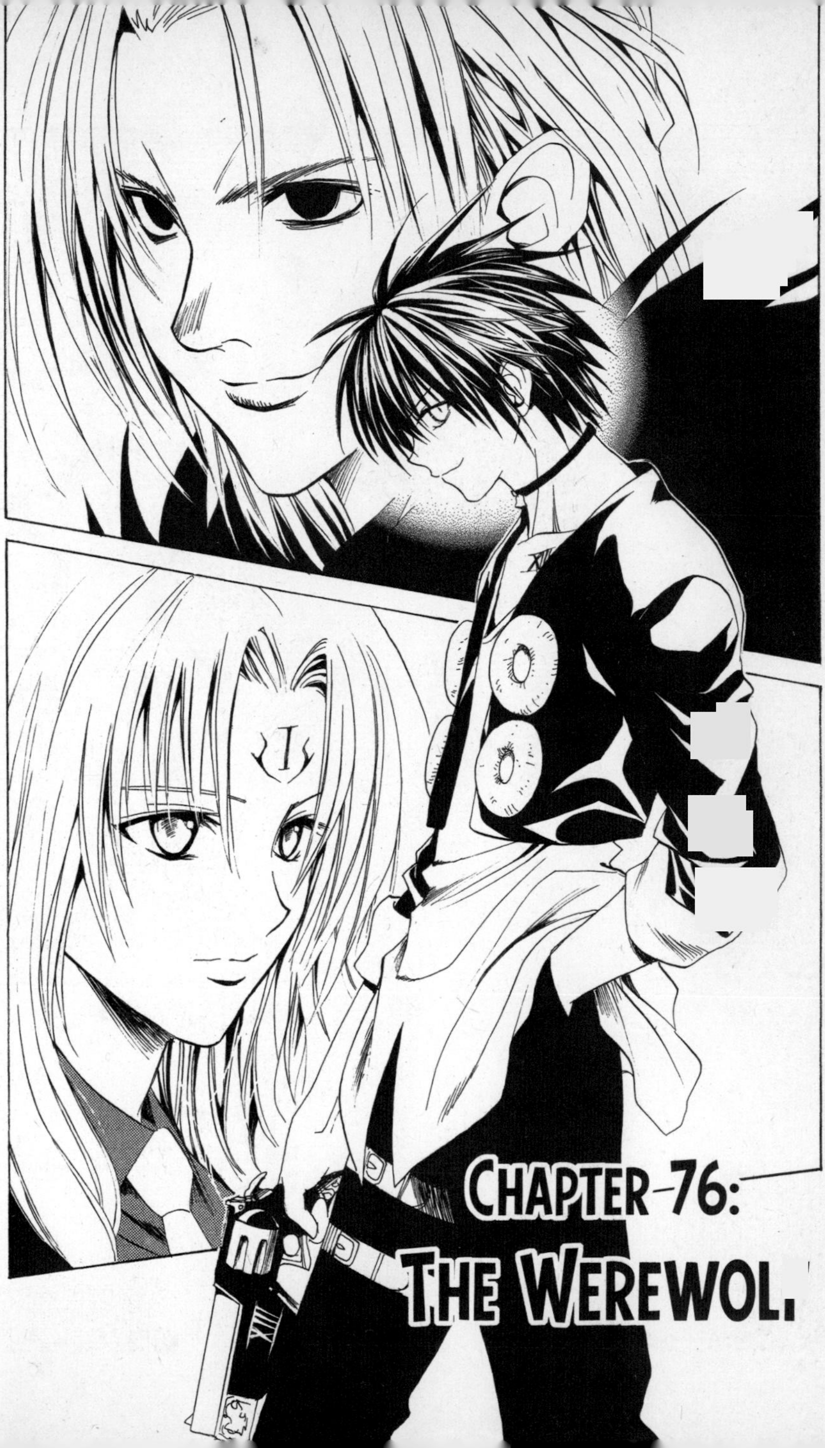
Chapter 76:
The Werewol

READ THIS WAY

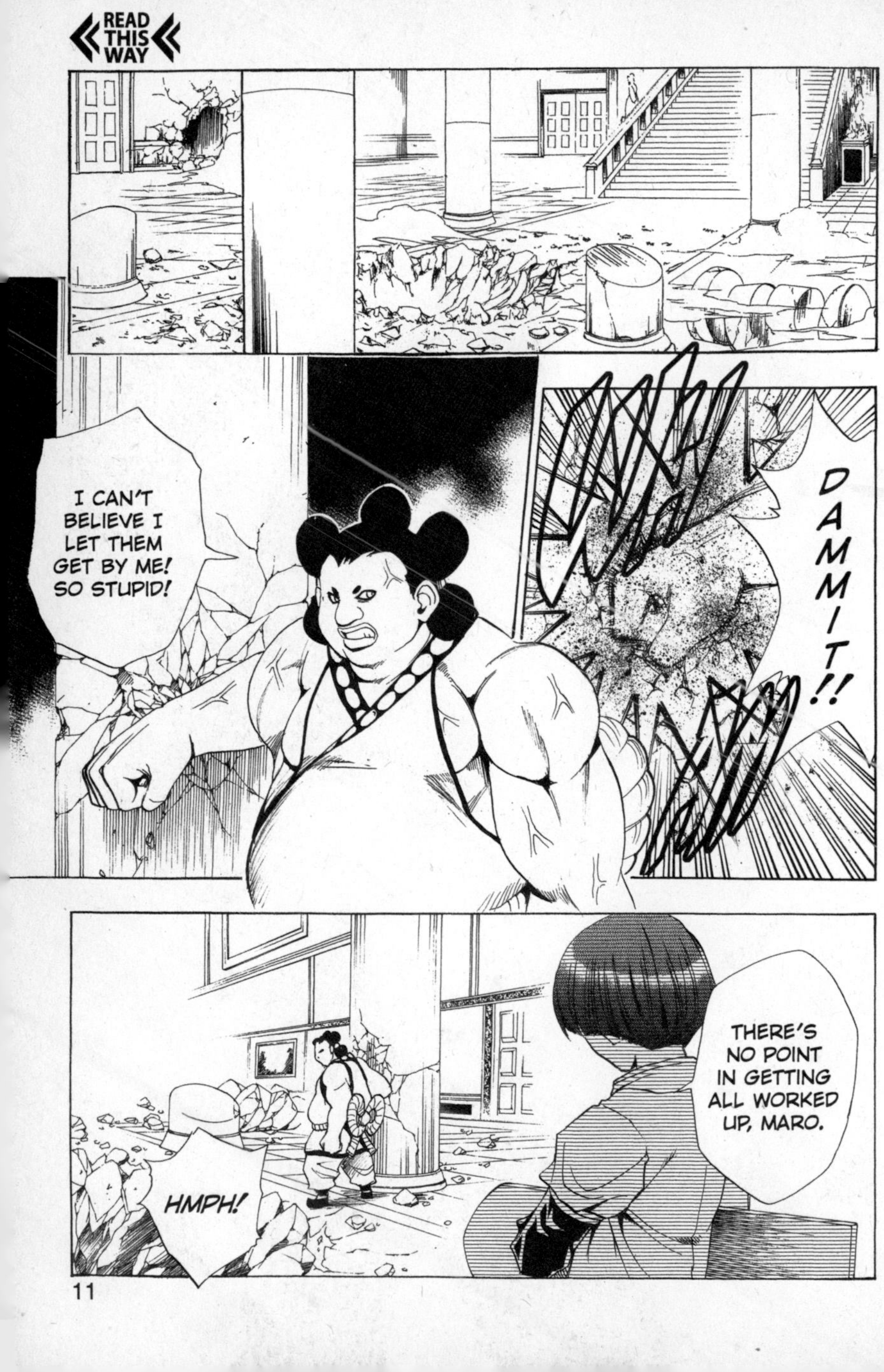
DAMMIT!!
I CAN'T BELIEVE I LET THEM GET BY ME! SO STUPID!
THERE'S NO POINT IN GETTING ALL WORKED UP, MARO.
HMPH!

INSTEAD OF TALKING, WE SHOULD GO AFTER THEM.

AGREED.

I *KNOW* THAT!!

SO HELP ME, I'M GONNA POUND THOSE...

WE'RE WASTING PRECIOUS TIME STANDING AROUND.

12

THAT WON'T BE NECESSARY, MARO.

?!

TSS

!

STTT

ECHIDNA!

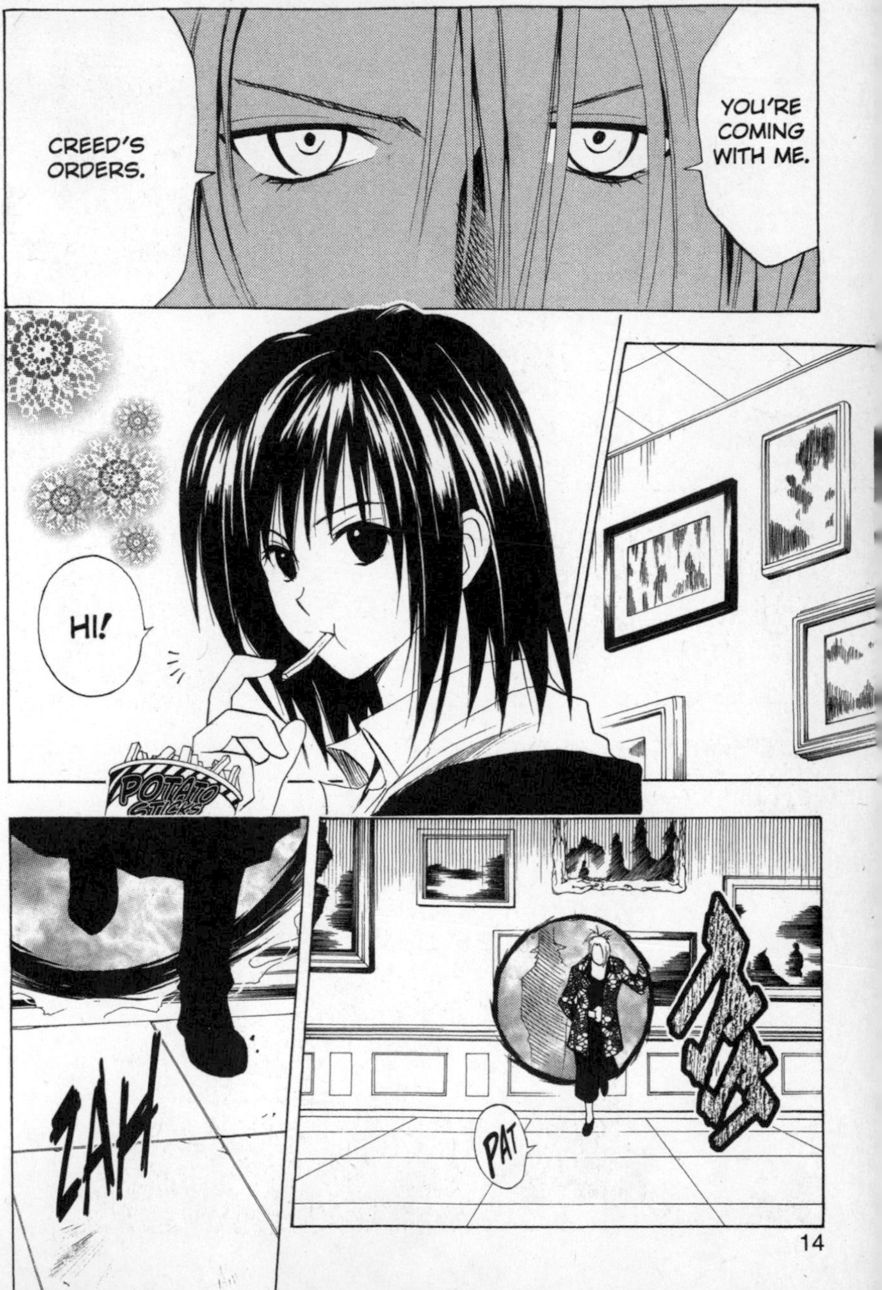
YOU'RE COMING WITH ME.
CREED'S ORDERS.
HI!
POTATO STICKS
ZAH
PAT

HE IS NOT HERE.

HE JUST LEFT WITH THAT RINSLET WOMAN.

WHERE IS CREED?

TO DO WHAT?

TO BEGIN TESTING A NEW WEAPON...

A HERETOFORE SECRET NANOTECH WEAPON.

15

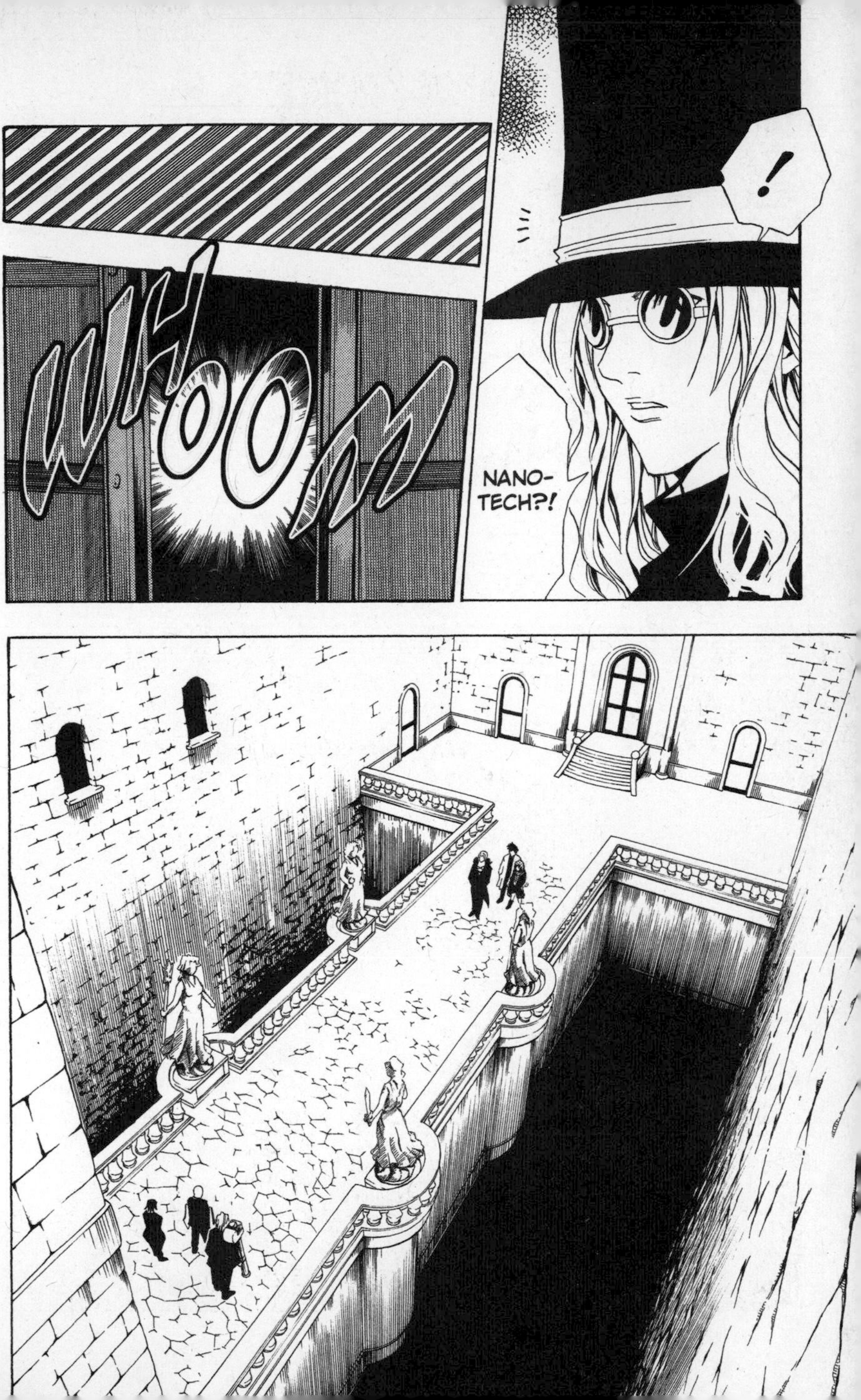
!
NANO-
TECH?!
WHOOM

...

YOU LOOK WELL.

CREED! LONG TIME NO SEE.

HMPH!

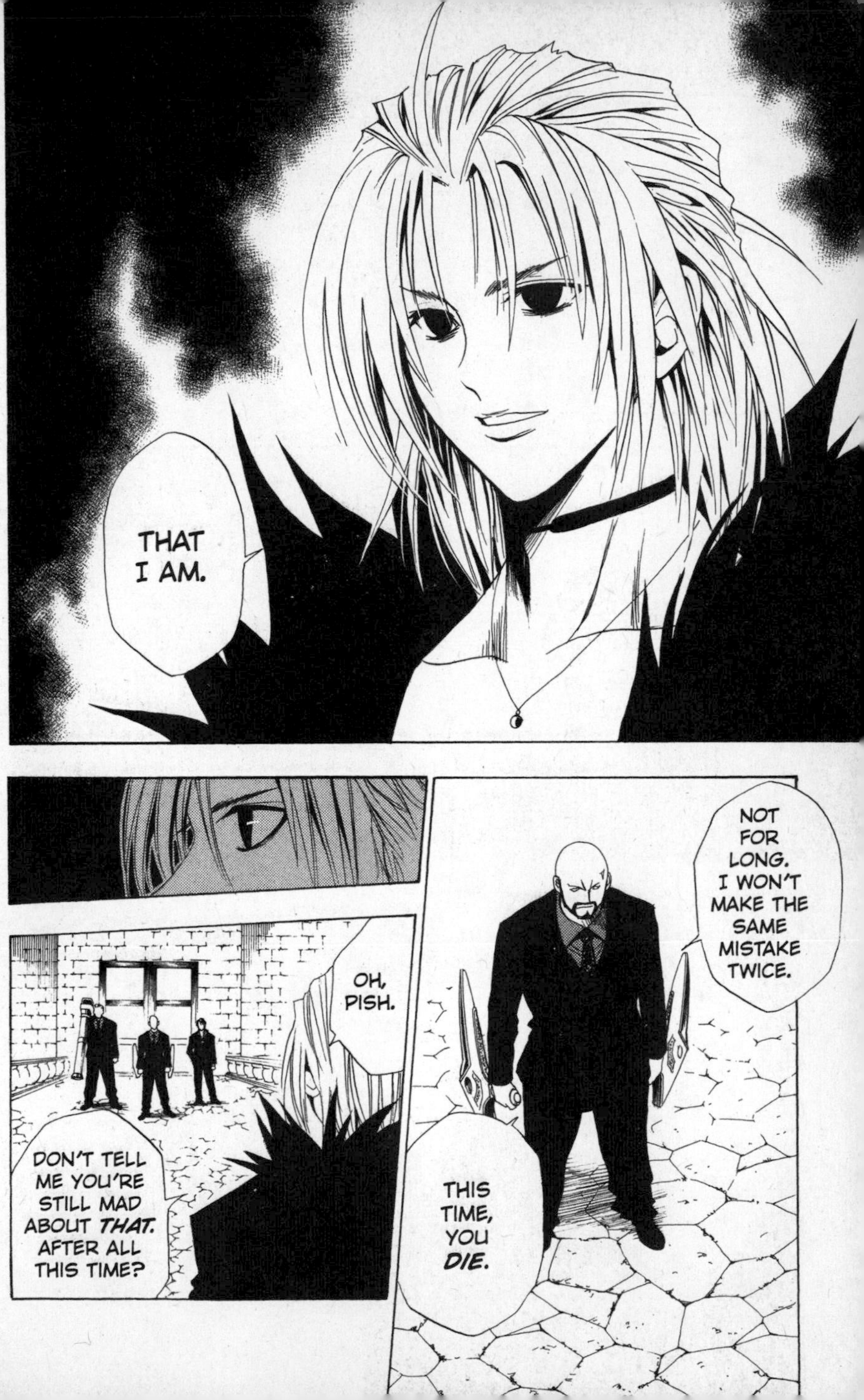
THAT I AM.
NOT FOR LONG. I WON'T MAKE THE SAME MISTAKE TWICE.
THIS TIME, YOU *DIE*.
OH, PISH.
DON'T TELL ME YOU'RE STILL MAD ABOUT *THAT*. AFTER ALL THIS TIME?

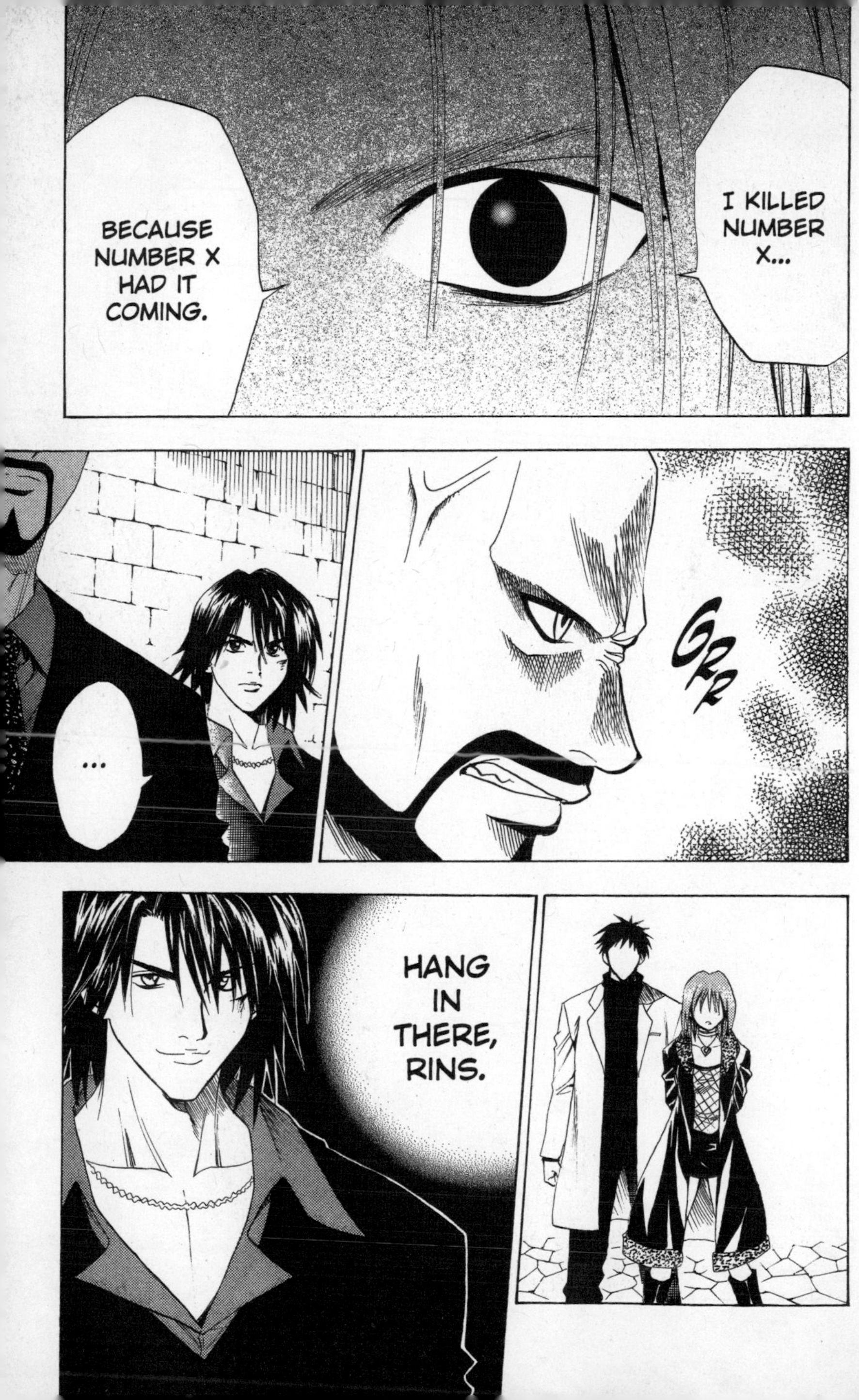
I KILLED NUMBER X...
BECAUSE NUMBER X HAD IT COMING.
GRR
...
HANG IN THERE, RINS.

SLIP

HUH?

PAT

PAT

Heh
Heh
Heh

Heh

Heh

TWITCH

WHO'S THIS?

ANOTHER OF YOUR APOSTLES?

20

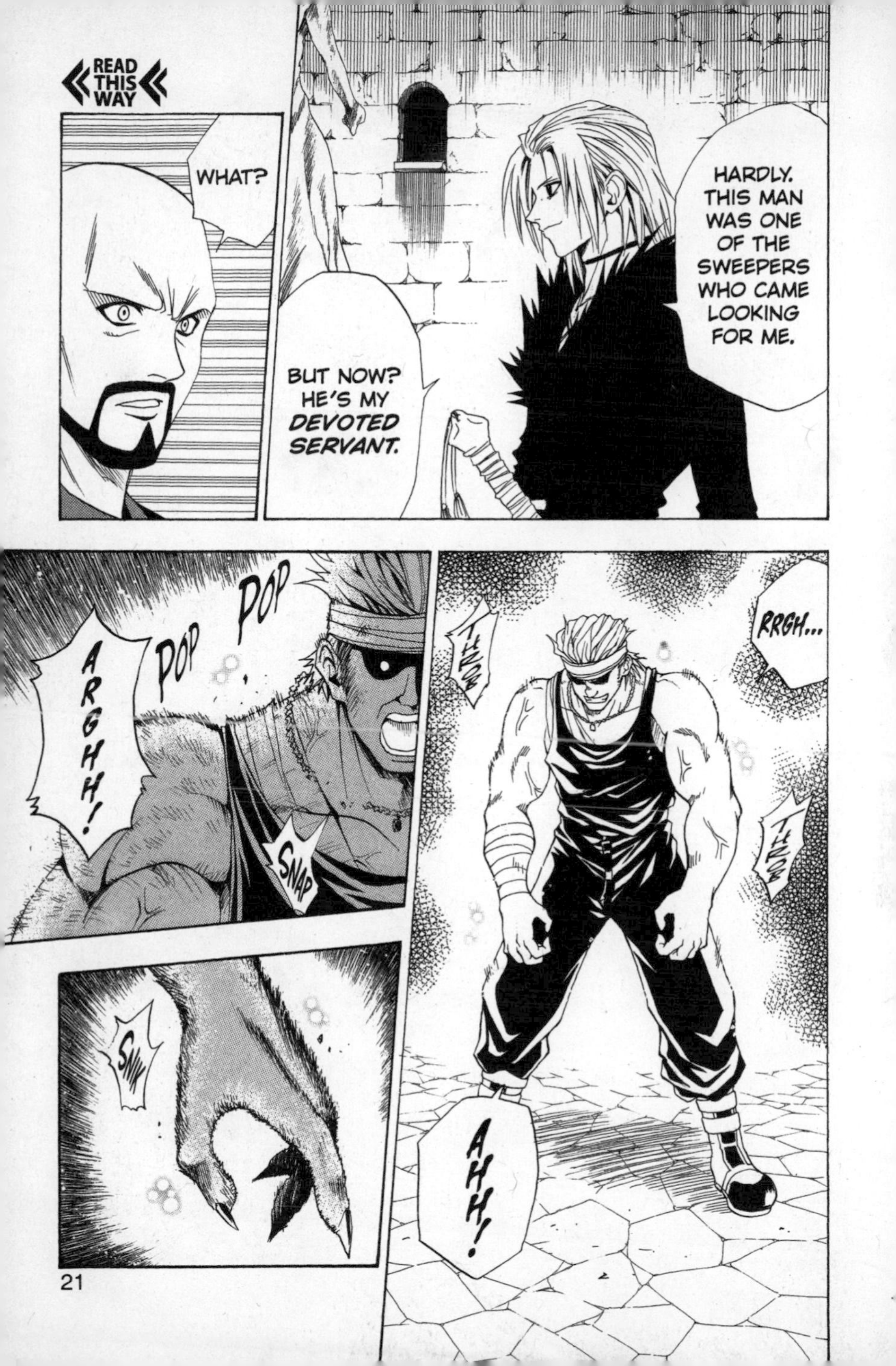
READ THIS WAY
HARDLY. THIS MAN WAS ONE OF THE SWEEPERS WHO CAME LOOKING FOR ME.
BUT NOW? HE'S MY *DEVOTED SERVANT.*
WHAT?
RRGH...
THROB
THROB
AHH!
POP
POP
POP
ARGHH!
SNAP
SNIK

THIS PARTICULAR SWEEPER WAS INJECTED WITH A VARIETY OF NANO-MACHINES...

...THAT TRIGGERED HIS TRANS-FORMATION INTO A DEADLY WOLF-BEAST.

ROOOOOAAAA!!

SNIK

SNIK

READ THIS WAY

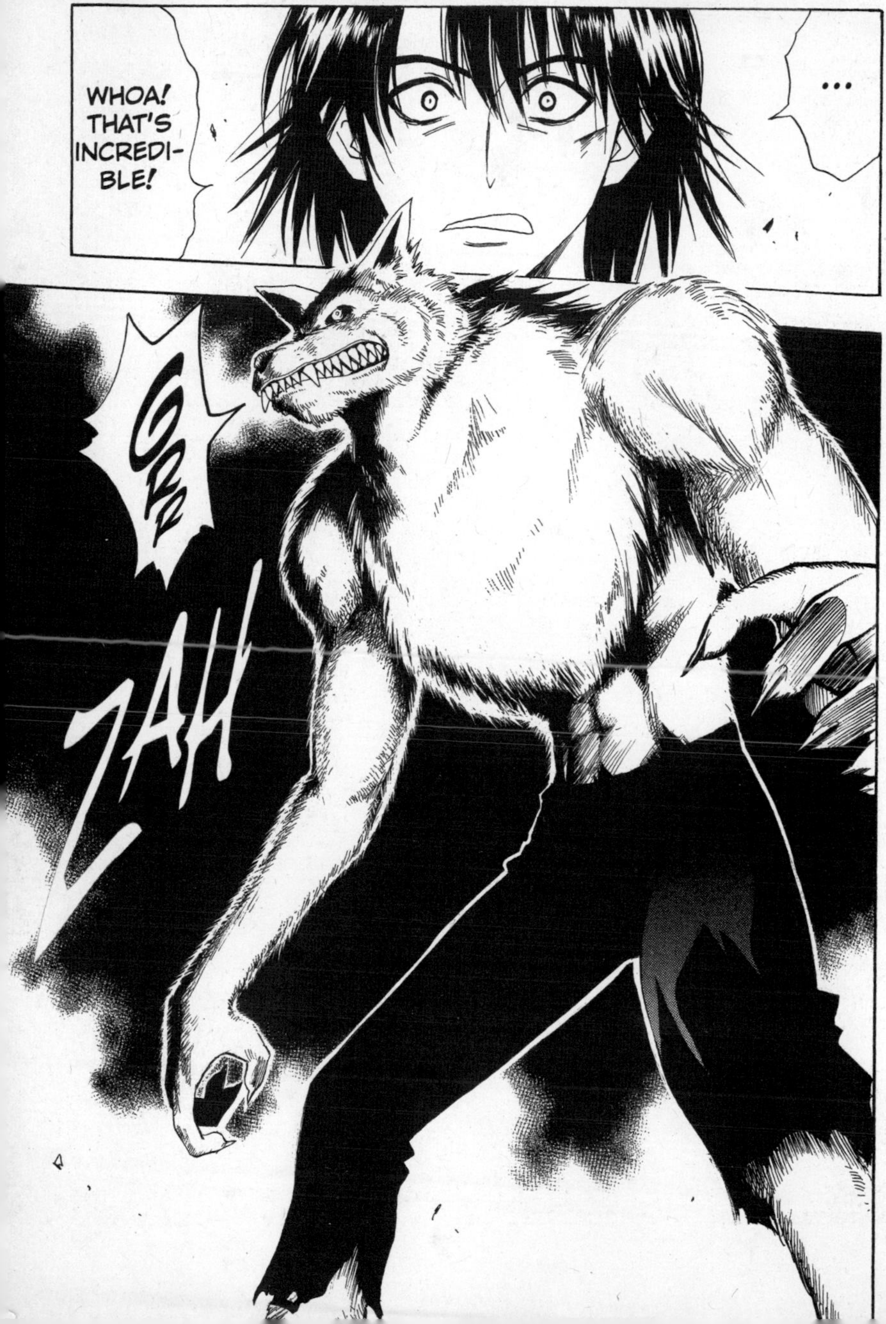

...
WHOA! THAT'S INCREDI-BLE!
ZAH

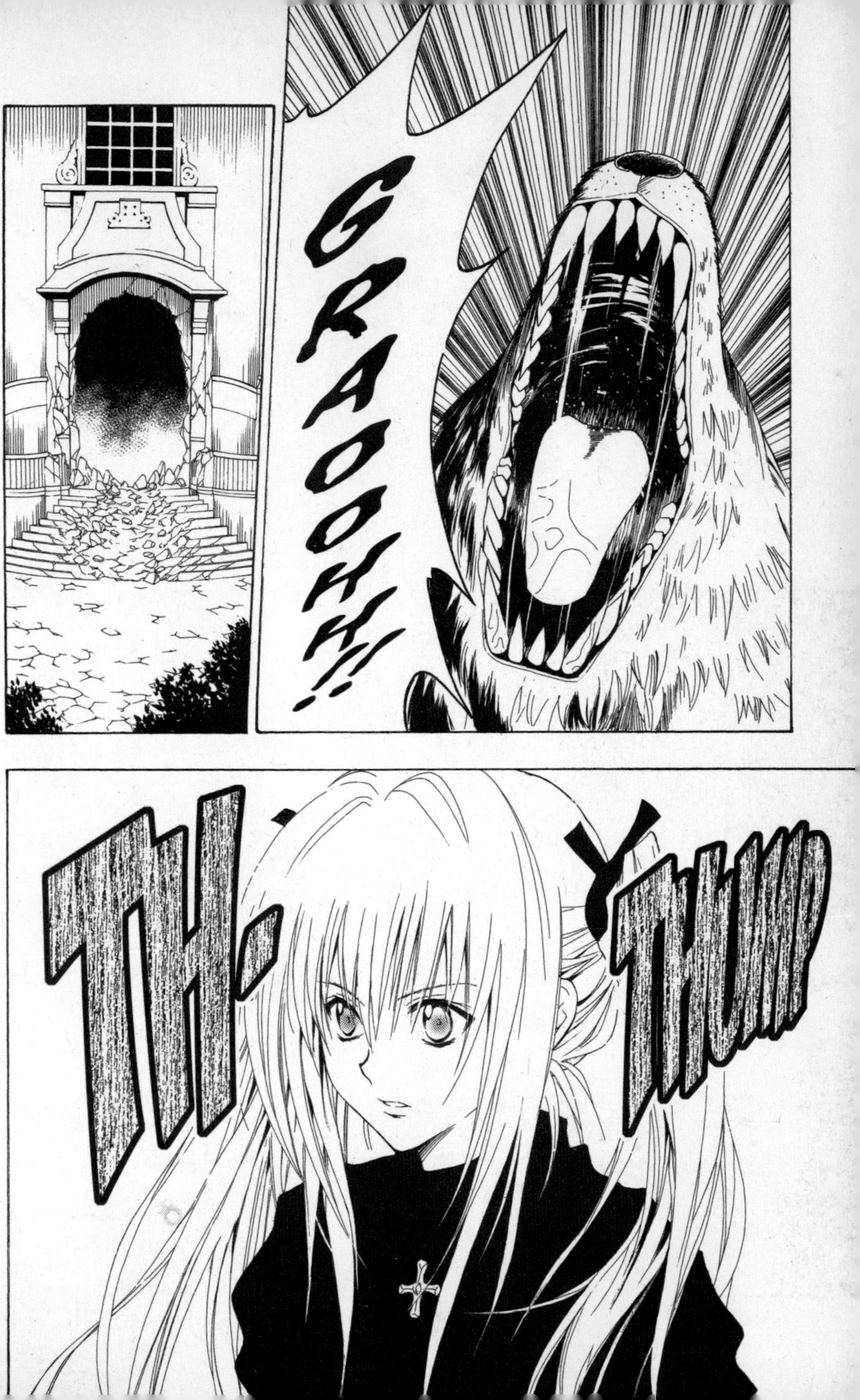
GRAOOHH!!
TH-THUMP

READ THIS WAY

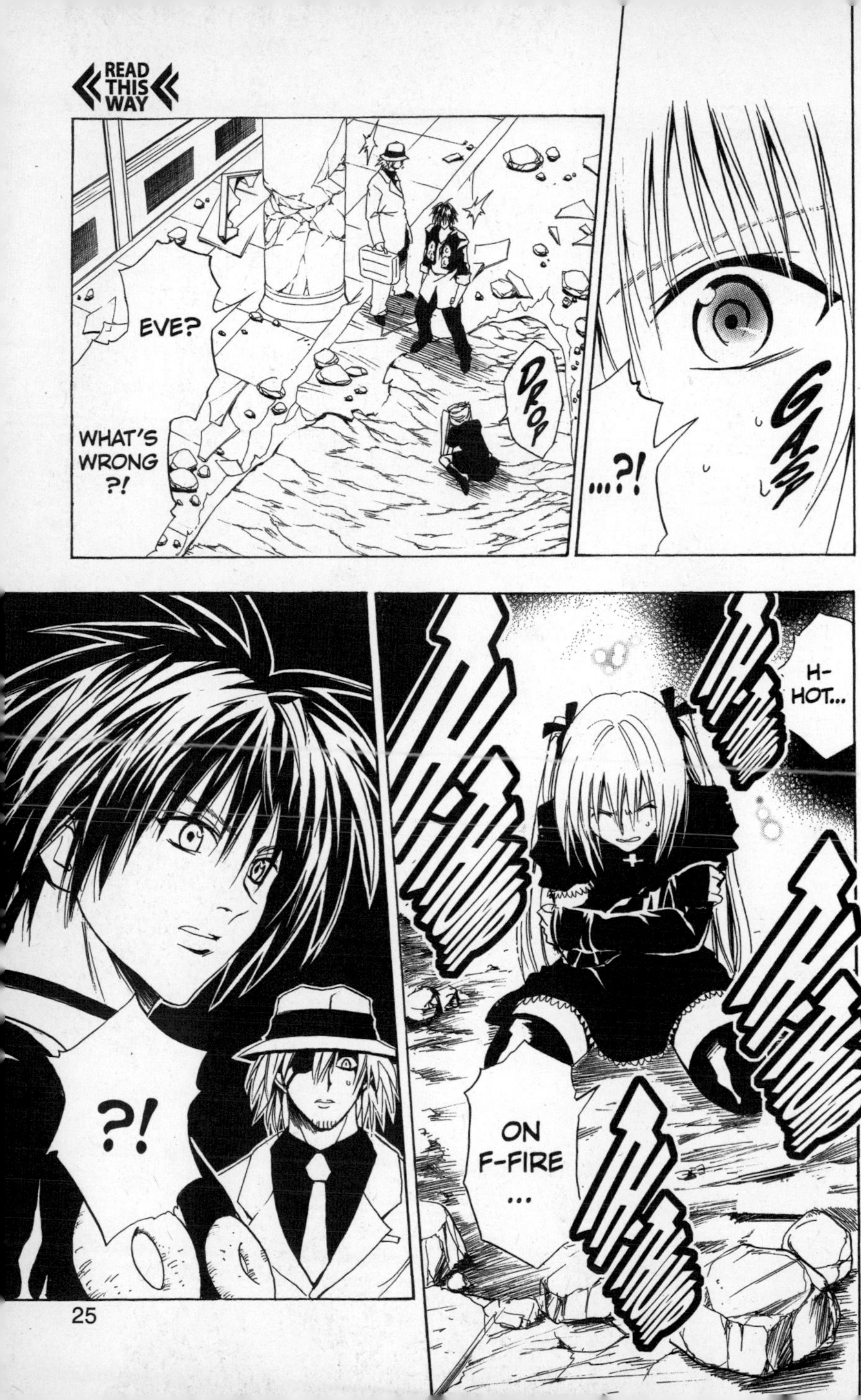
GASP
...?!
DROP
EVE?
WHAT'S WRONG ?!
H- HOT...
ON F-FIRE ...
?!

Chapter 77:
Nanotech Power

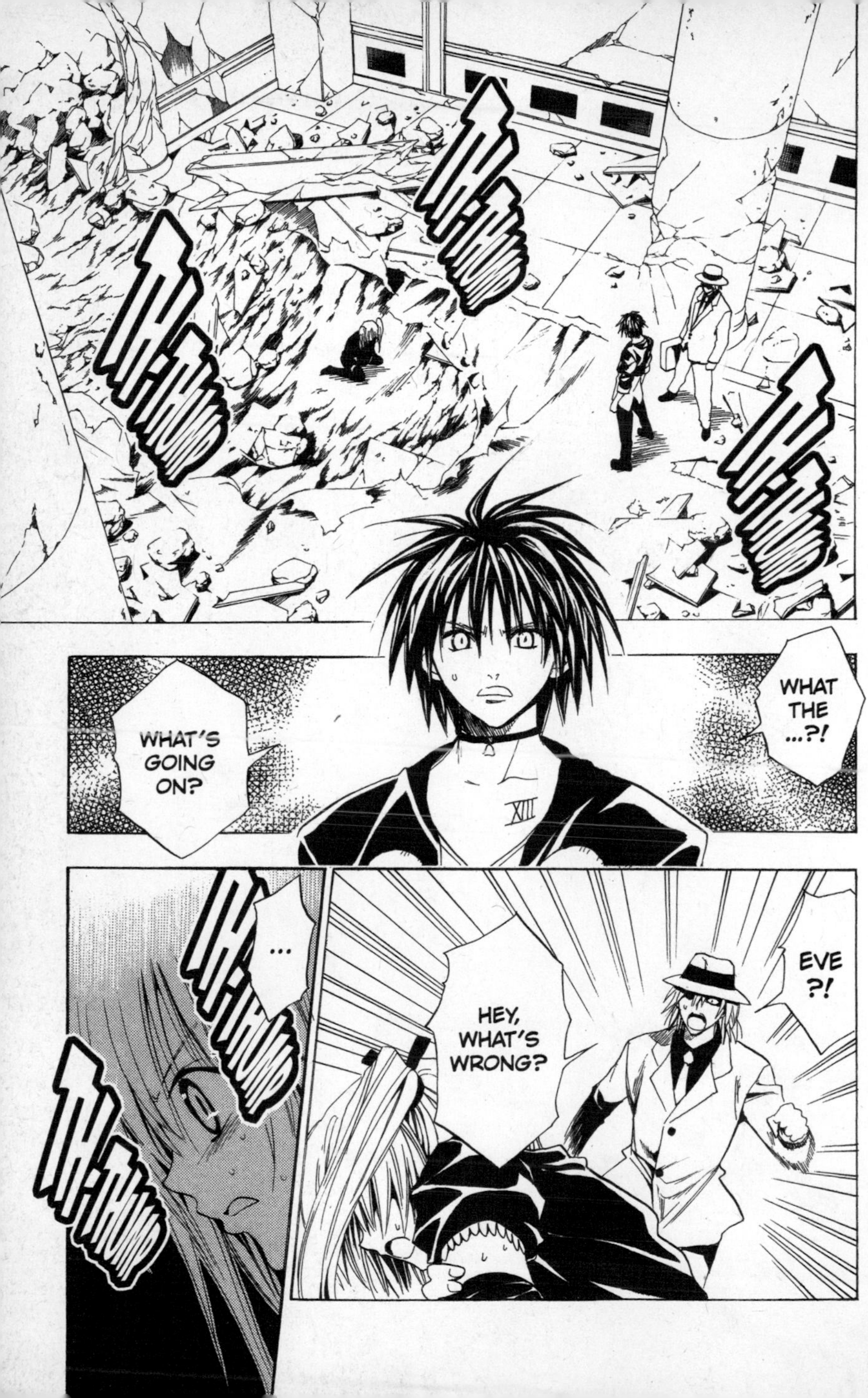
TH-THUMP
TH-THUMP
TH-THUMP
WHAT THE ...?!
WHAT'S GOING ON?
EVE ?!
HEY, WHAT'S WRONG?
...
TH-THUMP
TH-THUMP

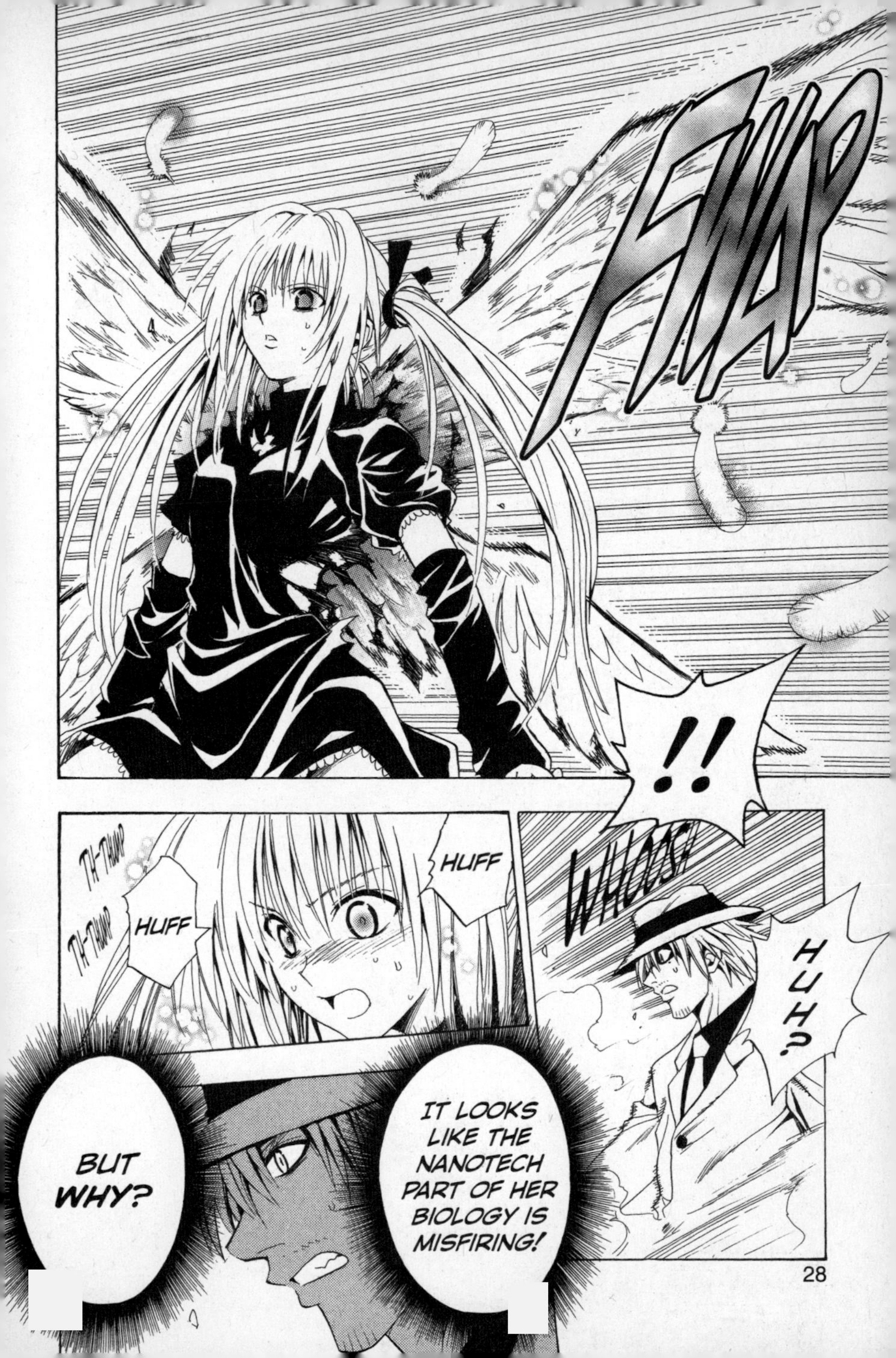
FWAP
!!
WHOOSH
HUH?
HUFF
HUFF
TH-THUMP TH-THUMP
IT LOOKS LIKE THE NANOTECH PART OF HER BIOLOGY IS MISFIRING!
BUT WHY?

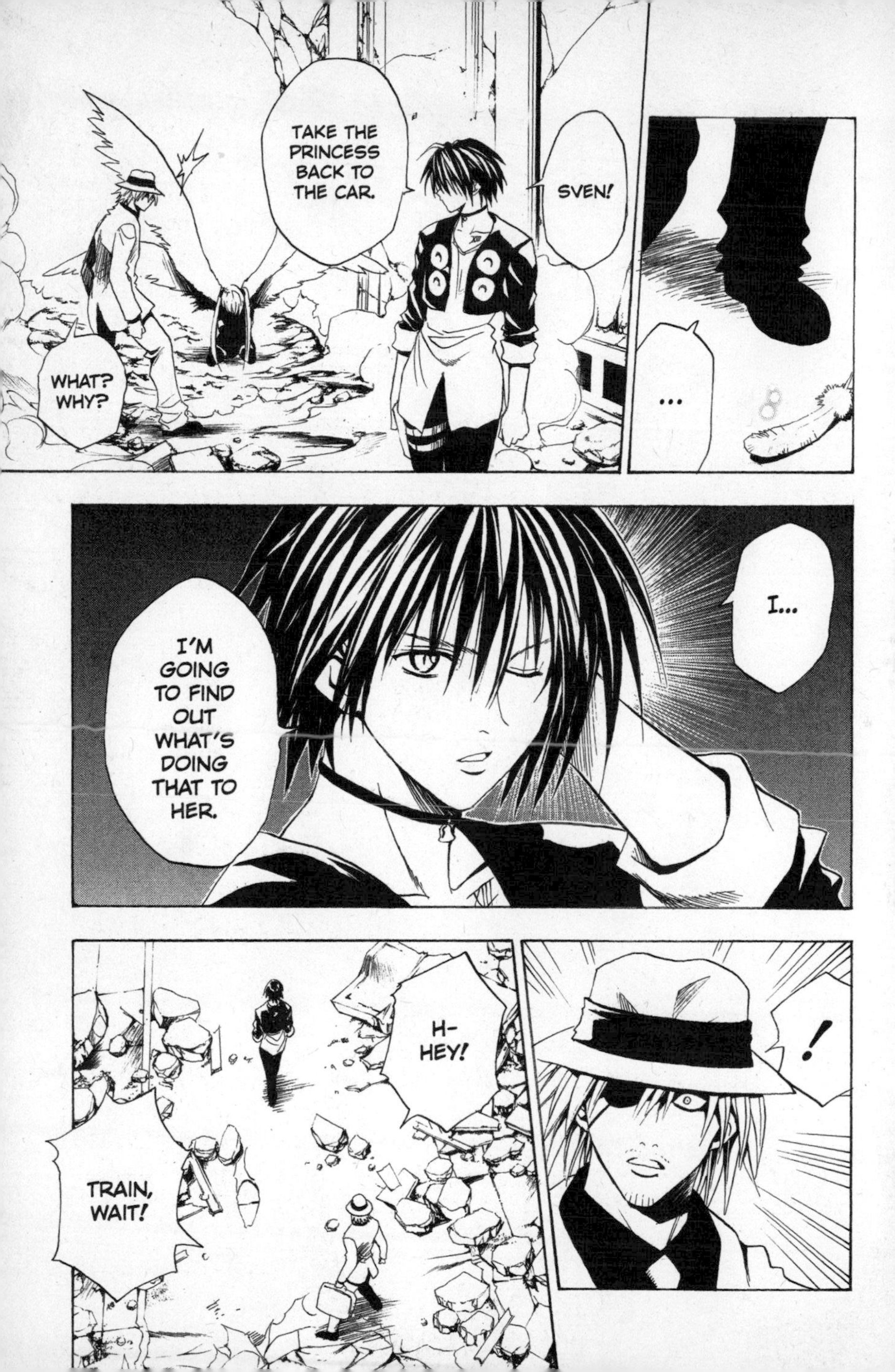
...
SVEN!
TAKE THE PRINCESS BACK TO THE CAR.
WHAT? WHY?
I...
I'M GOING TO FIND OUT WHAT'S DOING THAT TO HER.
!
H-HEY!
TRAIN, WAIT!

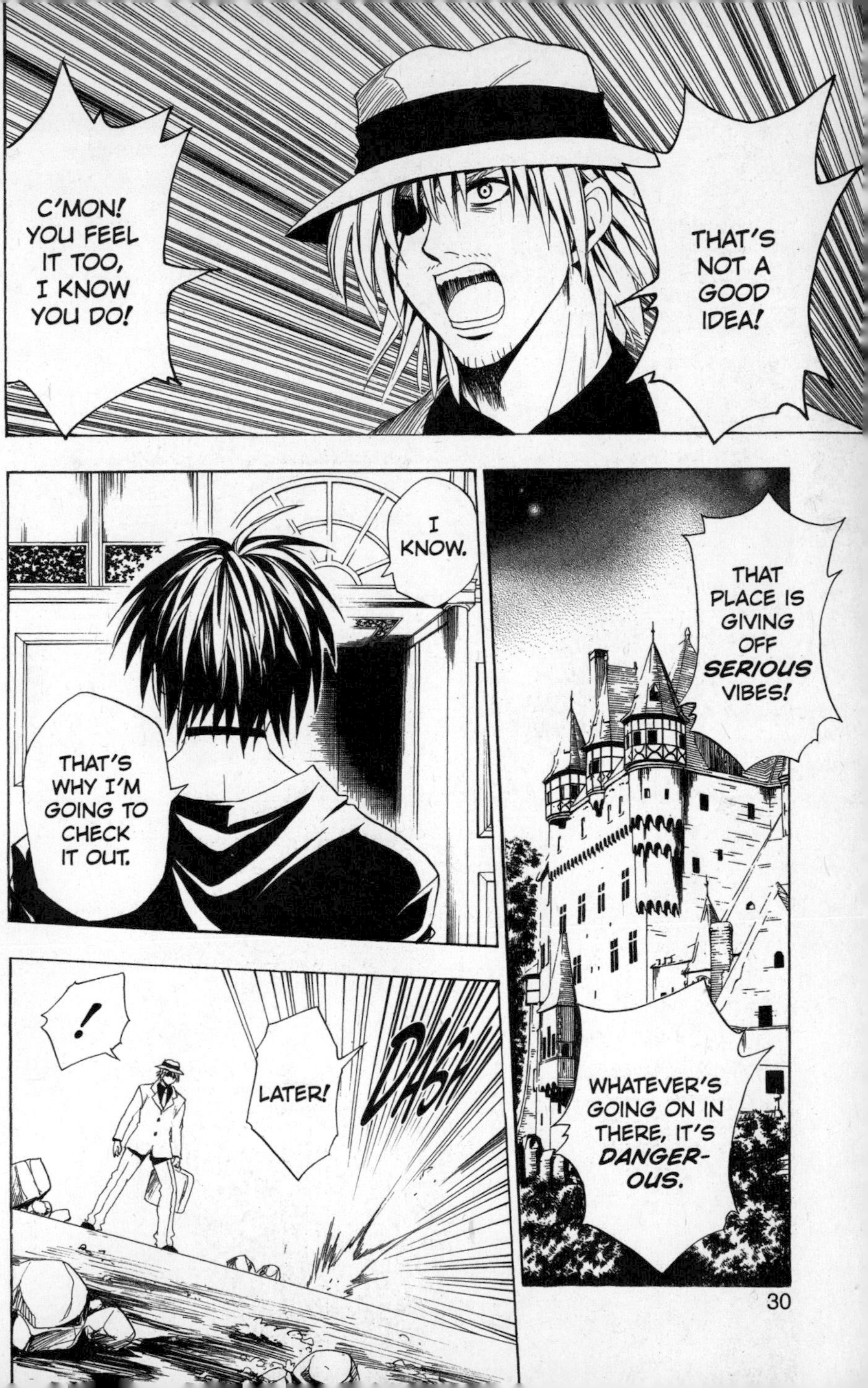
THAT'S NOT A GOOD IDEA!
C'MON! YOU FEEL IT TOO, I KNOW YOU DO!
THAT PLACE IS GIVING OFF SERIOUS VIBES!
WHATEVER'S GOING ON IN THERE, IT'S DANGEROUS.
I KNOW.
THAT'S WHY I'M GOING TO CHECK IT OUT.
DASH
LATER!
!

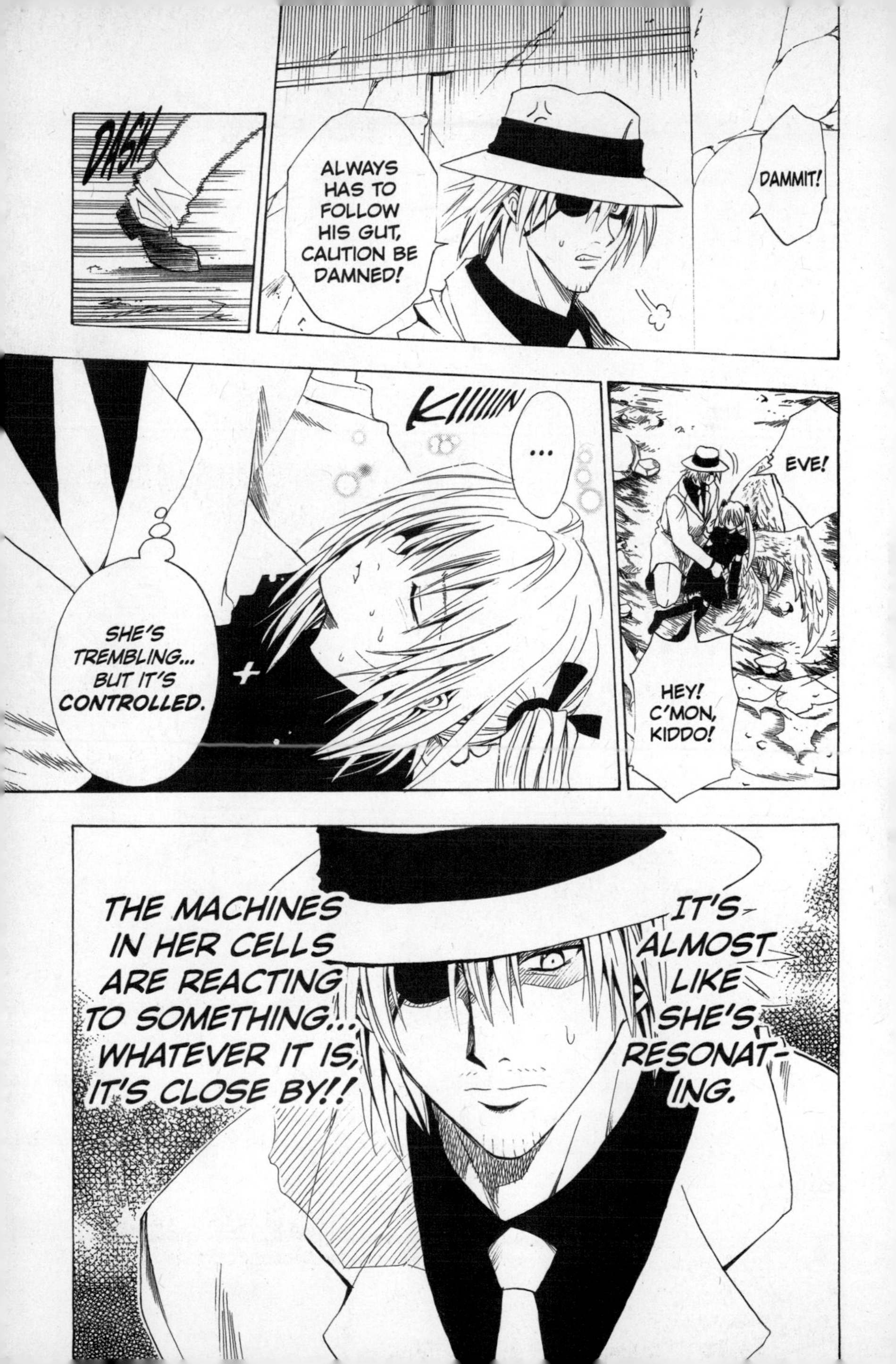
DAMMIT!
ALWAYS HAS TO FOLLOW HIS GUT, CAUTION BE DAMNED!
DASH
EVE!
HEY! C'MON, KIDDO!
KIIIIIIN
...
SHE'S TREMBLING... BUT IT'S CONTROLLED.
IT'S ALMOST LIKE SHE'S RESONATING.
THE MACHINES IN HER CELLS ARE REACTING TO SOMETHING... WHATEVER IT IS, IT'S CLOSE BY!!

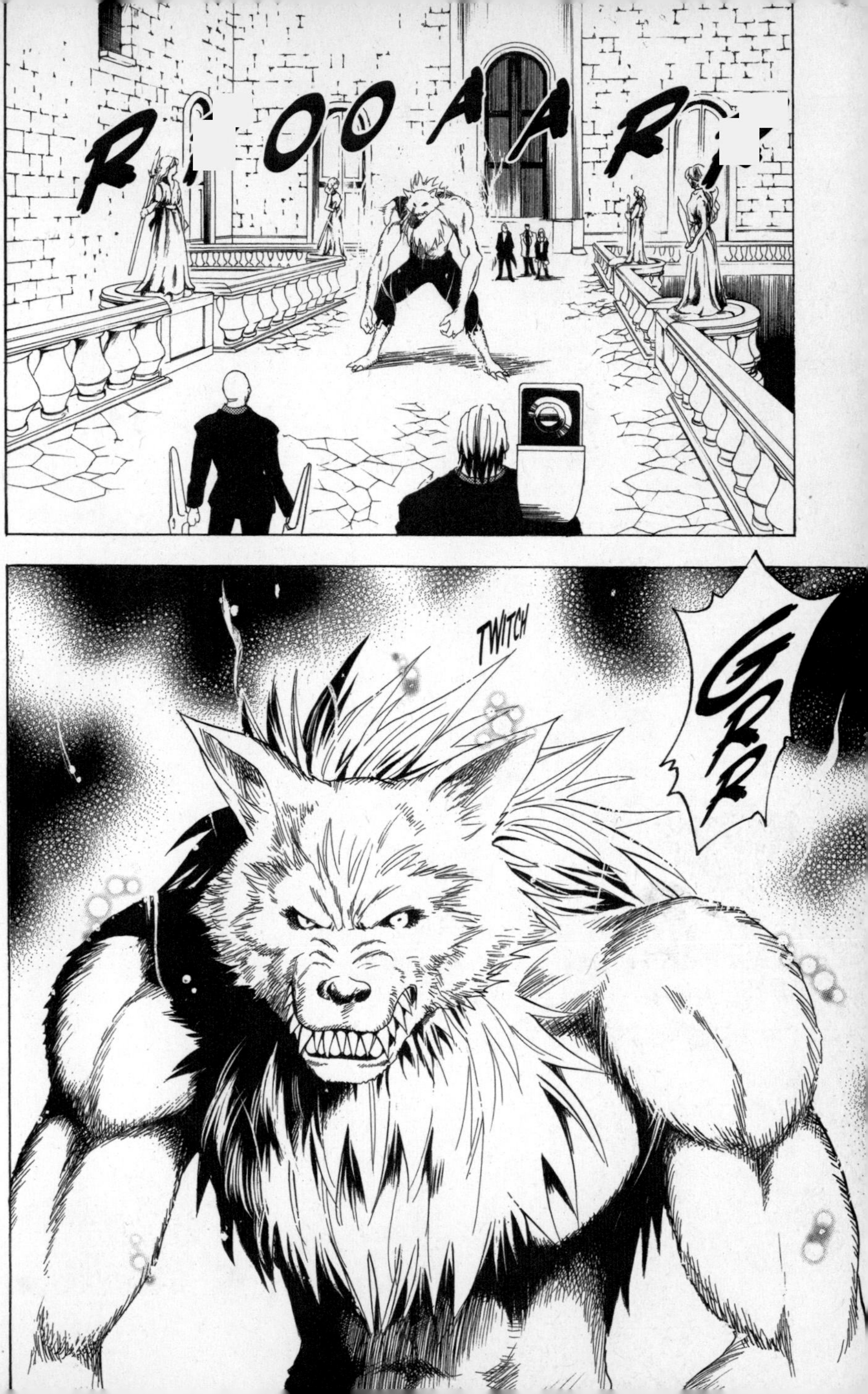
ROOAAR
TWITCH
GRRR

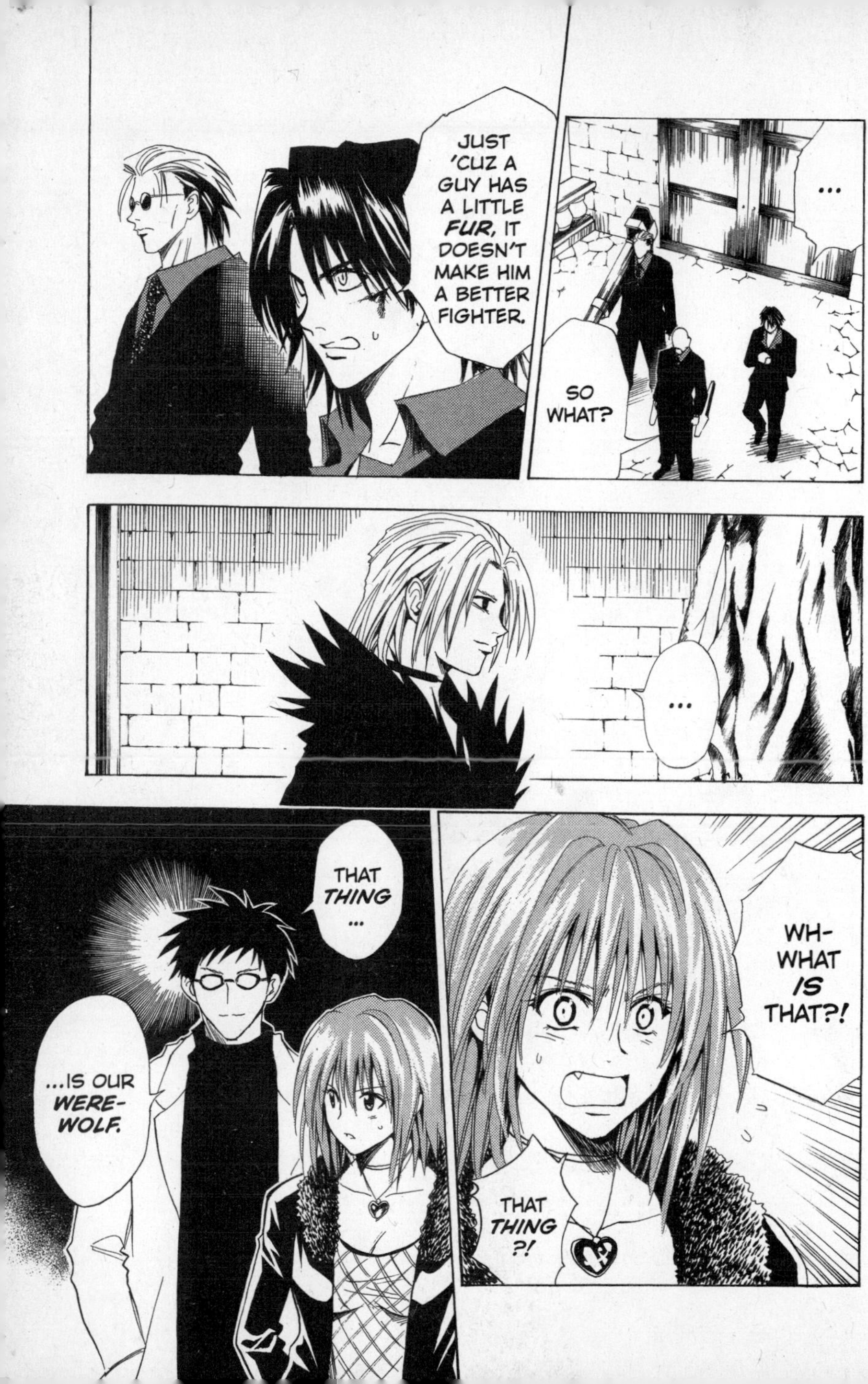
...
SO WHAT?
JUST 'CUZ A GUY HAS A LITTLE *FUR*, IT DOESN'T MAKE HIM A BETTER FIGHTER.
...
WH-WHAT *IS* THAT?!
THAT *THING* ?!
THAT *THING* ...
...IS OUR *WERE-WOLF.*

CELLULAR MACHINES TRIGGERED THE PROGRAMMING BURIED WITHIN HIS ANCESTRAL DNA.

NANOTECH POWER AT WORK!

...HOW TO BE A WOLF.

?!

HE'S REMEMBERING...

THOUGH IT'S COMMONLY HELD THAT *HOMO SAPIENS* EVOLVED FROM A *COMMON ANCESTOR* SHARED WITH THE *MODERN APE*...

EVEN THOSE *PRIMATES* WERE DESCENDED FROM *ANOTHER* COMMON ANCESTOR.

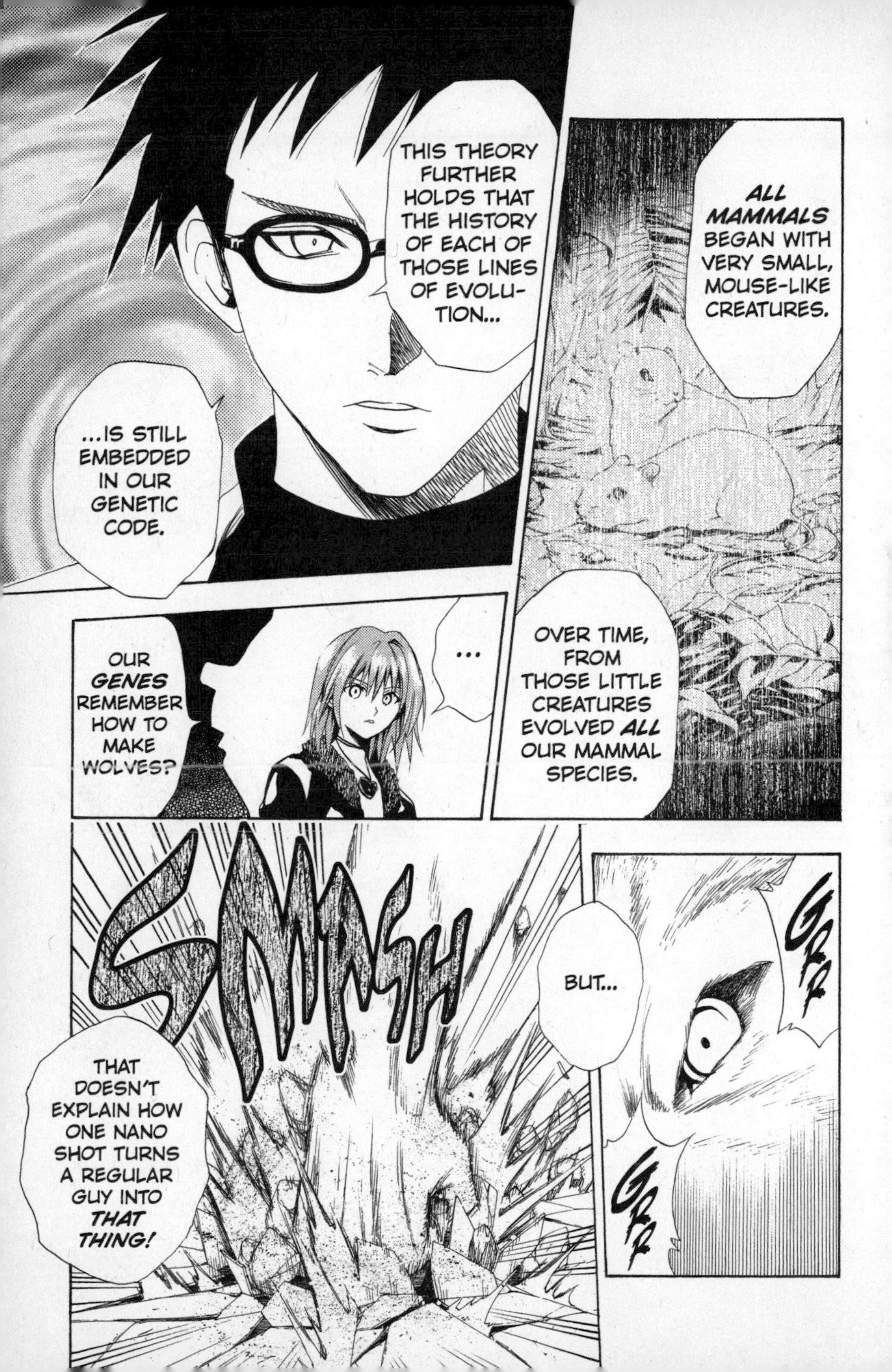
ALL MAMMALS BEGAN WITH VERY SMALL, MOUSE-LIKE CREATURES.
OVER TIME, FROM THOSE LITTLE CREATURES EVOLVED ALL OUR MAMMAL SPECIES.
THIS THEORY FURTHER HOLDS THAT THE HISTORY OF EACH OF THOSE LINES OF EVOLU-TION...
...IS STILL EMBEDDED IN OUR GENETIC CODE.
...
OUR GENES REMEMBER HOW TO MAKE WOLVES?
GRR
GRR
BUT...
SMASH
THAT DOESN'T EXPLAIN HOW ONE NANO SHOT TURNS A REGULAR GUY INTO THAT THING!

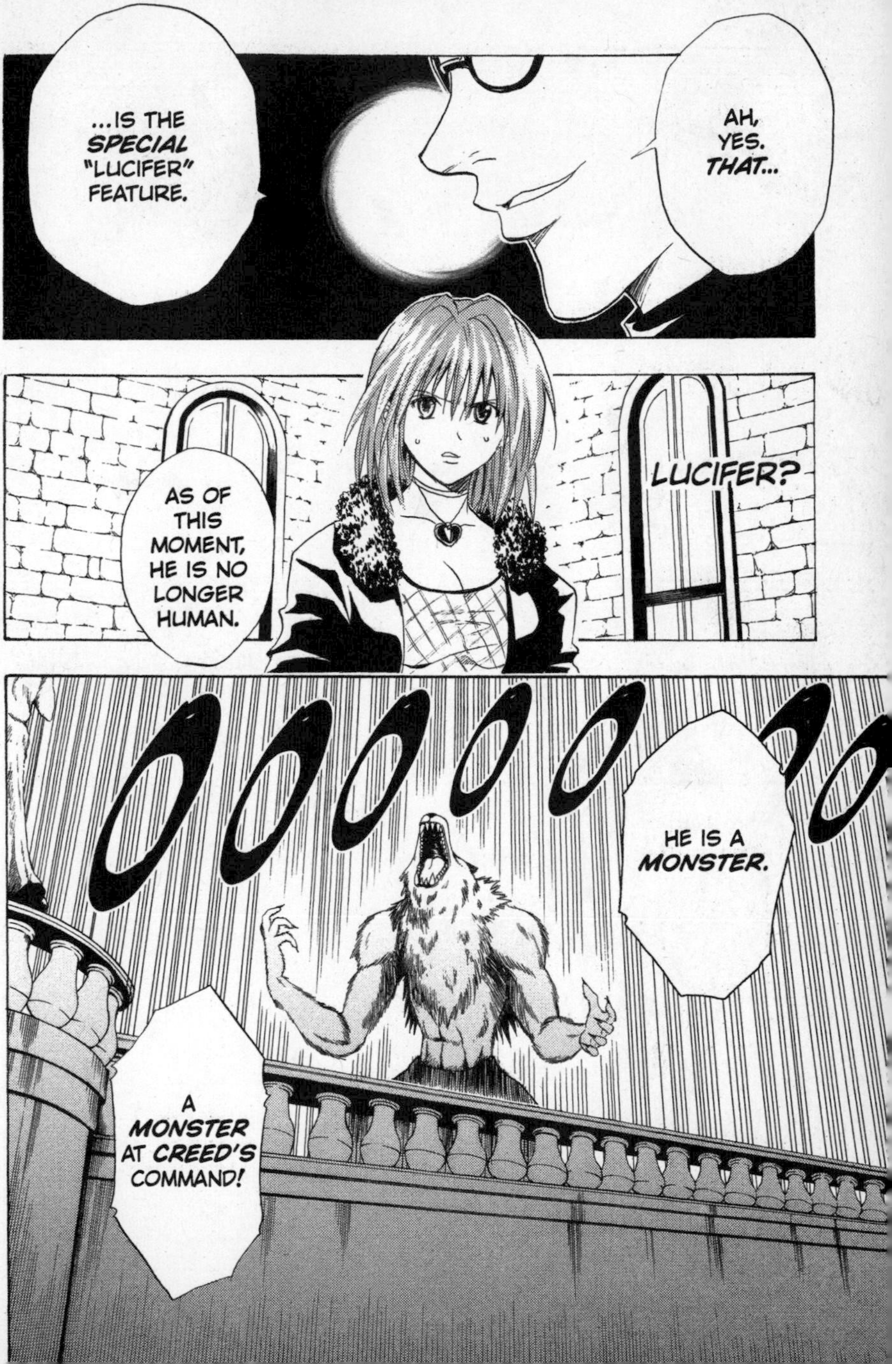
AH, YES. THAT...
...IS THE SPECIAL "LUCIFER" FEATURE.
LUCIFER?
AS OF THIS MOMENT, HE IS NO LONGER HUMAN.
HE IS A MONSTER.
A MONSTER AT CREED'S COMMAND!

TH-THEY'RE NUTS!

!!

THE DOCTOR, TOO!

NOT JUST CREED.

LIKE TRASH!

THEY THINK HUMANS ARE DISPOSABLE.

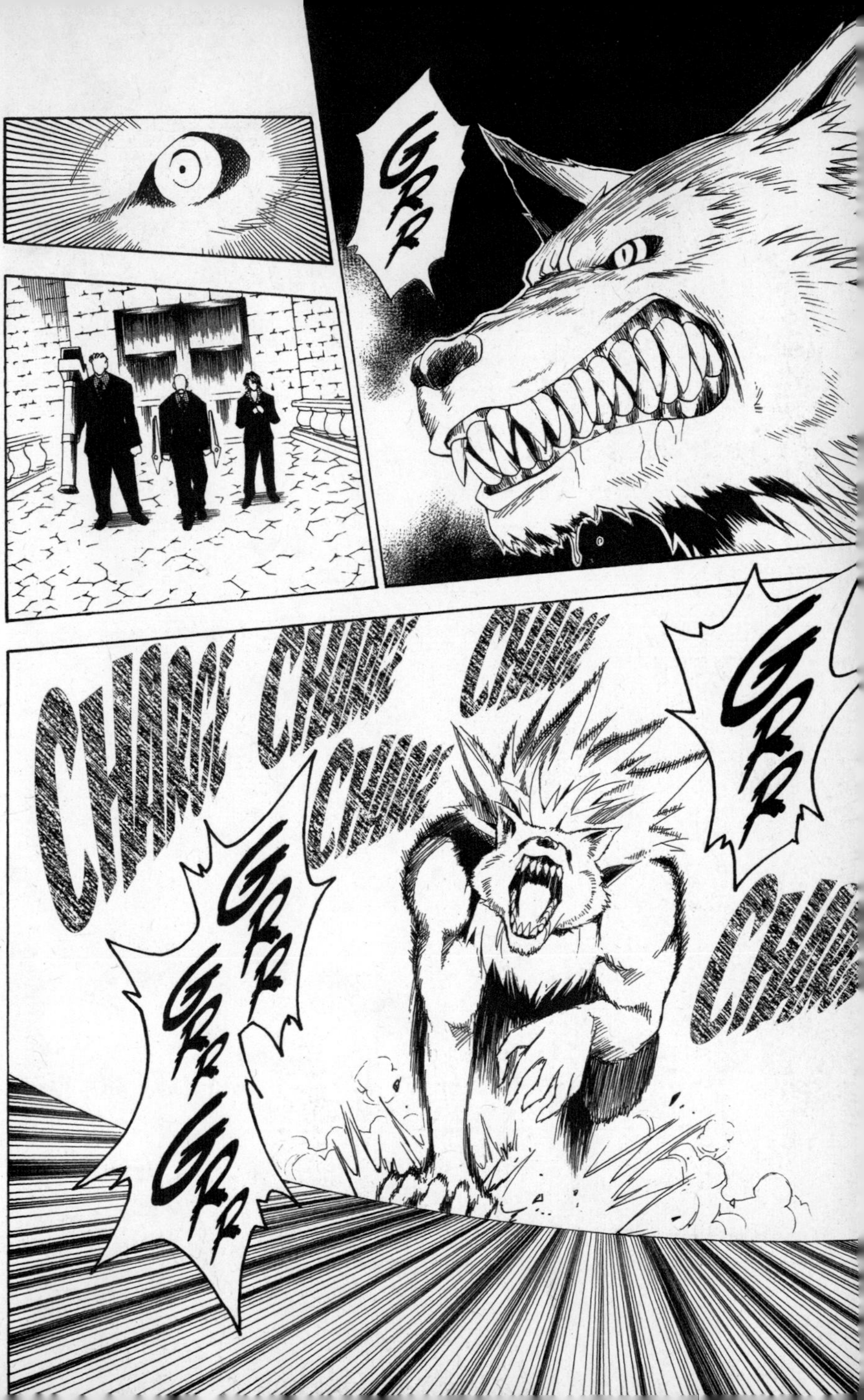
GRRR
GRRR
CHINK CHINK CHINK CHINK
GRRR GRRR GRRR

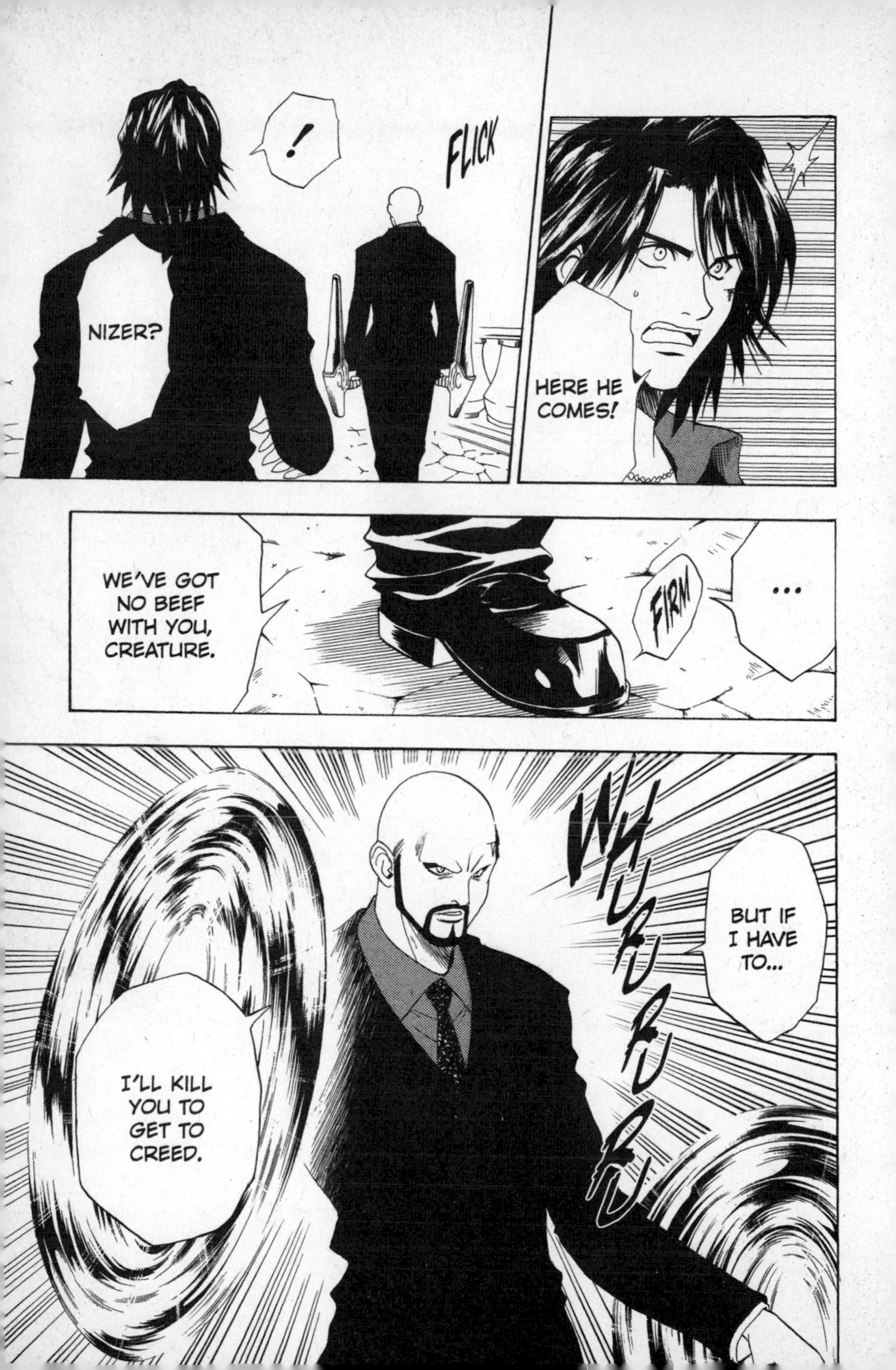

HERE HE COMES!
!
FLICK
NIZER?
...
FIRM
WE'VE GOT NO BEEF WITH YOU, CREATURE.
BUT IF I HAVE TO...
I'LL KILL YOU TO GET TO CREED.

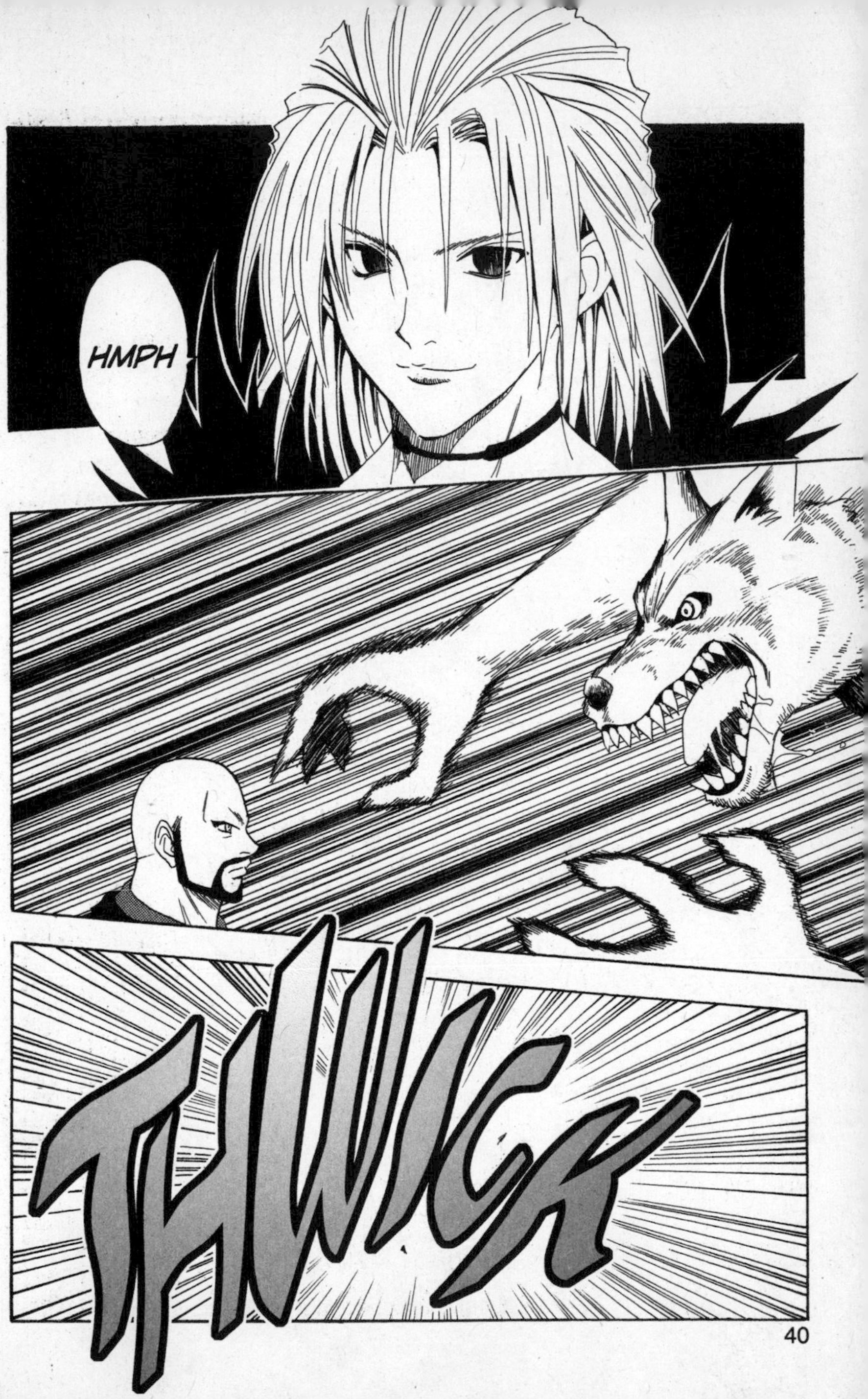
HMPH
THWICK

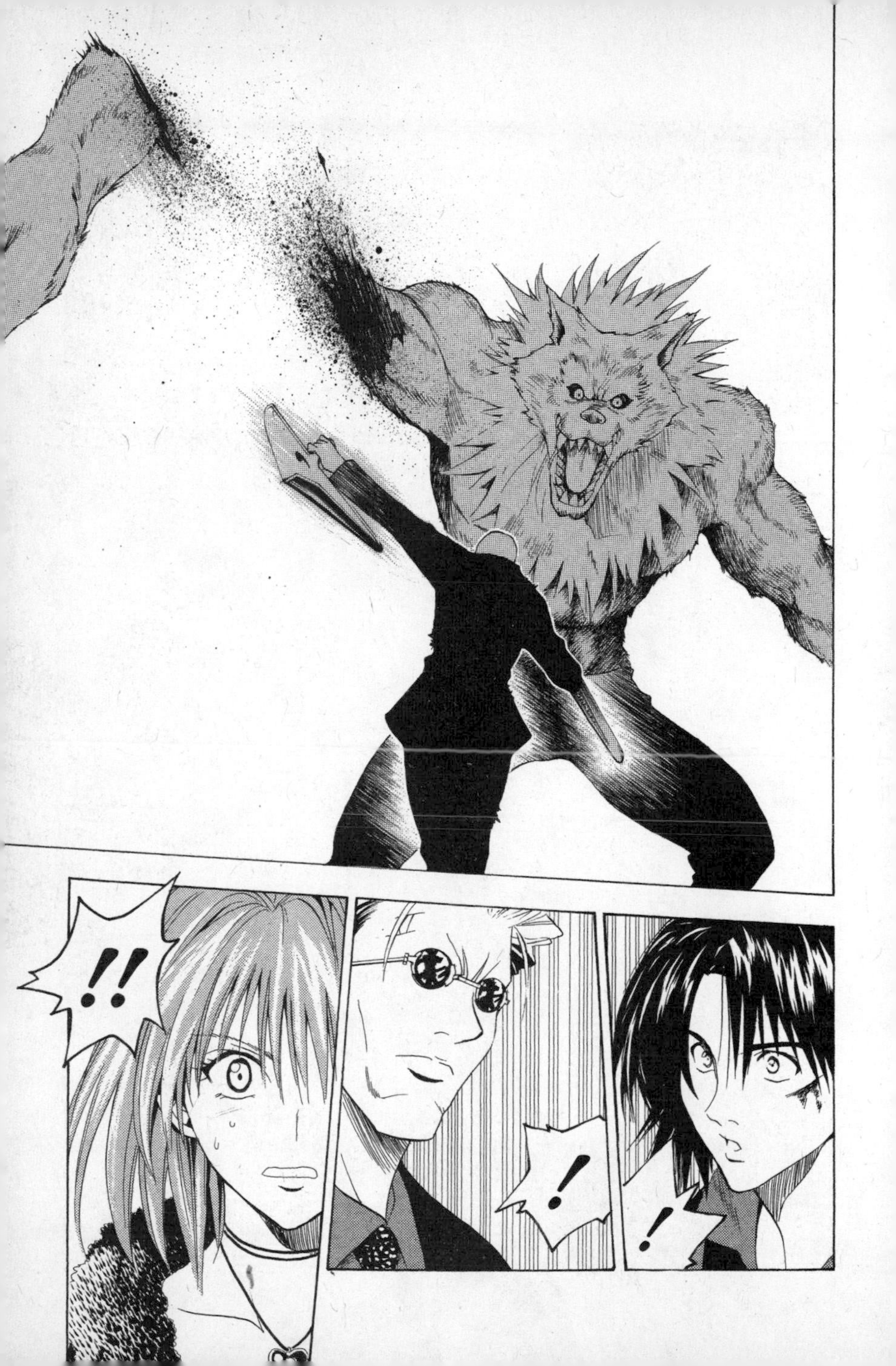
!!
!
!

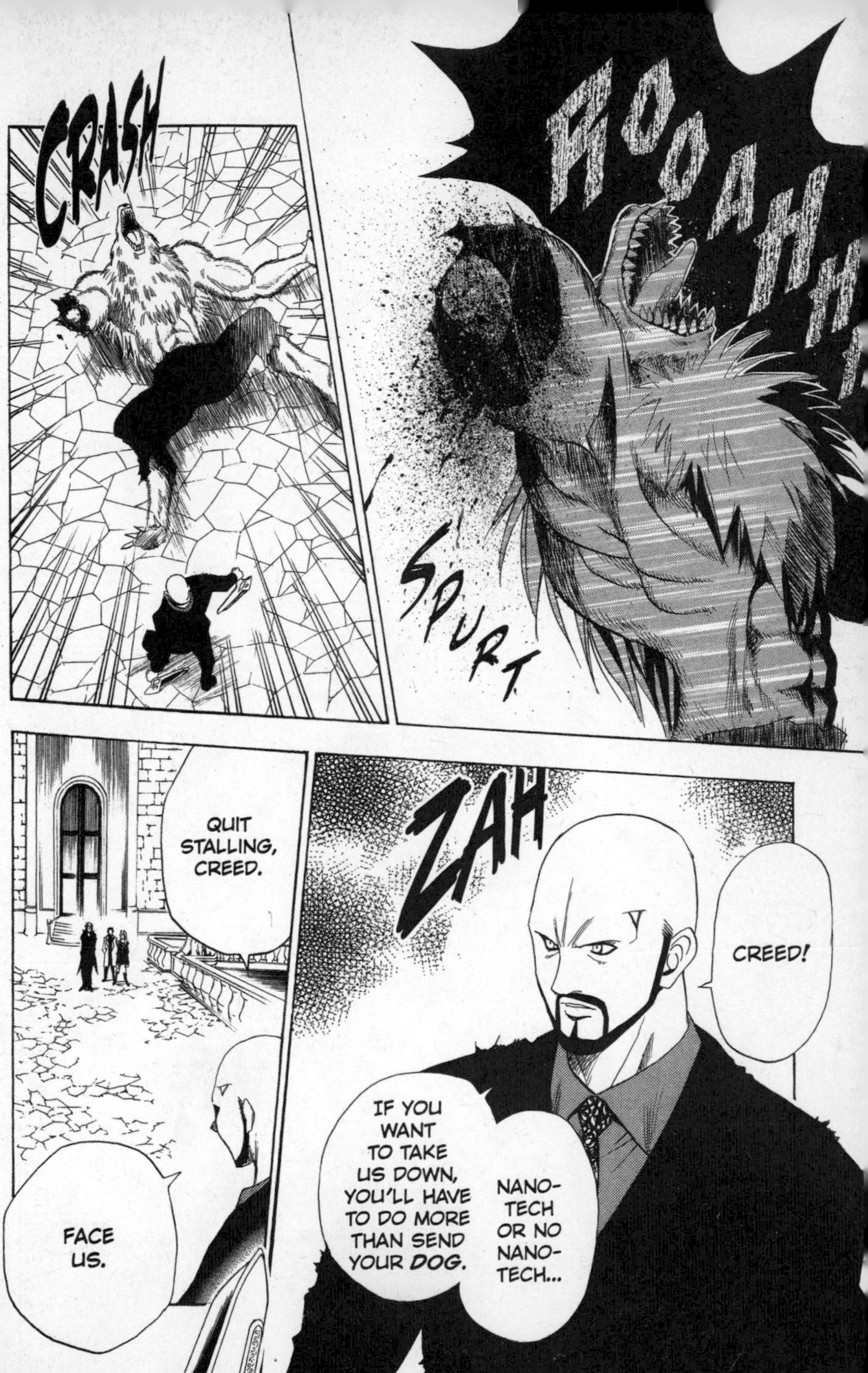
HOOAHH
SPURT
CRASH
ZAH
CREED!
NANO-TECH OR NO NANO-TECH...
IF YOU WANT TO TAKE US DOWN, YOU'LL HAVE TO DO MORE THAN SEND YOUR *DOG*.
QUIT STALLING, CREED.
FACE US.

READ THIS WAY

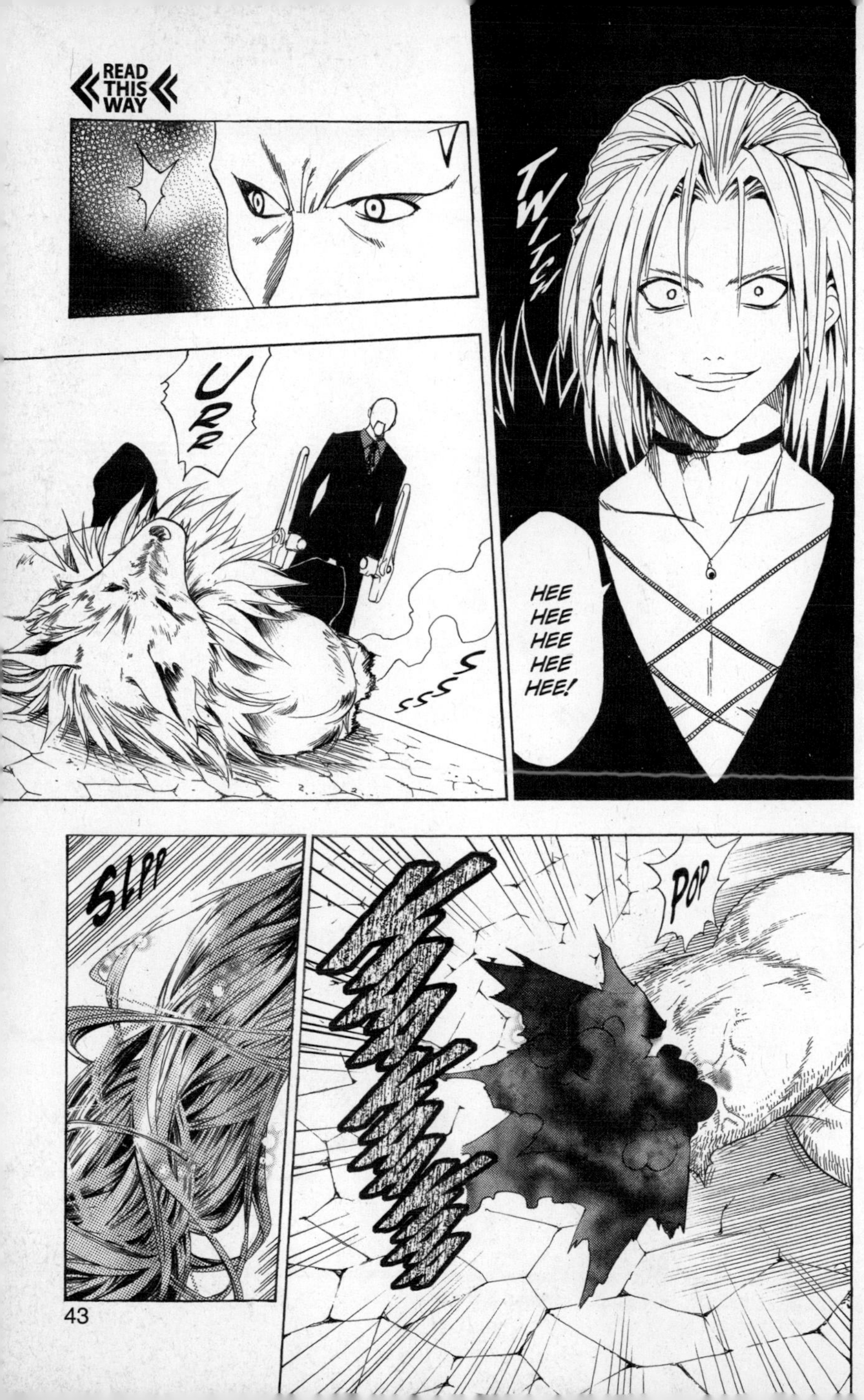

TWITCH
HEE HEE HEE HEE HEE!
URR
SSSS
POP
SLIP

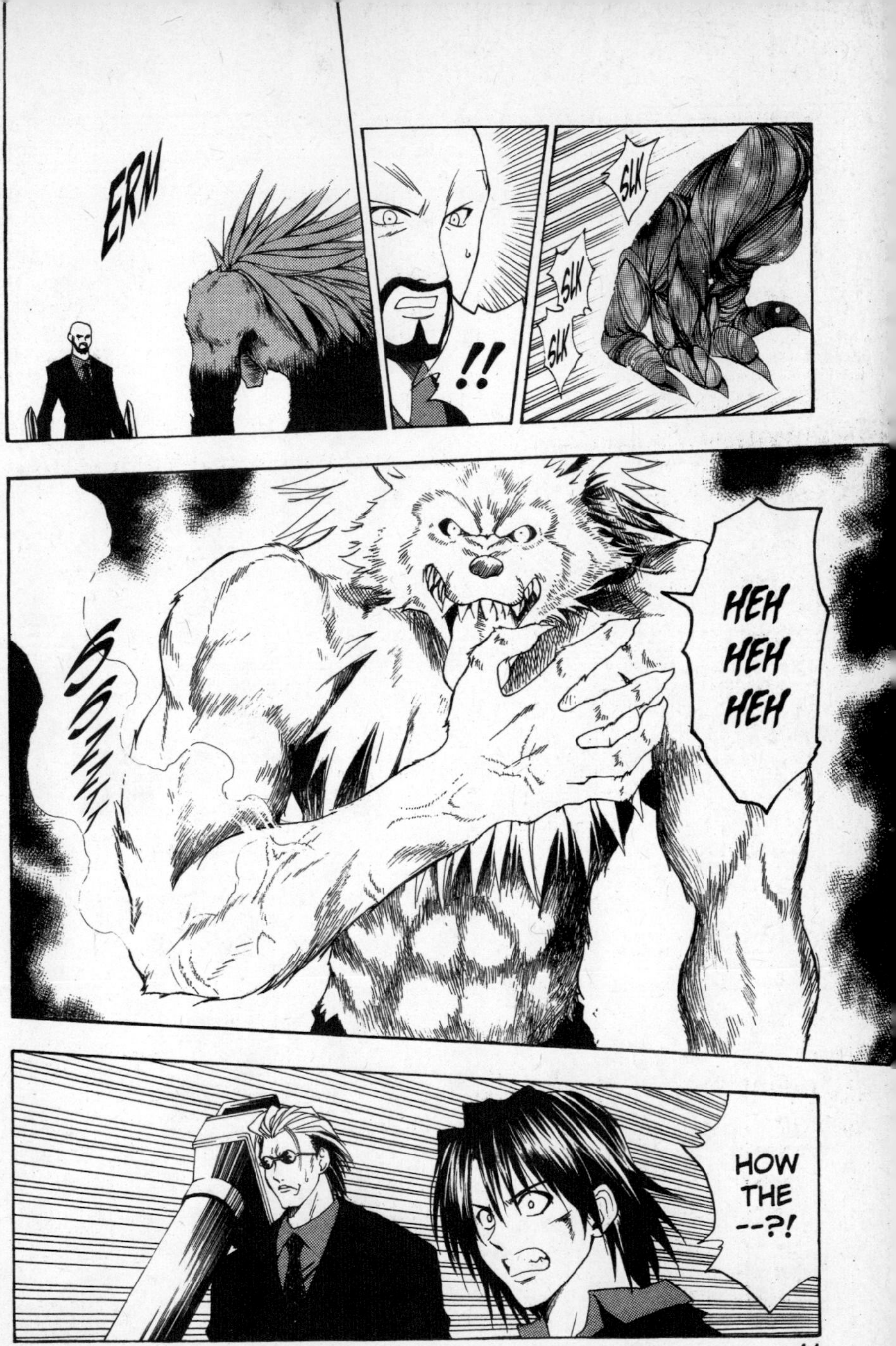
SLK
SLK
SLK
!!
ERM
HEH HEH HEH
SOOMM
HOW THE --?!

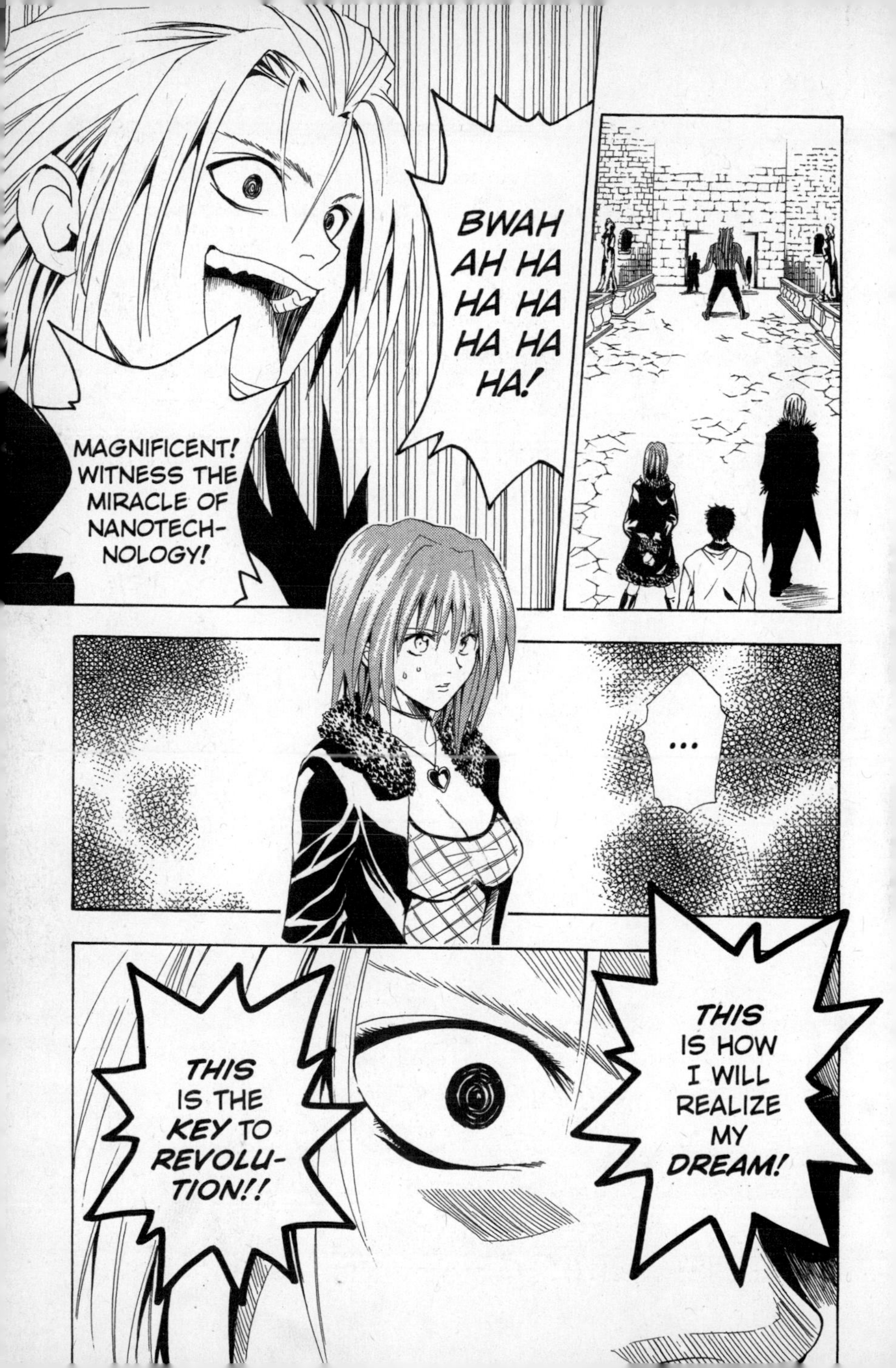
BWAH AH HA HA HA HA HA HA!
MAGNIFICENT! WITNESS THE MIRACLE OF NANOTECHNOLOGY!
...
THIS IS HOW I WILL REALIZE MY DREAM!
THIS IS THE KEY TO REVOLUTION!!

THE TAO POWER OF "GATE"

ECHIDNA'S TAO POWER ALLOWS HER TO
CREATE "GATES" IN THE ATMOSPHERE
WITH HIGHLY COMPRESSED AIR. THESE
"GATES" ENABLE HER TO INSTANTLY
TRANSPORT HERSELF UP TO A DISTANCE
OF FIFTEEN METERS. BY ADDING A TALISMAN
IN WHICH SHE HAS SEALED HER CHI TO
THE GATE, SHE CAN MAKE IT POSSIBLE
FOR SEVERAL PEOPLE TO PASS THROUGH.
ONCE A TALISMAN HAS BEEN USED,
SHE MUST RESEAL IT WITH CHI IN ORDER
TO USE IT AGAIN.

Chapter 78: Transcendent Power

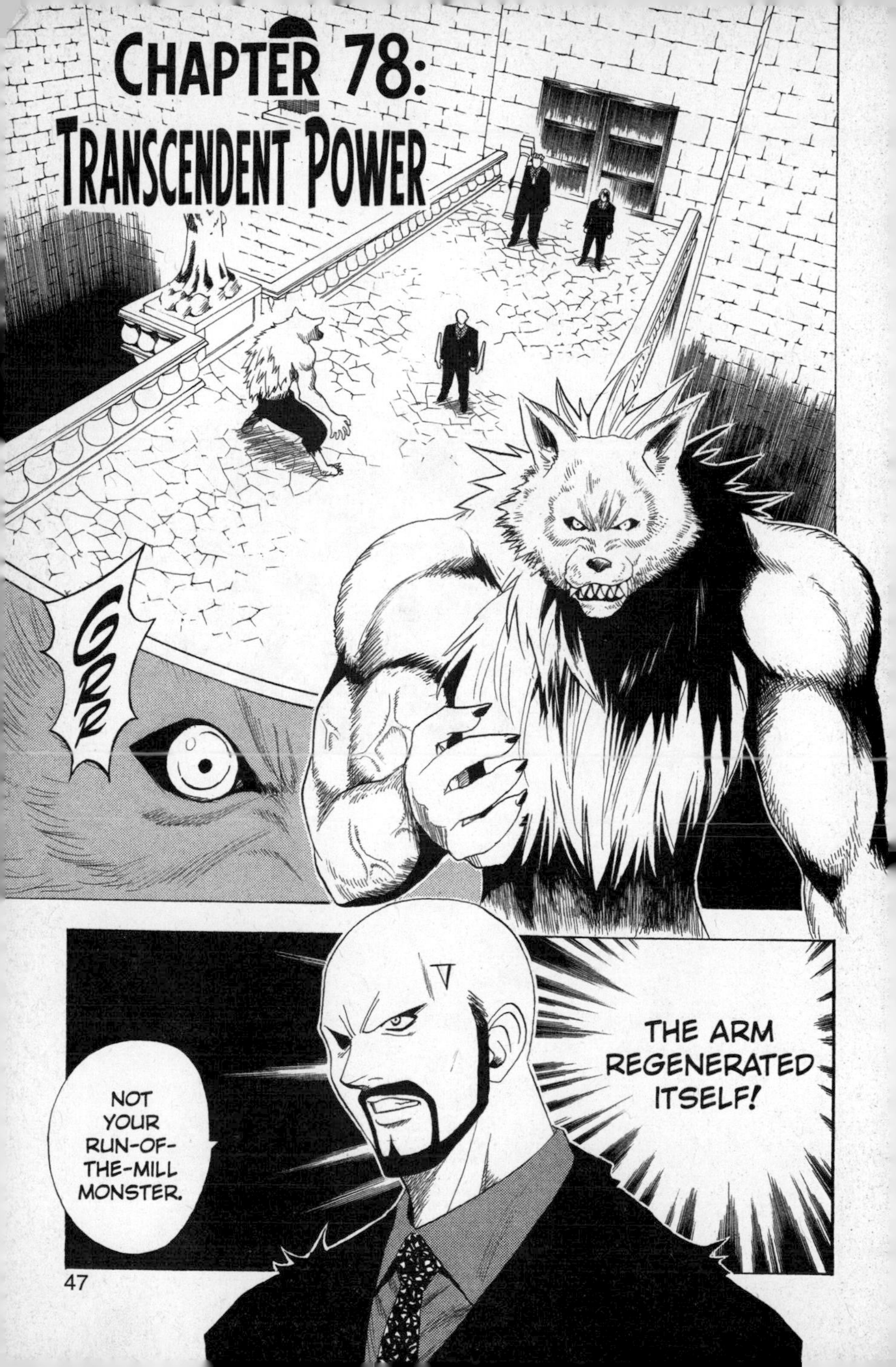
GRR
THE ARM REGENERATED ITSELF!
NOT YOUR RUN-OF-THE-MILL MONSTER.

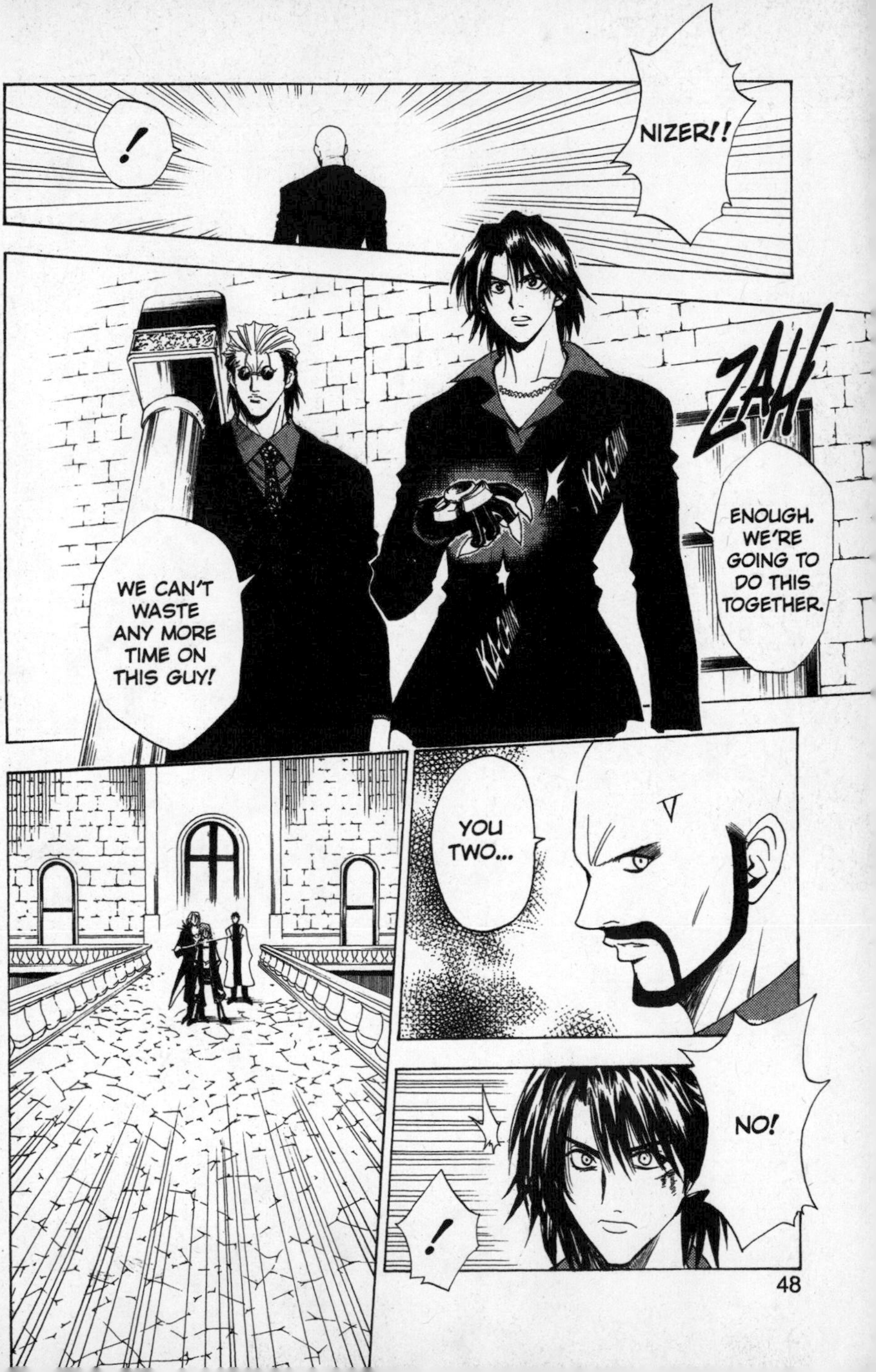
NIZER!!
!
ZAH
KA-CHIN
KA-CHIN
ENOUGH. WE'RE GOING TO DO THIS TOGETHER.
WE CAN'T WASTE ANY MORE TIME ON THIS GUY!
YOU TWO...
NO!
!

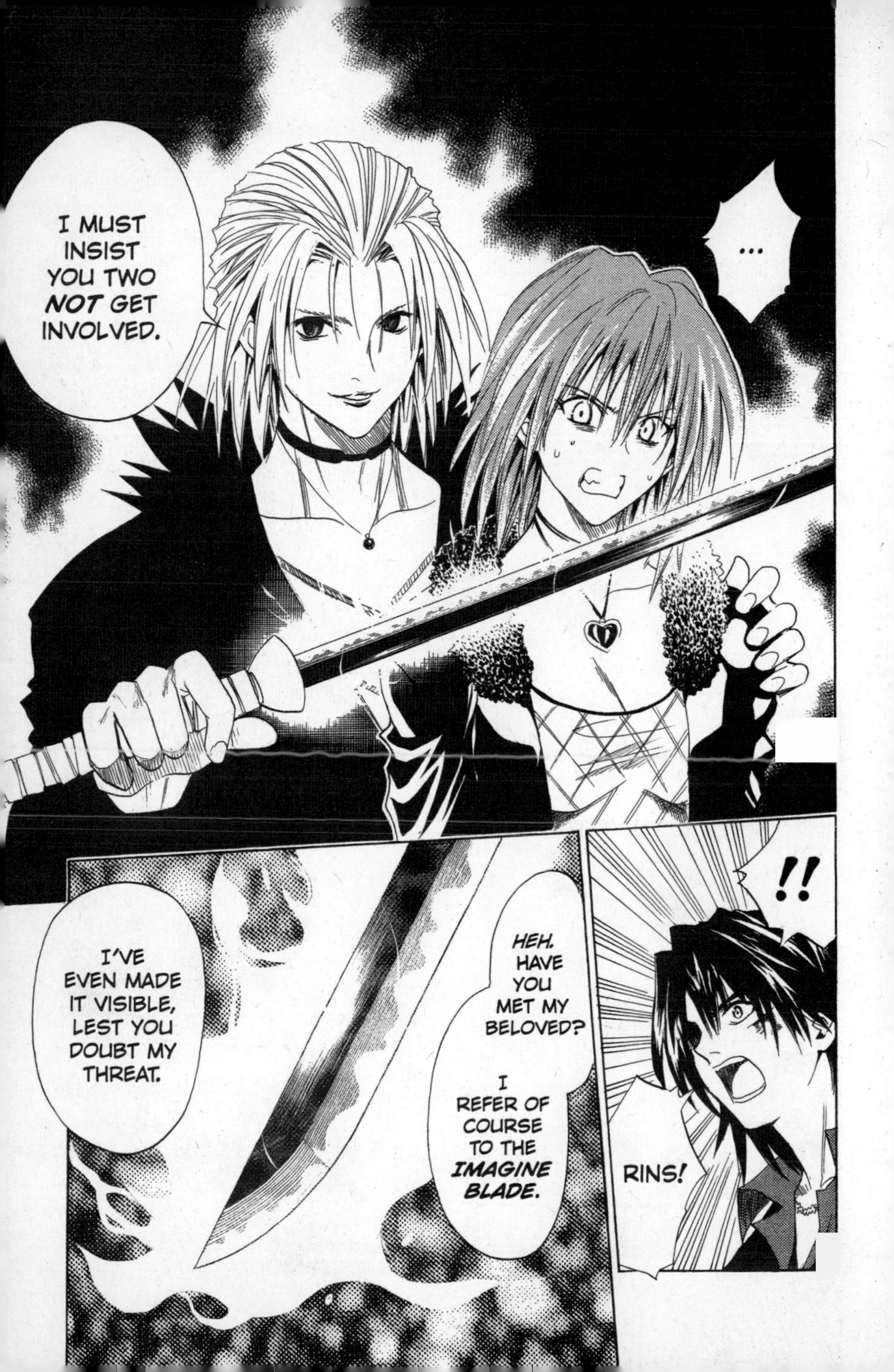
...
I MUST INSIST YOU TWO *NOT* GET INVOLVED.
!!
RINS!
HEH. HAVE YOU MET MY BELOVED?
I REFER OF COURSE TO THE *IMAGINE BLADE.*
I'VE EVEN MADE IT VISIBLE, LEST YOU DOUBT MY THREAT.

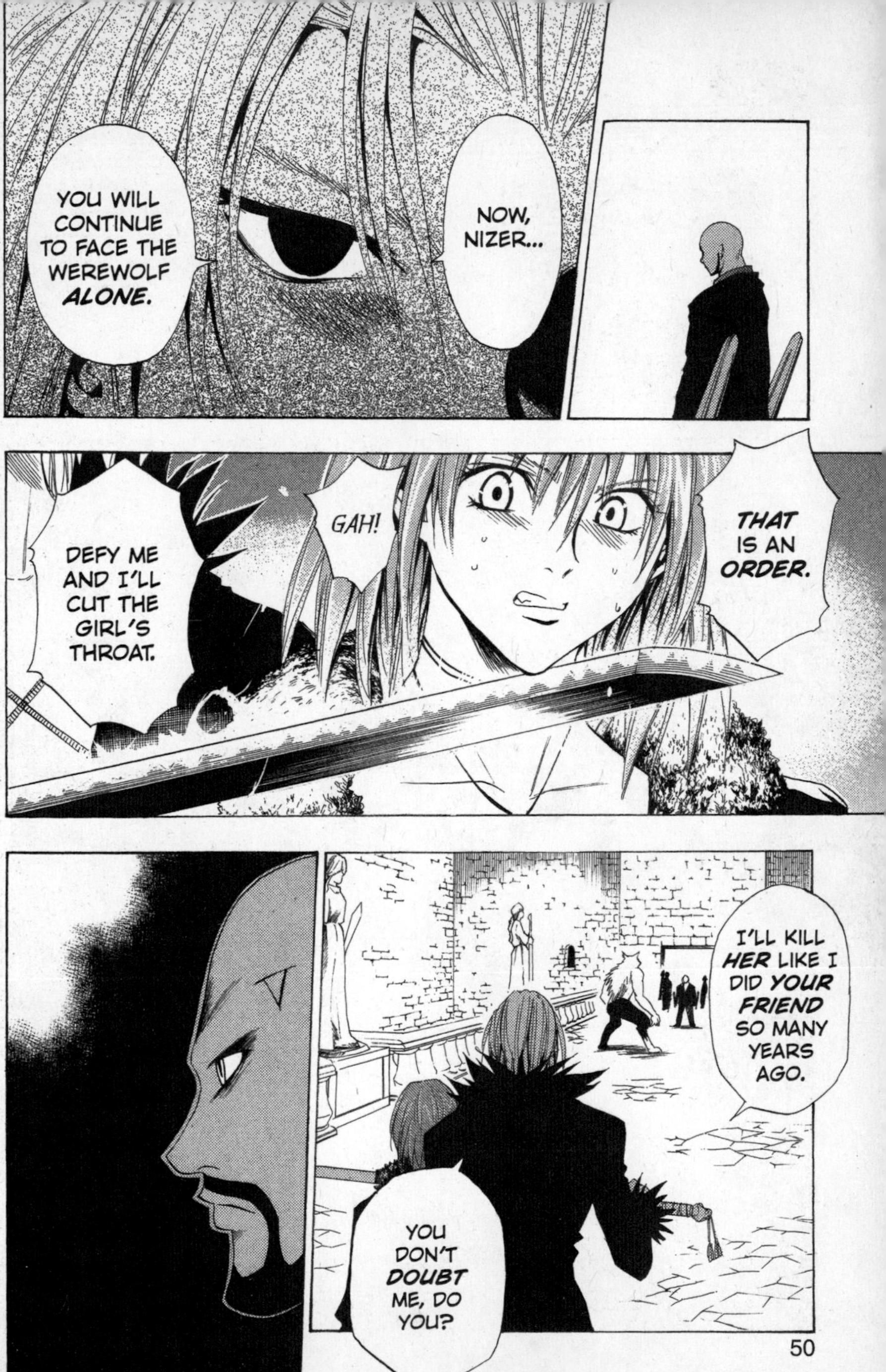
NOW, NIZER...
YOU WILL CONTINUE TO FACE THE WEREWOLF ALONE.
THAT IS AN ORDER.
GAH!
DEFY ME AND I'LL CUT THE GIRL'S THROAT.
I'LL KILL HER LIKE I DID YOUR FRIEND SO MANY YEARS AGO.
YOU DON'T DOUBT ME, DO YOU?

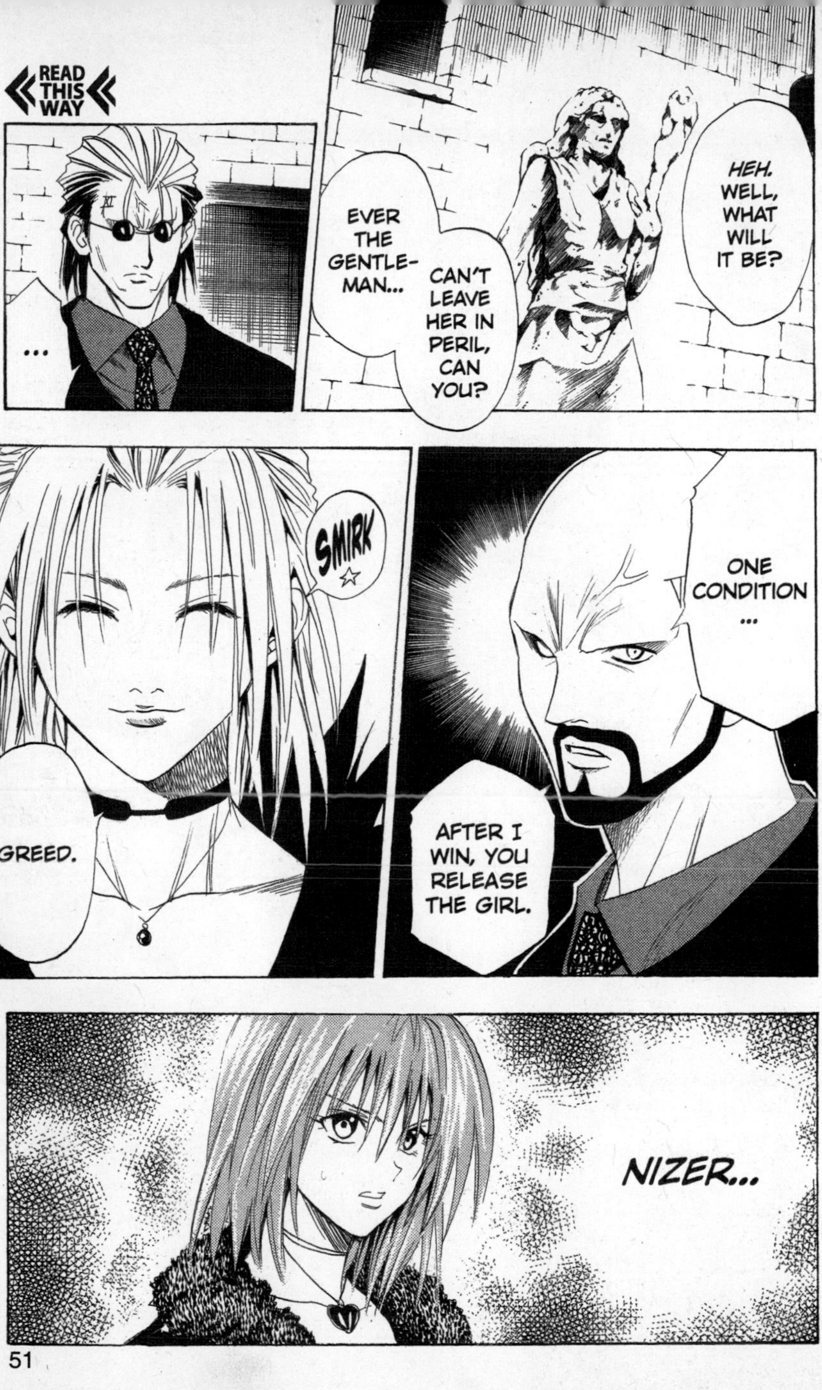
READ THIS WAY
HEH. WELL, WHAT WILL IT BE?
CAN'T LEAVE HER IN PERIL, CAN YOU?
EVER THE GENTLE-MAN...
...
ONE CONDITION ...
AFTER I WIN, YOU RELEASE THE GIRL.
SMIRK
AGREED.
NIZER...

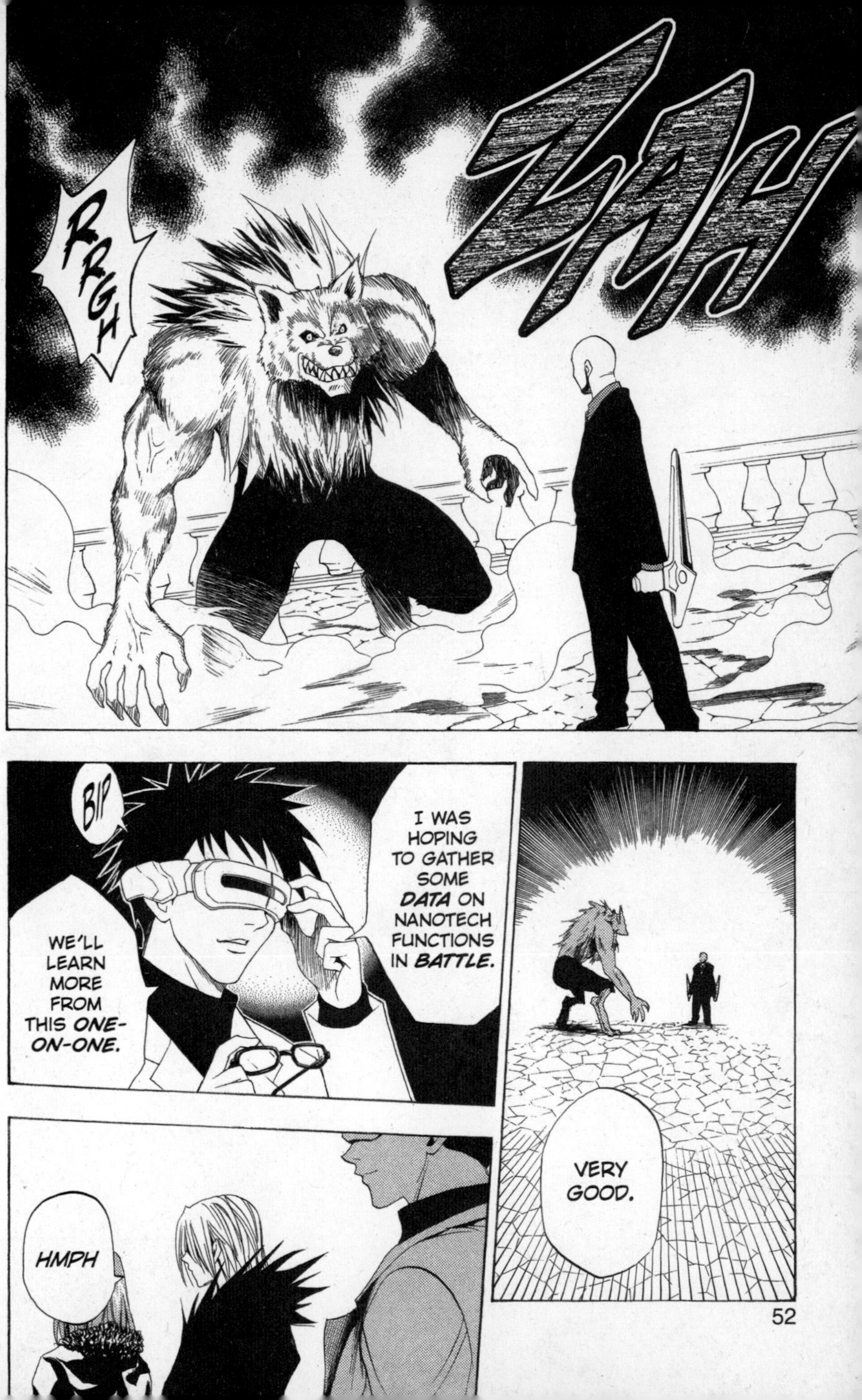
ZAAH
RRGH
BIP
I WAS HOPING TO GATHER SOME DATA ON NANOTECH FUNCTIONS IN BATTLE.
WE'LL LEARN MORE FROM THIS ONE-ON-ONE.
VERY GOOD.
HMPH

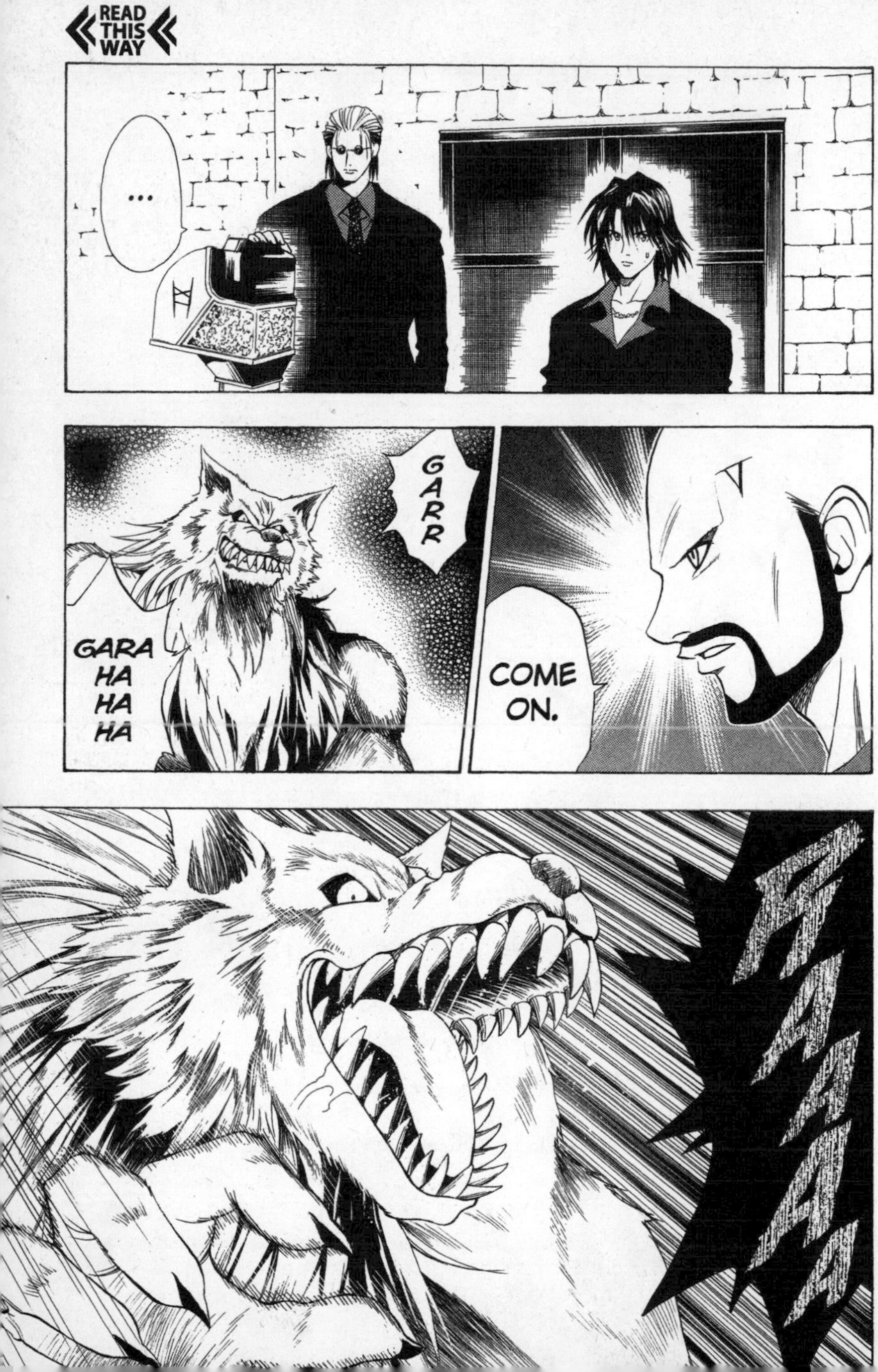
READ THIS WAY
...
COME ON.
GARR
GARA HA HA HA HA

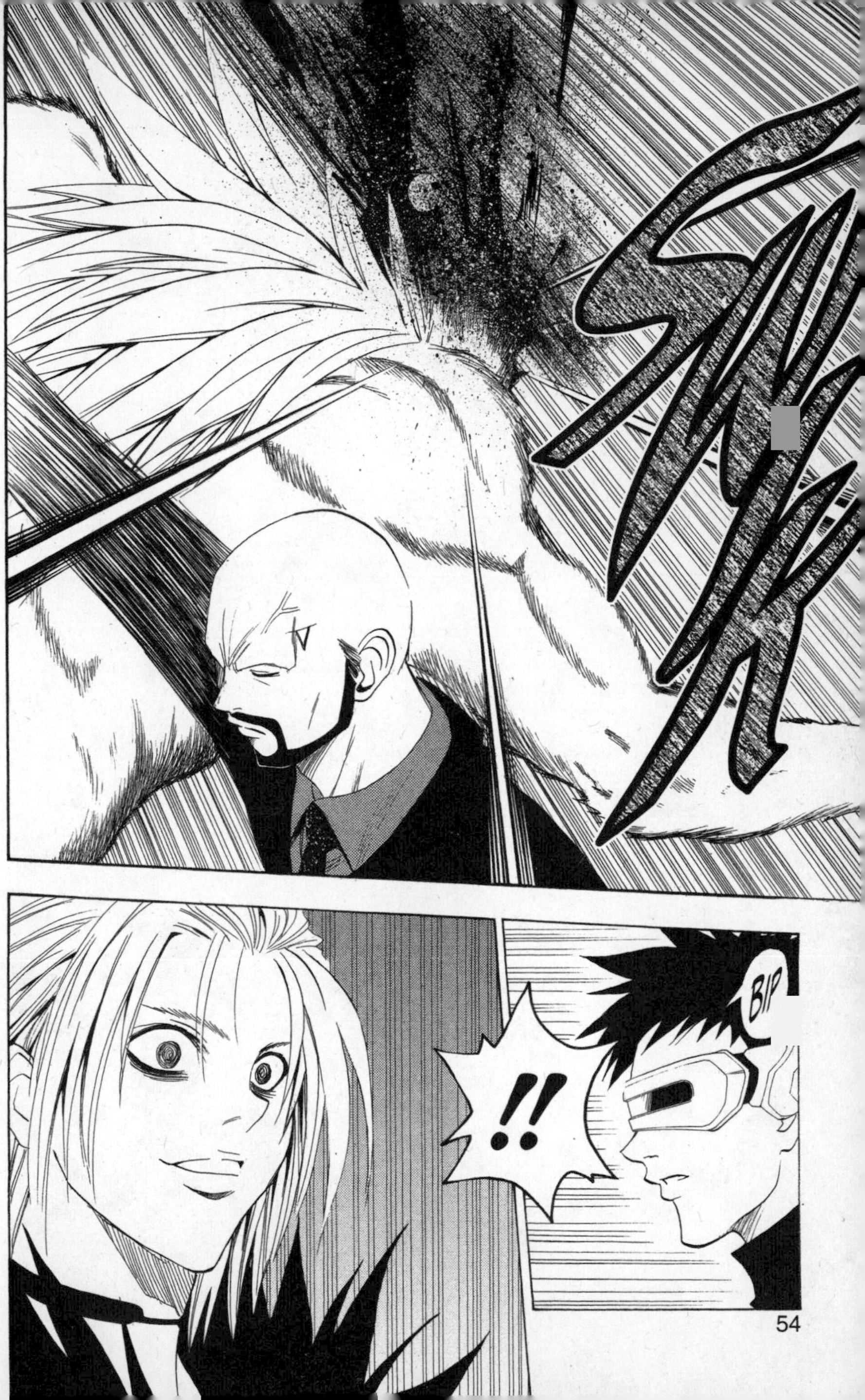
BIP
!!

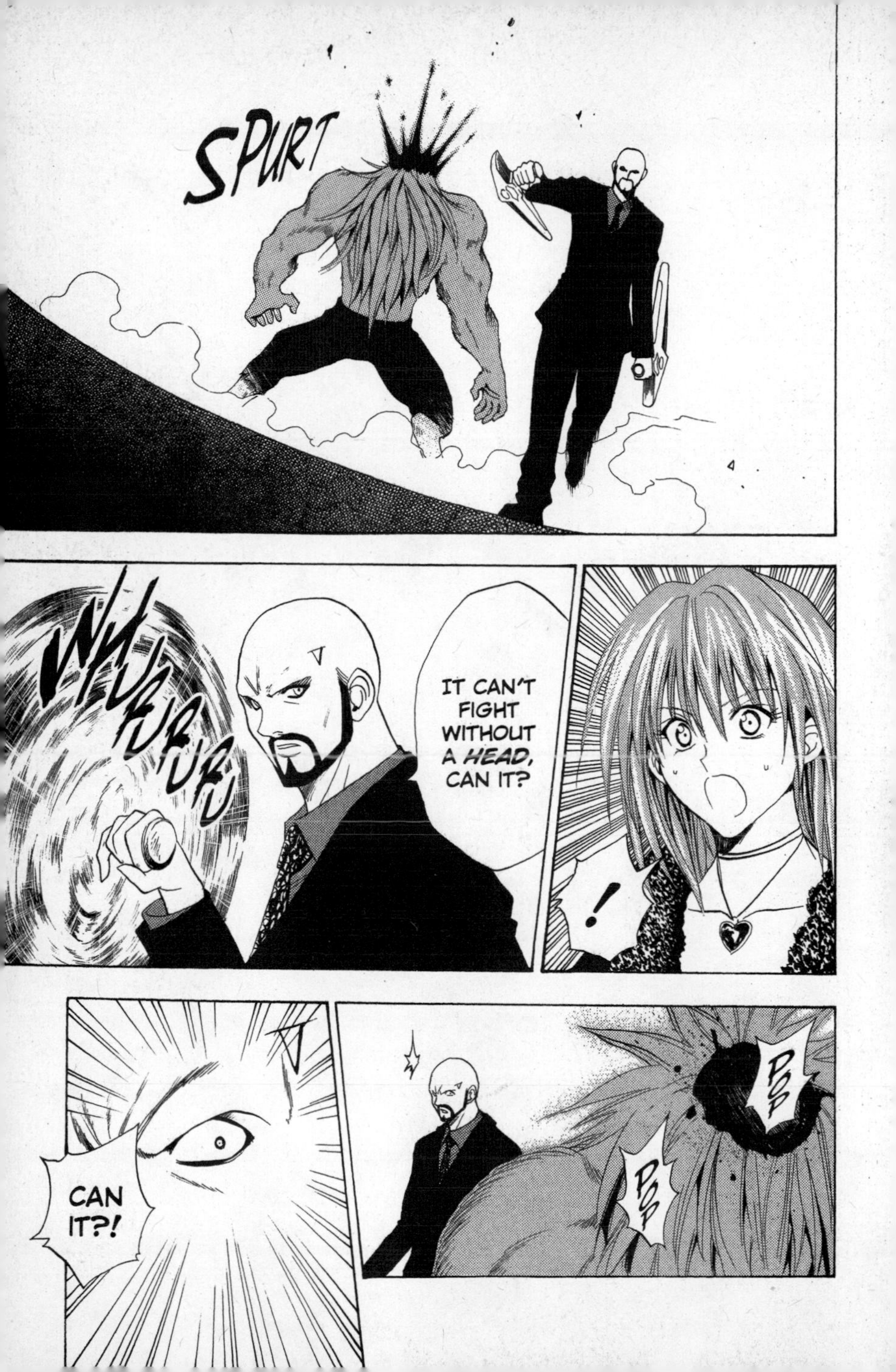
SPURT
WHUBUBUBU
IT CAN'T FIGHT WITHOUT A *HEAD*, CAN IT?
!
POP
POP
CAN IT?!

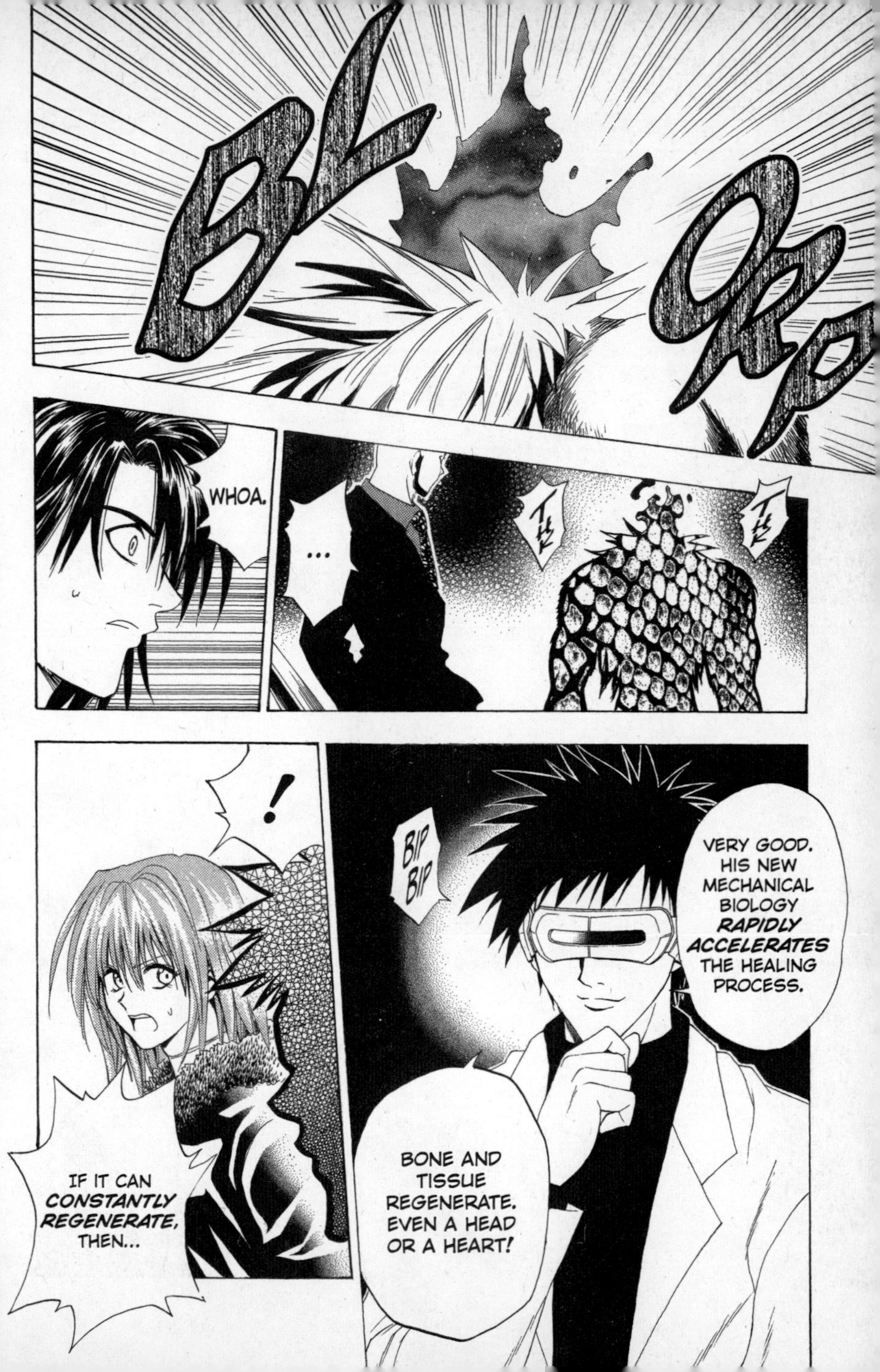
BLORP
THK
THK
...
WHOA.
BIP BIP
VERY GOOD. HIS NEW MECHANICAL BIOLOGY ***RAPIDLY ACCELERATES*** THE HEALING PROCESS.
BONE AND TISSUE REGENERATE. EVEN A HEAD OR A HEART!
!
IF IT CAN ***CONSTANTLY REGENERATE,*** THEN...

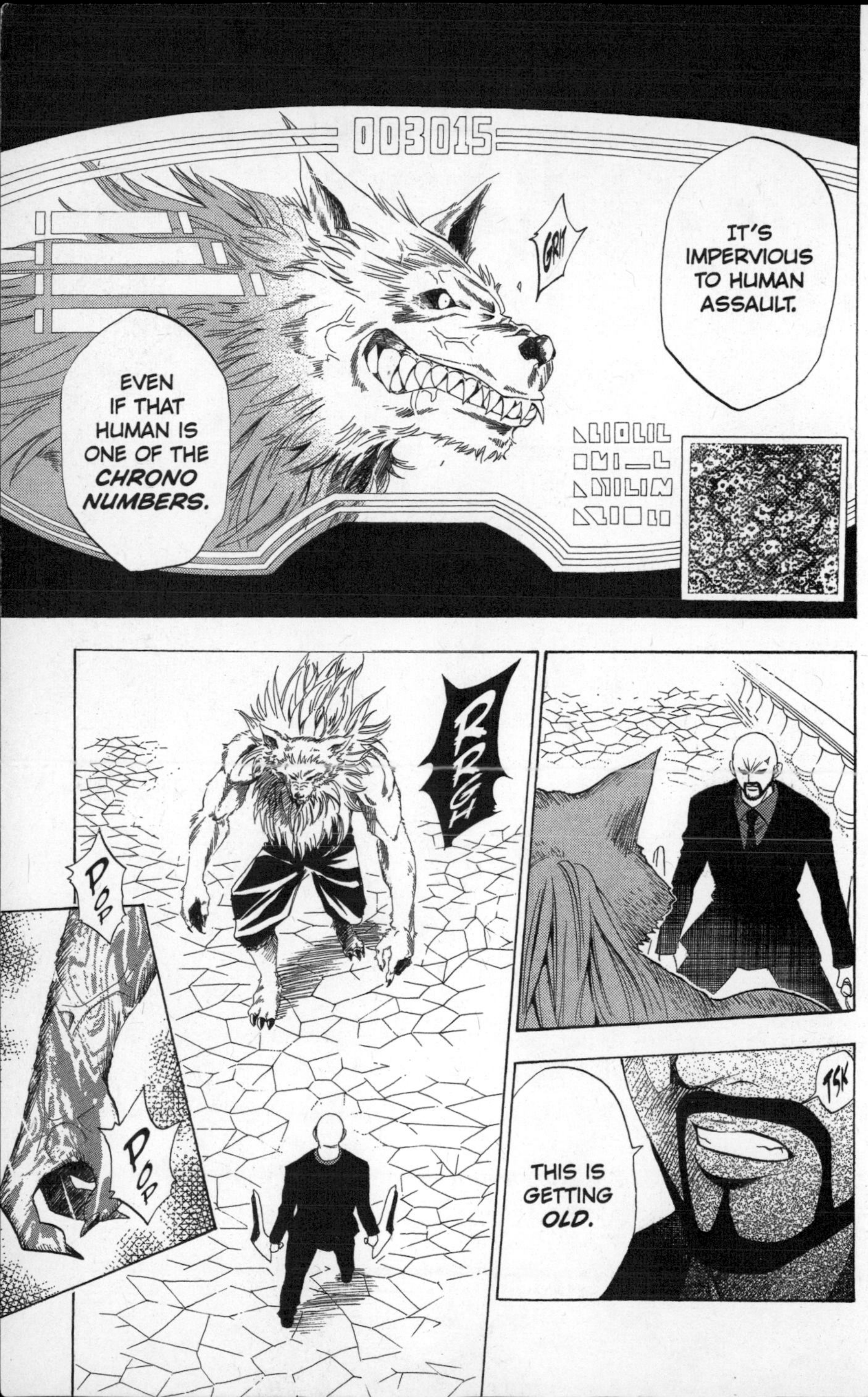
003015
IT'S IMPERVIOUS TO HUMAN ASSAULT.
GRR
EVEN IF THAT HUMAN IS ONE OF THE *CHRONO NUMBERS.*
RRGH
POP
POP
TSK
THIS IS GETTING *OLD.*

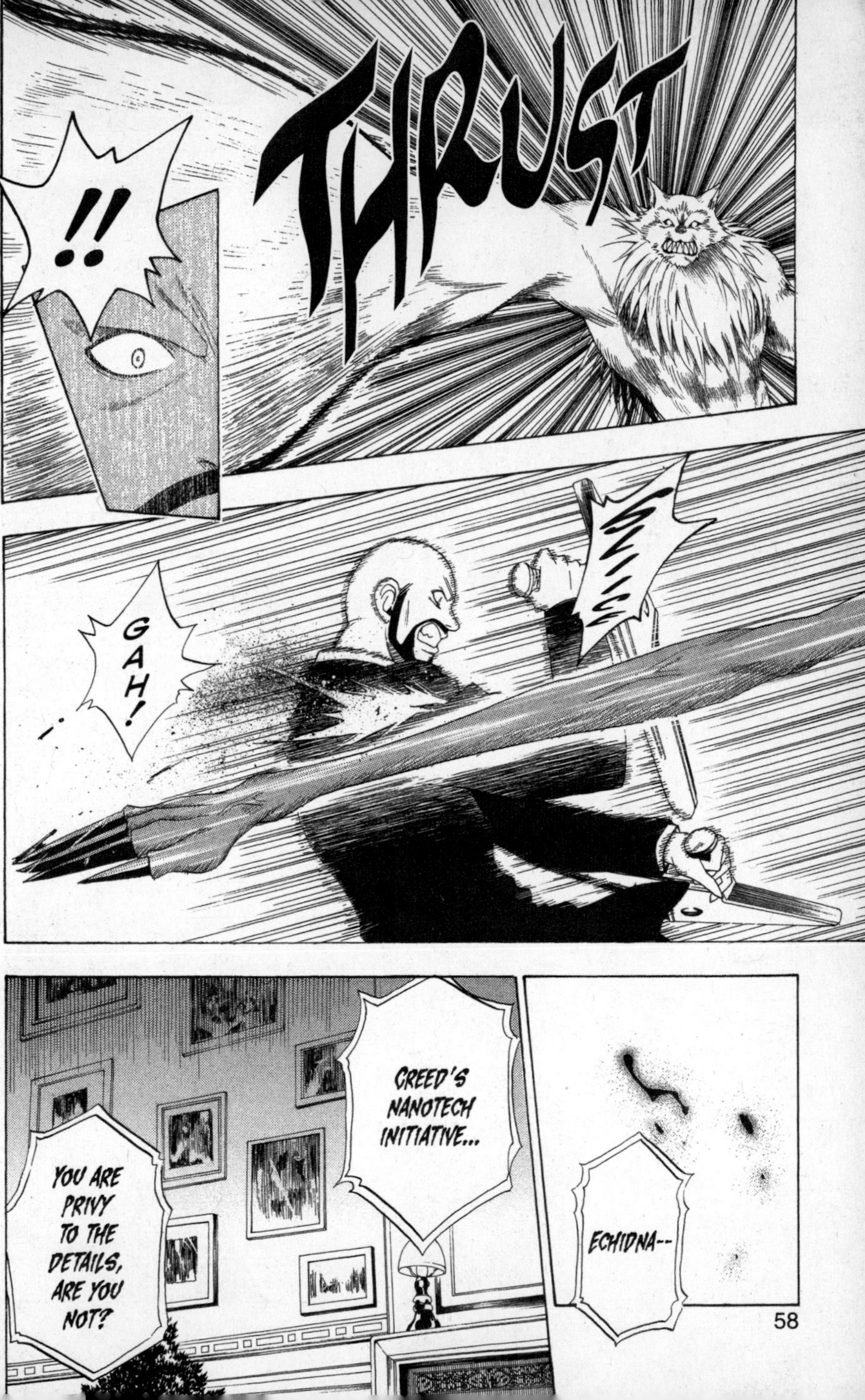
THRUST
!!
GAH!
ECHIDNA--
CREED'S NANOTECH INITIATIVE...
YOU ARE PRIVY TO THE DETAILS, ARE YOU NOT?

HAS CREED LOST HIS FAITH IN THE POWER OF TAO?

CAN YOU TELL US...

DON'T BE SILLY.

I'VE WONDERED THE SAME THING MYSELF.

WHAT'S THE STORY, ECHIDNA?

HEE HEE.

CREED NEVER INTENDED TO RELY SOLELY ON THE TAO TO BRING ABOUT REVOLUTION.

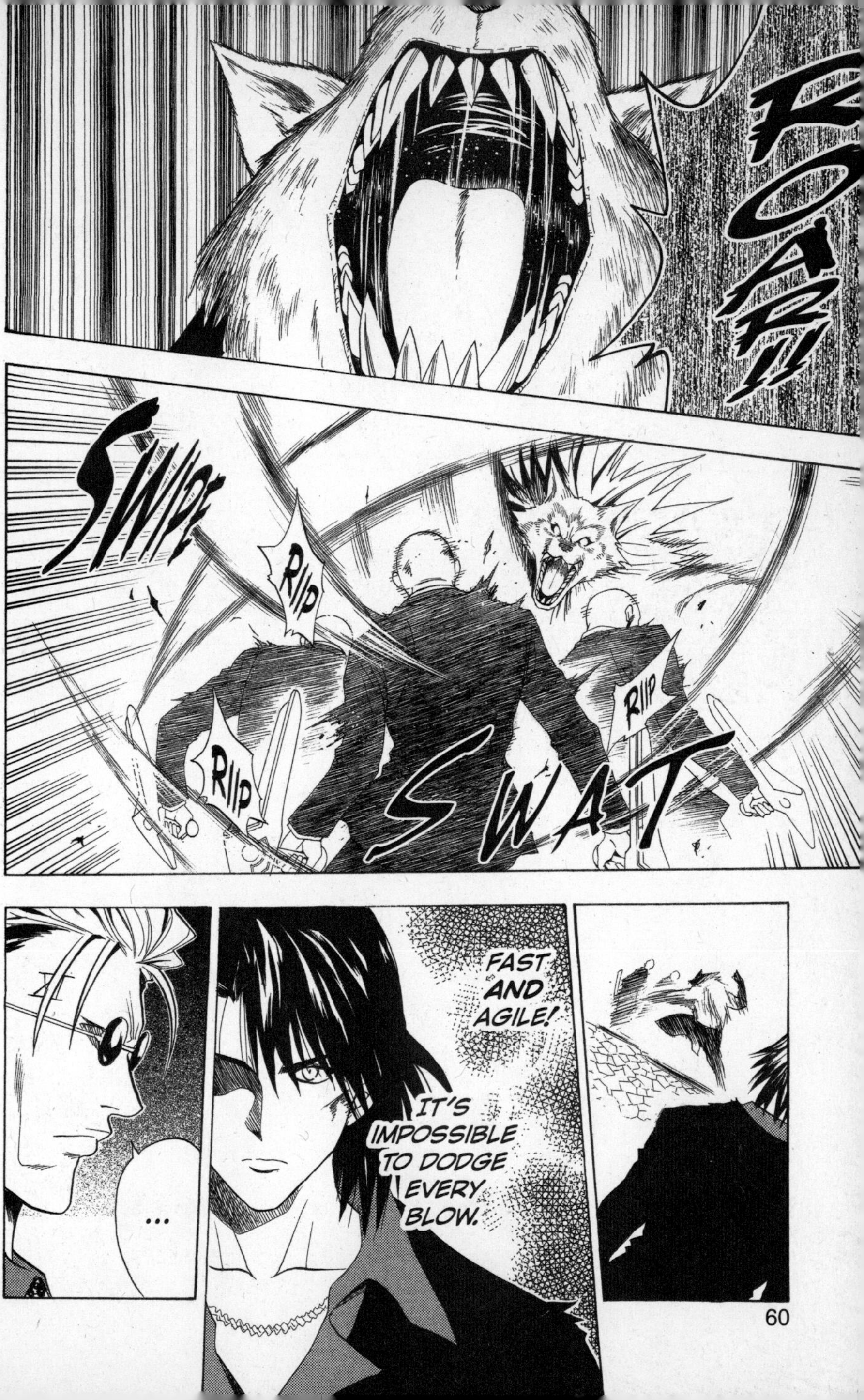
ROAR!!
SWIPE
RIIP
RIIP
RIIP
SWAT
FAST AND AGILE!
IT'S IMPOSSIBLE TO DODGE EVERY BLOW.
...

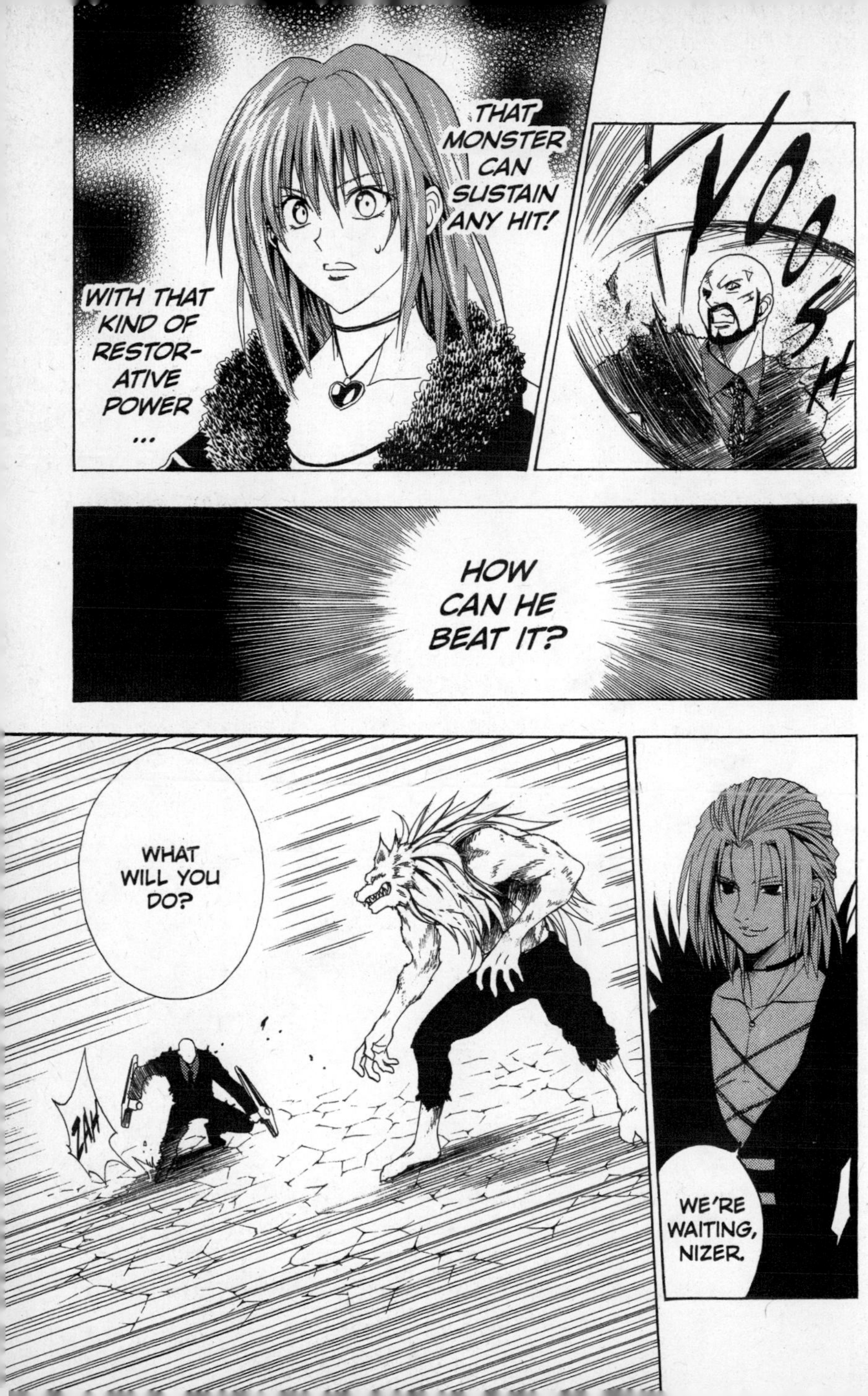
YVOOSH
THAT MONSTER CAN SUSTAIN ANY HIT!
WITH THAT KIND OF RESTOR-ATIVE POWER ...
HOW CAN HE BEAT IT?
WE'RE WAITING, NIZER.
WHAT WILL YOU DO?
ZAK

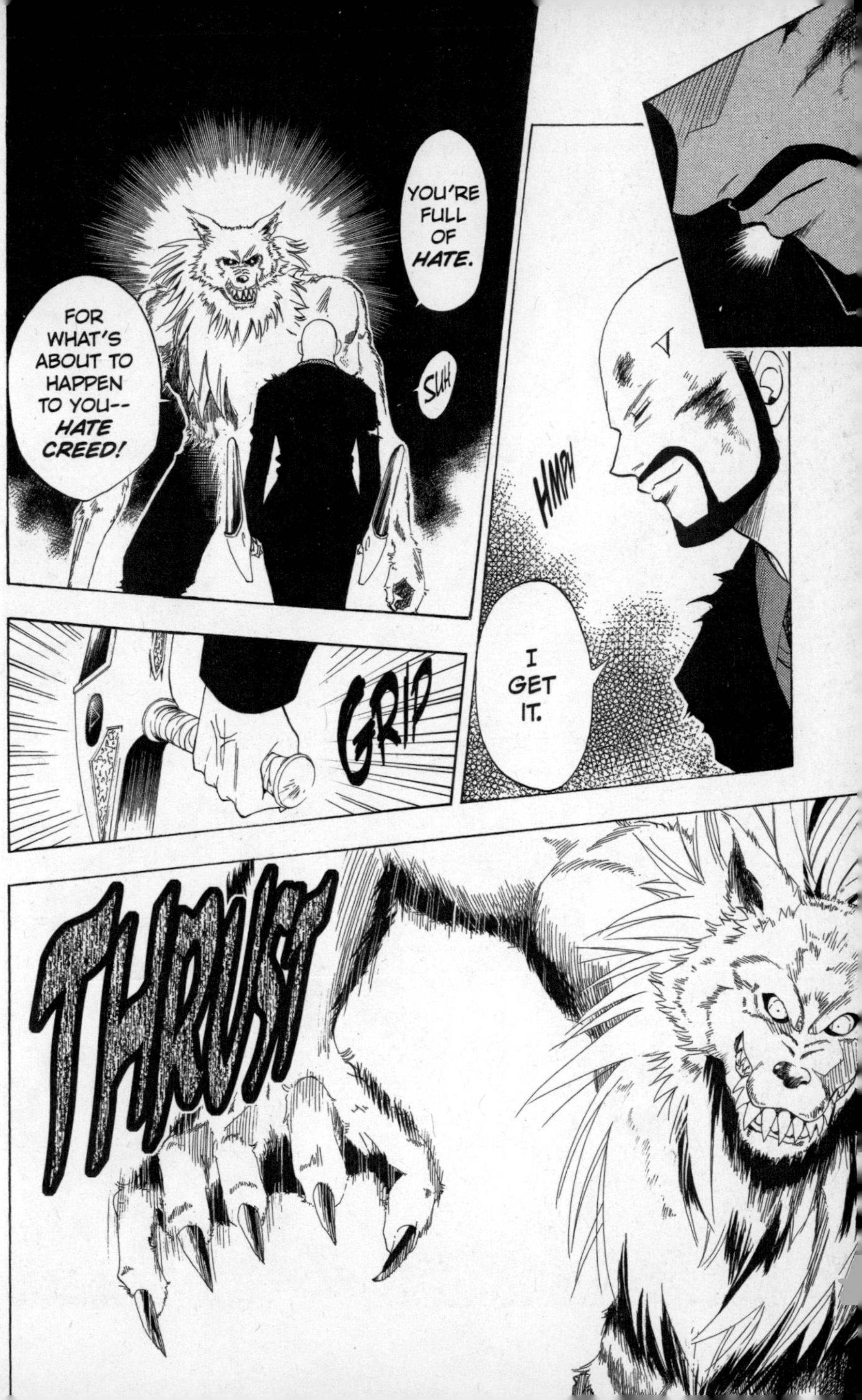
YOU'RE FULL OF *HATE.*
FOR WHAT'S ABOUT TO HAPPEN TO YOU-- *HATE CREED!*
SUH
HMPH
I GET IT.
GRIP
THRUST

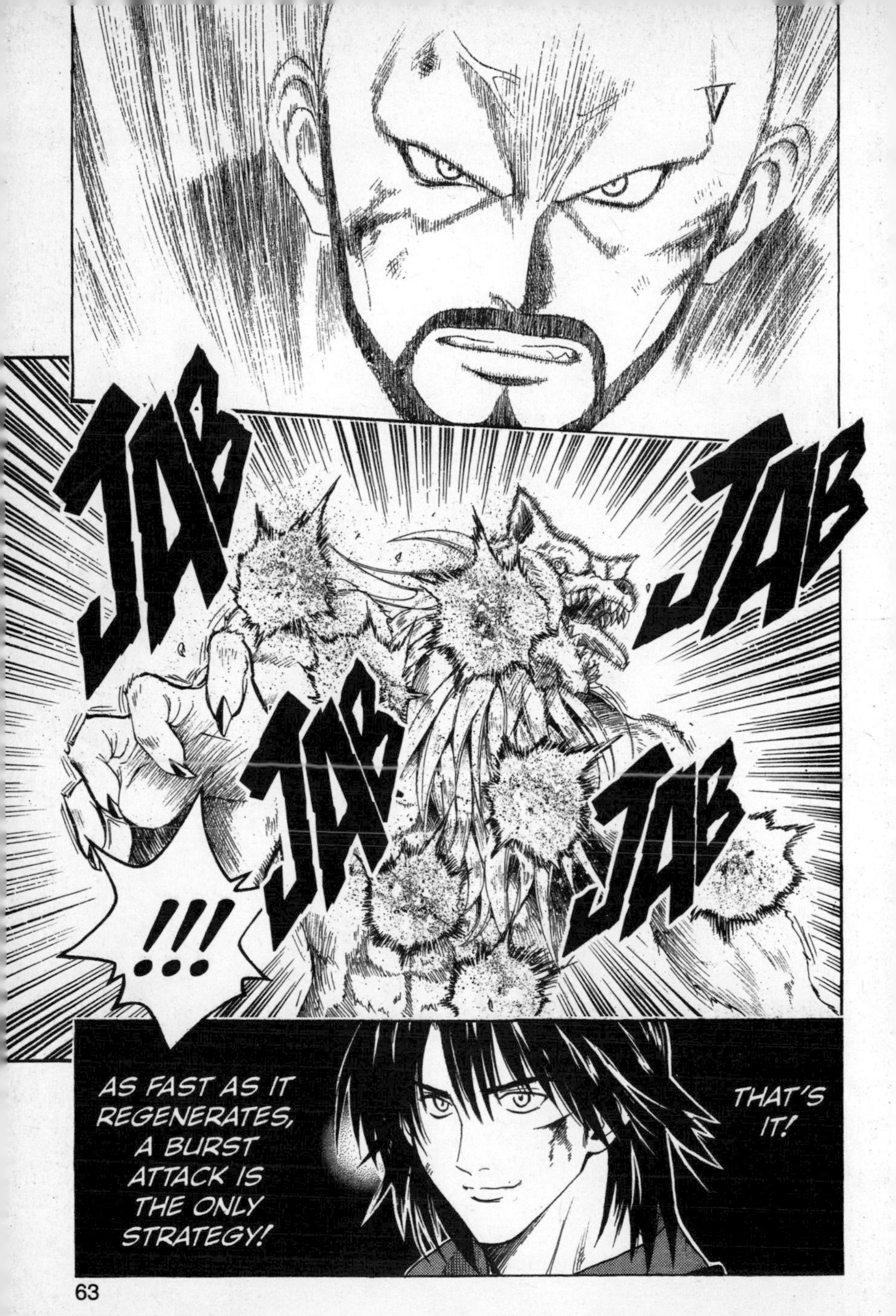
JAB
JAB
JAB
JAB
!!!
AS FAST AS IT REGENERATES, A BURST ATTACK IS THE ONLY STRATEGY!
THAT'S IT!

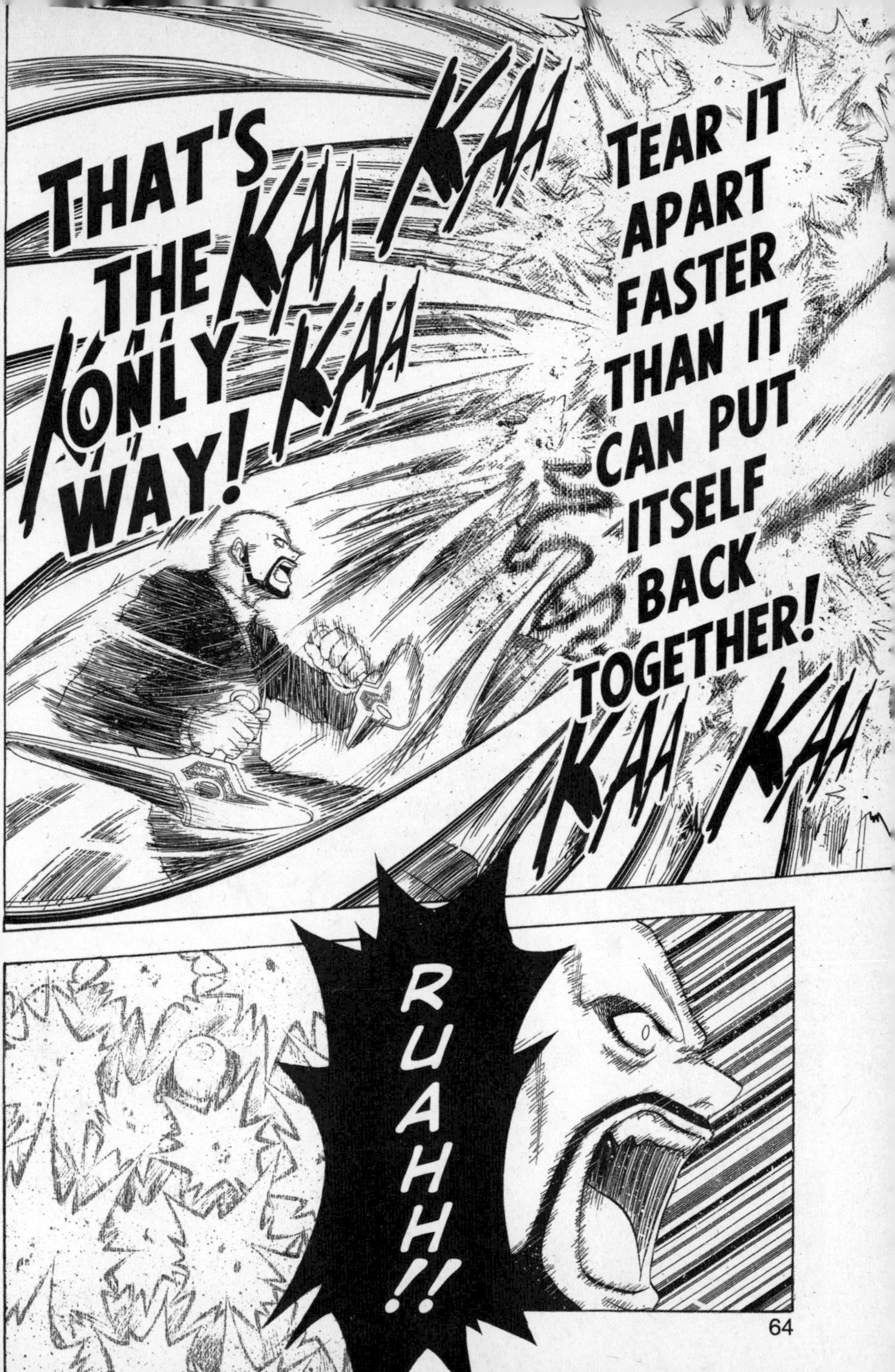
TEAR IT APART FASTER THAN IT CAN PUT ITSELF BACK TOGETHER!
THAT'S THE ONLY WAY!
KAA KAA KAA
KAA KAA
RUAHH!!

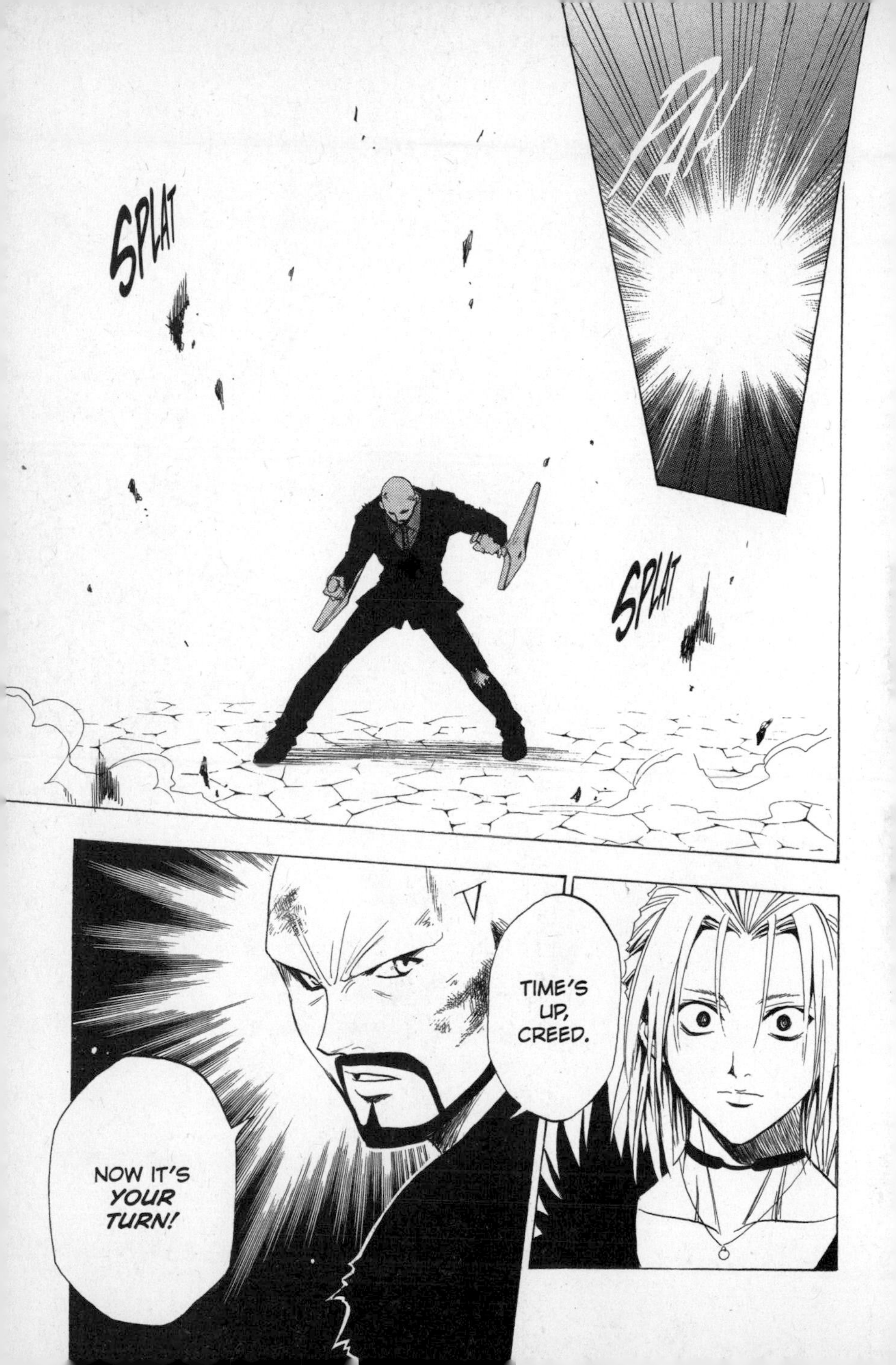
SPLAT
SPLAT
TIME'S UP, CREED.
NOW IT'S *YOUR TURN!*

◎ I DREW THIS COSPLAY FIGURE DEPICTING *DAIKOKUTEN*
OF THE SEVEN GODS OF FORTUNE AS A PIN-UP FOR *JUMP*.

I ENJOY LETTING MY IMAGINATION GO WILD AND DRAWING THINGS
I CAN'T JUSTIFY IN THE CONTEXT OF THE MANGA.

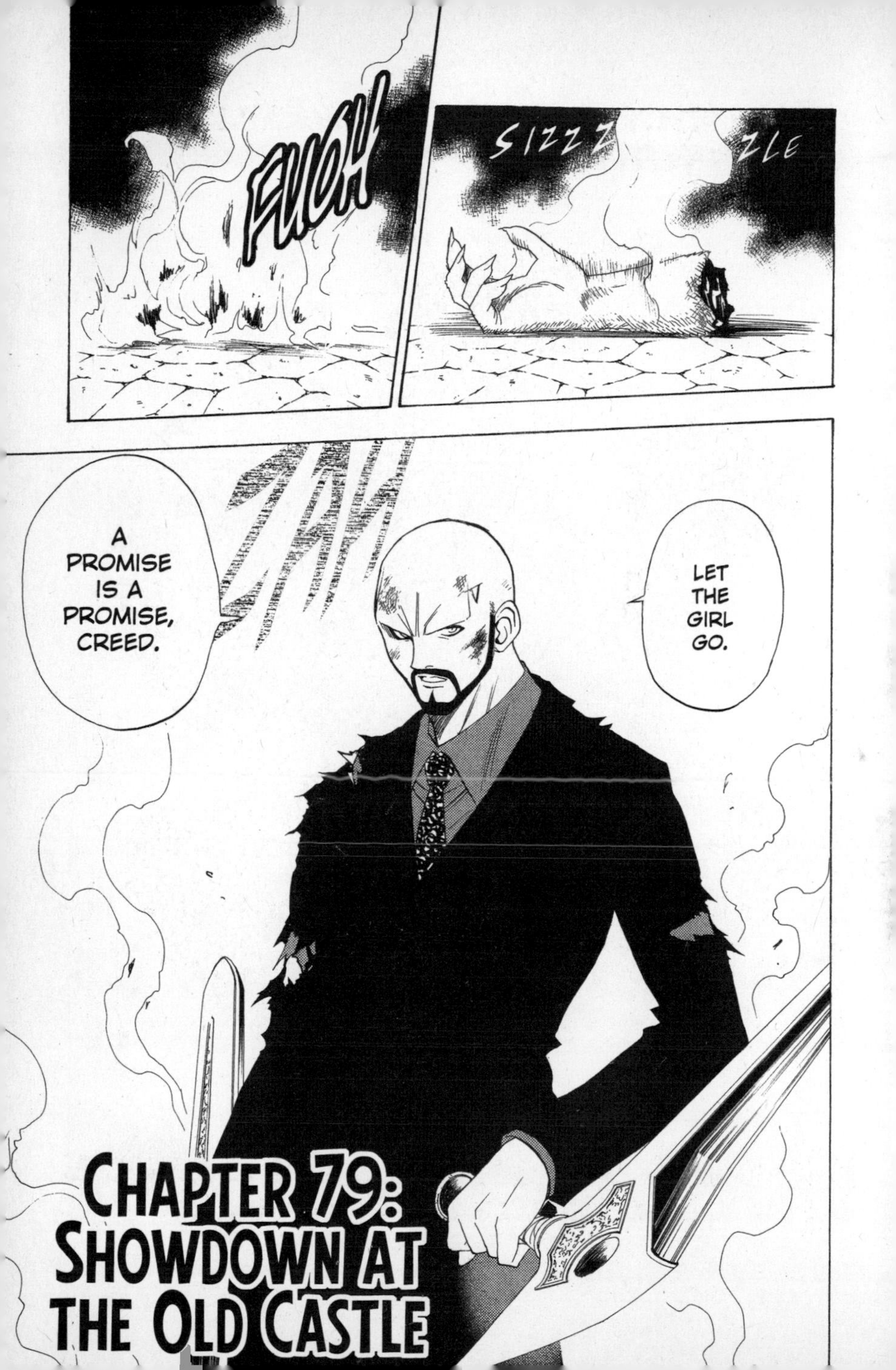
SIZZZ
ZLE
LET THE GIRL GO.
A PROMISE IS A PROMISE, CREED.
CHAPTER 79: SHOWDOWN AT THE OLD CASTLE

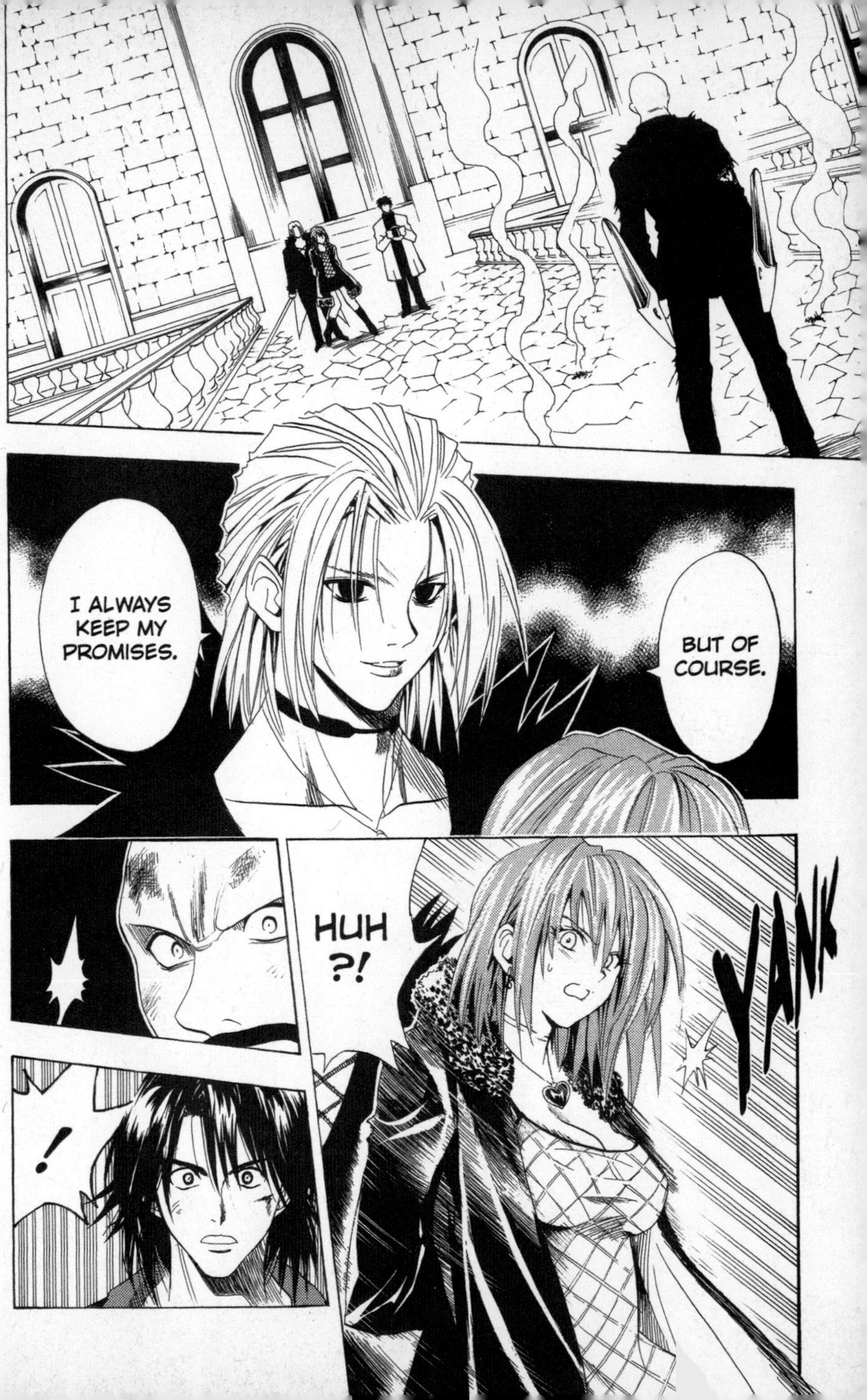
BUT OF COURSE.
I ALWAYS KEEP MY PROMISES.
YANK
HUH ?!
!

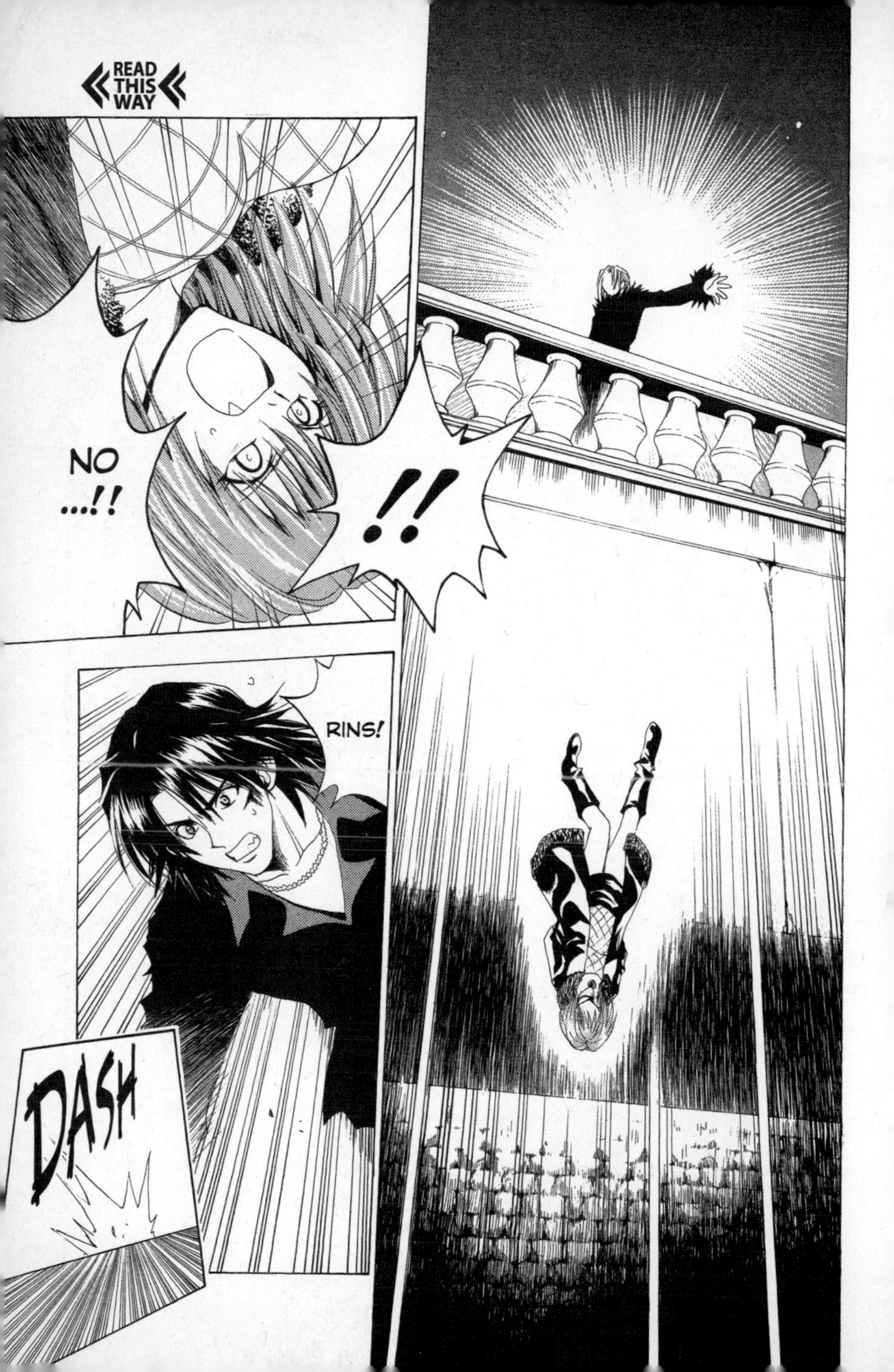
READ THIS WAY
!!
NO ...!!
RINS!
DASH

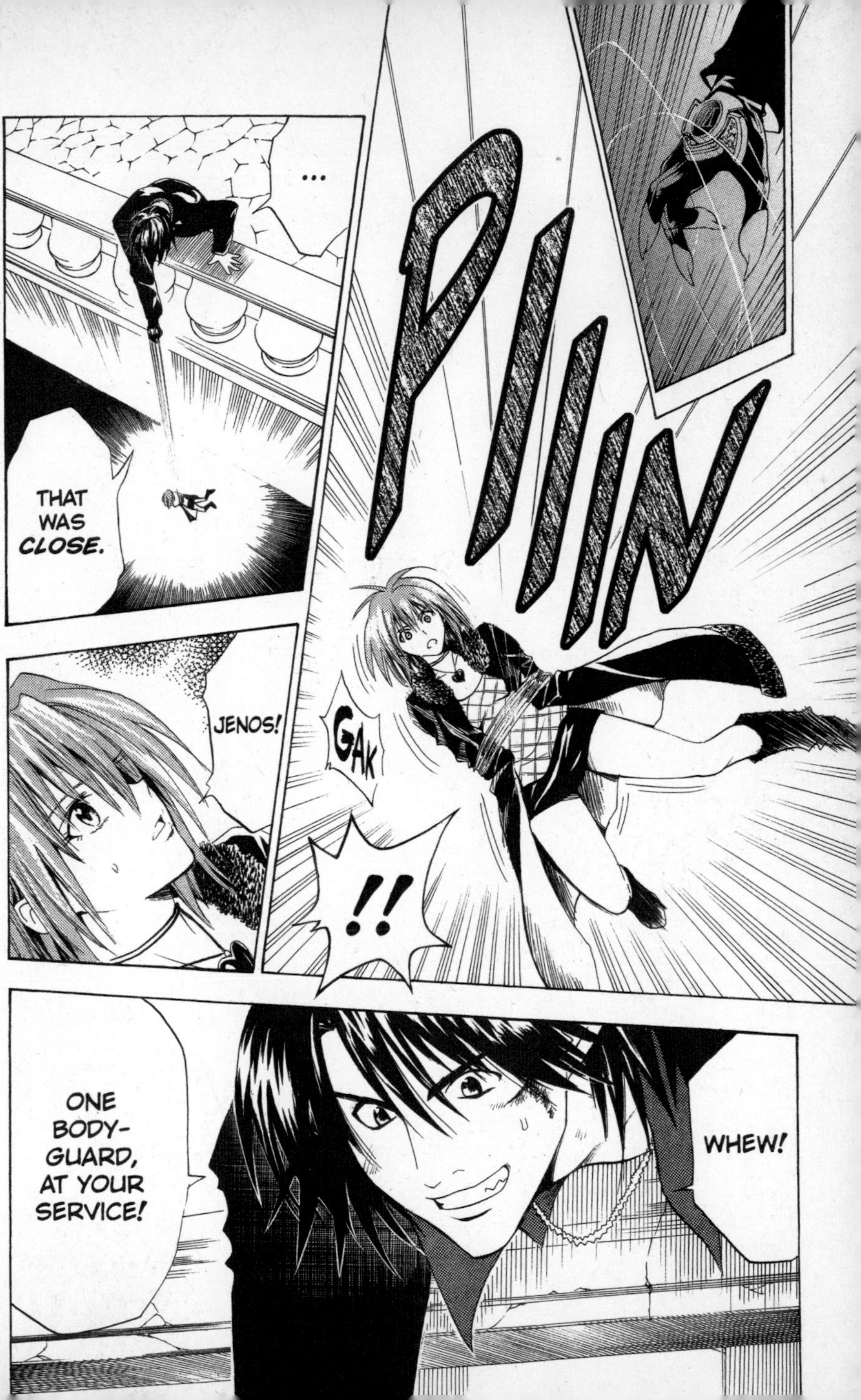
PIIIN
...
THAT WAS CLOSE.
GAK
!!
JENOS!
WHEW!
ONE BODY-GUARD, AT YOUR SERVICE!

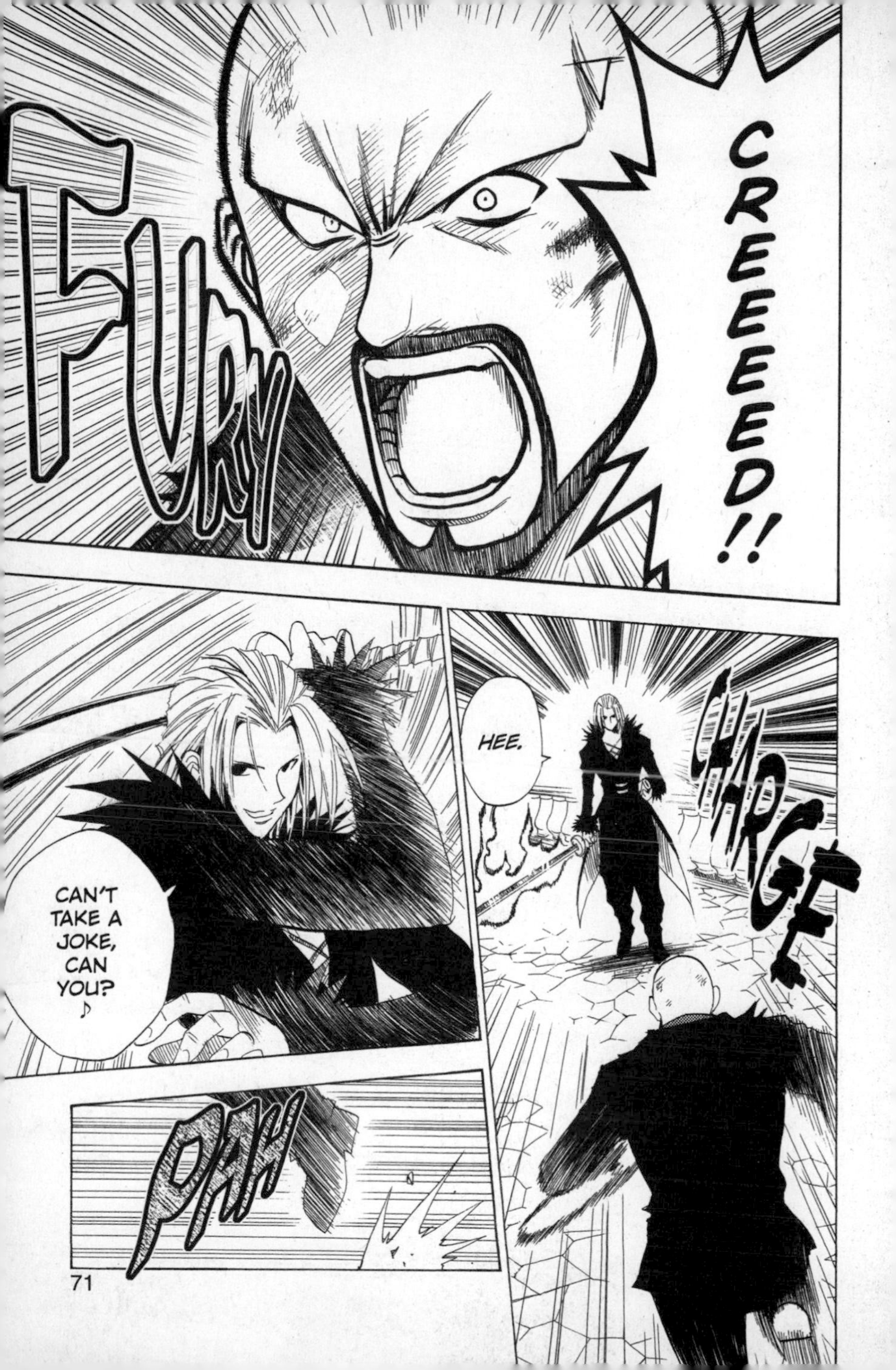
CREEEEED!!
FURY
HEE.
CHARGE
CAN'T TAKE A JOKE, CAN YOU? ♪
DAH

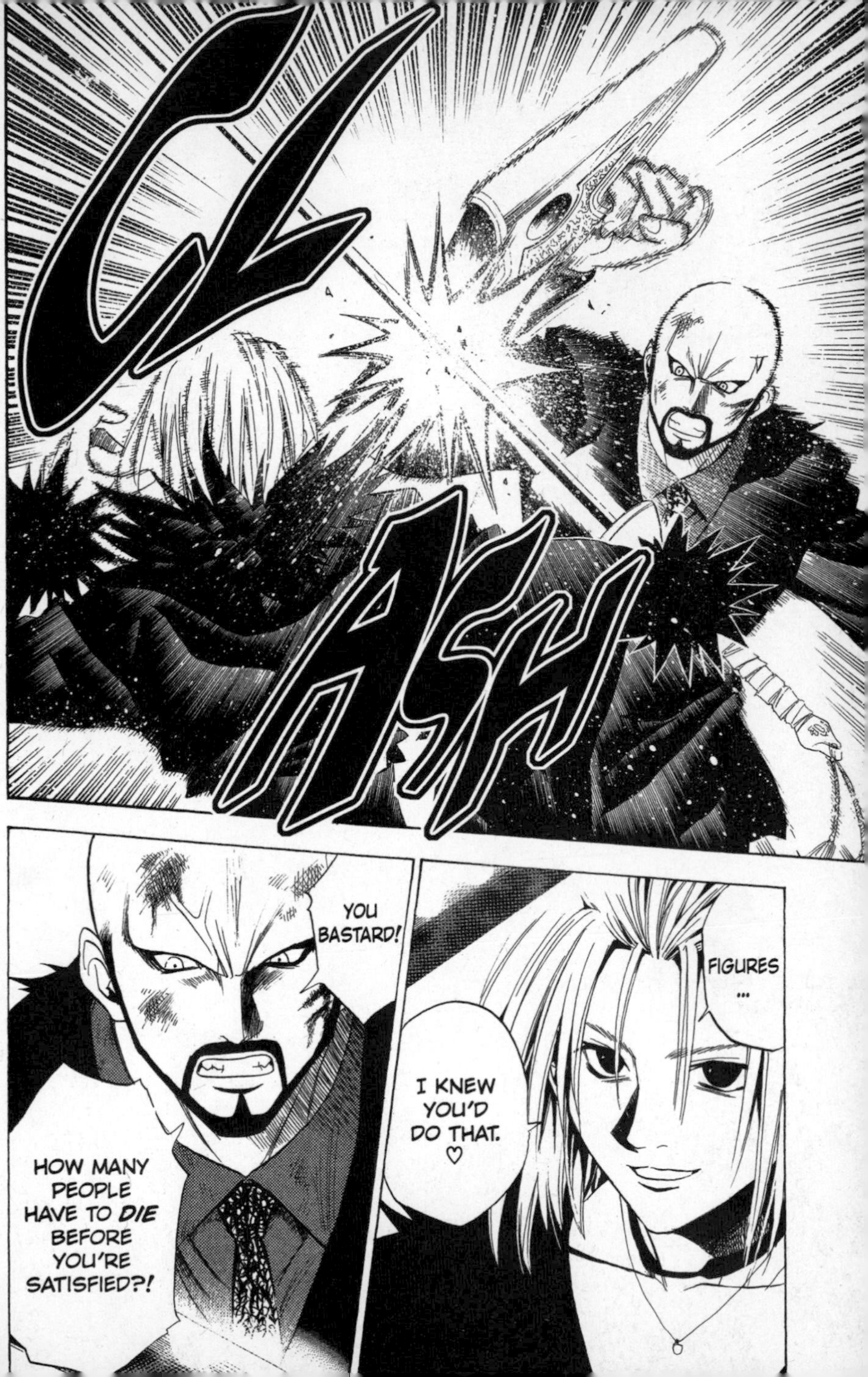
FIGURES ...
I KNEW YOU'D DO THAT. ♡
YOU BASTARD!
HOW MANY PEOPLE HAVE TO *DIE* BEFORE YOU'RE SATISFIED?!

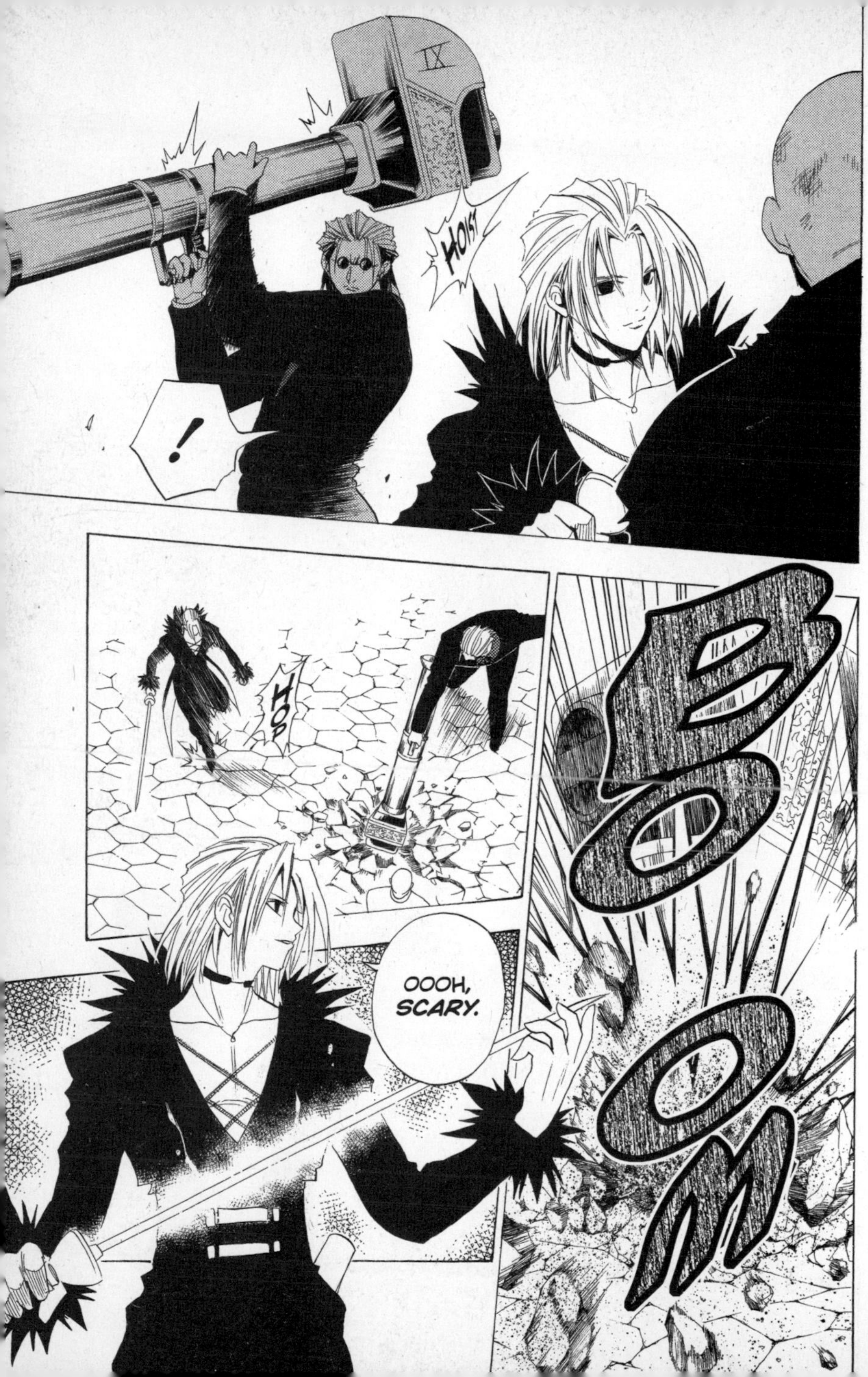
HOIST
!
BOOOM
HOP
OOOH, SCARY.

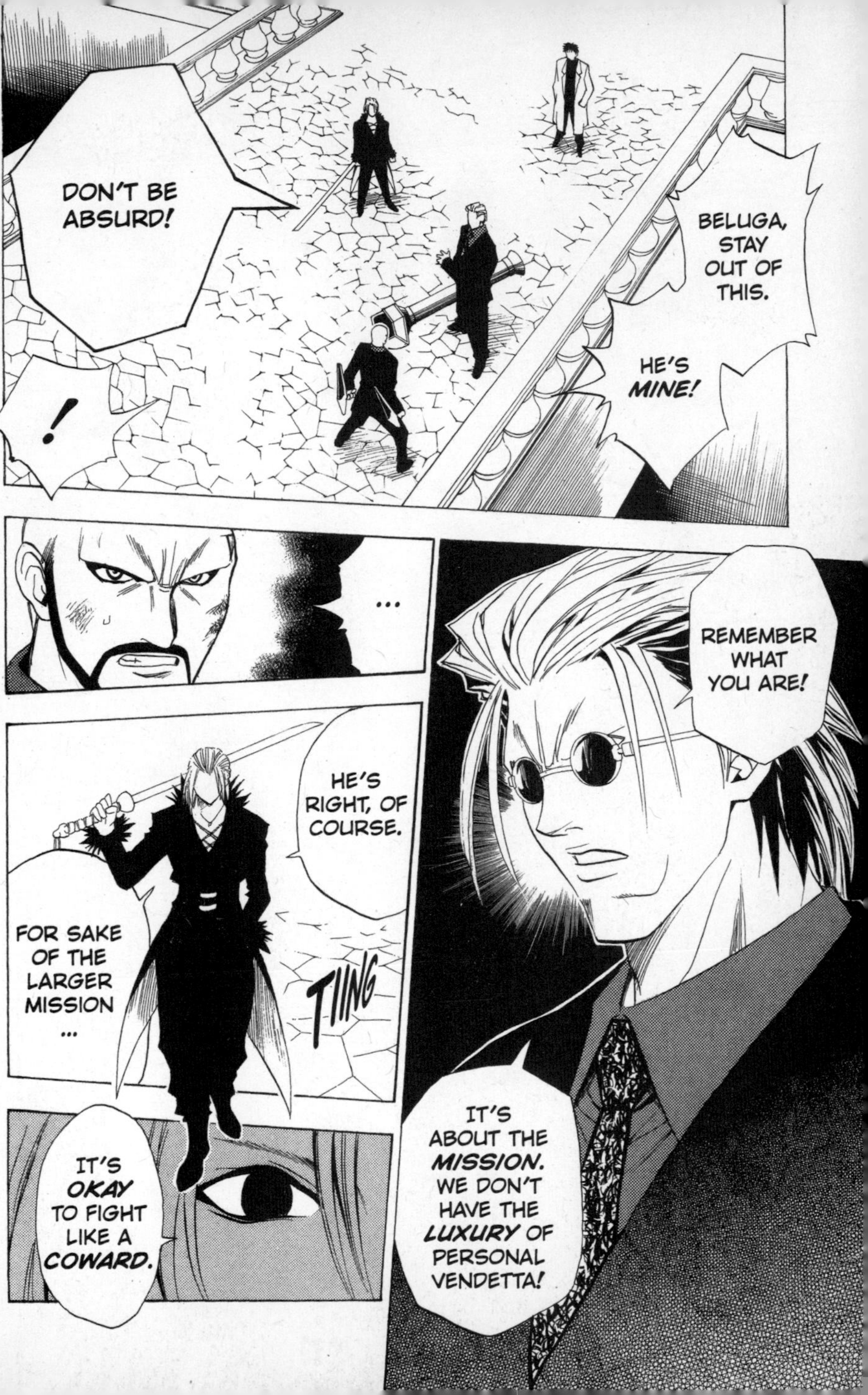
BELUGA, STAY OUT OF THIS.
HE'S MINE!
DON'T BE ABSURD!
!
REMEMBER WHAT YOU ARE!
...
HE'S RIGHT, OF COURSE.
FOR SAKE OF THE LARGER MISSION ...
TIING
IT'S ABOUT THE MISSION. WE DON'T HAVE THE LUXURY OF PERSONAL VENDETTA!
IT'S OKAY TO FIGHT LIKE A COWARD.

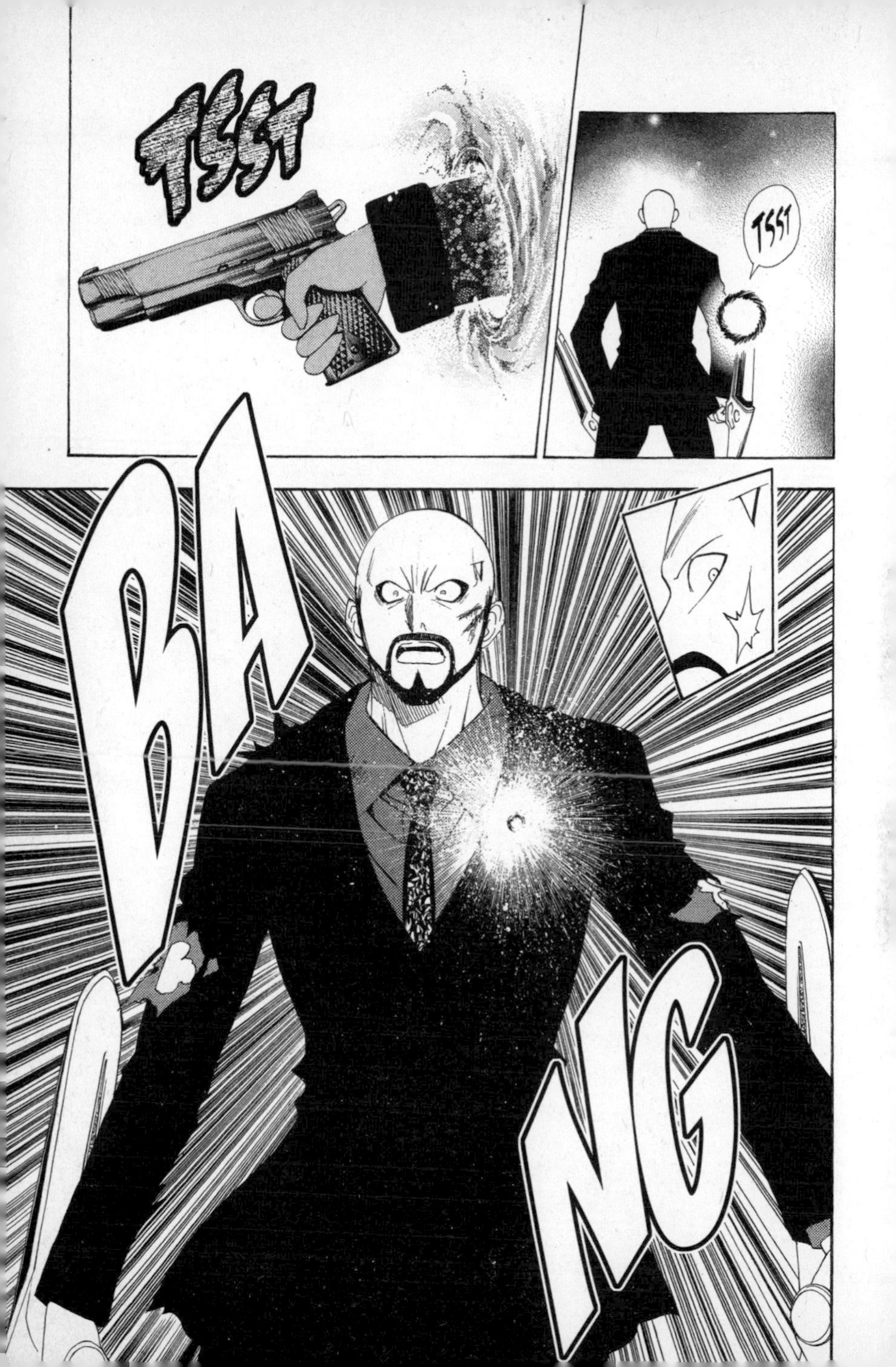
TSST
TSST
BANG

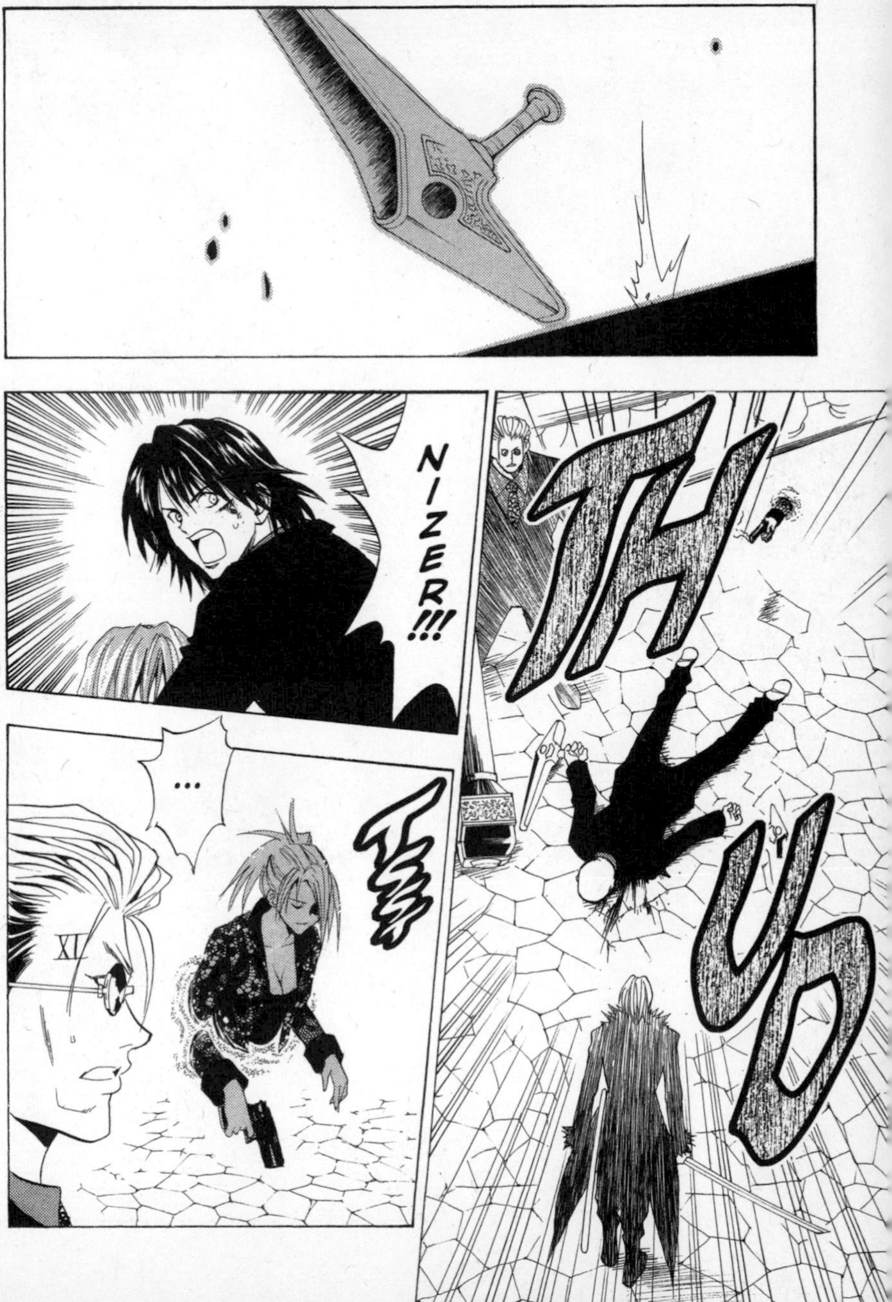

NIZER!!!
THUD
...
TMP

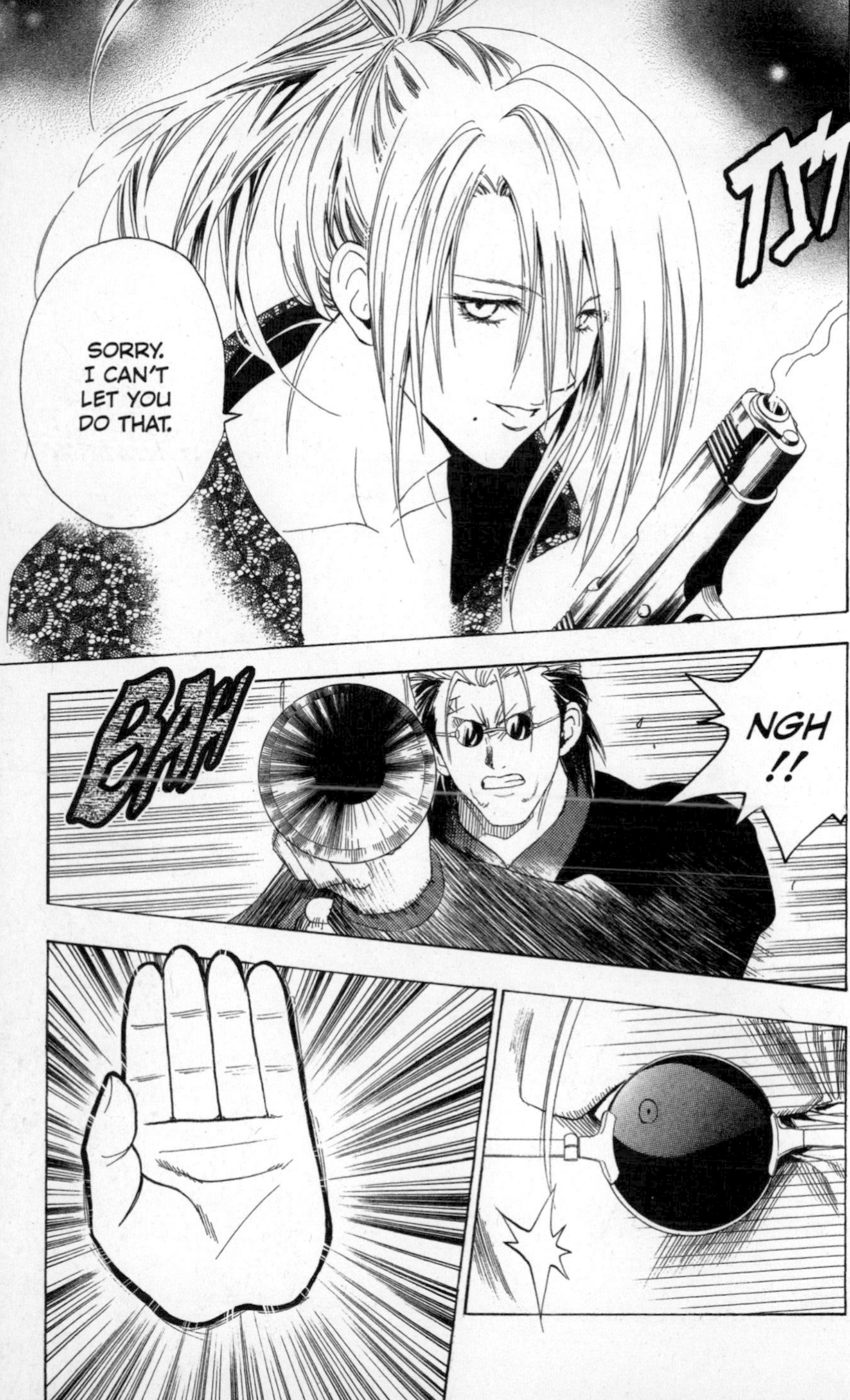
SORRY. I CAN'T LET YOU DO THAT.
NGH !!
BAM!

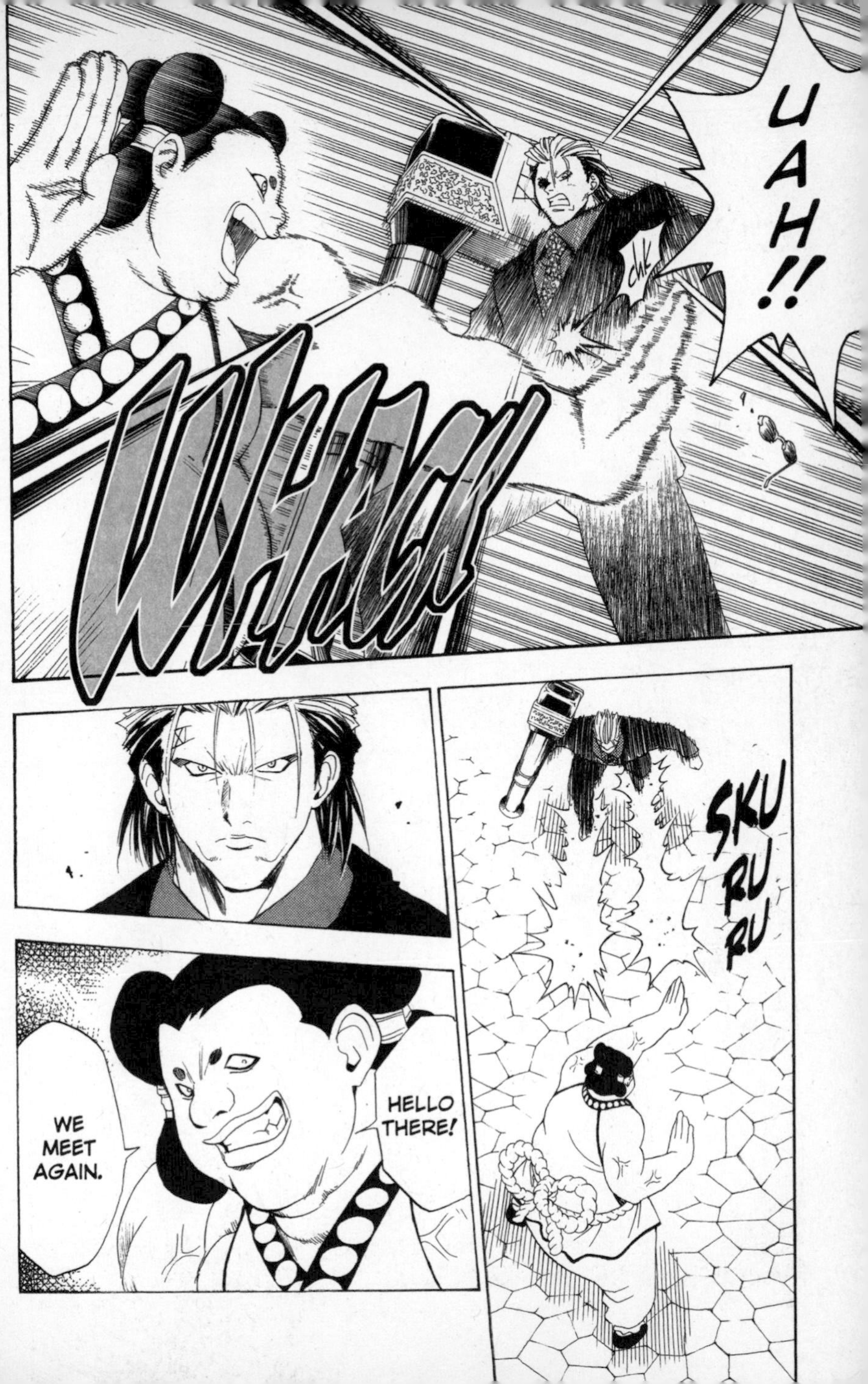
UAH!!
chk
WHACK
SKU RU RU
HELLO THERE!
WE MEET AGAIN.

READ THIS WAY

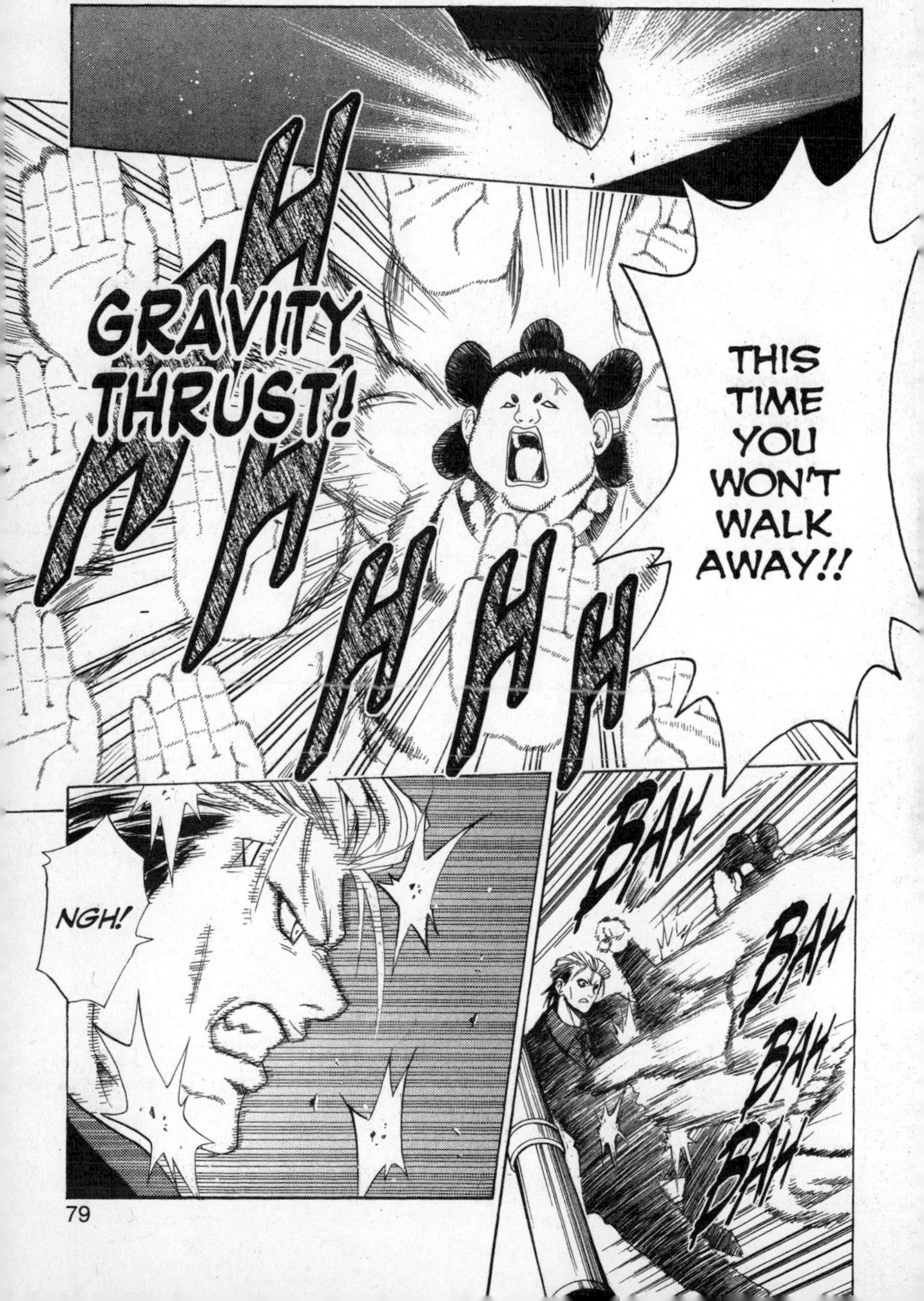
THIS TIME YOU WON'T WALK AWAY!!
GRAVITY THRUST!
BAH
BAH
BAH
BAH
NGH!

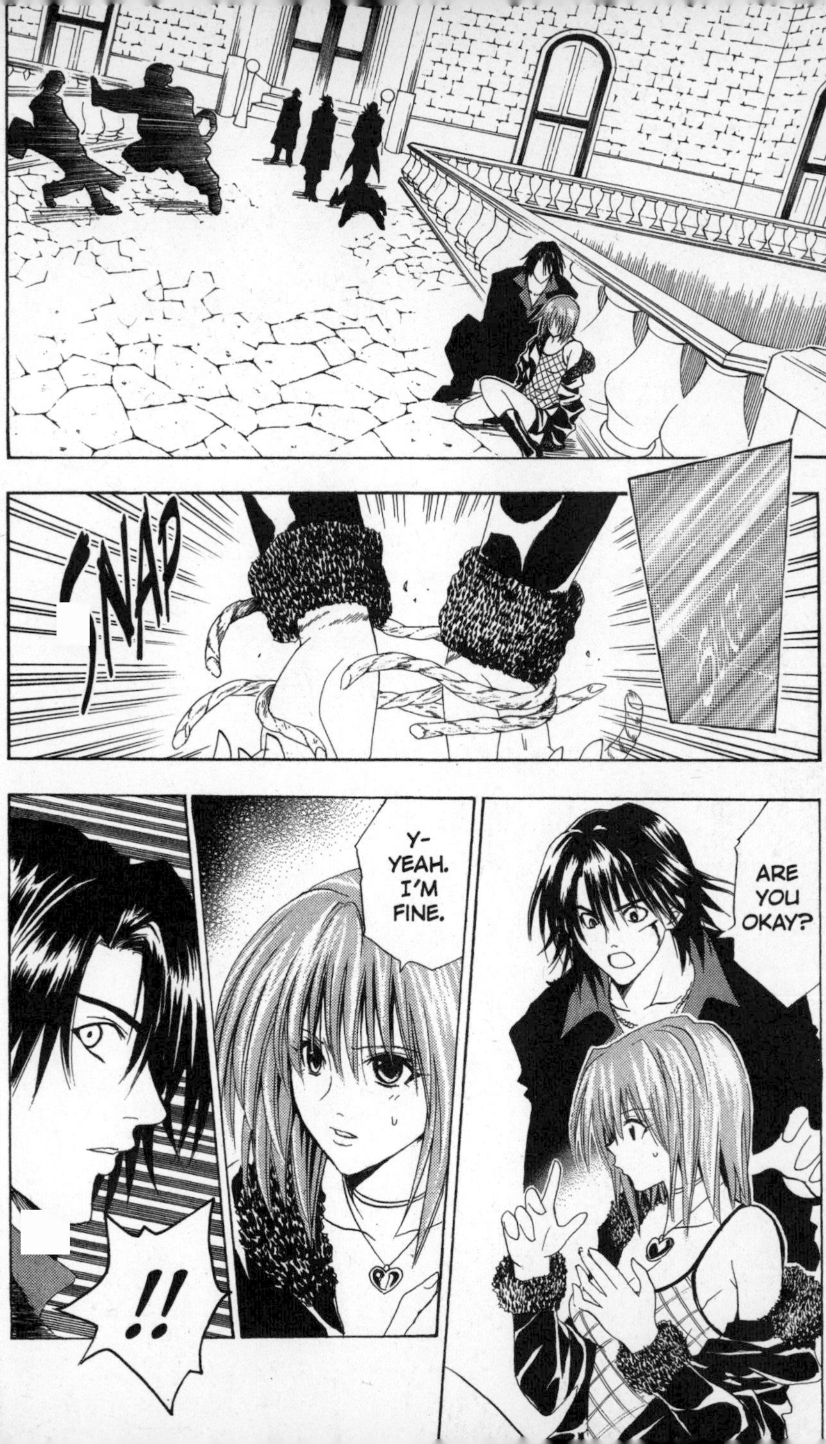
NAP
ARE YOU OKAY?
Y-YEAH. I'M FINE.
!!

ZA

HH

I HAVE UNANSWERED QUESTIONS.

BUT FIRST, THERE IS THE MATTER OF CERBERUS.

SHUUU

...

CREED...

ZURURURURU

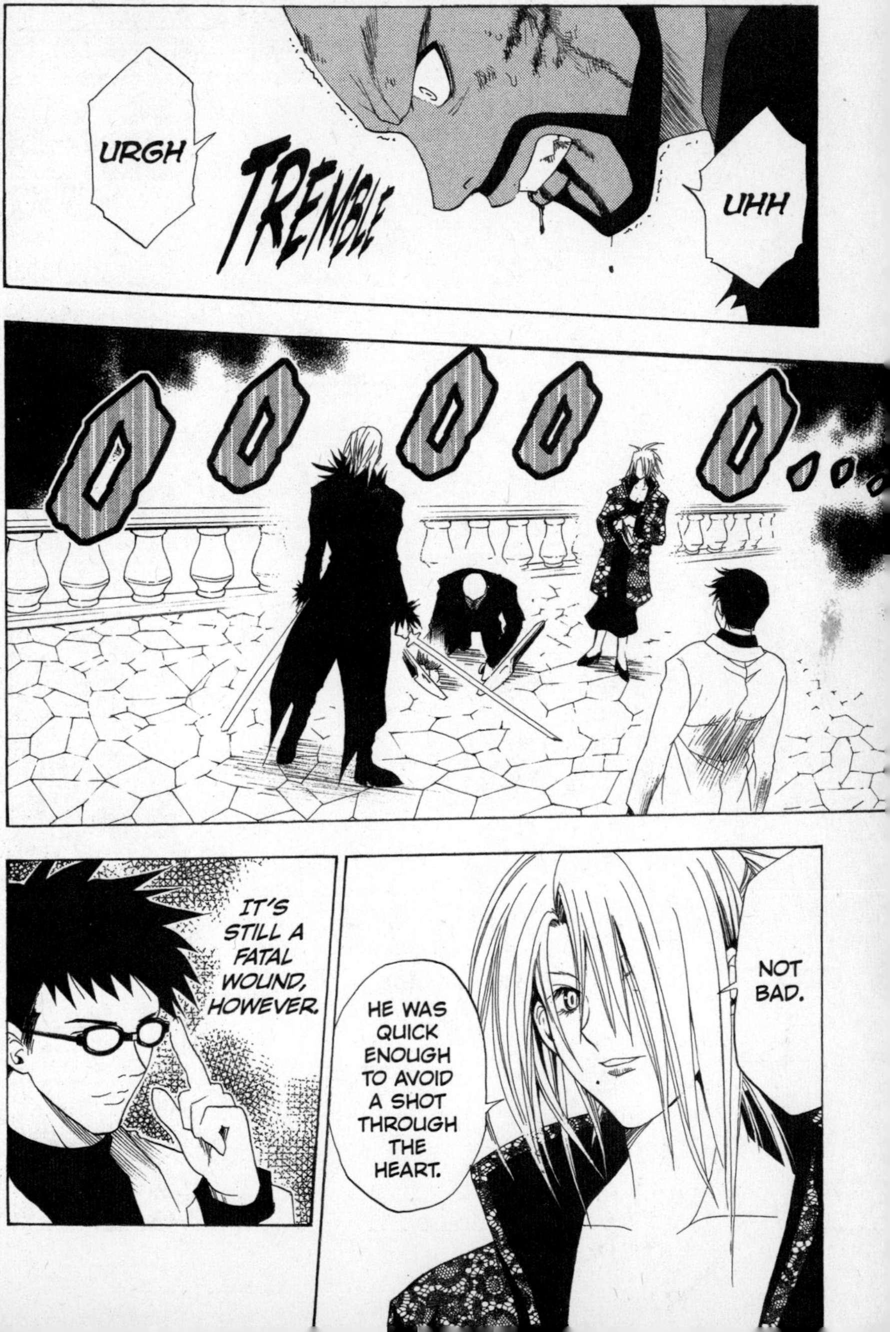
UHH
TREMBLE
URGH
OOOOO...
NOT BAD.
HE WAS QUICK ENOUGH TO AVOID A SHOT THROUGH THE HEART.
IT'S STILL A FATAL WOUND, HOWEVER.

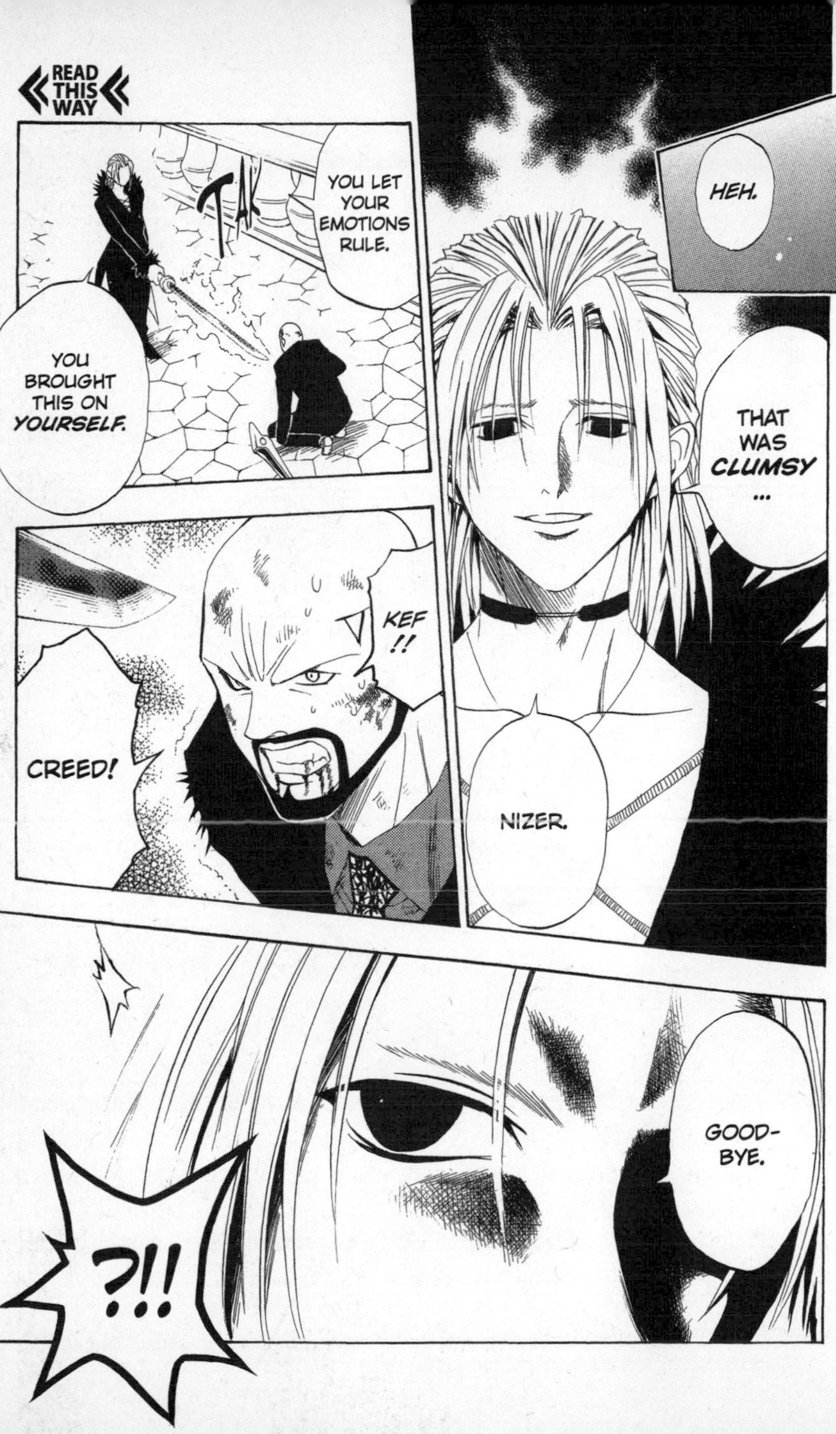
READ THIS WAY
HEH.
THAT WAS CLUMSY...
YOU LET YOUR EMOTIONS RULE.
TAK
YOU BROUGHT THIS ON YOURSELF.
KEF!!
CREED!
NIZER.
GOOD-BYE.
?!!

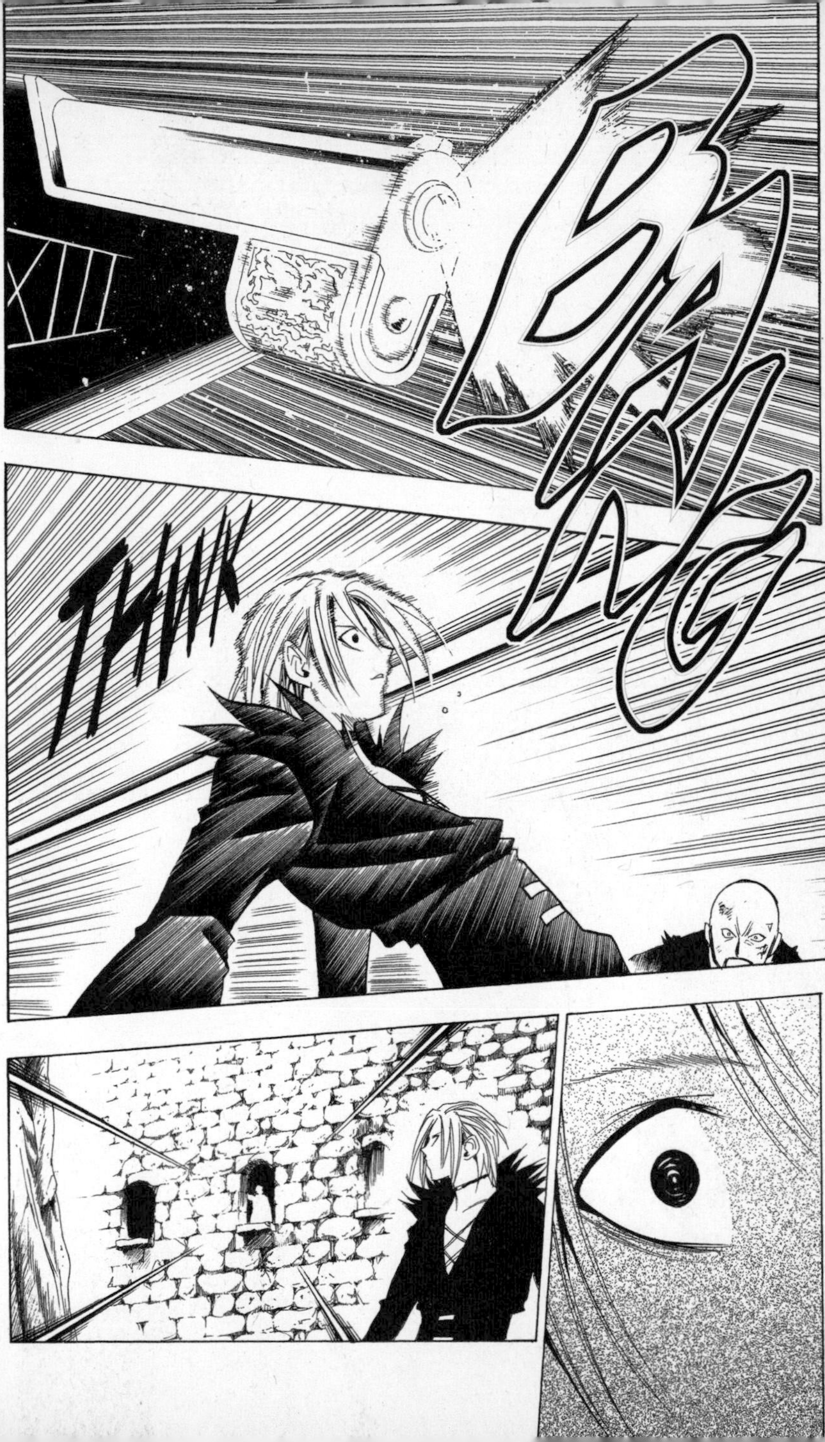

CLANG
THINK

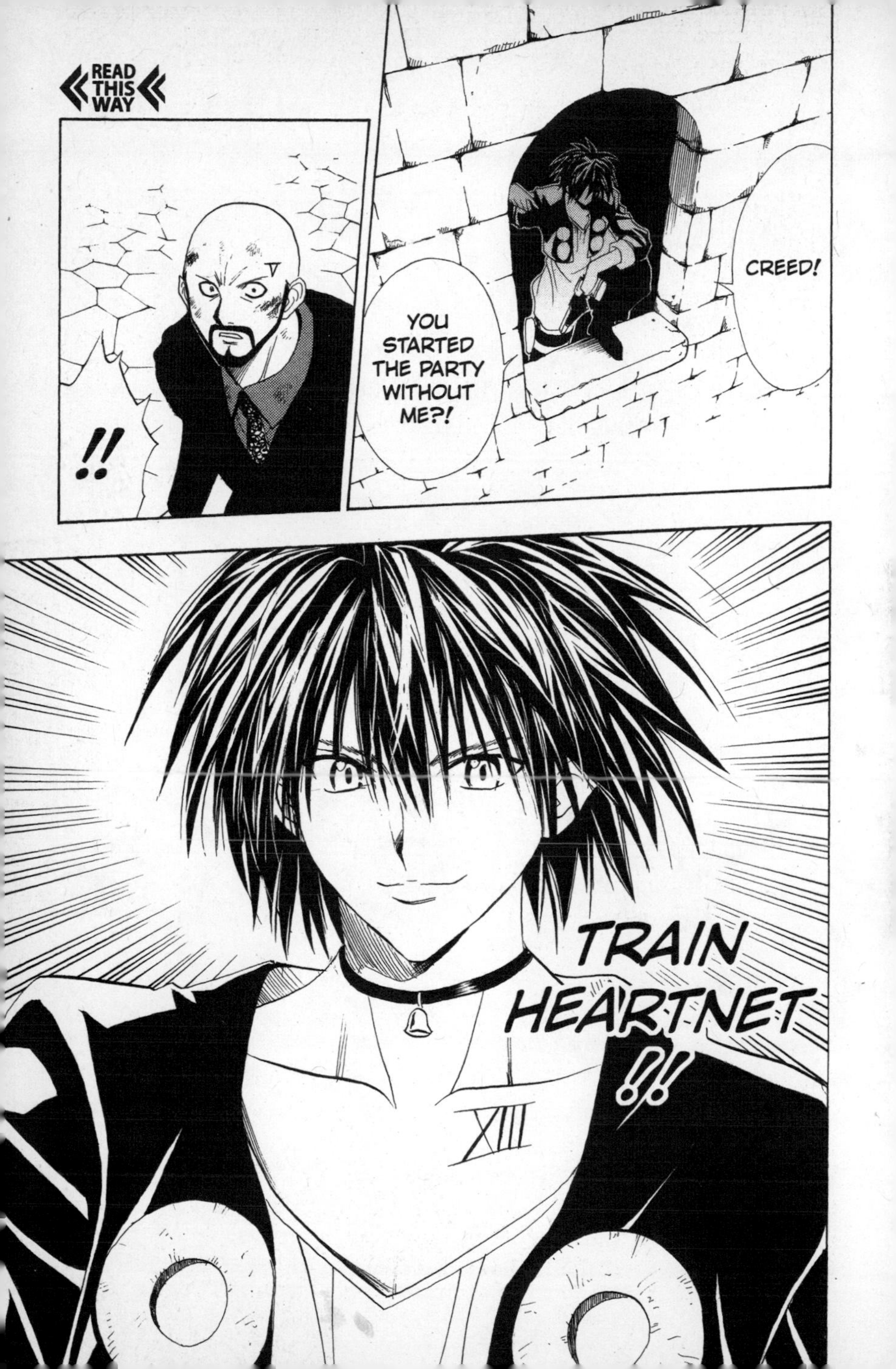
READ THIS WAY
CREED!
YOU STARTED THE PARTY WITHOUT ME?!
!!
TRAIN HEARTNET !!

 **QUICK HITS**

◎ **RINSLET'S MOMENT IN DANGER**
JENOS SAVED RINSLET WITH ORICHALCUM WIRES
THAT HE MANIPULATES WITH NIMBLE FINGERS.
HAD THAT FEAT BEEN ATTEMPTED BY ANYONE
ELSE, RINSLET WOULD HAVE BEEN CUT IN HALF.

◎ **VERETHRAGNA'S GIMMICK**
BELUGA'S BAZOOKA CAN TRANS-
FORM INTO A HAMMER IN A SINGLE
MOTION, ASSURING THAT EVEN
AFTER ITS THREE POWERFUL
CHARGES HAVE BEEN FIRED,
IT CAN STILL BE USED IN BATTLE.

◎ **THE GRAVITY THRUST (10GS)**
MARO'S AMAZING KILLING
TECHNIQUE. HE USES HIS TAO
POWER TO ADD ENORMOUS
GRAVITATIONAL FORCE TO HIS
THRUSTS. EACH BLOW PACKS
TEN TIMES THE AVERAGE FORCE.

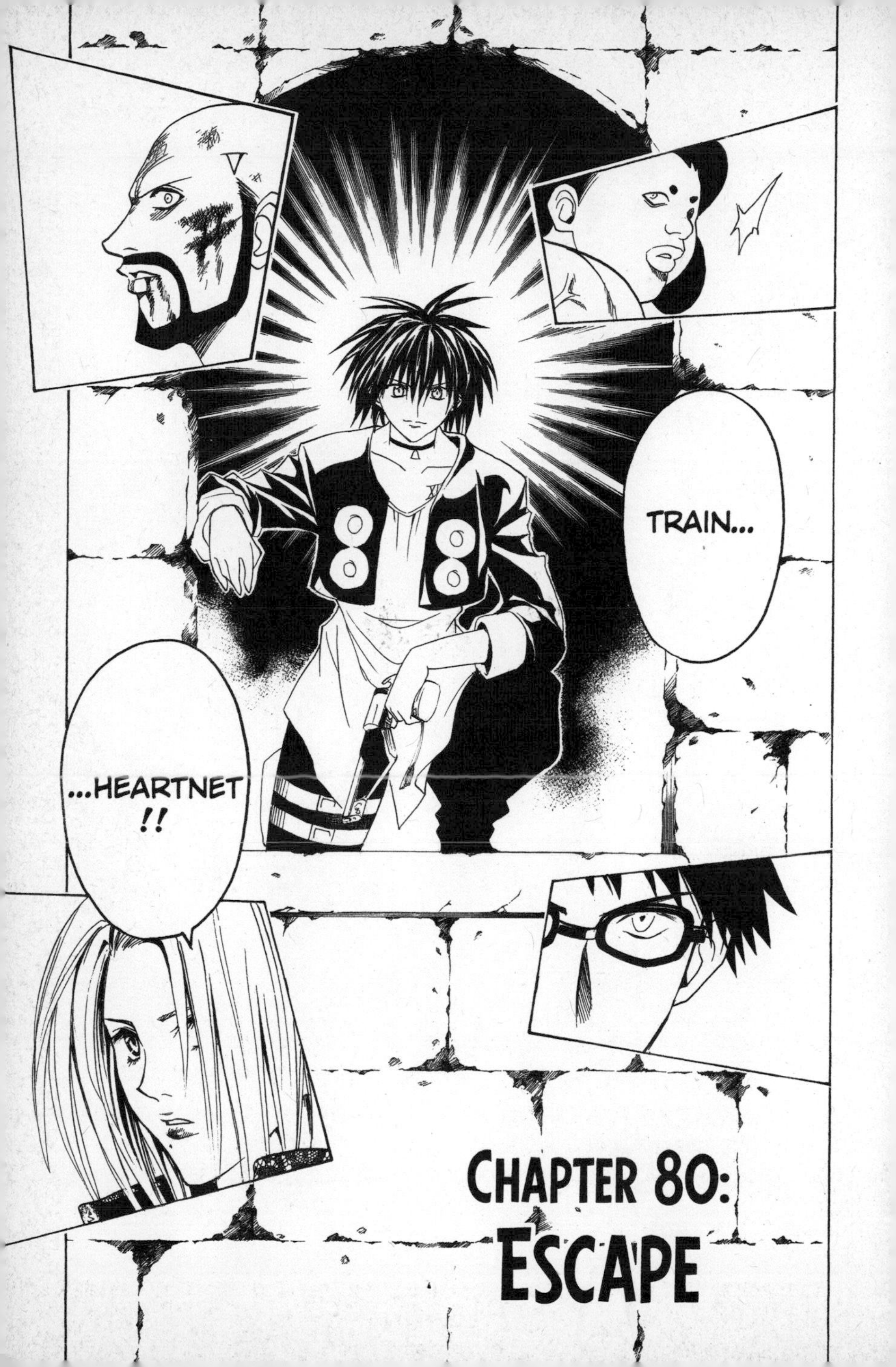
TRAIN...
...HEARTNET !!
CHAPTER 80:
ESCAPE

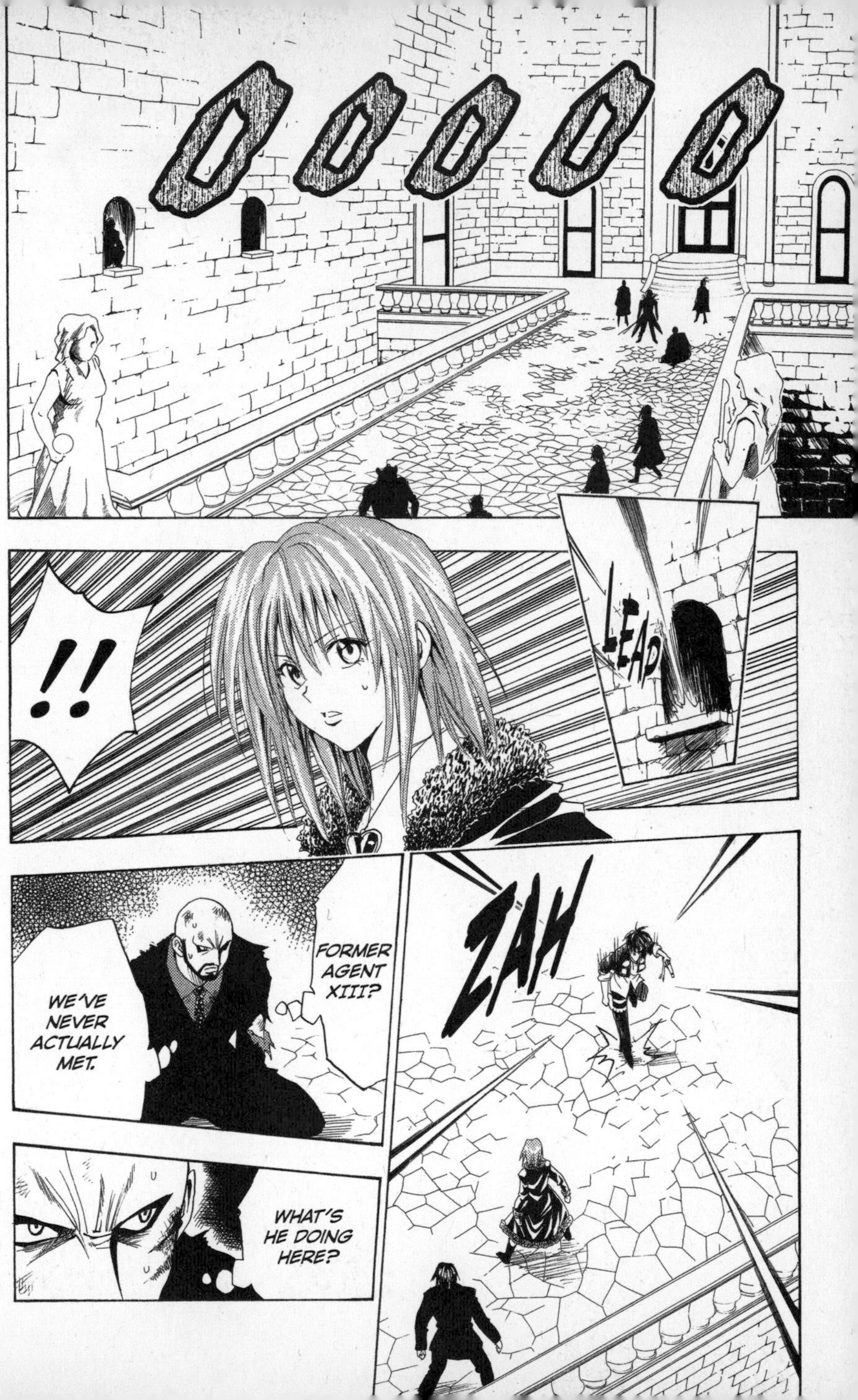
LEAD
!!
ZAH
FORMER AGENT XIII?
WE'VE NEVER ACTUALLY MET.
WHAT'S HE DOING HERE?

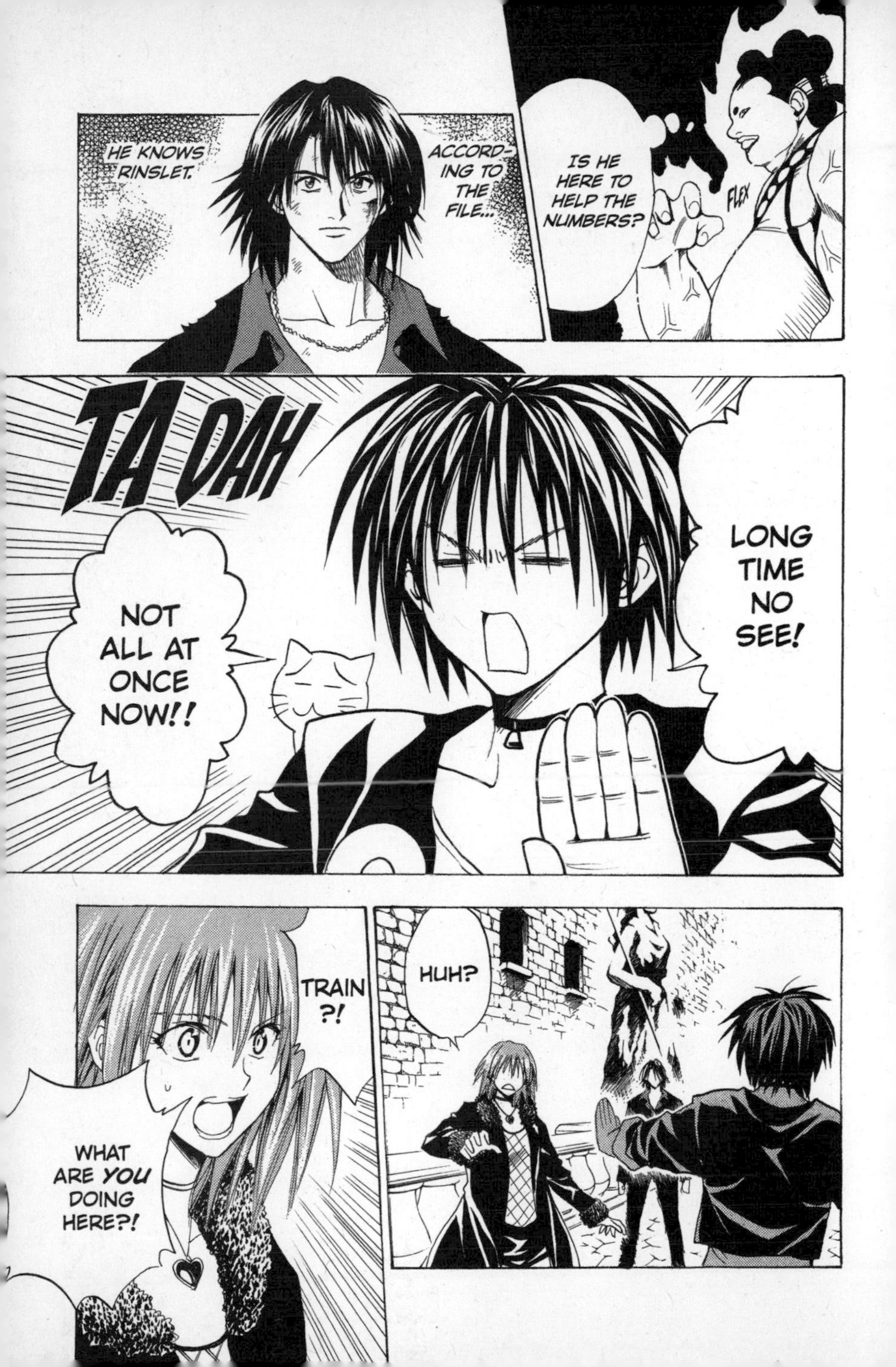

IS HE HERE TO HELP THE NUMBERS?
FLEX
ACCORD-ING TO THE FILE...
HE KNOWS RINSLET.
TA DAH
LONG TIME NO SEE!
NOT ALL AT ONCE NOW!!
HUH?
TRAIN?!
WHAT ARE YOU DOING HERE?!

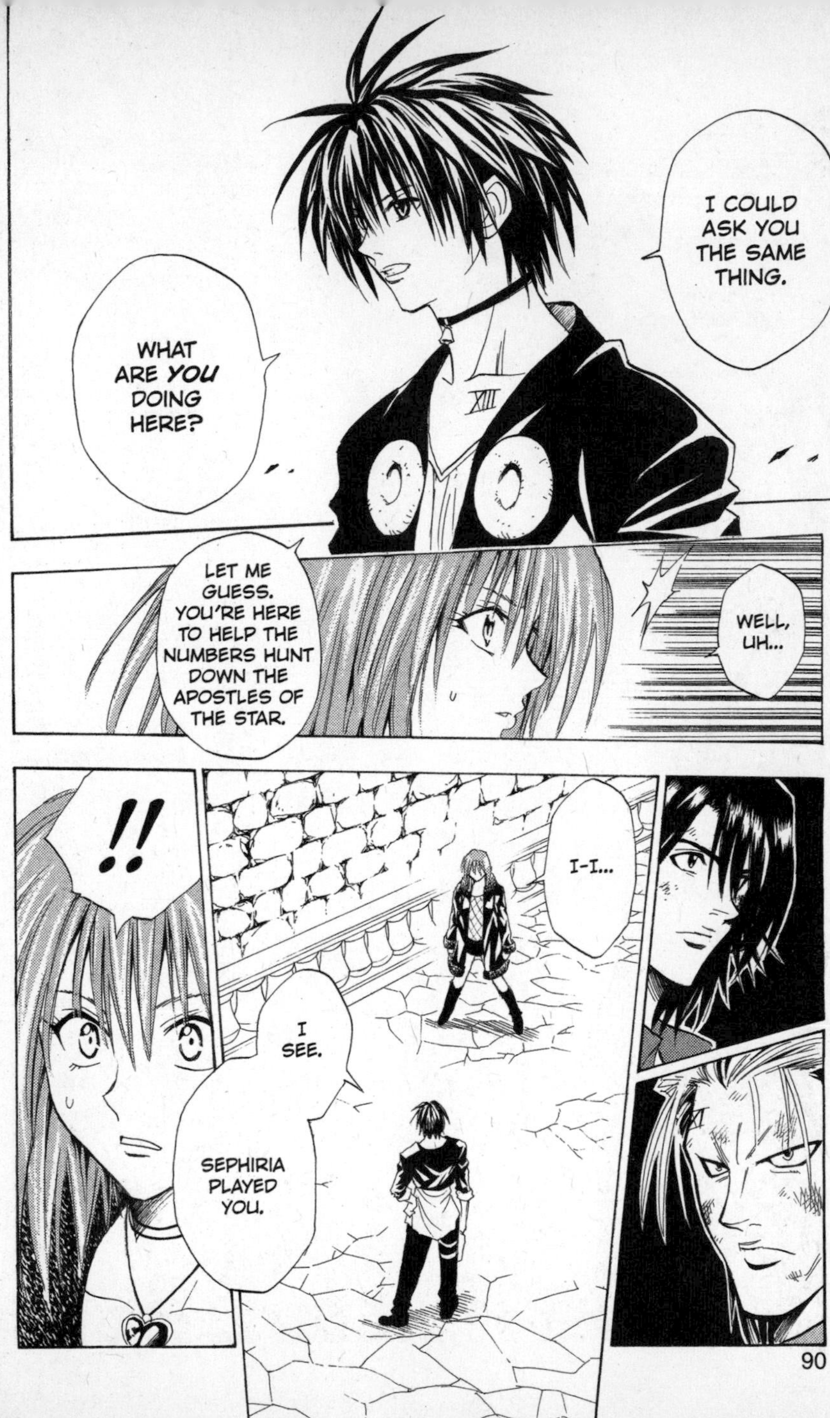
WHAT ARE *YOU* DOING HERE?
I COULD ASK YOU THE SAME THING.
LET ME GUESS. YOU'RE HERE TO HELP THE NUMBERS HUNT DOWN THE APOSTLES OF THE STAR.
WELL, UH...
!!
I SEE.
SEPHIRIA PLAYED YOU.
I-I...

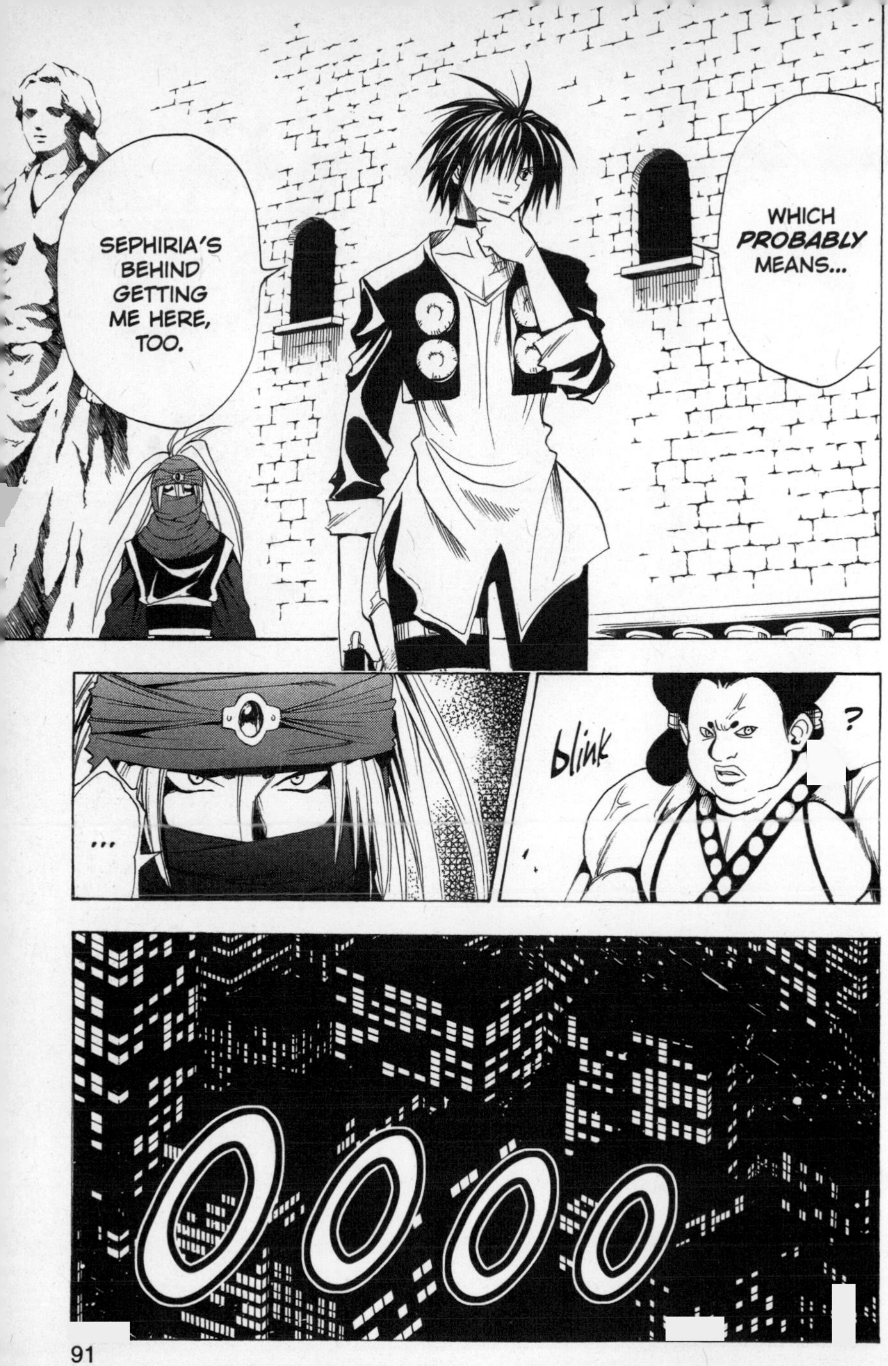
SEPHIRIA'S BEHIND GETTING ME HERE, TOO.
WHICH *PROBABLY* MEANS...
...
blink
?

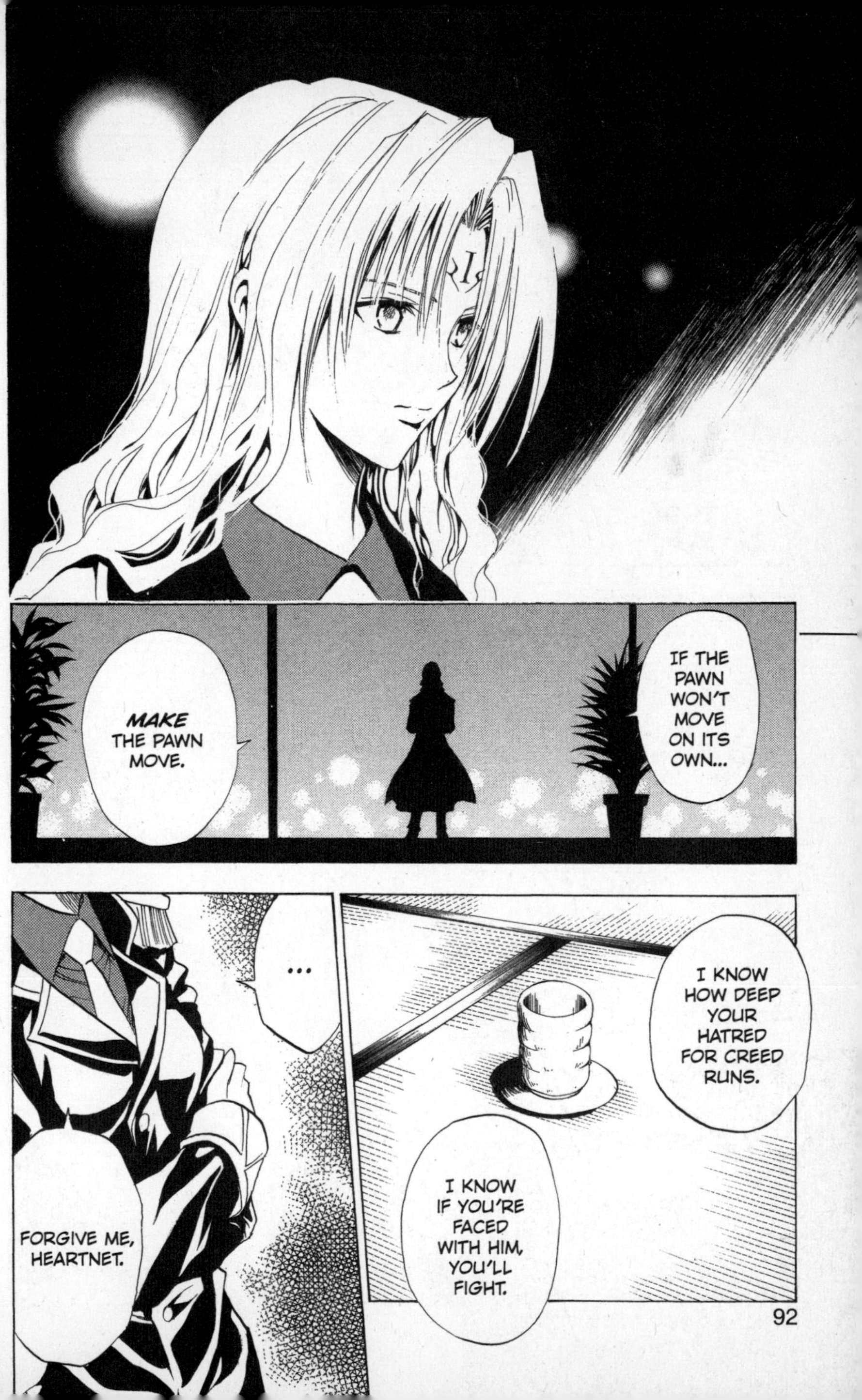
IF THE PAWN WON'T MOVE ON ITS OWN...
MAKE THE PAWN MOVE.
I KNOW HOW DEEP YOUR HATRED FOR CREED RUNS.
I KNOW IF YOU'RE FACED WITH HIM, YOU'LL FIGHT.
...
FORGIVE ME, HEARTNET.

YOU'RE BEING USED.

FOR THE SAKE OF THE MISSION...

CREED...

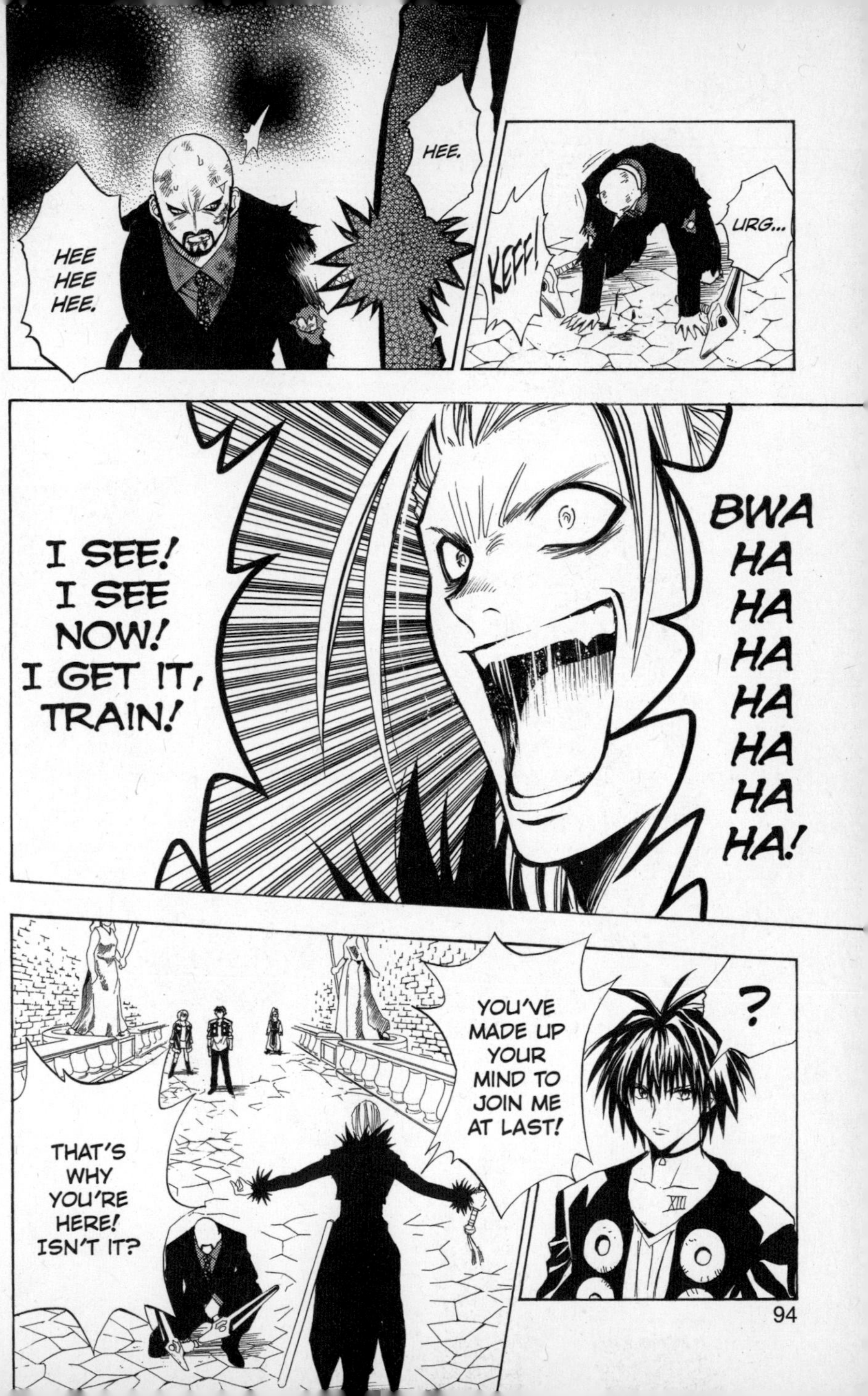
KEFF!
URG...
HEE.
HEE HEE HEE.
BWA HA HA HA HA HA HA HA!
I SEE! I SEE NOW! I GET IT, TRAIN!
?
YOU'VE MADE UP YOUR MIND TO JOIN ME AT LAST!
THAT'S WHY YOU'RE HERE! ISN'T IT?

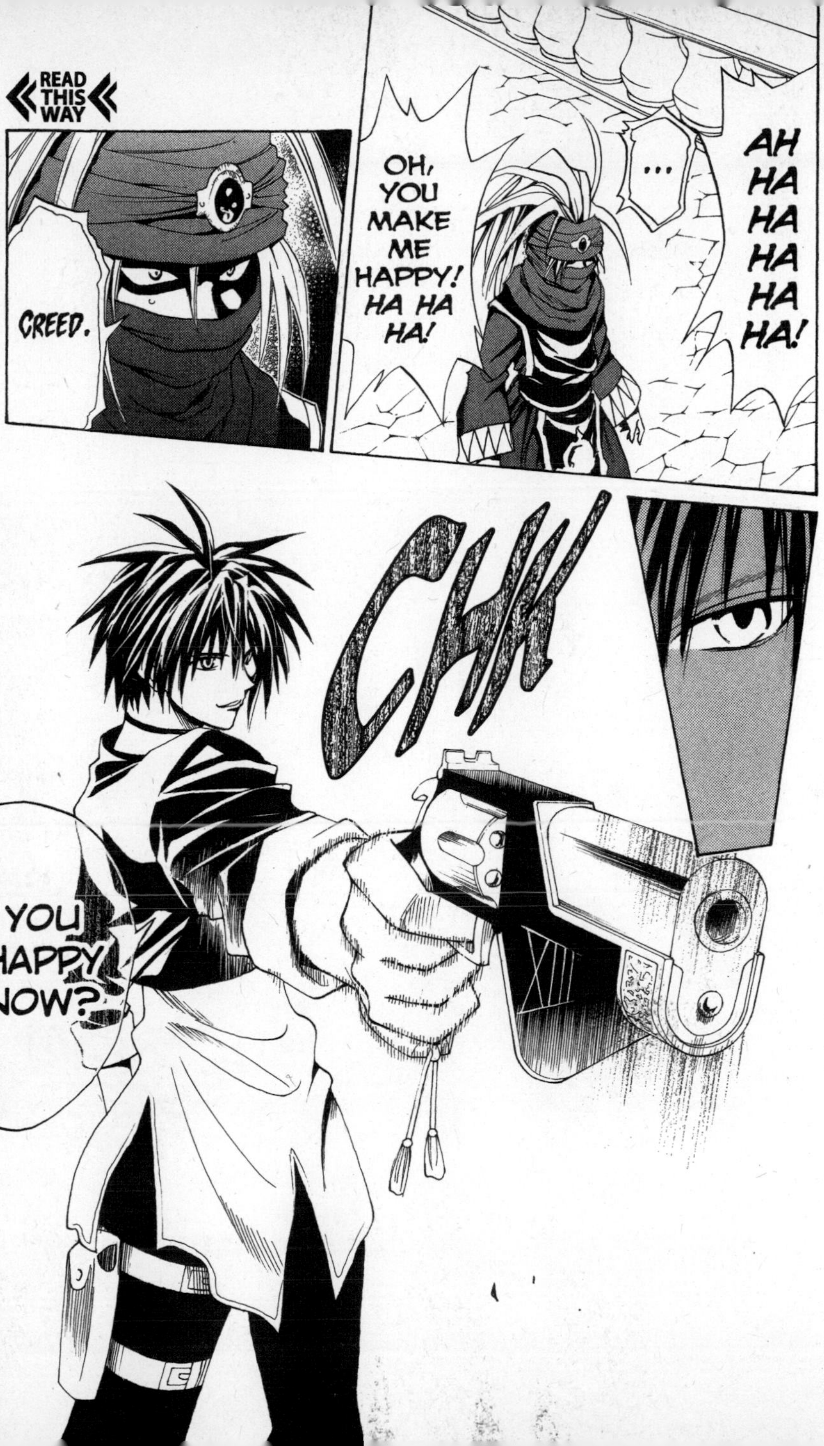
READ THIS WAY
AH HA HA HA HA HA HA!
...
OH, YOU MAKE ME HAPPY! HA HA HA!
CREED.
CHK
YOU HAPPY NOW?

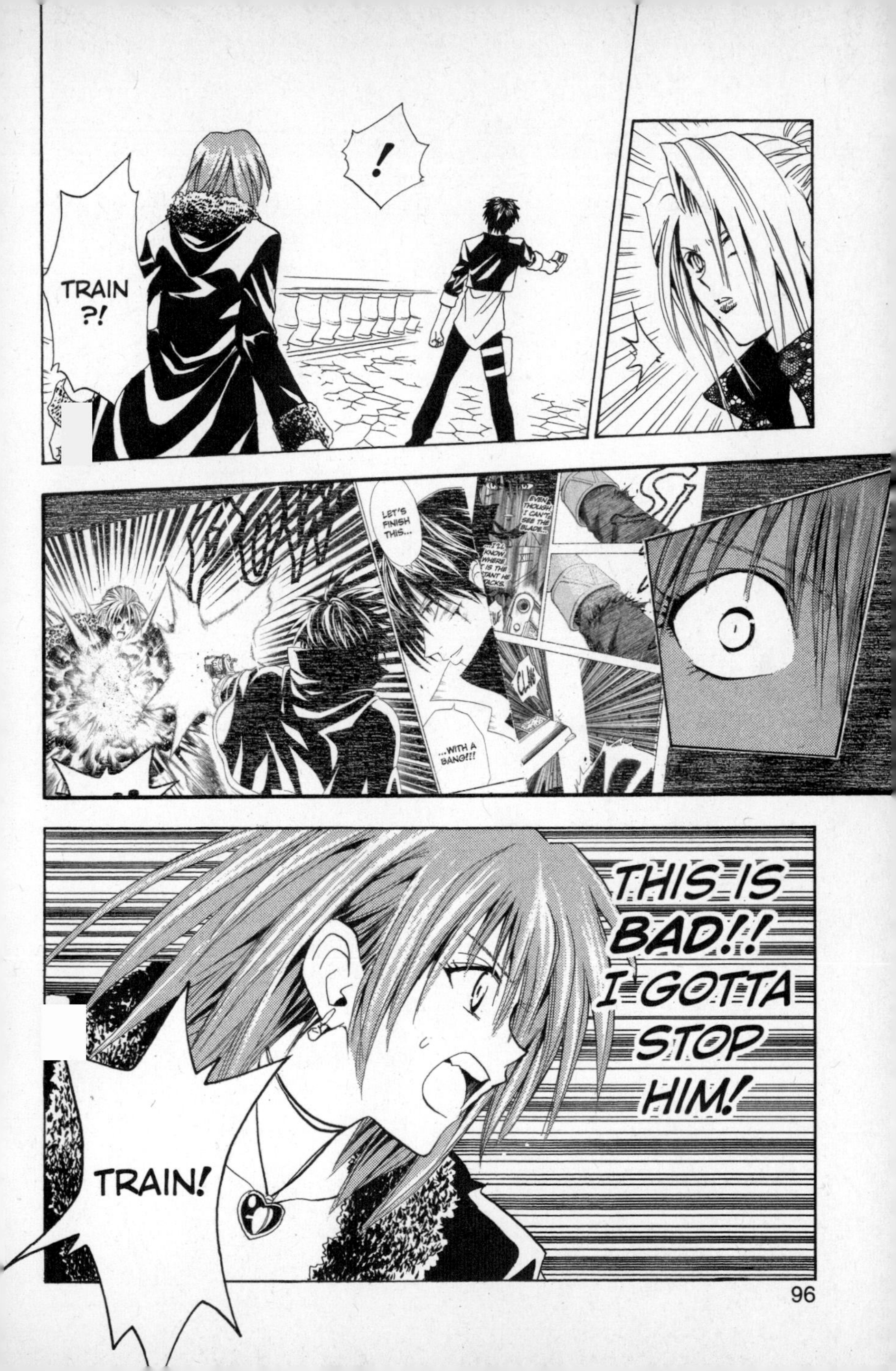
!
TRAIN ?!
EVEN THOUGH I CAN'T SEE THE BLADE...
LET'S FINISH THIS...
...WITH A BANG!!!
THIS IS BAD!! I GOTTA STOP HIM!
TRAIN!

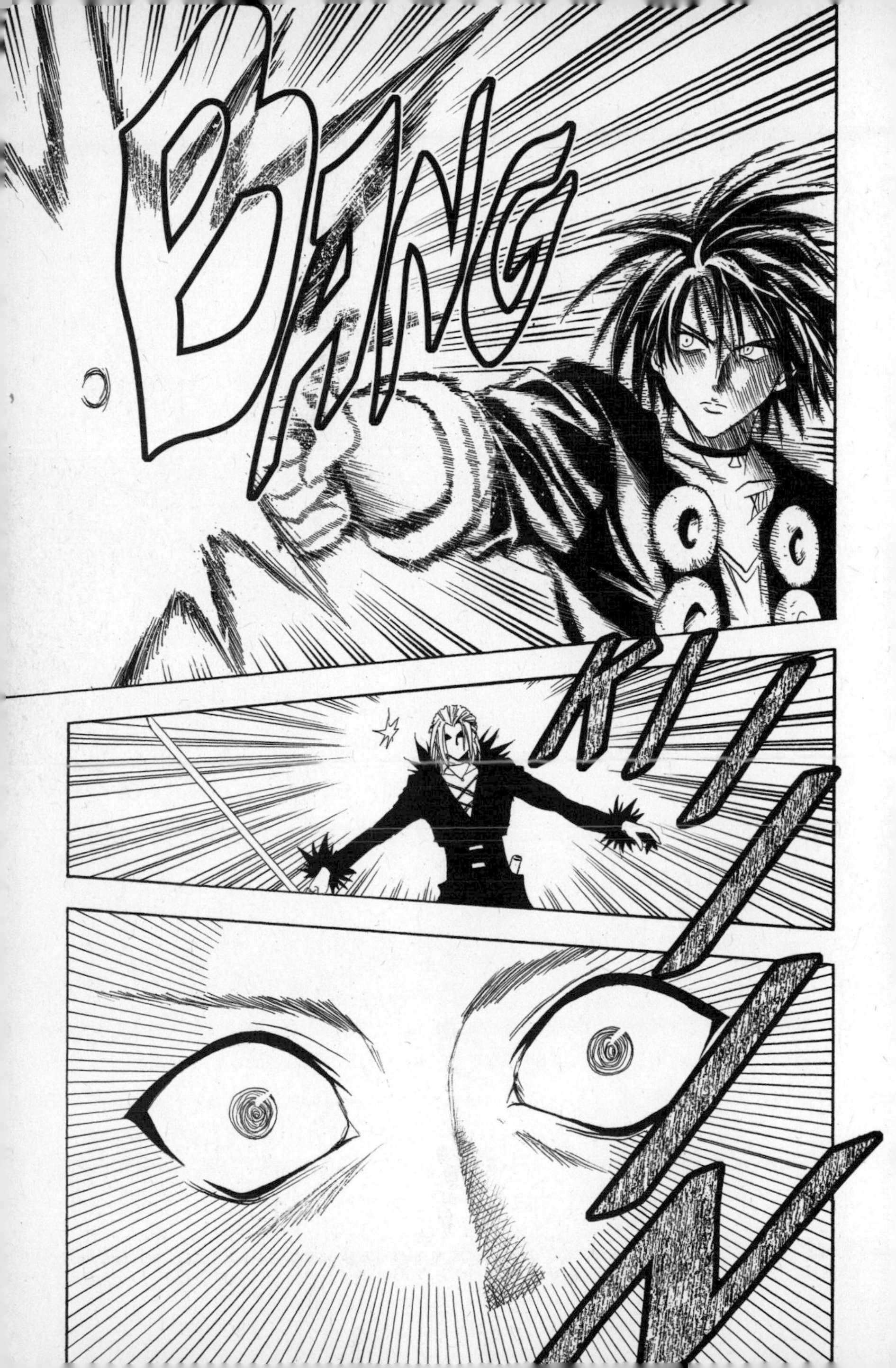
DANG
KIIIN

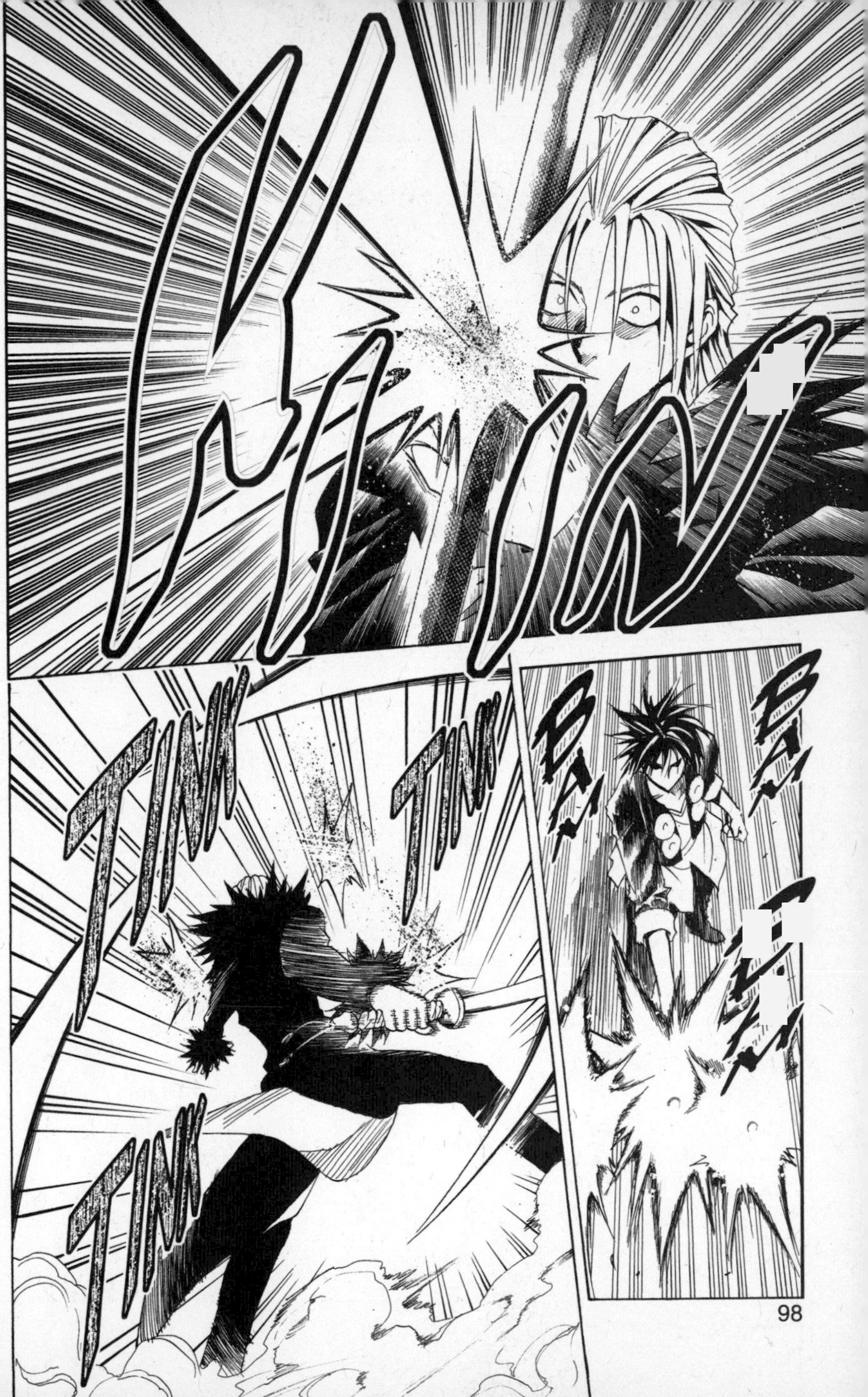
TINK
TINK
TINK
BA
BA

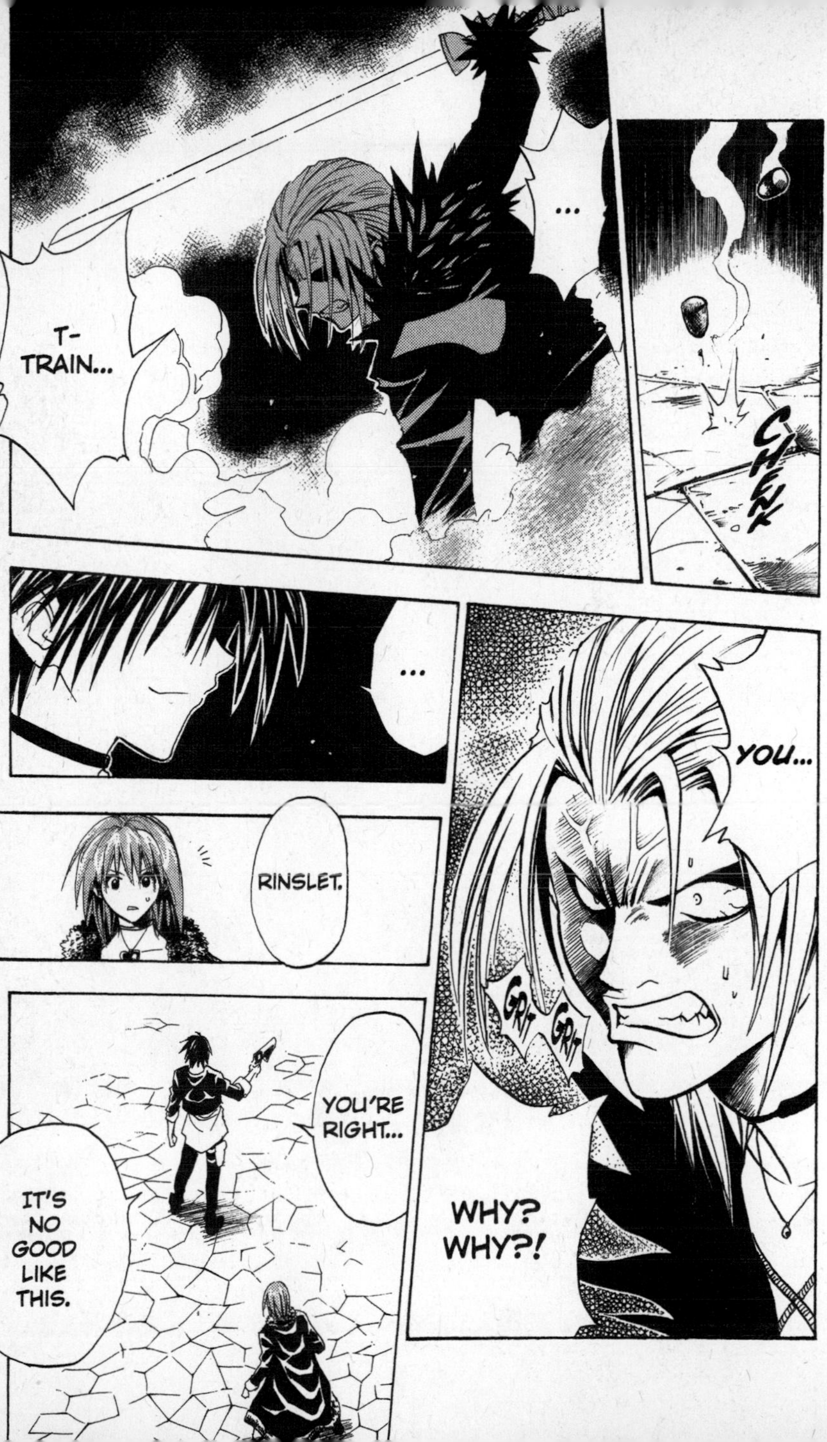
CHENK
...
T-TRAIN...
...
YOU...
GRIT GRIT
WHY? WHY?!
RINSLET.
YOU'RE RIGHT...
IT'S NO GOOD LIKE THIS.

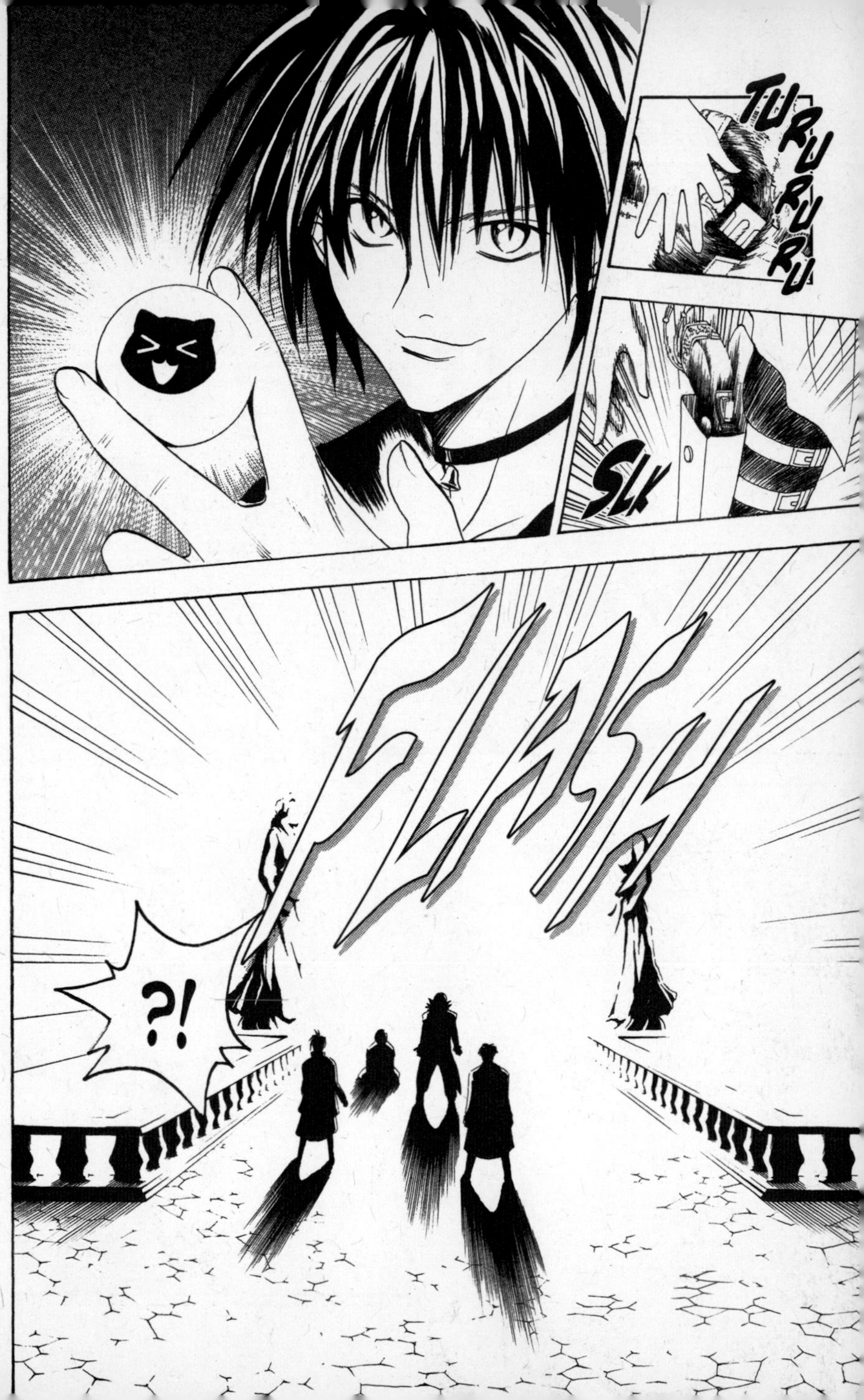
TURURURURU
SLK
FLASH
?!

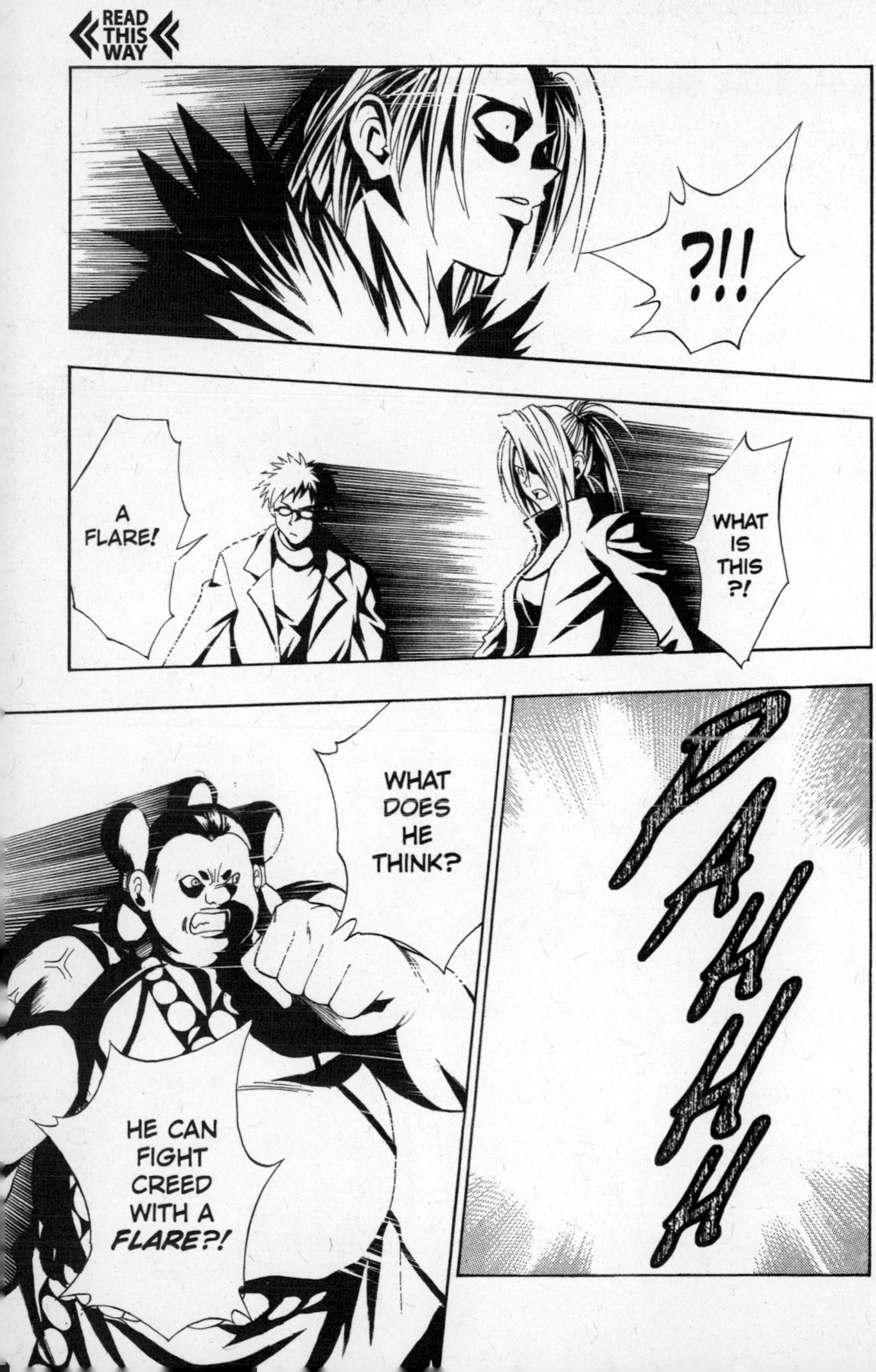
READ THIS WAY
?!!
A FLARE!
WHAT IS THIS ?!
WHAT DOES HE THINK?
HE CAN FIGHT CREED WITH A FLARE?!
DAHHHHH

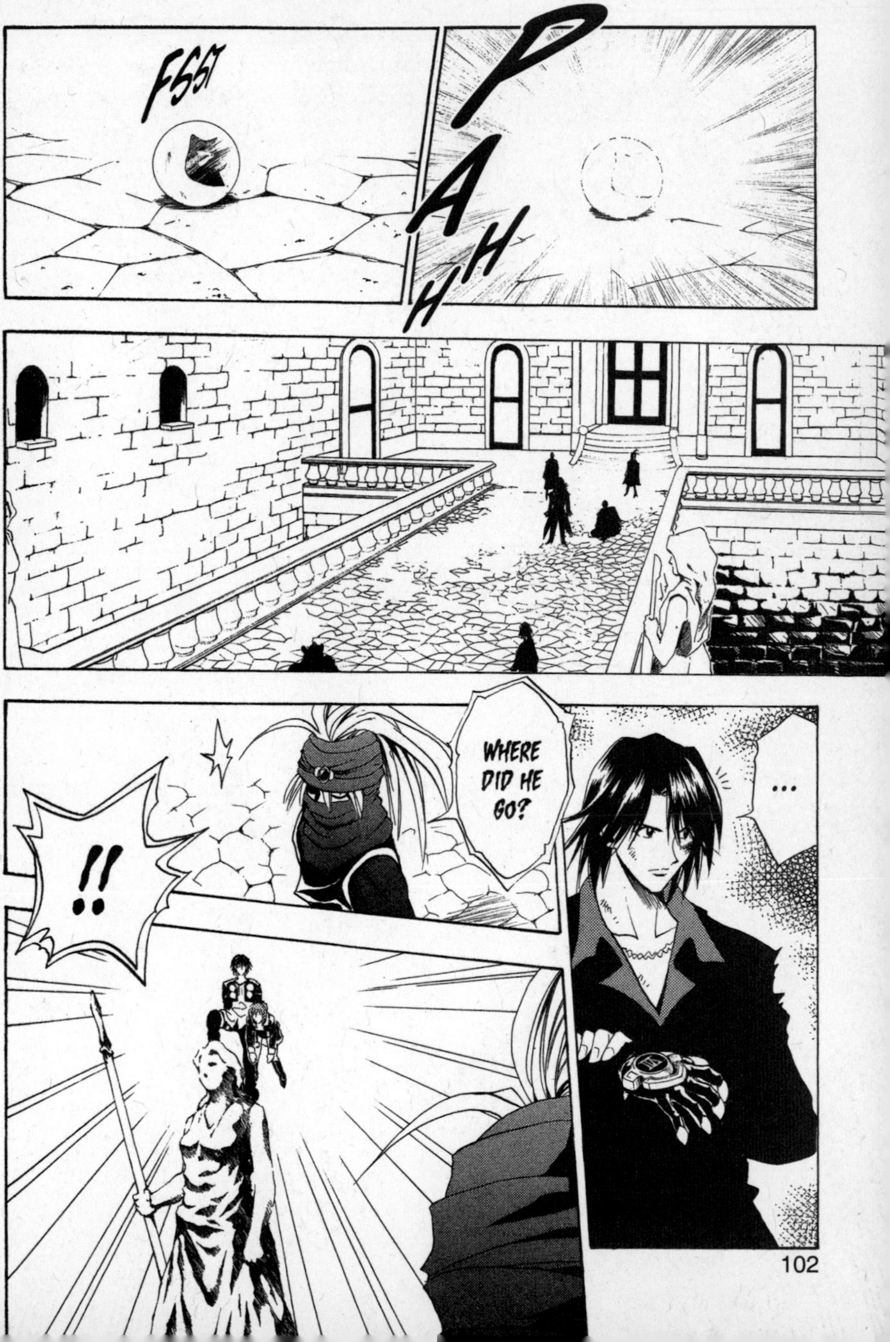
PAHHH
FSST
WHERE DID HE GO?
...
!!

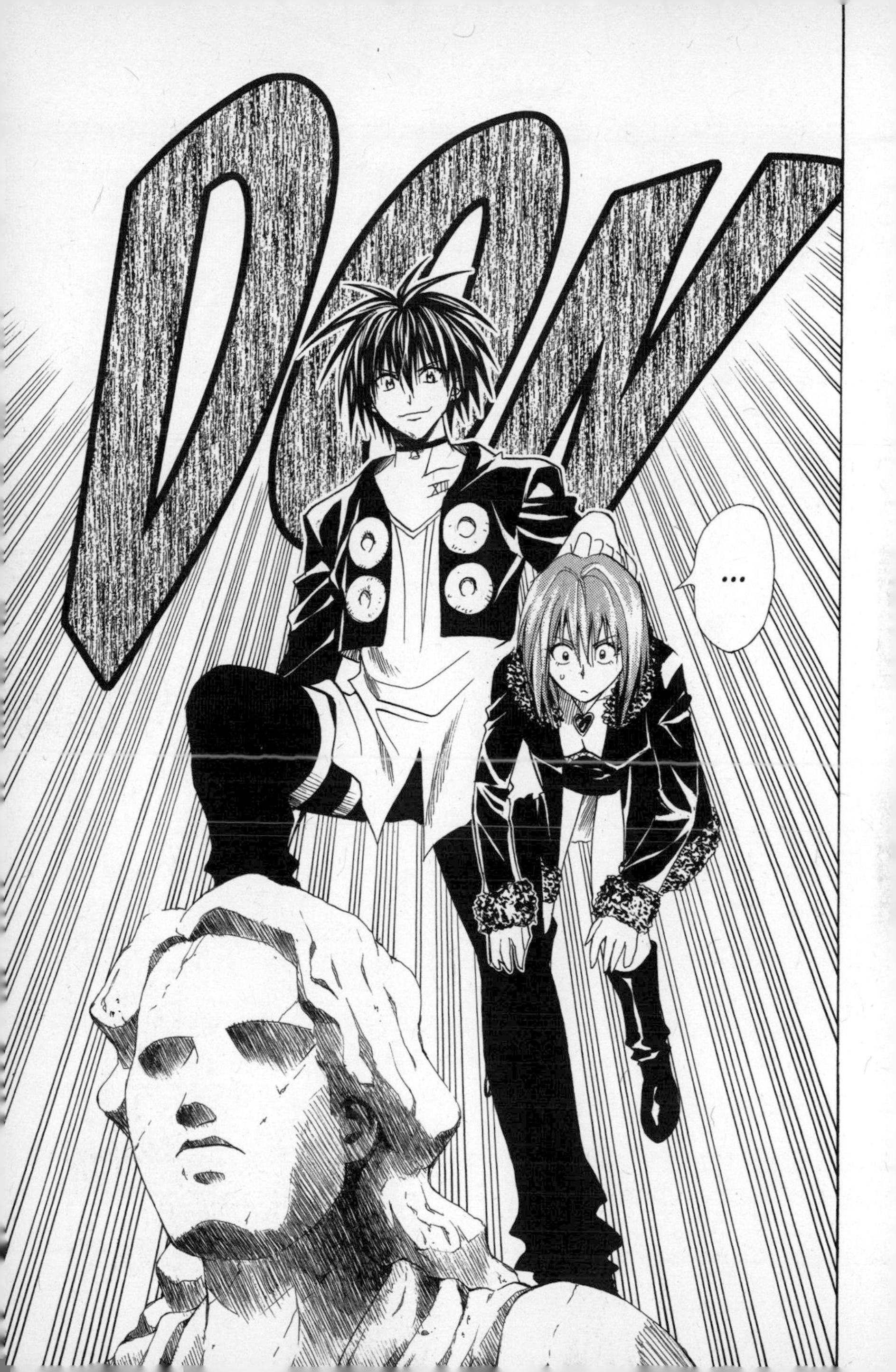
DON
...

BUT I GOTTA GO, CREED.

SEEMS A SHAME TO LET A CHANCE LIKE THIS SLIP PAST, I KNOW.

HEY! SHOW A GIRL SOME RESPECT!

?!

WHAT'S BETWEEN YOU AND CHRONOS DOESN'T INVOLVE ME.

SO...

WHAT?

HAVE AT IT. I'M OUT.

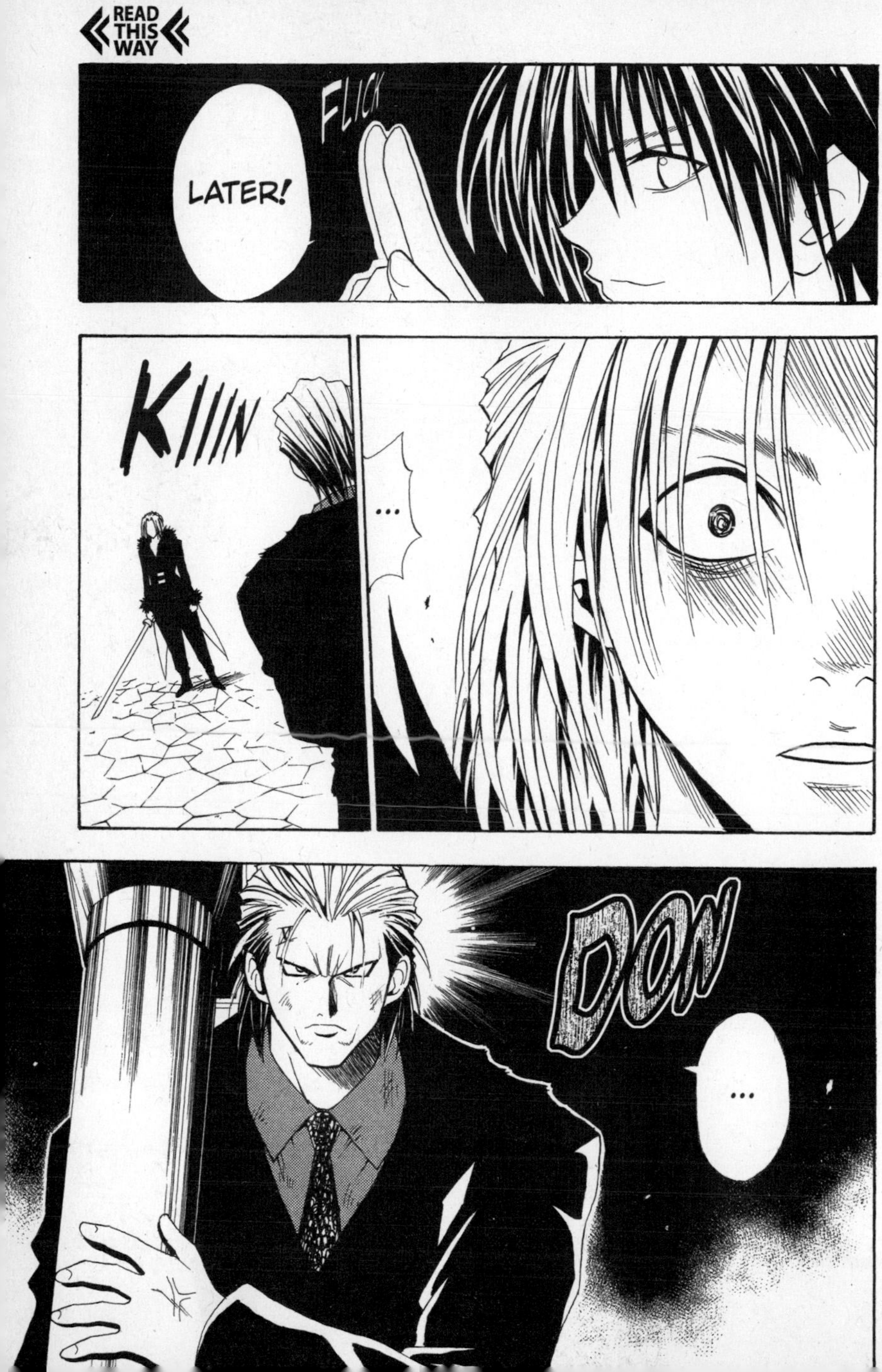
READ THIS WAY
FLICK
LATER!
KIIIN
...
DON
...

Maro's Lucky Smile

MAKE ENLARGEMENTS ON A COPY MACHINE AND HAVE FUN PINNING THE FACE ON MARO!

CHAPTER 81:
IMAGINE BLADE, LEVEL 2

SK!!!

...

HE LEFT?

WHY'D HE EVEN COME?

THIS IS MY CHANCE!

FURY

108

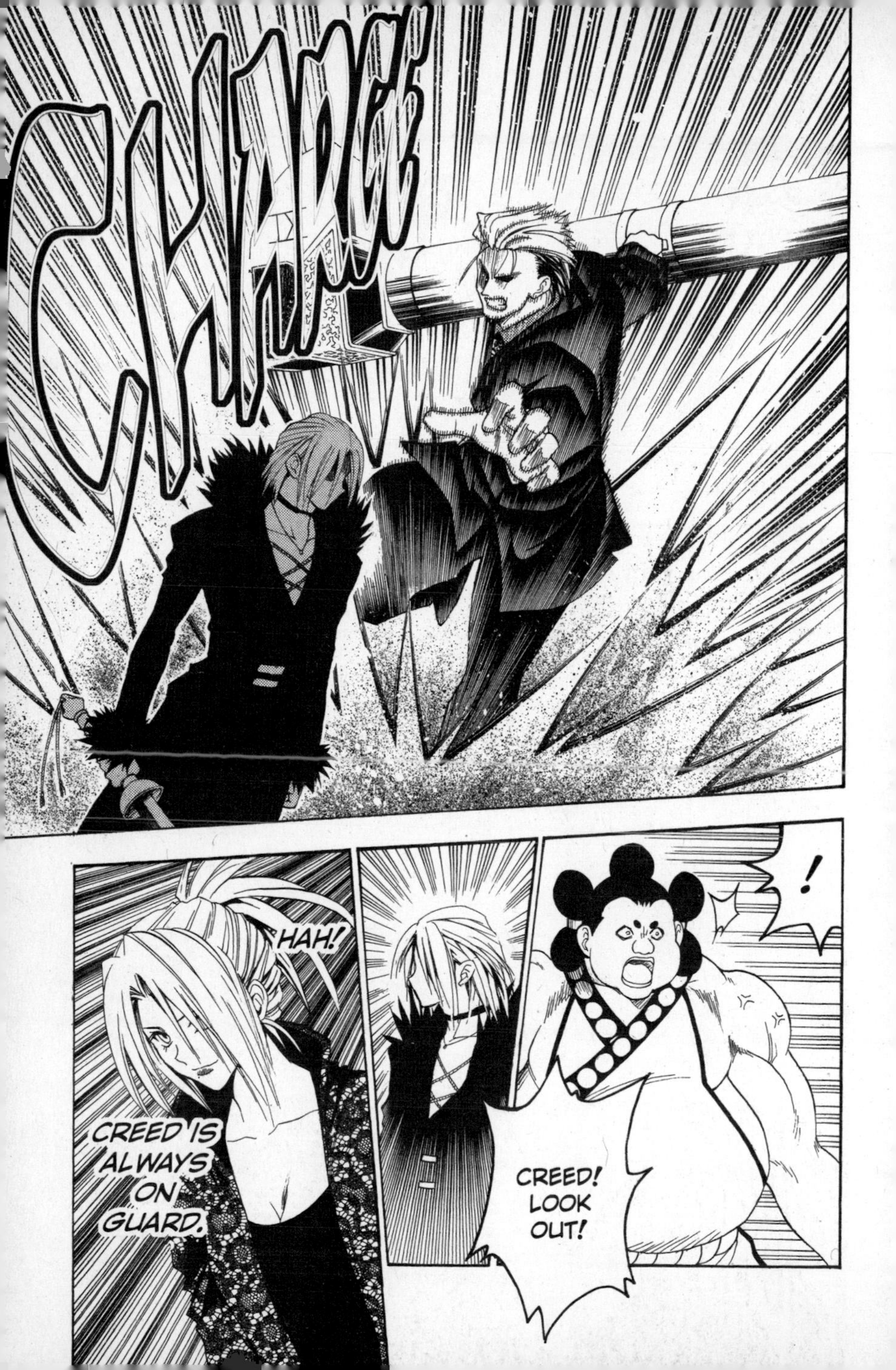
!
CREED! LOOK OUT!
HAH!
CREED IS ALWAYS ON GUARD.

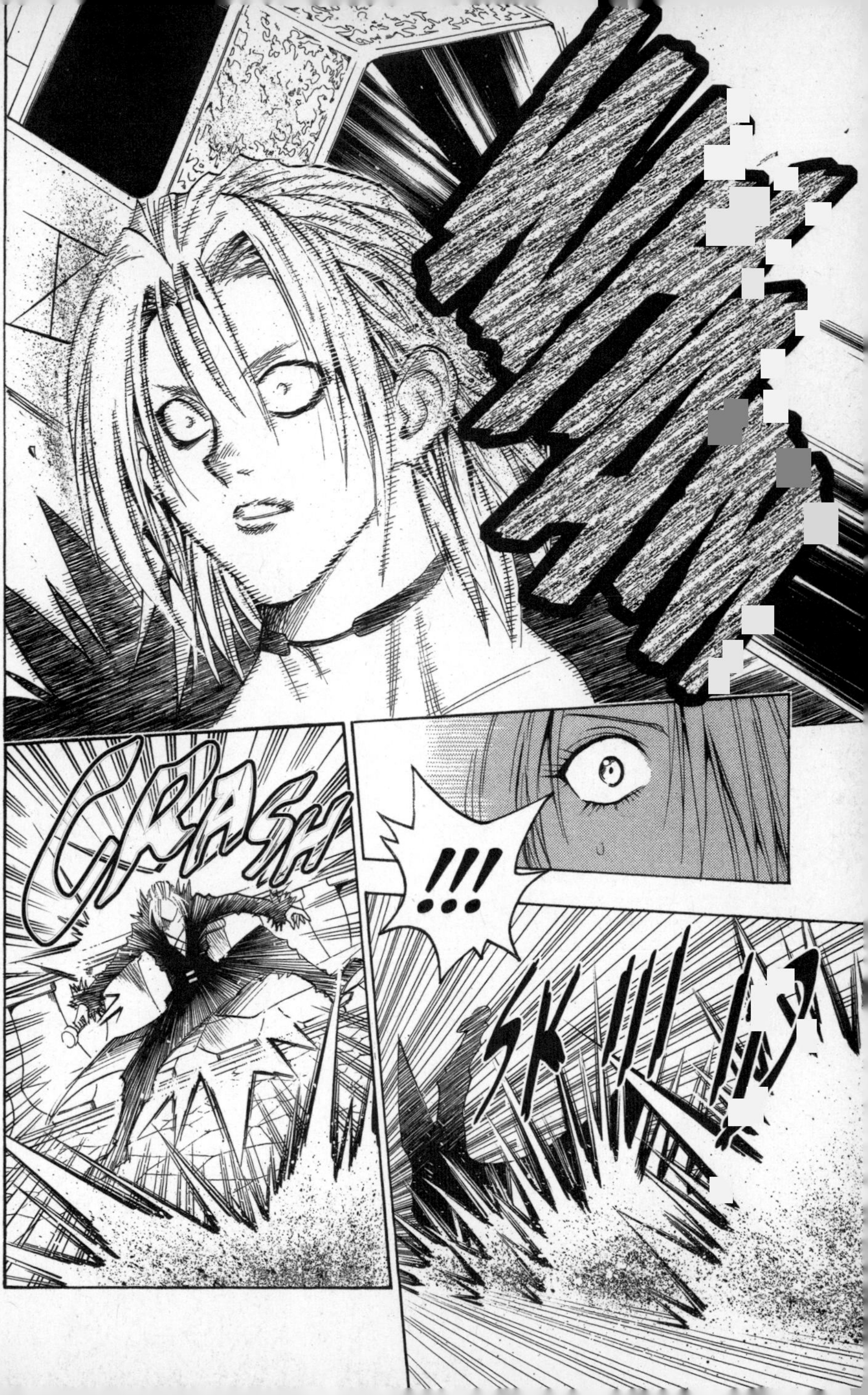
CRASH
!!!

DRIP   DRIP

I THOUGHT YOU'D CHANGED YOUR MIND.

SHUUUU

TRAIN...

I HOPED YOU'D COME TO YOUR SENSES.

I-I THOUGHT...

CREED!!

...

ZAH

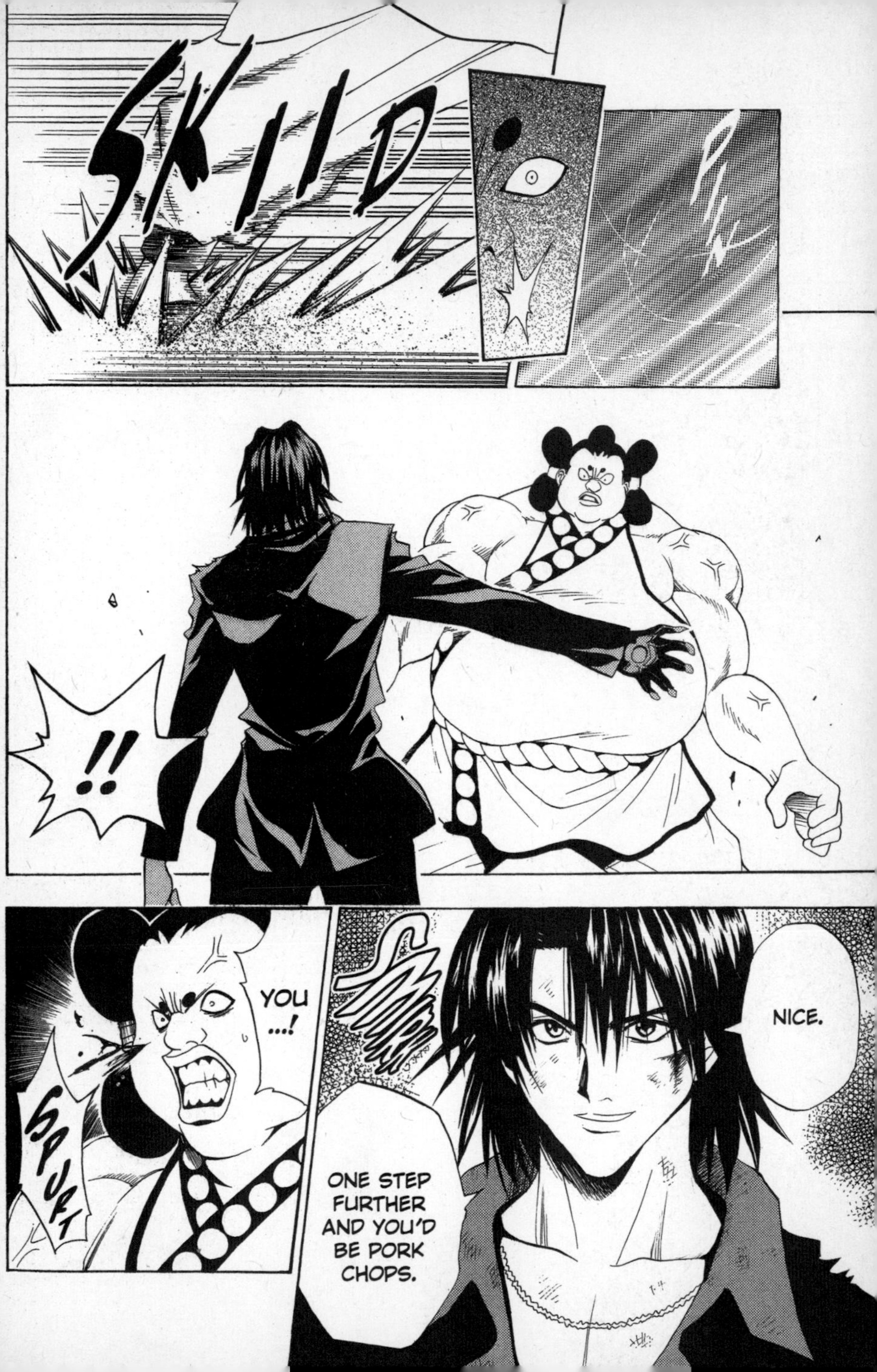
SKIID
!!
YOU ...!
SPURT
NICE.
ONE STEP FURTHER AND YOU'D BE PORK CHOPS.

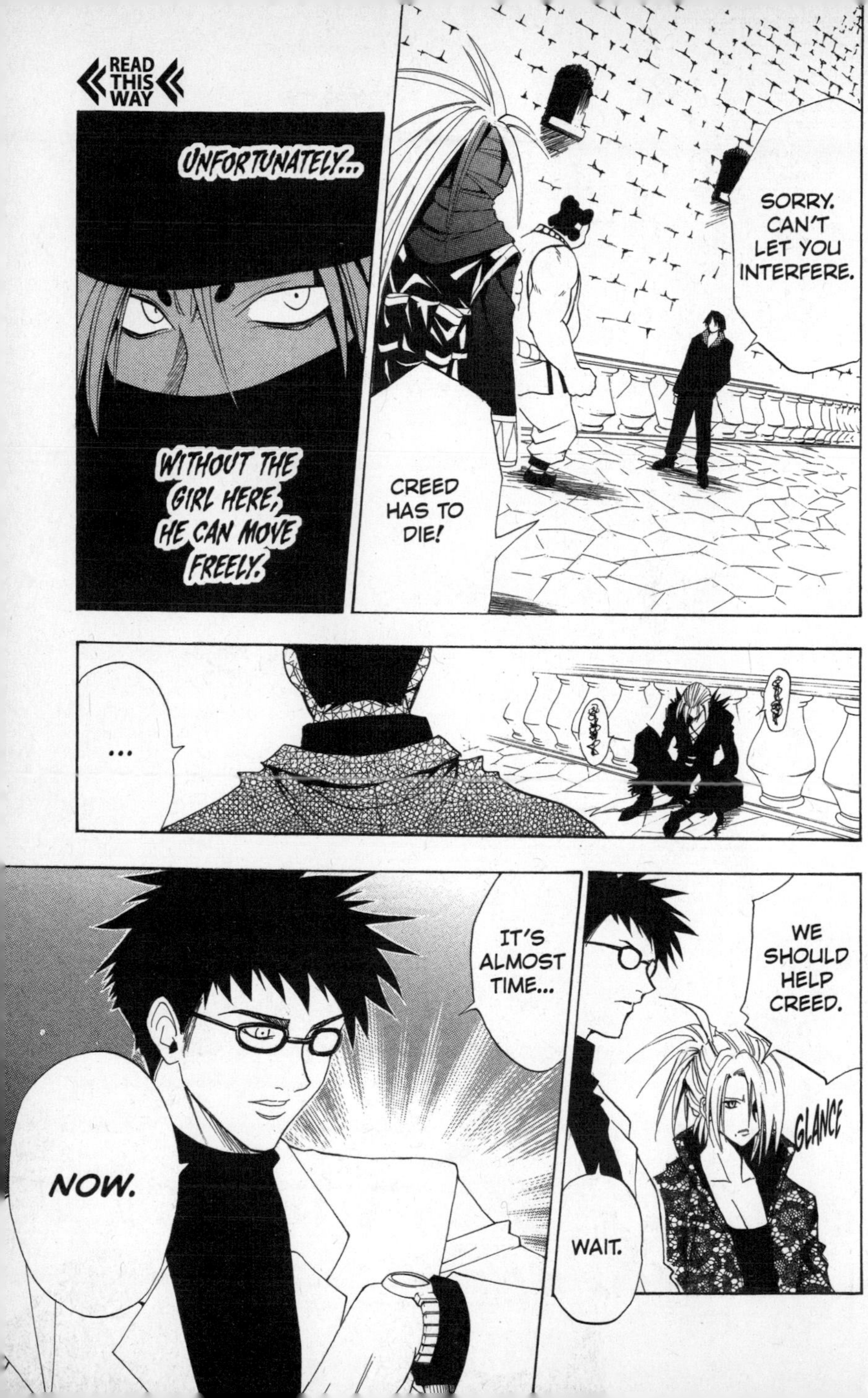
READ THIS WAY
SORRY. CAN'T LET YOU INTERFERE.
CREED HAS TO DIE!
UNFORTUNATELY...
WITHOUT THE GIRL HERE, HE CAN MOVE FREELY.
...
WE SHOULD HELP CREED.
GLANCE
IT'S ALMOST TIME...
WAIT.
NOW.

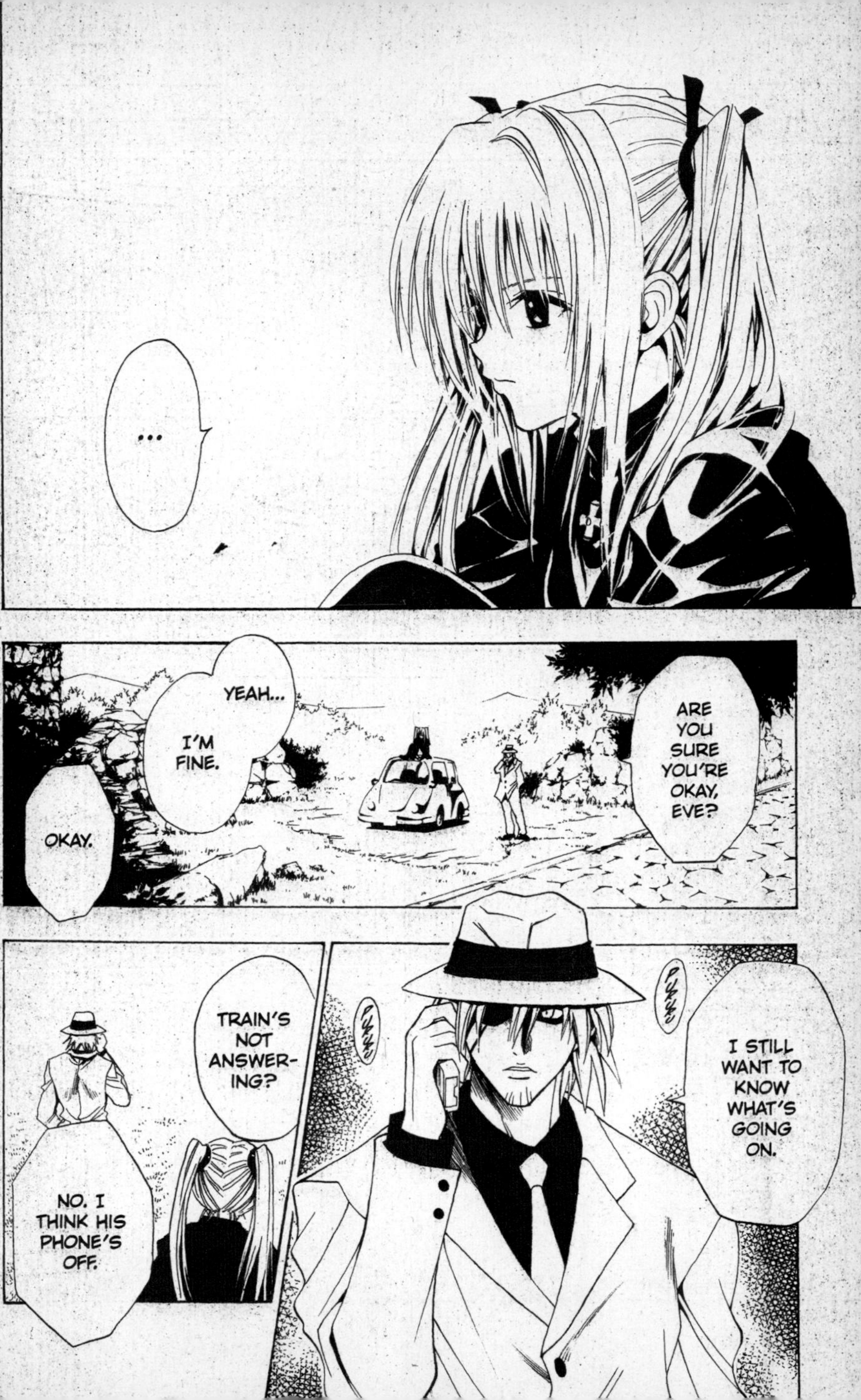
...
ARE YOU SURE YOU'RE OKAY, EVE?
YEAH... I'M FINE.
OKAY.
I STILL WANT TO KNOW WHAT'S GOING ON.
TRAIN'S NOT ANSWERING?
NO. I THINK HIS PHONE'S OFF.

READ THIS WAY

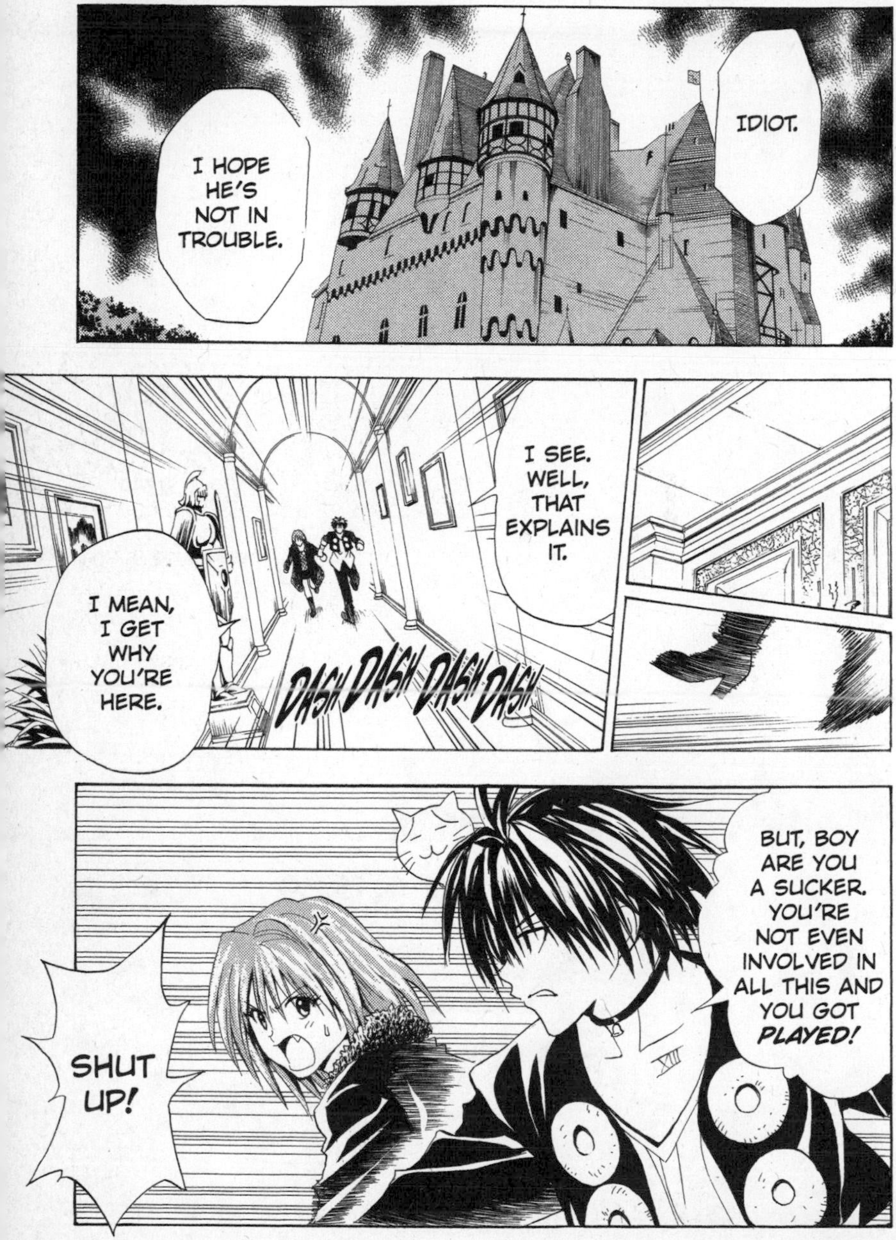
IDIOT.
I HOPE HE'S NOT IN TROUBLE.
I SEE. WELL, THAT EXPLAINS IT.
I MEAN, I GET WHY YOU'RE HERE.
DASH DASH DASH DASH
BUT, BOY ARE YOU A SUCKER. YOU'RE NOT EVEN INVOLVED IN ALL THIS AND YOU GOT PLAYED!
SHUT UP!

THEY'RE OKAY *NOW.*

ANY-WAY...

NOW?

I HOPE THOSE GUYS ARE OKAY.

YOU'RE STARTING TO GET ON MY NERVES!

SURE. NOTHING'S HOLDING THEM BACK NOW THAT *YOU'RE* GONE!

PFFT

HOW ARE YOU GOING TO FEEL IF THEY MANAGE IT?

IF CERBERUS KILLS CREED, I MEAN.

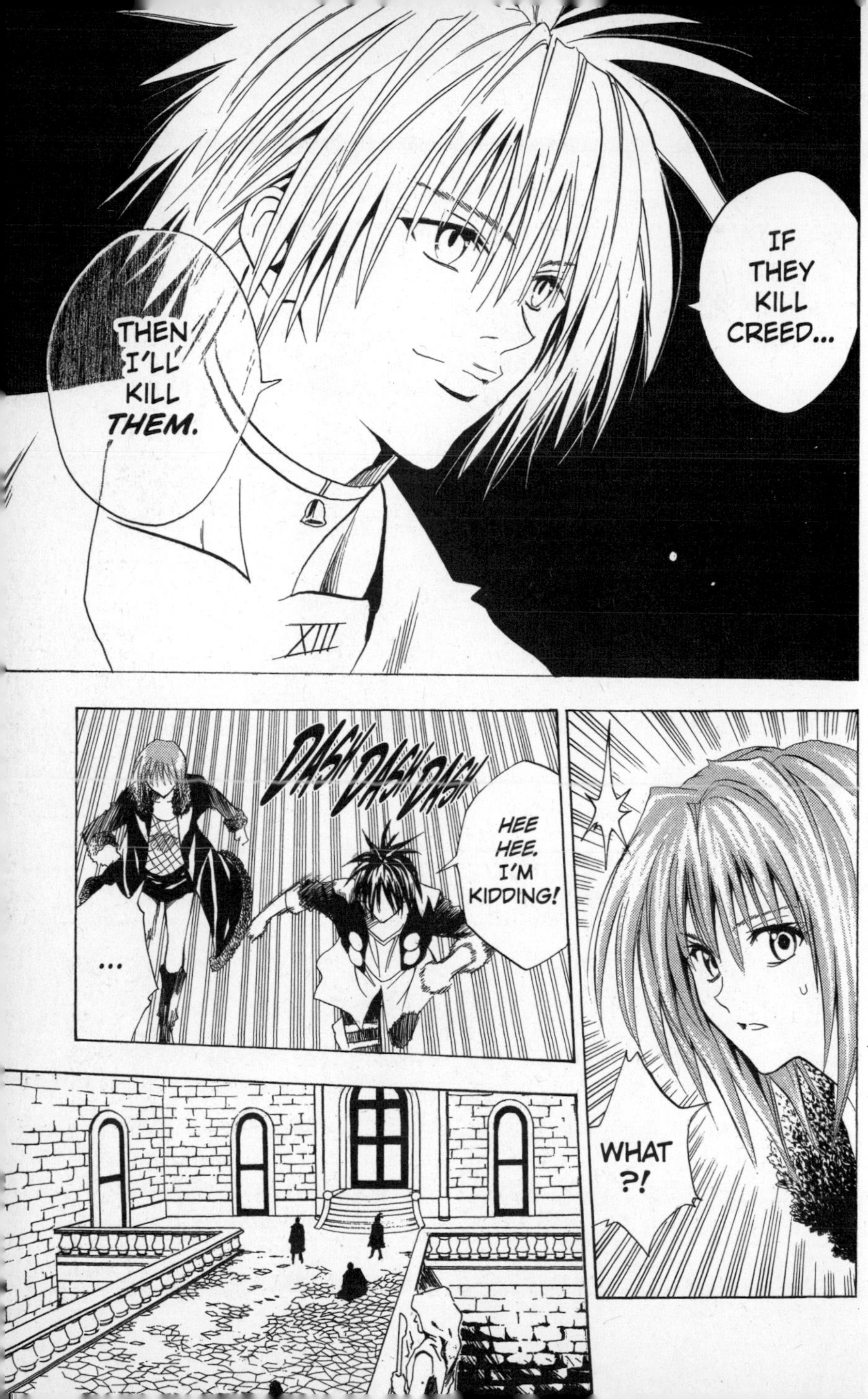
IF THEY KILL CREED...
THEN I'LL KILL *THEM.*
WHAT ?!
DASH DASH DASH
HEE HEE. I'M KIDDING!
...

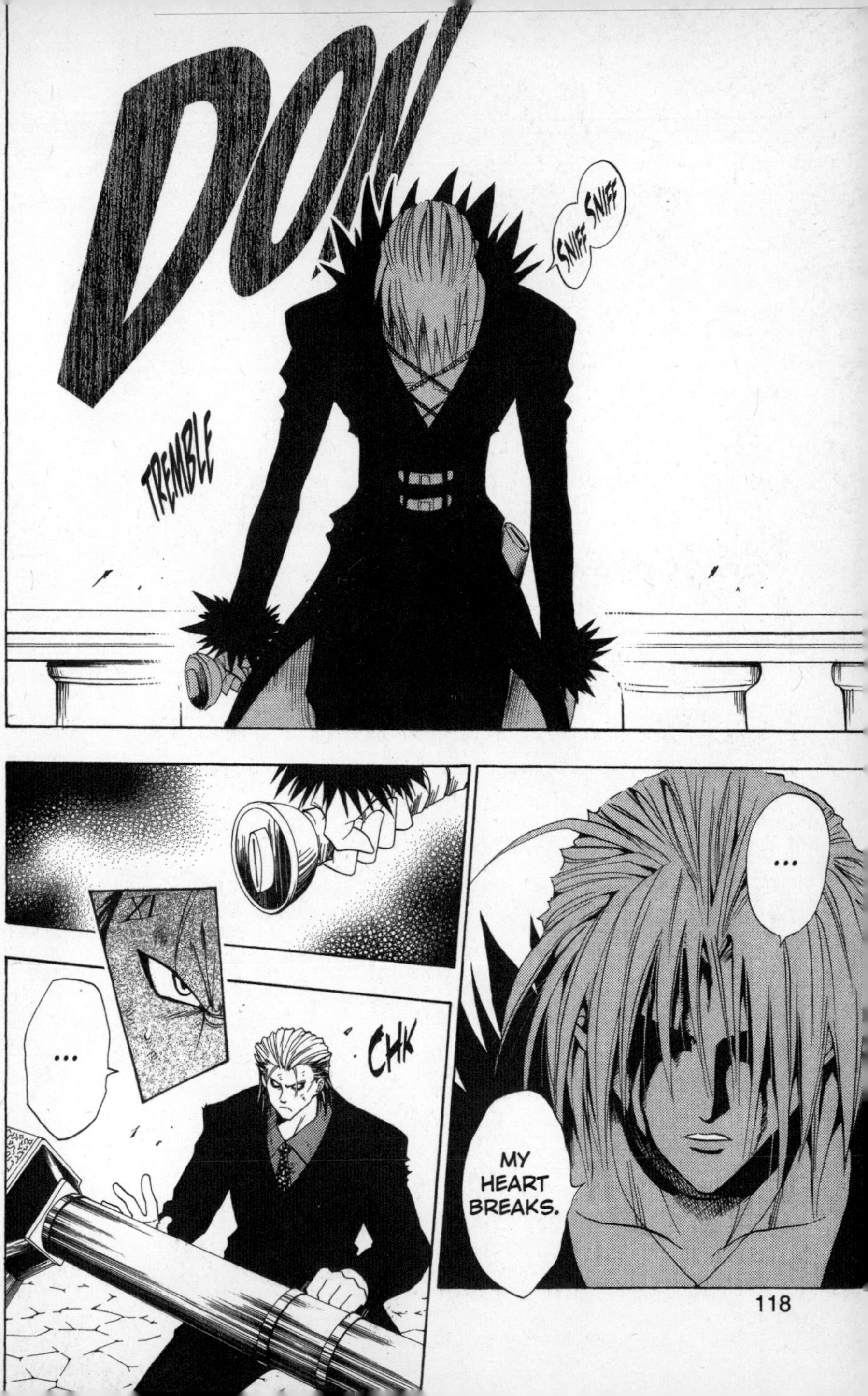
DON
SNIFF SNIFF
TREMBLE
...
MY HEART BREAKS.
CHK
...

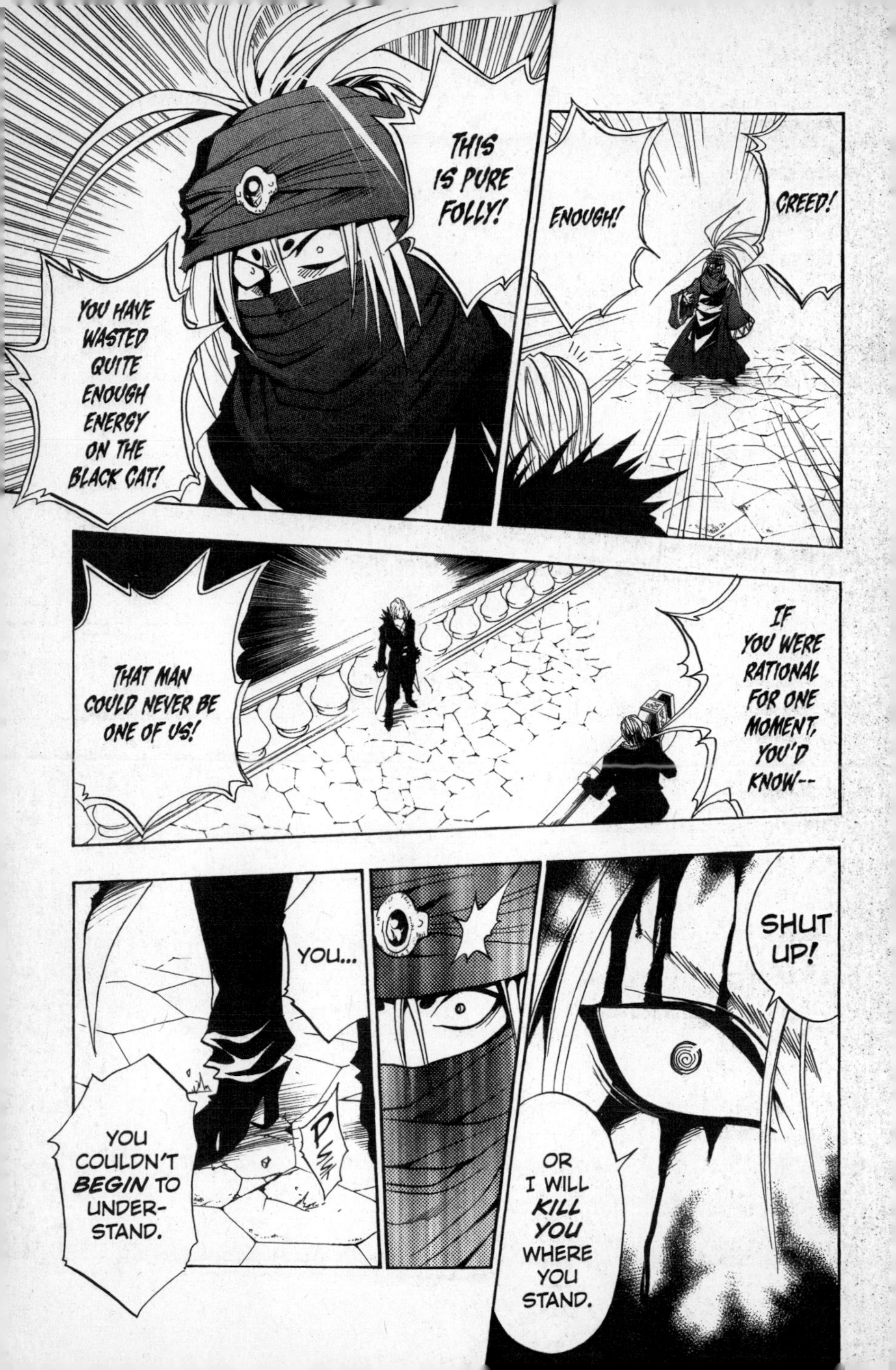
CREED!
ENOUGH!
THIS IS PURE FOLLY!
YOU HAVE WASTED QUITE ENOUGH ENERGY ON THE BLACK CAT!
IF YOU WERE RATIONAL FOR ONE MOMENT, YOU'D KNOW--
THAT MAN COULD NEVER BE ONE OF US!
SHUT UP!
OR I WILL *KILL YOU* WHERE YOU STAND.
YOU...
YOU COULDN'T *BEGIN* TO UNDER-STAND.

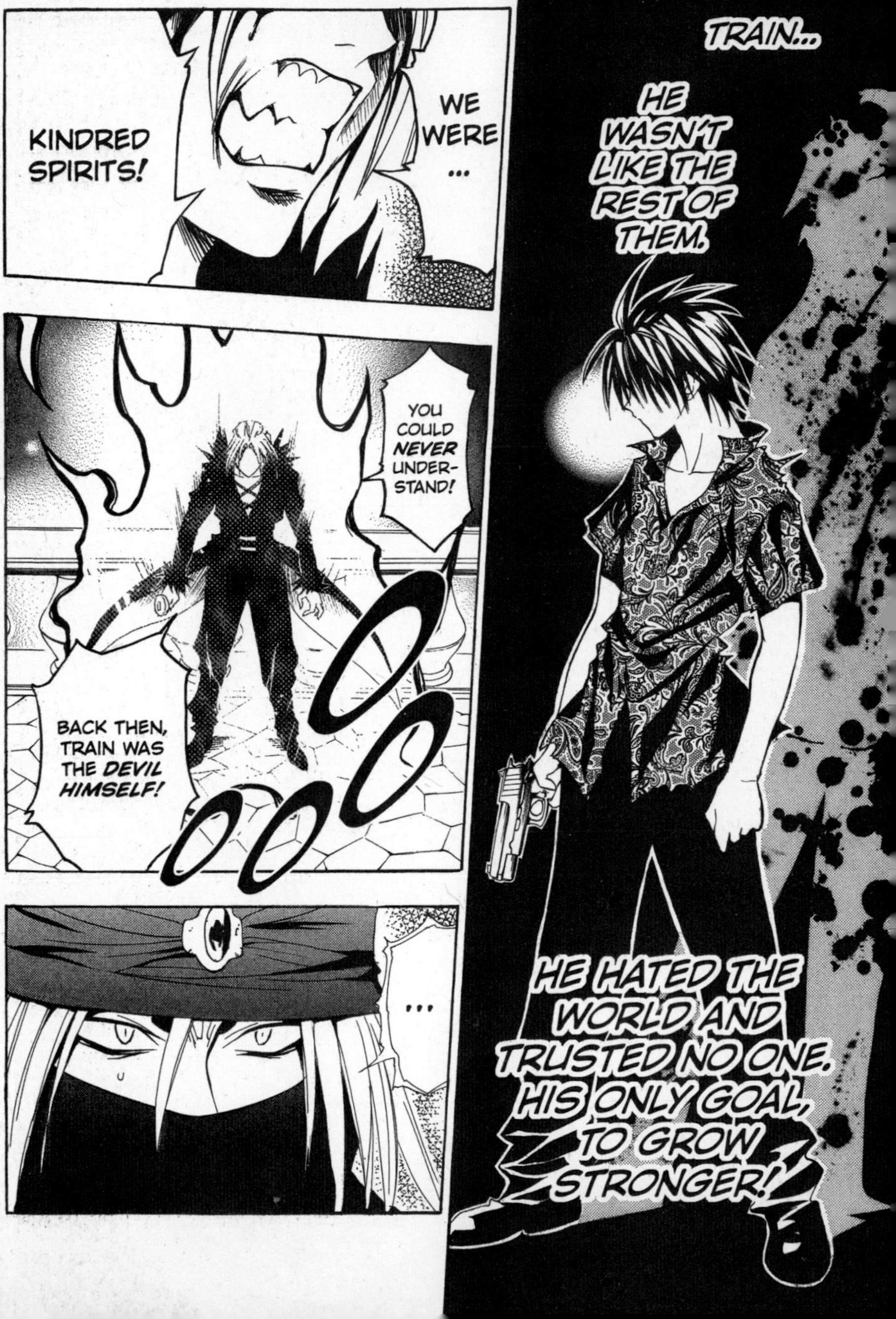
TRAIN...
HE WASN'T LIKE THE REST OF THEM.
WE WERE...
KINDRED SPIRITS!
YOU COULD NEVER UNDER-STAND!
BACK THEN, TRAIN WAS THE DEVIL HIMSELF!
...
HE HATED THE WORLD AND TRUSTED NO ONE. HIS ONLY GOAL, TO GROW STRONGER!

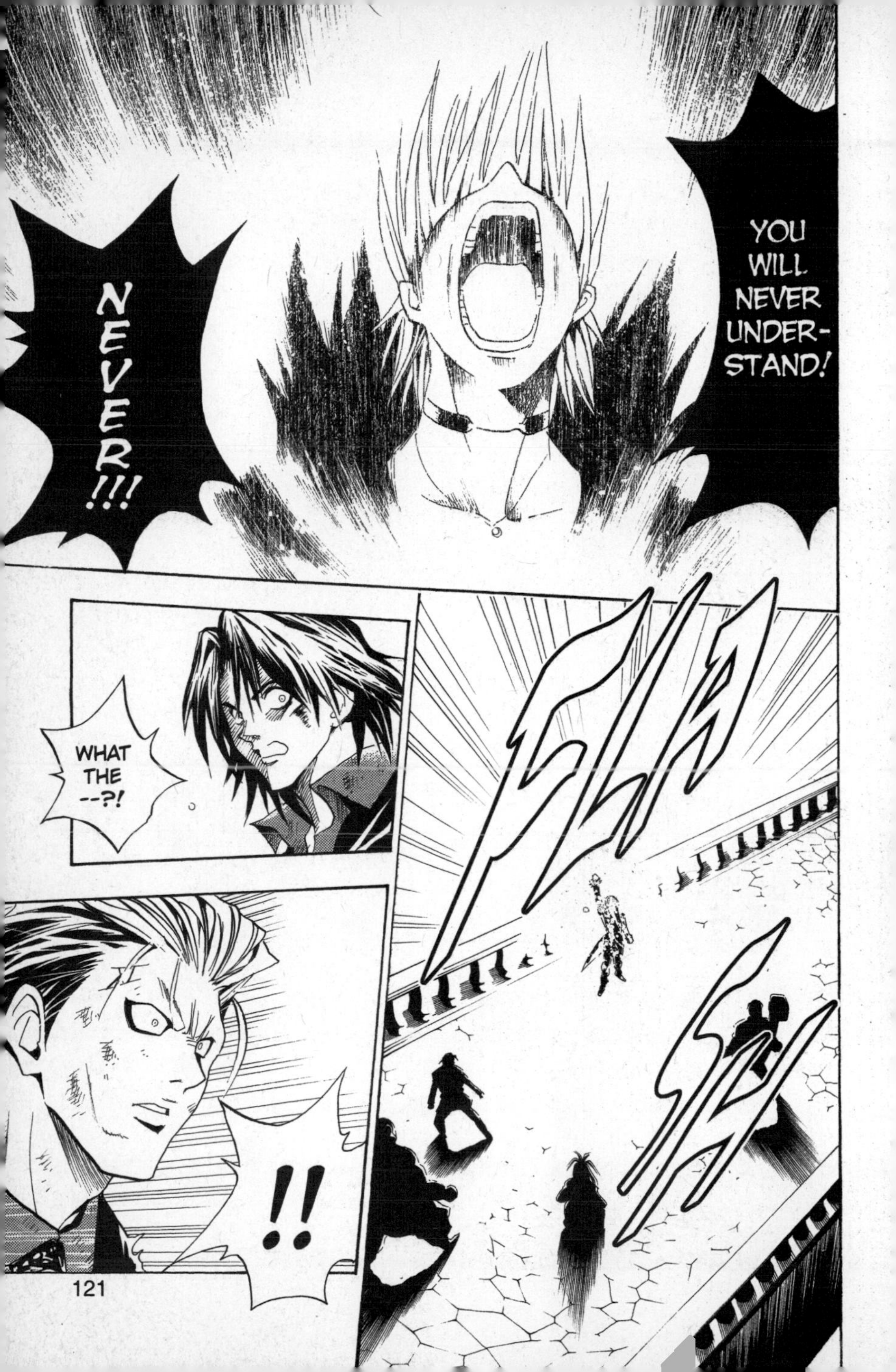
YOU WILL NEVER UNDER-STAND!
NEVER!!!
WHAT THE --?!
!!

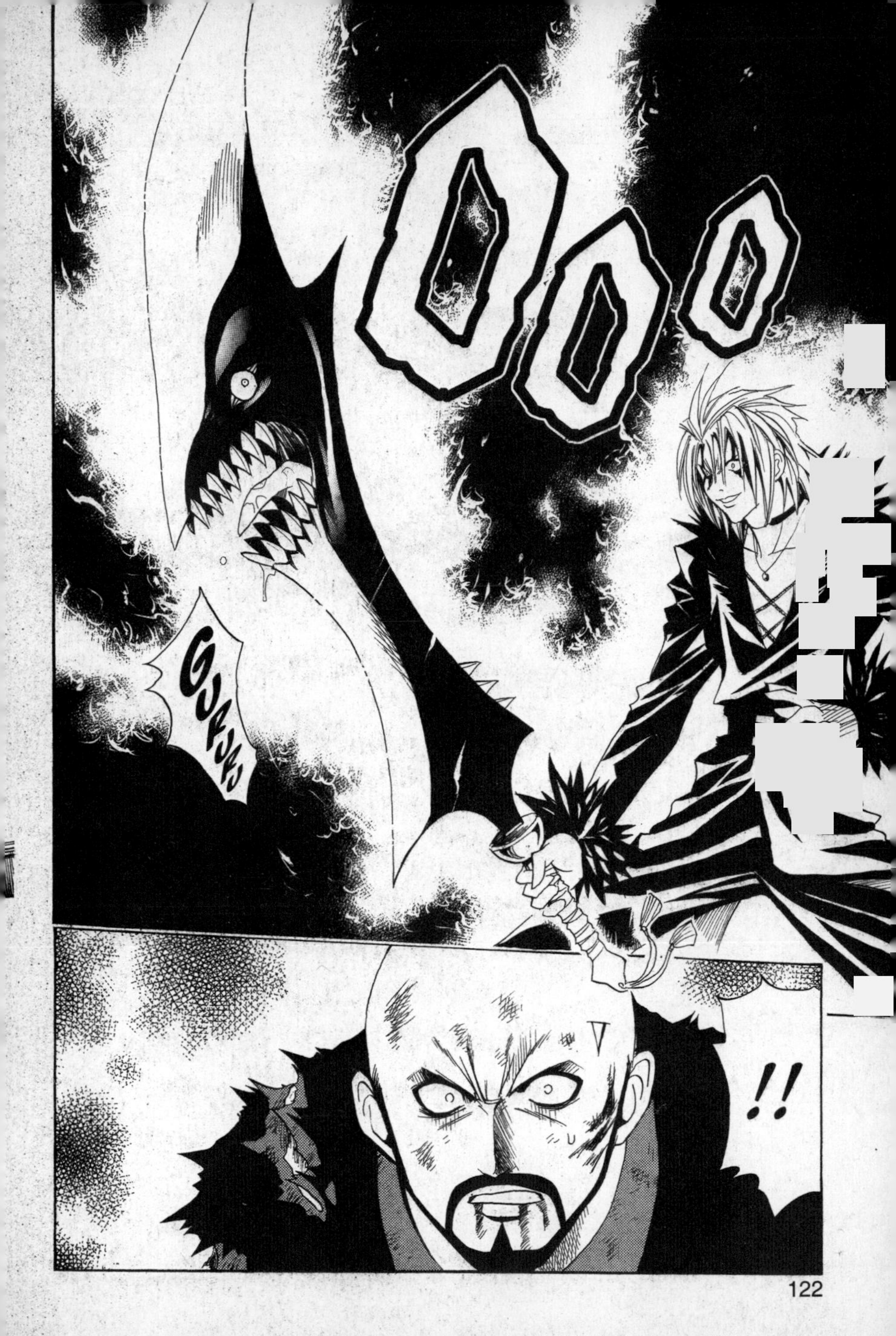
!!

READ THIS WAY

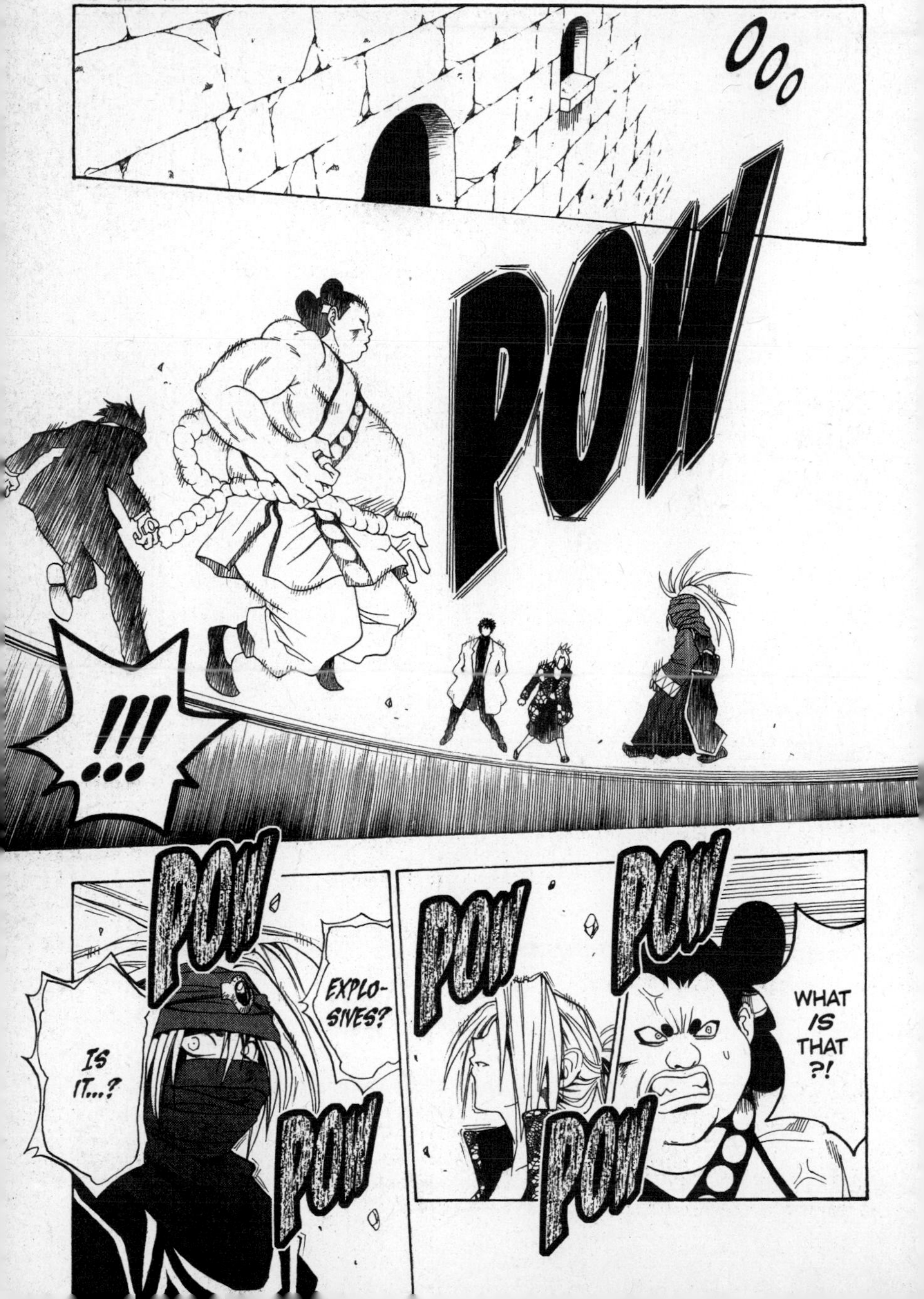
OOO
POW
!!!
...
POW
POW
POW
WHAT IS THAT?!
POW
POW
EXPLOSIVES?
IS IT...?

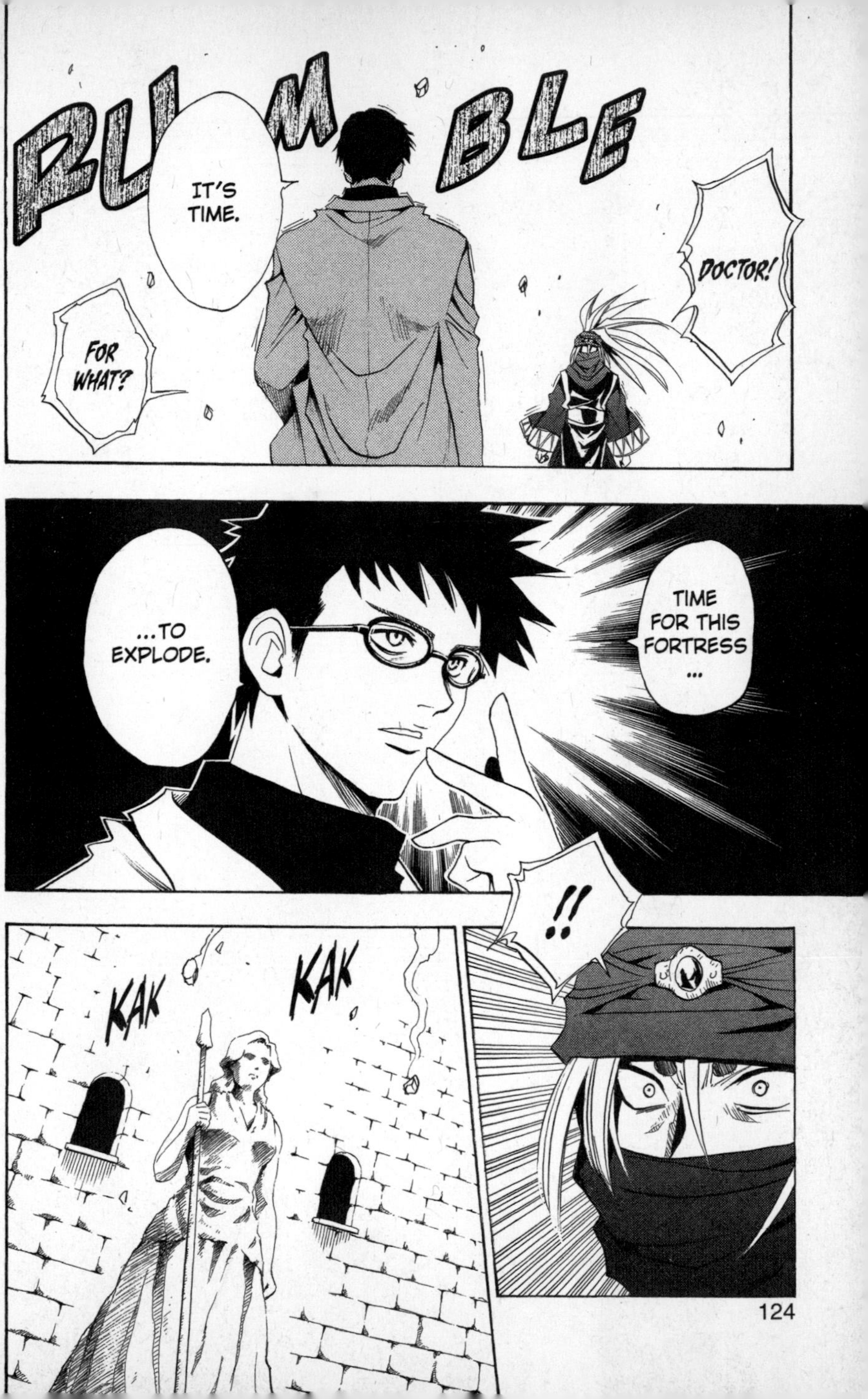
RUMBLE
IT'S TIME.
FOR WHAT?
DOCTOR!
TIME FOR THIS FORTRESS ...
...TO EXPLODE.
!!
KAK
KAK

READ THIS WAY

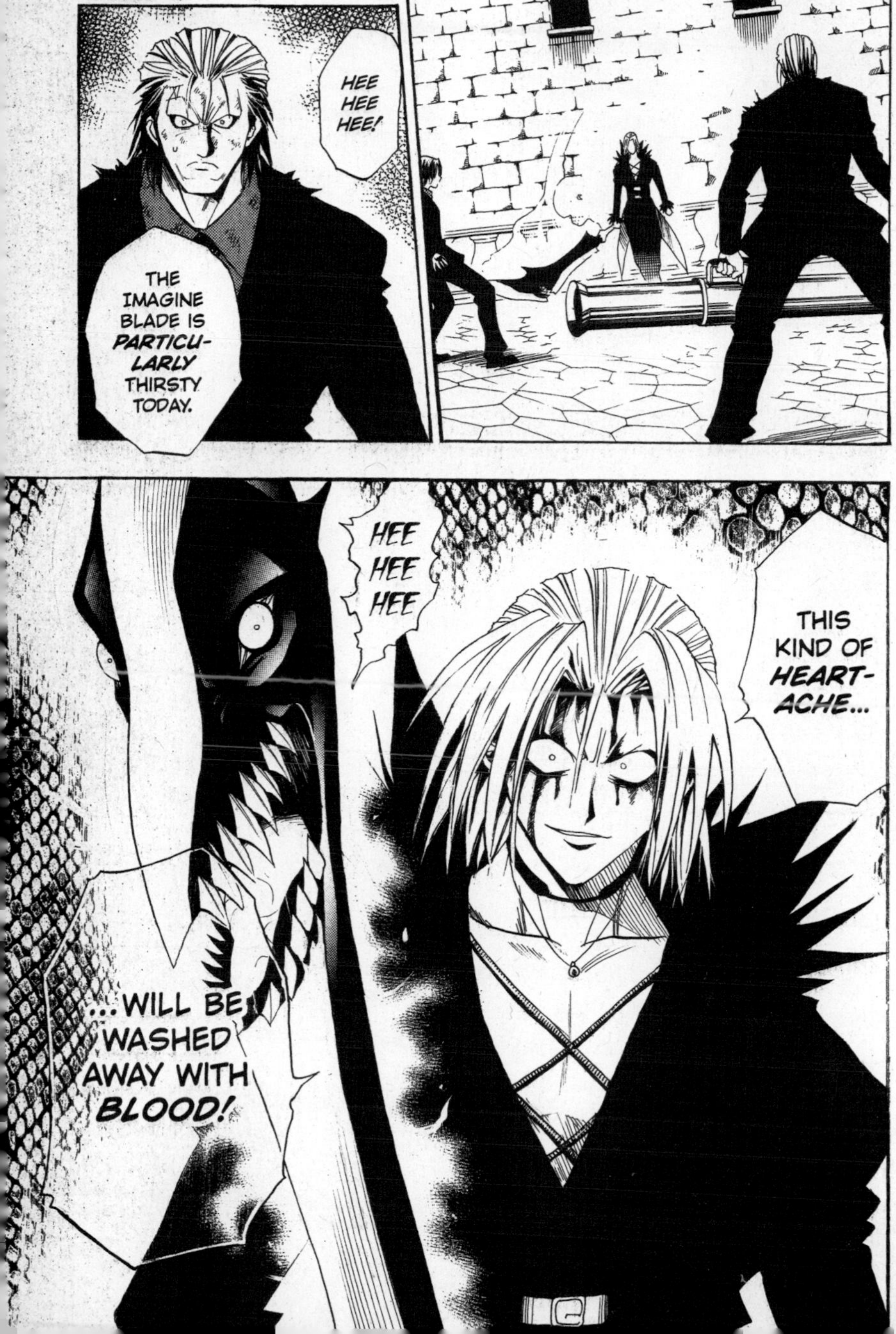
HEE HEE HEE!
THE IMAGINE BLADE IS *PARTICULARLY* THIRSTY TODAY.
THIS KIND OF *HEART-ACHE...*
HEE HEE HEE
...WILL BE WASHED AWAY WITH *BLOOD!*

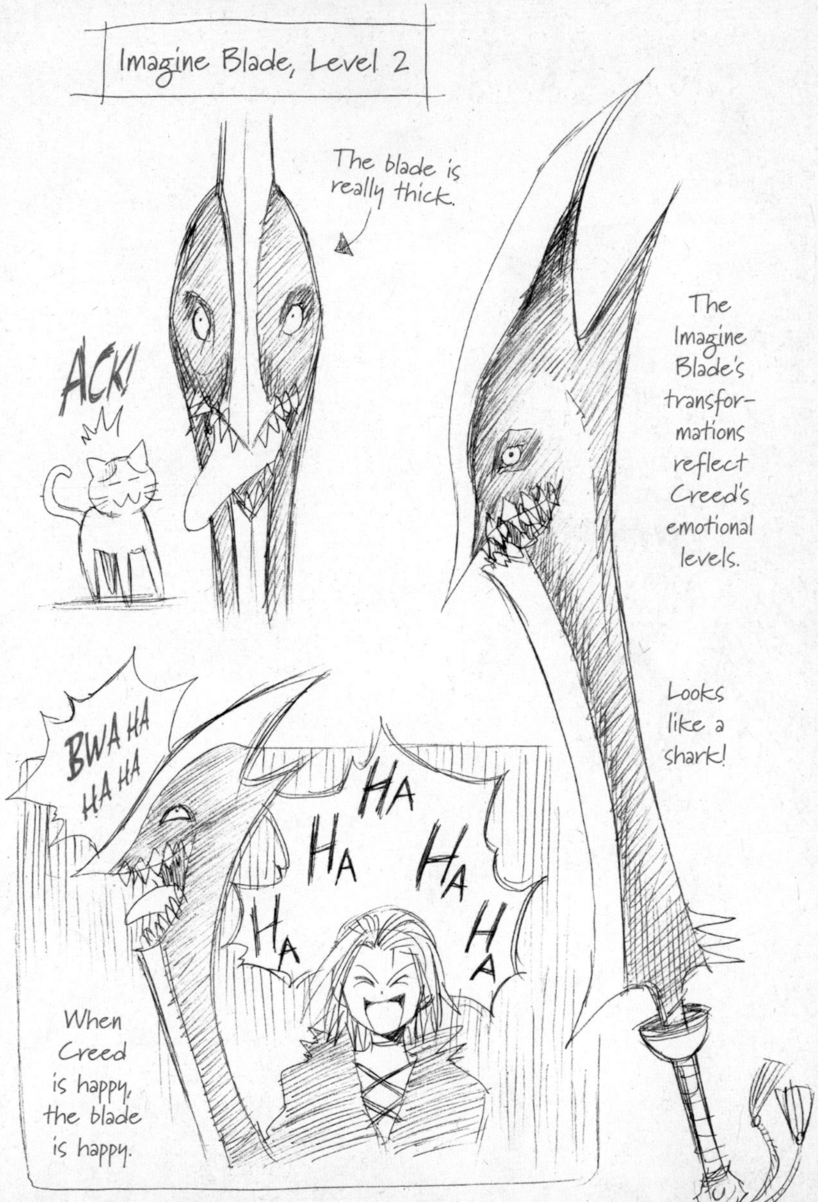
Imagine Blade, Level 2
The blade is really thick.
ACK!
The Imagine Blade's transfor-mations reflect Creed's emotional levels.
Looks like a shark!
BWA HA HA HA
HA HA HA HA HA
When Creed is happy, the blade is happy.

Chapter 82:
Nizer's Resolve

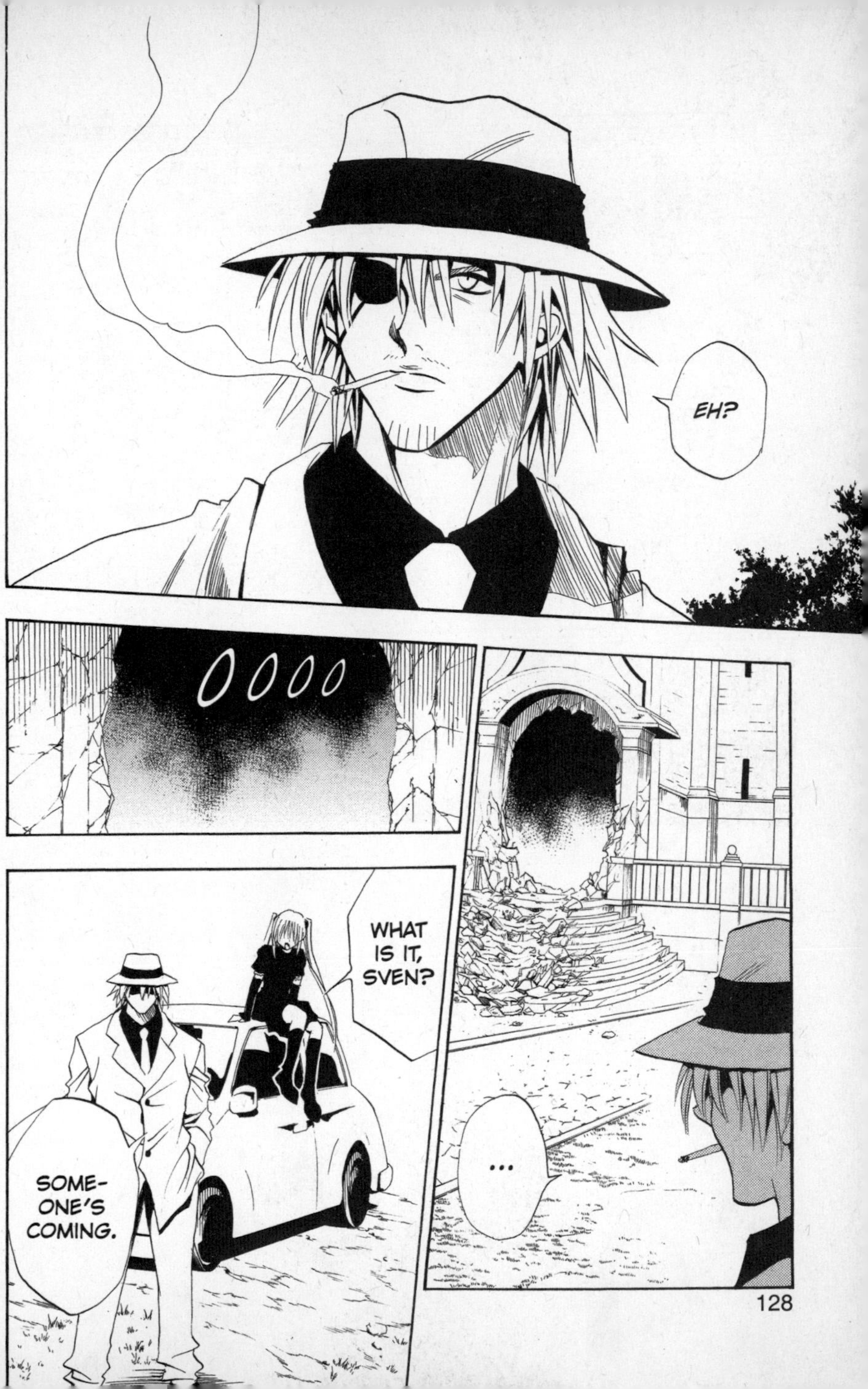

EH?
...
OOOO
WHAT IS IT, SVEN?
SOME-ONE'S COMING.

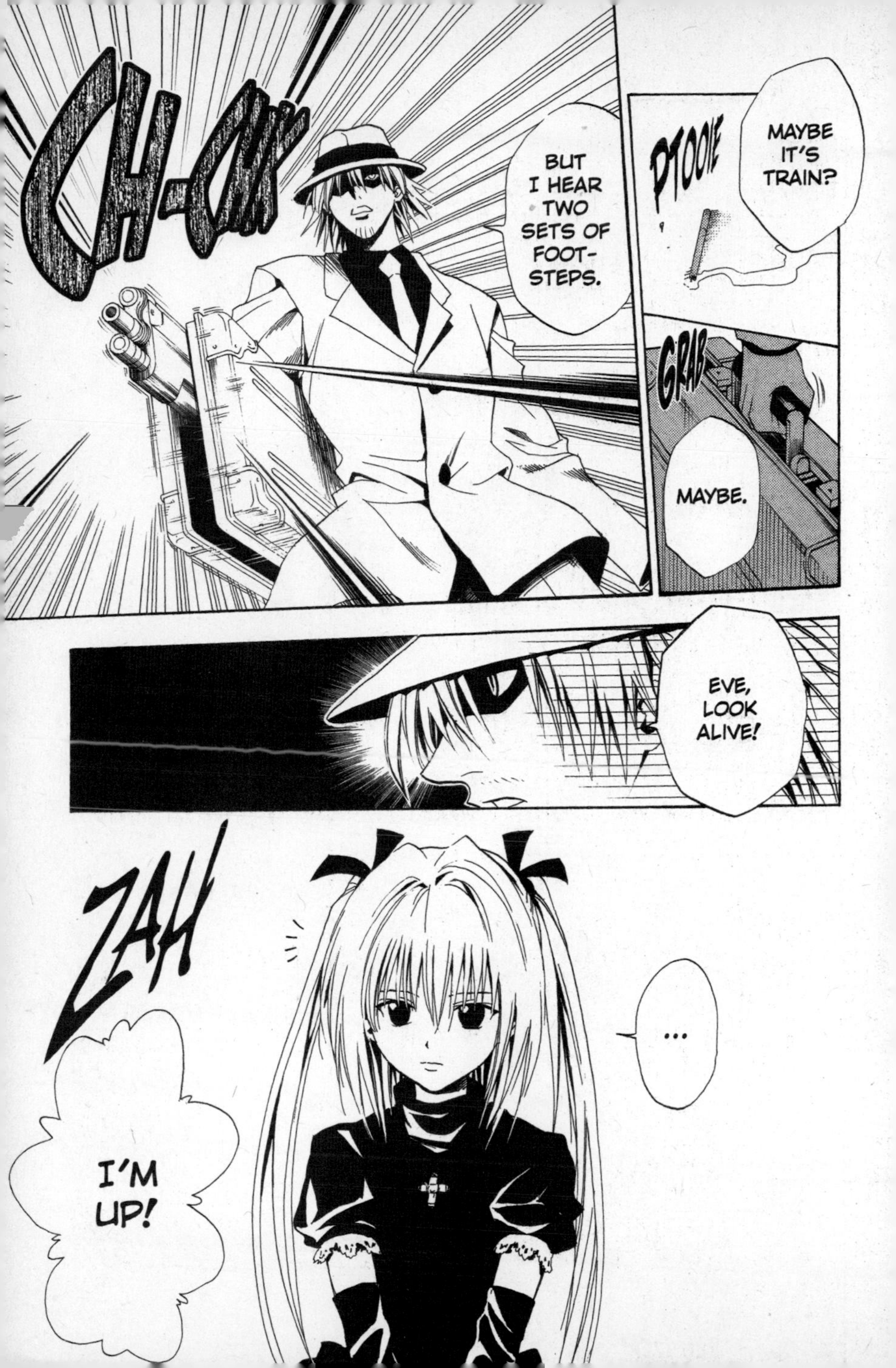
MAYBE IT'S TRAIN?
PTOOIE
BUT I HEAR TWO SETS OF FOOT-STEPS.
CH-CHK
GRAB
MAYBE.
EVE, LOOK ALIVE!
...
ZAH
I'M UP!

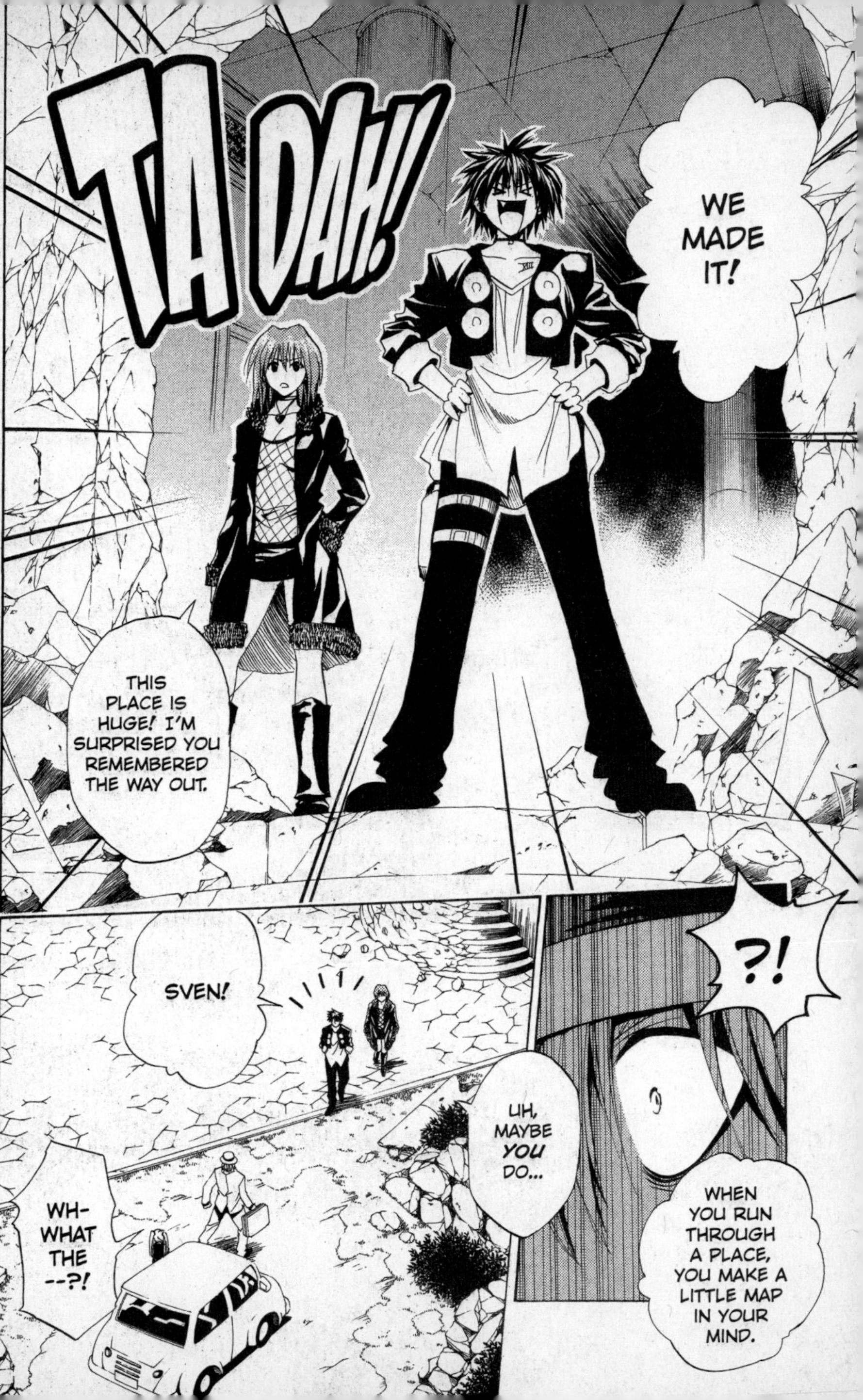

TA DAH!
WE MADE IT!
THIS PLACE IS HUGE! I'M SURPRISED YOU REMEMBERED THE WAY OUT.
WHEN YOU RUN THROUGH A PLACE, YOU MAKE A LITTLE MAP IN YOUR MIND.
UH, MAYBE *YOU* DO...
?!
SVEN!
WH- WHAT THE --?!

LONG TIME NO SEE, BIG GUY. ♡

CHARMING, AS EVER.

WHAT'S *SHE* DOING HERE?

?

Rinslet's Field of View

WHAT A PAIR.

SO RUDE!

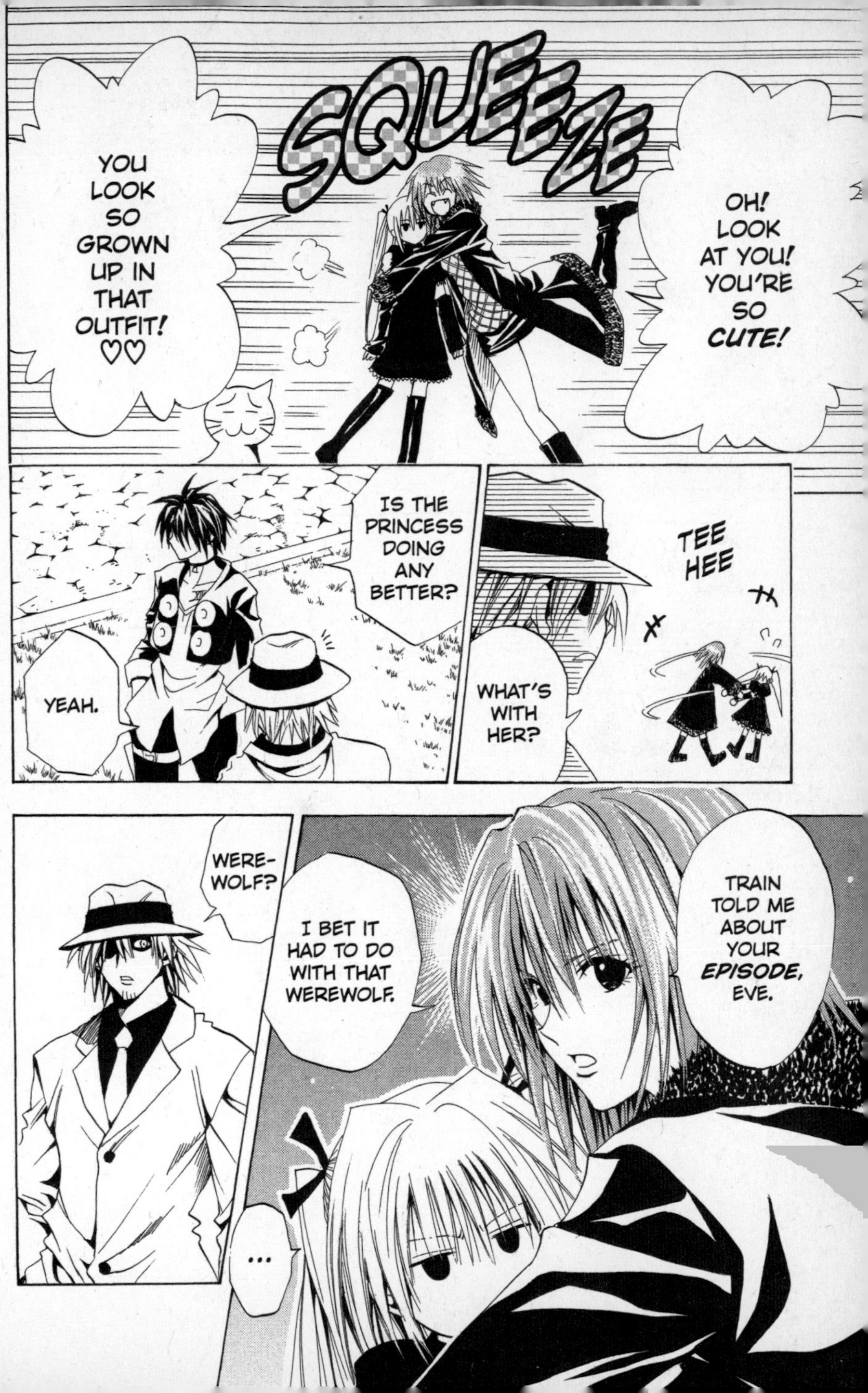
OH! LOOK AT YOU! YOU'RE SO CUTE!
SQUEEZE
YOU LOOK SO GROWN UP IN THAT OUTFIT! ♡♡
TEE HEE
WHAT'S WITH HER?
IS THE PRINCESS DOING ANY BETTER?
YEAH.
TRAIN TOLD ME ABOUT YOUR EPISODE, EVE.
I BET IT HAD TO DO WITH THAT WEREWOLF.
WERE-WOLF?
...

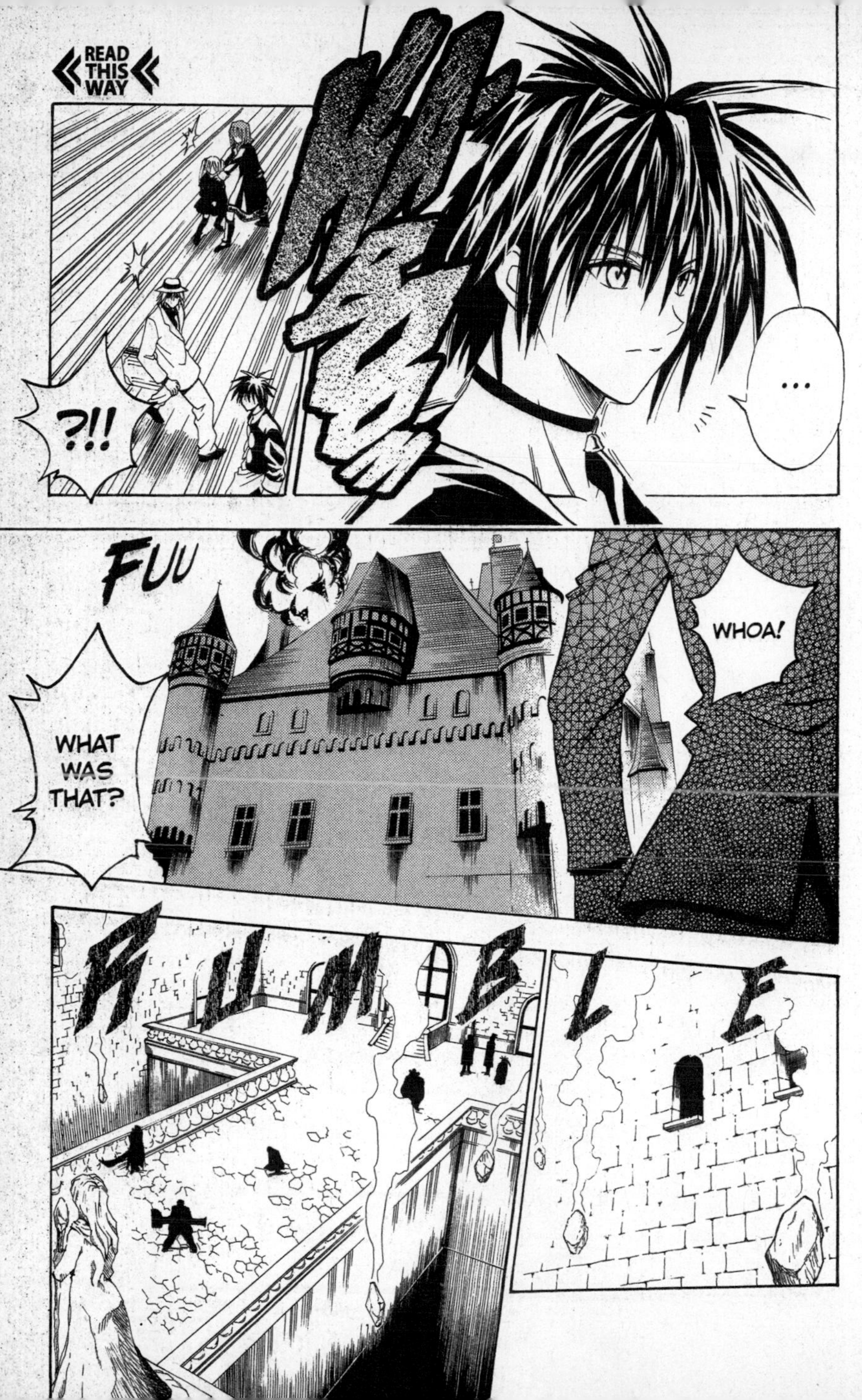
READ THIS WAY
...
?!!
WHOA!
FUU
WHAT WAS THAT?
RUMBLE

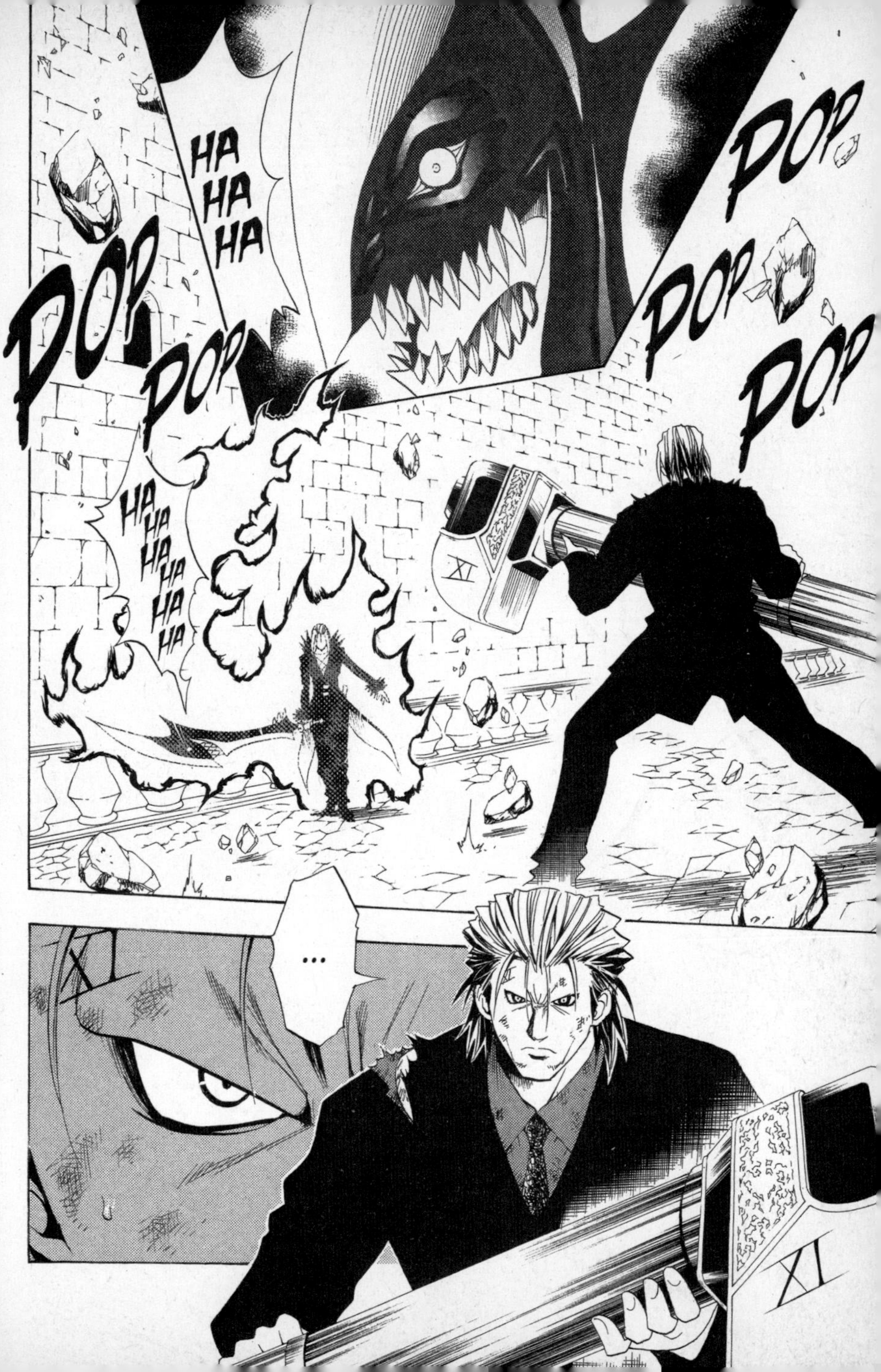

POP
POP
POP
HA HA HA
POP
POP
HA HA HA HA HA HA HA
...
XI

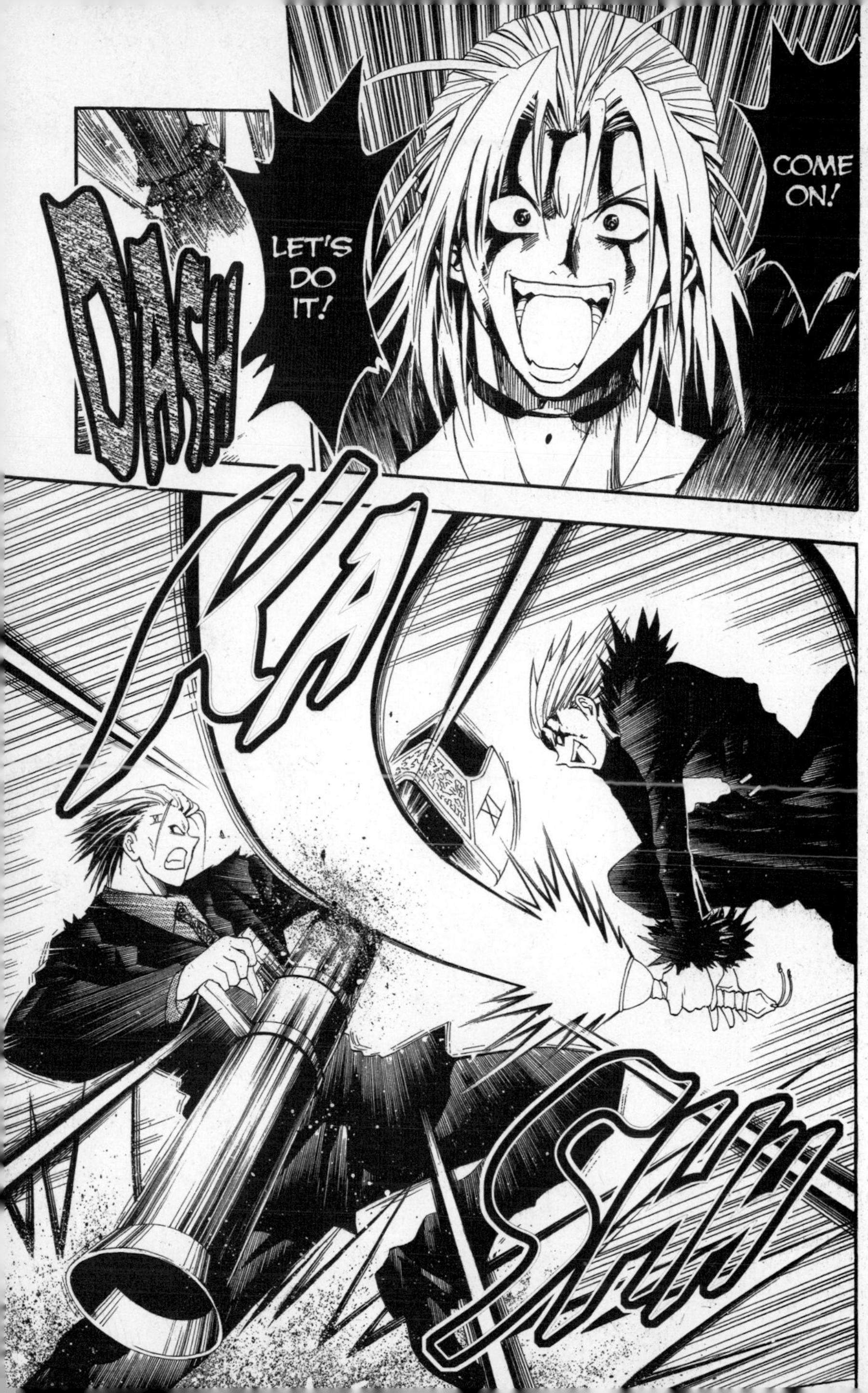
COME ON!
LET'S DO IT!

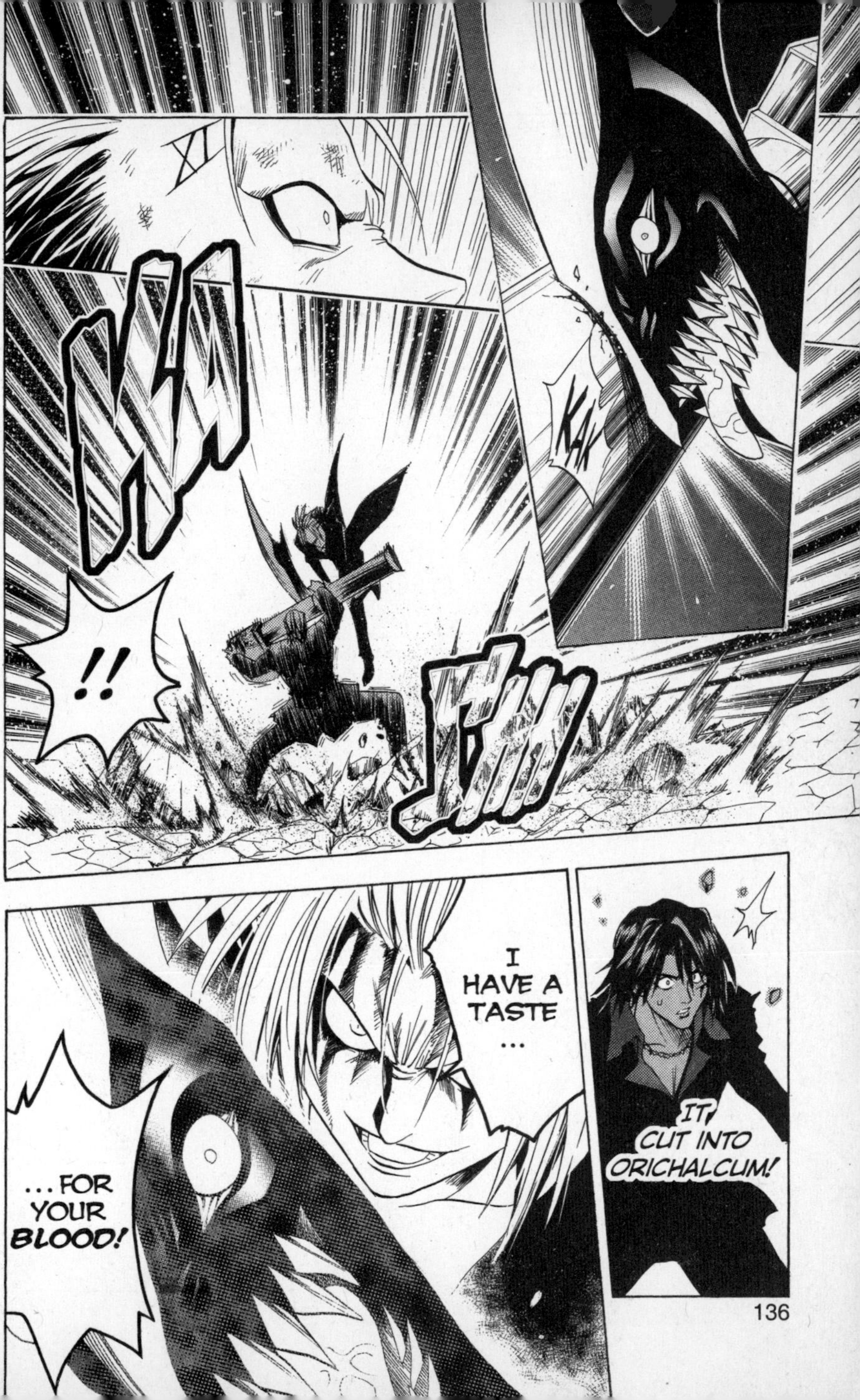

KAK
!!
I HAVE A TASTE ...
IT CUT INTO ORICHALCUM!
... FOR YOUR BLOOD!

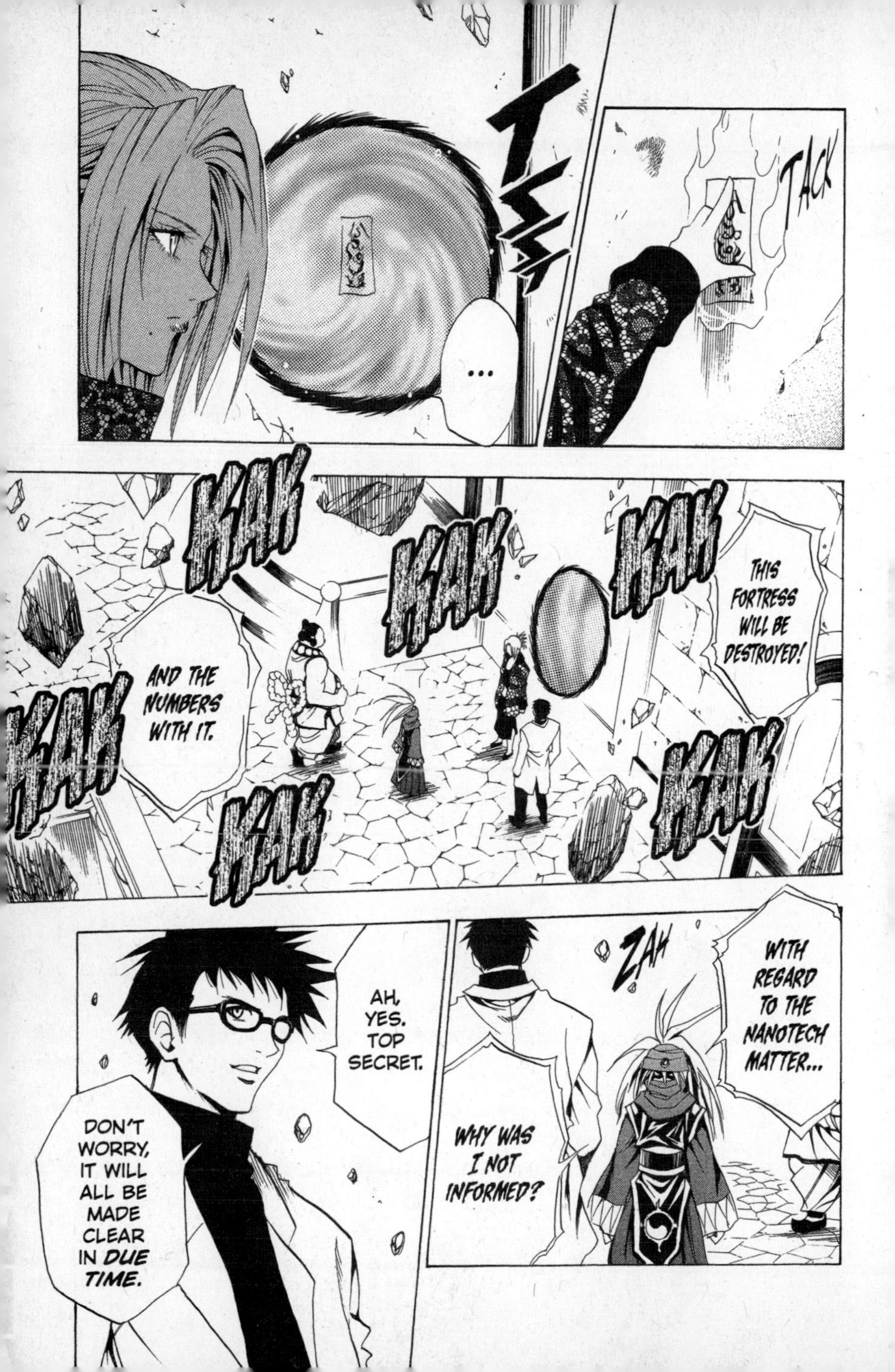
TACK
...
KAK KAK KAK KAK KAK KAK
THIS FORTRESS WILL BE DESTROYED!
AND THE NUMBERS WITH IT.
ZAK
WITH REGARD TO THE NANOTECH MATTER...
WHY WAS I NOT INFORMED?
AH, YES. TOP SECRET.
DON'T WORRY, IT WILL ALL BE MADE CLEAR IN DUE TIME.

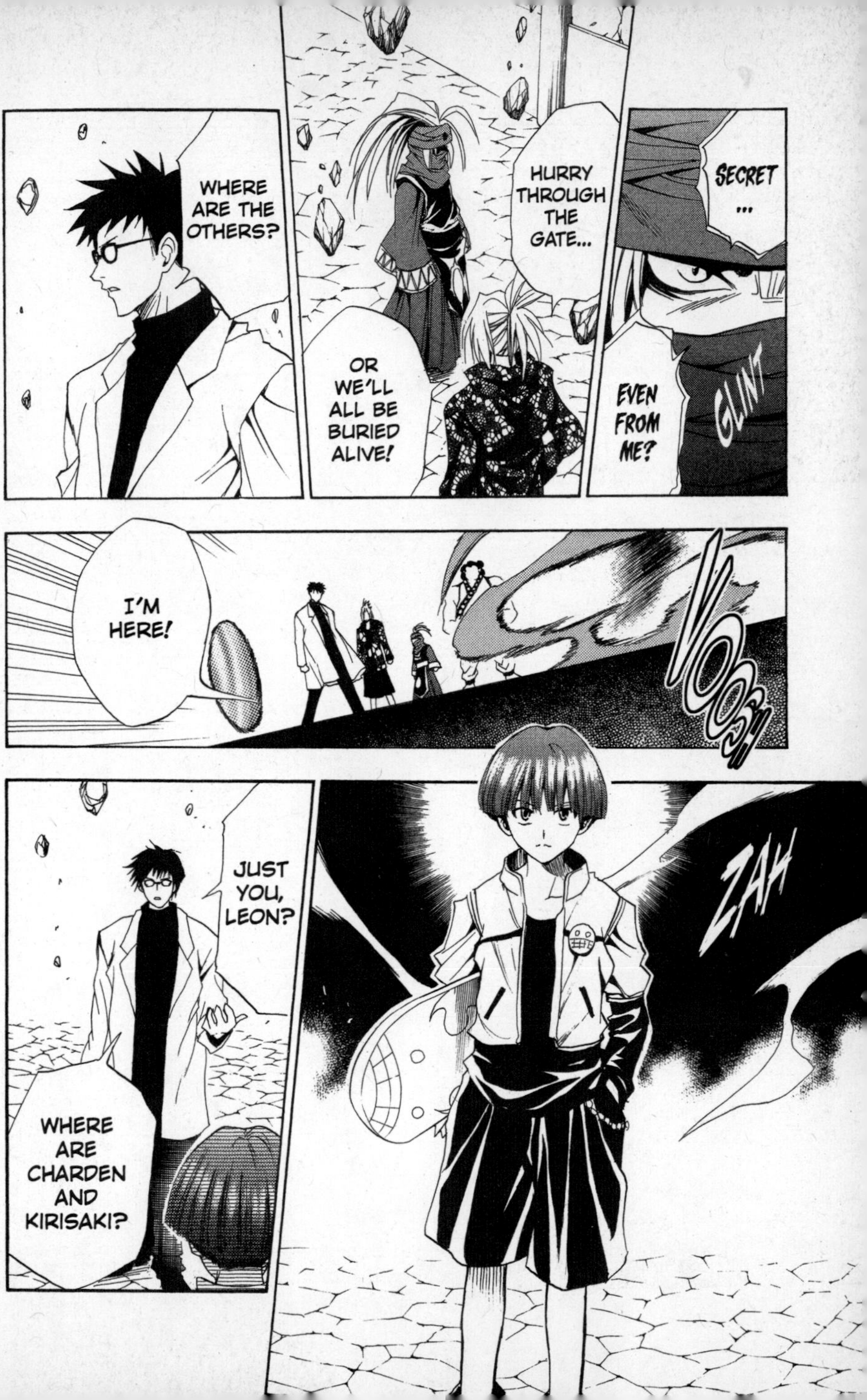
SECRET ...
EVEN FROM ME?
GLINT
HURRY THROUGH THE GATE...
OR WE'LL ALL BE BURIED ALIVE!
WHERE ARE THE OTHERS?
VOOSH
I'M HERE!
ZAH
JUST YOU, LEON?
WHERE ARE CHARDEN AND KIRISAKI?

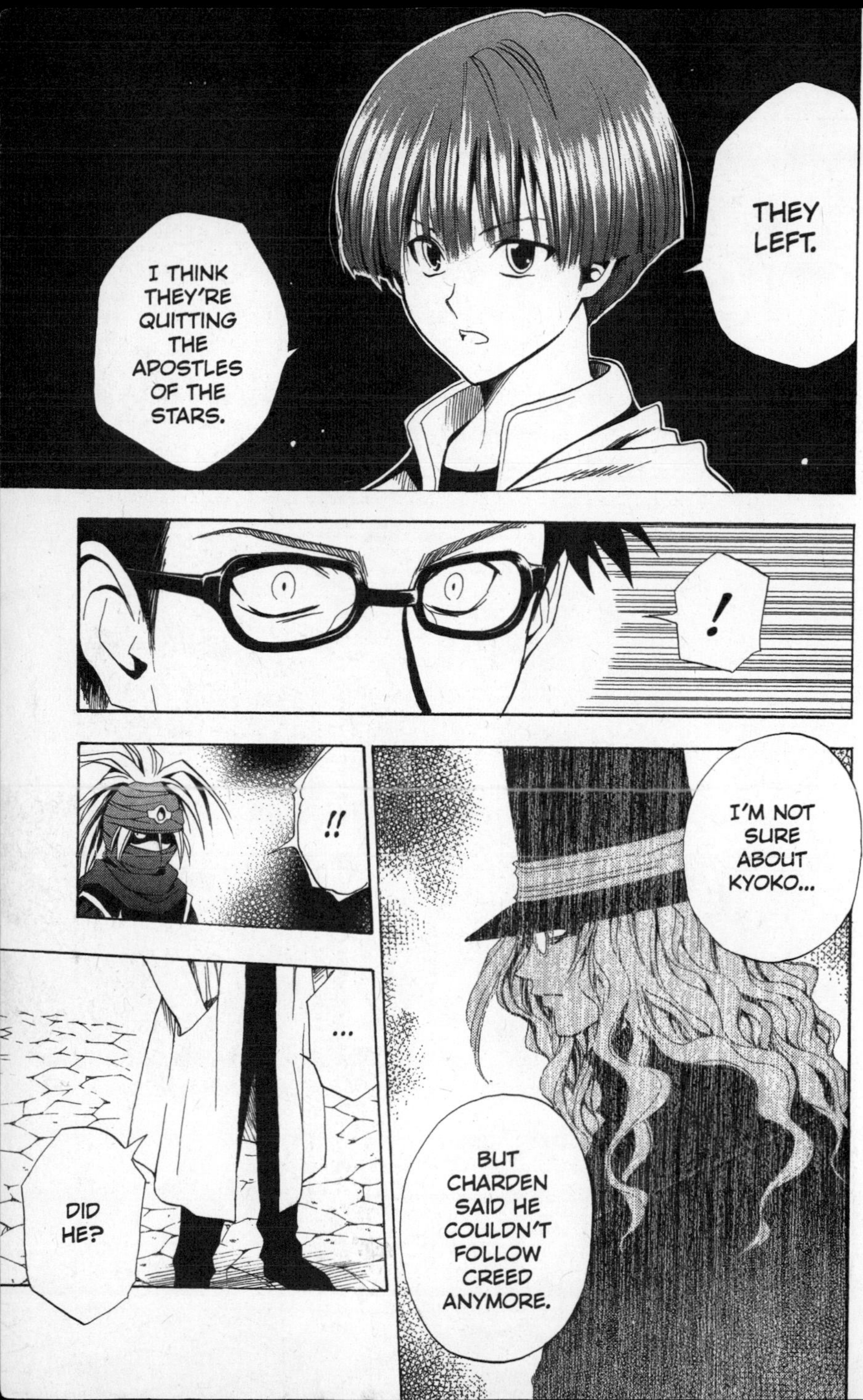
THEY LEFT.
I THINK THEY'RE QUITTING THE APOSTLES OF THE STARS.
!
!!
I'M NOT SURE ABOUT KYOKO...
...
BUT CHARDEN SAID HE COULDN'T FOLLOW CREED ANYMORE.
DID HE?

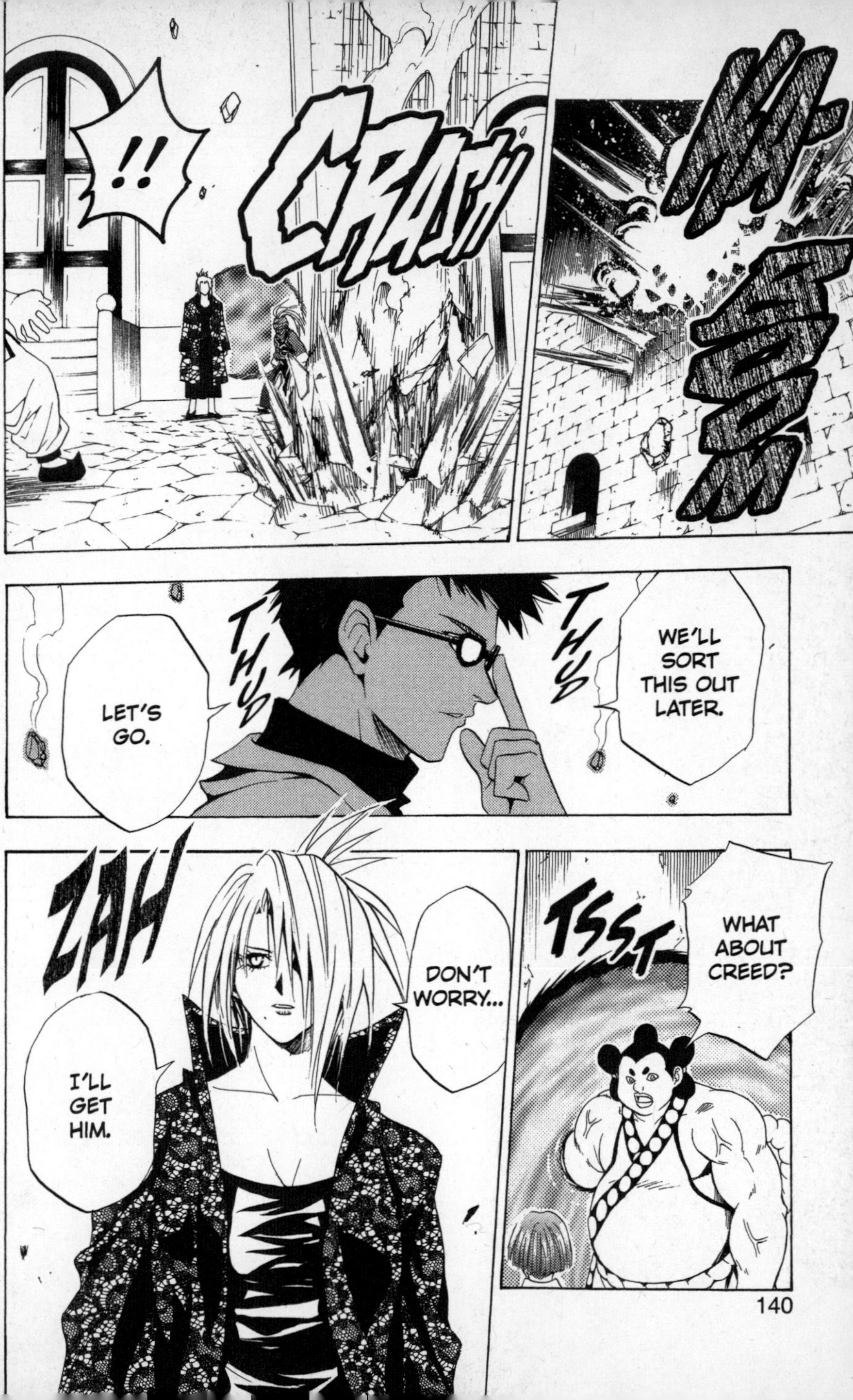
CRASH
!!
THUD
WE'LL SORT THIS OUT LATER.
THUD
LET'S GO.
WHAT ABOUT CREED?
TSST
DON'T WORRY...
I'LL GET HIM.
ZAH

READ THIS WAY

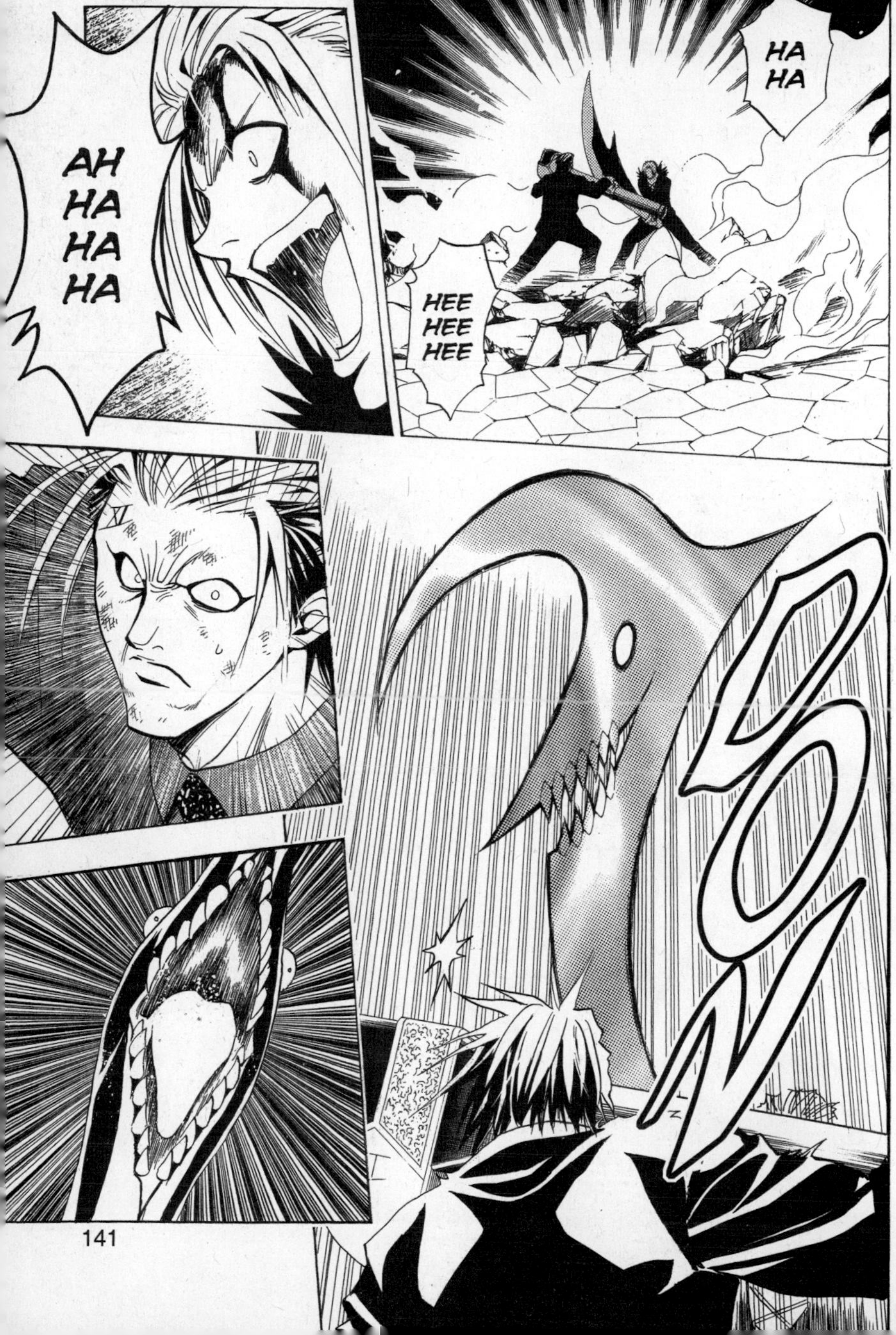
HA HA
HEE HEE HEE
AH HA HA HA

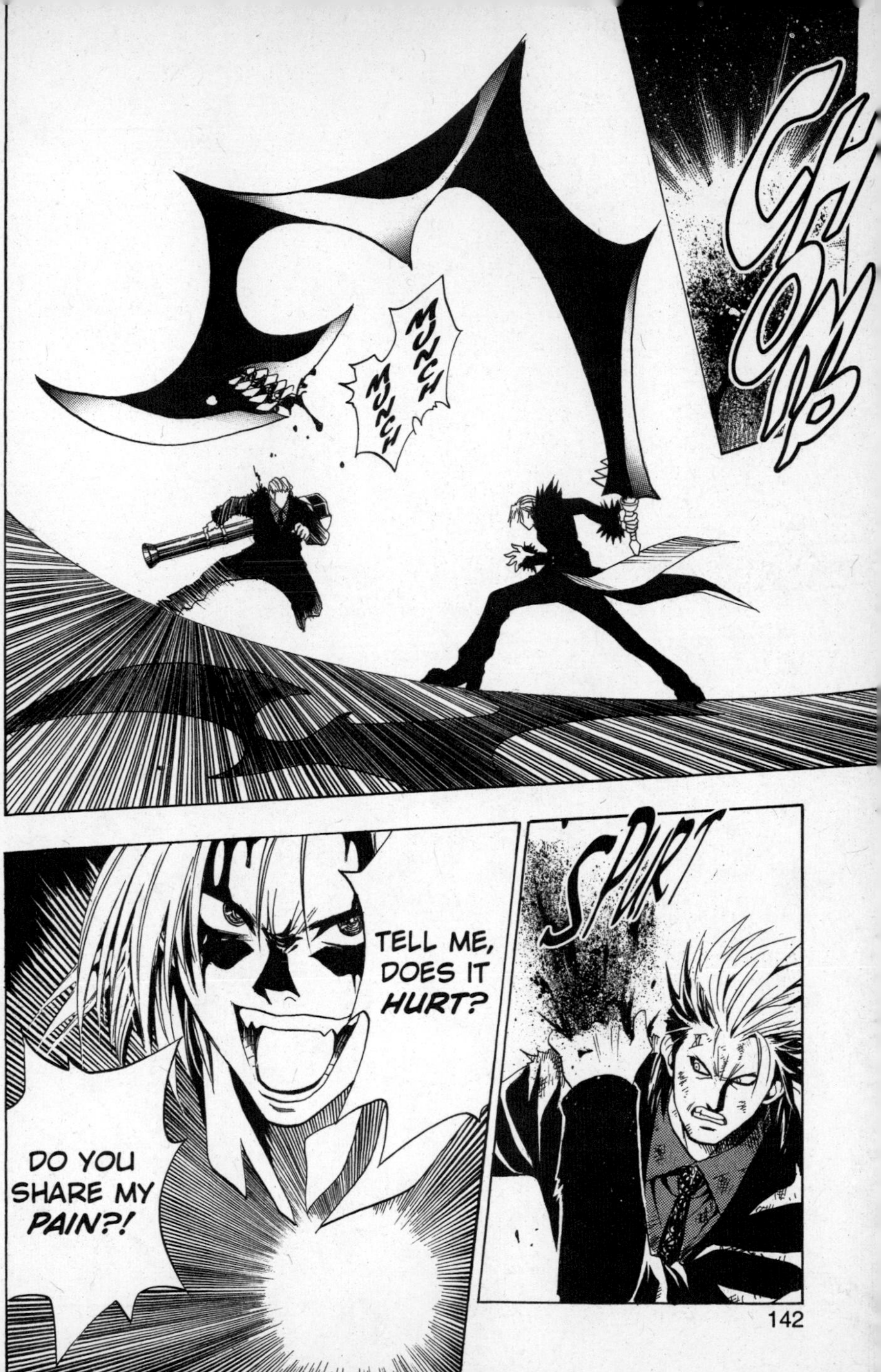
CHOMP
MUNCH MUNCH
SPURT
TELL ME, DOES IT *HURT?*
DO YOU SHARE MY *PAIN?!*

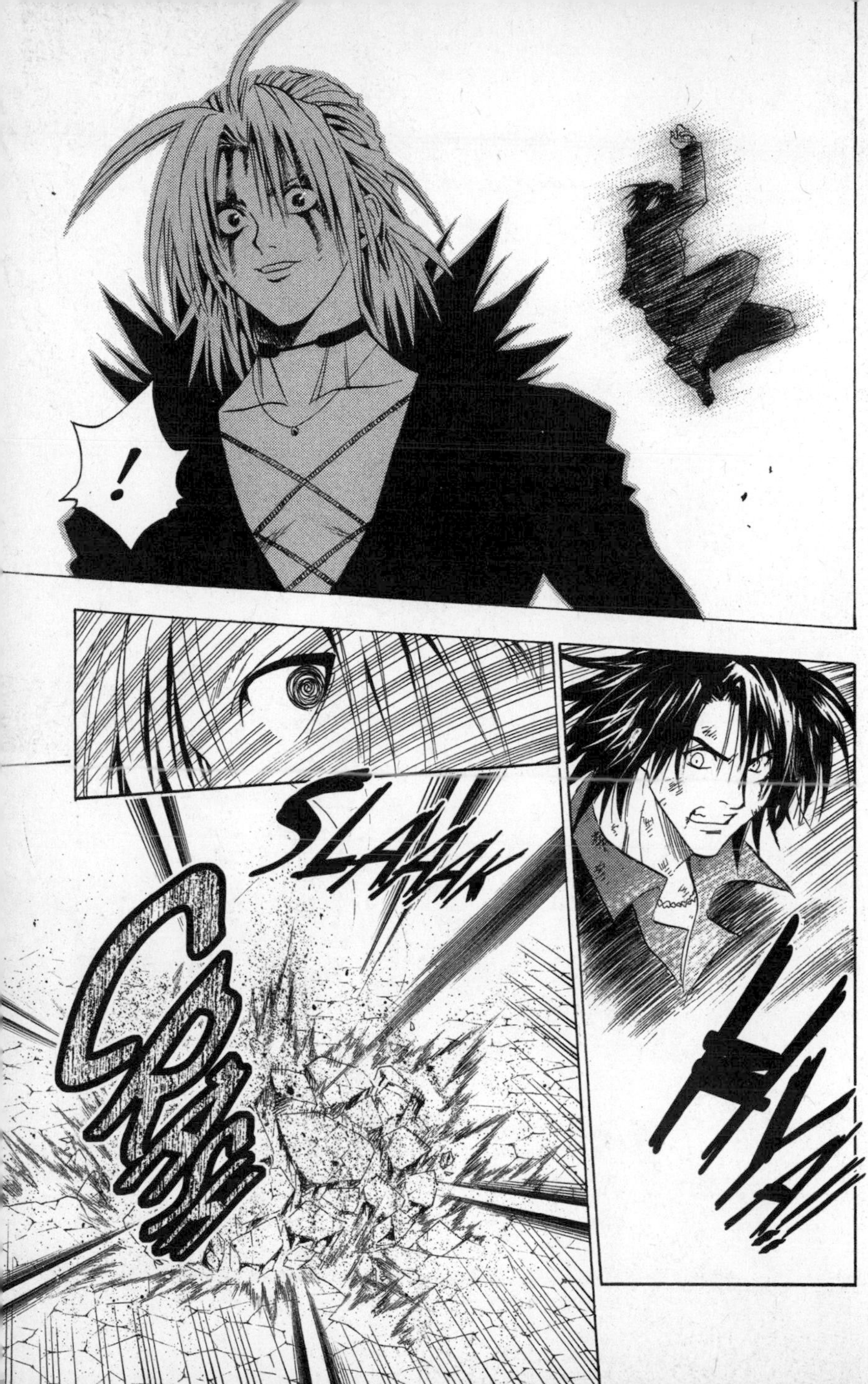
!
HYA!!
SLAAAK
CRASH

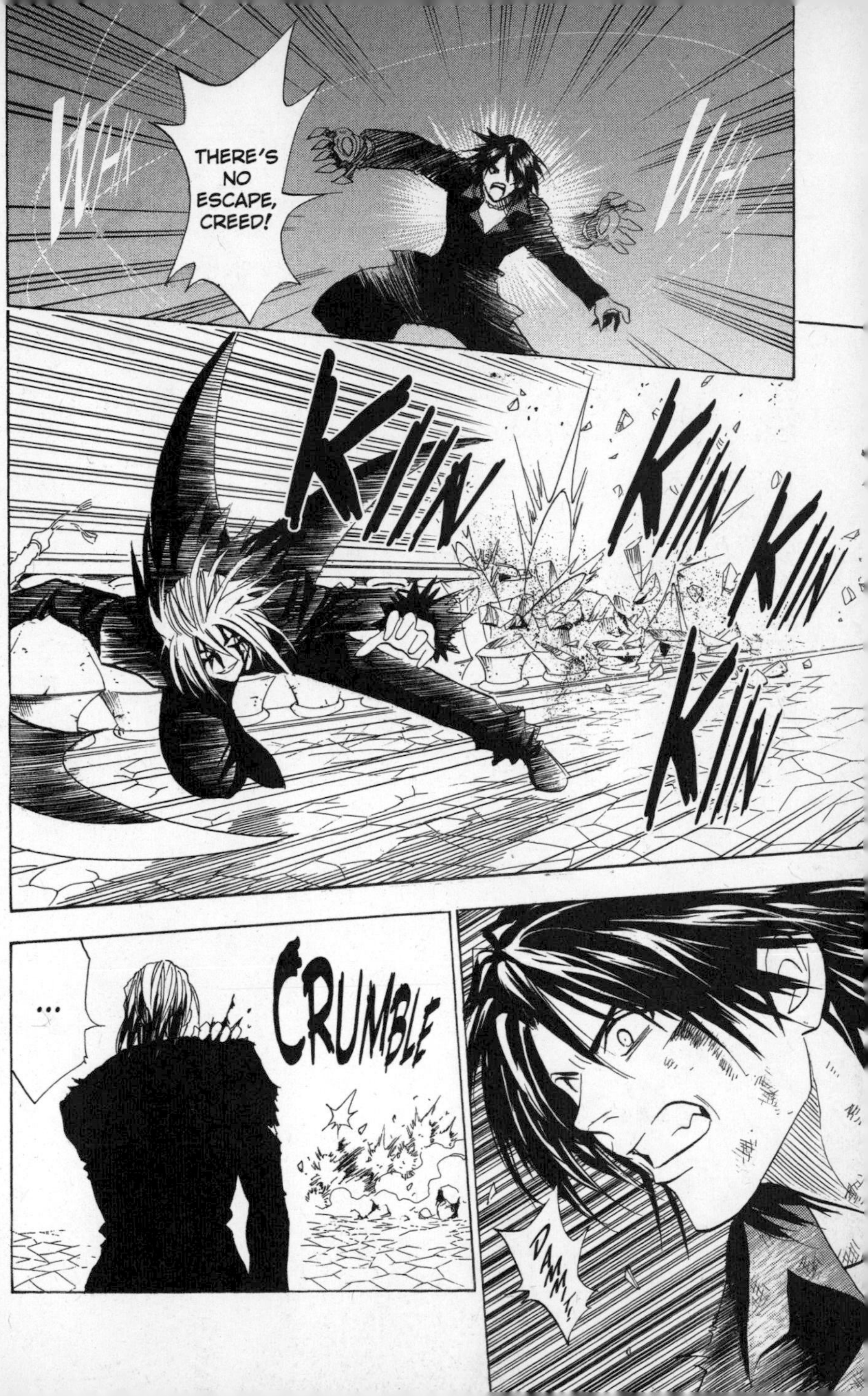
WHAK
THERE'S NO ESCAPE, CREED!
WHAK
KIIIN
KIIN KIIN KIIN
KIIN
...
CRUMBLE
DAMN...!

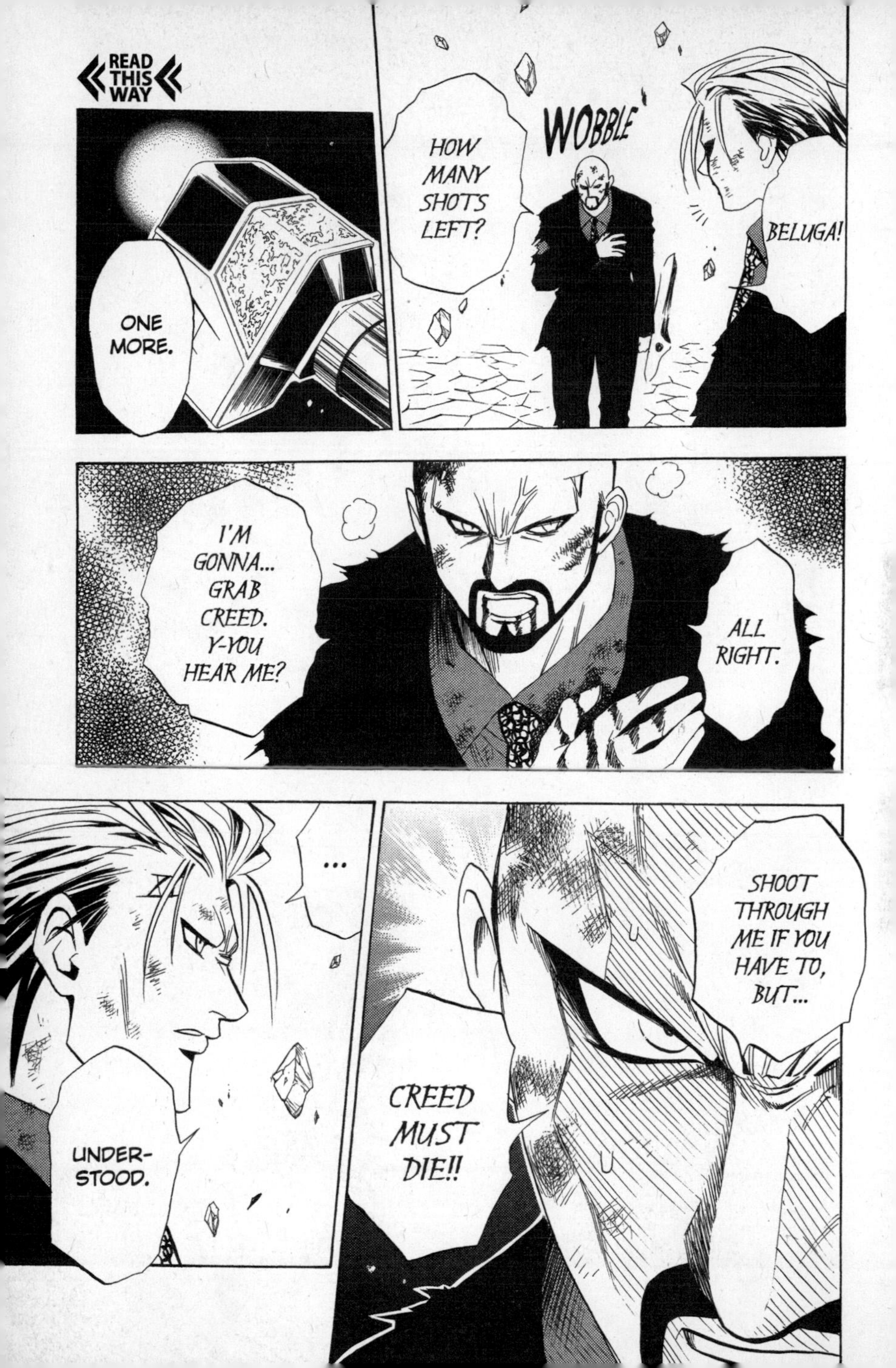
READ THIS WAY
BELUGA!
WOBBLE
HOW MANY SHOTS LEFT?
ONE MORE.
ALL RIGHT.
I'M GONNA... GRAB CREED. Y-YOU HEAR ME?
SHOOT THROUGH ME IF YOU HAVE TO, BUT...
CREED MUST DIE!!
...
UNDER-STOOD.

SKETCHES NO. 1

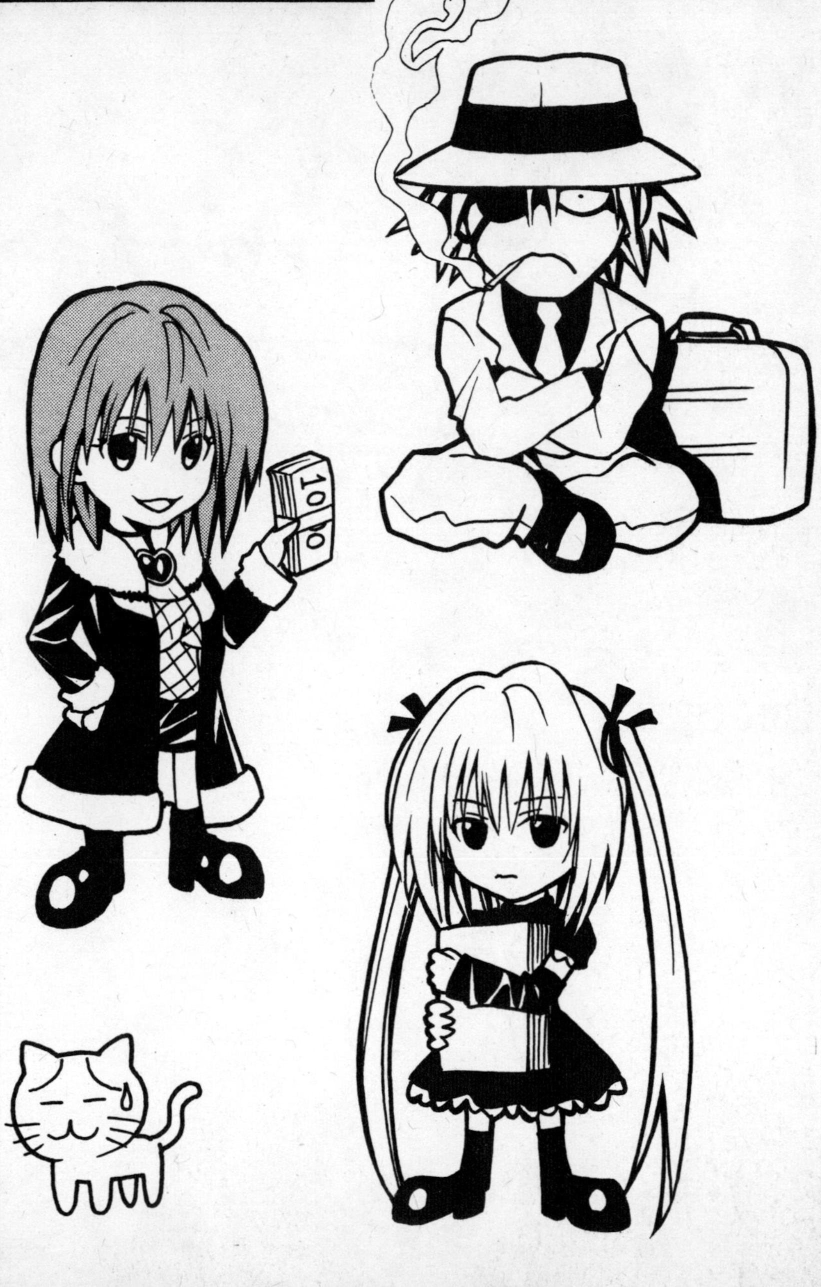

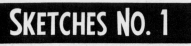

CHAPTER 83:
THE WAY OF THE NUMBERS

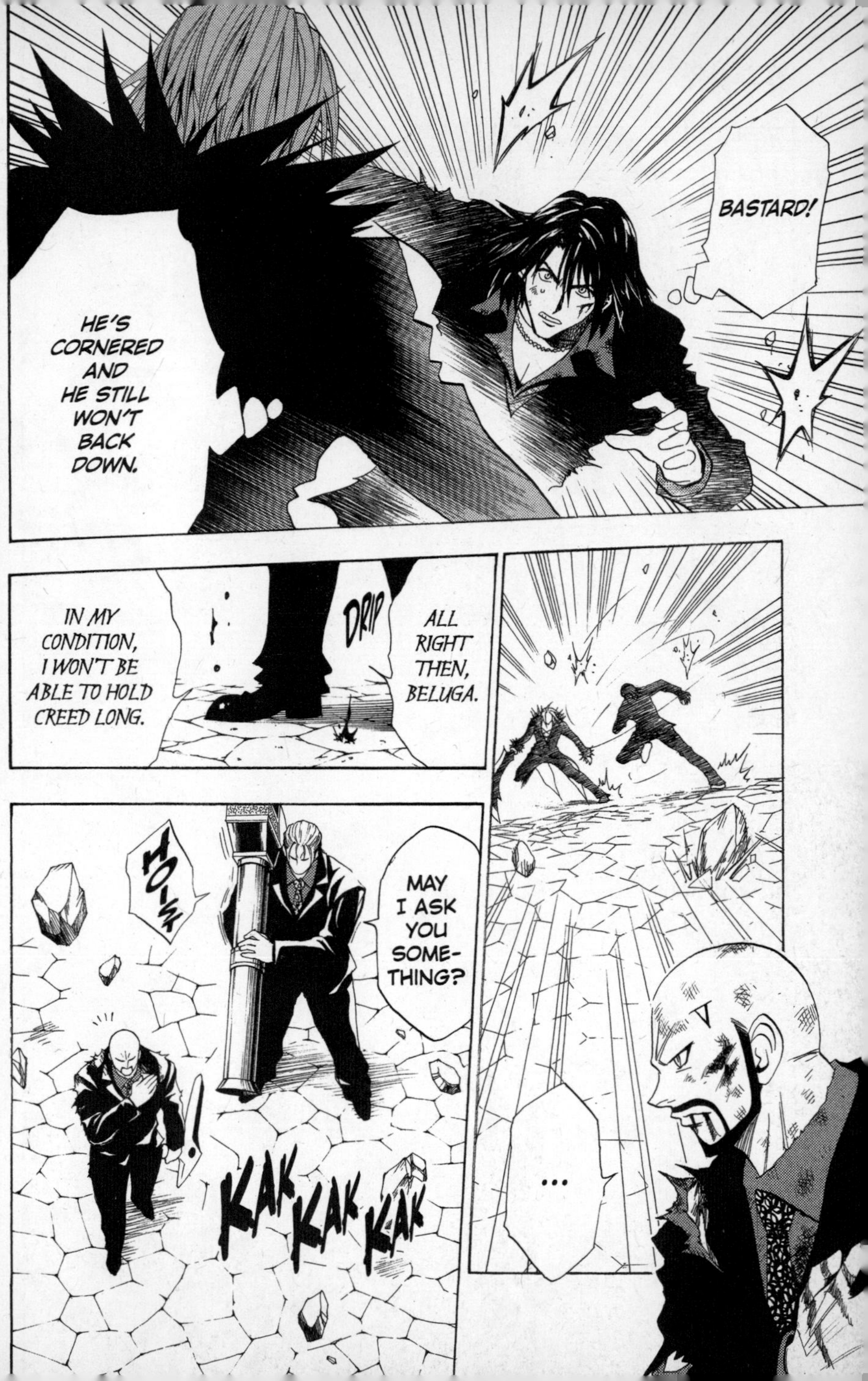
BASTARD!
HE'S CORNERED AND HE STILL WON'T BACK DOWN.
ALL RIGHT THEN, BELUGA.
DRIP
IN MY CONDITION, I WON'T BE ABLE TO HOLD CREED LONG.
...
MAY I ASK YOU SOMETHING?
HOIST
KAK KAK KAK

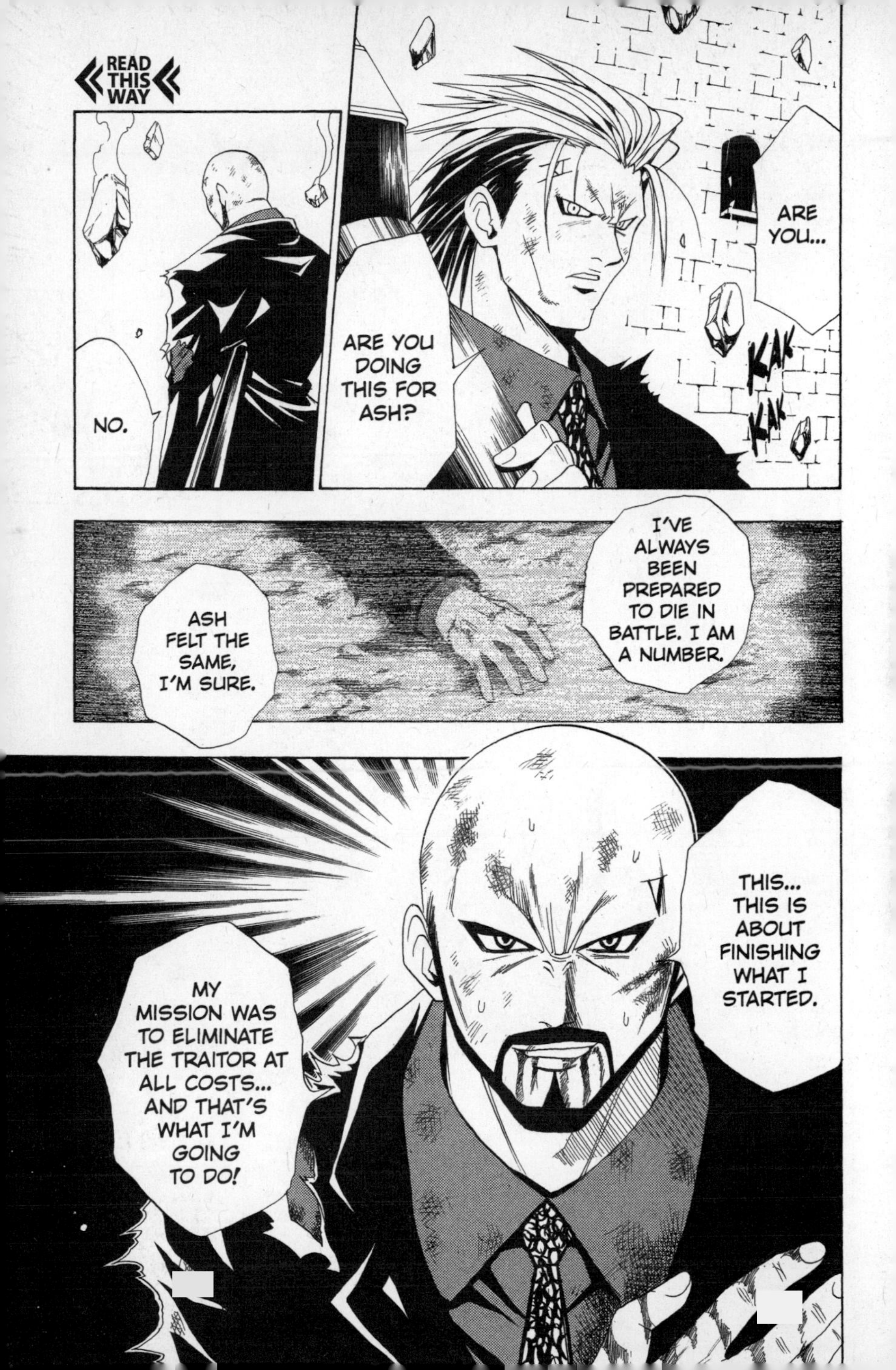
READ THIS WAY
ARE YOU...
KAK KAK
ARE YOU DOING THIS FOR ASH?
NO.
I'VE ALWAYS BEEN PREPARED TO DIE IN BATTLE. I AM A NUMBER.
ASH FELT THE SAME, I'M SURE.
THIS... THIS IS ABOUT FINISHING WHAT I STARTED.
MY MISSION WAS TO ELIMINATE THE TRAITOR AT ALL COSTS... AND THAT'S WHAT I'M GOING TO DO!

Chapter 83:
The Way of the Numbers

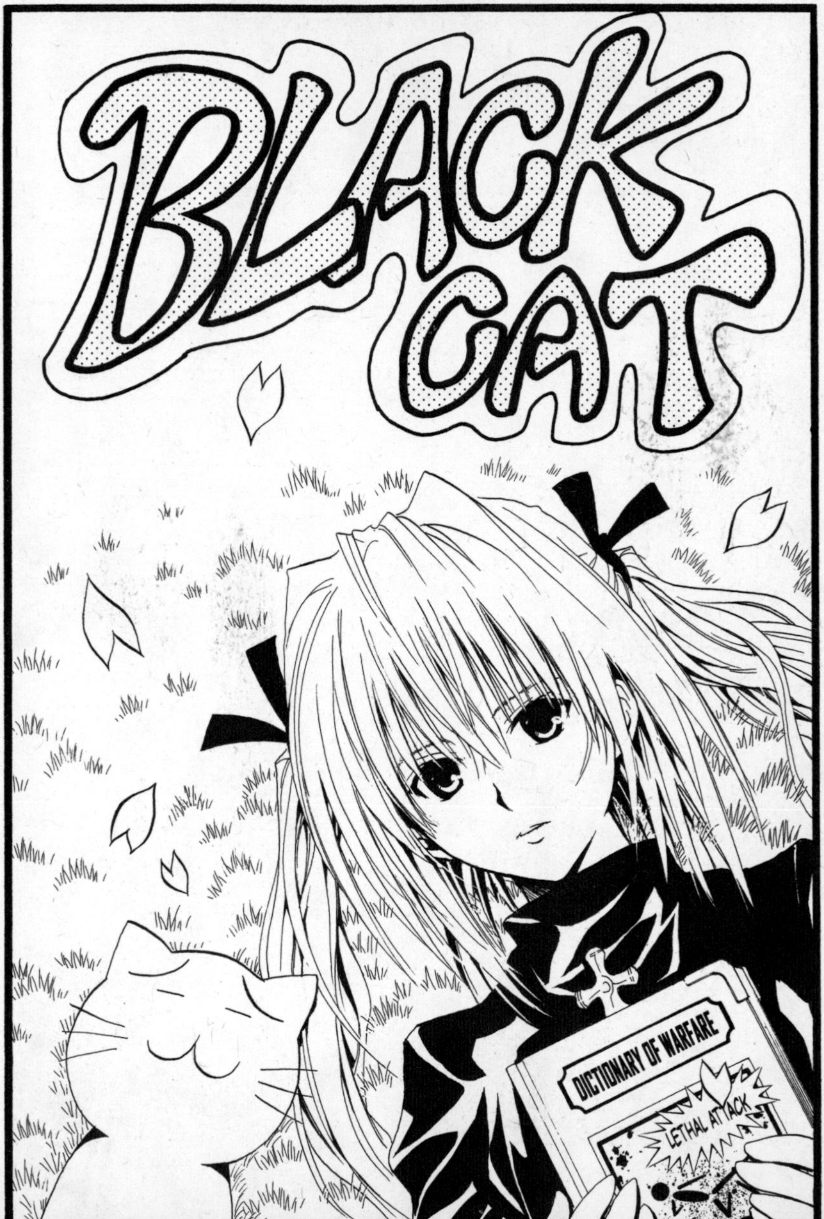
BLACK CAT
DICTIONARY OF WARFARE
LETHAL ATTACK

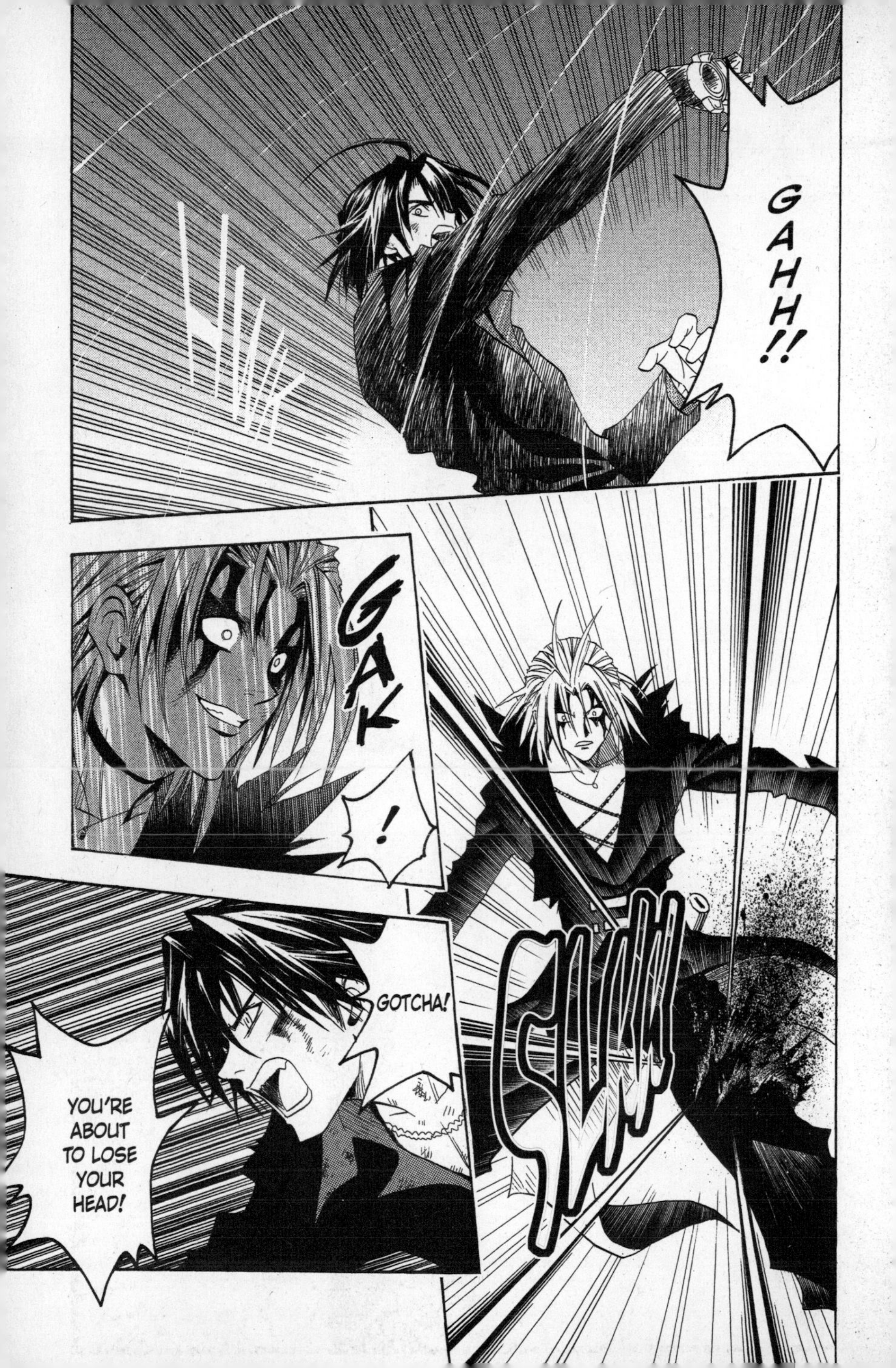
GAHH!!
GAK
!
GOTCHA!
YOU'RE ABOUT TO LOSE YOUR HEAD!

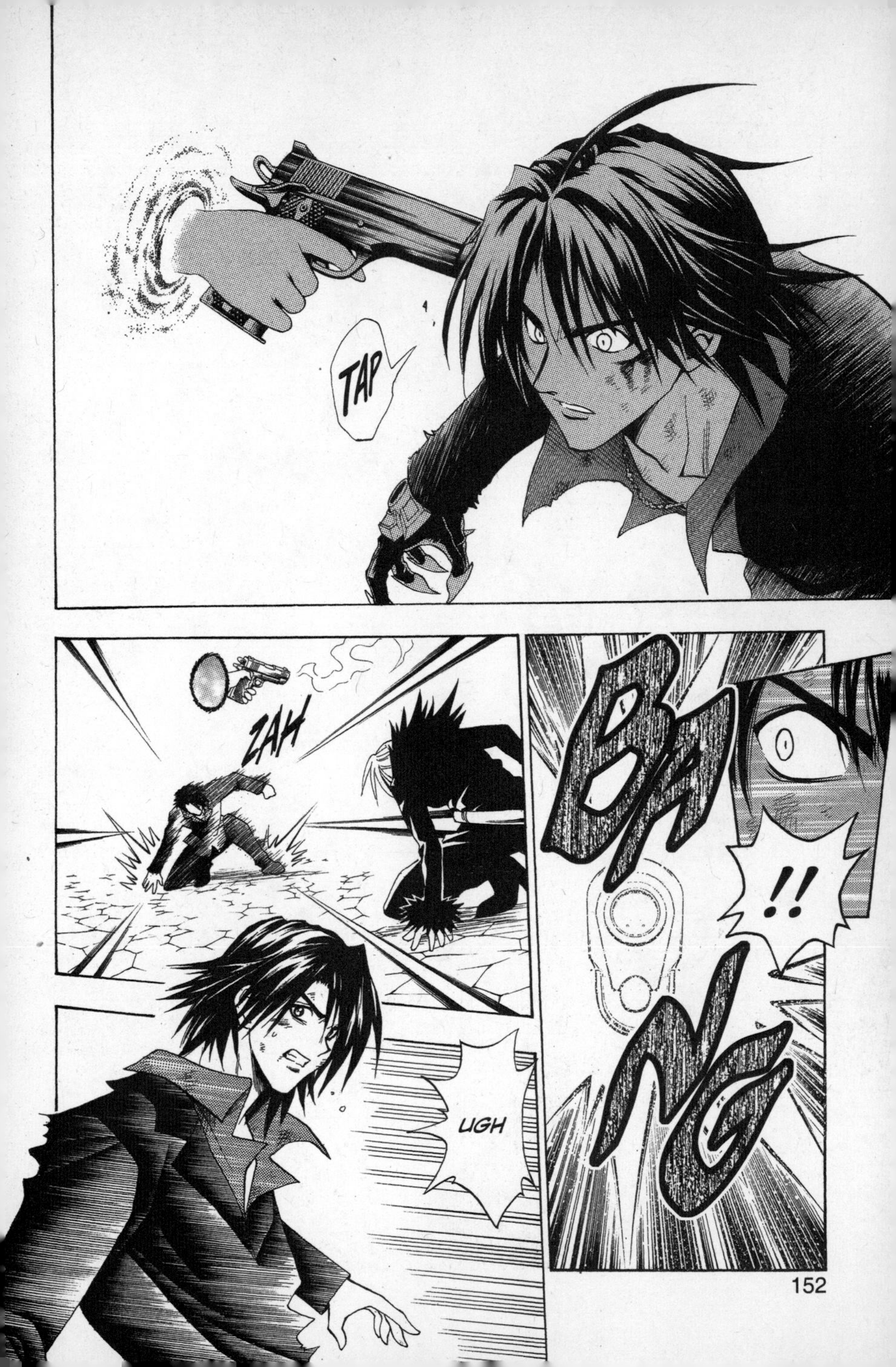
TAP
BANG
!!
ZAH
UGH

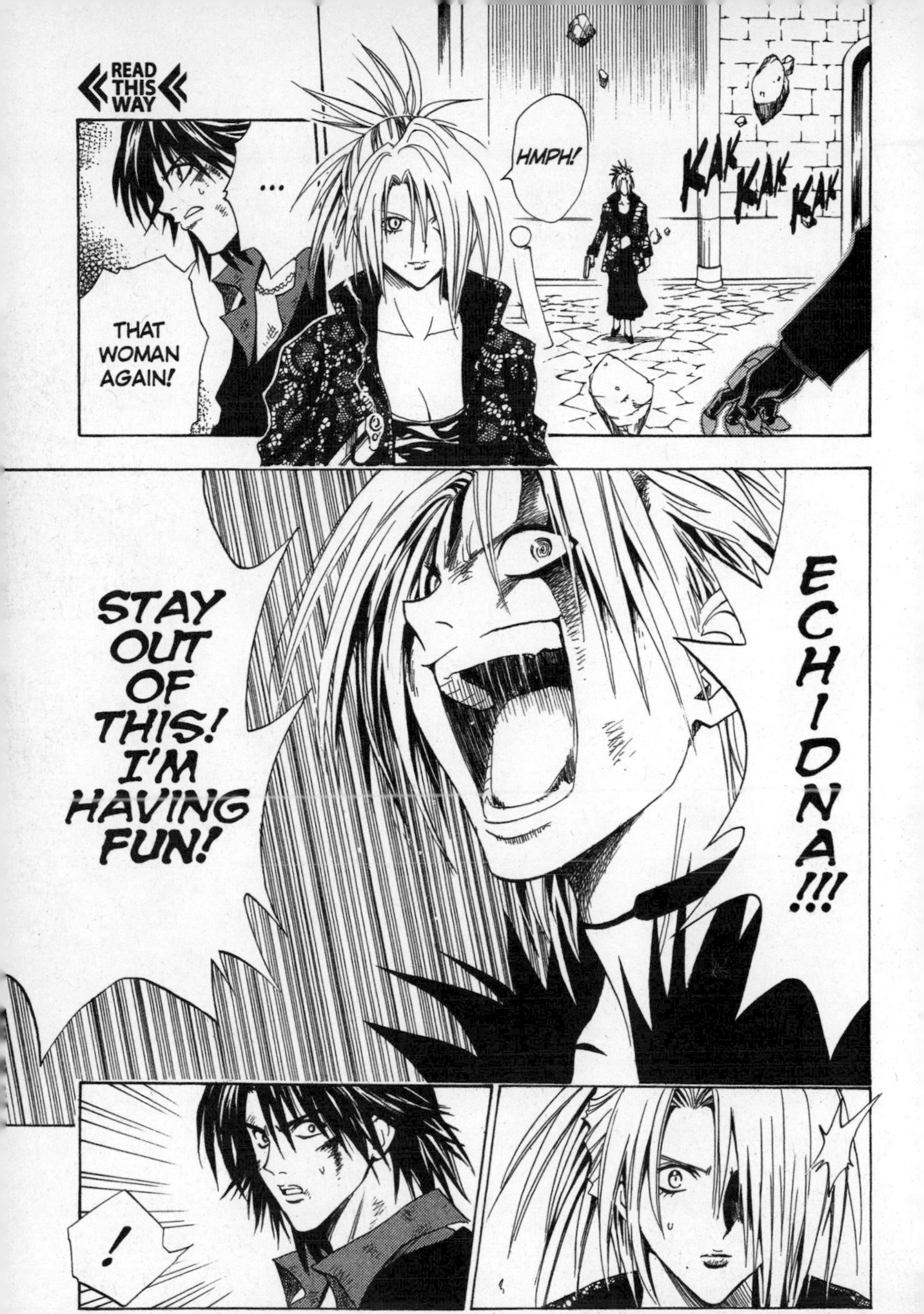
READ THIS WAY
HMPH!
KAK KAK KAK KAK
...
THAT WOMAN AGAIN!
ECHIDNA!!!
STAY OUT OF THIS! I'M HAVING FUN!
!

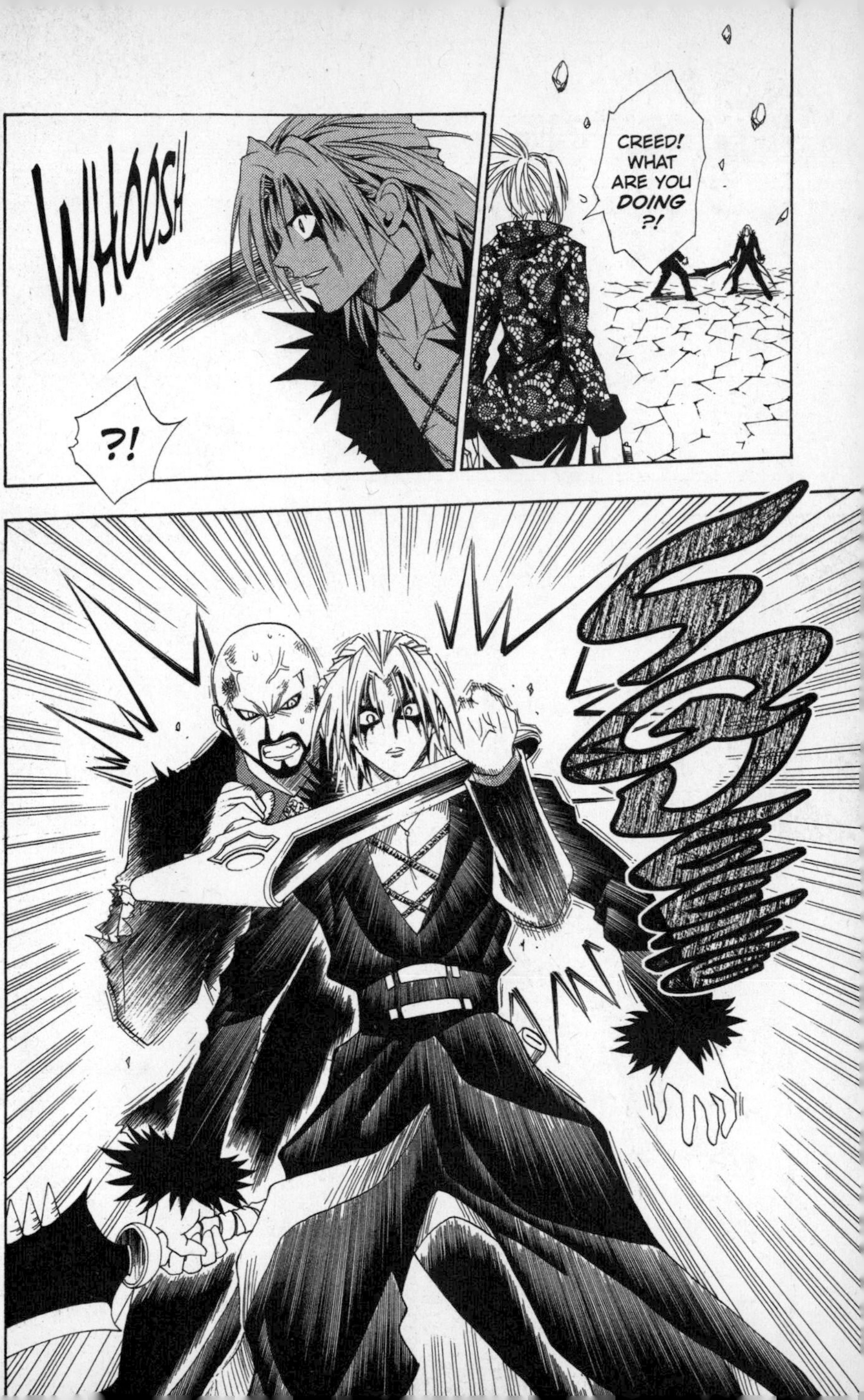
CREED! WHAT ARE YOU DOING ?!
WHOOSH
?!

READ THIS WAY

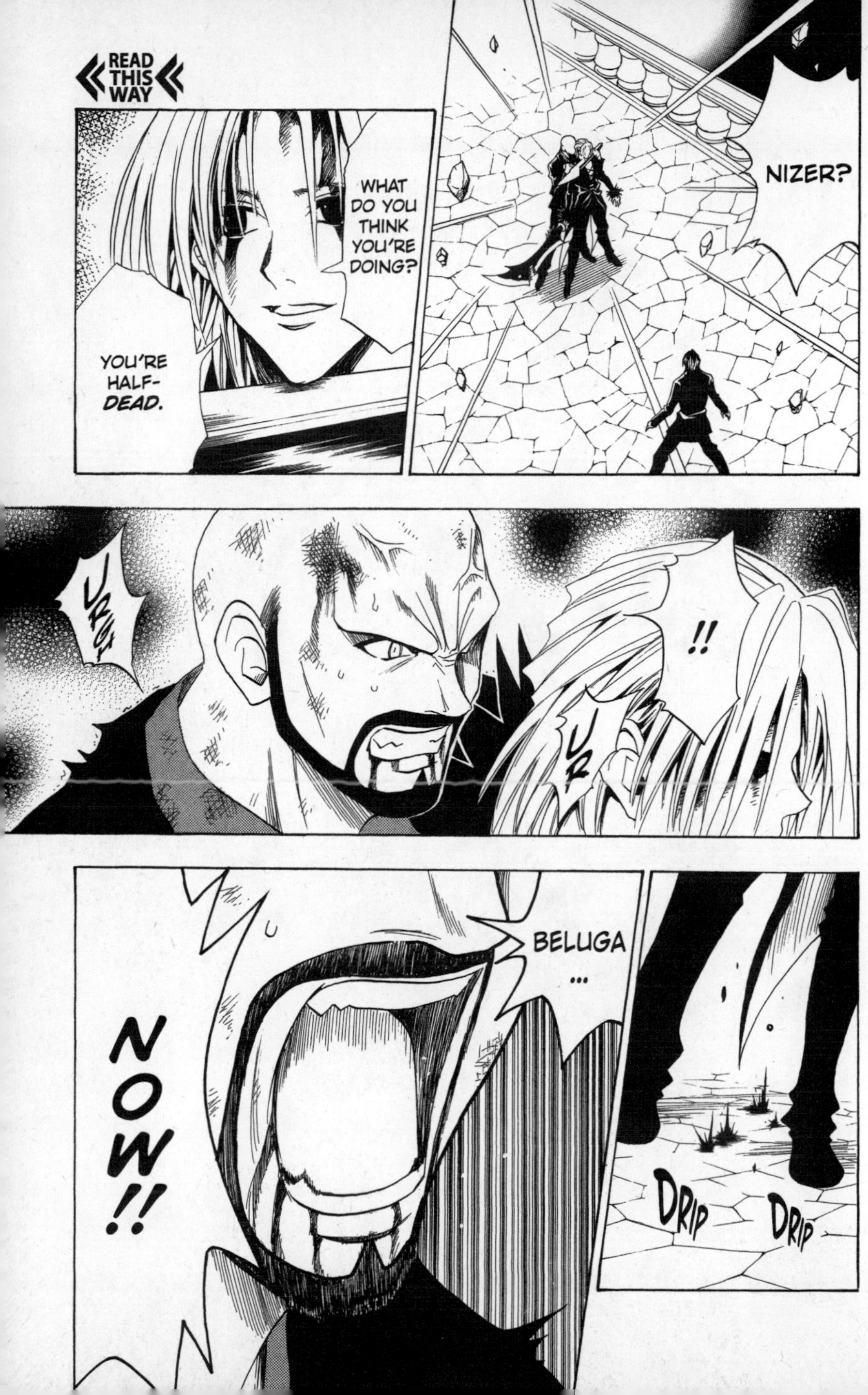
NIZER?
WHAT DO YOU THINK YOU'RE DOING?
YOU'RE HALF-DEAD.
!!
UR
URGH
DRIP
DRIP
BELUGA ...
NOW!!

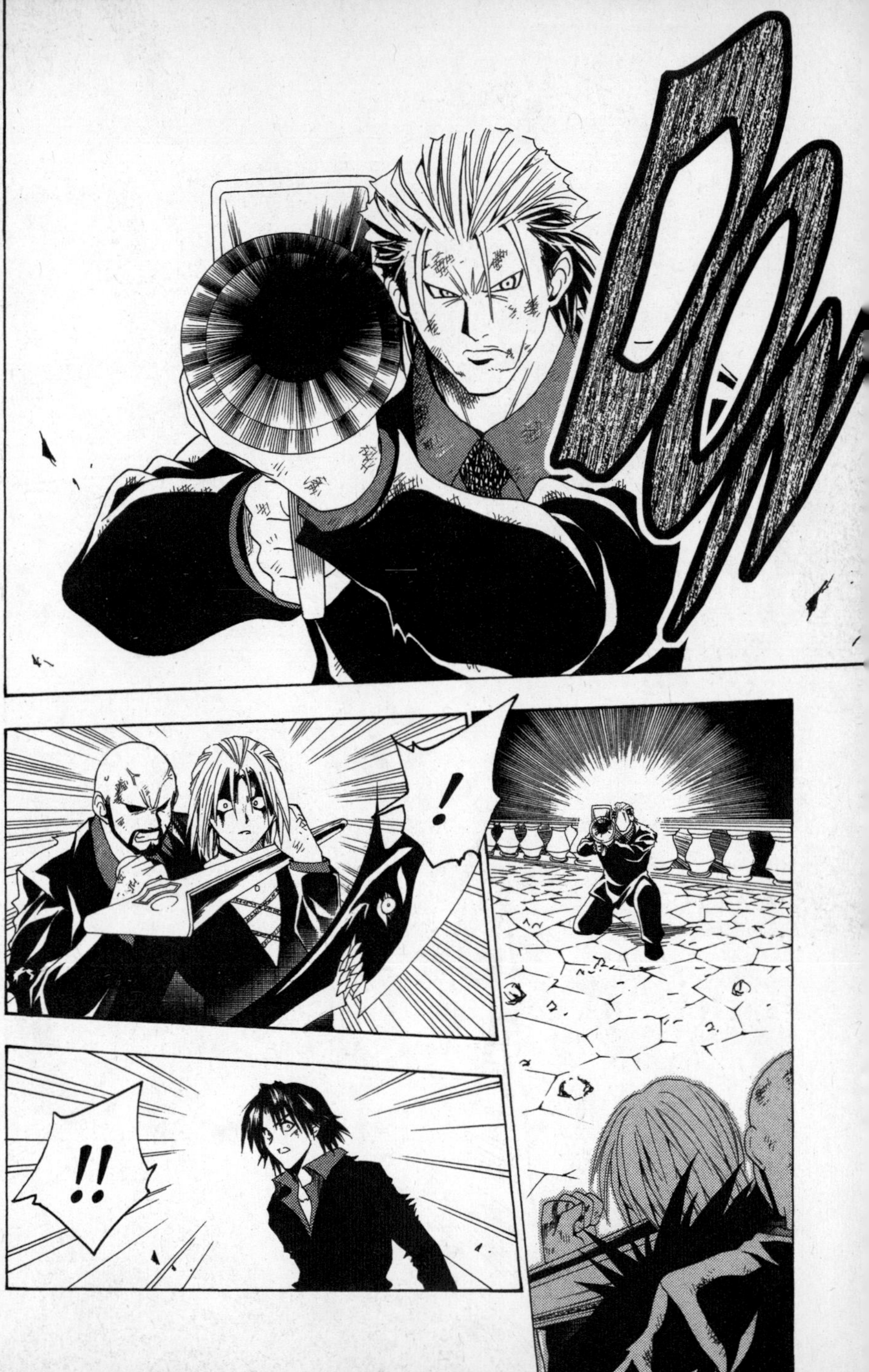
!
!!

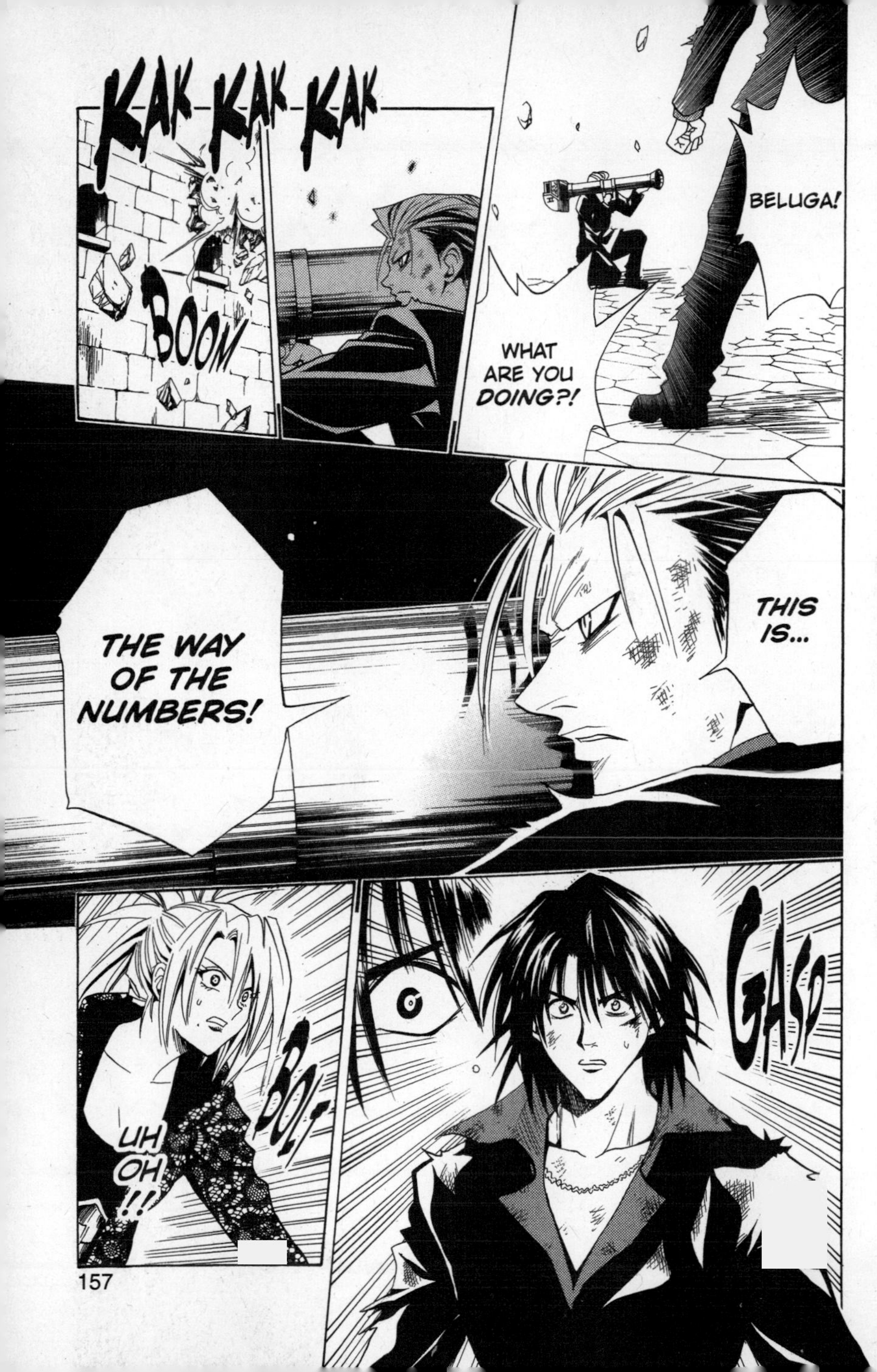

BELUGA!
WHAT ARE YOU DOING?!
KAK KAK KAK
BOOM
THIS IS...
THE WAY OF THE NUMBERS!
GASP
BOI
UH OH!!

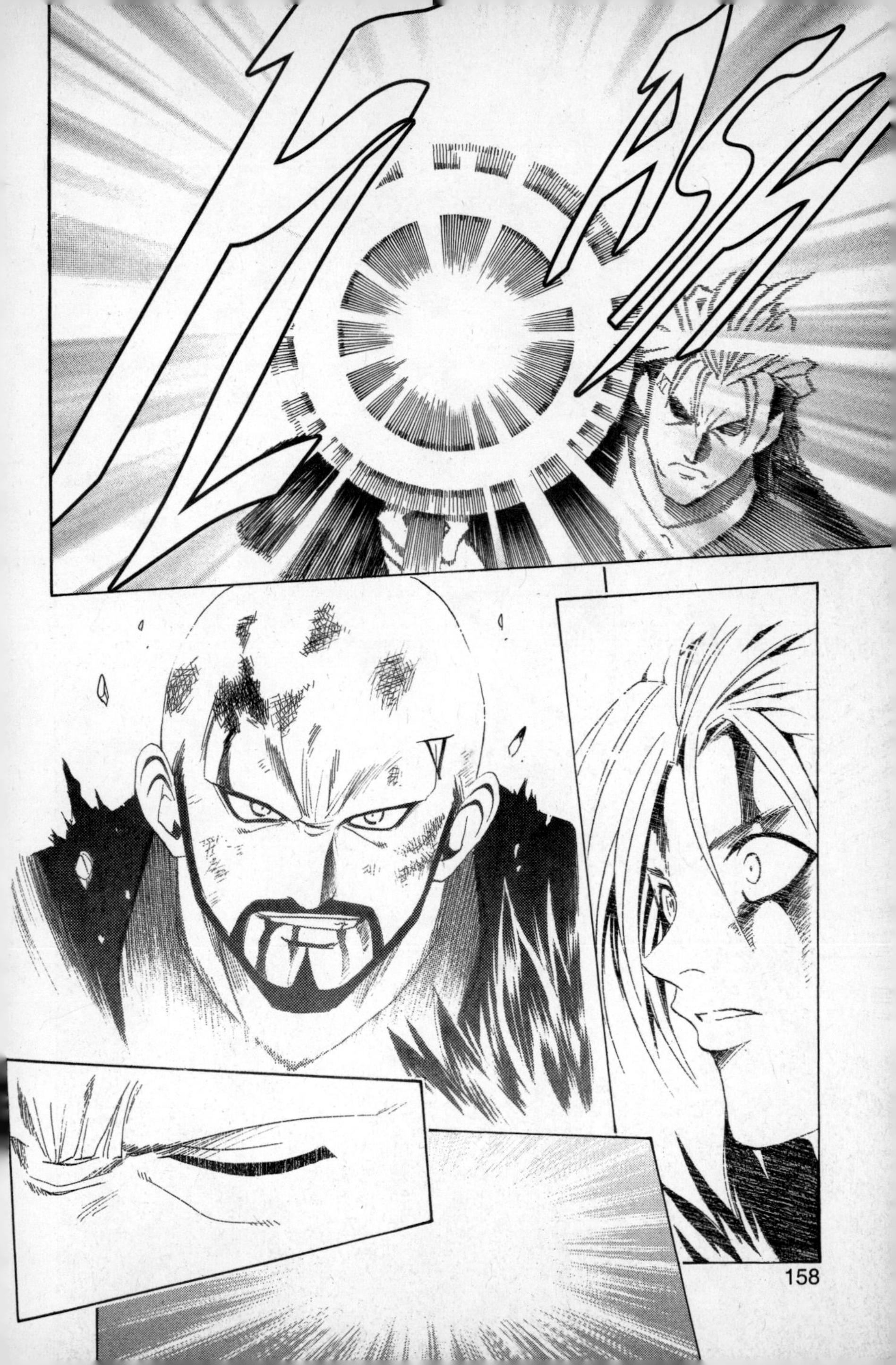
FLASH

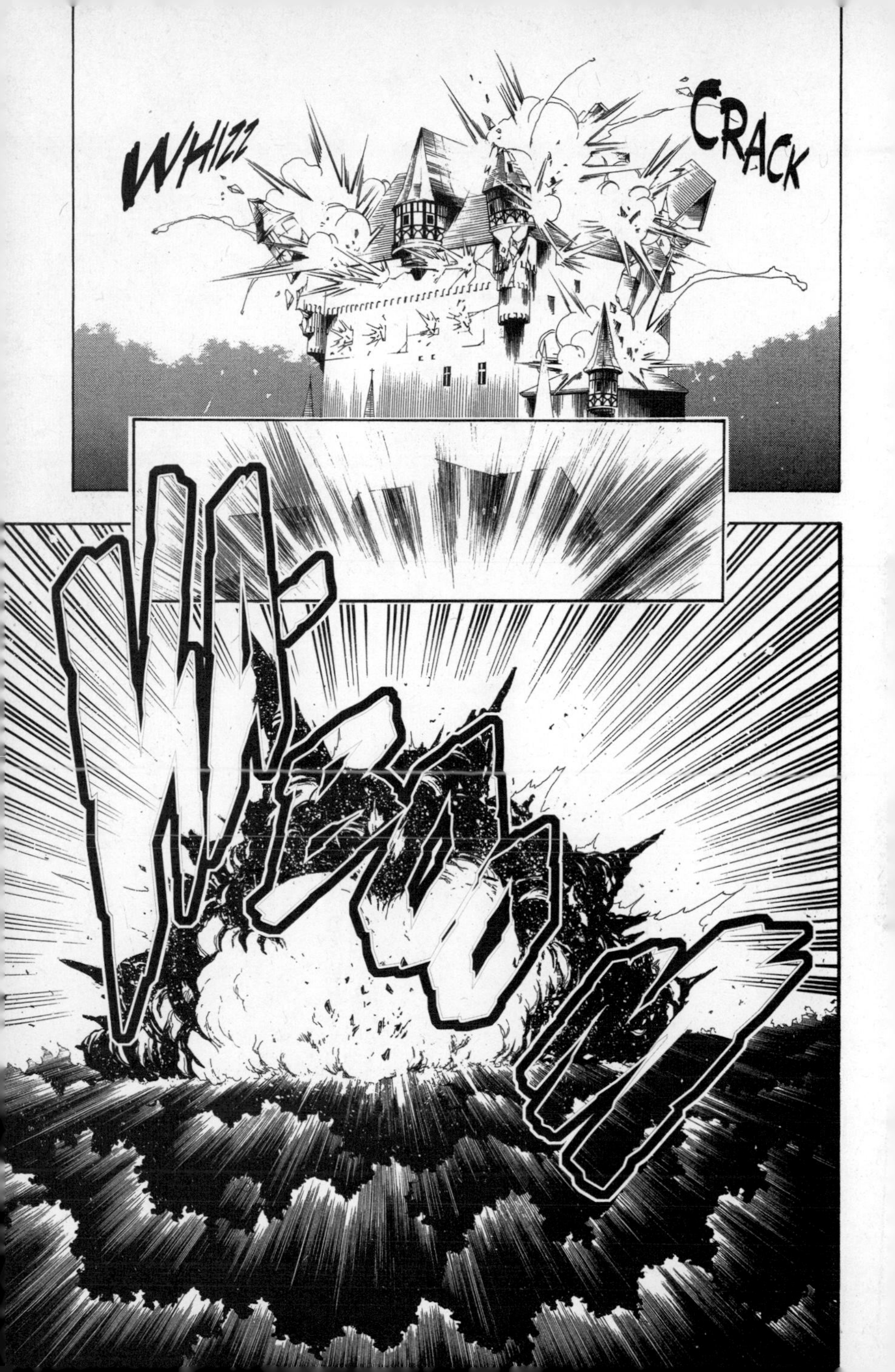

CRACK
WHIZZ

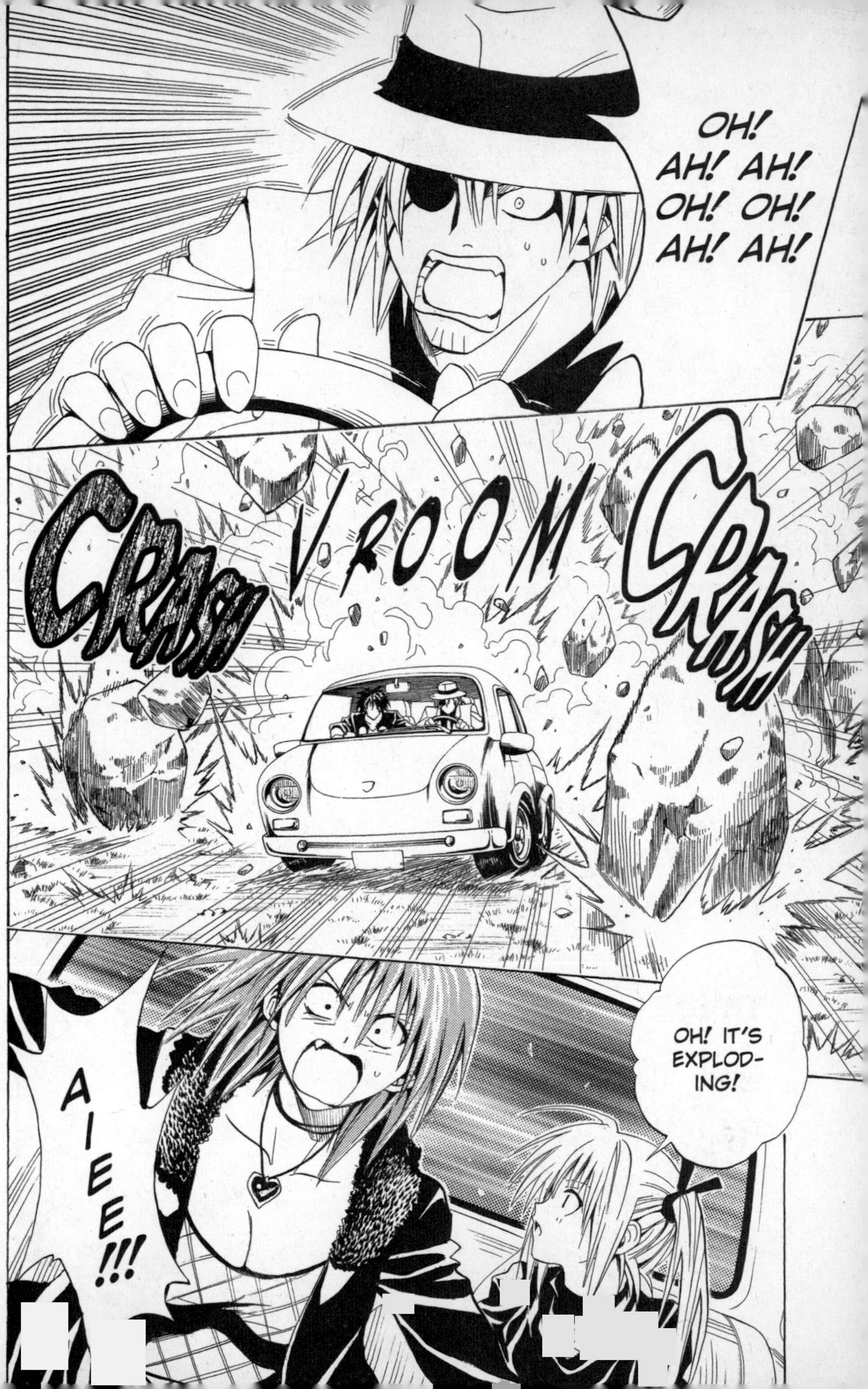
OH! AH! AH! OH! OH! AH! AH!
CRASH
VROOM
CRASH
OH! IT'S EXPLOD-ING!
AIEE!!!

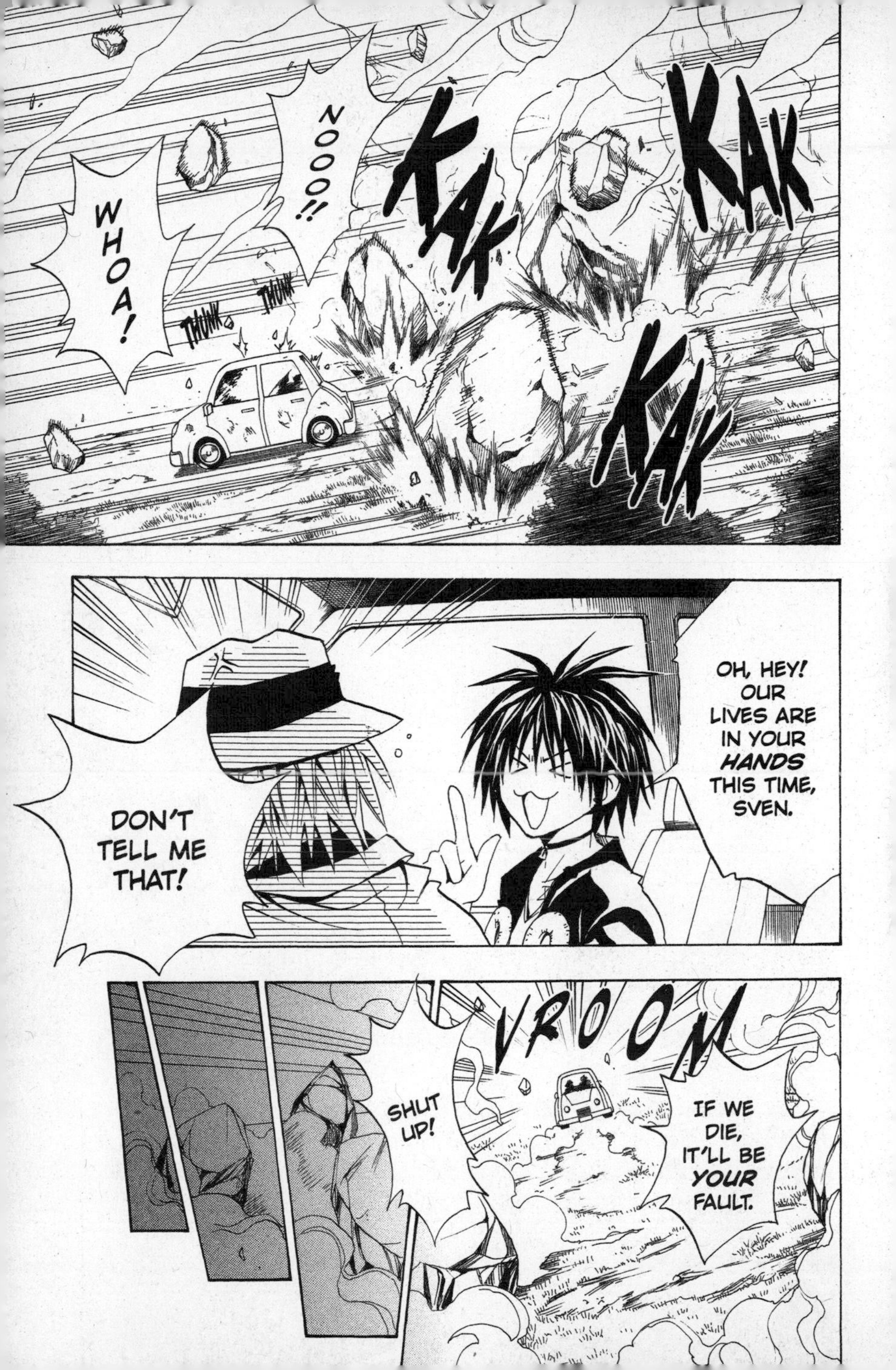
KAK
KAK
KAK
NOOOO!!
WHOA!
THUNK
THUNK
OH, HEY! OUR LIVES ARE IN YOUR *HANDS* THIS TIME, SVEN.
DON'T TELL ME THAT!
IF WE DIE, IT'LL BE *YOUR* FAULT.
VROOM
SHUT UP!

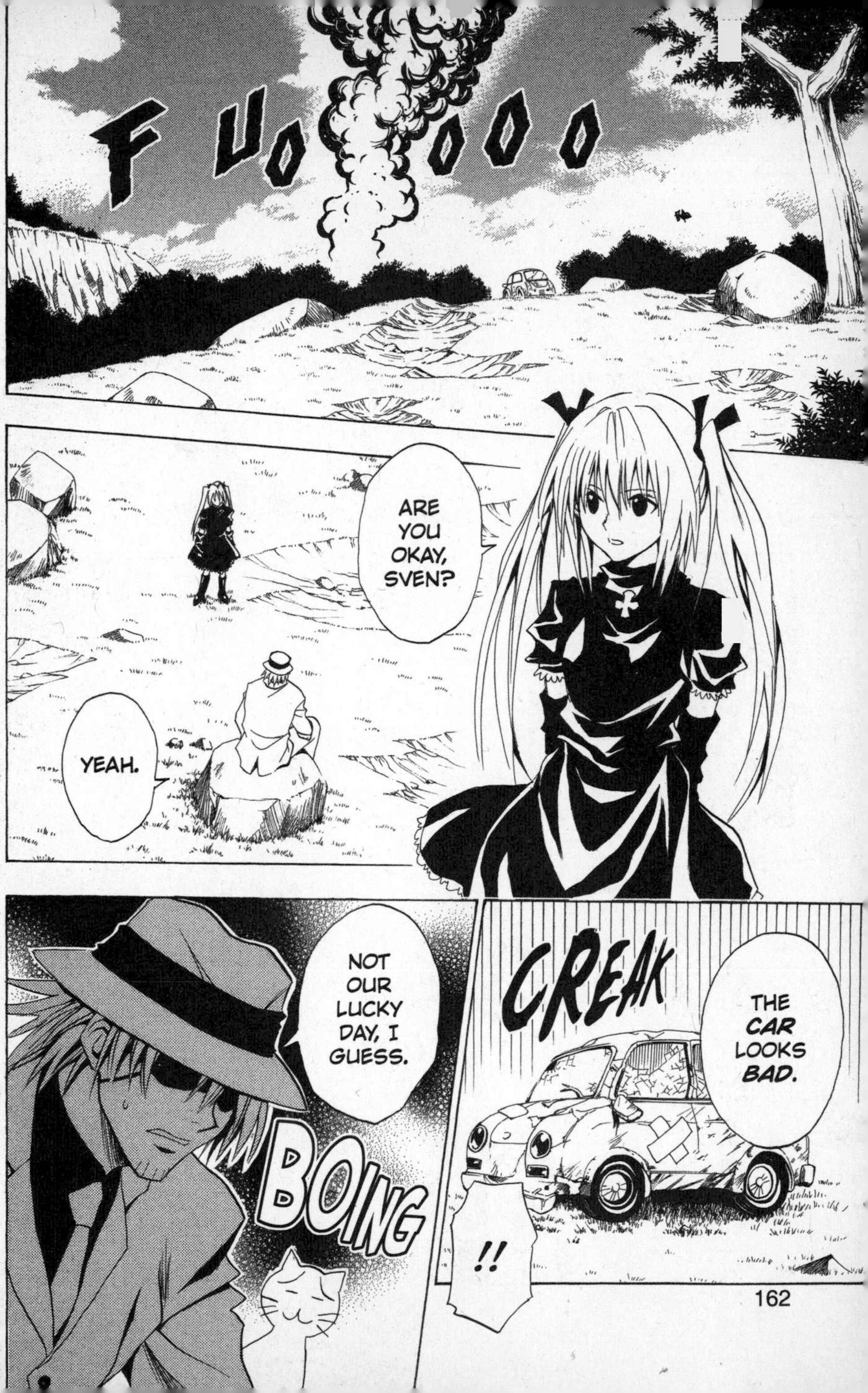
FUOOOOO
ARE YOU OKAY, SVEN?
YEAH.
THE CAR LOOKS BAD.
CREAK
!!
NOT OUR LUCKY DAY, I GUESS.
BOING

Trying to make him feel better.

OH! I THINK IT LOOKS GOOD! *DISTRESSED.* KIND OF VINTAGE-Y!

THINK SO?

YOU WORRIED?

YOU MEAN ABOUT THE NUMBERS?

FUUU

...

HEH.

I OWE THEM MY LIFE.

YEAH, I AM.

IF IT'S BEEN DESTROYED, DOES THAT MEAN THE APOSTLES LOST?

SO, THAT WAS THE APOSTLES OF THE STARS HIDEOUT?

...

I DON'T KNOW.

DO YOU THINK THE NUMBERS HAD TIME TO GET OUT?

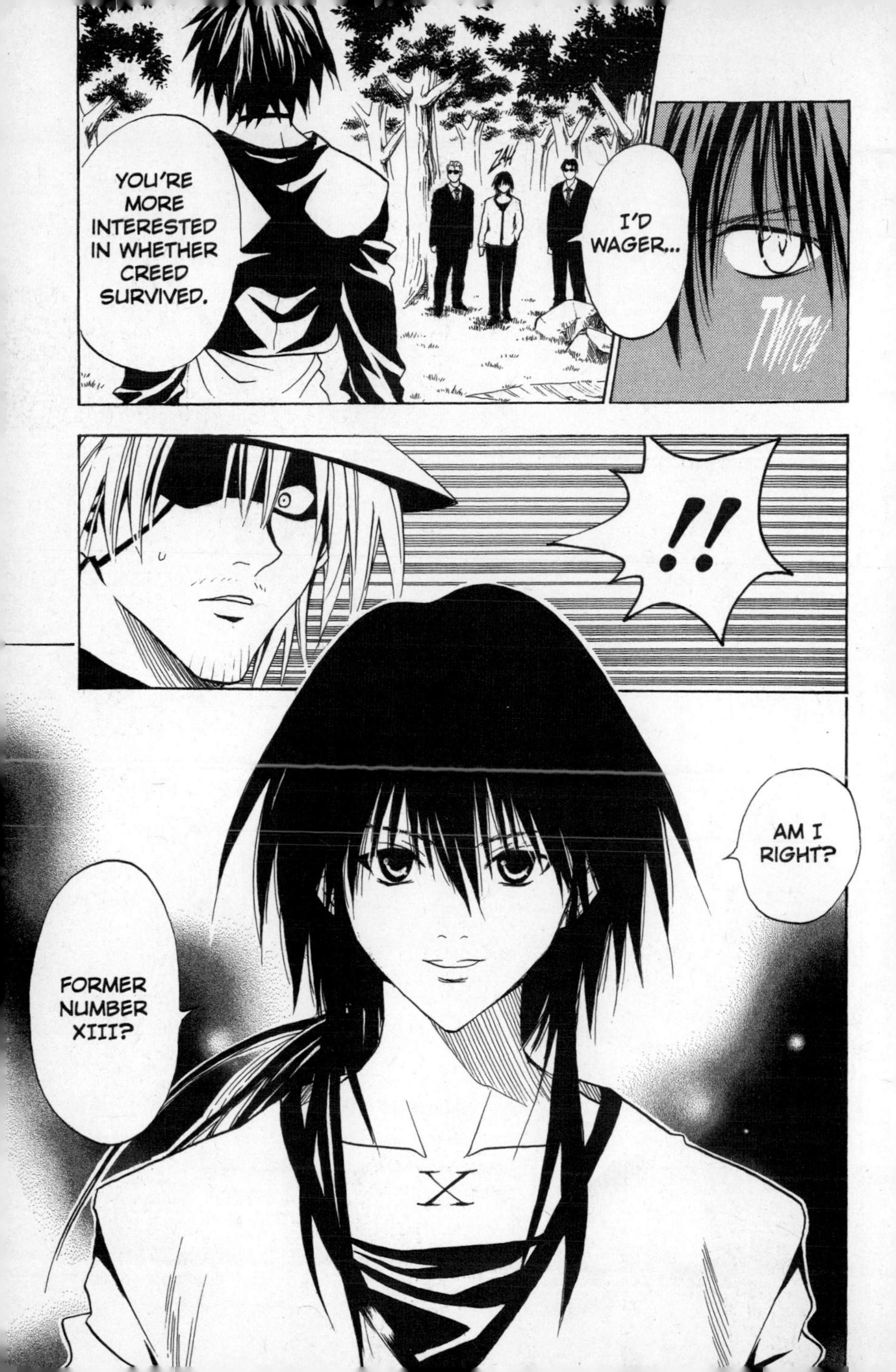
I'D WAGER...
TWITCH
ZAH
YOU'RE MORE INTERESTED IN WHETHER CREED SURVIVED.
!!
AM I RIGHT?
FORMER NUMBER XIII?
X

SKETCHES NO. 2

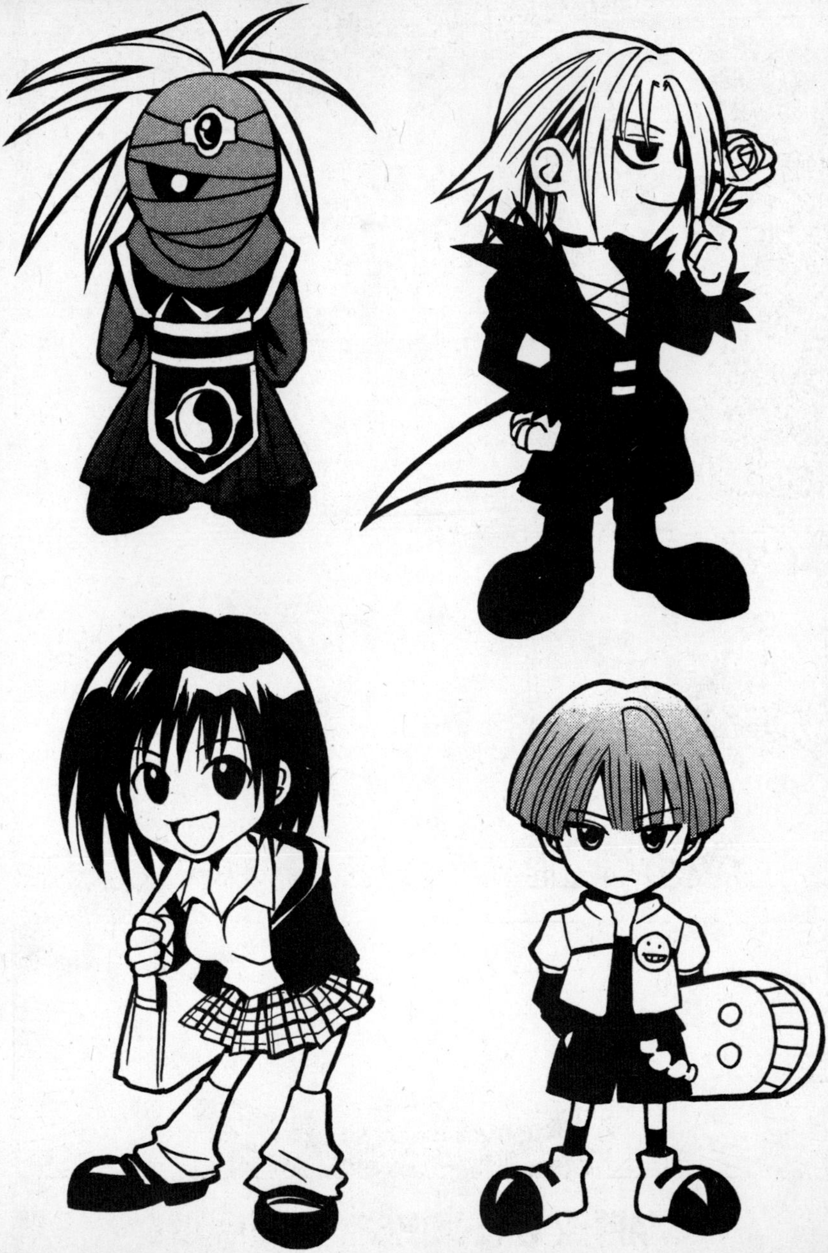

CHAPTER 84: NUMBER X, SHAOLEE

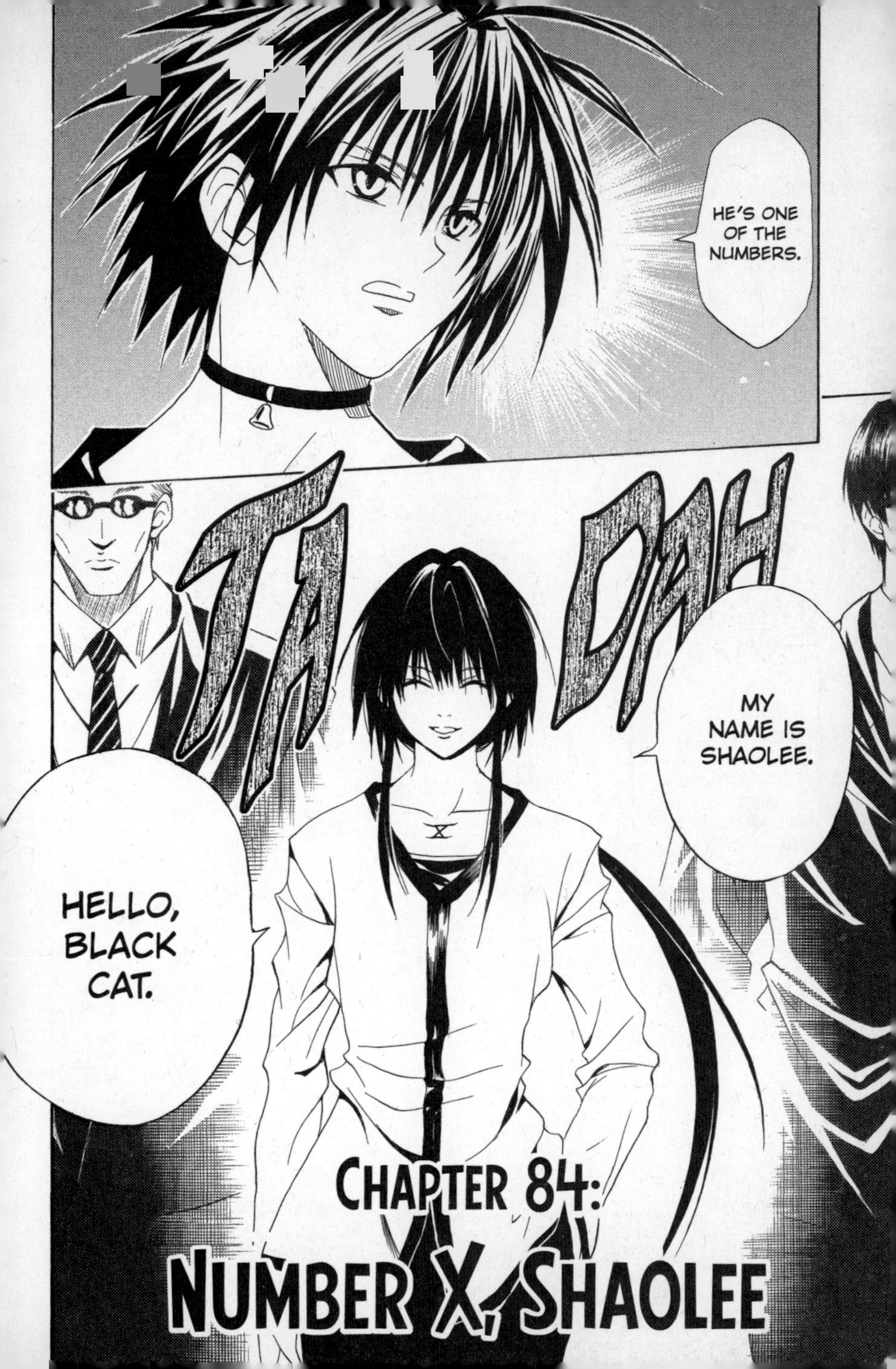
HE'S ONE OF THE NUMBERS.
TA DAH
MY NAME IS SHAOLEE.
HELLO, BLACK CAT.
CHAPTER 84:
NUMBER X, SHAOLEE

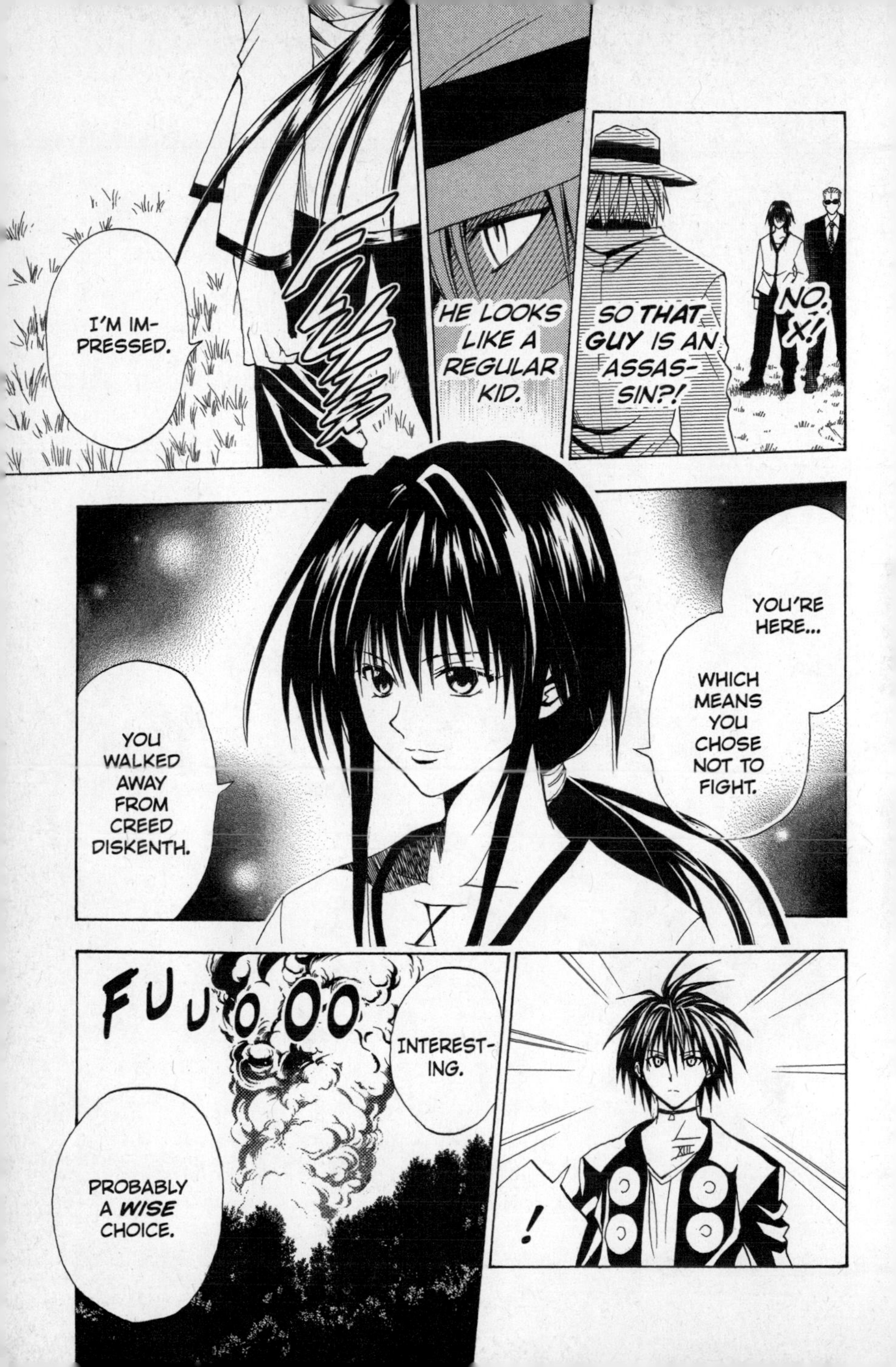
NO. X!
SO THAT GUY IS AN ASSAS-SIN?!
HE LOOKS LIKE A REGULAR KID.
I'M IM-PRESSED.
YOU'RE HERE...
WHICH MEANS YOU CHOSE NOT TO FIGHT.
YOU WALKED AWAY FROM CREED DISKENTH.
!
FUUOOO
INTEREST-ING.
PROBABLY A WISE CHOICE.

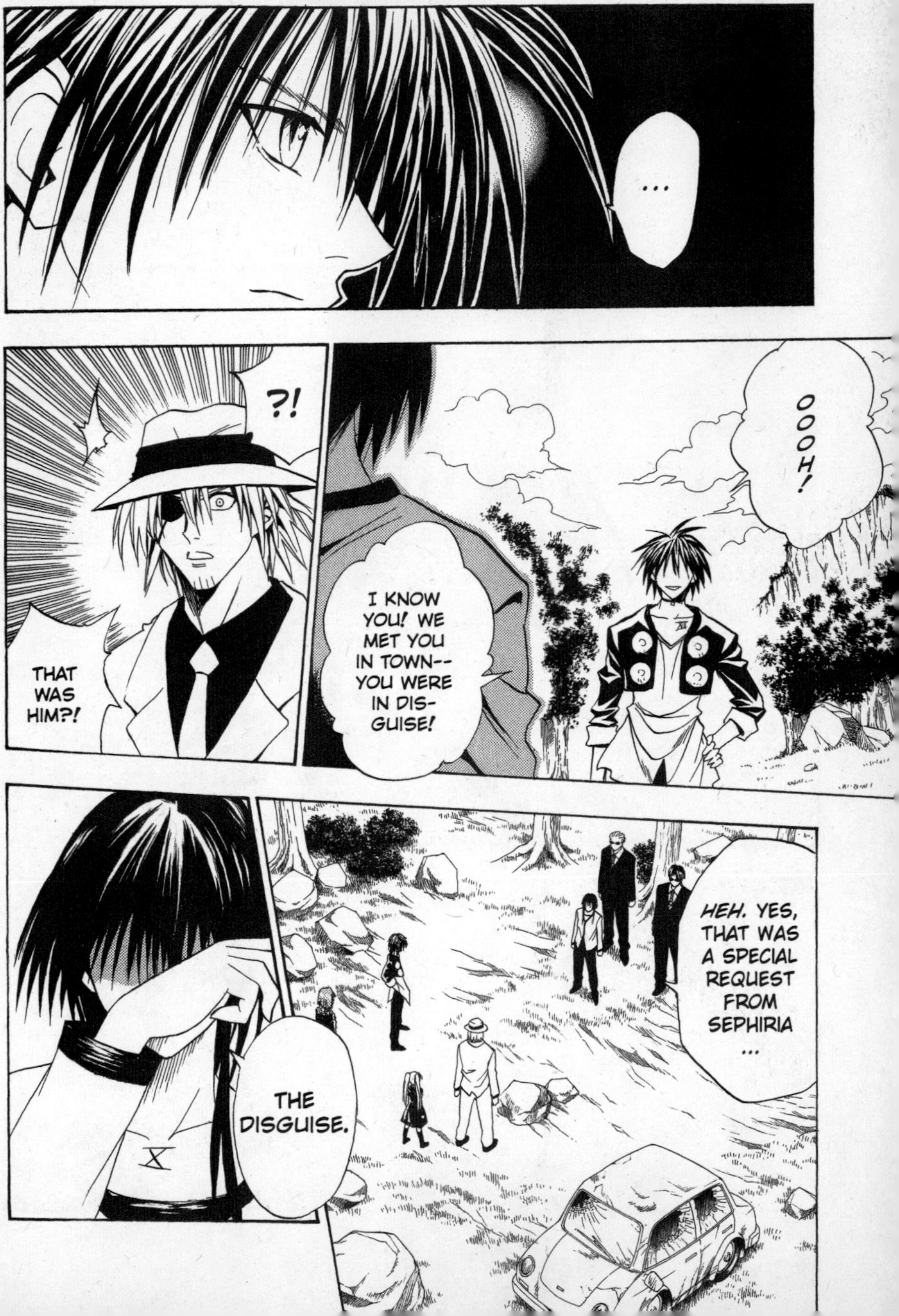
...
OOOH!
I KNOW YOU! WE MET YOU IN TOWN--YOU WERE IN DISGUISE!
?!
THAT WAS HIM?!
HEH. YES, THAT WAS A SPECIAL REQUEST FROM SEPHIRIA ...
THE DISGUISE.

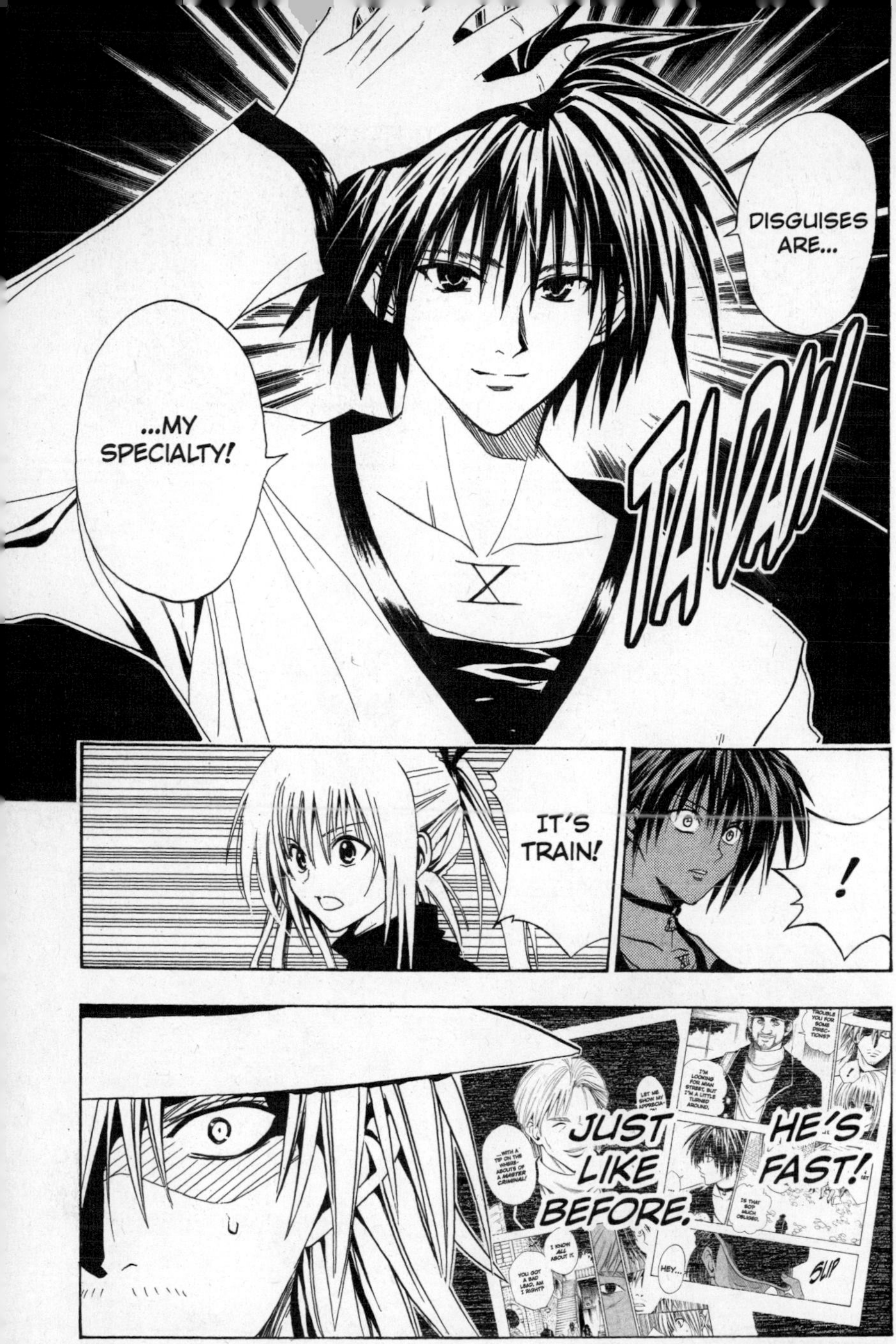
DISGUISES ARE...
...MY SPECIALTY!
TADAH
IT'S TRAIN!
!
HE'S FAST!
JUST LIKE BEFORE.
I'M LOOKING FOR MIAN STREET, BUT I'M A LITTLE TURNED AROUND.
IS THAT SO? MUCH OBLIGED.
HEY...
SLIP
I KNOW ALL ABOUT IT.
YOU GOT A BAD LEAD, AM I RIGHT?
...WITH A TIP ON THE WHERE-ABOUTS OF A MASTER CRIMINAL!

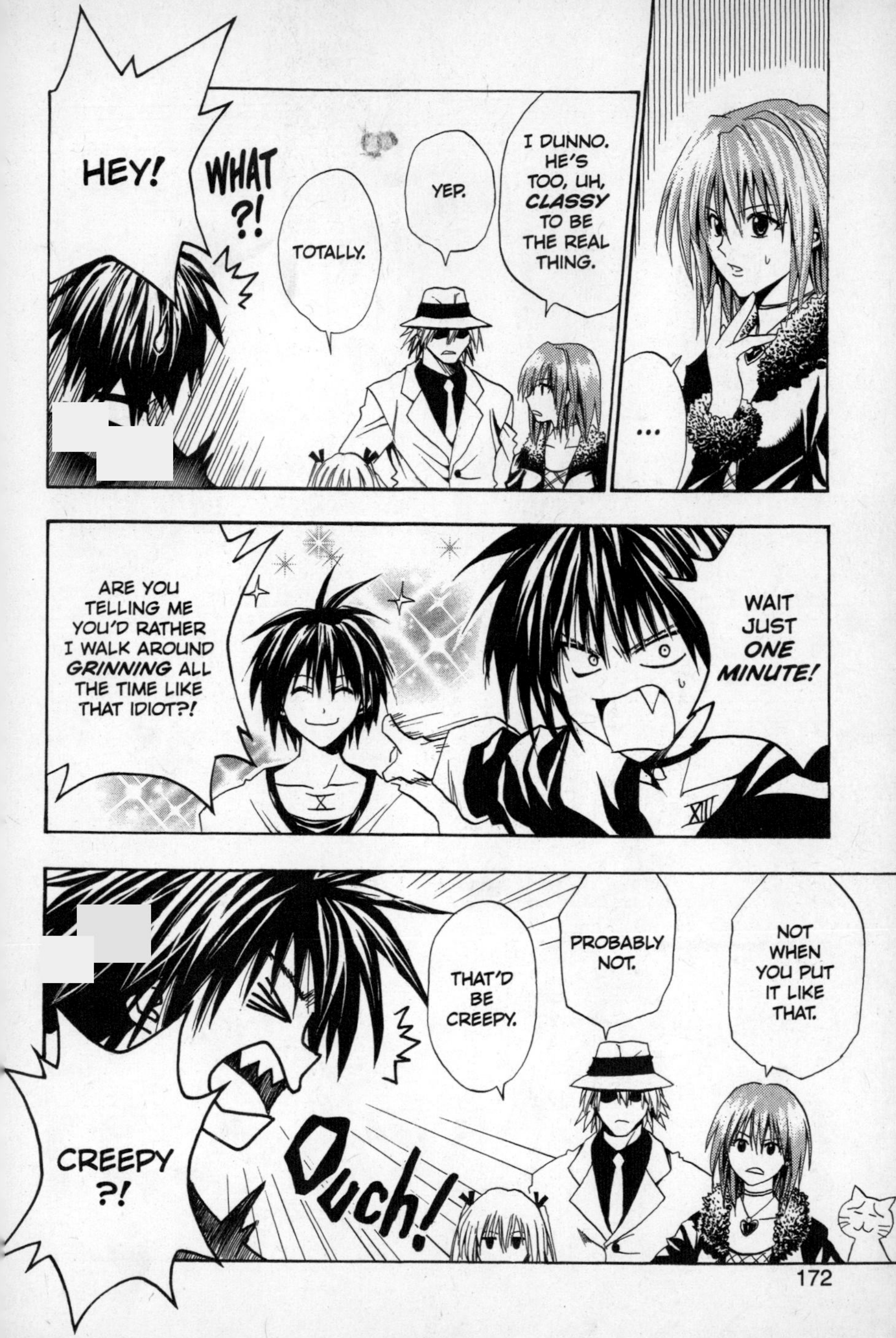
...
I DUNNO. HE'S TOO, UH, CLASSY TO BE THE REAL THING.
YEP.
TOTALLY.
WHAT?!
HEY!
WAIT JUST ONE MINUTE!
ARE YOU TELLING ME YOU'D RATHER I WALK AROUND GRINNING ALL THE TIME LIKE THAT IDIOT?!
NOT WHEN YOU PUT IT LIKE THAT.
PROBABLY NOT.
THAT'D BE CREEPY.
CREEPY?!
Ouch!

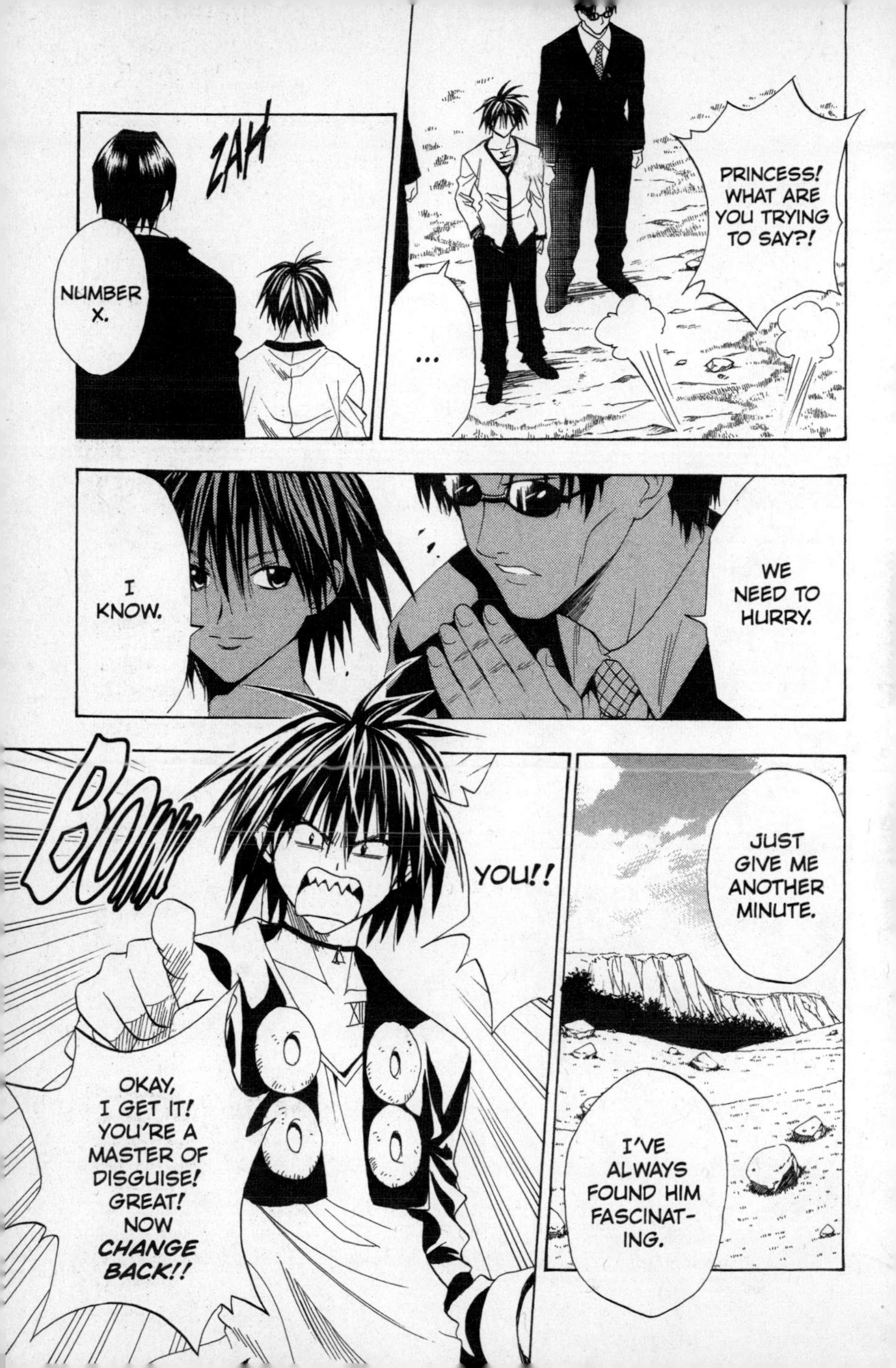
PRINCESS! WHAT ARE YOU TRYING TO SAY?!
...
ZAK
NUMBER X.
WE NEED TO HURRY.
I KNOW.
JUST GIVE ME ANOTHER MINUTE.
I'VE ALWAYS FOUND HIM FASCINATING.
YOU!!
BOM
OKAY, I GET IT! YOU'RE A MASTER OF DISGUISE! GREAT! NOW CHANGE BACK!!

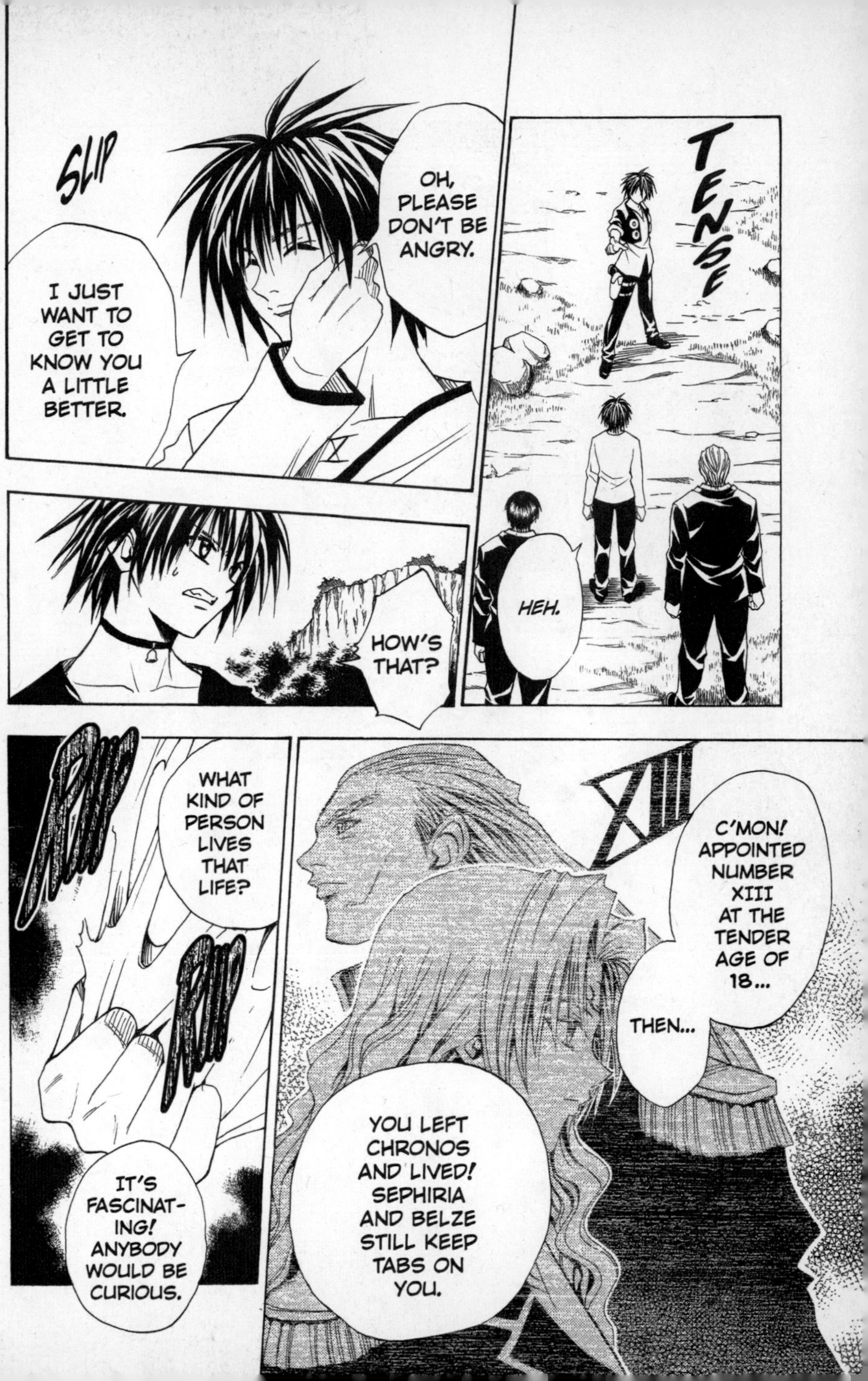
TENSE
HEH.
OH, PLEASE DON'T BE ANGRY.
I JUST WANT TO GET TO KNOW YOU A LITTLE BETTER.
SLIP
HOW'S THAT?
C'MON! APPOINTED NUMBER XIII AT THE TENDER AGE OF 18...
THEN...
YOU LEFT CHRONOS AND LIVED! SEPHIRIA AND BELZE STILL KEEP TABS ON YOU.
WHAT KIND OF PERSON LIVES THAT LIFE?
IT'S FASCINAT-ING! ANYBODY WOULD BE CURIOUS.

WOULDN'T YOU AGREE?

IT'S MY UNDER-STAND-ING...

THAT YOU AND CREED SHARE AN *AFFINITY* OF SORTS.

TRAIN?

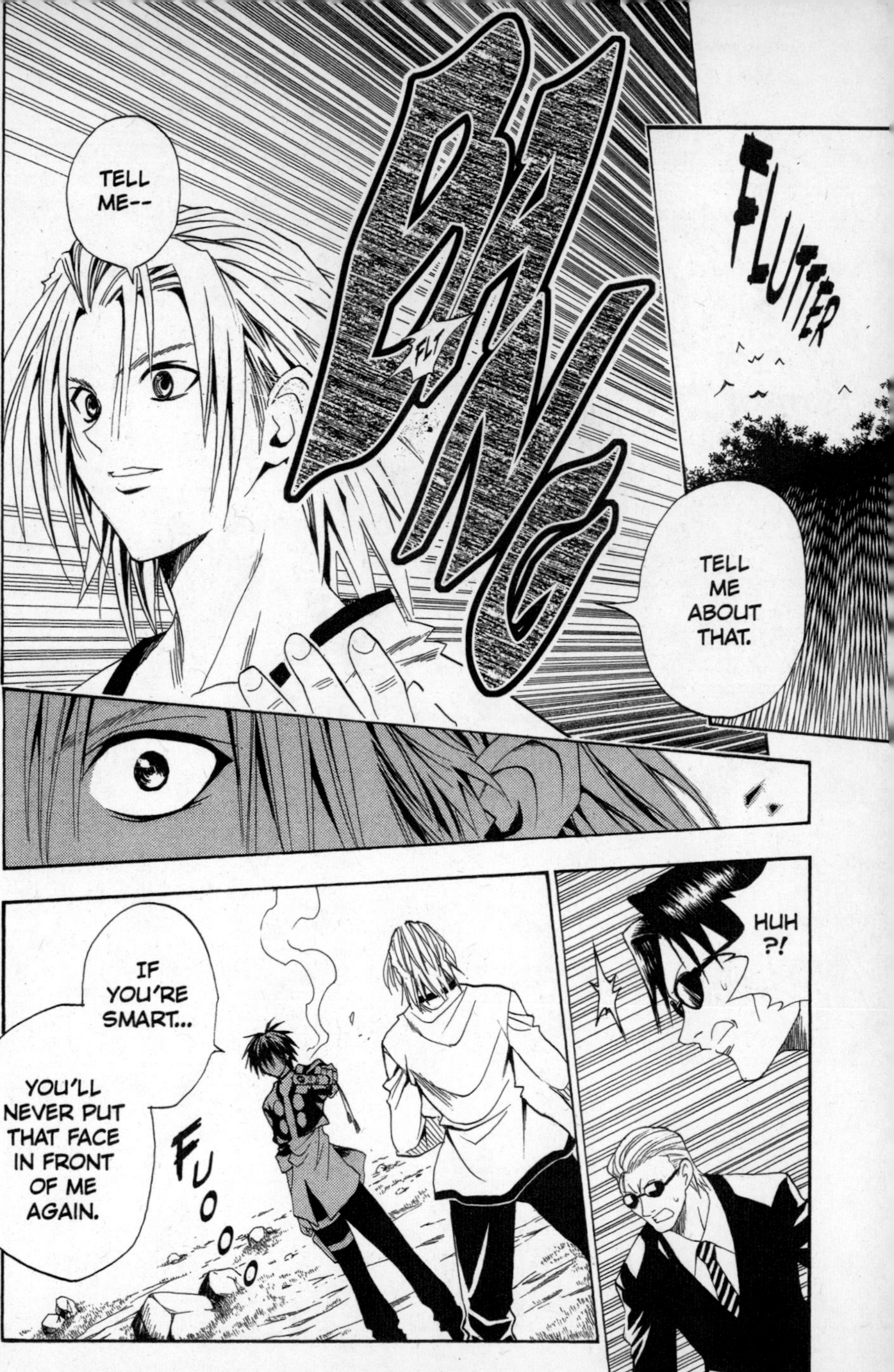
FLUTTER
TELL ME--
FLT
TELL ME ABOUT THAT.
HUH ?!
IF YOU'RE SMART...
YOU'LL NEVER PUT THAT FACE IN FRONT OF ME AGAIN.
FUOOO

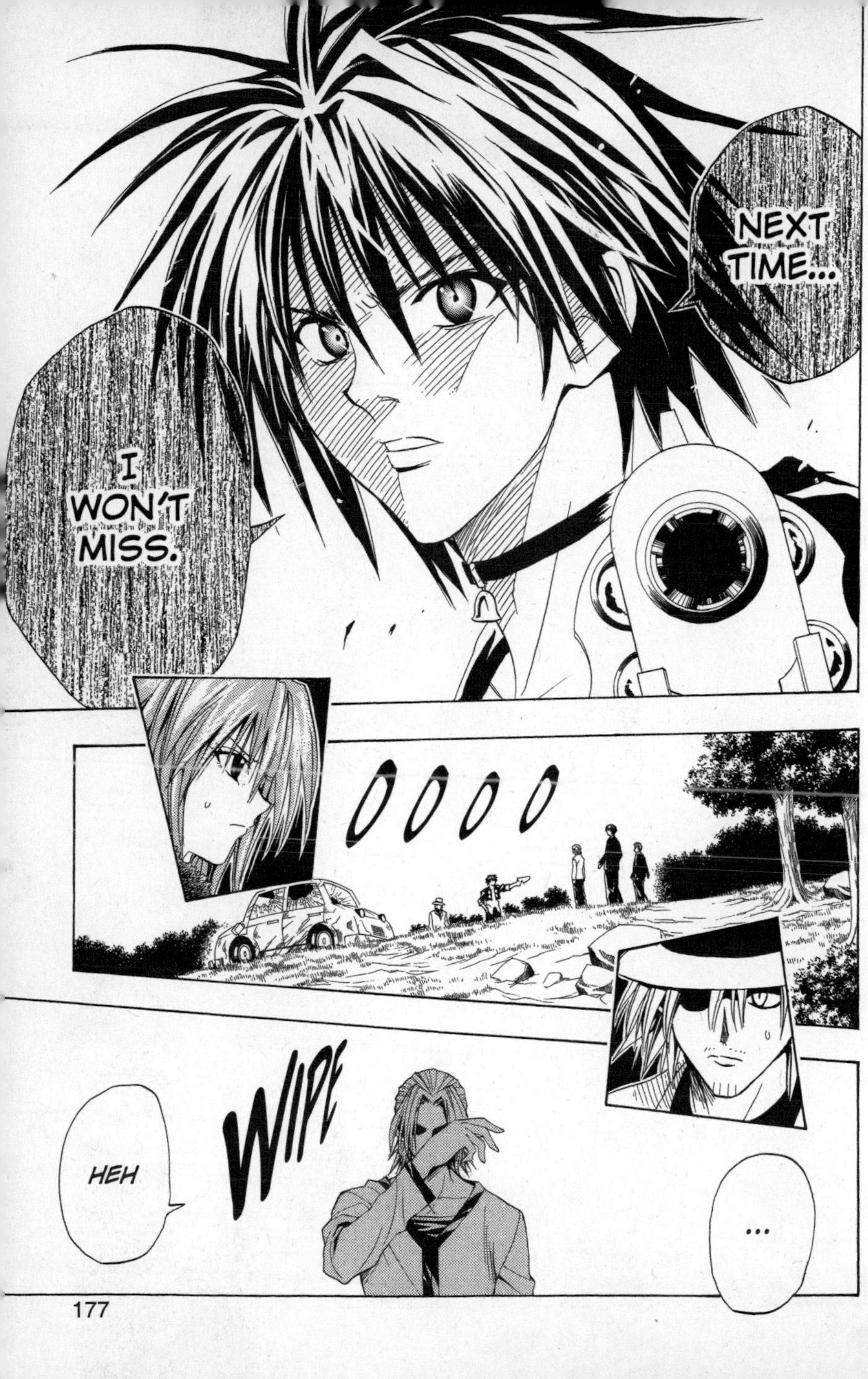
NEXT TIME...
I WON'T MISS.
...
WIPE
HEH

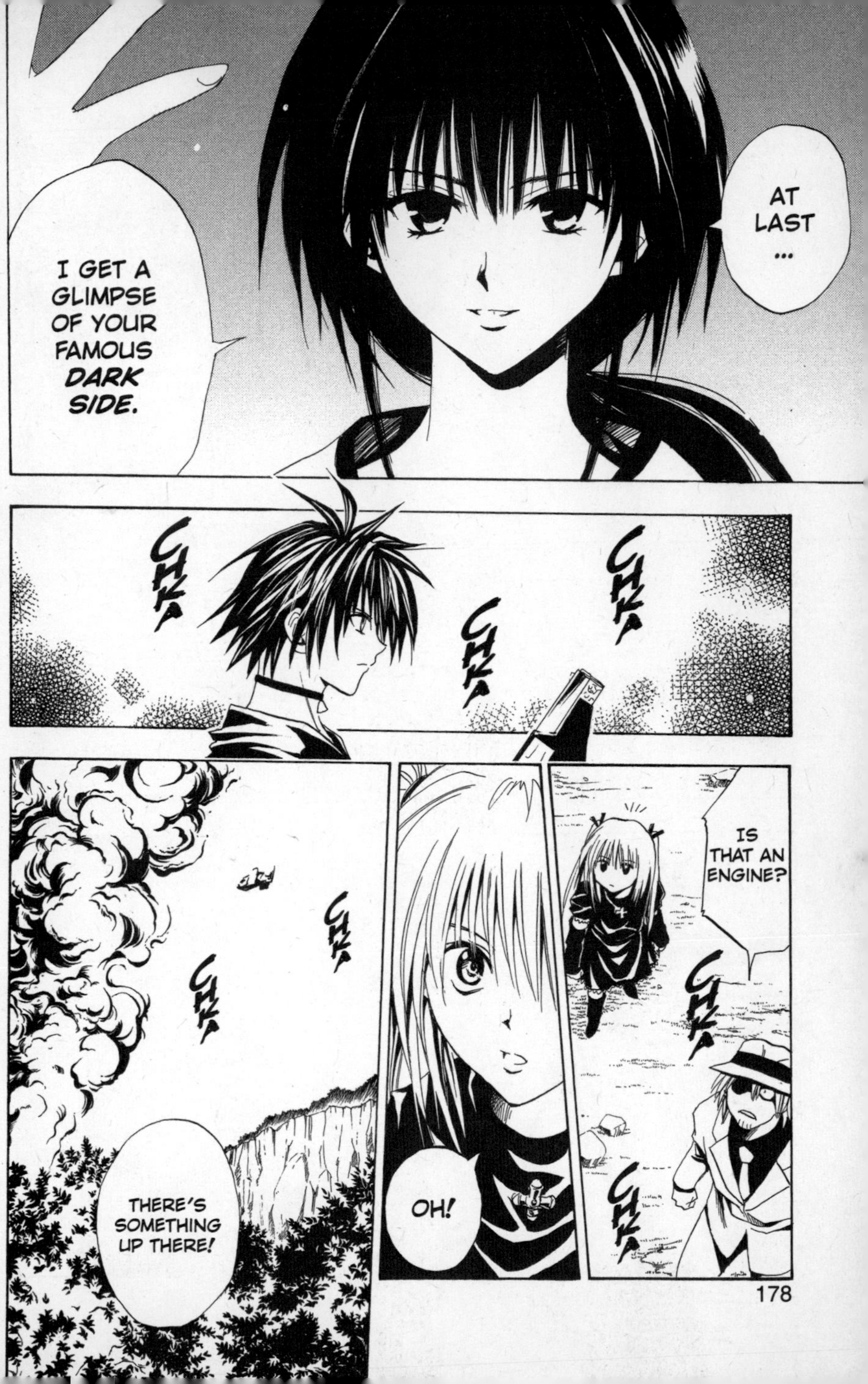
AT LAST ...
I GET A GLIMPSE OF YOUR FAMOUS ***DARK SIDE.***
CHKA
CHKA
CHKA
IS THAT AN ENGINE?
CHKA
CHKA
OH!
CHKA
CHKA
THERE'S SOMETHING UP THERE!

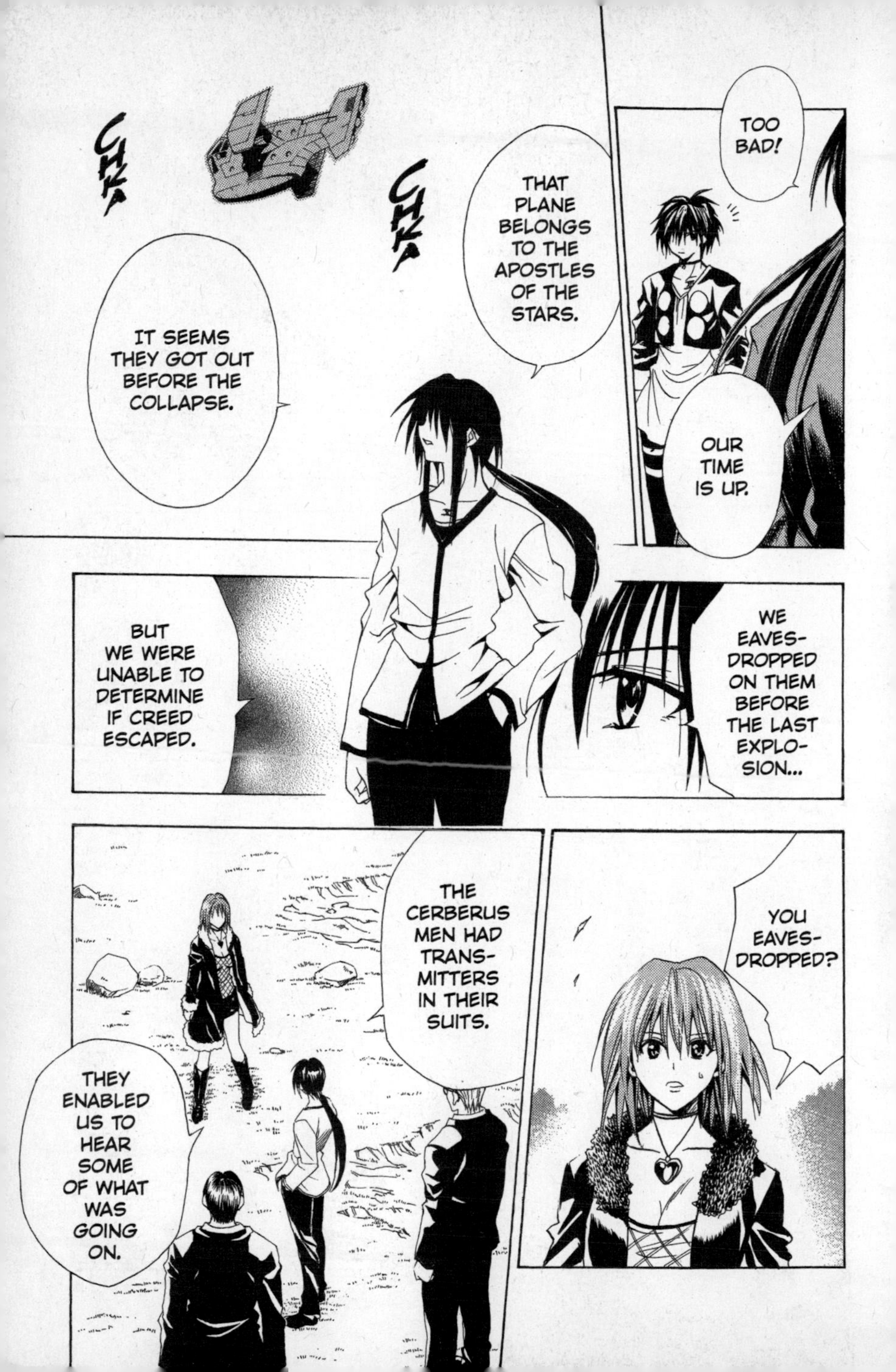
TOO BAD!
OUR TIME IS UP.
THAT PLANE BELONGS TO THE APOSTLES OF THE STARS.
CHKA
CHKA
IT SEEMS THEY GOT OUT BEFORE THE COLLAPSE.
WE EAVES-DROPPED ON THEM BEFORE THE LAST EXPLO-SION...
BUT WE WERE UNABLE TO DETERMINE IF CREED ESCAPED.
YOU EAVES-DROPPED?
THE CERBERUS MEN HAD TRANS-MITTERS IN THEIR SUITS.
THEY ENABLED US TO HEAR SOME OF WHAT WAS GOING ON.

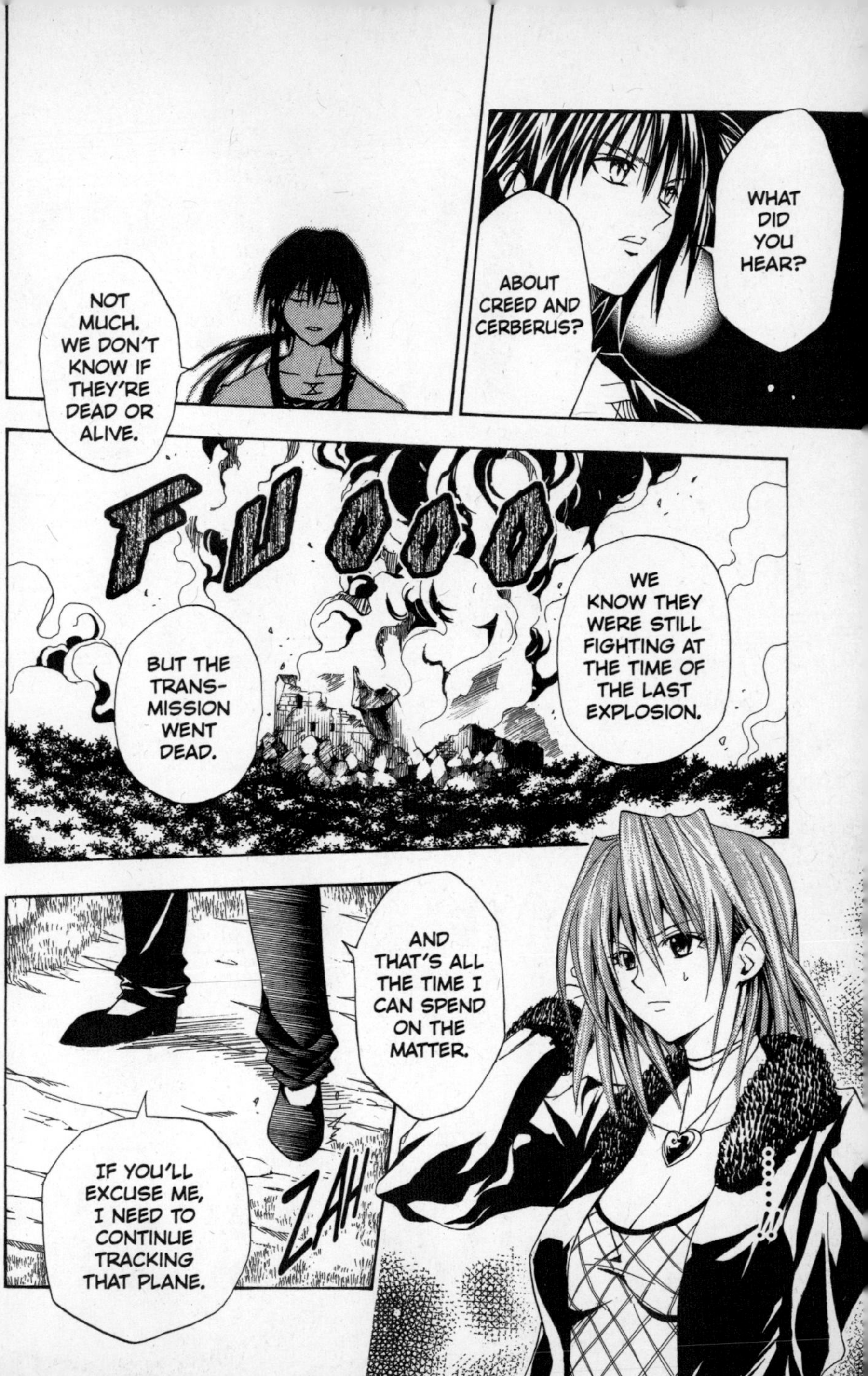
WHAT DID YOU HEAR?
ABOUT CREED AND CERBERUS?
NOT MUCH. WE DON'T KNOW IF THEY'RE DEAD OR ALIVE.
FUOOO
WE KNOW THEY WERE STILL FIGHTING AT THE TIME OF THE LAST EXPLOSION.
BUT THE TRANS-MISSION WENT DEAD.
AND THAT'S ALL THE TIME I CAN SPEND ON THE MATTER.
ZAH
IF YOU'LL EXCUSE ME, I NEED TO CONTINUE TRACKING THAT PLANE.

I HOPE WE'LL PICK UP WHERE WE LEFT OFF.

NEXT TIME, BLACK CAT...

SO COLD.

YOU DIRTY LITTLE SNEAK!

NO CHANCE!

BLECH

BYE.

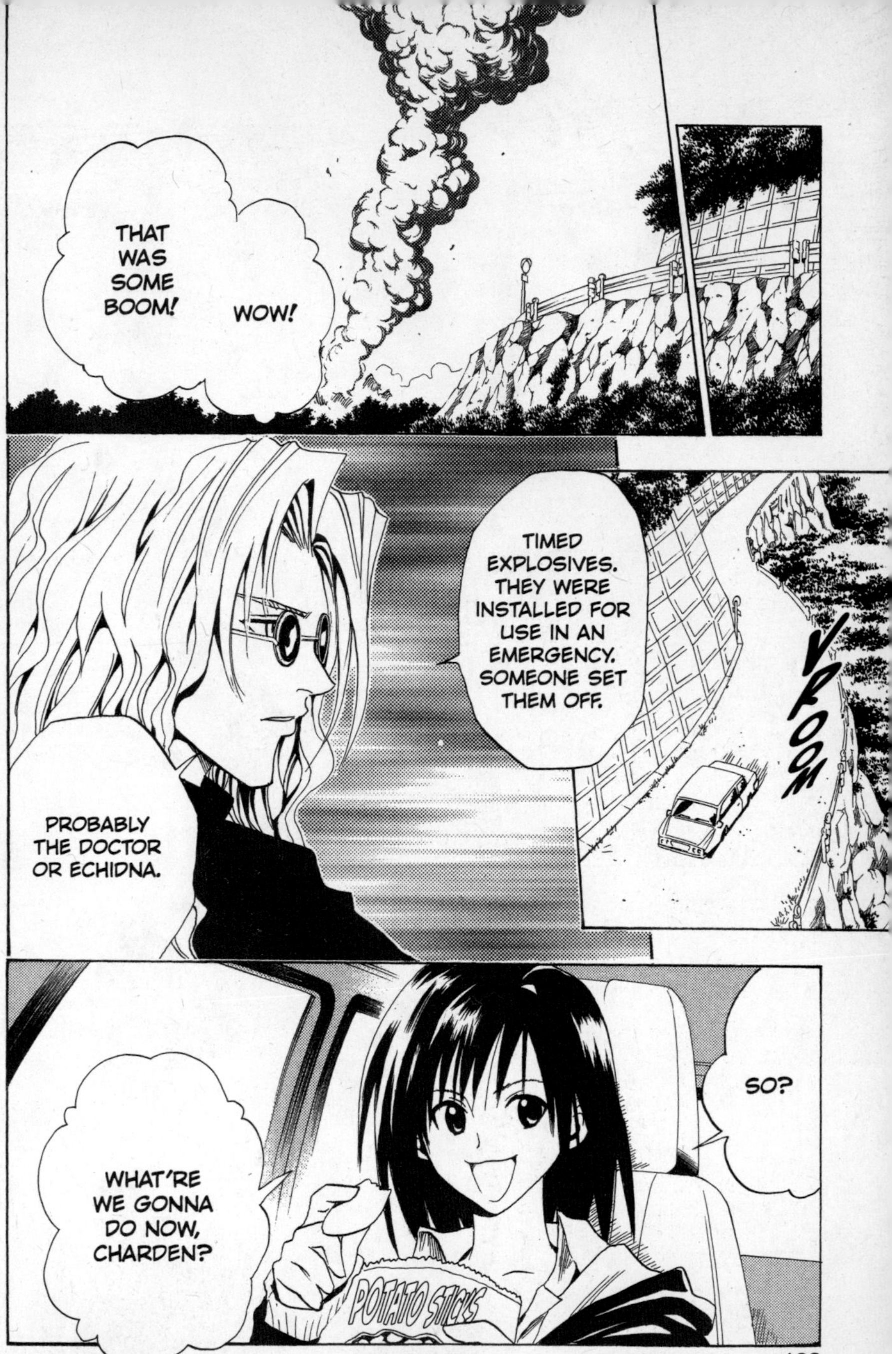
WOW!
THAT WAS SOME BOOM!
VROOM
TIMED EXPLOSIVES. THEY WERE INSTALLED FOR USE IN AN EMERGENCY. SOMEONE SET THEM OFF.
PROBABLY THE DOCTOR OR ECHIDNA.
SO?
WHAT'RE WE GONNA DO NOW, CHARDEN?
POTATO STICKS

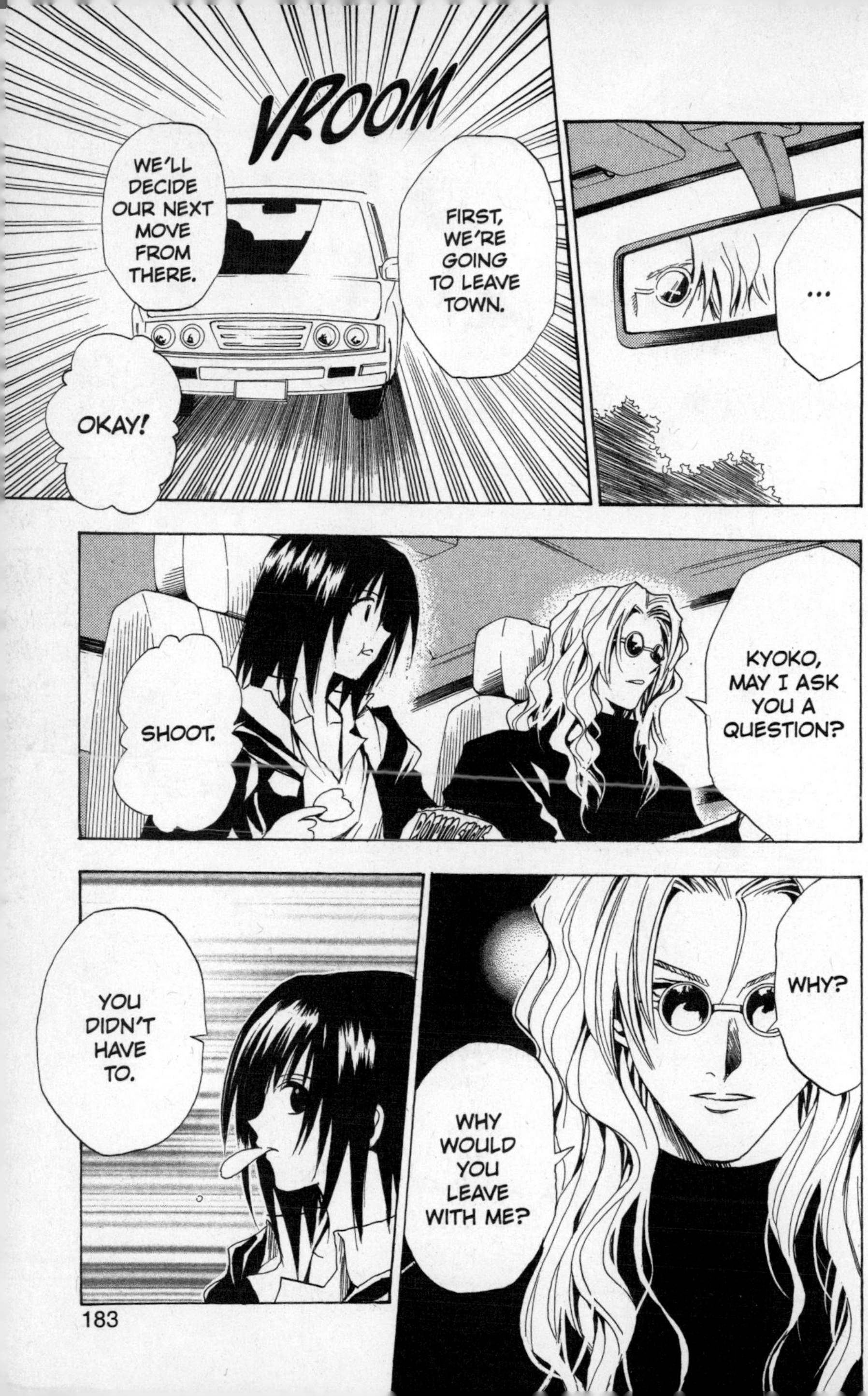
VROOM
FIRST, WE'RE GOING TO LEAVE TOWN.
WE'LL DECIDE OUR NEXT MOVE FROM THERE.
OKAY!
...
KYOKO, MAY I ASK YOU A QUESTION?
SHOOT.
WHY?
WHY WOULD YOU LEAVE WITH ME?
YOU DIDN'T HAVE TO.

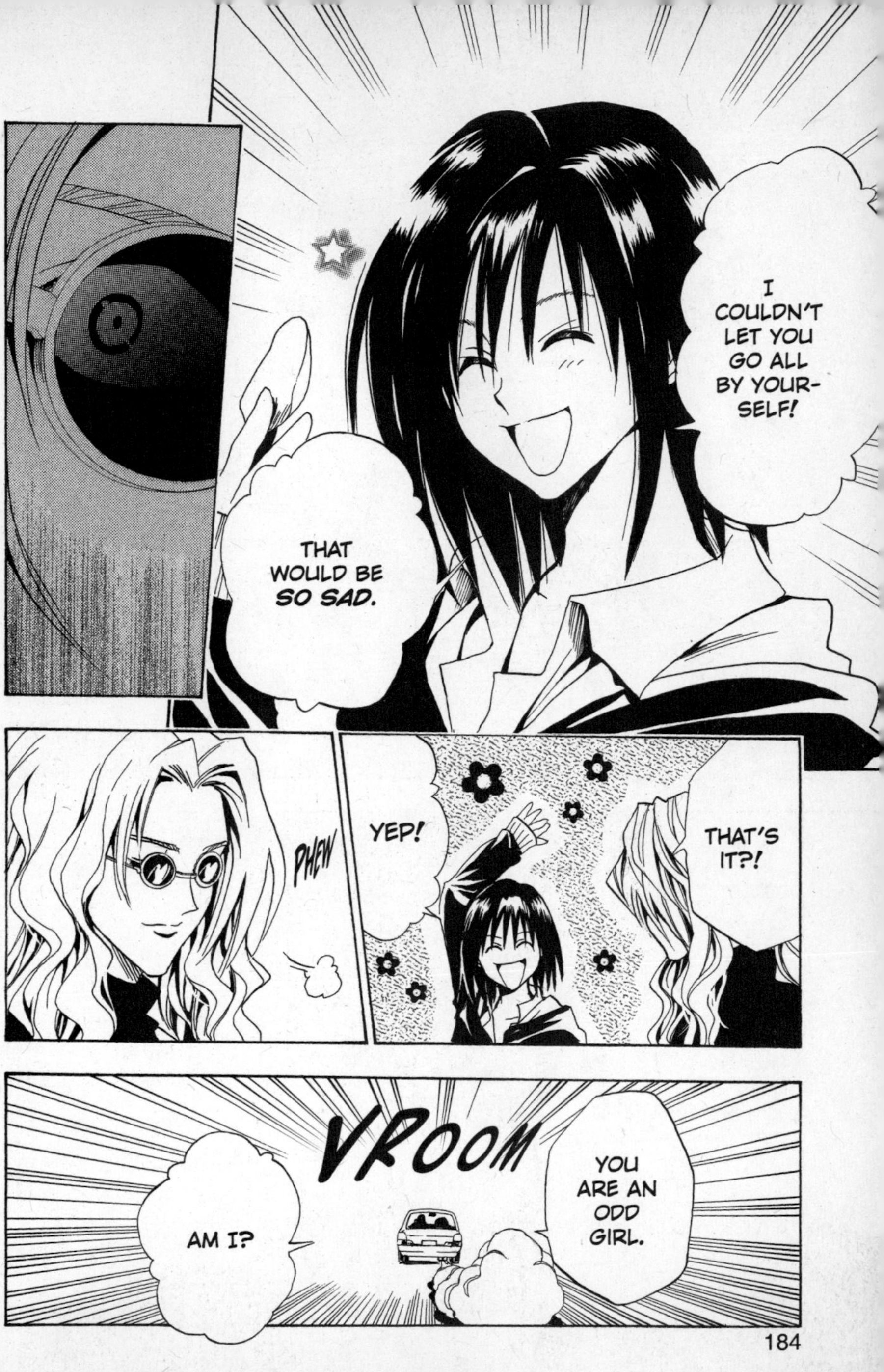
I COULDN'T LET YOU GO ALL BY YOUR-SELF!
THAT WOULD BE SO SAD.
THAT'S IT?!
YEP!
PHEW
VROOM
YOU ARE AN ODD GIRL.
AM I?

SHOWDOWN AT THE OLD CASTLE (THE END)

BLACK CAT

ブラック・キャット

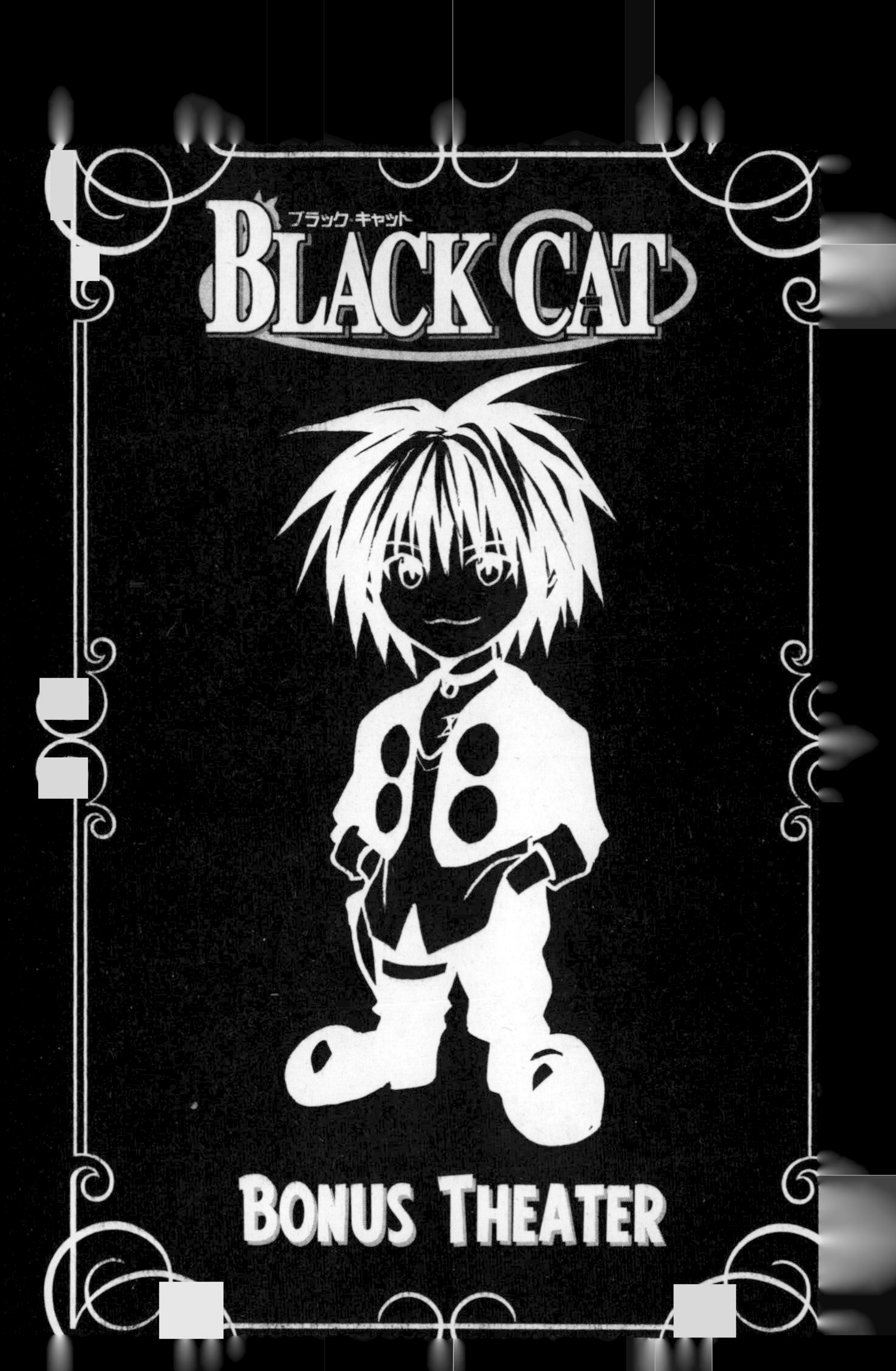

BONUS THEATER

A Day at KY Productions (BY KENTARO HONNA)

THIS IS A WORK OF FICTION.

NO. X Shaolee ♥♥♥

BY SHIKO KASHIWAGI

This is what happens when I call for take-out.

The food doesn't come. | Fried rice, green-peppers, and... | I'm very nice on the phone, but...
I'm starving.

So it's not coming, huh? | Sorry. We have a big order from a school.

So it's not coming, huh? | It's raining and it's cold.

So it's not coming, huh? | The chef went home to cook for her kids.

They give reasons, so that's nice. And the chef's sweet.

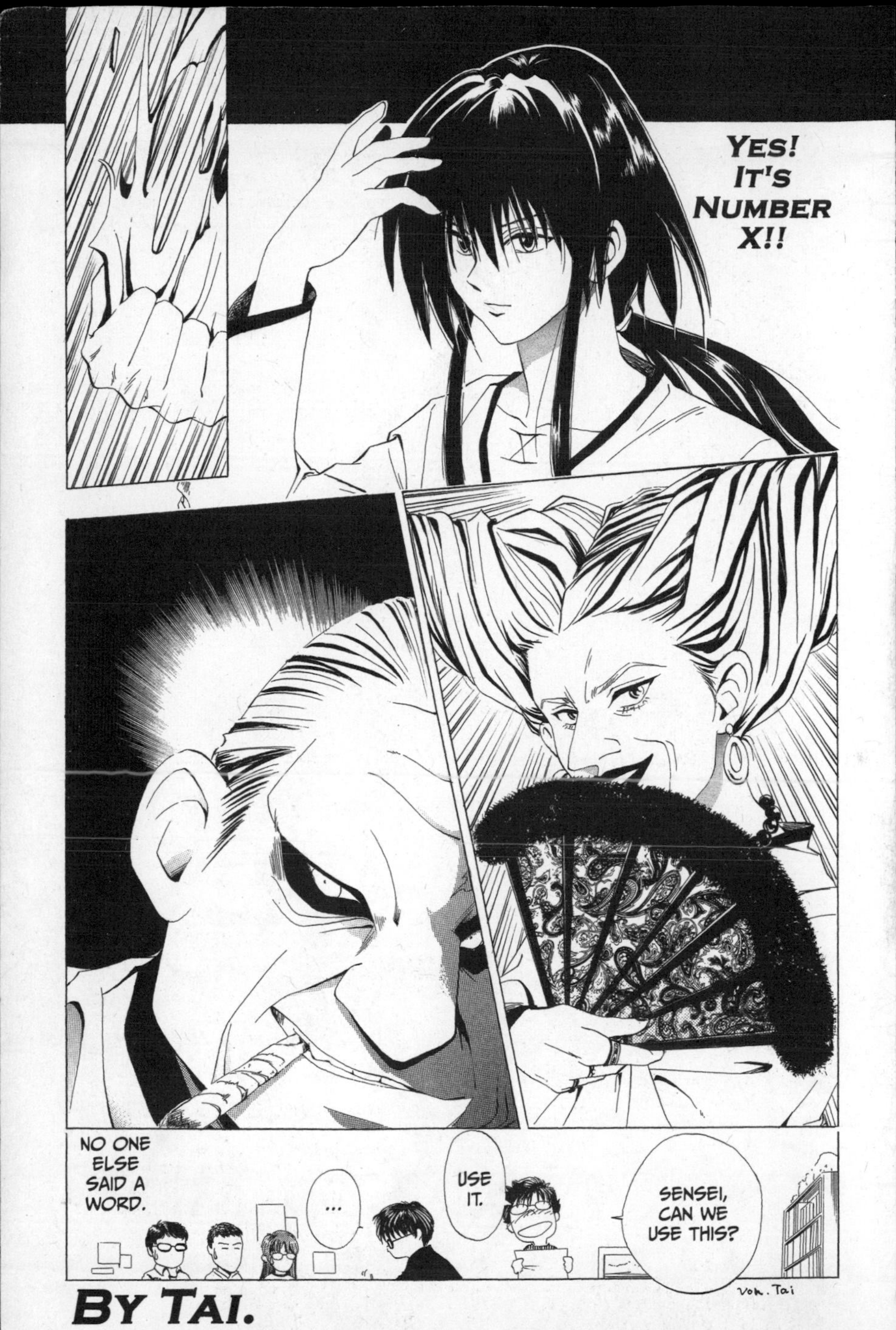
YES! IT'S NUMBER X!!
SENSEI, CAN WE USE THIS?
USE IT.
...
NO ONE ELSE SAID A WORD.
von. Tai

BY TAI.

BLACK CAT EXTRA
ABOUT CATS

I THINK HE'S A SPY ROBOT FROM ANOTHER COUNTRY.

MAYBE HE THINKS I'M A STRAY CAT?

HE'S AN ALIEN DISGUISED AS A TOY CAT.

NOW THAT'S ABSURD!

HIS IDENTITY REMAINS A MYSTERY.

NOT THAT ABSURD...

HA HA HA HA HA

BLACK CAT EXTRA

THE END

IN THE NEXT VOLUME...

Just when Train thinks his battles with Chronos and the Apostles have come to a halt, Sven and Eve are captured by Creed, who believes that their deaths will incite Train to join him in his lethal crusade. Now Train has figure out how to save his only friends.

AVAILABLE SEPTEMBER 2007! ◁ ◁ ◁ ◁ ◁ ◁ ◁

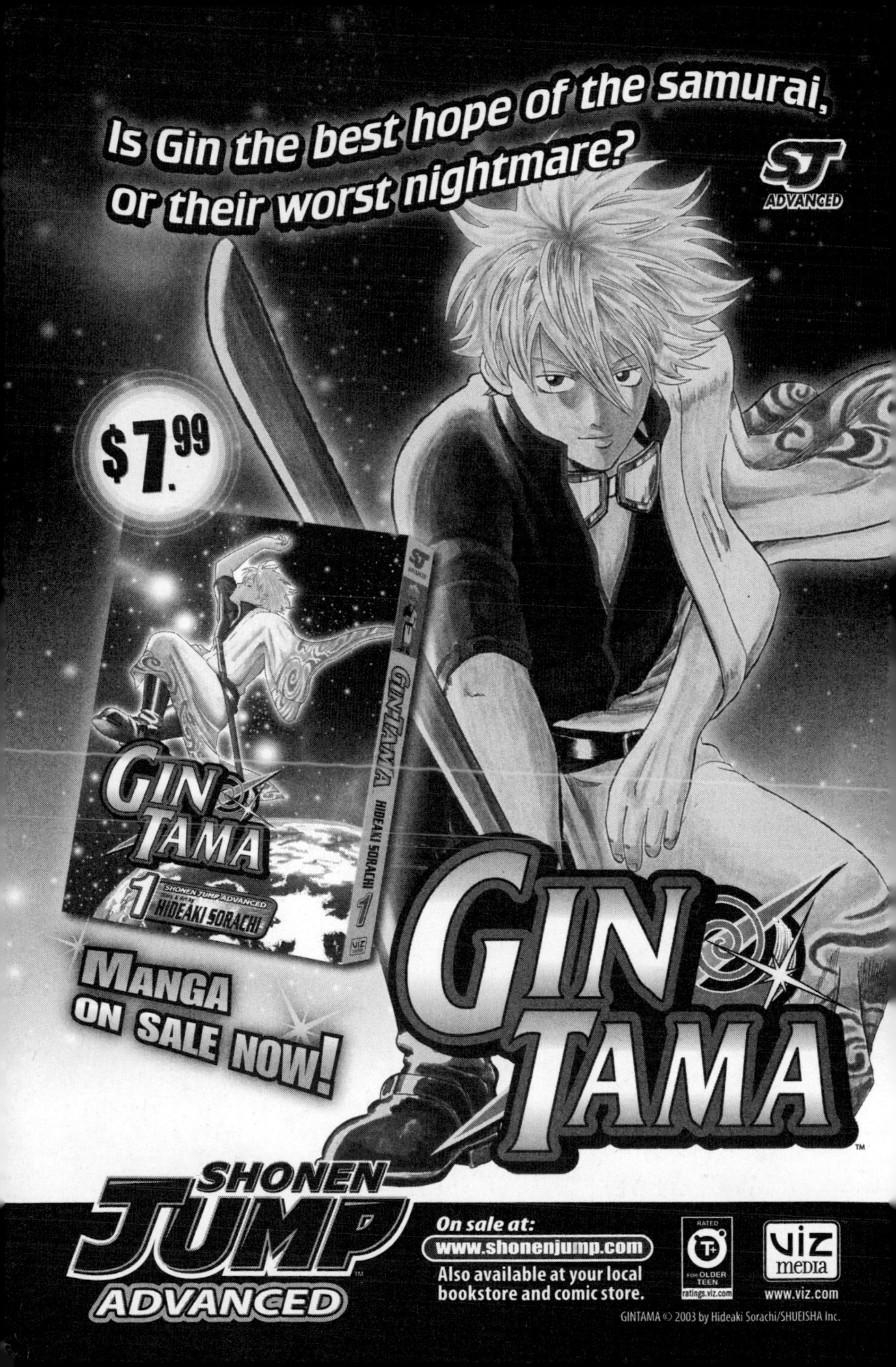

Is Gin the best hope of the samurai,
or their worst nightmare?
SJ ADVANCED
$7.99
GIN TAMA
1 SHONEN JUMP ADVANCED
HIDEAKI SORACHI
GINTAMA HIDEAKI SORACHI 1
MANGA ON SALE NOW!
GIN TAMA™
SHONEN JUMP ADVANCED
On sale at:
www.shonenjump.com
Also available at your local bookstore and comic store.
RATED T+ FOR OLDER TEEN ratings.viz.com
VIZ media
www.viz.com
GINTAMA © 2003 by Hideaki Sorachi/SHUEISHA Inc.

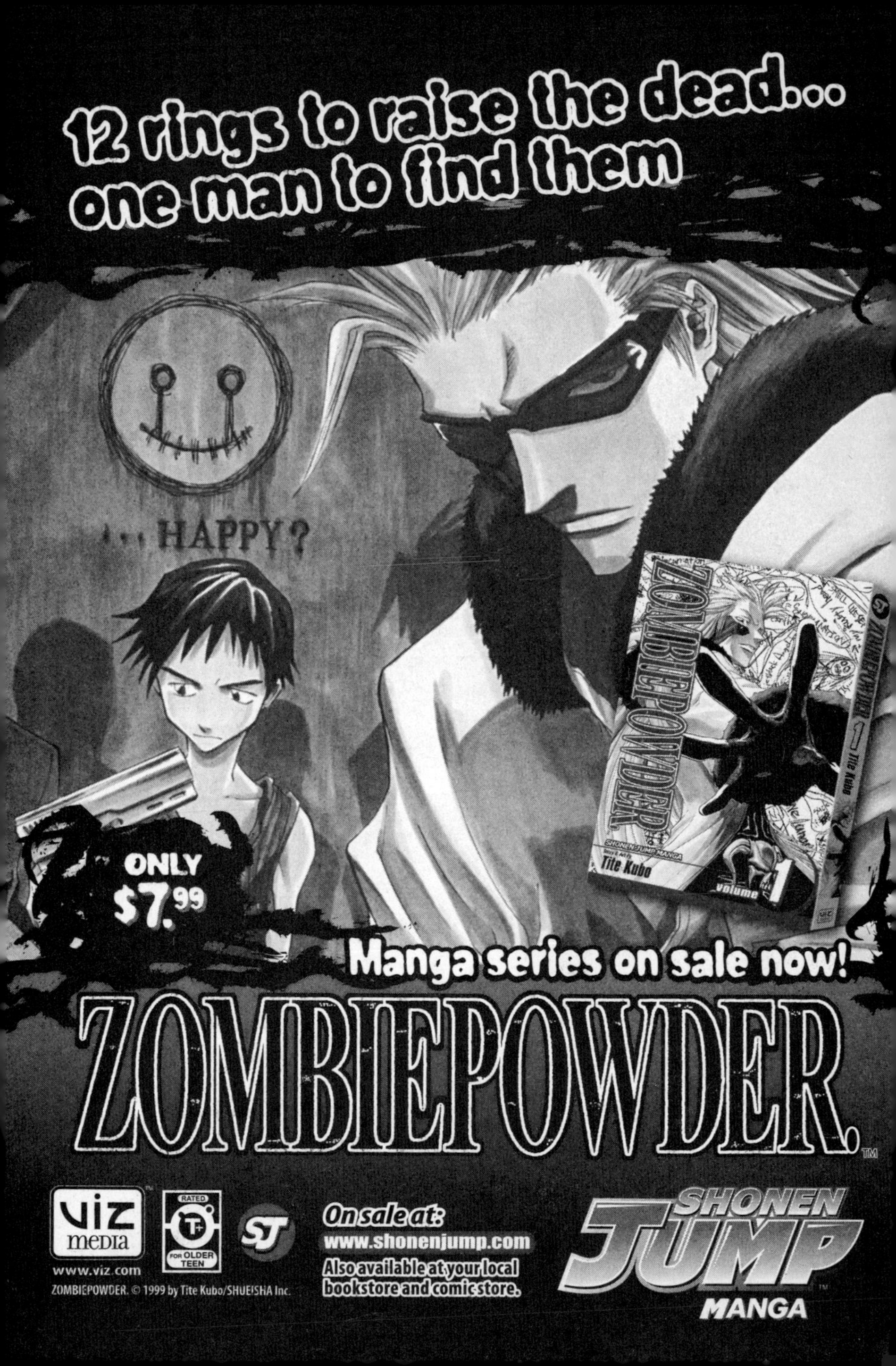
12 rings to raise the dead...
one man to find them
...HAPPY?
ZOMBIEPOWDER
SHONEN JUMP MANGA
Tite Kubo
volume 1
ONLY $7.99
Manga series on sale now!
ZOMBIEPOWDER.™
viz media
www.viz.com
RATED T+ FOR OLDER TEEN
SJ
On sale at:
www.shonenjump.com
Also available at your local bookstore and comic store.
SHONEN JUMP MANGA
ZOMBIEPOWDER. © 1999 by Tite Kubo/SHUEISHA Inc.

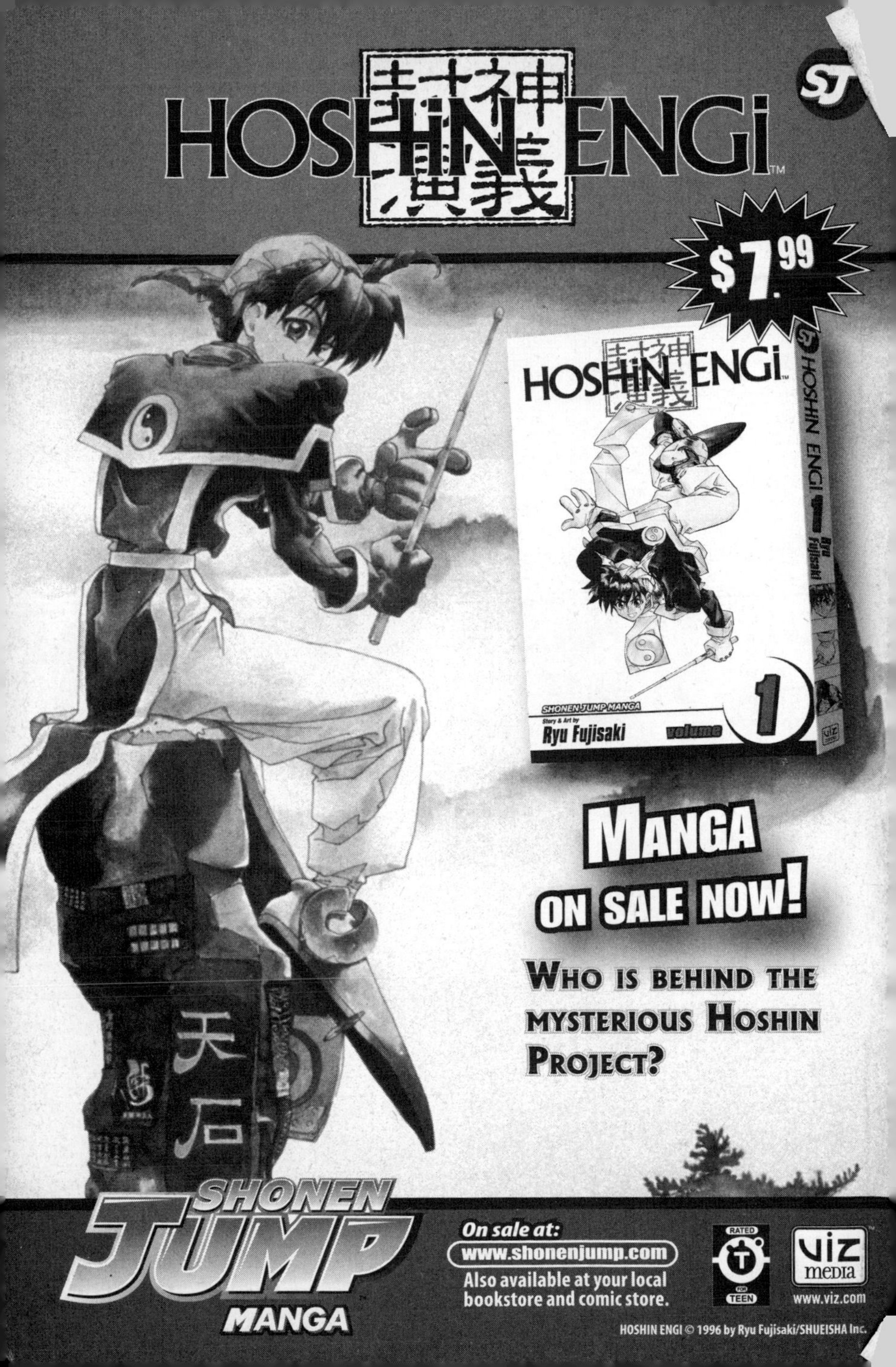
HOSHIN ENGI
封神演義
SJ
$7.99
HOSHIN ENGI
SHONEN JUMP MANGA
Story & Art by
Ryu Fujisaki
volume 1
MANGA
ON SALE NOW!
WHO IS BEHIND THE MYSTERIOUS HOSHIN PROJECT?
SHONEN JUMP MANGA
On sale at:
www.shonenjump.com
Also available at your local bookstore and comic store.
RATED T FOR TEEN
viz media
www.viz.com
HOSHIN ENGI © 1996 by Ryu Fujisaki/SHUEISHA Inc.

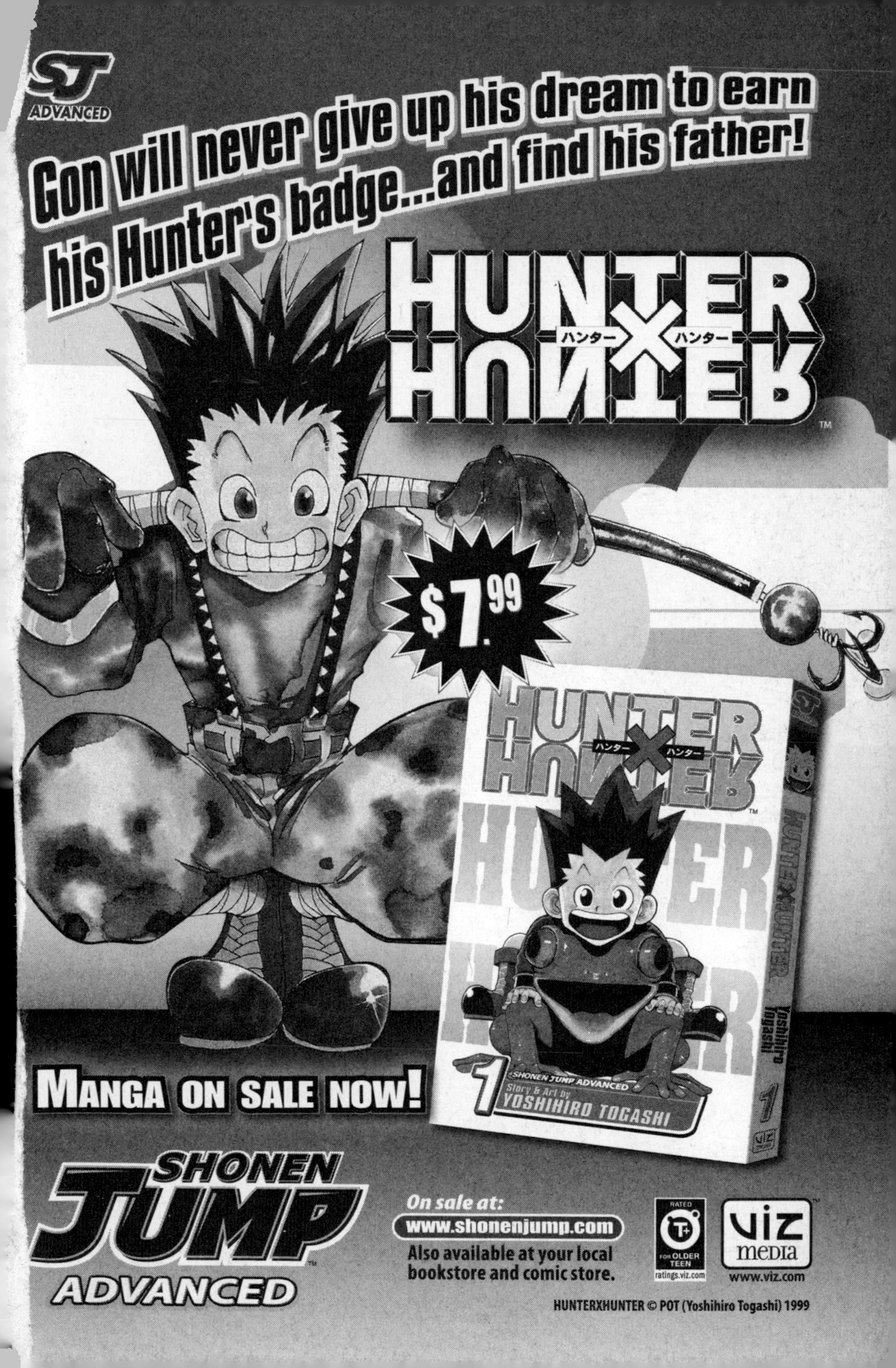

SJ ADVANCED
Gon will never give up his dream to earn his Hunter's badge...and find his father!
HUNTER×HUNTER
ハンター ハンター
$7.99
HUNTER×HUNTER
SHONEN JUMP ADVANCED
Story & Art by YOSHIHIRO TOGASHI
Yoshihiro Togashi
MANGA ON SALE NOW!
SHONEN JUMP ADVANCED
On sale at:
www.shonenjump.com
Also available at your local bookstore and comic store.
RATED T+ FOR OLDER TEEN
ratings.viz.com
viz media
www.viz.com
HUNTERXHUNTER © POT (Yoshihiro Togashi) 1999

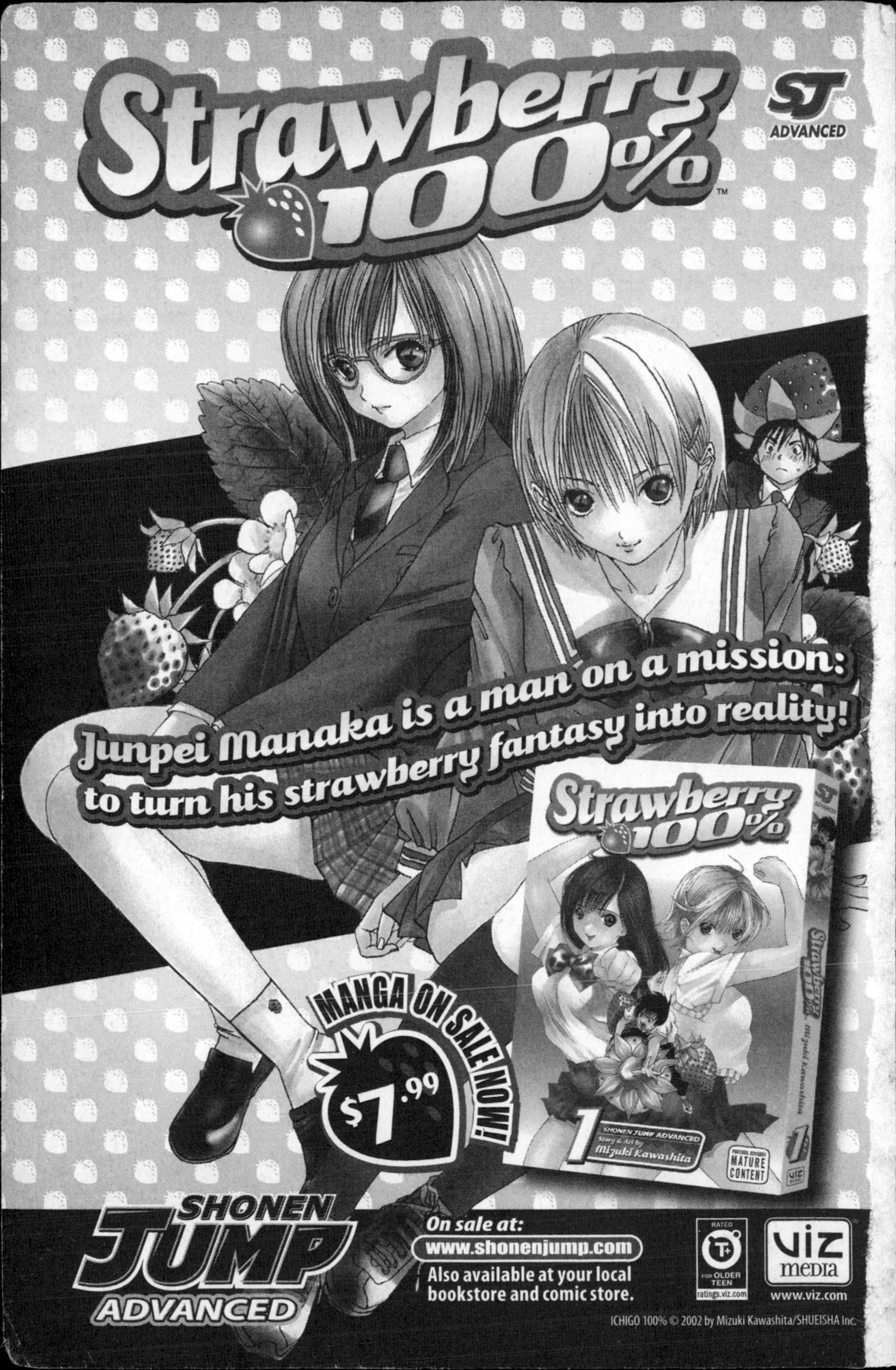

Strawberry 100%™
SJ ADVANCED
Junpei Manaka is a man on a mission: to turn his strawberry fantasy into reality!
Strawberry 100%
1 SHONEN JUMP ADVANCED Story & Art by Mizuki Kawashita
MATURE CONTENT
MANGA ON SALE NOW!
$7.99
SHONEN JUMP ADVANCED
On sale at:
www.shonenjump.com
Also available at your local bookstore and comic store.
RATED T+ FOR OLDER TEEN
ratings.viz.com
VIZ media
www.viz.com
ICHIGO 100% © 2002 by Mizuki Kawashita/SHUEISHA Inc.

Tell us what you think about SHONEN JUMP manga!

Our survey is now available online.
Go to: **www.SHONENJUMP.com/mangasurvey**

Help us make our product offering better!

WITHDRAWN

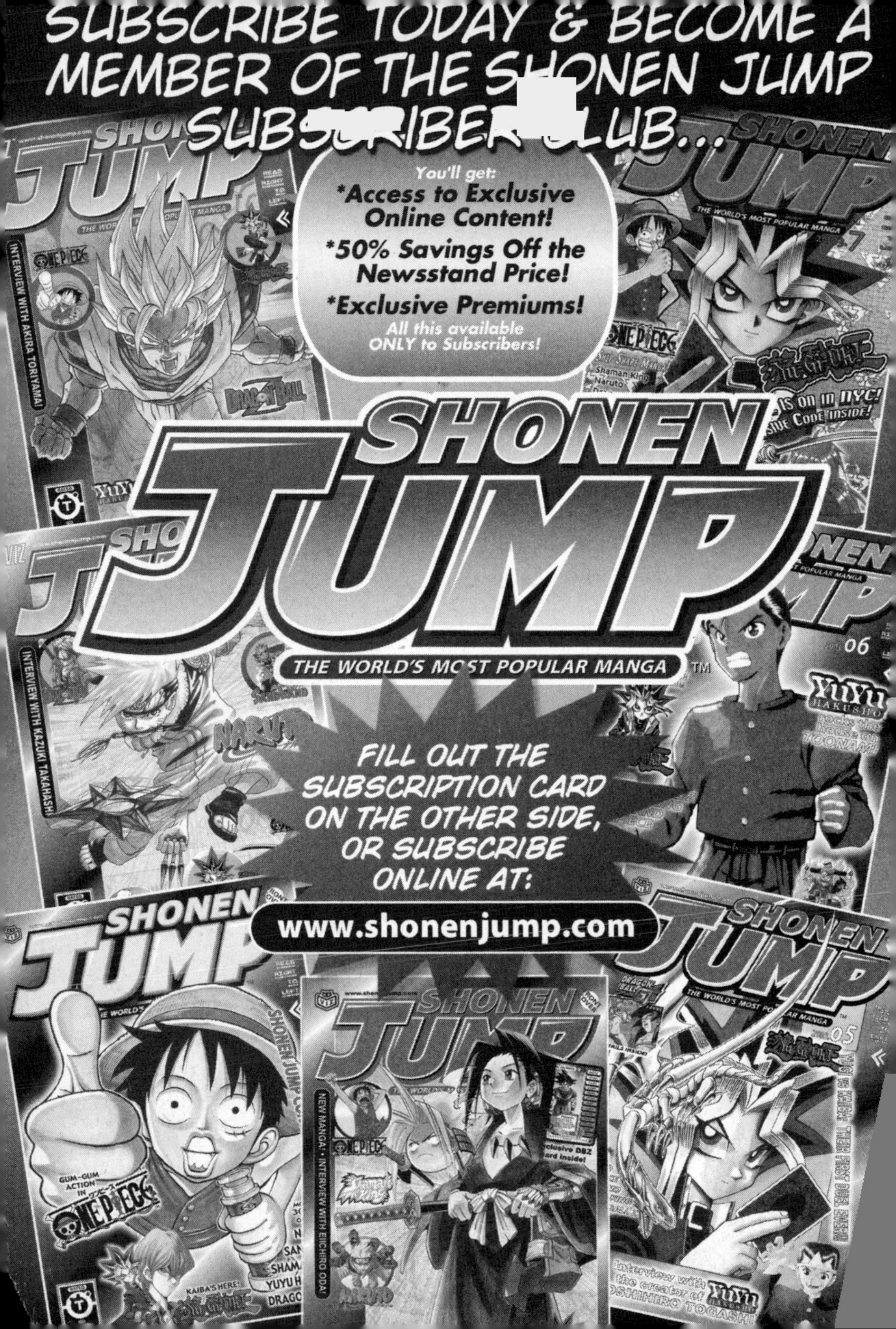
SUBSCRIBE TODAY & BECOME A MEMBER OF THE SHONEN JUMP SUBSCRIBER CLUB...
You'll get:
*Access to Exclusive Online Content!
*50% Savings Off the Newsstand Price!
*Exclusive Premiums!
All this available ONLY to Subscribers!
SHONEN JUMP
THE WORLD'S MOST POPULAR MANGA ™
FILL OUT THE SUBSCRIPTION CARD ON THE OTHER SIDE, OR SUBSCRIBE ONLINE AT:
www.shonenjump.com

THE CONQUEROR SERIES

LORDS OF
THE BOW

CONN IGGULDEN

HARPER

Harper
An Imprint of HarperCollins*Publishers*
77–85 Fulham Palace Road,
Hammersmith, London W6 8JB

www.harpercollins.co.uk

This paperback edition 2010
1

First published in Great Britain by HarperCollins*Publishers* 2008

A catalogue record for this book is available from the British Library

ISBN: 978 0 00 735326 2

Set in Minion by Palimpsest Book Production Limited
Grangemouth, Stirlingshire

Printed and bound in Great Britain by Clays Ltd, St Ives plc

Mixed Sources

Product group from well-managed forests and other controlled sources
www.fsc.org Cert no. SW-COC-001806
© 1996 Forest Stewardship Council

FSC is a non-profit international organisation established to promote the responsible management of the world's forests. Products carrying the FSC label are independently certified to assure consumers that they come from forests that are managed to meet the social, economic and ecological needs of present and future generations.

Find out more about HarperCollins and the environment at
www.harpercollins.co.uk/green

To my daughter Sophie

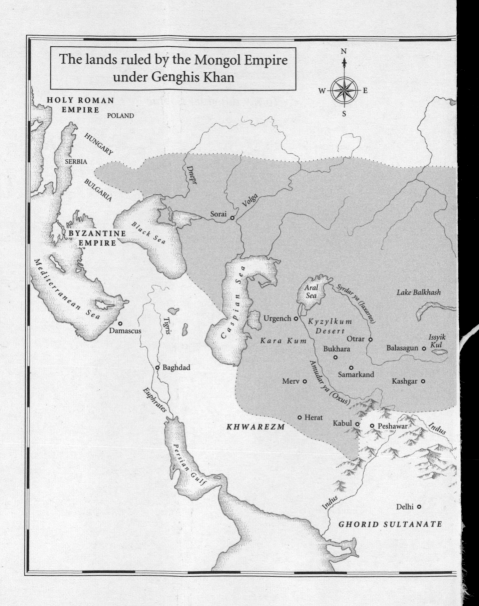

The lands ruled by the Mongol Empire under Genghis Khan

N
W   E
S

HOLY ROMAN
EMPIRE
POLAND

HUNGARY

SERBIA

BULGARIA

BYZANTINE
EMPIRE

Black Sea

Dnepr

Volga

Sorai

Mediterranean Sea

Caspian Sea

Damascus

Tigris

Aral
Sea

Syrdar ya (Jaxartes)

Lake Balkhash

Urgench

Kyzylkum
Desert

Kara Kum

Otrar

Bukhara

Balasagun

Issyik
Kul

Baghdad

Euphrates

Amudar ya (Oxus)

Merv

Samarkand

Kashgar

Persian Gulf

KHWAREZM

Herat

Kabul

Peshawar

Indus

Delhi

Indus

GHORID SULTANATE

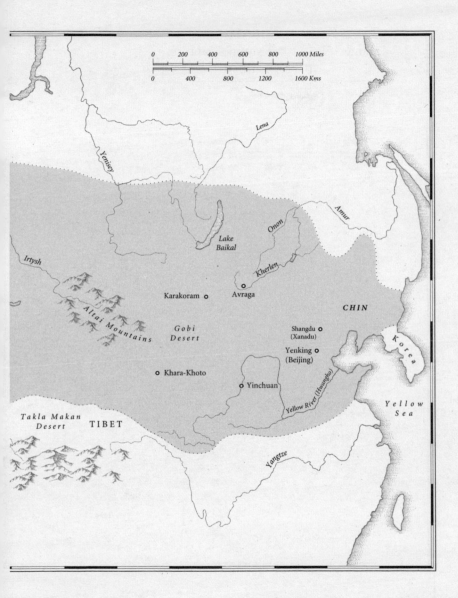

Scale:
0 — 200 — 400 — 600 — 800 — 1000 Miles
0 — 400 — 800 — 1200 — 1600 Kms

Lena

Yenisey

Amur

Onon

Lake
Baikal

Kherlen

Irtysh

Karakoram ○   ○ Avraga

Altai Mountains

CHIN

Gobi
Desert

Shangdu ○
(Xanadu)

Korea

Yenking ○
(Beijing)

○ Khara-Khoto

○ Yinchuan

Yellow River (Hwangho)

Yellow
Sea

Takla Makan
Desert   TIBET

Yangtze

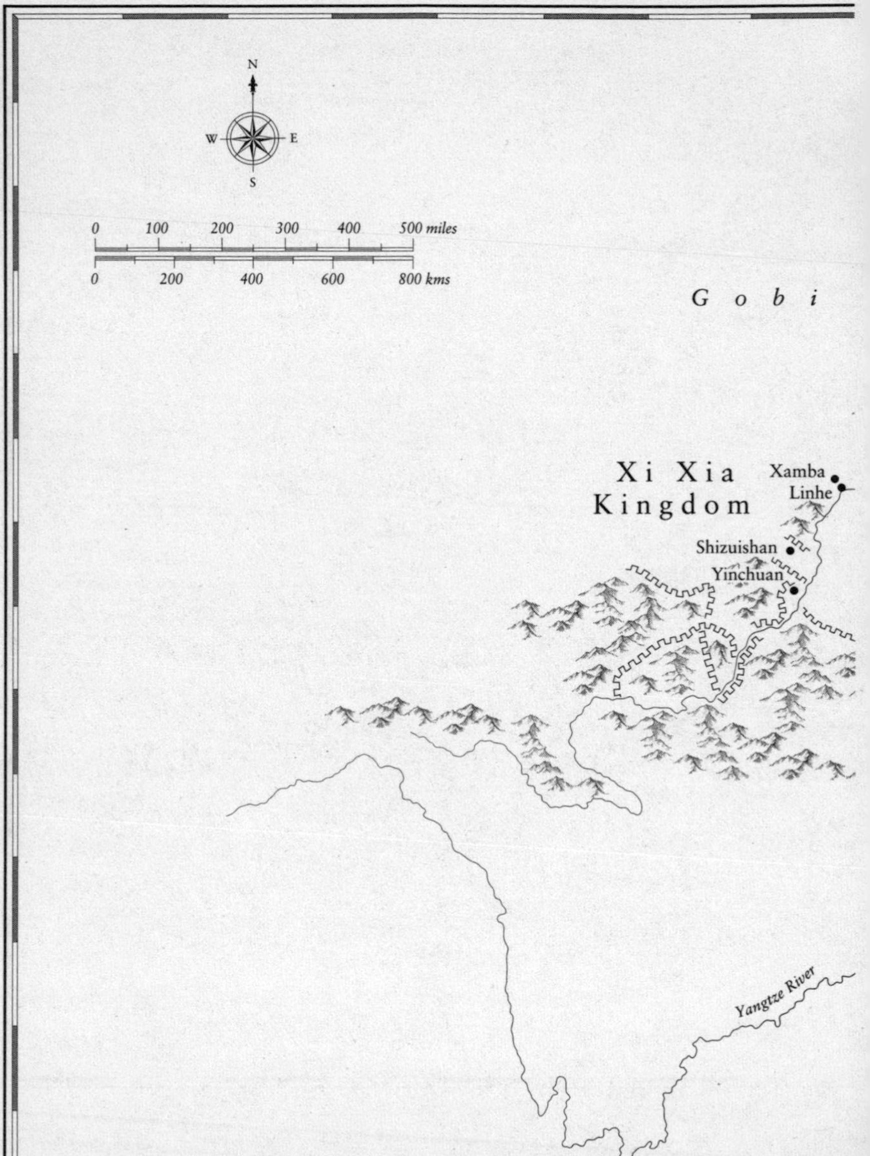
N
W
E
S
0
100
200
300
400
500 miles
0
200
400
600
800 kms
G o b i
Xi Xia
Kingdom
Xamba
Linhe
Shizuishan
Yinchuan
Yangtze River

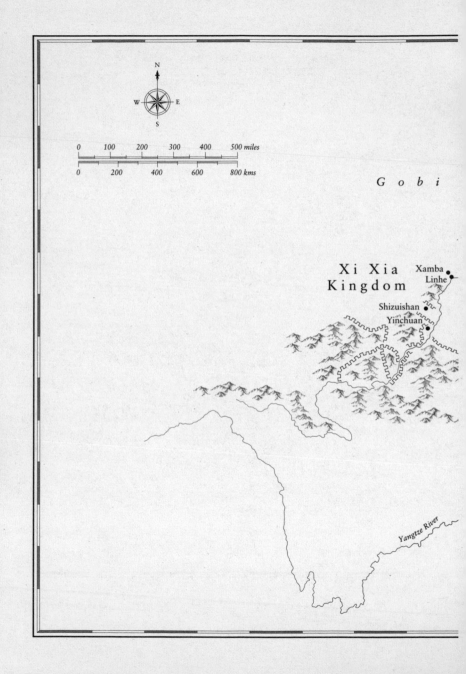

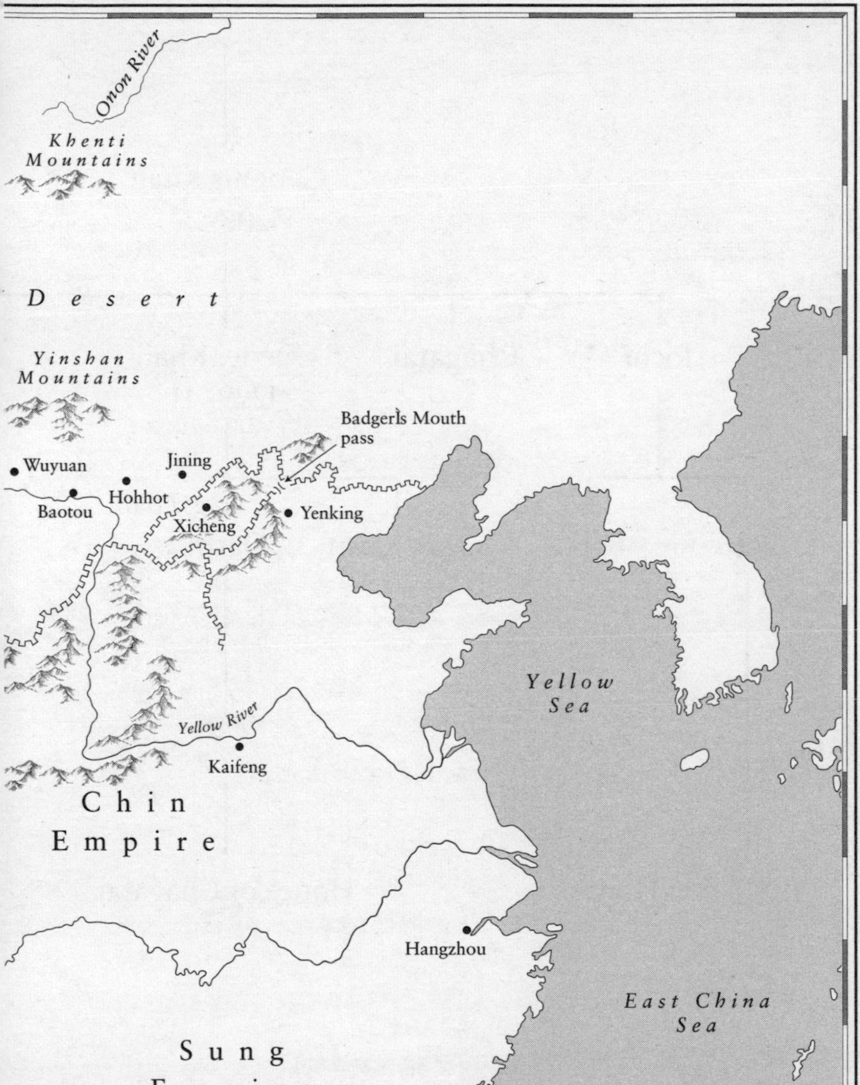
Onon River
Khenti Mountains
Desert
Yinshan Mountains
Badger's Mouth pass
Wuyuan
Jining
Hohhot
Baotou
Xicheng
Yenking
Yellow Sea
Yellow River
Kaifeng
Chin Empire
Hangzhou
East China Sea
Sung Empire

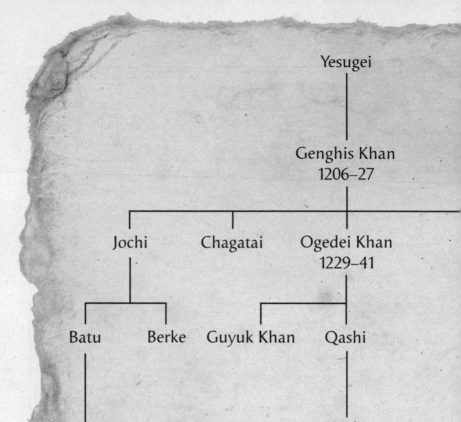

Yesugei

Genghis Khan
1206–27

Jochi   Chagatai   Ogedei Khan
1229–41

Batu   Berke   Guyuk Khan   Qashi

Kaidu

The Golden Horde   House of Chagatai

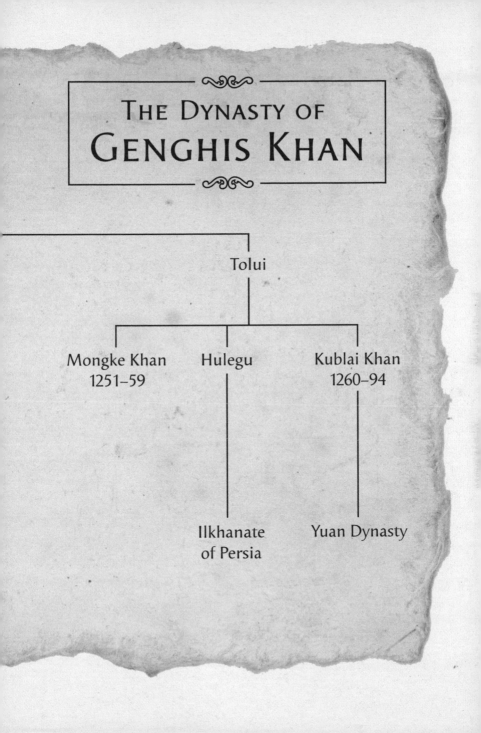

THE DYNASTY OF GENGHIS KHAN

Tolui

Mongke Khan
1251–59

Hulegu

Kublai Khan
1260–94

Ilkhanate
of Persia

Yuan Dynasty

PROLOGUE

The khan of the Naimans was old. He shivered in the wind as it blew over the hill. Far below, the army he had gathered made its stand against the man who called himself Genghis. More than a dozen tribes stood with the Naimans in the foothills as the enemy struck in waves. The khan could hear yelling and screams on the clear mountain air, but he was almost blind and could not see the battle.

'Tell me what is happening,' he murmured again to his shaman.

Kokchu had yet to see his thirtieth year and his eyes were sharp, though shadows of regret played over them.

'The Jajirat have laid down their bows and swords, my lord. They have lost their courage, as you said they might.'

'They give him too much honour with their fear,' the khan said, drawing his deel close around his scrawny frame. 'Tell me of my own Naimans: do they still fight?'

Kokchu did not respond for a long time as he watched the roiling mass of men and horses below. Genghis had caught them all by surprise, appearing out of the grasslands at dawn when the best scouts said he was still hundreds of miles away. They had struck the Naiman alliance with all the ferocity of men used to victory, but there had been a chance to break their charge. Kokchu silently cursed the Jajirat tribe, who had brought

1

so many men from the mountains that he had thought they might even win against their enemies. For a little time, their alliance had been a grand thing, impossible even a few years before. It had lasted as long as the first charge and then fear had shattered it and the Jajirat had stepped aside.

As Kokchu watched, he swore under his breath, seeing how some of the men his khan had welcomed even fought against their brothers. They had the mind of a pack of dogs, turning with the wind as it blew strongest.

'They fight yet, my lord,' he said at last. 'They have stood against the charge and their arrows sting the men of Genghis, hurting them.'

The khan of the Naimans brought his bony hands together, the knuckles white.

'That is good, Kokchu, but I should go back down to them, to give them heart.'

The shaman turned a feverish gaze on the man he had served all his adult life.

'You will die if you do, my lord. I have seen it. Your bondsmen will hold this hill against even the souls of the dead.' He hid his shame. The khan had trusted his counsel, but when Kokchu watched the first Naiman lines crumple, he had seen his own death coming on the singing shafts. All he had wanted then was to get away.

The khan sighed. 'You have served me well, Kokchu. I have been grateful. Now tell me again what you see.'

Kokchu took a quick, sharp breath before replying.

'The brothers of Genghis have joined the battle now. One of them has led a charge into the flanks of our warriors. It is cutting deeply into their ranks.' He paused, biting his lip. Like a buzzing fly, he saw an arrow darting up towards them and watched it sink to its feathers in the ground just a few feet below where they crouched.

'We must move higher, my lord,' he said, rising to his feet without looking away from the seething mass of killing far below.

The old khan rose with him, aided by two warriors. They were cold-faced as they witnessed the destruction of their friends and brothers, but they turned up the hill at Kokchu's gesture, helping the old man to climb.

'Have we struck back, Kokchu?' he asked, his voice quavering. Kokchu turned and winced at what he saw. Arrows hung in the air below, seeming to move with oily slowness. The Naiman force had been split in two by the charge. The armour Genghis had copied from the Chin was better than the boiled leather the Naimans used. Each man wore hundreds of finger-width lengths of iron sewn onto thick canvas over a silk tunic. Even then, it could not stop a solid hit, though the silk often trapped the arrowhead. Kokchu saw the warriors of Genghis weather the storm of shafts. The horsetail standard of the Merkit tribe was trampled underfoot and they too threw down their weapons to kneel, chests heaving. Only the Oirat and Naimans fought on, raging, knowing they could not hold for long. The great alliance had come together to resist a single enemy and with its end went all hope of freedom. Kokchu frowned to himself, considering his future.

'The men fight with pride, my lord. They will not run from these, not while you are watching.' He saw a hundred warriors of Genghis had reached the foot of the hill and were staring balefully up at the lines of bondsmen. The wind was cruelly cold at such a height and Kokchu felt despair and anger. He had come too far to fail on a dry hill with the cold sun on his face. All the secrets he had won from his father, surpassed even, would be wasted in a blow from a sword, or an arrow, to end his life. For a moment, he hated the old khan who had tried to resist the new force on the plains. He had failed and that

3

made him a fool, no matter how strong he had once seemed. In silence, Kokchu cursed the bad luck that still stalked him.

The khan of the Naimans was panting as they climbed and he waved a weary hand at the men who held his arms.

'I must rest here,' he said, shaking his head.

'My lord, they are too close,' Kokchu replied. The bondsmen ignored the shaman, easing their khan down to where he could sit on a ledge of grass.

'Then we have lost?' the khan said. 'How else could the dogs of Genghis have reached this hill, if not over Naiman dead?'

Kokchu did not meet the eyes of the bondsmen. They knew the truth as well as he, but no one wanted to say the words and break the last hope of an old man. Below, the ground was marked in curves and strokes of dead men, like a bloody script on the grass. The Oirat had fought bravely and well, but they too had broken at the last. The army of Genghis moved fluidly, taking advantage of every weakness in the lines. Kokchu could see groups of tens and hundreds race across the battlefield, their officers communicating with bewildering speed. Only the great courage of the Naiman warriors remained to hold back the storm and it would not be enough. Kokchu knew a moment's hope when the warriors retook the foot of the hill, but it was a small number of exhausted men and they were swept away in the next great charge against them.

'Your bondsmen still stand ready to die for you, my lord,' Kokchu murmured. It was all he could say. The rest of the army that had stood so bright and strong the night before lay shattered. He could hear the cries of dying men.

The khan nodded, closing his eyes.

'I thought we might win this day,' he said, his voice little more than a whisper. 'If it is over, tell my sons to lay down their swords. I will not have them die for nothing.'

The khan's sons had been killed as the army of Genghis

roared over them. The two bondsmen stared at Kokchu as they heard the order, their grief and anger hidden from view. The older man drew his sword and checked the edge, the veins in his face and neck showing clearly, like delicate threads under the skin.

'I will take word to your sons, lord, if you will let me go.'

The khan raised his head.

'Tell them to live, Murakh, that they might see where this Genghis takes us all.'

There were tears in Murakh's eyes and he wiped them away angrily as he faced the other bondsman, ignoring Kokchu as if he were not there.

'Protect the khan, my son,' he said softly. The younger man bowed his head and Murakh placed a hand on his shoulder, leaning forward to touch foreheads for a moment. Without a glance at the shaman who had brought them to the hill, Murakh strode down the slope.

The khan sighed, his mind full of clouds.

'Tell them to let the conqueror through,' he whispered. Kokchu watched as a bead of sweat hung on his nose and quivered there. 'Perhaps he will be merciful with my sons once he has killed me.'

Far below, Kokchu saw the bondsman Murakh reach the last knot of defenders. They stood taller in his presence; exhausted, broken men who nonetheless raised their heads and tried not to show they had been afraid. Kokchu heard them calling farewell to one another as they walked with a light step towards the enemy.

At the foot of the hill, Kokchu saw Genghis himself come through the mass of warriors, his armour marbled in blood. Kokchu felt the man's gaze pass over him. He shivered and touched the hilt of his knife. Would Genghis spare a shaman who had drawn it across his own khan's throat? The old man sat with his head bowed, his neck painfully thin. Perhaps such a murder would win Kokchu's life for him and, at that moment, he was desperately afraid of death.

Genghis stared up without moving for a long time and Kokchu let his hand fall. He did not know this cold warrior who came from nowhere with the dawn sun. Kokchu sat at the side of his khan and watched the last of the Naimans go down to die. He chanted an old protective charm his father had taught him, to turn enemies to his side. It seemed to ease the tension in the old khan to hear the tumbling words.

Murakh had been first warrior to the Naimans and had not fought that day. With an ululating yell, he tore into the lines of Genghis' men without a thought for his defence. The last of the Naimans shouted in his wake, their weariness vanishing. Their arrows sent the men of Genghis spinning, though they rose quickly and snapped the shafts, showing their teeth as they came on. As Murakh killed the first who stood against him, a dozen more pressed him on all sides, making his ribs run red with their blows.

Kokchu continued the chant, his eyes widening as Genghis blew a horn and his men pulled back from the panting Naiman survivors.

Murakh still lived, standing dazed. Kokchu could see Genghis call to him, but he could not hear the words. Murakh shook his head and spat blood on the ground as he raised his sword once more. There were only a few Naimans who still stood and they were all wounded, their blood running down their legs. They too raised their blades, staggering as they did so.

'You have fought well,' Genghis shouted. 'Surrender to me and I will welcome you at my fires. I will give you honour.'

Murakh grinned at him through red teeth.

'I spit on Wolf honour,' he said.

Genghis sat very still on his pony before finally shrugging and dropping his arm once more. The line surged forward and Murakh and the others were engulfed in the press of stamping, stabbing men.

High on the hill, Kokchu rose to his feet, his chant dying in his throat as Genghis dismounted and began to climb. The battle was over. The dead lay in their hundreds, but thousands more had surrendered. Kokchu did not care what happened to them.

'He is coming,' Kokchu said softly, peering down the hill. His stomach cramped and the muscles in his legs shuddered like a horse beset with flies. The man who had brought the tribes of the plains under his banners was walking purposefully upwards, his face without expression. Kokchu could see his armour was battered and more than a few of its metal scales hung by threads. The fight had been hard, but Genghis climbed with his mouth shut, as if the exertion was nothing to him.

'Have my sons survived?' the khan whispered, breaking his stillness. He reached out and took hold of the sleeve of Kokchu's deel.

'They have not,' Kokchu said with a sudden surge of bitterness. The hand fell away and the old man slumped. As Kokchu watched, the milky eyes came up once more and there was strength in the way he held himself.

'Then let this Genghis come,' the khan said. 'What does he matter to me now?'

Kokchu did not respond, unable to tear his gaze from the warrior who climbed the hill. The wind was cold on his neck and he knew he was feeling it more sweetly than ever before. He had seen men faced with death; he had given it to them

with the darkest rites, sending their souls spinning away. He
saw his own death coming in the steady tread of that man and
for a moment he almost broke and ran. It was not courage
that held him there. He was a man of words and spells,
more feared amongst the Naimans than his father had ever
been. To run was to die with the certainty of winter coming.
He heard the whisper as Murakh's son drew his sword, but
took no comfort from it. There was something awe-inspiring
about the steady gait of the destroyer. Armies had not stopped
him. The old khan lifted his head to watch him come, sensing
the approach in the same way his sightless eyes could still seek
out the sun.

Genghis paused as he reached the three men, gazing at them.
He was tall and his skin shone with oil and health. His eyes
were wolf-yellow and Kokchu saw no mercy in them. As Kokchu
stood frozen, Genghis drew a sword still marked with drying
blood. Murakh's son took a pace forward to stand between the
two khans. Genghis looked at him with a spark of irritation
and the young man tensed.

'Get down the hill, boy, if you want to live,' Genghis said. 'I
have seen enough of my people die today.'

The young warrior shook his head without a word and
Genghis sighed. With a sharp blow, he knocked the sword aside
and swept his other hand across, plunging a dagger into the
young man's throat. As the life went out of Murakh's son, he fell
onto Genghis with open arms. Genghis gave a grunt as he
caught the weight and heaved him away. Kokchu watched the
body tumble limply down the slope.

Calmly, Genghis wiped his knife and replaced it in a sheath
at his waist, his weariness suddenly evident.

'I would have honoured the Naimans, if you had joined me,'
he said.

The old khan stared up at him, his eyes empty.

'You have heard my answer,' he replied, his voice strong. 'Now send me to my sons.'

Genghis nodded. His sword came down with apparent slowness. It swept the khan's head from his shoulders and sent it rolling down the hill. The body hardly jerked at the tug of the blade and only leaned slightly to one side. Kokchu could hear the blood spattering on the rocks as every one of his senses screamed to live. He paled as Genghis turned to him and he spoke in a desperate torrent of words.

'You may not shed the blood of a shaman, lord. You may not. I am a man of power, one who understands power. Strike me and you will find my skin is iron. Instead, let me serve you. Let me proclaim your victory.'

'How well did you serve the khan of the Naimans to have brought him here to die?' Genghis replied.

'Did I not bring him far from the battle? I saw you coming in my dreams, lord. I prepared the way for you as best I could. Are you not the future of the tribes? My voice is the voice of the spirits. I stand in water, while you stand on earth and sky. Let me serve you.'

Genghis hesitated, his sword perfectly still. The man he faced wore a dark brown deel over a grubby tunic and leggings. It was decorated with patterns of stitching, swirls of purple worn almost black with grease and dirt. The boots Kokchu wore were bound in rope, the sort a man might wear if the last owner had no more use for them.

Yet there was something in the way the eyes burned in the dark face. Genghis remembered how Eeluk of the Wolves had killed his father's shaman. Perhaps Eeluk's fate had been sealed on that bloody day so many years before. Kokchu watched him, waiting for the stroke that would end his life.

'I do not need another storyteller,' Genghis said. 'I have three men already who claim to speak for the spirits.'

Kokchu saw the curiosity in the man's gaze and he did not hesitate.

'They are children, lord. Let me show you,' he said. Without waiting for a reply, he reached inside his deel and removed a slender length of steel bound clumsily into a hilt of horn. He sensed Genghis raise his sword and Kokchu held up his free palm to stay the blow, closing his eyes.

With a wrenching effort of will, the shaman shut out the wind on his skin and the cold fear that ate at his belly. He murmured the words his father had beaten into him and felt the calm of a trance come sharper and faster than even he had expected. The spirits were with him, their caress slowing his heart. In an instant, he was somewhere else and watching.

Genghis opened his eyes wide as Kokchu touched the dagger to his own forearm, the slim blade entering the flesh. The shaman showed no sign of pain as the metal slid through him and Genghis watched, fascinated, as the tip raised the skin on the other side. The metal showed black as it poked through and Kokchu blinked slowly, almost lazily, as he pulled it out.

He watched the eyes of the young khan as the knife came free. They were fastened on the wound. Kokchu took a deep breath, feeling the trance deepen until a great coldness was in every limb.

'Is there blood, lord?' he whispered, knowing the answer.

Genghis frowned. He did not sheathe his sword, but stepped forward and ran a rough thumb over the oval wound in Kokchu's arm.

'None. It is a useful skill,' he admitted grudgingly. 'Can it be taught?'

Kokchu smiled, no longer afraid.

'The spirits will not come to those they have not chosen, lord.'

Genghis nodded, stepping away. Even in the cold wind, the shaman stank like an old goat and he did not know what to make of the strange wound that did not bleed.

With a grunt, he ran his fingers along his blade and sheathed it.

'I will give you a year of life, shaman. It is enough time to prove your worth.'

Kokchu fell to his knees, pressing his face into the ground.

'You are the great khan, as I have foretold,' he said, tears staining the dust on his cheeks. He felt the coldness of whispering spirits leave him then. He shrugged his sleeve forward to hide the fast-growing spot of blood.

'I am,' Genghis replied. He looked down the hill at the army waiting for him to return. 'The world will hear my name.' When he spoke again, it was so quiet that Kokchu had to strain to hear him.

'This is not a time of death, shaman. We are one people and there will be no more battles between us. I will summon us all. Cities will fall to us, new lands will be ours to ride. Women will weep and I will be pleased to hear it.'

He looked down at the prostrate shaman, frowning.

'You will live, shaman. I have said it. Get off your knees and walk down with me.'

At the foot of the hill, Genghis nodded to his brothers, Kachiun and Khasar. Each of them had grown in authority in the years since they had begun the gathering of tribes, but they were still young and Kachiun smiled as his brother walked amongst them.

'Who is this?' Khasar asked, staring at Kokchu in his ragged deel.

'The shaman of the Naimans,' Genghis replied.

Another man guided his pony close and dismounted, his eyes fastened on Kokchu. Arslan had once been swordsmith to the Naiman tribe and Kokchu recognised him as he approached. The man was a murderer, he remembered, forced into banishment. It was no surprise to find such as he amongst Genghis' trusted officers.

'I remember you,' Arslan said. 'Has your father died then?'

'Years ago, oathbreaker,' Kokchu replied, nettled by the tone. For the first time, he realised he had lost the authority he had won so painfully with the Naimans. There were few men in that tribe who would have looked on him without lowering their eyes, for fear that they would be accused of disloyalty and face his knives and fire. Kokchu met the gaze of the Naiman traitor without flinching. They would come to know him.

Genghis watched the tension between the two men with something like amusement.

'Do not give offence, shaman. Not to the first warrior to come to my banners. There are no Naimans any longer, nor ties to tribe. I have claimed them all.'

'I have seen it in the visions,' Kokchu replied immediately. 'You have been blessed by the spirits.'

Genghis' face grew tight at the words.

'It has been a rough blessing. The army you see around you has been won by strength and skill. If the souls of our fathers were aiding us, they were too subtle for me to see them.'

Kokchu blinked. The khan of the Naimans had been credulous and easy to lead. He realised this new man was not as open to his influence. Still, the air was sweet in his lungs. He lived and he had not expected even that an hour before.

Genghis turned to his brothers, dismissing Kokchu from his thoughts.

12

'Have the new men give their oath to me this evening, as the sun sets,' he said to Khasar. 'Spread them amongst the others so that they begin to feel part of us, rather than beaten enemies. Do it carefully. I cannot be watching for knives at my back.'

Khasar dipped his head before turning away and striding through the warriors to where the defeated tribes still knelt.

Kokchu saw a smile of affection pass between Genghis and his younger brother Kachiun. The two men were friends and Kokchu was beginning to learn everything he could. Even the smallest detail would be useful in the years to come.

'We have broken the alliance, Kachiun. Did I not say we would?' Genghis said, clapping him on the back. 'Your armoured horses came in at the perfect time.'

'As you taught me,' Kachiun replied, easy with the praise.

'With the new men, this is an army to ride the plains,' Genghis said, smiling. 'It is time to set the path, at last.' He thought for a moment.

'Send out riders in every direction, Kachiun. I want the land scoured of every wanderer family and small tribe. Tell them to come to the black mountain next spring, near the Onon River. It is a flat plain that will hold all the thousands of our people. We will gather there, ready to ride.'

'What message shall they take?' Kachiun asked.

'Tell them to come to me,' he said softly. 'Tell them Genghis calls them to a gathering. There is no one to stand against us now. They can follow me or they can spend their last days waiting for my warriors on the horizon. Tell them that.' He looked around him with satisfaction. In seven years, he had gathered more than ten thousand men. With the survivors of the defeated allied tribes, he had almost twice that number. There was no one left on the plains who could challenge his

13

leadership. He looked away from the sun to the east, imagining the bloated, wealthy cities of the Chin.

'They have kept us apart for a thousand generations, Kachiun. They have ridden us until we were nothing more than savage dogs. That is the past. I have brought us together and they will be trembling. I'll give them cause.'

PART ONE

'Behold, a people shall come from the north, and a great nation. They shall hold the bow and the lance; they are cruel and will not show mercy; their voice shall roar like the sea, and they shall ride upon horses, every one put in array, like a man to the battle.'

– Jeremiah 50:41, 42

CHAPTER ONE

In the summer dusk, the encampment of the Mongols stretched for miles in every direction, the great gathering still dwarfed by the plain in the shadow of the black mountain. Ger tents speckled the landscape as far as the eye could see and around them thousands of cooking fires lit the ground. Beyond those, herds of ponies, goats, sheep and yaks stripped the ground of grass in their constant hunger. Each dawn saw them driven away to the river and good grazing before returning to the gers. Though Genghis guaranteed the peace, tension and suspicion grew each day. None there had seen such a host before and it was easy to feel hemmed in by the numbers. Insults imaginary and real were exchanged as all felt the pressure of living too close to warriors they did not know. In the evenings, there were many fights between the young men, despite the prohibition. Each dawn found one or two bodies of those who had tried to settle an old score or grudge. The tribes muttered among themselves while they waited to hear why they had been brought so far from their own lands.

In the centre of the army of tents and carts stood the ger of Genghis himself, unlike anything seen before on the plains. Half as high again as the others, it was twice the width and built of stronger materials than the wicker lattice of the gers around it. The construction had proved too heavy to dismantle easily and was mounted on a wheeled cart drawn by eight oxen. As the night came, many hundreds of warriors directed their feet towards it, just to confirm what they had heard and to marvel.

Inside, the great ger was lit with mutton-oil lamps, casting a warm glow over the inhabitants and making the air thick. The walls were hung with silk war banners, but Genghis disdained any show of wealth and sat on a rough wooden bench. His brothers lay sprawled on piled horse blankets and saddles, drinking and chatting idly.

Before Genghis sat a nervous young warrior, still sweating from the long ride that had brought him amongst such a host. The men around the khan did not seem to be paying attention, but the messenger was aware that their hands were never far from their weapons. They did not seem tense or worried at his presence and he considered that their hands might always be near a blade. His people had made their decision and he hoped the elder khans knew what they were doing.

'If you have finished your tea, I will hear the message,' Genghis said.

The messenger nodded, placing the shallow cup back on the floor at his feet. He swallowed his last gulp as he closed his eyes and recited, 'These are the words of Barchuk, who is khan to the Uighurs.'

The conversations and laughter around him died away as he spoke and he knew they were all listening. His nervousness grew.

'It is with joy that I learned of your glory, my lord Genghis Khan. We had grown weary waiting for our people to know one another and rise. The sun has risen. The river is freed of ice. You are the gurkhan, the one who will lead us all. I will dedicate my strength and knowledge to you.'

The messenger stopped and wiped sweat from his brow.

When he opened his eyes, he saw that Genghis was looking at him quizzically and his stomach tightened in fear.

'The words are very fine,' Genghis said, 'but where are the Uighurs? They have had a year to reach this place. If I have to fetch them . . .' He left the threat dangling.

The messenger spoke quickly. 'My lord, it took months just to build the carts to travel. We have not moved from our lands in many generations. Five great temples had to be taken apart, stone by stone, each one numbered so that it could be built again. Our store of scrolls took a dozen carts by itself and cannot move quickly.'

'You have writing?' Genghis asked, sitting forward with interest.

The messenger nodded without pride.

'For many years now, lord. We have collected the writings of nations in the west, whenever they have allowed us to trade for them. Our khan is a man of great learning and has even copied works of the Chin and the Xi Xia.'

'So I am to welcome scholars and teachers to this place?' Genghis said. 'Will you fight with scrolls?'

The messenger coloured as the men in the ger chuckled.

'There are four thousand warriors also, my lord. They will follow Barchuk wherever he leads them.'

'They will follow me, or they will be left as flesh on the grass,' Genghis replied. For a moment, the messenger could only stare, but then he dropped his eyes to the polished wooden floor and remained silent.

Genghis stifled his irritation.

'You have not said when they will come, these Uighur scholars,' he said.

'They could be only days behind me, lord. I left three moons ago and they were almost ready to leave. It cannot be long now, if you will have patience.'

'For four thousand, I will wait,' Genghis said softly, thinking. 'You know the Chin writing?'

'I do not have my letters, lord. My khan can read their words.'

'Do these scrolls say how to take a city made of stone?'

The messenger hesitated as he felt the sharp interest of the men around him.

'I have not heard of anything like that, lord. The Chin write about philosophy, the words of the Buddha, Confucius and Lao Tzu. They do not write of war, or if they do, they have not allowed us to see those scrolls.'

'Then they are of no use to me,' Genghis snapped. 'Get yourself a meal and be careful not to start a fight with your boasting. I will judge the Uighurs when they finally arrive.'

The messenger bowed low before leaving the ger, taking a relieved breath as soon as he was out of the smoky atmosphere. Once more, he wondered if his khan understood what he had promised with his words. The Uighur ruled themselves no longer.

Looking around at the vast encampment, the messenger saw twinkling lights for miles. At a word from the man he had met, they could be sent in any direction. Perhaps the khan of the Uighurs had not had a choice.

Hoelun dipped her cloth into a bucket and laid it on her son's brow. Temuge had always been weaker than his brothers and it seemed an added burden that he fell sick more than Khasar or Kachiun, or Temujin himself. She smiled wryly at the thought that she must now call her son 'Genghis'. It meant the ocean and was a beautiful word twisted beyond its usual meaning by his ambition. He who had never seen the sea in his twenty-six years of life. Not that she had herself, of course.

Temuge stirred in his sleep, wincing as she probed his stomach with her fingers.

'He is quiet now. Perhaps I will leave for a time,' Borte said.

Hoelun glanced coldly at the woman Temujin had taken as a wife. Borte had given him four perfect sons and for a time Hoelun had thought they would be as sisters, or at least friends. The younger woman had once been full of life and excitement, but events had twisted her somewhere deep, where it could not be seen. Hoelun knew the way Temujin looked at the eldest boy. He did not play with little Jochi and all but ignored him. Borte had fought against the mistrust, but it had grown between them like an iron wedge into strong wood. It did not help that his three other boys had all inherited the yellow eyes of his line. Jochi's were a dark brown, as black as his hair in dim light. While Temujin doted on the others, it was Jochi who ran to his mother, unable to understand the coldness in his father's face when he looked at him. Hoelun saw the young woman glance at the door to the ger, no doubt thinking of her sons.

'You have servants to put them to bed,' Hoelun chided. 'If Temuge wakes, I will need you here.'

As she spoke, her fingers drifted over a dark knot under the skin of her son's belly, just a few fingerbreadths above the dark hair of his groin. She had seen such an injury before, when men lifted weights too heavy for them. The pain was crippling, but most of them recovered. Temuge did not have that kind of luck, and never had. He looked less like a warrior than ever as he had grown to manhood. When he slept, he had the face of a poet and she loved him for that. Perhaps because his father would have rejoiced to see the men the others had become, she had always found a special tenderness for Temuge. He had not grown ruthless, though he had endured as much as they. She sighed to herself and felt Borte's eyes on her in the gloom.

'Perhaps he will recover,' Borte said. Hoelun winced. Her son blistered under the sun and rarely carried a blade bigger than an eating knife. She had not minded as he began to learn the histories of the tribes, taking them in with such speed that the older men were amazed at his recall. Not everyone could be skilled with weapons and horses, she told herself. She knew he hated the sneers and jibes that followed him in his work, though there were few who dared risk Genghis hearing of them. Temuge refused to mention the insults and that was a form of courage all its own. None of her sons lacked spirit.

Both women looked up as the small door of the ger opened. Hoelun frowned as she saw Kokchu enter and bow his head to them. His fierce eyes darted over the supine figure of her son and she fought not to show her dislike, not even understanding her own reaction. There was something about the shaman that set her teeth on edge and she had ignored the messengers he had sent. For a moment, she drew herself up, struggling between indignation and weariness.

'I did not ask for you,' she said coldly.

Kokchu seemed oblivious to the tone.

'I sent a slave to beg a moment with you, mother to khans. Perhaps he has not yet arrived. The whole camp is talking of your son's illness.'

Hoelun felt the shaman's gaze fasten on her, waiting to be formally welcomed, as she looked at Temuge once more. Always he was watching, as if, inside, someone else looked out. She had seen how he pushed himself into the inner circles around Genghis and she could not like him. The warriors might reek of sheep turds, mutton fat and sweat, but those were the smells of healthy men. Kokchu carried an odour of rotting meat, though whether it was from his clothes or his flesh, she could not tell.

Faced with her silence, he should have left the ger, or risked her calling for guards. Instead, he spoke brazenly, somehow certain that she would not send him away.

'I have some healing skill, if you will let me examine him.'

22

Hoelun tried to swallow her distaste. The shaman of the Olkhun'ut had only chanted over Temuge, without result.

'You are welcome in my home, Kokchu,' she said at last. She saw him relax subtly and could not shake the feeling of being too close to something unpleasant.

'My son is asleep. The pain is very great when he is awake and I want him to rest.'

Kokchu crossed the small ger and crouched down beside the two women. Both edged unconsciously away from him.

'He needs healing more than rest, I think.' Kokchu peered down at Temuge, leaning close to smell his breath. Hoelun winced in sympathy as he reached out to Temuge's bare stomach and probed the area of the lump, but she did not stop him. Temuge groaned in his sleep and Hoelun held her breath.

After a time, Kokchu nodded to himself.

'You should prepare yourself, old mother. This one will die.'

Hoelun jerked out a hand and caught the shaman by his thin wrist. Her strength surprised him.

'He has wrenched his gut, shaman. I have seen it many times before. Even on ponies and goats have I seen it and they always live.'

Kokchu undid her shaking clasp with his other hand. It pleased him to see fear in her eyes. With fear, he could own her, body and soul. If she had been a young Naiman mother, he might have sought sexual favours in return for healing her son, but in this new camp, he needed to impress the great khan. He kept his face still as he replied.

'You see the darkness of the lump? It is a growth that cannot be cut out. Perhaps if it were on the skin, I would burn it off, but it will have run claws into his stomach and lungs. It eats him mindlessly and it will not be satisfied until he is dead.'

'You are wrong,' Hoelun snapped, but there were tears in her eyes.

23

Kokchu lowered his gaze so that she would not see his triumph glitter there.

'I wish I was, old mother. I have seen these things before and they have nothing but appetite. It will continue to savage him until they perish together.' To make his point, he reached down and squeezed the swelling. Temuge jerked and came awake with a sharp breath.

'Who are you?' Temuge said to Kokchu, gasping. He struggled to sit up, but the pain made him cry out and he fell back onto the narrow bed. His hands tugged at a blanket to cover his nakedness and his cheeks flushed hotly under Kokchu's scrutiny.

'He is a shaman, Temuge. He is going to make you well,' Hoelun said. Temuge broke into fresh sweat and she dabbed the cloth to his skin as he settled back. After a time, his breathing slowed and he drifted into exhausted sleep once more. Hoelun lost a little of her tension, if not the terror Kokchu had brought into her home.

'If it is hopeless, shaman, why are you still here?' she said. 'There are other men and women who need your healing skill.' She could not keep the bitterness from her voice and did not guess that Kokchu rejoiced in it.

'I have fought what eats him twice before in my life. It is a dark rite and dangerous for the man who practises it as well as for your son. I tell you this so you do not despair, but it would be foolish to hope. Consider him to have died and if I win him back, you will know joy.'

Hoelun felt a chill as she looked into the shaman's eyes. He smelled of blood, she realised, though no trace of it showed on his skin. The thought of him touching her perfect son made her clench her hands, but he had frightened her with his talk of death and she was helpless against him.

'What will you have me do?' she whispered.

24

He sat very still while he considered.

'It will take all my strength to bring the spirits to your son. I will need a goat to take in the growth and another to cleanse him with blood. I have the herbs I need, if I am strong enough.'

'What if you fail?' Borte asked suddenly.

Kokchu took a deep breath, letting it shudder from his lips.

'If my strength fails as I begin the chant, I will survive. If I reach the final stage and the spirits take me, then you will see me torn out of my body. It will live for a time, but without the soul it will be empty flesh. This is no small thing, old mother.'

Hoelun watched him, once more suspicious. He seemed so plausible, but his quick eyes were always watching, seeing how his words were received.

'Fetch two goats, Borte. Let us see what he can do.'

It was dark outside and while Borte brought the animals, Kokchu used the cloth to wipe Temuge's chest and belly. When he pressed his fingers into Temuge's mouth, the young man woke again, his eyes bright with terror.

'Lie still, boy. I will help you if I have the strength,' Kokchu told him. He did not look round as the bleating goats were brought in and dragged to his side, his attention fully on the young man in his care.

With the slowness of ritual, Kokchu took four brass bowls from his robe and placed them on the ground. He poured grey powder into each one and lit a taper from the stove. Soon, snakes of white-grey smoke made the air chokingly thick in the ger. Kokchu breathed deeply, filling his lungs. Hoelun coughed into her hand and flushed. The fumes were making her dizzy, but she would not leave her son alone with a man she did not trust.

In a whispering voice, Kokchu began to chant in the most ancient tongue of their people, almost forgotten. Hoelun sat back as she heard it, remembering the sounds from the healers

25

and shamans of her youth. It brought back darker memories for Borte, who had heard her husband recite the old words on a night long before, butchering men and forcing slivers of burned heart between her lips. It was a language of blood and cruelty, well suited to the winter plains. There was no word in it for kindness, or for love. As Borte listened, the ribbons of smoke seeped into her, making her skin numb. The tumbling words brought a rush of vicious images and she gagged.

'Be still, woman,' Kokchu growled at her, his eyes wild. 'Be silent while the spirits come.' His chant resumed with greater force, hypnotic as he repeated phrases over and over, growing in volume and urgency. The first goat bleated in desperation as he held it over Temuge, looking into the young man's terrified eyes. With his knife, Kokchu slit the goat's throat and held it while its blood poured and steamed over Hoelun's son. Temuge cried out at the sudden warmth, but Hoelun touched her hand to his lips and he quietened.

Kokchu let the goat fall, still kicking. His chant grew faster and he closed his eyes, reaching deep into Temuge's gut. To his surprise, the young man remained silent and Kokchu had to squeeze the lump hard to make him cry out. The blood hid the sharp twist as he undid the strangled piece of gut and shoved it back behind the wall of muscle. His father had shown him the ritual with a real tumour and Kokchu had seen the old man chanting while men and women screamed, sometimes yelling back over their open mouths so that his spittle entered their throats. Kokchu's father had taken them so far past exhaustion that they were lost and they were mad and they *believed*. He had seen obscene growths shrink and die after that point of agony and faith. If a man gave himself utterly to the shaman, sometimes the spirits rewarded that trust.

There was no honour in using the craft to fool a young man with a torn stomach, but the rewards would be great. Temuge was brother to the khan and such a man would always be a valuable ally. He thought of his father's warnings about those who abused the spirits with lies and tricks. The man had never understood power, or how intoxicating it could be. The spirits swarmed around belief like flies on dead meat. It was not wrong to make belief swell in the camp of the khan. His authority could only increase.

Kokchu breathed heavily as he chanted, rolling his eyes up in his head as he pushed his hand deeper into Temuge's belly. With a cry of triumph, he made a wrenching movement, pulling out a small piece of calf's liver he had hidden from sight. In his grip, it jerked like something alive and Borte and Hoelun recoiled from it.

Kokchu continued to chant as he yanked the second goat close. It too struggled, but he forced his hand past its yellow teeth, though they gnawed at his knuckles. He pushed the foul meat down the gullet until the animal could do nothing but swallow in jerking spasms. When he saw the throat move, he stroked it hard, forcing the liver into the goat's stomach before letting it go.

'Do not let her touch the other animals,' he said, panting, 'or it will spread and live again, perhaps even get back into your son.' Sweat dripped from his nose as he watched them.

'It would be better to burn the goat to ashes. She must not be eaten as the flesh contains the growth. Be sure with this. I do not have the strength to do it again.'

He let himself slump as if his senses had left him, though he still breathed like a dog in the sun.

'The pain has gone,' he heard Temuge say wonderingly. 'It is sore, but nothing like it was before.' Kokchu sensed Hoelun lean over her son and heard him gasp as she touched the place where his gut had come through his stomach muscle.

'The skin is whole,' Temuge said. Kokchu could hear the awe

27

in his voice and chose that moment to open his eyes and sit up. He was dull-eyed and squinted through the haze of smoke.

His long fingers hunted in the pockets of his deel, pulling out a piece of twisted horsehair stained with old blood.

'This has been blessed,' he told them. 'I will bind it over the wound so that nothing may enter.'

No one spoke as he took a grubby ribbon of cloth from his deel and made Temuge sit up. Kokchu chanted under his breath as he wound it around the young man's gut, covering the stiff piece of hair with line after line of cloth and heaving each one tight until it was hidden from view. When he had knotted it, Kokchu sat back, satisfied that the gut would not pop out and spoil all his work.

'Keep the charm in place for a turn of the moon,' he said wearily. 'Let it fall and perhaps the growth will find its home once more.' He closed his eyes, as if exhausted. 'I must sleep now, for tonight and most of tomorrow. Burn that goat before you leave her to spread the growth. She will be dead in a few hours at the most.' Given that he had laced the liver with enough poison to kill a full-grown man, he knew he spoke the truth. There would be no suspiciously healthy animal to spoil his achievement.

'Thank you for what you have done,' Hoelun said. 'I do not understand it . . .'

Kokchu smiled tiredly.

'It took me twenty years of study to begin my mastery, old mother. Do not think to understand it in a single evening. Your son will heal now, as he would have done if the growth had not begun to writhe in him.' He thought for a moment. He did not know the woman, but surely she would tell Genghis what had happened. To make certain, he spoke again.

'I must ask that you do not tell anyone of what you have seen. There are still tribes where they kill those who practise the old magic. It is seen as too dangerous.' He shrugged. 'Perhaps it is.' With that, he knew the tale would spread right through the camp before he woke the next day. There were always some who wanted a charm against illness, or a curse on an enemy. They would leave milk and meat at his ger, and with power came respect and fear. He longed for them to be afraid, for when they were, they would give him anything. What did it matter if he had not saved a life this time? The belief would be there when another life hung in his hands. He had dropped a stone in the river and the ripples would go far.

Genghis and his generals were alone in the great ger as the moon rose above the host of his people. The day had been busy for all of them, but they could not sleep while he remained awake and there would be yawns and bleary eyes the following day. Genghis seemed as fresh as he had that morning, when he had welcomed two hundred men and women from a Turkic tribe so far to the north-west that they could not understand more than a few words of what he said. Still, they had come.

'Every day brings more of them, with two moons left of summer,' Genghis said, looking round proudly at men who had been with him since the first days. At fifty years of age, Arslan was growing old after the years of war. He and his son Jelme had come to Genghis when he had nothing but his wits and his three brothers. Both had remained utterly loyal through hard years and Genghis had let them prosper and take wives and wealth. Genghis nodded to the swordsmith who had become his general, pleased to see the man's back as straight as ever.

Temuge did not attend their discussions, even when he was well. Of all the brothers, he had shown no aptitude for tactics. Genghis loved him, but he could not trust him to lead others. He shook his head, realising that his thoughts were wandering. He too was weary, though he would not allow it to show.

'Some of the new tribes have never even heard of the Chin,' Kachiun said. 'The ones who came this morning dress like nothing I've ever seen. They are not Mongols, as we are.'

'Perhaps,' Genghis said. 'But I will make them welcome. Let them prove themselves in war before we judge them. They are not Tartars, or blood enemies to any man here. At least I will not be called to untangle some grudge going back a dozen generations. They will be useful.'

He took a draught from a rough clay cup, smacking his lips at the bitterness of the black airag.

'Be wary in the camp, my brothers. They have come because *not* to come invites us to destroy them. They do not trust us yet. Many of them know only my name and nothing else.'

'I have men listening at every fire,' Kachiun said. 'There will always be some who seek an advantage in such a gathering. Even as we speak here, there will be a thousand other conversations discussing us. Even whispers will be heard. I will know if I have to act.'

Genghis nodded to his brother, proud of him. Kachiun had grown into a stocky man with an immense breadth of shoulder from his bow practice. They shared a bond that Genghis could claim with no one else, not even Khasar.

'Still, my back itches when I walk through the camp. While we wait, they grow restless, but there are more to come and I cannot move yet. The Uighurs alone will be valuable. Those who are already here may test us, so be ready and let no insult go unpunished. I will trust you in your judgement, even if you throw a dozen heads at my feet.'

The generals in the ger met each other's eyes without smiling. For every man they had brought to the great plain, two more had come. The advantage they held was that not one of the strongest khans knew the extent of their support. Anyone riding into the shadow of the black mountain saw a single host and gave no thought to the fact that it was composed of a hundred different factions, watching each other in mutual mistrust.

Genghis yawned at last.

'Get some sleep, my brothers,' he said wearily. 'Dawn is close and the herds have to be moved to new grass.'

'I will look in on Temuge before I sleep,' Kachiun said.

Genghis sighed.

'Let us hope the sky father makes him well. I cannot lose my only sensible brother.'

Kachiun snorted, throwing open the small door to the outside air. When they had all left, Genghis rose, cracking the stiffness out of his neck with a swift jerk of his hands. His family ger was nearby, though his sons would be asleep. It was one more night when he would thump into the blankets without his family knowing he had come home.

CHAPTER TWO

Genghis eyed his younger brother with disquiet. Temuge had spent the morning telling anyone who would listen about the cure Kokchu had wrought. The camp was a stifling place despite its size and any news spread quickly. By noon, it would be in the mouths of the newest wanderers off the plains.

'So how do you know it was *not* a strangled bit of gut?' Genghis said, watching him. Temuge seemed to stand a little taller than usual in the family ger and his face was lit with excitement and something more. Whenever he mentioned Kokchu's name, his voice would dip almost to a murmur. Genghis found his awe irritating.

'I saw him pull it out of me, brother! It squirmed and writhed in his hand and I nearly vomited to see it. When it was gone, the pain went with it.' Temuge touched his hand to the place and winced.

'Not completely gone, then,' Genghis noted.

Temuge shrugged. The area above and below the bandage was a mass of purple and yellow, though it was already beginning to fade.

'It was eating me alive before. This is no worse than a bruise.'

'Yet you say there is no cut,' Genghis said, wonderingly.

Temuge shook his head, his excitement returning. He had explored the area with his fingers in the darkness before dawn.

Under the tight cloth, he could feel a split in the muscle that was still incredibly tender. He felt sure it was from there the growth had been torn.

'He has power, brother. More than any one of the charlatans we have seen before. I trust what I saw. You know the eyes do not lie.'

Genghis nodded.

'I will reward him with mares, sheep and new cloth. Perhaps a new knife and boots. I cannot have the man who saved my brother looking like a beggar.'

Temuge winced in sudden doubt.

'He did not want the story to get out, Genghis. If you reward him, everyone will know what he did.'

'Everyone *does* know,' Genghis replied. 'Kachiun told me at dawn and three more have come to talk about it before I saw you. There are no secrets in this camp, you should know that.'

Temuge nodded thoughtfully.

'Then he cannot mind, or he will forgive if he does.' He hesitated before going on, nervous under his brother's gaze.

'With your permission, I will learn from him. I think he would take me as a pupil and I have never felt such a desire to know . . .' He broke off as Genghis frowned.

'I had hoped you would resume your duties with the warriors, Temuge. Do you not want to ride with me?'

Temuge flushed and looked at the floor.

'You know as well as I do that I will never be a great officer. Perhaps I could learn to be competent, but the men will always know I was raised for my blood and not my skill. Let me learn from this Kokchu. I do not think he would be unwilling.'

Genghis sat perfectly still as he considered. Temuge had more than once been the subject of mirth in the tribes. His archery was abysmal and he won no respect with his red-faced efforts with a sword. He could see his youngest brother was trembling, his face tight with fear that Genghis would refuse. Temuge was out of place in the tribes and there had been many evenings when Genghis had wished for him to find something he could do. Yet he was reluctant to let him go so easily. Men like Kokchu stood apart from the tribes. They were feared certainly, and that was good, but they were not part of the family. They were not made welcome and greeted as old friends. Genghis shook his head slightly. Temuge too had always been outside the tribes, a watcher. Perhaps this was the way his life would go.

'On the condition that you practise with a blade and bow for two hours each day. Give your word on that and I will confirm your choice, your path.'

Temuge nodded, smiling shyly.

'I will. Perhaps I will be more useful to you as a shaman than I ever was as a warrior.'

Genghis' eyes became cold.

'You are still a warrior, Temuge, though it has never been easy for you. Learn what you want from this man, but in your private heart, remember that you are my brother and our father's son.'

Temuge felt tears come to his eyes and dipped his head before his brother could see and be ashamed for him.

'I do not forget it,' he said.

'Then tell your new master to come to me and be rewarded. I will embrace him in front of my generals and let them know he is valuable to me. My shadow will ensure you are treated with courtesy in the camp.'

Temuge bowed low before turning away and Genghis was left alone, his thoughts twisting darkly. He had hoped Temuge would harden himself and ride with his brothers. He had yet to meet a shaman he liked and Kokchu had all the arrogance of his kind. Genghis sighed to himself. Perhaps it was justified. The healing had been extraordinary and he remembered how

Kokchu had passed a blade through his own flesh without a drop of blood. The Chin were said to have workers of magic, he recalled. It might be useful to have men to match them. He sighed again. Having his own brother as one of that breed had never been in his plans.

Khasar strolled through the camp, enjoying the bustle and noise. New gers were springing up on every spare bit of ground and Genghis had ordered deep latrine pits dug at every intersection. With so many men, women and children in one place, new problems had to be tackled each day and Khasar found no interest in the details. Kachiun seemed to enjoy the challenges and had organised a group of fifty strong men to dig the pits and help erect the gers. Khasar could see two of them building a shelter for bundles of new birch arrows to protect them from rain. Many warriors made their own, but Kachiun had ordered vast numbers for the army and every ger Khasar passed had women and children busy with feathers, thread and glue, bundling them up in fifties to be taken away. The forges of the tribes roared and spat all night to make the arrowheads and every dawn brought new bows to the ranges for testing.

The vast camp was a place of life and work and it pleased Khasar to see his people so industrious. In the distance, a newborn child started squalling and he smiled to hear it. His feet followed tracks in the grass that had been worn down to the clay beneath. When they left, the camp would look like a vast drawing of shapes and he struggled to picture it.

Relaxed as he was, he did not at first take notice of the disturbance at a meeting of paths ahead of him. Seven men stood in an angry knot, wrestling to pull a reluctant stallion to the ground. Khasar paused to watch them geld the animal, wincing

35

as one flailing hoof caught a man in the stomach and left him writhing on the earth. The pony was young and powerfully muscled. It fought the men, using its huge strength against the ropes they had on it. Once it was down, they would truss the legs and render it helpless for the gelding knife. They seemed hardly to know what they were doing and Khasar shook his head in amusement, beginning to walk past the struggling group.

As he edged around the kicking beast, it reared, pulling one of the men off his feet. The pony snorted in fury and backed up into Khasar, stepping on his foot so that he shouted in pain. The closest man to him reacted to the noise, back-handing him across the face to get him out of their way.

Khasar erupted with a fury to match the bound horse. He hammered a blow in return. The man staggered, dazed, and Khasar saw the others drop their ropes, their eyes dangerous. The pony took advantage of the unexpected freedom to bolt, racing away through the camp with its head down. All around them, the other stallions of the herd whinnied in response to its calls and Khasar was left facing furious men. He stood before them without fear, knowing they would recognise his armour.

'You are Woyela,' he said, looking to break the tension. 'I will have your horse recaptured and brought to you.'

They said nothing as they exchanged glances. Each of them shared a resemblance and Khasar realised they were the sons of the Woyela khan. Their father had arrived only a few days before, bringing five hundred warriors as well as the families. He had a reputation for quick temper and a prickly sense of honour. As the men crowded around Khasar, he thought the same traits had been passed to his sons.

Khasar hoped for a moment that they would let him go without a fight, but the one he had struck was wild with anger and it was he who pressed closest, bolstered by the presence of his brothers. A livid mark showed on the side of his face where Khasar had hit him.

'What right do you have to interfere?' one of the others snapped. They were deliberately crowding him and Khasar could see the bustle of the camp had stopped around them. There were many families watching the exchange and, with a sinking feeling, he knew he could not back away without shaming Genghis, perhaps even risking his hold on the camp.

'I was trying to get past,' he ventured through gritted teeth, readying himself. 'If your bullock of a brother had not struck me, you would have had that pony on the ground by now. Next time, truss his legs first.'

One of the largest spat on the ground near his feet and Khasar clenched his fists as a voice cut through the air.

'What is this?' The effect on the men was instant and they stood still. Khasar glanced at an older man who bore the same stamp of features. It could only be the khan of the Woyela and Khasar could do nothing but bow his head. It had not yet come to blades and he knew better than to insult the one man who might control his sons.

'You are brother to the man who calls himself Genghis,' the khan said. 'Yet this is a Woyela camp. Why are you here to anger my sons and spoil their work?'

Khasar flushed in irritation. No doubt Kachiun would have been informed of the confrontation and would have men on the way, but he did not trust himself to answer at first. The khan of the Woyela was clearly enjoying the situation and Khasar did not doubt he had seen it from the beginning. When he had mastered his temper, he spoke slowly and clearly to the khan.

'I struck the man who struck me. There is no cause to see blood spilled today.'

In reply, the khan's mouth twisted into a sneer. He had a

hundred warriors within easy call and his sons were ready to beat humility into the man who stood so proudly before him.

'I might have expected such a response. Honour cannot be set aside when it is not convenient. This part of the camp is Woyela land. You trespass upon it.'

Khasar assumed the cold face of the warrior to hide his irritation.

'My brother's orders were clear,' he said. 'All tribes may use the land while we gather. There is no Woyela ground here.'

The khan's sons muttered amongst themselves as they heard his words and the khan himself seemed to stiffen.

'I say there is and I see no one of rank to challenge my word. Yet you will hide in your brother's shadow.'

Khasar took a slow breath. If he claimed the protection of Genghis, the incident would end. The khan of the Woyela was not such a fool as to challenge his brother in the camp, with a vast army at his call. Yet the man watched him like a snake ready to strike and Khasar wondered if it had been chance that put the brothers and the wild stallion in his path that morning. There would always be those willing to test men who presumed to lead them in war. Khasar shook his head to clear it. Kachiun enjoyed politics and manoeuvring, but he had no taste for it, nor for the posturing of the khan and his sons.

'I will not spill blood here,' he began, seeing the triumph in the khan's eyes, 'but I will not need my brother's shadow.' As he spoke, he slammed his fist into the chin of the nearest brother, knocking him cold. The others roared and leaped at him almost as one. Blows rained on his head and shoulders as he moved backwards, then braced his legs and struck hard into a face, feeling the nose break. Khasar enjoyed fighting as much as any man who had grown up amongst brothers, but the odds were impossible and he almost went down as his head was snapped back and hard thumping blows crashed against his armour.

At least he was protected there and as long as he remained on his feet, he could duck and slip their punches while hammering back at them with everything he had.

Even as he formed the thought, one of them took him around the waist and dumped him on the ground. Khasar kicked out hard, hearing a yelp as he covered his head against their stamping boots. Where was Kachiun, by the spirits? Khasar could feel blood pouring from his nose and his lips had begun to swell. His head was ringing from a kick to his right ear. Much more of this and he would be permanently injured.

He felt the weight of one of them straddling him, trying to pull Khasar's arms away from his face. Khasar peered through a gap at the man. He chose his moment and shoved a thumb hard into his attacker's eye. It seemed to give under his strike, and he hoped he had blinded him. The Woyela son rolled off with a cry and, if anything, the kicks intensified.

A shout of pain came from somewhere close and, for a moment, Khasar was left alone to try to get to his feet. He saw a stranger had leaped among the Woyela brothers, knocking one to the ground and kicking another hard in the knee. The newcomer was little more than a boy, but he could punch with all his weight behind a blow. Khasar smiled at him through broken lips, but he was too dazed to rise.

'Stop this!' ordered a voice behind him and Khasar knew a moment of hope before he realised Temuge had not arrived with a dozen men to help him. His younger brother ran straight up to the struggling mass and heaved one of the Woyela men away.

'Get Kachiun,' Khasar shouted, his heart sinking. Temuge would accomplish nothing but getting himself beaten and then there would be blood. Genghis might accept one brother fighting, but a second would be a personal attack on his family too great to ignore. The khan of the Woyela seemed oblivious to the danger and Khasar heard him laugh as one of his sons smashed a fist into Temuge's face, knocking him to his knees. The young stranger too had lost the advantage of surprise and he was suffering under a rain of kicks and punches. The Woyela sons were laughing as they transferred their efforts to the two newcomers and Khasar raged to hear Temuge cry out in pain and humiliation, fending off their kicks as he struggled to rise.

Another sound came then, a series of hard cracks that had the sons of the Woyela yelping and falling back. Khasar continued to protect his head on the ground until he heard Kachiun's voice, tight with fury. He had brought men with him and it had been their sticks Khasar had heard.

'Stand, if you can, brother. Tell me who you want dead,' Kachiun snapped to Khasar. As Khasar lowered his hands, he spat red phlegm onto the grass and levered himself to his feet. His face was a mass of bruising and blood and the khan of the Woyela stiffened at the sight, his amusement fading.

'This was a private matter,' the khan said quickly as Kachiun glared at him. 'Your brother claimed no formal rank.'

Kachiun looked at Khasar, who shrugged, wincing as his bruised body protested.

Temuge too had regained his feet, looking as pale as milk. His eyes were cold and his shame made him angrier than Khasar or Kachiun had ever seen him. The third man straightened painfully and Khasar nodded to him in thanks. He too had been battered, but he grinned infectiously as he rested his hands on his knees and panted.

'Be careful,' Kachiun murmured to his brothers, barely loud enough to hear. He had brought a bare dozen of his workers, all he could grab when he heard of the fight. They would last only moments before the armed men of the Woyela. Hard eyes in the crowd watched the scene and the khan regained some of his confidence.

'Honour has been satisfied,' he declared. 'There is no grudge between us.' He turned to Khasar to see how his words had been received. Khasar stood smiling crookedly. He had heard the sound of marching feet coming closer. All of those who stood there stiffened in alarm at the jingling approach of armoured warriors. It could only be Genghis.

'There is no grudge?' Kachiun hissed at the khan. 'That is not for you to decide, Woyela.'

All eyes turned to see Genghis coming. He walked with Arslan and five other men in full armour. All carried drawn blades and the Woyela sons glanced at each other in dawning worry at what they had done. They had talked of testing one of the brothers of Genghis and that part had gone beautifully. Only the arrival of Temuge had dragged them into deeper water and none of them knew how it would be resolved.

Genghis took in the scene, his face a mask. His gaze lingered on Temuge and, for a moment, the yellow eyes tightened at the sight of his little brother's trembling hands. The khan of the Woyela spoke before anyone else.

'This is already settled, lord,' he said. 'It was merely a diversion, a fight over a horse.' He swallowed dryly. 'There is no need for you to rule on this.'

Genghis ignored him.

'Kachiun?'

Kachiun controlled his anger to reply in a calm voice.

'I do not know what started it. Khasar can tell you that.'

Khasar winced at hearing his name. Under Genghis' stare, he considered his words carefully. The entire camp would hear eventually and he could not be seen to complain like a child to his father. Not if he expected to lead them in war afterwards.

'I am satisfied with my part in this, brother,' he said through gritted teeth. 'If I have need to discuss it further with these men, I will do so on another day.'

41

'You will not,' Genghis snapped, understanding the implied threat as well as the Woyela sons did themselves. 'I forbid it.'

Khasar bowed his head.

'As you say, lord,' he replied.

Genghis looked at Temuge, seeing the shame at his public beating, coupled with the bright rage that had surprised Khasar and Kachiun before.

'You too are marked, Temuge. I cannot believe you were part of this.'

'He tried to stop it,' Kachiun replied. 'They knocked him to his knees and . . .'

'Enough!' Temuge snapped. 'In time, I will return every blow.' Blushing red, he seemed close to tears, like a child. Genghis stared at him and his own anger suddenly broke free. With a grunt, he shook his head and strode through the brothers of the Woyela. One of them was too slow and Genghis barged him down with his shoulder, barely seeming to feel the impact. The khan raised his hands in a plea, but Genghis grabbed his deel and yanked him forward. As he unsheathed his sword, the Woyela warriors drew their own in a rasp of metal.

'Hold!' Genghis roared at them, a voice that had carried across a hundred battles. They ignored the order and, as they closed, Genghis jerked the khan upwards like a marmot in his grip. In two quick slashes, he brought his sword across the man's thighs, gashing the muscles.

'If my brother was made to kneel, Woyela, you will not stand again,' he said. The khan was bellowing and blood poured over his feet as he fell. Before the warriors could reach him, Genghis raised his gaze to stare them down.

'If I see one sword in a hand in ten heartbeats more, not a single Woyela man, woman or child will live past this evening.'

The officers amongst the warriors hesitated, raising their arms to hold back the others. Genghis stood before them without a trace of fear while the khan at his feet fell to one side, moaning. The sons still stood frozen, horrified at what they had seen. With an effort of will, the khan made a gesture that his officers chose to interpret as assent. They sheathed their swords and the warriors followed, their eyes wide. Genghis nodded.

'When we ride, you Woyela will be the guards for my brother,' he said. 'If you will have them?' Khasar murmured assent, his swollen face blank.

'Then this is finished. There is no blood feud and I have seen justice served.'

Genghis caught the eyes of his brothers and they fell in with him as he strode back to the great ger and the business of the day. Khasar clapped a hand on the young man who had helped him, taking him along rather than leaving him to be beaten again.

'This one came to help me,' Khasar said as they walked. 'He knows no fear, brother.'

For an instant, Genghis glanced at the young man, seeing his pride.

'What is your name?' he asked gruffly, still seething at what he had seen.

'Tsubodai of the Uriankhai, lord.'

'Come and see me when you want a good horse and armour,' Genghis said. Tsubodai beamed and Khasar punched him lightly in the shoulder, approving. Behind them, the Woyela khan was left to be tended by his women. With such wounds, he would never stand straight, or perhaps even walk again.

As Genghis and his brothers strode through the tribes gathered in the shadow of the black mountain, there were many who looked on them with awe and approval. He had shown he would not be challenged and one more small victory had been won.

* * *

The Uighurs were sighted as the summer waned and the flood-waters from the hills swelled the Onon River to bursting point. The plains were still a vivid green and skylarks leaped and fluttered as the Uighur carts passed them.

It was an impressive display of strength and Genghis answered it with five thousand of his horsemen in ranks before the great camp. He did not come to meet them himself, knowing that his absence would be taken as subtle disapproval for their lateness. Instead, the Woyela took a position around Khasar as he rode to meet the new arrivals and none of the khan's sons dared do more than stare at the back of his head.

As the Uighurs drew close, Khasar approached the cart that led the dark snake of people and animals. His eyes flickered over the warriors, judging their quality. They were well armed and seemed fierce and alert, though he knew appearances could be deceiving. They would learn the tactics that had brought victory to Genghis, or be reduced to carrying messages amongst the host.

The Uighurs were horse traders as well as scholars and Khasar was pleased to see the vast herd that accompanied them. There had to be three ponies for every warrior and he knew the camp would be busy over the next month as the other tribes came to bargain and replenish their blood lines.

At his raised hand, the warriors around the lead cart drew up in a defensive position, their hands on the hilts of swords. The Uighurs must have had a good supply of ore for so many to carry blades, Khasar thought. Perhaps there would be trade in steel as well. There were still too many in the camp with nothing but a knife to complement their bows. Khasar directed his gaze to a small grey-haired man on the front of the cart. It was he who had held up an arm to halt the column and Khasar saw how the warriors looked to him for orders. Though the man's deel was of simple cut, it had to be the Uighur khan, Barchuk. Khasar decided to give him honour by speaking first.

'You are welcome in the camp, lord,' he said formally. 'You are the last of the great tribes to arrive, but my lord Genghis has received your message in goodwill and allocated grazing land for your families.'

The small man nodded thoughtfully as he looked past Khasar to the riders who waited in formation.

'I can see we must be the last. I can hardly believe there are any more warriors in the world, given the size of the host on this plain. You are the first men we have seen in many days of travel.' He shook his head in wonder at the thought. 'The Uighurs will pledge to Genghis, as I have promised. Show us where to pitch our gers and we will do the rest.'

In comparison to some of the pricklier khans, Khasar appreciated the man's bluntness. He smiled.

'I am his brother, Khasar,' he said. 'I will show you myself.'

'Step up beside me then, Khasar. I am hungry for news.' The khan patted the wooden bench of the cart and Khasar dismounted, sending his horse back to the first rank of Woyela warriors with a slap on its rump.

'If we are the last, perhaps it will not be long before Genghis points this great arrow at his enemies,' the khan said as Khasar clambered up beside him. Barchuk clicked in his cheek at the oxen and the cart moved off with a lurch. Khasar watched how the Uighur warriors kept formation around them and was pleased. They could ride, at least.

'Only he can say, lord.' The bruises he had taken from the Woyela had almost faded, though he felt Barchuk's eyes drift over them without comment. The camp had been quiet for a time after seeing the Woyela humbled, but with the end of summer, they were restless again and, now that the Uighurs had arrived, he thought his brother would move in just a few

45

days. He felt his own excitement mounting at the idea. They had the tribes and Genghis would take their oaths of loyalty. After that, war would come and he and his brothers would take the Chin foot off the necks of their people.

'You seem cheerful, Khasar,' Barchuk observed as he guided the cart around a hump in the grass. The older man was wiry with strength and his eyes seemed constantly amused.

'I was thinking that we have never before come together, lord. Always there has been some blood feud, or Chin bribery to keep us at each other's throats.' He waved an arm to encompass the camp on the plain. 'This? This is a new thing.'

'It may end in destruction for our people,' Barchuk murmured, watching him closely. Khasar grinned. He remembered Kachiun and Genghis debating the same point and he echoed their words.

'Yes, but not one of us, not one man, woman or child will be alive in a hundred years. Everyone you see here will be bones.'

He saw Barchuk frown in puzzlement and wished he had Kachiun's ability to speak as he went on.

'What is the purpose of life if not to conquer? To steal women and land? I would rather be here and see this than live out my life in peace.'

Barchuk nodded.

'You are a philosopher, Khasar.'

Khasar chuckled.

'You are the only one who thinks it. No, I am the great khan's brother and this is our time.'

CHAPTER THREE

Barchuk of the Uighurs spoke for hours as the sun set outside the great ger. Genghis was fascinated by the man's knowledge and if he came across a concept he did not understand, he made the khan go over and over it until the meaning was clear.

Of all subjects, anything to do with the Chin had Genghis leaning forward in his seat like a hawk, his eyes bright with interest. The Uighurs had come from land to the far south-west, bordering the Gobi Desert and the Chin kingdom of Xi Xia. Genghis revelled in every detail Barchuk could provide of Chin trade caravans, their dress and customs, and, most of all, their weapons and armour. It was true that merchants may not have had the best of guards, but each scrap of information fell upon the desert of Genghis' imagination like spring water, vanishing deep.

'Peace has brought you wealth and security,' Genghis said as Barchuk paused to clear his throat with a gulp of tea. 'Perhaps you could have approached the king of the Xi Xia to ally against me. Did you consider it?'

'Of course,' Barchuk replied, disarming him with honesty. 'But if I have given you the impression of their friendship, it is false. They trade with us because they have markets for the skins of snow leopards from the mountains, for hard woods, even seeds of rare plants to aid them in their study of healing.

In return, they sell us raw iron, carpets, tea and sometimes a scroll they have already copied many times.' He paused and smiled wryly at the gathering of men. 'They bring their litters and their guards into Uighur towns, but their distaste can be read on every face, even those they call slaves.' The memories had brought a flush of irritation to his face and he wiped his brow before continuing. 'Since I have learned their language, I know them too well to ask for support. You have to see them to understand, lord. They care nothing for those who are not Xi Xia subjects. Even the Chin regard them as a separate people, though they share many of the same customs. They pay tribute to the Chin emperor and, though under his protection, still consider themselves apart from their powerful neighbour. Their arrogance is colossal, lord.'

Barchuk leaned forward, reaching out to tap Genghis on his knee. He did not seem to notice the way the surrounding men bristled.

'We have had their scraps for many generations, lord, while they kept the best meat behind their forts and walls.'

'And you would see them broken,' Genghis murmured.

'I would. All I ask is that their libraries are turned over to the Uighurs for study. In addition, we have seen rare gems and a stone that is like milk and fire. They do not trade such items no matter what we offer.'

Genghis watched the khan closely as he spoke. Barchuk knew he had no right to demand spoils from war. The tribes were not paid to fight and anything they won or looted was theirs by tradition. Barchuk asked a great deal, but Genghis could not think of another group who might want the libraries of the Xi Xia. The very idea made him want to smile.

'You may have the scrolls, Barchuk. My word on it. Anything else goes to the victors and is in the hands of the sky father. I can give you no special claim.'

Barchuk sat back and gave a reluctant nod.

'It is enough, with everything else we will win from them. I have seen my people ridden down in the road by their horses, lord. I have seen them starve while the Xi Xia grew fat on crops they would not share. I have brought my warriors to extract a price for their arrogance and our towns and fields are empty behind us. The Uighurs are with you, gers, horses, salt and blood.'

Genghis reached out and the two men bound the oath with a quick clasp that hid the seriousness of such a declaration. The tribes waited outside the ger and Genghis would demand a similar oath from them all as soon as he was ready. To offer it in private was a demonstration of support that Genghis did not treat lightly.

'I ask one thing of you, Barchuk, before we go out to them,' he said. Barchuk paused in the middle of rising and his face became a mask as he realised the talk was not over.

'My youngest brother has expressed an interest in learning,' Genghis said. 'Stand, Temuge, where he can see you.' Barchuk looked round at the slender young man who rose and bowed to him. He acknowledged the gesture with a stiff dip of his head before turning back to Genghis.

'My shaman, Kokchu, will lead him in this, when the time comes, but I would like them to read and learn whatever they think is worthwhile. I include the scrolls you already own as well as any we might win from our enemies.'

'The Uighurs are yours to command, lord,' Barchuk said. It was not too much to ask and he did not understand why Genghis seemed ill at ease bringing up the subject. Temuge beamed at his back and Kokchu bowed his head as if he had received a great honour.

'It is settled then,' Genghis said. His eyes were shadowed, flickering in the lamps that had been lit against the evening gloom. 'If the Xi Xia are as rich as you say, they will be the first to see us on the move. Will the Chin support them?'

Barchuk shrugged.

'I cannot say for certain. Their lands border one another, but the Xi Xia have always been separate in their kingdom. The Chin may raise an army against you to counter any later threat. Or they may let them die to the last man without lifting a hand. No one can say how their minds work.'

Genghis shrugged.

'If you had told me ten years ago that the Kerait were facing a great host, I would have laughed and counted myself lucky not to be in the path of the battle. Now I call them brothers. It does not matter if the Chin come against us. If they do, I will break them all the faster. In truth, I would rather face them on a plain than have to climb the walls of their cities.'

'Even cities can fall, lord,' Barchuk said softly, his own excitement mounting.

'And they will,' Genghis replied. 'In time, they will. You have shown me the underbelly of the Chin in these Xi Xia. I will gut them there and then pull their heart out.'

'I am honoured to serve, lord,' Barchuk replied. He stood and bowed low, holding the pose until Genghis made a gesture for him to rise.

'The tribes have assembled,' Genghis said, standing and stretching his back. 'If we are to cross the desert, we will need to collect water and feed for the horses. Once I have the oath, there is nothing more holding us to this place.' He paused for a moment.

'We came here as tribes, Barchuk. We leave as a nation. If you are recording events in those scrolls as you describe, be sure to write that.'

Barchuk's eyes shone, fascinated by the man who commanded the great host.

'I will see it done, lord. I will teach the script to your shaman and your brother that they might read them to you.'

Genghis blinked in surprise, intrigued at the image of his brother repeating words trapped on stiff calfskin.

'It would be interesting to see such a thing,' he said. He took Barchuk by the shoulder, giving him honour by letting him leave the great ger in his company. The generals fell in behind. Outside, they could hear the hushed murmur of the gathered tribes as they waited for the one who would lead them.

Even in the summer darkness, the camp glowed yellow under the stars, lit by ten thousand fluttering flames. The centre had been cleared in a vast ring around the ger of Genghis, and the warriors of a hundred factions had left their families to stand together in the flickering light. From one man to the next, their armour could be a piece of stiff leather or the helmets and neat sets of iron scales copied from the Chin. Some carried the stamp of their tribes, while most were blank, showing that they were new and that there was only one tribe under the sky. Many of them held swords, fresh from the forges that had been working night and day since coming to the plain. Huge holes had been dug by sweating men under the sun as they carted ore back to the flames and watched in excitement as the sword-smiths turned out weapons they could hold. More than one man had burned his fingers reaching for them before they had cooled properly, but they had never dreamed of owning a long blade and they did not mind.

The wind always blew across the plain, but that evening the breeze was gentle as they waited for Genghis.

When he came, Barchuk of the Uighurs was guided down the steps of the cart and stood in the first rank around the wheels of wood and iron. Genghis stood for a moment, looking over the heads of the crowd and marvelling at the size of it. His brothers, Arslan and Jelme and last the shaman, Kokchu, stepped down from the height, each one pausing to take in the ranks stretching away in pools of light.

Then he was alone and he closed his eyes for a moment. He gave thanks to the sky father for bringing him to that place, with such an army to follow him. He said a few brief words to the spirit of his father in case that man could see him. Yesugei would be proud of his son, he knew. He had broken new ground for his people and only the spirits could tell where the path would end. As he opened his eyes, he saw Borte had brought his four sons to stand in the front rank, three of them too young to be left on their own. Genghis nodded sharply to them, his gaze lingering on the eldest, Jochi, and Chagatai whom he had named after the shaman of the Wolves. At almost nine, Jochi was in awe of his father and he lowered his eyes while Chagatai merely stared, his nervousness obvious.

'We came here from a hundred different tribes,' Genghis roared. He wanted his voice to carry, but even a throat trained on the field of battle could only reach so far. Those who could not hear would have to follow the lead of those who could.

'I have brought Wolves to this plain, Olkhun'ut and Kerait. I have brought Merkit and Jajirat, Uirat and Naimans. Woyela have come here, Tuvan, Uighurs and Uriankhai.' As he named each group, there was a stir from where they sat. He noticed how they remained together even for that night. There would be no easy assimilation for those who counted tribal honour above all else. It did not matter, he told himself. He would raise their gaze higher. His memory was faultless as he named each tribe that had ridden to join him in the shadow of the black mountain. He left no one out, knowing that the omission would be noted and remembered.

'More, I have called those who had no tribe,' he went on,

'but still had honour and heeded the call of blood to blood. They rode to us in trust. And I say to you all, there are no tribes under the sky father. There is only one Mongol nation and it begins this night, in this place.'

Some of those who listened cheered, while others remained stony-faced. Genghis kept the warrior's mask on his own features. He needed them to understand there was no loss of honour in what he asked.

'We are brothers in blood, separated too long ago for anyone here to know. I claim a greater family of all tribes, a blood tie to you all. I call you as brothers to my standard and we will ride as one family, one nation.' He paused, judging the response. They had heard the idea before, whispered in the gathering from tribe to tribe. Still, it shook them to hear it from him. The bulk of the men did not cheer and he had to crush a sudden spike of irritation. The spirits knew he loved them, but his own people were maddening at times.

'We will pile spoils enough to equal the mountain at your backs. You will have ponies and wives and gold, oils and sweetmeats. You will take lands for your own and you will be feared wherever they hear your names. Every man here will be a khan to those who bow to him.'

They cheered that, at least, and Genghis risked a small smile, pleased he had found the right tone. Let the lesser khans worry about the ambition of those around them. He meant every word of it.

'To the south is the great desert,' he called to them. Silence fell on the instant and he could feel their attention like a force. 'We will cross it at a speed the Chin kingdoms cannot imagine. We will fall on the first of them like wolves on lambs and they will scatter before our swords and bows. I will give you their riches and their women for your own. That is where I will plant my standard and the ground will shake as I do. The earth mother will know her sons and brothers have found their inheritance and she will rejoice to hear thunder on the plains.'

The cheering came again and Genghis raised his arms for quiet, though it pleased him.

'We will ride into the dry country, taking all the water we need for one sudden strike. After that, we will not stop until the sea bounds us in every direction. I am Genghis who say this and my word is iron.'

They roared in appreciation and Genghis snapped his fingers at Khasar, who stood waiting on the ground below. Khasar handed up a heavy pole of silver birch onto which eight horsetails had been tied. The crowd murmured as they saw it. Some recognised the black of the Merkit, or the red tail of the Naimans, bound with the others. Every one of them had been the khan's standard for one of the great tribes and Genghis had them all on the plain. As he took the staff, Khasar handed up a horsetail dyed with Uighur blue.

Barchuk's eyes narrowed at this most potent of symbols, but with the host at his back, he was still filled with excitement and the vision of the future. As he felt Genghis' eyes flicker over him, he bowed his head.

With nimble fingers, Genghis bound the tip of the last horsetail to the others and planted the butt on the wood at his feet. The breeze caught the coloured standard, so that the tails whipped and twisted as if alive.

'I have bound the colours,' he called to them. 'When they are bleached white, there will be no differences between them. They will be the standard of a nation.'

At his feet, his officers raised their swords and the host responded, caught up in the moment. Thousands of weapons jabbed the sky and Genghis nodded to them, overwhelmed. It took a long time for the noise to end, though he held up his free hand and patted the air with it.

'The oath you will take is binding, my brothers. Yet it is no stronger than the blood that binds us already. Kneel to me.'

The front ranks dipped immediately and the rest followed in ripples outward as they saw what was happening. Genghis watched closely for hesitation, but there was none. He had them all.

Kokchu climbed the steps back up to the cart, his expression carefully blank. In his wildest ambition, he had not dreamed of such a moment. Temuge had put in the word for him and Kokchu congratulated himself on bringing the young man to the point where he would make the suggestion.

As the tribes knelt, Kokchu revelled in his status. He wondered if Genghis had considered he would be the only one amongst them who did not take the oath. Khasar, Kachiun and Temuge knelt on the grass with all the others, khans and warriors alike.

'Under one khan, we are a nation,' Kokchu called over their heads, his heart pounding in excitement. The words echoed back to him, filling the valley in waves as those behind repeated them. 'The khan offers gers, horses, salt and blood, in all honour.'

Kokchu gripped the railing of the cart as they chanted. After that night, they would all know the shaman to the great khan. He glanced upwards as the words came in surges from further and further back. Under those clear skies, the spirits would be writhing in wild and simple joy, unseen and unfelt by anyone but the most potent of his calling. In the chant of thousands, Kokchu sensed them swirling in the air and he exulted. At last, the tribes fell silent and he let out a long breath.

'Now you, shaman,' Genghis murmured at his back. Kokchu started in surprise, before falling to his knees and repeating the same oath.

When Kokchu had rejoined the others around the cart, Genghis drew his father's sword. For those who could see, his eyes glittered with satisfaction.

'It is done. We are a nation and we will ride. Tonight, let no man think of his tribe and mourn. We are a greater family and all lands are ours to take.'

He dropped his arm as they bellowed, this time as one. The smell of roasting mutton was strong on the breeze and his step was light as the warriors prepared for a night of drink and enough food to make their bellies swell. There would be a thousand children begun by drunken warriors before dawn. Genghis considered returning to Borte in his tent and masked the discomfort at the thought of her accusing eyes. She had done her duty to him, no man could deny it, but the paternity of Jochi remained a doubt, like a thorn in his skin.

He shook his head to clear it of idle thoughts and accepted a skin of black airag from Kachiun. Tonight, he would drink himself to insensibility, as khan to all the tribes. In the morning, they would prepare to cross the dry lands of the Gobi Desert and walk the path he had chosen for them.

CHAPTER FOUR

The wind screamed around the carts, carrying a fine mist of sand that made the men and women spit constantly and wince at the grit in their food. Flies tormented them all, tasting the salt from their sweat and leaving red marks where they had bitten. During the day, the Uighurs had shown them how to protect their faces with cloth, leaving only their eyes to peer out at the bleak landscape, shimmering with heat. Those who wore armour found their helmets and neckpieces too hot to touch, but they did not complain.

After a week, the army of Genghis climbed a range of rust-coloured hills to enter a vast plain of rippled dunes. Though they had hunted in the foothills, game had become rare as the heat increased. On the blistering sand, the only sign of life was tiny black scorpions scuttling away from their ponies and vanishing into holes. Time and again the carts became bogged down and had to be dug out in the full heat of the day. It was backbreaking work, but every hour lost was one that brought them closer to running out of water.

They had filled thousands of bloated goatskins, tied with sinew and baked hard in the sun. With no other source, the supply dwindled visibly and, in the heat, many of the skins were found to have burst under the weight of the rest. They had carried only enough for twenty days and already twelve had passed. The warriors drank the blood of their mounts every second day, as well as a few cupfuls of warm, brackish water, but they were close to the edge of endurance and became dazed and listless, their lips dry enough to bleed.

Genghis rode with his brothers at the head of the army, squinting into the glare for some sign of the mountains he had been told to expect. The Uighurs had traded deep into the desert and he depended on Barchuk to guide them. He frowned to himself as he considered the endless flat basin of rippled black and yellow, stretching all the way to the horizon. The heat of the day was the worst he had known, but his skin had darkened and his face was seamed in new lines of dirt and sand. He had almost been glad of the cold on the first night, until it grew so biting that the furs in the gers gave little protection. The Uighurs had shown the other tribesmen how to heat rocks in the fire and then sleep on a layer of them as they cooled. More than a few warriors had brown patches on their backs where the rocks had burned their deels, but the cold had been beaten and, if they survived the constant thirst, the desert held nothing else that could stop them coming. Genghis wiped his mouth at intervals as he rode, shifting a pebble in his cheek to keep the spittle flowing.

He glanced behind him as Barchuk rode up to his side. The Uighurs had covered the eyes of their ponies with cloth and the animals rode blind. Genghis had tried that with his own mounts, but those who had not experienced it before bucked and snorted at the cloth until it was removed, then suffered through the hot days. Many of the animals had developed crusts of whitish-yellow muck on their eyelids and would need healing salves if they ever found their way out of the desert. Hardy as they were, they had to be given their share of precious water. On foot, the new nation would die in the desert.

Barchuk pointed to the ground, jabbing his hand and raising his voice over the unremitting wind.

'Do you see the blue flecks in the sand, lord?'

Genghis nodded, working his dry mouth so that he could reply.

'They mark the beginning of the last stage before the Yinshan Mountains. There is copper here. We have traded it with the Xi Xia.'

'How much further then before we see these mountains?' Genghis asked hoarsely, refusing to let his hopes rise.

Barchuk shrugged with Mongol impassivity.

'We have no certain knowledge, but merchants from Xi Xia are still fresh when they cross our trails in this place, their horses barely marked with dust. It cannot be far now.'

Genghis looked back over his shoulder at the silent mass of riders and carts. He had brought sixty thousand warriors into the desert, as many again of their wives and children. He could not see the end of the tail that stretched back for miles, the forms blurring into one another until they were no more than a dark smear wavering in the heat. The water was almost gone and soon they would have to slaughter the herds, taking only what meat they could carry and leaving the rest on the sands. Barchuk followed his gaze and chuckled.

'They have suffered, lord, but it will not be long now before we are knocking at the doors of the Xi Xia kingdom.'

Genghis snorted wearily to himself. The Uighur khan's knowledge had brought them into this bleak place, but they still had only his word that the kingdom was as rich and fertile as he said. No warriors of the Uighurs had been allowed to travel beyond the mountains that bordered the desert to the south and Genghis had no way to plan his attack. He considered this irritably as his horse sent another scorpion skittering over the sand. He had staked them all on the chance of a weak point in the Chin defences, but he still wondered what it would be like to see a great city of stone, as tall as a mountain. Against such a thing, his horsemen might only stare in frustration.

The sand under his pony's hooves grew blue-green as they rode, great stripes of the strange colours stretching away in all directions. When they stopped to eat, the children threw it into the air and drew pictures with sticks. Genghis could not share their pleasure as the supply of water dwindled and each night was spent shivering despite the hot rocks.

There was little to amuse the army before they fell into weary sleep. Twice in twelve days, Genghis had been called to settle some dispute between tribes as heat and thirst made tempers flare. Both times, he had executed the men involved and made it clear that he would not allow anything to threaten the peace of the camp. He considered them to have entered enemy lands and if the officers could not handle a disturbance, his involvement meant a ruthless outcome. The threat was enough to keep most of the hot-headed warriors from outright disobedience, but his people had never been easy to rule and too many hours in silence made them fractious and difficult.

As the fourteenth dawn brought the great heat once more, Genghis could only wince as he threw off his blankets and scattered the stones under him to be collected for the next night by his servants. He felt stiff and tired, with a film of grit on his skin that made him itch. When little Jochi stumbled into him in some game with his brothers, Genghis cuffed him hard, sending him weeping to his mother for solace. They were all short-tempered in the desert heat and only Barchuk's promises of a green plain and a river at the end kept their eyes on the horizon, reaching out to it in imagination.

On the sixteenth day, a low rise of black hills appeared. The Uighur warriors riding as scouts came back at a canter, their mounts sending up puffs of sand and labouring through its grip. Around them, the land was almost green with copper and black rocks poked through like sharp blades. Once more, the families could see lichen and scrub bushes clinging to life in the shadow of the rocks and, at dawn, the hunters brought hares and voles caught in their night traps. The mood of the families lifted subtly, but they were all suffering from thirst and sore eyes so that tempers remained foul in the camp. Despite their tiredness, Genghis increased the patrols around the main force and had the men drill and practise with their bows and swords. The warriors were dark and whip-thin from the desert, but they took to the work with grim endurance, each man determined not to fail under the eyes of the great khan. Slowly, imperceptibly the pace increased once more, while the heavier carts drifted to the rear of the procession.

As they drew closer to the hills, Genghis saw that they were far higher than he had realised. They were made of the same black rock that broke through the sand around him, sharp and steep. Climbing them was impossible and he knew there would have to be a pass through the peaks or he would be forced to travel right around their length. With their water supply almost gone, the carts were lighter, but he knew they had to find Barchuk's valley quickly or they would begin to die. The tribes had accepted him as khan, but if he had brought them to a place of heat and death, if he had killed them, they would take revenge while they still had the strength. Genghis rode straight-backed in the saddle, his mouth a mass of sores. Behind him, the tribes muttered sullenly.

Kachiun and Khasar squinted through the heat-hazed air at the foot of the cliffs. With two of the scouts, they had ridden ahead of the main army to look for a pass. The scouts were experienced men and the sharp eyes of one had pointed out a promising cut between peaks. It started well enough as the steep slopes gave way into a narrow canyon that echoed to the hooves of the four riders. On either side, the rocks extended up towards the sky, too high for a man to climb alone, never mind with carts and horses. It took no special skill in tracking to see the ground had been worn away in a wide path and the small group kicked their mounts into a canter, expecting to be able to report a way through to the Xi Xia kingdom beyond the hills.

As they rode around a kink in the trail, the scouts drew rein in astonishment, awed to silence. The end of the canyon was blocked by a huge wall of the same black stone as the mountains themselves. Each block on its own would have been heavier than anything the tribes could move and the wall seemed strange, somehow *wrong* to their eyes. They had no craftsmen who worked in stone. With its neat lines and smooth surfaces, it was clearly the work of man, but the sheer size and scale was something they had only seen in wild rocks and valleys. At the base was the final proof that it was not a natural thing. A gate of black iron and wood was set into the base of the wall, ancient and strong.

'Look at the size of it!' Kachiun said, shaking his head. 'How are we going to get through that?'

The scouts merely shrugged and Khasar whistled softly to himself.

'It would be easy to trap us in this spiritless place. Genghis must be told quickly, before he follows us in.'

'He'll want to know if there are warriors up there, brother. You know it.'

Khasar eyed the steep slopes at either side, suddenly feeling vulnerable. It was easy to imagine men dropping stones from the top and there would be no way to avoid them. He considered the pair of scouts who had accompanied them into the canyon. They had been warriors of the Kerait before Genghis had claimed them. Now, they waited impassively for orders, hiding their awe at the size of the wall ahead.

'Perhaps they just built it to block an army from the desert,' Khasar said to his brother. 'It might be unmanned.'

As he spoke, one of the scouts pointed, directing their gaze to a tiny figure moving along the top of the wall. It could only be a soldier and Khasar felt his heart sink. If there was another pass, Barchuk did not know of it and finding a way past the mountains would see the army of Genghis begin to wither. Khasar made his decision, knowing it could mean the lives of the two scouts.

'Ride to the foot of the wall, then come straight back,' he said to them. The two men bowed their heads, exchanging a glance in expressionless faces. As one, they dug in their heels and called 'Chuh!' to make their mounts run. Sand spattered into the air as they began their race to the foot of the black wall and Khasar and Kachiun watched through eyes slitted against the glare.

'Do you think they will reach it?' Kachiun asked. Khasar shrugged without speaking, too intent on watching the wall.

Kachiun thought he saw a sharp gesture from the distant guard. The scouts had the sense not to ride together, taking a split path at full gallop and veering right and left to spoil the aim of any archers. For a long time, there was no sound but the echoes of their hooves and the brothers watched with held breath.

Kachiun swore as a line of archers appeared on the wall.

'Come *on*,' he urged under his breath. Dark specks flashed down at the two scouts riding wildly in and Kachiun saw one of them swerve recklessly as he reached the great gate. They could see him slam his fist into the wood as he turned his mount, but the archers were loosing in waves and, an instant later, he and his horse were pinned with a dozen shafts. The dying man cried out and his mount began the trip back, missing a step and stumbling as it was hit again and again. They fell at last almost together, lying still on the sand.

The second scout was luckier, though he had not touched the wall. For a time, it looked as if he might escape the shafts and Khasar and Kachiun shouted to him. Then he jerked in the saddle and his horse reared and collapsed, its legs kicking as it rolled over him.

The horse made it to its feet and limped back to the brothers, leaving the scout's body broken behind it.

Khasar dismounted and took the loose reins. The leg was broken and the pony would not be ridden again. In silence, Khasar tied the reins to his saddle. He wasn't going to leave the animal behind with so many mouths to feed in the camp.

'We have our answer, brother,' Khasar muttered, 'though it's not the one I wanted. How are we going to get through them?'

Kachiun shook his head.

'We will find a way,' he said, glancing back to the dark line of archers watching them. Some of them raised their arms, though whether in mockery or salute, he could not tell. 'Even if we have to take it down, stone by stone.'

As soon as Khasar and Kachiun were sighted riding alone, the forces of Genghis were halted in their tracks. Before they could reach the outer lines of mounted warriors, the brothers passed skirmishing groups who remained staring outwards at the mountains they left behind. Genghis and his officers had learned hard lessons in the years of building the tribes into a single army and galloping boys raced ahead to tell him they were coming in.

Neither man replied to those who called to them. Grim and silent, they rode to their brother's ger, sitting like a white limpet on its cart. When they reached it, Khasar dismounted in a jump and glanced at the man who stepped forward to take the reins.

'Tsubodai,' he said in greeting, forcing a smile. The young

warrior seemed nervous and Khasar recalled he had been promised armour and a good horse. He grimaced at the timing.

'We have many things to discuss with the khan. Claim your
horse another time.'

Tsubodai's face fell with disappointment and Khasar snorted,
catching him by the shoulder as he turned away. He recalled
the boy's courage in leaping among the sons of the Woyela. It
was a favour he could repay.

'Perhaps there will be a moment when we are done. Come
with me then, if you can be silent.' Tsubodai regained his grin
on the instant, tinged with nervousness at meeting the great
khan himself. With a dry mouth, he climbed the steps of the
cart and followed the brothers into the shadowed interior.

Genghis was ready for them, his young messenger still
panting at his side.

'Where are the scouts?' he demanded, taking in their serious
expressions.

'Dead, brother. And the pass is guarded by a wall of black
stone as high as a hundred gers, maybe more.'

'We saw perhaps fifty archers drawn out,' Kachiun added.
'They were not skilled, as we know it, but they could hardly
miss. The wall lies at the end of a narrow pass, a gorge between
steep sides of rock. I could not see a way to flank them.'

Genghis frowned, rising from his seat. He made a clicking
sound in his throat as he stepped across the ger and passed out
into the bright sun. Khasar and Kachiun followed him out,
hardly noticing the wide-eyed Tsubodai on their heels.

Genghis stood on the blue-green sand below them, looking
up. He held a stick in his hands and gestured with it, drawing
a line on the ground.

'Show me,' he ordered. It was Kachiun who took the stick
and drew in neat strokes. Khasar watched in fascination as his
brother recreated the canyon he had seen a few hours before.

To one side, Kachiun drew a copy of the arched gate and Genghis rubbed his chin in irritation.

'We could tear the carts up to make wooden shields to get men close,' he said doubtfully.

Kachiun shook his head.

'That would bring us to the gate against their shafts, but once we were there, they could drop stones on us. From that height, a few planks would be smashed to pieces.'

Genghis raised his head, gazing over the ranks of the families to the treeless expanse of the desert in all directions. They had nothing with which to build.

'Then we will have to draw them out,' he said. 'A staged retreat, with valuable items left in our wake. I will send in men in the best armour and they will survive the arrows, but be driven back by them in panic, with much shouting.' He smiled at the prospect. 'It will teach our warriors a little humility, perhaps.'

Kachiun rubbed his boot along the edge of the drawing.

'It might work if we could know when they open the gate, but the canyon twists. As soon as we are out of sight, we'll have no way of knowing when they come out. If I could get a couple of boys onto the crags at the sides, they could signal to us, but it is a vicious climb and there's no cover on those rocks. They would be seen.'

'May I speak, lord?' Tsubodai said suddenly.

Khasar started in indignation.

'I told you to be silent. Can you not see this is important?' The gaze of all three men turned on the young warrior and he blushed darkly.

'I am sorry. I thought of a way we might know when they come out.'

'Who are you?' Genghis asked.

Tsubodai's voice wavered as he bowed his head.

66

'Tsubodai of the Uriankhai, lord.' He caught himself in embarrassment. 'Of the nation, lord. I . . .'

Genghis held up a hand.

'I remember. Tell me what you are thinking.'

With a visible effort, Tsubodai swallowed his nervousness and told them. It surprised him that they had not thought of it. The gaze of Genghis in particular seemed to bore into him and he ended staring away into the middle distance.

Tsubodai suffered in silence while the three men considered. After an age, Genghis nodded.

'That could work,' he said, grudgingly. Tsubodai seemed to grow a little taller.

Khasar flashed a smile at the younger man, as if he was responsible for his cleverness.

'See to it, Kachiun,' Genghis said. He grinned at Tsubodai's pride. 'Then I will ride to see this place you describe.' His mood changed as he considered destroying some of the carts that had carried the families across the desert. With wood so scarce, each one was much mended and handed down through the generations. There was no help for it.

'Take the first ten carts you see and join the wood into a barricade that can be held and moved.'

He saw Kachiun's gaze drift over the khan's ger at his back and snorted.

'Begin with the next cart you see, brother. Do not think to have mine.'

Kachiun moved quickly away to gather the men and materials he would need. Genghis remained, facing the young warrior.

'I have promised you a horse and armour. What else would you have from me?'

Tsubodai's face paled in confusion. He had not thought to add to the khan's debt, only to solve a problem that had intrigued him.

'Nothing, lord. It is enough to ride with my people.'

Genghis stared at him and scratched the side of his face.

'He has courage and intelligence, Khasar. Give him ten men in the attack on the wall.' His yellow eyes flickered back to Tsubodai who stood rooted in shock.

'I will watch to see how you lead more experienced warriors.' He paused for the news to sink in and added a barb to prick the young man's swelling confidence.

'If you fail them, you will not live beyond the sunset of that day,' he said.

Tsubodai bowed deeply in response, the warning barely denting his excitement. Genghis grunted to himself.

'Have my horse brought, Khasar. I will see this wall and these archers who think to stand in my way.'

CHAPTER FIVE

The Xi Xia defenders could have no idea how many Mongols had crossed the desert against them. Though Genghis rode up to the edge of bow range with a dozen officers, he kept the main army well back in the twisting canyon. He had decided against sending climbers up the slopes. The plan depended on the defenders thinking of them as unsophisticated herdsmen. Watchers on the peaks would reveal at least some talent for planning and make the fort soldiers suspicious. Genghis chewed his lower lip as he stared up at the Xi Xia fort. Archers clustered like ants on the wall and at intervals one would send a shaft high into the air to get the range for any assault that might follow. Genghis watched the last of them sink into the ground a dozen paces ahead of him. His own men could fire further and he spat contemptuously in the enemy archers' direction.

The air was thick and still in the canyon where no winds could blow. The heat of the desert was still strong while the sun crossed overhead and cut their shadows almost to nothing. He touched the sword of his father for luck, then turned his pony and rode back to where a hundred warriors waited.

They were silent, as he had ordered, but excitement was visible in their young faces. Like all Mongols, they relished the idea of tricking an enemy even more than overwhelming him by force.

'The wooden shield is lashed together,' Khasar said at his shoulder. 'It's rough, but it will get them to the foot of the wall. I have given them forge hammers to try the gate. Who knows, they might break in.'

'If that happens, have another hundred ready to charge in support,' Genghis said. He turned to Kachiun, standing nearby to oversee the last details. 'Hold the rest back, Kachiun. It would be an easy killing ground for them to be packed in tight while only a few can climb through. I do not want them running wild.'

'I'll put Arslan at the head of the second group,' Kachiun replied. It was a good choice and Genghis nodded assent. The swordsmith could follow orders in a storm of arrows.

At their backs, the wall seemed to loom still, though it was lost to direct sight. Genghis had no idea what lay behind the dark stones, or how many men defended the pass. It did not matter. In less than two days, the last water skins would be empty. The tribes would start to drop after that, dying from thirst and his ambitions. The fort had to fall.

Many of the men carried beautiful swords and spears to leave on the sand, anything that might catch the eye of the defenders and make them come out. To a man, they wore the best armour, copies of a Chin design. In the heat, the finger-width iron scales stung bare skin and their silk undertunics were soon sour with sweat. They gulped from skins of the dwindling water supply. Genghis had imposed no ration on men about to risk their lives.

'We have done all we can, brother,' Khasar said, interrupting his thoughts. Both men watched as Kokchu appeared among the warriors, scattering precious water over them and chanting. Many of the men bowed their heads to receive his blessing and Genghis frowned to himself. He imagined Temuge doing the same thing in the future and could find no glory in it.

'I should be among the attackers,' Genghis murmured.

Kachiun heard and shook his head.

'You cannot be seen to run from anything, brother. Perhaps the plan will go wrong and the tribes will be routed. You cannot be seen as a coward and not half the army knows the plan here, not yet. It is enough for them to see you watching. I have chosen most for nerve and courage. They will follow orders.'

'They must,' Genghis replied.

His brothers moved apart to clear the trail for the assault group and the wide wooden shelter. The men bore it above their heads with pride and the tension built in silence.

'I would see this wall brought down,' Genghis said to them. 'If not with blades and hammers, then with guile. Some of you will die, but the sky father loves the warrior spirit and you will be welcomed. You will open a way to the sweet kingdom beyond. Sound the drums and horns. Let them hear and worry in their precious fort. Let the sound carry right to the heart of the Xi Xia and even the Chin in their cities.'

The warriors took deep breaths, readying themselves for the sprint to come. In the distance a bird called shrilly, high on the thermals above the hills. Kokchu exclaimed that it was a good omen and most of the men looked up to the blue bowl above their heads. A dozen drummers began to pound the rhythms of battle and the familiar sound lifted them all, making hearts beat faster. Genghis swept his arm down and the army roared and horns wailed. The first group jogged to the point where they could turn into the main canyon and then accelerated, calling a raucous challenge. Echoing back came the warning cries from the fort.

'Now we will see,' Genghis said, clenching and unclenching his sword hand.

* * *

71

The voices of the warriors crashed against the sides of the pass as they ran. They were suffering under the weight of the barricade above their heads, already half blind with sweat. It proved its worth in moments as it bristled with black shafts, the coloured feathers quivering. The archers were well disciplined, Genghis saw, loosing together after a barked order. One or two shots were lucky and by the time the barricade reached the wall, there were three still figures lying face down on the sand in their wake.

A dull booming filled the pass as the hammer men attacked the door in the wall. Archers swarmed above, leaning over to send their arrows straight down at the smallest gaps. Men cried out and fell away from the edges of the wooden shield, their bodies jerking as they were hit again and again.

Genghis swore under his breath as he saw heavy stones being raised to the parapet. He had discussed the possibility with his generals, but still winced in anticipation as an officer wearing a plumed helmet raised his arm and screamed an order. The first stone seemed to fall for a long time and Genghis heard the crack as it drove those below to their knees. As they struggled up, the hammer men struck even harder, their blows coming as fast as the drummers they had left behind.

Two more stones fell before the wooden barricade broke apart. The hammers were thrown to the sand and a great roar of panic went up as the archers above found fresh targets. Genghis clenched his fists as he watched his men scatter. The door in the wall had held and they could do nothing but shake their weapons in rage at the enemy over their heads. Man after man fell and, without warning, they broke back down the pass, racing each other in desperation.

As they ran, more of them were knocked from their feet by waves of buzzing arrows. Barely more than a dozen made it out of range, resting their hands on their knees and panting.

Behind them, the pass was littered with everything they had dropped in the retreat, the bodies marked by shafts sticking out of them.

Genghis walked slowly to the centre of the path, staring up at the jubilant defenders. He could hear their cheering and it was hard to make himself turn his back to them. When he did, the sound intensified and he walked stiffly away until he knew he was lost to sight.

On the highest point of the wall, Liu Ken watched him go, his satisfaction straining the impassive mask he showed the soldiers around him. They were smiling openly and clapping each other on the back as if they had won a great victory. He felt his temper rising at their foolishness.

'Change the shift and get five *sui* of fresh archers up here,' he snapped. The smiles vanished. 'We've lost a thousand shafts in the gorge, so make sure the quivers are full once again. Give every man a drink of water.'

Liu rested his hands on the ancient stone, looking into the pass. They had killed almost all of those who had come into range and he was pleased with the archers. He made a note to congratulate the officer of the wall. The sound of hammers had worried him, but the door had held. Liu Ken smiled tightly to himself. If it hadn't, the Mongols would have run straight into a high-walled compound with archers on every side above them. The fort was beautifully designed and he was pleased his tour of duty had not ended before he had seen this test of its construction.

He frowned at the broken pieces of wood on the sand. Everything he had been told of the tribes suggested that if they came at all, they would attack like wild animals. The barricade showed shrewd planning and it nagged at him. He would be sure to put it in his report to the governor of the province. Let him decide how best to respond. Liu mused to himself as he looked down at the scattered dead. The stones had never been used before. Most were moss-covered from years of lying ready on the wall. Those too would have to be replenished from the stores, though there were clerks for that sort of mundane activity. It was about time they did more than allocate food and water for the men, he considered.

Liu turned at the clatter of sandals and swallowed his dismay at the sight of the fort commander coming up the steps to the wall. Shen Ti was an administrator rather than a soldier and Liu braced himself to answer his inane questions. The climb up to the wall had left the fat man gasping, so Liu had to look away rather than acknowledge his superior's weakness. He waited without speaking as Shen Ti joined him at the wall and looked down with bright eyes, his breathing still laboured.

'We have sent the dogs running,' Shen Ti said, recovering.

Liu inclined his head in silent agreement. He had not seen the commander during the attack. No doubt he had been cowering with his concubines in his private rooms on the other side of the fort. With wry humour, Liu thought of the words of Sun Tzu on defensive war. Shen Ti was certainly adept at hiding in 'the recesses of the earth', but only because Liu had been there to scatter the attackers. Still, he owed courtesy to the man's rank.

'I will leave the bodies for the rest of the day, lord, to be certain none of them are faking death. I will send men out to gather weapons and collect shafts at dawn.'

Shen Ti peered down at the bodies in the canyon. He could see boxes lying on the ground as well as a beautiful spear as long as a man. He knew that if he left it to the soldiers, anything valuable would vanish into private collections. Something sparkled in the green and gold sand and he squinted at it.

'You will supervise them, Liu. Send men down now to check the gate is not damaged. Have them bring anything valuable to me to examine.'

Liu hid a wince at the fat commander's naked greed. The Uighurs never had anything of value, he thought. There was no reason to expect more than a few bits of shiny metal from those ragged tribesmen. Yet he was not a noble and he bowed as low as he could in full armour.

'As you command, lord.' He left Shen Ti still staring down, a faint smile touching his fleshy lips. Liu snapped his fingers to attract the attention of a group of archers who were taking turns drinking from a water bucket.

'I am going out to strip the dead.' He took a deep breath, aware that he had allowed his bitterness at the shameful order to show. 'Get back to your positions and be ready for another attack.'

The men scurried to obey, the water bucket landing with a clang and spinning untended as they rushed back to the wall. Liu sighed to himself, before concentrating on the task at hand. No doubt the Uighurs would be made to pay for the attack when the king heard about it. In the peaceful lands of the Xi Xia, it would be the talk of the court, perhaps for months. Trade would be strangled for a generation and punishment raids would be sent out against every Uighur settlement. Liu had no taste for that sort of war and he considered asking for a transfer back to Yinchuan city. They always needed good guards with experience.

He gave crisp orders to a dozen spearmen to follow him and walked down the cool steps to the outer gate. From the inside, it looked untouched by the assault and, in the shadow of the walls, he considered the fate of anyone foolish enough to break it down. He would not like to be among them, he thought. It was second nature to him to check the inner gate was secure before he raised his hand to the outer locking bar. Sun Tzu was perhaps the greatest military thinker the Chin had ever produced, but he did not consider the difficulties of greedy men like Shen Ti giving the orders.

Liu took a deep breath and pushed open the door, letting in a beam of hard sunlight. The men behind him shuffled in readiness and he nodded to their captain.

'I want two men to stay and guard the door. The rest of you are to collect useable shafts and anything else that might be valuable. If there is trouble, drop it all and run for the gate. There will be no talking and not one of you will go more than fifty paces, even if there are emeralds the size of duck eggs lying in the sand. Acknowledge my orders.'

The soldiers saluted as one and their captain tapped two on the shoulder to remain on guard. Liu nodded, squinting out into the sun as his eyes adjusted. He could not expect high standards from the sort of soldier who ended up in the fort. Almost to a man, they had made some error in the standing army, or offended someone with influence. Even Shen Ti had made some secret error in his political past, he was sure, though the fat man would never unburden himself to a common soldier, no matter what rank he held.

Liu let out a long, low breath, checking a mental list of the defences. He had done all he could, but still there was a feeling in his bones that he did not like. He stepped over a body, noting that the man wore armour very similar to his own. He frowned at that. There was no record of the Uighurs copying Chin armour. It was rough, but of serviceable quality and Liu found his sense of unease growing.

Ready to leap back, he trod heavily on an outstretched hand. He heard a bone break and, at the lack of movement, he nodded and went further out. The dead lay thickest near the gate and he could see two sprawling men with arrows through their throats. Heavy hammers had fallen near them and Liu picked one up, propping it against the wall to be taken in on his return. It too was well made.

As he narrowed his eyes on the end of the pass, his men fanned out, stooping to pick up weapons from the sand. Liu began to relax a little, seeing two of them yanking arrows from a body that resembled a porcupine from the density of the strikes. He strode out of the wall's shadow, wincing at the sudden brightness. Thirty paces ahead of him lay two boxes and he knew Shen Ti would be watching to see if he found something of worth in them. Why the tribesmen would have brought gold or silver to an attack Liu could not fathom, but he walked across the baking sand towards them, his hand ready on his sword. Could they contain snakes or scorpions? He had heard of such things being used to attack cities, though usually they were thrown over the walls. The tribesmen had brought no catapults or ladders on their assault.

Liu drew his blade and dug the point into the sand, levering the box onto its side. Birds erupted from the confined space, soaring upwards as he threw himself back in shock.

For a moment, Liu stood and stared at the birds, unable to understand why they had been left to bake on the sand. He raised his head to watch them fly and then comprehension dawned and his eyes widened in sudden panic. The birds were the signal. A dull rumbling came to his ears and the ground seemed to vibrate under his feet.

'Get back to the gate!' Liu shouted, waving his sword. Around him, he saw his soldiers staring in shock, some of them with armfuls of arrows and swords. 'Run! Get back!' Liu bellowed again. Glancing down the pass, he saw the first dark lines of galloping horses and he turned to the gate himself. If the fools were too slow, they had only themselves to blame, he thought, his mind racing.

He skidded to a halt in horror before he had run more than a few paces. Around the gate, some of the bodies were leaping up, still with shafts lodged in them. One of them had lain perfectly still while Liu broke his hand under his sandal. Liu swallowed his panic at the thunder growing at his back and he began to run again. He saw the gate begin to close, but one of the enemy was there to shove his arm into the gap. The tribesman cried out in agony as his hand was hacked to pieces inside, but there were others with him to wrench it open and fall on the defenders.

Liu raised his voice in a howl of rage and never saw the arrow that took him in the back of the neck. He tumbled onto the sand, feeling its sting even as the darkness came for him. The inner gate was shut, he was certain. He had seen it closed behind him and there was still a chance. His own blood choked off his thoughts and the sound of hooves faded to nothing.

Tsubodai rose from where he had lain in the sand. The arrow that had felled him had been followed by two more lodged in his armour. His ribs were agony and every step brought fresh pain and the warm sensation of blood trickling down his thigh. The canyon was filled with a sound like thunder as the galloping line came in at full speed. Tsubodai looked upwards as he heard bows thrumming and saw black shafts darting down. A horse screamed behind him as Tsubodai saw the gate was jammed open by bodies and staggered towards it.

He looked around him for the ten men Genghis had placed under his command. He recognised four of the figures rushing at the gate, while the others lay still on the sand, truly dead. Tsubodai swallowed painfully as he stepped over a man he had known from the Uriankhai.

The sound of riders grew into a force at his back until he

expected to be hammered from his feet. He thought his wounds had dazed him, for everything seemed to be happening slowly and yet he could hear each laboured breath from his open mouth. He shut it, irritated at this show of weakness. Ahead of him, those who had survived the assault were rushing through the gate with swords drawn. Tsubodai heard the snap of bows, muffled by the thick stone of the wall. He had a glimpse of men falling as they went through, spitted on arrows as they looked up and cried out. At that instant, his mind cleared and his senses sharpened. Arrows still sank into the sand around him, but he ignored them. He roared an order to stand back as his warriors reached the gate. His voice was rough, but to his relief, the men responded.

'Make shields of the wood. Take the hammers,' Tsubodai told them, pointing. He heard the jingle of armour as men leaped to the sand all around him. Khasar landed running and Tsubodai grabbed his arm.

'There are archers inside. We can still use the broken wood.'

Arrows vanished into the sand around them, leaving only the black feathers. Calmly, Khasar glanced down at Tsubodai's hand just long enough to remind the young warrior of his status. As Tsubodai released his grip, Khasar snapped out orders. All around them, men picked up pieces of the original shield and held them over their heads as they rushed through the gate.

As the hammers were taken up again, archers above their heads shot into the pit between the two gates. Even with the rough shield, some of the shafts found their marks. On the hot sand outside, Khasar ordered waves of arrows up against the archers on the outer wall, keeping the Chin soldiers down and spoiling their aim until the army could move. He bit his lip at the exposed position, but until the inner gate was broken, they were all stuck. The dull thump of hammers sounded over the cries of dying men.

'Get in there and make sure they aren't enjoying a quick rest while we wait,' Khasar shouted to Tsubodai. The young warrior bowed his head and ran to join his men.

He passed under a band of shadow into bright sunlight and had a glimpse of a line of cold-eyed archers shooting shaft after shaft into the killing hole.

Tsubodai barely had time to duck under a piece of broken planking. An arrow scratched his arm as he did and he swore aloud. He recognised only one of his original ten men still alive.

The space between the gates was deliberately small and no more than a dozen warriors could stand inside at a time. Except for those who wielded hammers with desperate force, the others stood with pieces of wood above their heads, wedged together as best they could. The ground was still sandy and bristled with spent shafts, thicker than the hairs on a dog. Still more were shot down and Tsubodai heard orders shouted in an alien language above his head. If they had stones to drop, the entire assault would be crushed before the inner gate gave way, he thought, fighting terror. He felt enclosed, trapped. The man closest to him had lost his helmet in the attack. He gave a shriek of pain and fell with an arrow's feathers standing upright in his neck, loosed from almost directly above. Tsubodai caught the planking he had held and raised it, wincing with every shuddering impact. The hammer blows went on with maddening slowness and, suddenly, Tsubodai heard a grunt of satisfaction from one of the warriors and the sound changed as those closest began kicking at the cracking timbers.

The gate gave way, sending men sprawling on the dusty ground beyond it. The first ones through died instantly as they were met with a volley of crossbow shafts from a line of soldiers. Behind them, Khasar's men roared in savage anticipation, sensing there was a way in. They pushed forward, compressing the group at the gate as they stumbled over dead men.

Tsubodai could not believe he was still alive. He drew the sword Genghis himself had given him and ran forward in a mass of raging men, freed at last from the confines of the killing ground. The crossbowmen never had a chance to reload and Tsubodai killed his first enemy with a straight thrust to the throat as the soldier froze in horror. Half of those who came into the fort were wounded and bloody, but they had survived and they exulted as they met the first lines of defenders. Some of the first ones inside climbed wooden steps to a higher level and grinned as they saw the archers still firing down into the killing hole. Mongol bows snapped shafts across the fighting below, striking the Xi Xia bowmen from their feet as if they had been hit by hammers.

The army of Genghis began to funnel through the gate, exploding into the fort. There was little order to the assault in the first charge. Until senior men like Khasar or Arslan took charge, Tsubodai knew he was free to kill as many as he could and he shouted wildly, filled with excitement.

Without Liu Ken to organise the defence, the Xi Xia warriors broke and ran before the invaders, scattering in panic. Leaving his horse in the pass, Genghis walked through the gate and ducked through the broken inner gate. His face was alight with triumph and pride as his warriors tore through the fort soldiers. In all their history, the tribes had never had a chance to strike back at those who held them down. Genghis did not care that the Xi Xia soldiers thought themselves different from the Chin. To his people, they were all part of that ancient, hated race. He saw that some of the defenders had laid down their weapons and he shook his head, calling Arslan to him as the swordsman strode past.

'No prisoners, Arslan,' Genghis said. His general bowed his head.

The slaughter became methodical after that. Men were discovered hiding in the fort's cellars and dragged out for execution. As the day wore on, the dead soldiers were piled on the red stones of a central courtyard. A well there became the eye of the storm as every dry-throated man found time to quench his thirst in water, bucket by bucket, until they were gasping and soaked. They had beaten the desert.

As the sun began to set, Genghis himself walked to the well, stepping over the piles of twisted dead. The warriors fell silent at his step and one of them filled the leather bucket and handed it to the khan. As Genghis drank at last and grinned, they roared and bayed in voices loud enough to echo back from the walls all around. They had found their way through the maze of rooms and halls, cloisters and walkways, all strange to their eyes. Like a pack of wild dogs, they had reached right to the far side of the fort, leaving the black stones bloody behind them.

The commander of the fort was discovered in a suite of rooms hung with silk and priceless tapestries. It took three men to batter down the door of iron and oak to reveal Shen Ti, hiding with a dozen terrified women. As Khasar strode into the room, Shen Ti tried to take his own life with a dagger. In his terror, the blade slipped in his sweating hands and merely scored a line in his throat. Khasar sheathed his sword and took hold of the man's fleshy hand over the hilt, guiding it back to the neck a second time. Shen Ti lost his nerve and tried to struggle, but Khasar's grip was strong and he drew the dagger sharply across, stepping back as blood spurted out and the man flailed in death.

'That is the last of them,' Khasar said. He looked the women over and nodded to himself. They were strange creatures, their skin powdered as white as mare's milk, but he found them attractive. The scent of jasmine mingled with the stench of blood in the room and Khasar smiled wolfishly at them. His brother Kachiun had won an Olkhun'ut girl for his wife and had two children already in his ger. Khasar's first wife had died and he had no one. He wondered if Genghis would let him marry two or three of these foreign women. The idea pleased him enormously and he stepped to the far window, looking out on the lands of the Xi Xia.

The fort was high in the mountains and Khasar had a view of a vast valley, with cliffs stretching away into the haze on either side. Far below, he saw a green land, studded with farms and villages. Khasar breathed deeply in appreciation.

'It will be like picking ripe fruit,' he said, turning to Arslan as the older man entered. 'Send someone to fetch my brothers. They should see this.'

CHAPTER SIX

The king sat in the highest room of his palace, looking over the flat valley of the Xi Xia. With the dawn mist rising off the fields, it was a landscape of great beauty. If he did not know there was an army out there beyond sight, the land might have seemed as peaceful as any other morning. The canals shone in the sun like lines of gold, carrying precious water to the crops. There were even distant figures of farmers out there, working without thought for the army that had entered their country from the northern desert.

Rai Chiang adjusted his robe of green silk, patterned in gold. Alone, his expression was calm, but as he stared out into the dawn, his fingers picked nervously at a thread, worrying at it until it caught in his nails and snapped. He frowned, looking down at the damage. The robe was a Chin weave, worn to bring him luck in the matter of reinforcements. He had sent a letter with two of his fastest scouts as soon as he heard of the invasion, but the reply was long in coming.

He sighed to himself, his fingers resuming their picking without him being aware of it. If the old Chin emperor had lived, there would be fifty thousand soldiers marching to defend his little kingdom, he was sure of it. The gods were fickle to have taken his ally at the very moment when he needed aid. Prince Wei was a stranger and Rai Chiang did not know whether the arrogant son would have the generosity of his father.

Rai Chiang considered the differences between their lands, wondering if he could have done more to ensure Chin support. His most distant ancestor had been a Chin prince and ruled the province as a personal fiefdom. He would have seen no shame in asking for aid. The Xi Xia kingdom had been forgotten in the great conflict centuries before, unnoticed as greater princes struggled against each other until the Chin empire had been cut in two. Rai Chiang was the sixty-fourth ruler since that bloody period. Since the death of his father, he had spent almost three decades keeping his people free of the Chin shadow, cultivating other allies and never giving offence that could lead to his kingdom being forcibly returned to the fold. One of his sons would one day inherit that uneasy peace. Rai Chiang paid his tribute, sent his merchants to trade and his warriors to swell the ranks of the Imperial army. In return, he was treated as an honoured ally.

It was true Rai Chiang had ordered a new script for his people, one that bore little resemblance to Chin writing. The old Chin emperor had sent him rare texts by Lao Tzu and the Buddha Sakyamuni to be translated. Surely that was a sign of acceptance, if not approval. The Xi Xia valley *was* separate from the Chin lands, bordered by mountains and the Yellow River. With a new language, the Xi Xia would move further from the influence of the Chin. It was a dangerous and delicate game, but he knew he had the vision and energy to find the right future for his people. He thought of the new trade routes he had opened into the west and the wealth that was flowing back along them. All that was endangered by these tribes roaring out of the desert.

Rai Chiang wondered if Prince Wei would realise the Mongols had come round his precious wall in the north-east by entering the Xi Xia kingdom. It would do the Chin no good now the wolf had found the gate to the field.

'You *must* support me,' he whispered to himself. It galled him to depend on the Chin for military aid, after so many generations easing his people away from their dependence. He did not know yet if he could bear the price Prince Wei would ask for that support. The kingdom could be saved only to become a province again.

Rai Chiang tapped his fingers in irritation at the thought of a Chin army on his land. He needed them desperately, but what if they did not leave when the battle was over? What if they did not come at all?

Two hundred thousand people already sheltered within the walls of Yinchuan, with thousands more gathered outside the closed gates. In the night, the most desperate tried to climb into the city and the king's guards were forced to drive them off with swords, or shoot a volley of arrows into their midst. The sun rose each day on fresh corpses and more soldiers had to leave Yinchuan to bury them before they could spread disease, labouring under the sullen stares of the rest. It was a grim and unpleasant business, but the city could feed only so many and the gates remained closed. Rai Chiang worried at the golden threads until beads of blood appeared under his fingernails.

Those who had found sanctuary slept in the streets, the beds of every inn and lodging house long taken. The price of food was rising every day and the black market thrived, though the guards hanged anyone caught hoarding. Yinchuan was a city of fear as they waited for the barbarians to attack, but three months had gone by with nothing but reports of destruction as the army of Genghis laid waste to everything in their path. They had not yet come to Yinchuan, though their scouts had been seen riding in the far distance.

A gong sounded, making Rai Chiang start. He could hardly

86

believe it was the hour of the dragon already. He had been lost in contemplation, but it had not brought him the usual sense of peace before the day truly began. He shook his head against the malicious spirits that sapped the will of strong men. Perhaps the dawn would bring better news. Preparing himself to be seen, he straightened in his throne of lacquered gold and tucked the sleeve with the broken thread under the other. When he had spoken to his ministers, he would have a new robe brought and a cooling bath to make his blood flow with less turbulence.

The gong sounded again and the doors to the chamber opened in perfect silence. A line of his most trusted advisers walked in, their footsteps muffled by shoes of felt so the polished floor would not be scratched. Rai Chiang regarded them impassively, knowing that they took their confidence from his manner. Let him but show one trace of nervousness and they would feel the storms of panic that blew through the slums and streets of the city below.

Two slaves took up positions on either side of their king, creating a gentle breeze from large fans. Rai Chiang hardly noticed their presence as he saw his first minister could barely maintain his calm. He forced himself to wait until the men had touched their foreheads to the floor and proclaimed their oath of loyalty. The words were ancient and comforting. His father and grandfather had heard them many thousand times in this very room.

At last, they were ready to begin the business of the day and the great doors shut behind them. It was foolish to think they were completely private, Rai Chiang reflected. Anything of note in the throne room became market gossip before the sun set. He watched the ministers closely, looking for some sign that they felt the fear curdling in his breast. Nothing showed and his mood lightened a fraction.

'Imperial Majesty, Son of Heaven, king and father to us all,' his first minister began, 'I bear a letter from Emperor Wei of the Chin.' He did not approach himself, but handed the scroll to a bearer slave. The young man knelt and held out the roll of precious paper and Rai Chiang recognised the personal chop of Prince Wei. Rai Chiang hid the stirring of hope in his breast as he took it and broke the wax seal.

It did not take long to read the message and, despite his control, Rai Chiang frowned. He could sense the hunger for news in the room and his calm had been affected badly enough for him to read it aloud.

'It is to our advantage when our enemies attack one another. Wherein lies the danger to us? Bleed these invaders and the Chin will avenge your memory.'

There was utter silence in the room as the ministers digested the words. One or two of them had paled, visibly disturbed. There would be no reinforcements. Worse, the new emperor had described them as enemies and could no longer be considered the ally his father had been. It was possible that they had heard the end of the Xi Xia kingdom in those few words.

'Our army is ready?' Rai Chiang said softly into the silence.

His first minister bowed deeply before replying, hiding his fear. He could not bring himself to tell his king how poorly prepared the soldiers were for war. Generations of peace had made them more adept at bullying favours from city prostitutes than martial skills.

'The barracks are full, Majesty. With your royal guards to lead them, they will send these animals back into the desert.'

Rai Chiang sat perfectly still, knowing no one there would dare to interrupt his thoughts.

'Who will keep the city safe if my personal guard goes out onto the plains?' he said at last. 'The peasants? No, I have sheltered and fed the militia for years. It is time they *earned* what they have had from my hand.' He ignored the taut expression of his first minister. The man was merely a cousin and, though he ran the city's scribes with rigid discipline, he was out of his depth with anything requiring original thought.

'Send for my general, that I may plan an attack,' Rai Chiang said. 'The time for talk and letters is over, it seems. I will consider the words of . . . Emperor Wei, and my response, when we have dealt with the closer threat.'

The ministers filed out, their nervousness showing in their stiff bearing. The kingdom had been at peace for more than three centuries and no one there could remember the terrors of war.

'This place is perfect for us,' Kachiun said, looking out over the plain of the Xi Xia. At his back, the mountains loomed, but his gaze lingered over green and gold fields, lush with growing crops. The tribes had covered ground at incredible speed over the previous three months, riding hard from village to village with almost no opposition. Three large towns had fallen before the news had gone ahead and the people of the tiny kingdom began to flee the invaders. At first, the tribes had taken prisoners, but when they had close to forty thousand, Genghis had grown tired of their wailing voices. His army could not feed so many and he would not leave them behind him, though the miserable farmers did not look like any kind of threat. He had given the order and the slaughter had taken an entire day. The dead had been left to rot in the sun and Genghis had visited the hills of the dead only once to see that his orders had been carried out. After that, he thought no more of them.

Only the women had been left alive to be taken as prizes

and Kachiun had found a couple of rare beauties that very morning. They waited for him in his ger and he found his thoughts straying in that direction instead of to the next move in the assault. He shook his head to clear it.

'The peasants don't seem warlike at all and these canals are perfect for watering our horses,' he went on, glancing at his older brother.

Genghis sat on a pile of saddles next to his ger, resting his chin on his hands. The mood of the tribes was cheerful around the two men and he saw a group of boys setting wands of birch into the ground. He raised his head in interest as he saw his two eldest sons were part of the chattering gang, pushing and shoving each other as they argued over how best to set the sticks. Jochi and Chagatai were dangerous company for the boys of the tribes, often leading them into trouble and scuffles that resulted in them being slapped apart by the women of the gers.

Genghis sighed, running his tongue over his lower lip as he thought.

'We're like a bear with his paw in honey, Kachiun, but they will rouse themselves. Barchuk tells me the Xi Xia merchants boasted of a huge standing army. We have not met them yet.'

Kachiun shrugged, unworried at the prospect.

'Perhaps. There is still their great city. They may be hiding behind the walls there. We could starve them out, or break the walls down around their ears.'

Genghis frowned at his brother.

'It will not be so easy, Kachiun. I expect rashness from Khasar. I keep you close to be the voice of caution and sense when the warriors get too full of themselves. We have not fought a single battle in this realm and I do not want the men to be fat and slow when it comes. Get them back on the training field and burn the laziness out of them. You too.'

Kachiun flushed at the rebuke.

'Your will, my brother,' he said, bowing his head. He saw Genghis was watching his sons as they mounted their shaggy ponies. It was a game of skill learned from the Olkhun'ut and Genghis was distracted as Jochi and Chagatai readied themselves to gallop past the row of wands in the soil.

Jochi turned his pony faster and raced along the line with his child's bow fully bent. Genghis and Kachiun watched as he loosed his arrow at full speed, sending the head slicing through the slender stick. It was a good strike and, in the same instant, Jochi reached down with his left hand and snatched the falling piece of wood, raising it triumphantly as he turned back to his companions. They cheered him, though Chagatai merely snorted before beginning his own run.

'Your son will be a fine warrior,' Kachiun murmured. Genghis winced at the words and Kachiun did not look at him, knowing the expression he would see.

'While they can retreat behind walls five times higher than a man,' Genghis said stubbornly, 'they can laugh at us riding around on the plains. What does their king care for a few hundred villages? We have barely stung him while this Yinchuan city sits safe and he resides in it.'

Kachiun did not respond as Chagatai rode the line. His arrow cut the wand, but his flailing hand failed to snatch it before it fell. Jochi laughed at his brother and Kachiun saw Chagatai's face darken in anger. They knew their father was watching of course.

At his back, Genghis made his decision, rising to his feet.

'Get the men sober and ready to march. I will see this city of stone that so impressed the scouts. Somehow or other there must be a way in.' He did not show his brother the worries that plagued him. He had never seen a city girdled in high walls as his scouts described. He hoped that the sight of it would bring some insight into how he could enter without seeing his army dash itself uselessly against the stone.

As Kachiun left to relay the orders, he saw Chagatai had said something to his older brother. Jochi leaped from his pony as he passed, sending them both thumping into the ground in a flurry of elbows and bare feet. Kachiun grinned as he passed them, remembering his own childhood.

The land they had found beyond the mountains was fertile and rich. Perhaps they would have to fight to keep it, but he could not imagine a force capable of defeating the army they had brought a thousand miles from their home. As a boy, he had once levered a huge rock free on a hillside and seen the way it gathered speed. At first, it was slow, but after only a little time, it was unstoppable.

Scarlet was the Xi Xia colour for war. The king's soldiers wore armour lacquered in vivid red and the room where Rai Chiang met his general was unadorned except for polished walls of the same shade. Only a single table spoiled the echoing emptiness and both men stood to gaze down at maps of the region, held with lead weights. The original secession from the Chin had been planned within those red walls; it was a place to save and win a kingdom, rich with its own history. General Giam's lacquered armour was such a perfect match for the room that he almost vanished against the walls. Rai Chiang himself wore a tunic of gold over black silk trousers.

The general was white-haired, a man of dignity. He could feel the history of the Xi Xia hanging heavy in the air of that ancient room, as heavy as the responsibility he would bear himself.

He placed another marker of ivory on the lines of dark blue ink.

'Their camp is here, Majesty, not far from where they entered the kingdom. They send their warriors out to raid a hundred *li* in every direction.'

'A man cannot ride further in a day, so they must make other camps for the night,' Rai Chiang murmured. 'Perhaps we can attack them there.'

His general shook his head slightly, unwilling openly to contradict his king.

'They do not rest, Majesty, or stop for food. We have scouts who say they ride that far and then back from dawn to sunset. When they take prisoners, they are slower, driving them before them. They have no infantry and carry supplies with them from the main camp.'

Rai Chiang frowned delicately, knowing that would be enough criticism to make the general sweat in his presence.

'Their camp is not important, general. The army must engage and break these riders who have caused so much destruction. I have a report of a pile of dead peasants as high as a mountain. Who will gather the crops? The city could starve even if these invaders left us today!'

General Giam made his face a mask rather than risk further anger.

'Our army will need time to form and prepare the ground. With the royal guard to lead them, I can have the fields sown with spikes that will destroy any charge. If the discipline is good, we will crush them.'

'I would have preferred to have Chin soldiers with my own militia,' Rai Chiang said as if to himself.

The general cleared his throat, knowing it was a sensitive subject.

'All the more need for your own guards, Majesty. The militia are little better than peasants with weapons. They cannot stand on their own.'

Rai Chiang turned his pale eyes on his general.

'My father had forty thousand trained soldiers to man the walls of Yinchuan. As a child, I watched the red ranks parade through the city on his birthday and there seemed no end to them.' He grimaced irritably. 'I have listened to fools and counted the cost of so many over the dangers we could face. There are barely twenty thousand in my own guard and you would have me send them out? Who then would defend the city? Who would form the teams for the great bows and hold the walls? Do you think the peasants and merchants will be of any use to us once my guard have gone out? There will be food riots and fires. Plan to win without them, general. There is no other way.'

General Giam had been born to one of the king's uncles and promotion had come easily. Yet he had courage enough to face Rai Chiang's disapproval.

'If you give me ten thousand of your guard, they will steady the others. They will be a core the enemy cannot break.'

'Even ten thousand is too many,' Rai Chiang snapped.

General Giam swallowed.

'Without cavalry, I cannot win, my lord. With even five thousand guards and three thousand of those on heavy horse, I would have a chance. If you cannot give me that, you should execute me now.'

Rai Chiang raised his eyes from the map and found General Giam's gaze steady. He smiled, amused at the bead of sweat that was making its way down the man's cheek.

'Very well. It is a balance between giving you the best we have and still keeping enough to defend the city. Take a thousand crossbowmen, two of cavalry and two more of heavy pikes. They will be the core that leads the others against the enemy.'

General Giam closed his eyes in silent thanks for an instant. Rai Chiang did not notice as he turned back to the map.

'You may empty the stores of armour. The militia may not be my red guards, but perhaps looking like them will give them courage. It will relieve the boredom of hanging profiteers and whitewashing the barracks, I have no doubt. Do not fail me in this, general.'

'I will not, Your Majesty.'

Genghis rode at the head of his army, a vast line of horsemen that stretched across the plain of the Xi Xia. As they came to canals, the line would bulge as men raced each other over the drop, laughing and calling to anyone who fell into the dark water and had to ride hard to catch up.

The city of Yinchuan had been a smear on the horizon for hours before Genghis gave the order to halt. Horns sounded up and down the line and the host came to a stop, with echoing orders passing down to alert men on the wings. This was hostile country and they would not be taken by surprise.

The city loomed in the distance. Even miles away, it seemed a massive construction, intimidating in its sheer size. Genghis squinted into the haze of the afternoon sun. The stone the builders had used was a dark grey and he could see columns that could have been towers inside the walls. He could not guess their purpose and strove not to show his awe in front of the men.

He looked around him, seeing that his people could not be ambushed on such a flat piece of ground. The crops could have hidden crawling soldiers, but his scouts would sight them long before they were close. It was as safe as anywhere could be to set up camp and he made the decision, dismounting as he gave his orders.

Behind him, the tribes scurried in the routines they knew.

Gers were lashed together and raised by individual families long used to the work. A village, a town, a city of their own sprang out of the carts and herds of bleating animals. It was not long before Genghis' own cart came up and the smell of frying mutton filled the air.

Arslan walked along the line with his son Jelme. Under their eyes, the warriors of all the tribes stood tall and kept their chatter to a minimum. Genghis approved and he was ready with a smile as they reached him.

'I have never seen such a flat land,' Arslan said. 'There is nowhere to hold, nowhere to retreat to if we are overwhelmed. We are too exposed here.'

His son Jelme raised his eyes at the words, but did not speak. Arslan was twice the age of the other generals and he led cautiously and with intelligence. He would never be a firebrand amongst the tribes, though his skill was respected, and his temper feared.

'We will not be turned, Arslan. Not from here,' Genghis replied, clapping him on the shoulder. 'We will make them come out from that city, or if they will not, perhaps I will just build a ramp of earth to the top of their walls and ride in. That would be a thing to see, would it not?'

Arslan's smile was tight. He had been one of those who had ridden closer to Yinchuan, close enough for them to waste arrows on him.

'It is like a mountain, lord. You will see when you ride close to the walls. Each corner has a tower and the walls are set with slits where archers poke their faces through to watch you pass. It would be hard to hit them, while they have an easy shot against us.'

Genghis lost some of his good humour.

'I will see it first before I decide. If it will not fall to us, I will starve them out.'

Jelme nodded at the idea. He had ridden with his father close enough to feel the shadow of the city on his back. For a man used to the open steppes, he found himself irritated at the thought of such an ant hill of men. The very idea offended him.

'The canals pass into the city, lord,' Jelme said, 'through tunnels barred with iron. I am told they wash away the dung of so many people and animals. There may be a weakness there.'

Genghis brightened. He had ridden all day and he was weary. There would be time to plan the assault tomorrow when he had eaten and rested.

'We will find a way,' he promised.

CHAPTER SEVEN

With no sign of opposition, the younger warriors under Genghis spent their days riding as close as they dared to the city, testing their courage. The bravest of them galloped under the shadow of the walls as arrows whipped overhead. Their whooping cries echoed over the fields in challenge, yet only one Xi Xia archer managed a clean strike in three days. Even then, the tribesman recovered his seat and rode clear, pulling the arrow out of his armour and throwing it contemptuously to the ground.

Genghis too rode close, with his generals and officers. What he saw brought him no inspiration. Even the canals into the city were protected by iron bars as thick as a man's forearm, set deep into stone. He thought they might still batter their way in, though the thought of crawling down dank tunnels was unpleasant to a man of the plains.

As night fell, his brothers and generals gathered in the great ger to eat and discuss the problem. Genghis' mood had grown dark once more, but Arslan had known him from the beginning of his rise and did not fear to speak bluntly.

'With the sort of wooden shield we used against the fort, we could protect men long enough to hammer through the canal openings,' Arslan said, chewing. 'Though I do not like the look of those constructions on the walls. I would not have believed a bow could be so large. If they're real, they must fire arrows as long as a man. Who knows how much damage they can do?'

'We cannot stay out here for ever, while they send messages to their allies,' Kachiun murmured, 'and we cannot pass by and leave their army free to strike at our back. We must enter the city, or return to the desert and give up everything we have won.'

Genghis glanced at his younger brother, his expression sour.

'That will not happen,' he said with more confidence than he felt. 'We have their crops. How long can a city last before the people are eating each other? Time is on our side.'

'We are not hurting them yet, I think,' Kachiun replied. 'They have the canals to bring water and, for all we know, the city is stuffed with grain and salted meat.' He saw Genghis frown at the image, but continued. 'We could be here for years, waiting, and who knows how many armies are marching to support them? By the time they are starving, we could be facing the Chin themselves and be caught between them.'

'Then give me an answer!' Genghis snapped. 'The Uighur scholars tell me that every city in Chin lands is like this one, or even larger, if you can imagine it. If they have been built by men, they can be destroyed by men, I am certain of it. Tell me how.'

'We could poison the water in the canals,' Khasar said, reaching for another piece of meat with his knife. He speared it in sudden silence and looked round at the others.

'What? This is not our land.'

'That is an evil thing to say,' Kachiun chided his brother, speaking for all of them. 'What would we drink ourselves, then?'

Khasar shrugged. 'We would drink clean water from further up.'

Genghis listened, considering.

'We need to sting them into coming out,' he said. 'I will not see clean water poisoned, but we can break the canals and let the city go thirsty. Let them see the work of generations being destroyed and perhaps they will meet us on the plain.'

'I will see it done,' Jelme said.

Genghis nodded to him. 'And you, Khasar. You will send a hundred men to break through the bars where the canals enter the city.'

'Protecting them will mean more carts taken apart. The families will not like that at all,' Khasar said.

Genghis snorted.

'I will build more when we are in that cursed city. They will thank us then.'

All the men in the ger heard galloping hoofbeats coming closer. Genghis paused with a piece of greasy mutton in his fingers. He looked up as a clatter sounded on the steps outside and the door to the ger opened.

'They are coming out, lord.'

'In the darkness?' Genghis said incredulously.

'There is no moon, but I was close enough to hear them, lord. They chattered like birds and made more noise than children.'

Genghis tossed the meat down into the platter in the centre of the ger.

'Return to your men, my brothers. Make them ready.' His gaze flickered around the ger to Arslan and Jelme, the father and son sitting together.

'Arslan, you will keep five thousand to protect the families. The rest will ride with me.' He grinned at the prospect and they responded.

'Not years, Kachiun. Not one more *day*. Get the fastest scouts riding. I want to know what they are doing as soon as dawn comes. I will have orders for you then.'

* * *

So far south, the autumn was still hot, the uncut crops drooping under their own weight as they began to rot in the fields. The Mongol scouts shouted challenges to the red army that had marched from the safety of Yinchuan, while others rode back to Genghis with details. They entered the great ger in groups of three, passing on what they had learned.

Genghis strode back and forth, listening to each man as he described the scene.

'I do not like this business with the baskets,' he said to Kachiun. 'What could they be sowing on this ground?' He had heard of hundreds of men walking together in patterns before the host from Yinchuan. Each had carried a basket on his shoulders while a man behind him reached into it, over and over, casting his arms wide.

The khan of the Uighurs had been summoned to explain the mystery. Barchuk had questioned the scouts closely, demanding every scrap of information they could recall.

'It could be something to slow our horses, lord,' he said at last. 'Sharp stones, perhaps, or iron. They have sown a wide band of these seeds outside the army and they show no sign of crossing it. If they are intent on drawing us in, perhaps they expect the charge to founder.'

Genghis clapped him on the shoulder.

'Whatever it is, I will not let them choose the ground,' he said. 'You will have your scrolls yet, Barchuk.' He looked around him at the bright faces of his most trusted men. None of them could truly know the enemy they faced. The slaughter at the fort to enter Xi Xia lands bore little relation to the fighting formations of the king's own city. He could feel his heart beating quickly at the thought of finally standing against his people's enemies. Surely they would not fail, after so long in preparation? Kokchu said the stars themselves proclaimed a new destiny for his people. With the shaman attending him, Genghis had sacrificed a white

101

goat to the sky father, using the name in the most ancient shaman's tongue. Tängri would not refuse them. They had been weak for too long, made so by the Chin in their cities of gold. Now they were strong and he would see the cities fall.

The generals stood perfectly still as Kokchu reached into tiny pots and drew lines on their faces. When they looked at each other, they could not see the men they knew. They saw only the masks of war and eyes that were fierce and terrible.

The shaman left Genghis until last, dragging a red line from high on the khan's forehead, over the eyes and down on each side of his mouth.

'Iron will not touch you, lord. Stone will not break you. You are the Wolf and the sky father watches.'

Genghis stared without blinking, the blood somehow hot on his skin. At last, he nodded and left the ger, mounting his pony with the lines of warriors drawn up on either side. He could see the city in the distance and, before it, a blurry mass of red men waiting to see his ambitions humbled. He looked left and right along the line and raised his arm.

The drums started, carried by a hundred unarmed boys. Each one of them had fought his fellows for the right to ride with the warriors and many of them bore the marks of their struggle. Genghis felt his strength as he touched the hilt of his father's sword for luck. He dropped his arm and, as one, they thundered forward over the plain of the Xi Xia, towards the city of Yinchuan.

'They are coming, lord,' Rai Chiang's first minister said excitedly. The vantage point from the king's tower offered the best view of the plain from anywhere in the city and Rai Chiang had not objected to the presence of his councillors in his private chambers.

In their lacquered armour, the soldiers resembled a bright splash of blood on the ground before the city. Rai Chiang thought he could see the distant white-bearded figure of General Giam riding up and down the lines. Pikes gleamed in the morning sun as the regiments formed up and he could see his own royal guard held the wings. They were the best horsemen of the Xi Xia and he did not regret giving them to this task.

It had hurt him deeply to hide in the city while his lands were ravaged. Just the sight of an army facing the invader lifted his spirits. Giam was a solid thinker, a dependable man. It was true that he had not seen battle in his rise to power in the army, but Rai Chiang had reviewed his plans and found no fault with them. The king drank a pale white wine as he waited, relishing the thought of seeing his enemies destroyed before his eyes. News of the victory would reach Emperor Wei and he would know bitterness. If the Chin had reinforced them, Rai Chiang would have been in his debt for ever. Emperor Wei was subtle enough to know when he had given up an advantage in trade and power and the thought was intoxicating to Rai Chiang. He would see to it that the Chin were informed of every detail of the battle.

General Giam watched the dust cloud as the enemy advanced. The ground was drying out, he realised, with no farmers daring to water their crops. Those who had tried had been cut down by the scouts of the invader, apparently for sport or to blood the younger men. That would stop today, Giam thought.

His orders were relayed to the ranks on high poles, fluttering in the breeze for all to see. As he glanced up and down the lines, black crosses mingled with the red pennants, a symbol that meant they would hold the ground. Beyond the army, the fields were sown with a hundred thousand spikes of iron, hidden in the grass. Giam waited impatiently for the tribesmen to hit them. It would be carnage and then he would raise flags to attack in close formation, while the Mongols were still dazed.

The royal cavalry held the wings and he nodded to himself at the sight of their fine horses, snorting and pawing at the ground in excitement. The king's pike guards stood resolute in the centre of his army, splendid in their scarlet, like the scales of exotic fish. Their grim faces helped to steady the others as the dust cloud grew larger and they all felt the earth tremble under their feet. Giam saw one of the flag pikes dip and sent a man over to chastise the bearer. The army of Xi Xia was nervous, he could see it in their faces. When they saw the enemy line crumple, it would encourage them. Giam felt his bladder complain and swore softly under his breath, knowing he could not dismount with the enemy rushing towards them. In the ranks, he saw many of the men urinating onto the dusty ground, readying themselves.

He had to shout his orders over the swelling thunder of galloping horses. The guard officers were spread along the line and they repeated the command to stand and wait.

'Just a little longer,' he murmured. He could see individuals amongst the enemy and his stomach tightened at the sight of so many. He felt the gaze of the citizens on his back and he knew the king would be watching with every other man and woman who could find a place on the walls. Yinchuan depended on them for survival, but they would not be found lacking.

His second in command stood ready to relay Giam's orders.

'It will be a great victory, general,' he said. Giam could hear the strain in the man's voice and forced himself to turn away from the enemy.

'With the king's eye on us, the men must not lose heart. They know he watches?'

'I have made certain of it, general. They . . .' The man's eyes widened and Giam snapped his gaze back to the charging line hammering across the plain.

From the centre of it, a hundred galloping ponies moved forward, their riders forming a column like an arrow shaft. Giam watched without understanding as they approached the hidden line of spikes in the grass. He hesitated, unsure how the new formation affected his plans. He felt a line of sweat trickle from his hair and drew his sword to steady his hands.

'Nearly there . . .' he whispered. The horsemen were low on the backs of their ponies, their faces straining against the wind. Giam watched as they passed the line he had created and, for a terrifying instant, he thought they would somehow ride straight through the spikes. Then the first horse screamed, tumbling over itself in a great crash. Dozens more went down as the spikes pierced the soft part of their hooves and men were thrown to their death. The thin column faltered and Giam knew a moment of fierce joy. He saw the galloping line waver as the mass of following warriors yanked savagely on their reins. Almost all of those who had run full tilt into the spikes lay crippled or dead on the grass and a cheer went up from the red ranks.

Giam saw the pike flags were standing proud and he clenched his left fist in excitement. Let them come on foot and see what he had for them!

Beyond the screaming men and horses, the bulk of the enemy milled without formation, having lost all impetus in the death of their brothers. As Giam watched, the untrained tribesmen panicked. They had no tactics except for the wild charge and they had lost that. Without warning, hundreds turned away to race back through their own lines. The rout spread with extraordinary speed and Giam saw Mongol officers bawling conflicting orders at their fleeing men, striking at them with the flats of their swords as they passed. Behind him, the people of Yinchuan roared at the sight.

Giam jerked round in the saddle. His entire first rank took a half-step forward, straining like dogs on a leash. He could see the blood lust rising in them and knew it had to be controlled.

'Stand!' he bellowed. 'Officers, hold your men. The order is to stand!' They could not be held. Another step broke the last restraint and the yelling red ranks surged forward, their new armour shining. The air filled with dust. Only the king's guard held their positions and, even then, the cavalry on the wings were forced to come forward with the others or leave them vulnerable. Giam shouted again and again in desperation and his own officers raced up and down the lines, trying to hold the army back. It was impossible. They had seen the enemy riding in the shadow of the city for almost two months. Here at last was a chance to make them bleed. The militia screamed defiance as they reached the barrier of iron spikes. These were no danger to men and they passed through quickly, killing those warriors who still lived and stabbing the dead over and over until they were bloody rags on the grass.

Giam used his horse to block lines of men as best he could. In fury, he had the signal horns blow retreat, but the men were deaf and blind to everything except the enemy and the king who watched them. They could not be called back.

On horseback, Giam saw the sudden change in the tribes before any of his running men. Before his eyes, the wild rout vanished and perfect new Mongol lines formed, the discipline terrifying. The scarlet army of the Xi Xia had come half a mile past the traps and pits they had dug the night before and still raced onwards to bloody their swords and send these enemies away from their city. Without warning, they faced a confident army of horsemen on exposed ground. Genghis gave a single order and the entire force moved into a trot. The Mongol warriors pulled bows from shaped leather holders on the saddles, taking the first long arrows from the quivers on their hips or backs. They guided the ponies with their knees alone, riding with the arrows pointing down. At another barked order from Genghis, they brought their lines to a canter and then instantly to full gallop, the arrows coming up to their faces for the first volley.

Caught out in the open, fear swept through the massed red ranks. The Xi Xia lines compressed and some at the rear were still cheering ignorantly as the Mongol army swept back in. Giam roared desperate orders to increase the space between the ranks, but only the king's guard responded. As they faced a massed charge for the second time, the militia bunched even tighter, terrified and confused.

Twenty thousand buzzing arrows smashed the red lines to their knees. They could not return the volleys in the face of such destruction. Their own crossbowmen could only shoot blindly towards the enemy, hampered by the scramble of their own companions. The Mongols drew and shot ten times in every sixty heartbeats and their accuracy was crushing. The red armour saved some, but as they rose screaming, they were hit again and again until they stayed down. As the Mongols darted in for the close killing, Giam dug in his heels and raced across the face of the bloody lines to the king's pikemen, desperate to have them hold. Somehow, he came through unscathed.

The king's guards looked no different from the militia in their red armour. As Giam took command, he saw some of the militia rushing back through their ranks, chased down by screaming Mongol riders. The guards did not run and Giam gave a sharp order to raise pikes, passed on down the line. The tribesmen saw too late that these were not panicking like the others. Pike blades held up at an angle could cut a man in half as he charged and dozens of Mongol riders went down as they tried to gallop through. Giam felt hope rise in him that he could yet salvage the day.

The guard cavalry had moved out to defend the wings against the mobile enemy. As the militia was crushed, Giam was left with only the few thousand of the king's trained men and a few hundred stragglers. The Mongols seemed to delight in hitting the Xi Xia riders. Whenever the guard cavalry tried to charge, the tribesmen would spear in at high speed and pick men off with bows. The wildest of them engaged the guards with swords, looping in and out again like stinging insects. Though the cavalry kept their discipline, they had been trained to ride down infantry on the open field and could not respond to attacks from all directions. Caught away from the city, it was slaughter.

The pikemen survived the first charges against them, gutting the Mongol horses. When the king's cavalry were crushed and scattered, those who fought on foot were exposed. The pikemen could not turn to face the enemy easily and every time they tried, they were too slow. Giam bawled orders hopelessly, but the Mongols encircled them and cut them to pieces in a storm of arrows that still failed to claim him with them. Each man who died fell with a dozen shafts in him, or was cut from his saddle by a sword at full gallop. Pikes were broken and trampled in the press. Those who still survived tried to run to the shadow of the walls where archers could protect them. Almost all were ridden down.

The gates were shut. As Giam glanced back at the city, he found himself hot with shame. The king would be watching in horror. The army was shattered, ruined. Only a few battered, weary men had made it to the walls. Somehow, Giam had remained in the saddle, more aware than ever of his king's gaze. In misery, he raised his sword and cantered gently towards the Mongol lines until they spotted him.

Shaft after shaft broke against his red armour as he closed on them. Before he reached the line, a young warrior galloped out to meet him, his sword raised. Giam shouted once, but the warrior ducked under his blow, carving a great gash under the general's right arm. Giam swayed in the saddle, his horse slowing to a walk. He could hear the warrior circling back, but his arm hung on sinews and he could not raise his sword. Blood rushed across his thighs and he looked up for a moment, never feeling the blow that took his head and ended his shame.

Genghis rode triumphantly through the mounds of scarlet dead, their armour resembling the gleaming carcases of beetles. In his right hand, he held a long pike with the head of the Xi Xia general on top, the white beard twitching in the breeze. Blood ran down the shaft onto his hand and dried there, gumming his fingers together. Some of the army had escaped by running back through the spikes where his riders could not follow. Even then, he had sent warriors to lead their horses on foot. It had been a slow business and perhaps a thousand of the enemy in all had made it close enough to the city to be covered by archers. Genghis laughed at the sight of the bedraggled men standing in the shadow of Yinchuan. The gates remained closed and they could do nothing but stare in blank despair at his warriors as they rode among the dead, laughing and calling to each other.

Genghis dismounted as he reached the grass and rested the bloody pike against his horse's heaving flank. He bent down and picked up one of the spikes, examining it with curiosity. It was a simple thing of four nails joined together so one remained upright no matter how it fell. If he had been forced to take the defensive position, he thought he would have laid bands of them in widening circles around the army, but even then, the defenders had not been warriors as he knew them. His own men had better discipline, taught by a harder land than the peaceful valley of the Xi Xia.

As Genghis walked, he could see fragments of torn and broken armour on the ground. He examined a piece of it with interest, seeing how the red lacquer had chipped and flaked away at the edges. Some of the Xi Xia soldiers had fought well, but the Mongol bows took them even so. It was a good omen for the future and the final confirmation that he had brought them to the right place. The men knew it, as they looked on their khan in awe. He had brought them through the desert and given them enemies who fought poorly. It was a good day.

His gaze fell on ten men wearing deels marked in Uighur blue stitching as they walked amongst the dead. One of them carried a sack and he saw the others reach down to bodies and make a quick jerking motion with a knife.

'What are you doing?' he called to them. They stood proudly when they saw who addressed them.

'Barchuk of the Uighurs said you would want to know the numbers of the dead,' one of them replied. 'We are cutting ears to be tallied later on.'

Genghis blinked. Looking around, he saw that many of the bodies nearby had a red gash where an ear had been that morning. The sack bulged already.

'You may thank Barchuk on my behalf,' he began, then his voice trailed away. As the men shared nervous glances, Genghis took three strides through the corpses, sending flies buzzing into the air around him.

'There is a man here without any ears at all,' Genghis said. The Uighur warriors hurried over and, as they saw the earless soldier, the man with the sack began to curse his companions.

'You miserable offal! How can we keep a straight count if you cut off both ears?'

110

Genghis took one look at their faces and burst into laughter as he returned to his pony.

He was still chuckling as he took up the pike and tossed the cluster of black nails into the grass. He strolled towards the walls with his grisly trophy, judging where the archers of the Xi Xia could reach.

In full view of the city walls, he jammed the pike into the ground with all his weight, standing back from it as he stared upwards. As he had expected, thin arrows soared out towards him, but the range was too far and he did not flinch. Instead, he drew his father's sword and raised it towards them, while his army chanted and roared at his back.

Genghis' expression became grim once more. He had blooded the new nation. He had shown they could stand even against Chin soldiers. Yet, he still had no way to enter a city that mocked him with its strength. He rode slowly to where his brothers had gathered. Genghis nodded to them.

'Break the canals,' he said.

CHAPTER EIGHT

With every able-bodied man working with stones and iron hammers, it still took six days to reduce the canals around Yinchuan to rubble. At first, Genghis looked on the destruction with savage pleasure, hoping the mountain rivers might flood the city.

It disturbed him to see how the waters rose so quickly on the plain, until his warriors were ankle deep before they had finished destroying the last of the canals. The sultry days brought huge quantities of snow melt down from the mountain peaks and he had not truly considered where all the water might go once it wasn't channelled down towards the city and the crops.

Even gently sloping ground became sodden mud by noon of the third day and, though the crops were flooded, the waters continued to rise. Genghis could see the amusement on the faces of his generals as they realised the error. At first, the hunting was excellent as small animals escaping the flood could be seen splashing from far away. Hundreds of hares were shot and brought back to the camp in slick bundles of wet fur, but by then, the gers were in danger of being ruined. Genghis was forced to move the camp miles to the north before water flooded the entire plain.

By evening, they had reached a point above the broken

canal system where the ground was still firm. The city of Yinchuan was a dark spot in the distance and, in between, a new lake had sprung from nothing. It was no more than a foot deep, but it caught the setting sun and shone gold for miles.

Genghis was sitting on the steps leading up to his ger when his brother Khasar came by, his face carefully neutral. No one else had dared to say anything to the man who led them, but there were many strained faces in the camp that evening. The tribes loved a joke and flooding themselves off the plain appealed to their humour.

Khasar followed his brother's irritated gaze out onto the expanse of water.

'Well, that taught us a valuable lesson,' Khasar murmured. 'Shall I have the guards watch for enemy swimmers, creeping up on us?'

Genghis looked sourly at his brother. They could both see children of the tribes frolicking at the water's edge, black with stinking mud as they threw each other in. Jochi and Chagatai were in the centre of them as usual, delighted with the new feature of the Xi Xia plain.

'The water will sink into the ground,' Genghis replied, frowning.

Khasar shrugged.

'If we divert the waters, yes. I think it will be too soft for riders for some time after that. It occurs to me that breaking the canals may not have been the best plan we have come up with.'

Genghis turned to see his brother watching him with a wry expression and barked a laugh as he rose to his feet.

'We learn, brother. So much of this is new to us. Next time, we *don't* break the canals. Are you satisfied?'

'I am,' Khasar replied cheerfully. 'I was beginning to think my brother could not make an error. It has been an enjoyable day for me.'

'I am pleased for you,' Genghis said. Both of them watched as the boys on the water's edge began to fight again. Chagatai threw himself at his brother and they thrashed together in the muddy shallows, first one on top, then the other.

'We cannot be attacked from the desert and no army can reach us here with that new lake in the way. Let us feast tonight and celebrate our victory,' Genghis said.

Khasar nodded, grinning.

'Now that, my brother, is a fine idea.'

Rai Chiang gripped the arms of his gilded chair, staring out over the drowned plain. The city had warehouses of salted meat and grain, but with the crops rotting, there would be no more. He turned the problem over and over in his mind, despairingly. Though they did not yet know it, many in the city would starve to death. His remaining guards would be overwhelmed by the hungry mob when winter came and Yinchuan would be ruined from within.

As far as his eye could see, the waters stretched back to the mountains. Behind the city to the south, there were still fields and towns where neither the invaders nor the flood had yet reached, but they were not enough to feed the people of the Xi Xia. He thought of the militia in those places. If he stripped every last man from those towns, he could assemble another army, but he would lose the provinces to banditry as soon as the famine began to bite. It was infuriating, but he could not see a solution to his troubles.

He sighed to himself, causing his first minister to look up.

'My father told me always to keep the peasants fed,' Rai Chiang said aloud. 'I did not understand its importance at the time. What does it matter if a few starve each winter? Does it not show the displeasure of the gods?'

The first minister nodded solemnly.

'Without the example of suffering, Majesty, our people will not work. While they can see the results of laziness, they toil in the sun to feed themselves and their families. It is the way the gods have ordered the world and we cannot stand against their will.'

'But now, they will *all* go hungry,' Rai Chiang snapped, tired of the man's droning voice. 'Instead of a just example, a moral lesson, half our people will be clamouring for food and fighting in the streets.'

'Perhaps, Majesty,' the minister replied, unconcerned. 'Many will die, but the kingdom will remain. The crops will grow again and, next year, there will be an abundance for the mouths of the peasants. Those who survive the winter will grow fat and bless your name.'

Rai Chiang could not find the words to argue. He stared down from the tower of his palace at the throng in the streets. The lowest beggars had heard the news of the crops being left to spoil in the water from the mountains. They were not hungry yet, but they would be thinking of the cold months and already there were riots. His guard had been ruthless on his order, culling hundreds at the slightest sign of unrest. The people had learned to fear the king and yet, in his private thoughts, he feared them more.

'Can anything be saved?' he asked at last. Perhaps it was his imagination, but he thought he could smell the rich odour of dying vegetation on the breeze.

The first minister considered, looking through a list of events in the city as if he might find inspiration there.

'If the invaders left today, Majesty, we could no doubt salvage some of the hardier grains. We could sow rice in the waterlogged

115

fields and take one crop. The canals could be rebuilt, or we could direct the course of the water around the plain. Perhaps a tenth of the yield could be saved or replaced.'

'But the invaders will *not* leave,' Rai Chiang went on. He thumped his fist into the arm of the chair.

'They have beaten us. Lice-ridden, stinking tribesmen have cut right to the heart of the Xi Xia and I am meant to sit here and preside over the stench of rotting wheat.'

The first minister bowed his head at the tirade, frightened to speak. Two of his colleagues had been executed that very morning as the king's temper mounted. He did not want to join them.

The king rose and clasped his hands behind his back.

'I have no choices left. If I strip the south of the militia in every town, it will not equal the numbers who failed against them. How long would it be before those towns become strongholds for bandits without the king's soldiers to keep them quiet? I would lose the south as well as the north and then the city would fall.' He swore under his breath and the minister paled.

'I will not sit and wait for the peasants to riot, or this sickly smell of rot to fill every room in the city. Send out messengers to the leader of these people. Tell him I will grant him an audience that we may discuss his demands on my people.'

'Majesty, they are little better than savage dogs,' the minister spluttered. 'There can be no negotiation with them.'

Rai Chiang turned furious eyes on his servant.

'Send them out. I have not been able to destroy this army of savage dogs. All I have is the fact that he cannot take my city from me. Perhaps I can bribe him into leaving.'

The minister flushed with the shame of the task, but he bowed to the floor, pressing his head against the cool wood.

* * *

As evening came, the tribes were drunk and singing. The story-tellers had been busy with tales of the battle and how Genghis had drawn the enemy past their ring of iron. Comic poems had the children in fits of giggles and, before the light faded, there were many contests of wrestling and archery, the champions wearing a grass wreath on their heads until they drank themselves to insensibility.

Genghis and his generals presided over the celebration. Genghis blessed a dozen new marriages, giving weapons and ponies from his own herd to warriors who had distinguished themselves. The gers were packed with women captured from the towns, though not all the wives welcomed the newcomers. More than one fight between women had ended in bloodshed, each time with the sinewy Mongol women victorious over their husbands' captives. Before nightfall, Kachiun had been called to the site of three different killings as anger flared with the airag liquor in their veins. He had ordered two men and a woman to be tied to a post and beaten bloody. He did not care about those who had been killed, but he had no desire to see the tribes descend into an orgy of lust and violence. Perhaps because of his iron hand, the mood of the tribes remained light as the stars came out and, though some of them missed the plains of home, they looked upon their leaders with pride.

Beside the ger where Genghis met his generals was his family home, no larger or more ornate than any other raised by the families of the new nation. While he cheered the wrestling bouts, and torches were lit around the vast camp, his wife Borte sat with her four sons, crooning to them as they ate. With the coming of dusk, Jochi and Chagatai had made themselves difficult to find, preferring the noise and fun of the feast to sleep. Borte had been forced to send out three warriors to scour the gers for them and they had been brought back still struggling under their arms. Both boys sat glaring at one another in the little ger while Borte sang Ogedai and little Tolui to sleep. The day had been exhausting for them and it did not take long before both younger boys were dreaming in their blankets.

Borte turned to Jochi, frowning at the anger in his face.

'You have not eaten, little man,' she said to him. He sniffed without replying and Borte leaned closer to him.

'That cannot be airag I smell on your breath?' she demanded. Jochi's manner changed in an instant and he drew up his knees like a barrier.

'It would be,' Chagatai said, delighted at the chance to see his brother squirm. 'Some of the men gave him a drink and he was sick on the grass.'

'Keep your mouth still!' Jochi shouted, springing up. Borte grabbed him by the arm, her strength easily a match for the little boy's. Chagatai grinned, thoroughly satisfied.

'He is bitter because he broke his favourite bow this morning,' Jochi snapped, struggling in his mother's grasp. 'Let me go!'

In response, Borte slapped Jochi across the face and dropped him back onto the blankets. It was not a hard blow, but he raised his hand to his cheek in shock.

'I have heard your squabbling all day,' she said angrily. 'When will you realise you cannot fight like puppies with the tribes watching? Not you. Do you think it pleases your father? If I tell him, you will . . .'

'Don't tell him,' Jochi said quickly, fear showing on his face.

Borte relented immediately. 'I will not, if you behave and work. You will inherit nothing from him simply because you are his sons. Is Arslan his blood? Jelme? If you are fit to lead, he will choose you, but do not expect him to favour you over better men.'

Both boys were listening intently and she realised she had

not spoken to them in this way before. It surprised her to see how they hung on every word and she considered what else she might say before they were distracted.

'Eat your food while you listen,' she said. To her pleasure, both boys took the plates of meat and wolfed into them, though they had long gone cold. Their eyes never left hers as they waited for their mother to continue.

'I had thought your father might have explained this to you by now,' she murmured. 'If he were khan of a small tribe, perhaps his eldest would expect to inherit his sword, his horse and his bondsmen. He once expected the same from your grandfather, Yesugei, though his brother Bekter was oldest.'

'What happened to Bekter?' Jochi asked.

'Father and Kachiun killed him,' Chagatai said with relish. Borte winced as Jochi's eyes widened in surprise.

'Truly?'

His mother sighed.

'That is a story for another day. I don't know where Chagatai heard it, but he should know better than to listen to the gossip of the campfires.'

Chagatai nodded briskly at Jochi behind her back, grinning at his brother's discomfort. Borte shot him an irritable glance, catching him before he could freeze.

'Your father is not some small khan from the hills,' she said. 'He has more tribes than can be counted on the hands. Will you expect him to hand them over to a weakling?' She turned to Chagatai. 'Or a fool?' She shook her head. 'He will not. He has younger brothers and they will all have sons. The next khan may come from them, if he is dissatisfied with the men you become.'

Jochi lowered his head as he thought this through.

'I am better with a bow than anyone else,' he muttered. 'And my pony is only slow because he is so small. When I have a man's mount, I will be faster.'

Chagatai snorted.

'I am not talking about the skills of war,' Borte said, nettled. 'You will both be fine warriors, I have seen it in you.' Before they could begin to preen at the rare compliment, she went on.

'Your father will look to see if you can lead men and think quickly. Did you see the way he raised Tsubodai to command a hundred? The boy is unknown, of no blood line that matters, but your father respects his mind and his skill. He will be tested, but he could be a general when he has his full growth. He could command a thousand, even ten thousand warriors in war. Will you do the same?'

'Why not?' Chagatai said instantly.

Borte turned to him.

'When you are playing with your friends, are you the one the others look to? Do they follow your ideas or do you follow theirs? Think hard now, for there will be many who flatter you because of your father. Think of those *you* respect. Do they listen?'

Chagatai bit his lip as he thought. He shrugged.

'Some of them. They are children.'

'Why would they follow you when you spend your days fighting with your brother?' she said, pressing him.

The little boy looked resentful as he struggled with ideas too big for him. He raised his chin in defiance.

'They won't follow Jochi. He thinks they should, but they never will.'

Borte felt a coldness touch her chest at the words.

'Really, my son?' she said softly. 'Why would they not follow your older brother?'

Chagatai turned his head away and Borte reached out and gripped him painfully by his arm. He did not cry out, though tears showed at the corners of his eyes.

'Are there secrets between us, Chagatai?' Borte asked, her voice grating. 'Why would they never follow Jochi?'

'Because he is a Tartar bastard!' Chagatai shouted. This time, the slap that Borte landed on her son was not gentle. It knocked his head to one side and he sprawled on the bed, dazed. Blood trickled from his nose and he began to wail in shock.

Jochi spoke quietly behind her.

'He tells them that all the time,' he said. His voice was dark with fury and despair and Borte found tears in her own eyes at the pain he was suffering. Chagatai's crying had wakened her two youngest sons and they too began to sob, affected by the scene in the ger without understanding it.

Borte reached out to Jochi and enfolded him in her arms.

'You cannot wish it back into your brother's foolish mouth,' she murmured into his hair. She pulled back then to look into Jochi's eyes, wanting him to understand. 'Some words can be a cruel weight on a man, unless he learns to ignore them. You will have to be better than all the others to win your father's approval. You know it now.'

'Is it true then?' he whispered, looking away. He felt the stiffness in her back as she considered her answer and he began to sob gently himself.

'Your father and I begat you on a winter plain, hundreds of miles from the Tartars. It is true that I was lost to him for a time and he . . . killed the men who had taken me, but you are his son and mine. His first-born.'

'My eyes are different, though,' he said.

Borte snorted.

'So were Bekter's when they were young. He was a son of Yesugei, but his eyes were as dark as yours. No one ever *dared* to question his blood. Do not think of it, Jochi. You are a grandson of Yesugei and a son of Genghis. You will be a khan one day.'

As Chagatai snuffled and wiped blood onto his hand, Jochi grimaced, leaning back to look at his mother. Visibly, he summoned his courage, taking a deep breath before speaking. His voice quavered, humiliating him in front of his brothers.

'He killed his brother,' he said, 'and I have seen the way he looks at me. Does he love me at all?'

Borte pressed the little boy into her breast, her heart breaking for him.

'Of course he does. You will make him see you as his heir, my son. You will make him proud.'

CHAPTER NINE

It took five thousand warriors even longer to divert the canals with earth and rubble than it had to break them. Genghis had given the order when he saw the flood levels were threatening even the rising ground of the new camp. When the work was done, the water formed new lakes to the east and west, but at last the way to Yinchuan was drying in the sun. The ground was thick with greasy black plants and swarms of biting flies that irritated the tribes. Their ponies sank to the knees in sticky mud, making it hard to scout and adding to a feeling of confinement in the gers. There were many arguments and fights among the tribes each evening and Kachiun was hard pressed to keep the peace.

The news that eight riders were toiling across the sodden plain was welcomed by all those who had grown tired of their inactivity. They had not come through the desert to remain in one place. Even the children had lost interest in the floodwaters and many of them had become ill from drinking stagnant water.

Genghis watched the Xi Xia horsemen struggle through the mud. He had assembled five thousand of his warriors to face them on the dry ground, placing them right on the edge of the mud so that his enemy would have no place to rest. The Xi Xia horses were already blowing with the effort of pulling each leg from the clotted soil and the riders were hard pressed to keep their dignity as they risked a fall.

To Genghis' enormous pleasure, one of them did slip from the saddle when his mount lurched into a hole. The tribes hooted in derision as the man yanked savagely on his reins and remounted, soaked in filth. Genghis glanced at Barchuk at his side, noting the man's expression of satisfaction. He was there as an interpreter, but Kokchu and Temuge stood with them as well to hear what the king's messenger had to say. Both men had taken to their studies of the Chin language with what Genghis considered to be indecent enjoyment. The shaman and Genghis' younger brother were clearly excited at the chance to test their new-found knowledge.

The riders halted as Genghis raised a flat palm. They had come just close enough for him to hear their words and, though they seemed unarmed, he was not a trusting man. If he were in the position of the Xi Xia king, an attempt at assassination would certainly be something he considered at that time. At his back, the tribes watched in silence, their double-curved bows ready in their hands.

'Are you lost?' Genghis called to them. He watched as they glanced to one of their number, a soldier in fine armour that extended to a headpiece of iron scales. Genghis nodded to himself, knowing the man would speak for them all. He was not disappointed.

'I bear a message from the king of the Xi Xia,' the soldier replied. To the disappointment of Temuge and Kokchu, the words were perfectly clear in the language of the tribes.

Genghis looked questioningly at Barchuk and the Uighur khan spoke in a murmur, barely moving his lips.

'I have seen him before, at the trading days. He is an officer of some middle rank, very proud.'

'He looks it, in that fine armour,' Genghis replied, before raising his voice to address the soldiers.

'Dismount if you would talk to me,' Genghis called.

124

The riders exchanged resigned glances and Genghis masked his amusement as they stepped down into thick mud. They were held almost immobile by its grip and their expressions raised his spirits.

'What does your king have to say?' Genghis continued, staring at the officer. The man had flushed in anger as the mud ruined his fine boots and took a moment to master his emotions before replying.

'He bids you meet him in the shadow of the walls of Yinchuan, under truce. His honour will guarantee no attack while you are there.'

'What does he have to say to me?' Genghis said again, as if there had been no reply.

The man's flush deepened.

'If I knew his mind, there would be little point in such a meeting,' he snapped. Those with him glanced nervously at the host of Mongol warriors waiting with bows. They had seen the extraordinary accuracy of those weapons and their eyes pleaded with their spokesman not to give any offence that might lead to an attack.

Genghis smiled.

'What is your name, angry man?'

'Ho Sa. I am Hsiao-Wei of Yinchuan. You might call me a khan, perhaps, a senior officer.'

'I would not call you a khan,' Genghis replied. 'But you are welcome in my camp, Ho Sa. Send these goats home and I will welcome you in my ger and share tea and salt with you.'

Ho Sa turned to his companions and jerked his head back at the city in the distance. One of them spoke a string of meaningless syllables that made Kokchu and Temuge crane forward to hear. Ho Sa shrugged at his companion and Genghis watched as the other seven mounted and turned back to the city.

'Those are beautiful horses,' Barchuk said at his shoulder.

Genghis looked at the Uighur khan. He nodded, catching the eye of Arslan where he stood along the line of warriors. Genghis jerked two fingers at the retreating group, like a snake striking.

An instant later, a hundred shafts flashed through the air to take the seven riders neatly from their saddles. One of the horses was killed and Genghis heard Arslan barking at an unfortunate warrior for his incompetence. As Genghis watched, Arslan took the man's bow and cut the string with a jerk of his knife before handing it back to him. The warrior took it with his head bowed in humiliation.

Bodies lay still on the plain, face down in the mud. On such ground, the horses could not bolt easily. Without their riders to urge them on, they stood listlessly, looking back at the tribes. Two of them nuzzled the bodies of the men they had known, whickering nervously at the smell of blood.

Ho Sa stared in thin-lipped fury as Genghis turned to face him.

'They were good horses,' Genghis said. The soldier's expression did not change and the khan shrugged. 'Words are not heavy. It does not take more than one of you to carry my reply.'

He left Ho Sa to be taken to the great ger and given salt tea. Genghis remained behind to see the horses as they were captured and brought back.

'I will have first choice,' he said to Barchuk. The Uighur khan nodded, raising his eyes for a moment. First choice would give Genghis the best of them, but they were good mounts and still worth having.

Despite the late season, the sun was hot in the valley of the Xi Xia and the ground had been baked into a thin crust by the time Genghis rode towards the city. The king had requested he bring only three companions, but another five thousand rode with him for the first few miles. By the time he was close enough to make out details of the pavilion erected in front of the city, Genghis' curiosity had become overwhelming. What could the king want with him?

He left his escort behind with some reluctance, though he knew Khasar would ride to his aid if he signalled. He had considered the chances of a surprise attack on the king while they talked, but Rai Chiang was not a fool. The peach-coloured awning had been erected very close to the walls of the city. Huge bows armed with iron-tipped shafts as long as a man could destroy it in moments and ensure Genghis would not survive. The king was more vulnerable outside the walls, but the balance was delicate.

Genghis sat straight in the saddle as he rode ahead with Arslan, Kachiun and Barchuk of the Uighurs. They were well armed and carried extra blades hidden in their armour in case the king insisted on removing their swords.

Genghis tried to lighten his grim expression as he took in every detail of the peach awning. He liked the colour and wondered where he could find silk of that width and quality. He ground his teeth together at the thought of the untouched city in plain sight. If he had found a way in, he would not have come to meet the king of the Xi Xia. The thought nagged at him that every city in Chin lands was said to be as well protected and he had not yet discovered a way to counter the defence.

The four riders did not speak as they passed into the cool peach shade and dismounted. The awning hid them from view of the archers on the walls and Genghis found himself relaxing, standing in grim silence before the king's guards.

No doubt they had been chosen to impress, he thought, staring at them. Someone had given thought to the difficulties of the meeting. The entrance to the pavilion was wide so that he could see no assassins waited to catch him as he entered. The guards were powerfully built and they did not acknowledge the man who stood before them. Instead, they stared back like statues at the line of mounted warriors he had gathered in the far distance.

Though there were chairs within, the pavilion held only one man and Genghis nodded to him.

'Where is your king, Ho Sa? Is it too early in the morning for him?'

'He comes, my lord khan. A king does not arrive first.'

Genghis raised an eyebrow as he considered taking offence.

'Perhaps I should leave. I did not ask him to come to me, after all.'

Ho Sa flushed and Genghis smiled. The man was easy to irritate, but he had found he liked him, for all his prickly honour. Before he could respond, horns sounded on the walls of the city and the four Mongols reached for their swords. Ho Sa held up a hand.

'The king guarantees the peace, my lord khan. The horns are to let me know he is leaving the city.'

'Go out and watch him come,' Genghis said to Arslan. 'Tell me how many men ride with him.' He made an effort to relax his muscles where they had tightened. He had met khans before and he had killed them in their own gers. There was nothing new in this, he told himself, but still there was a touch of awe in him, an echo of Ho Sa's manner. Genghis smiled at his own foolishness, realising it was a part of being so far from home. Everything was new and different from the plains he remembered, but he would have chosen no other place to stand on that morning.

Arslan returned quickly.

'He comes in a litter carried by slaves. It looks much like the one Wen Chao used.'

'How many slaves?' Genghis replied, frowning. He would be outnumbered and his irritation showed on his face.

Ho Sa replied before Arslan.

'They are eunuchs, my lord. Eight men of strength, but not warriors. They are no more than beasts of burden and forbidden to carry weapons.'

Genghis considered. If he left before the king arrived, those in the city would believe his nerve had failed. Perhaps his own warriors would think the same. He held himself still. Ho Sa wore a long blade at his belt and the two guards were well armoured. He weighed the risks and then dismissed them. Sometimes, a man could worry too much about what might happen. He chuckled, making Ho Sa blink in surprise, then seated himself to wait for the king.

The bearer slaves held their precious burden at waist level as they approached the pavilion of silk. From inside, Genghis and his three companions watched with interest as they lowered the palanquin to the ground. Six of them stood in silence, while two unrolled a length of black silk across the mud. To Genghis' surprise, they drew wooden pipes from the sashes at their waist and began to play a subtle melody as the curtains were pulled open. It was strangely peaceful to hear the music over the breeze and Genghis found himself fascinated as Rai Chiang stepped out.

The king was a slightly built man, though he wore a set of armour perfectly fitted to his frame. The scales had been polished to a high sheen so that he gleamed in the sun. At his hip, he wore a sword with a jewelled hilt and Genghis wondered if he had ever drawn it in anger. The music swelled at his appearance and Genghis found he was enjoying the performance.

The king of the Xi Xia nodded to the two guards and they stepped away from the pavilion to take positions at his side.

Only then did he walk the few steps into the pavilion. Genghis and his companions rose to greet him.

'Lord khan,' Rai Chiang said, inclining his head. His accent was strange and he said the words as if he had memorised them without understanding.

'Majesty,' Genghis replied. He used the Xi Xia word that Barchuk had taught him. To his pleasure, he saw a glint of interest come into the king's eyes. For a fleeting moment, Genghis wished his father could have lived to see him meet kings in a foreign land.

The two guards took positions opposite Kachiun and Arslan, clearly marking their men in the event of trouble. For their part, the two generals stared back impassively. They were mere spectators at the meeting, but neither man would be taken by surprise. If the king planned their deaths, he would not survive the attempt.

Arslan frowned at a sudden thought. None of them had seen the king before. If this were an impostor, the army of Yinchuan could smash the pavilion flat from the walls and lose only a few loyal men. He stared at Ho Sa to see if he was unusually tense, but the man showed no sign of expecting imminent destruction.

Rai Chiang began to speak in the language of his people. His voice was firm, as might be expected of one so used to authority. He held Genghis' stare with his own and neither man seemed to blink. When the king had finished speaking, Ho Sa cleared his throat, his face carefully blank as he translated the king's words.

'Why do the Uighurs ravage the land of the Xi Xia? Have we not dealt fairly with you?'

Barchuk made a sound in his throat, but the king's gaze never left Genghis.

'I am khan of all the tribes, Majesty,' Genghis replied, 'the

Uighurs among them. We ride because we have the strength to rule. Why else?'

The king's brow furrowed as he listened to Ho Sa's translation. His reply was measured and betrayed no hint of his anger.

'Will you sit outside my city until the end of the world? It is not acceptable, lord khan. Do your people not bargain in war?'

Genghis leaned forward, his interest roused.

'I will not bargain with the Chin, Majesty. Your people are enemies as old as the land and I will see your cities broken into dust. Your lands are mine and I will ride the length and breadth of them as I please.'

Genghis waited patiently as Ho Sa rendered the words for his king. All the men in the tent could see the sudden animation that sparked into Rai Chiang as he heard them. He sat up straight and his voice became clipped. Genghis tensed warily, waiting for Ho Sa to speak. Instead, it was Barchuk who took up the translation.

'He says that his people are not of the Chin race,' Barchuk said. 'If *they* are your enemy, why do you delay here in the Xi Xia valley? Great Chin cities lie to the north and east.' Barchuk nodded to himself as the king spoke again.

'I think they are not the friends they once were, my lord khan. This king would not be displeased if you make war on the Chin cities.'

Genghis pursed his lips in thought.

'Why would I leave an enemy at my back?' he said.

Rai Chiang spoke again once he understood. Ho Sa had paled as he listened, but spoke before Barchuk could.

'Leave an ally, lord khan. If your true enemy is the Chin, we will send tribute to your tribes for as long as we are bound together as friends.' Ho Sa swallowed nervously. 'My king offers silk, falcons and precious stones, supplies and armour.'

He took a deep breath. 'Camels, horses, cloth, tea and a thousand coins of bronze and silver to be paid each year. He makes the offer to an ally, where he could not consider it to an enemy.'

Rai Chiang spoke again, impatiently, and Ho Sa listened. He grew very still as his king spoke and dared to ask a question. Rai Chiang made a sharp gesture with his hand and Ho Sa bowed his head, clearly disturbed.

'In addition, my king offers you his daughter, Chakahai, to be your wife.'

Genghis blinked, considering. He wondered if the girl was too ugly to marry off amongst the Xi Xia people. The bounty would please the tribes and keep the small khans from their plotting. The idea of tribute was not a new one for the tribes, though they had never been in a position to demand it from a truly wealthy enemy. He would have preferred to see the stone city smashed, but not one of his men could suggest a plan that might work. Genghis shrugged to himself. If he ever found out how, he could come back. Until then, let them believe they had bought peace. Goats could be milked many times but killed only once. All that remained was to get the best bargain he could.

'Tell your master his generosity is well received,' he said wryly. 'If he can add two thousand of his best soldiers, well armed and mounted, I will leave this valley before the moon turns. My men will dismantle the fort across the desert pass. Allies need no walls between them.'

As Ho Sa began to translate, Genghis remembered Barchuk's interest in the libraries of the Xi Xia. Ho Sa paused to hear as Genghis spoke again, interrupting the flow of his words.

'Some of my men are scholars,' Genghis said. 'They would enjoy the chance to read scrolls of the Xi Xia writing.' As Ho Sa opened his mouth, he went on. 'But not philosophy. Practical matters, subjects that would interest a warrior, if you have them.'

Rai Chiang's expression was unreadable as Ho Sa struggled to repeat everything he had heard. The meeting seemed to be at an end and Rai Chiang made no counter-offer. In that, Genghis saw his desperation. He was about to rise when he decided to push his luck.

'If I am to enter the cities of the Chin, I will need weapons that will break walls. Ask your king if he can supply those with all the rest.'

Ho Sa spoke nervously, sensing Rai Chiang's anger as he understood. Reluctantly, he shook his head.

'My king says he would have to be a fool,' Ho Sa said, unable to look Genghis in the eye.

'Yes, he would have been,' Genghis replied with a smile. 'The ground has dried and you can load up the gifts on new carts, with axles well greased for a long trip. You may tell your king that I am pleased by his offer. I will show that pleasure to the Chin.'

Ho Sa translated and Rai Chiang's face showed no sign of his satisfaction. All the men rose together and Genghis and his companions departed first, leaving Rai Chiang and Ho Sa alone with the guards. They watched the Mongol generals mount and ride away.

Ho Sa considered keeping silent, but he had one more question he had to ask.

'Majesty, have we not brought war to the Chin?'

Rai Chiang turned a cold gaze on his officer.

'Yenking is a thousand miles away and guarded by mountains and fortresses that make Yinchuan look like a provincial town. He will not take their cities.' The king's mouth quirked slightly, though his expression was stony. 'Besides, "It is to our advantage when our enemies attack one another. Wherein lies the danger to us?"'

Ho Sa had not been present for the meeting of ministers and did not recognise the words.

The mood among the tribes was almost that of a festival. It was true they had not taken the stone city that sat in the distance, but if the warriors grumbled at that, their families were thrilled with the silk and spoils that Genghis had won for them. A month had passed since the meeting with the king, and the carts had come from the city. Young camels snorted and spat among the herds of sheep and goats. Barchuk had disappeared into his ger with Kokchu and Temuge to decipher the strange writing of the Xi Xia people. Rai Chiang had provided scrolls with the Chin script under their own, but it was a laborious business.

Winter had come at last, though it was mild in that valley. Khasar and Kachiun had begun to drill the warriors Rai Chiang had given to them. The Xi Xia soldiers had protested the loss of their fine mounts, but those animals were far too good to waste on men who could not ride as well as Mongol children. Instead, they were given spare ponies from the herds. As the weeks fled and the air turned colder, they learned how to handle the bad-tempered, hardy beasts in a line of war. The army readied itself to move, but Genghis fretted in his ger as he waited for Rai Chiang to send out the last of the tribute and his daughter. He was not able to predict how Borte would receive the news. He hoped this Xi Xia princess would be attractive, at least.

She came on the first day of a new moon, borne in a litter very similar to the one her father had used for the meeting. Genghis watched as the honour guard of a hundred men kept close formation around her. He was amused to see that the mounts were not of the high quality he had come to expect.

Rai Chiang did not intend to lose these ones as well, even to escort a daughter.

The litter was placed on the ground just a few paces from Genghis as he waited in full armour. His father's sword was on his hip and he touched it for luck, mastering his impatience. He could see the soldiers of the city were angry at having to give her up and he smiled with genuine pleasure at them, drinking in their frustration. As he had requested, Ho Sa had come out of the city with them. He, at least, wore a cold expression of which Genghis could approve, showing nothing of his inner feelings.

When the daughter of the king stepped out onto the ground, there was a murmur of appreciation from the warriors who had gathered to witness this last sign of their triumph. She was dressed in white silk embroidered with gold, so that she shone in the sun. Her hair was bound high on her head with pins of silver and Genghis took in a breath at the flawless beauty of her white skin. In comparison to the women of his people, she was a dove amongst crows, though he did not say it aloud. Her eyes were dark pools of despair as she walked to him. She did not look at him, but instead lowered herself elegantly to the ground with her wrists crossed in front of her.

Genghis felt the anger in her father's soldiers swell, but he ignored them. If they moved, his archers would kill them before they could draw a blade.

'You are welcome in my ger, Chakahai,' he said softly. Ho Sa murmured a translation, his voice almost a whisper. Genghis reached down to touch her shoulder and she rose, her face carefully blank. She had none of the wiry strength he had come to expect from his women and he felt himself becoming aroused as a faint trace of her perfume reached his nostrils.

'I think you are worth more than all the rest of your father's gifts,' he said, giving her honour in front of his warriors, though she could not understand the words. Ho Sa began to speak, but Genghis silenced him with a sharp gesture.

He reached out with a sun-darkened hand, marvelling at the contrast as he raised her chin so that she had to look at him. He could see her fear and also a flash of disgust as she felt his rough skin touch hers.

'I have made a good bargain, girl. You will bear fine children for me,' he said. It was true that they could not be his heirs, but he found himself intoxicated with her. He could hardly keep her in the same ger as Borte and his sons, he realised. So fragile a girl would not survive. He would have another ger built for her alone and the children she would have.

He became aware he had been standing in silence for a long time and the tribes were watching his reaction with growing interest. More than a few grinning warriors nudged each other and whispered to their friends. Genghis raised his gaze to the officer standing with Ho Sa. Both men were pale with anger, but when Genghis gestured back to the city, Ho Sa turned as sharply as the others. The officer snapped an order at him and Ho Sa's mouth fell open in surprise.

'You I need, Ho Sa,' Genghis told him, delighted with his astonishment. 'Your king has given you to me for a year.'

Ho Sa drew his mouth into a thin line as he understood. With bitter eyes, he watched the rest of the escort riding back to the city, leaving him there with the shivering girl he had come to give away to wolves.

Genghis turned to face the wind from the east, breathing in the scent of it and imagining the cities of the Chin over the horizon. They had walls he could not break and he would not risk his people again in ignorance.

'Why did you ask for me?' Ho Sa said suddenly, the words wrenched out of him in the silence that Genghis seemed not to feel.

'Perhaps we will make a warrior of you.' Genghis seemed to find the idea amusing and slapped his leg. Ho Sa looked stonily at him until Genghis shrugged.

'You will see.'

The camp was noisy with the sound of the gers being dismantled as the tribes made ready to move. As midnight came, only the khan's ger stood untouched on its great cart, lit from within by oil lamps so that it glowed in the darkness and could be seen by all those who settled down in their rugs and furs to sleep under the stars.

Genghis stood over a low table, squinting down at a map. It had been drawn on thick paper and Ho Sa at least could see that it had been copied in haste from Rai Chiang's collection. The king of the Xi Xia was too canny a man to let a map marked with his seal fall into the hands of Emperor Wei of the Chin. Even the lettering was in the Chin language, carefully redone.

Genghis tilted his head one way and then the other as he tried to imagine the lines and drawings of cities as actual places. It was the first real map he had ever seen, though with Ho Sa present, he would not reveal his inexperience.

With a dark finger, Genghis traced along a blue line towards the north.

'This is the great river the scouts reported,' he said. He raised his pale eyes to Ho Sa, questioningly.

'Huang He,' Ho Sa replied. 'The Yellow River.' He stopped himself then, unwilling to become garrulous in the company of the Mongol generals. They filled the ger: Arslan, Khasar, Kachiun, others he did not know. Ho Sa had recoiled from Kokchu when Genghis had introduced him. The skinny shaman reminded him of the insane beggars of Yinchuan and he carried

137

a smell with him that seeped into the air until Ho Sa was forced to breathe shallowly.

All those present watched as Genghis drew his finger further north and east along the river until it rested on a tiny symbol and tapped.

'This city here is on the edge of Chin lands,' Genghis murmured. Once more he looked to Ho Sa for confirmation and he nodded reluctantly.

'Baotou,' Kokchu said, reading the script under the tiny drawing. Ho Sa did not look at the shaman, his gaze held by Genghis as the khan smiled.

'These marks to the north, what are they?' Genghis asked.

'It is a section of the outer wall,' Ho Sa replied.

Genghis frowned, puzzled.

'I have heard of this thing. The Chin hide from us behind it, do they not?'

Ho Sa repressed his irritation.

'They do not. Neither wall was built for you, but to keep separate the kingdoms of the Chin. You have passed through the weaker of the two. You will not pass the inner wall around Yenking. No one ever has.' Genghis grinned at that, before turning back to study the map. Ho Sa stared at him, irritated by the khan's easy confidence.

When he was a boy, Ho Sa had travelled with his father to the Yellow River. The old man had shown him the Chin wall to the north and, even back then, there had been holes in it and sections reduced to rubble. There had been no work done in the decades since. As Genghis traced a line with his finger on the parchment, Ho Sa wondered how the Chin had ever become so careless with their peace. Their outer wall was worthless. He swallowed nervously. Especially as the tribes were already behind it. Xi Xia had been the weak point and the tribes had poured south. Shame burned in him as he studied Genghis, wondering what he was planning.

'Will you attack Baotou?' Ho Sa blurted out without warning.

Genghis shook his head.

'And howl outside the gates as I did here? No. I am going home to the Khenti Mountains. I will ride the hills of my childhood, fly my eagle and marry your king's daughter.' His fierce expression eased at the thought. 'My sons should know the land that birthed me and they will grow strong there.'

Ho Sa looked up from the map in confusion.

'Then what is this talk of Baotou? Why am I here?'

'I said *I* was going home, Ho Sa. *You* are not. This city is too far from here to fear my army. They will have their gates open and merchants will come and go as they please.' Ho Sa saw Arslan and Khasar were grinning at him and he forced himself to concentrate.

Genghis clapped him on the shoulder.

'A walled city like Baotou will have builders, masters of their trade, will it not? Men who understand every aspect of the defences.'

Ho Sa did not reply and Genghis chuckled.

'Your king would not give them to me, but you will find them there, Ho Sa. You will travel to this Baotou with Khasar and my brother Temuge. Three men can enter where an army cannot. You will ask questions until you find these men who build walls and know so many clever things. And you will bring them to me.'

Ho Sa saw they were all smiling then, amused at his appalled expression.

'Or I will kill you now and ask for another from your king,' Genghis said softly. 'A man must always have the final choice in life and in death. Anything else can be taken from him, but never that.'

Ho Sa remembered how his companions had been killed for the horses they rode and he did not doubt his life hung on a single word.

'I am bound to you by my king's order,' he said at last.

Genghis grunted, turning back to the map.

'Then tell me of Baotou and its walls. Tell me everything you have heard or seen.'

The camp was quiet at dawn, but the light still flickered gold in the ger of the khan and those who lay close on the cold grass could hear the murmur of voices like the distant drums of war.

CHAPTER TEN

The three riders approached the edge of the dark river, dismounting as their ponies began to drink. A heavy moon hung low above the hills, casting a grey light that illuminated the expanse of water. It was bright enough to create black shadows behind the men as they gazed out at the shapes of small boats at anchor, rocking and creaking in the night.

Khasar pulled a linen bag from where it sat under his saddle. The day's ride had softened the meat inside and he dipped his hand into the fibrous mush, pulling a piece of it out and putting it in his mouth. It smelled rancid, but he was hungry and chewed idly as he watched his companions. Temuge was weary enough to sway slightly as he stood by his brother, his eyes hooded as he longed for sleep.

'The boatmen stay well away from the shore at night,' Ho Sa murmured. 'They are wary of bandits in the dark and they will have heard of your army to the west. We should find a place to sleep and go on in the morning.'

'I still don't understand why you want to use the river to reach Baotou,' Khasar said. Ho Sa swallowed his anger. He had explained half a dozen times since leaving the tribes, but the Mongol warrior's attachment to his pony was proving difficult to overcome.

'We were told not to call attention to ourselves, to enter

Baotou like merchants or pilgrims,' he replied, keeping his voice calm. 'Merchants do not ride in like Chin nobility and pilgrims would not have a horse between them.'

'It would be faster though,' Khasar said stubbornly. 'If the map I saw was accurate, we could cut across the bow of the river and be there in just a few days.'

'And have our passing noted by every peasant in the fields and every traveller on the roads,' Ho Sa snapped. He sensed Khasar stiffen angrily at his tone, but he had endured his complaining long enough. 'I do not think your brother welcomes the thought of riding a thousand *li* across open land.'

Khasar snorted, but it was Temuge who replied.

'He has the right of it, brother. This great river will take us north to Baotou and we will be lost in the mass of travellers. I do not want us to fight our way through suspicious Chin soldiers.'

Khasar did not trust himself to reply. At first, he had been excited at the thought of stealing among the Chin peoples, but Temuge rode like an old woman with stiff joints and was no fit companion for a warrior. Ho Sa was a little better, but away from Genghis, his fury at the task he had been given made him a surly companion. It was worse when Temuge had Ho Sa chattering in the language of bird-clucking and Khasar could not join in. He had asked Ho Sa to teach him curses and insults, but the man had only glared at him. Far from being an adventure, the journey was turning into a bickering contest and he wanted it over as soon as possible. The thought of drifting slowly up on one of the shadowy boats made his mood sink even further.

'We could swim the horses across the river tonight, then . . .' he began.

Ho Sa hissed out a sharp breath.

'You would be swept away!' he snapped. 'This is the Yellow

River, a full *li* from one bank to the next and this a narrow point. It is not one of your Mongol streams. There are no ferries here and by the time we reached Shizuishan to buy a place on one, our progress would have been reported. The Chin are not fools, Khasar. They will have spies watching the borders. Three men on horses will be too interesting for them to ignore.'

Khasar sniffed as he worked another piece of old mutton into his cheek and sucked on it.

'The river is not so wide,' he said. 'I could send an arrow over it.'

'You could not,' Ho Sa replied immediately. He clenched his fists as Khasar reached for his bow. 'And we would not see it land in the dark.'

'Then I will show you in the morning,' Khasar retorted.

'And how will that help us?' Ho Sa demanded. 'Do you think the boatmen will ignore a Mongol archer firing arrows over their river? Why *did* your brother send you for this work?'

Khasar let his hand fall from where he had grasped his bow. He turned to Ho Sa in the moonlight. In truth, he had wondered the same thing, but he would never admit it to Ho Sa or his studious brother.

'To protect Temuge, I imagine,' he said. 'He is here to learn the Chin language and check you are not betraying us when we reach the city. You are only here to talk and you have proved that enough times today already. If we are attacked by Chin soldiers, my bow will be more valuable than your mouth.'

Ho Sa sighed. He had not wanted to broach the subject, but his own temper was barely in check and he too was weary.

'You will have to leave your bow here. You can bury it in the river mud before dawn.'

Khasar was rendered speechless at that. Before he could express his indignation, Temuge laid a calming hand on his shoulder, feeling him jerk.

'He knows these people, brother, and he has kept faith with us so far. We must take the river, and your bow would raise suspicions from the start. We have bronze and silver to buy goods along the way so that we have something to trade in Baotou. Merchants would not carry a Mongol bow.'

'We could pretend to be selling it,' Khasar replied. In the gloom, he rested his hand on the weapon where it was tied to his saddle as if that touch brought him comfort. 'I will turn my pony loose, yes, but I will not give up my bow, not for a dozen secret river trips. Do not test me on this, my answer will be the same no matter what you say.'

Ho Sa began to argue again, but Temuge shook his head, tired of them both.

'Let it rest, Ho Sa,' he said. 'We will wrap the bow in cloth and perhaps it will not be noticed.' He dropped his hand from Khasar's shoulder and moved away to free his pony from the burdens of saddle and reins. It would take time to bury those and he could not risk falling asleep until the work had been done. He wondered again why Genghis had chosen him for the task of accompanying the two warriors. There were others in the camp who knew the Chin tongue, Barchuk of the Uighurs among them. Perhaps that one was too old, Temuge thought. He sighed as he undid the ropes on his mount. Knowing his brother as he did, Temuge suspected Genghis still hoped to make a warrior of him. Kokchu had shown him a different path and he wished his master were there to help him meditate before sleep.

As he led the pony away into the darkness of the river trees, Temuge could hear his companions resume their argument in fierce whispers. He wondered if they had a chance of surviving the trip to the city of Baotou. When he had buried the saddle and lain down, he tried hard to shut out the strained voices, repeating the phrases Kokchu had told him would bring calm. They did not, but sleep came while he was still waiting.

In the morning, Ho Sa raised his arm to another boat as it tacked against the wind to come upriver. Nine times the gesture had been ignored, though he held a leather purse of coins and jingled the contents. All three breathed in relief as the latest boat swung across the water towards them. On board, six sun-darkened faces stared suspiciously in their direction.

'Say nothing to them,' Ho Sa murmured to Temuge as they stood in the mud and waited for the boat to come closer. He and the two brothers wore simple robes tied at the waist that would not look too strange to the river crews. Khasar bore a roll of saddlecloth over one shoulder that contained his bow in its leather half-case and a full quiver. He stared at the boat in some interest, never having seen such a thing in daylight. The sail was almost as high as the boat was long, perhaps forty feet from end to end. He could not see how it could come close enough for them to step onto its small deck.

'The sail looks like a bird-wing. I can see the bones of it,' he said.

Ho Sa turned sharply towards him.

'If they ask, I will say you are a mute, Khasar. You must not speak to any one of them. Do you understand?'

Khasar scowled at the Xi Xia soldier.

'I understand that you want me to spend days without opening my mouth. I tell you, when this is over, you and I are going to go somewhere quiet . . .'

'Hush!' Temuge said. 'They are close enough to hear.' Khasar subsided, though he held Ho Sa's gaze long enough to nod ominously at him.

The boat manoeuvred close to the bank and Ho Sa did not

wait for his companions, stepping into the shallow water and wading out to it. He ignored Khasar's muttered curse behind him as strong hands drew him over the side.

The master of the boat was a short, wiry man with a red cloth tied around his head to keep the sweat from his eyes. Apart from that, he was naked except for a brown loincloth, with two knives slapping against his bare thigh. Ho Sa wondered for an instant if they had been taken in by one of the pirate crews said to raid villages along the river, but it was too late for misgivings.

'Can you pay?' the master demanded, reaching out to slap Ho Sa on the chest with the back of his hand. As Khasar and Temuge were dragged on board, Ho Sa pressed three warm bronze coins into the outstretched palm. The little man peered through the hole in the centre of each one, before stringing them on a cord under his belt.

'I am Chen Yi,' he said, staring as Khasar straightened. The Mongol was a head taller than the largest crewman and frowned around him as if affronted. Ho Sa cleared his throat and Chen Yi glanced at him, cocking his head to one side.

'We are going as far as Shizuishan,' Chen Yi said. Ho Sa shook his head and reached for more coins. Chen Yi watched closely as he heard the sound of metal.

'Three more to take us to Baotou,' Ho Sa said, holding them out.

The captain took the coins quickly, adding them to the line at his waist with practised skill.

'Three more to go so far upriver,' he said.

Ho Sa struggled to master his temper. He had already paid more than enough for a passage to the city. He doubted the man would return the money if he decided to wait for another boat.

'You have had enough,' he said firmly.

Chen Yi's eyes dropped to where Ho Sa kept his money under his belt and he shrugged.

'Three more or I have you thrown back,' he said.

Ho Sa stood very still and sensed Khasar's irritable confusion as the conversation went on. At any moment, he would blurt out some question, Ho Sa was certain.

'Where will you find yourself next on the wheel of life, I wonder?' Ho Sa murmured. To his surprise, Chen Yi seemed unconcerned and only shrugged. Ho Sa shook his head in bewilderment. Perhaps he was too used to the army, where his authority was never challenged. There was an air of confidence about Chen Yi that sat oddly with his rags and the grubby little boat. Ho Sa glared as he handed over more coins.

'Beggars do not go to Baotou,' Chen Yi said cheerfully. 'Now stay out of the way of my men while we work the river.' He indicated a pile of grain sacks in the stern of the little boat by the rudder and Ho Sa saw Khasar settling himself on them before he could nod.

Chen Yi cast a suspicious glance at Temuge and Khasar, but he had new coins on his cord that jingled as he moved. He gave orders to turn the sail across the wind, making the first cut across the river that would take them north to their destination. The boat was cramped with so many and there were no cabins. Ho Sa guessed the crew lay down on the deck at night. He began to relax just as Khasar stepped up to the rail and urinated into the river with a great sigh of relief. Ho Sa raised his eyes to heaven as the sound of spattering water went on and on.

Two of the crew pointed at Khasar and made an obscene joke, slapping each other on the back with hoots of laughter. Khasar flushed and Ho Sa moved swiftly to stand between the warrior and the crew, warning him with a glare. The sailors watched the exchange with wide grins before Chen Yi barked an order and they scurried to the prow to heave the sail over.

'Yellow dogs,' Khasar said after them. Chen Yi had been in the middle of guiding the sail over his head when he heard the words. Ho Sa's heart sank as the master of the boat came strolling back to them.

'What was that he said?' Chen Yi asked.

Ho Sa spoke quickly. 'He is a Moslem. He does not speak a civilised tongue. Who can understand the ways of such a people?'

'He does not look like a Moslem,' Chen Yi replied. 'Where is his beard?' Ho Sa sensed the eyes of the crew on them and this time each man rested a hand near his knife.

'All merchants have secrets,' Ho Sa said, holding Chen Yi's stare. 'Do I care for a man's beard when I have his wealth to trade? Silver speaks its own language, does it not?'

Chen Yi grinned. He held out a hand and Ho Sa pressed a silver coin into it, his face showing nothing.

'It does,' Chen Yi said, wondering how many more coins the warrior carried in his pouches. Whatever the three men claimed to be, they were not merchants. Chen Yi indicated Khasar with a jerk of a grimy thumb.

'Is he a fool then to trust you? Will you be throwing him over the side one night with a dagger across his throat?' To Ho Sa's discomfort, the little man drew his finger over his own throat, a gesture that Khasar watched with growing interest. Temuge too was frowning and Ho Sa wondered how much he had understood of the fast exchange.

'I betray no man, once I have given my word,' Ho Sa told the master quickly, as much for Temuge as anyone else. 'And though he is certainly a fool, he is a fighter of great skill. Be careful not to insult him, or I will not be able to hold him back.'

Chen Yi cocked his head again, a habitual gesture. He did

not trust the men he had taken on board and the tall, stupid one seemed to burn with anger. He shrugged at last. All men slept and, if they caused him trouble, they would not be the first passengers he had slipped into the wake of his little boat. He turned his back on them after pointing to the pile of sacks. Relieved beyond words, Ho Sa joined the other two in the stern. He tried hard to look as if the incident had not been a strain.

Khasar did not look at all apologetic.

'What did you tell him?' he asked.

Ho Sa took a deep breath.

'I told him you are a traveller from thousands of miles away. I thought perhaps he would never have heard of the followers of Islam, but he has met at least one in the past. He thinks I am lying, but he will not ask too many questions. Still, it explains why you cannot speak the Chin language.'

Khasar let out a breath, satisfied.

'So I am not a mute then,' he said, pleased. 'I did not think I could keep that up.' He settled himself back on the sacks, nudging Temuge out of the way to find a comfortable position. As the boat drifted upriver, Khasar closed his eyes and Ho Sa thought he had gone to sleep.

'Why did he draw his finger across his throat?' Khasar said without opening his eyes.

'He wanted to know if I intended to kill you and throw you overboard,' Ho Sa snapped. 'The idea had occurred to me.'

Khasar chuckled.

'I am beginning to like that little man,' he said drowsily. 'I am glad we took a boat.'

Genghis walked through the vast camp in the shadow of mountains he had known as a boy. Snow had fallen in the night and he took a deep breath of the chilled air, enjoying the way it filled his lungs. He could hear the whinnying of mares calling to their mates and, in the distance, someone was singing a child to sleep. With the families around him, he was at peace and his mood was light. It was easy to remember the days when his father still lived and he and his brothers knew nothing of the world around them. He shook his head in the gloom as he considered the lands that had been shown to him. The sea of grass was larger than he had ever realised and part of him hungered to see new things, even the cities of the Chin. He was young and strong and ruled a vast army of men with the skills to take what they wanted. He smiled to himself as he reached the ger he had built for his second wife, Chakahai. His father had been content with his mother, it was true, but Yesugei had been khan of a small tribe and had not had beautiful women offered to him in tribute.

Genghis ducked his head as he entered. Chakahai was waiting for him and her eyes were wide and dark in the glow from a single lamp. Genghis said nothing as she rose to greet him. He did not know how she had procured two young girls from her own people to serve her. Presumably they had been captured by his warriors and she had bought or bargained for them. As they slipped out of the ger, Genghis could smell the perfume they wore and he shuddered slightly as one of them brushed silk past his bare arms. He heard their whispering voices dwindle into the distance and he was alone.

Chakahai stood proudly before him, her head raised. The first weeks with the tribes had been hard for her, but he sensed a fine spirit in her flashing eyes long before she had learned the first words of his people. She walked as he would have expected a king's daughter to walk and the sight of her always aroused him. It was a strange thing, but her perfect posture was the greatest part of her beauty.

She smiled as his gaze travelled over her, knowing she had

his full attention. Choosing her moment, she knelt before him, bowing her head and then glancing up to see if he still watched the display of humility. He laughed at that and took a wrist to raise her up once more, lifting her into the air to lay her down on the bed.

He held her head in both hands as he kissed her then, his fingers lost in her black hair. She moaned into his mouth and he felt her hands lightly touching his thighs and waist, exciting him. The night was warm and he did not mind waiting while she opened up her silk tunic and revealed whiteness down to a flat belly and the silk belt and trousers she wore like a man. She gasped as he kissed her breasts and bit softly. The rest of the clothes followed swiftly after that and the camp drowsed around them as he took a princess of the Xi Xia, her cries echoing far in the gloom.

CHAPTER ELEVEN

It took a week for Chen Yi's boat to reach Shizuishan on the western bank of the river. The days were grey and cold and the silt-laden water darkened until it deserved its name, curling creamily under the prow. For a time, a family of dolphins had stayed with them before Khasar struck one with an oar in his excitement and they vanished as quickly as they had come. Ho Sa had formed his own opinions of the little boat master and he suspected the hold was stuffed with untaxed goods, perhaps even luxuries that would fetch high prices for the owner. He had no opportunity to test his suspicions, as the crew never seemed to tire of watching the passengers. It was likely that they were in the employ of a wealthy merchant and should not have risked the cargo by taking passengers. Ho Sa judged Chen Yi was an experienced man who seemed to know the river far better than the emperor's tax collectors. More than once they had taken a tributary off the main route, looping far around before returning to it. On the last of these occasions, Ho Sa had seen the dim shadow of an official barge in mid-stream behind them. The tactic suited his needs and he did not comment on the loss of time, though he slept with his knife in his sleeve and then only lightly, waking at the slightest sound.

Khasar snored at astonishing volume. To Ho Sa's irritation,

the crew seemed to like him and had already taught him phrases that would have little use outside a dockyard whorehouse. He swallowed his anger as Khasar arm-wrestled three of the burlier sailors, winning a skin of fiery rice wine which he then refused to share.

Of the three of them, it was Temuge who seemed to take no pleasure at all from the peaceful journey. Though the river was rarely choppy, he had vomited over the side on the second morning, earning hoots of derision from the crew. Mosquitoes found him at night so that he had a new crop of red bites on his ankles each morning. He watched Khasar's cheerful camaraderie with a tight expression of disapproval, but made no attempt to join in, despite his greater command of the language. Ho Sa could only wish the journey was at an end, but Shizuishan was merely a stopping point to replenish their supplies.

Long before the city came into view, the river grew crowded with small boats crossing from bank to bank and carrying with them the gossip and news of a thousand miles. Chen Yi did not seek anyone out, but as he tied up at a wooden post near the docks, boat after boat came close to exchange words with him. Ho Sa realised the little man was well known on the river. More than a few questions were called about the passengers and Ho Sa endured their stares. No doubt their descriptions would race the length of the river before they even saw Baotou. He began to consider the entire enterprise doomed and it did not help to see Khasar standing on the prow and shouting foul insults at other captains. In different circumstances, it might have earned him a beating or even a knife in his throat, but Chen Yi roared with laughter and something about Khasar's expression seemed not to give offence. Instead, they replied with worse and Khasar traded a couple of coins for fresh fruit and fish before the sun set. Ho Sa watched in glowering silence, punching a grain bag to make a depression for his head as he tried to find sleep.

Temuge awoke as something bumped against the side of the boat. The night air was thick with insects and he was heavy with sleep. He stirred drowsily, calling out a question to Ho Sa. There was no reply, and when Temuge raised his head, he saw Ho Sa and his brother were awake and staring into the blackness.

'What is happening?' Temuge whispered. He could hear creaking, and muffled sounds of movement, but the moon had yet to rise and he realised he could only have been asleep for a short time.

Light shone out without warning as one of the crew removed the shutters from a tiny oil lamp on the prow. Temuge saw the man's arm lit in gold, then the night erupted in shouts and confusion. Khasar and Ho Sa vanished into the gloom and Temuge rose to his feet, rooted in fear. Dark bodies crashed into the boat, coming over the sides. He scrabbled for his knife, hunching down behind the sacks so they could not see him.

A cry of pain sounded somewhere near and Temuge cursed aloud, convinced they had been discovered by Imperial soldiers. He heard Chen Yi shouting orders and all around were the grunts and gasps of men struggling with each other in near total darkness. Temuge crouched lower, waiting to be attacked. As he strained his eyes, he saw the tiny golden lamp swing up into the air, leaving a trail that remained in his vision. Instead of hissing into the river, he heard it thump onto wood. The oil spilled in a bloom of light and Temuge gasped in fear.

The thrown lamp had landed on the deck of a second boat, rocking wildly as men leaped from it. Like Chen Yi and his crew, the attackers wore little more than a strip of cloth at their waists. They carried knives as long as their forearms and fought with vicious grunts and curses. Behind them, flames grew on the dry wood and Temuge could see the sweating bodies locked together, some of them showing dark gashes and pouring with blood.

As he watched in horror, Temuge heard a sound he knew above all others, the slap of a double-curved bow. He jerked round to see Khasar standing steady on the prow, shooting arrow after arrow. Every shaft found its mark bar one that went into the water when Khasar was forced to duck a thrown knife. Temuge shuddered as a dead man fell face down near him, the impact shoving the arrow feathers further into his chest so that the point stuck out of his back.

Even then, they might have been overwhelmed if the flames had not begun to spread on the attackers' boat. Temuge saw some of them jump the gap to their craft, grabbing at leather buckets. They too fell with Khasar's arrows in them before they could quench the fire.

Chen Yi sawed through two thick ropes that bound the craft together and braced himself on a wooden rail to shove the other boat away. It drifted without control onto the dark river and Temuge could see struggling shadows of men fighting flames. It was too late for the boat and in the distance he heard splashes as they sought safety in the water.

The fire made its own sound, a coughing, spitting roar that dwindled as the current carried the burning boat downriver. A finger of bright sparks reached up into the darkness, taller than a sail. Temuge stood at last, his chest heaving. He jumped as someone came close, but it was Ho Sa, stinking of smoke and blood.

'Are you hurt?' Ho Sa said.

Temuge shook his head, then realised his companion was blind in the dark after staring at the flames.

'I am fine,' Temuge murmured. 'Who were those people?'

'River rats, perhaps, after whatever Chen Yi has in the hold. Criminals.' He fell silent as Chen Yi's voice barked in the night and the sail turned across the wind once more. Temuge heard the hiss of water as they began to move away from Shizuishan docks into the deepest part of the channel. At another order from Chen Yi, the crew fell silent and they moved unseen across the water.

The moon seemed to take an age to rise, but it was still half full and lit the river silver, casting shadows from the surviving crew. Two of Chen Yi's men had been killed in the fight and Temuge watched as they were dropped over the stern without ceremony.

Chen Yi had come back with Khasar to oversee the work and he nodded to Temuge, his expression unreadable in the half-light. Temuge watched him turn to go back to his place by the sail, but the man paused, clearly making a decision. He stood before the looming figure of Khasar, staring up at him.

'This merchant of yours is not a follower of Islam,' Chen Yi said to Ho Sa. 'Moslems pray endlessly and I have never yet seen him drop to his knees.'

Ho Sa tensed as he waited for the little master to continue. Chen Yi shrugged visibly.

'But he fights well, as you said. I can be blind in the dark or the day, do you understand?'

'I do,' Ho Sa replied. Chen Yi reached out and clapped Khasar on the shoulder. He mimicked the sound of the bow with his throat, making a hissing sound with obvious satisfaction.

'Who were they?' Ho Sa asked softly.

Chen Yi fell silent for a moment, considering his answer.

'Fools, and now dead fools. It is not your concern.'

'That depends on whether we will be attacked again, before Baotou,' Ho Sa replied.

'No man may know his fate, soldier-merchant, but I do not think so. They had a chance to steal from us and they wasted it. They will not catch us twice.' Once more he copied the sound of Khasar's bow and grinned.

'What is it in the hold that they wanted?' Temuge said suddenly. He had prepared the words carefully, but Chen Yi still looked surprised at the strange sounds. Temuge was about to try again when the little master replied.

'They were curious and now they are dead. Are you curious?'

Temuge understood and flushed unseen in the darkness. He shook his head.

'No, I am not,' he replied, looking away.

'You are lucky to have friends who can fight for you,' Chen Yi said. 'I did not see you move when we were attacked.' He chuckled as Temuge frowned. He could comprehend the scornful tone if not all the words, but Chen Yi turned to Khasar before he could formulate an answer, grasping his brother by the arm.

'You. Whore's blanket,' he said. 'You want a drink?' Temuge could see the whiteness of his brother's teeth as he recognised the word for the fiery spirit. Chen Yi led him away to the prow to toast the victory. The tension remained as Ho Sa and Temuge stood together.

'We are not here to fight river thieves,' Temuge said at last. 'With just a knife, what could I have done?'

'Get some sleep, if you can,' Ho Sa replied gruffly. 'I do not think we will be stopping again for a few days.'

It was a beautiful winter's day in the mountains. Genghis had ridden with his wife and sons to a river he had known as a boy, far from the vast camp of the tribes. Jochi and Chagatai had their own ponies, while Borte walked her mount behind them with Ogedai and Tolui perched high on the saddle.

As they had left the tribes, Genghis felt his mood lighten. He knew the land under his mare's hooves and he had been surprised at the wave of emotion that had struck him on first returning from the desert. He had known the mountains had a hold on him, but to his astonishment, feeling the turf of his childhood under his feet had brought tears to his eyes, quickly blinked away.

When he had been young, such a trip would always have had an element of danger. Wanderers or thieves could have roamed the hills around the stream. Perhaps there were still a few who had not joined him in his journey south, but he had a nation at his heels in the encampment and the hills were empty of flocks and herdsmen.

He smiled as he dismounted, watching with approval as Jochi and Chagatai pulled bushes together and tied the reins of their mounts. The river ran fast and shallow at the foot of a steep hill nearby. Jagged shards of ice tumbled past from where they had broken free in the peaks. Genghis looked up the slopes, remembering his father and how he had once climbed for eagles on the red hill. Yesugei had brought him to the same place and Genghis had seen no joy in the man, though perhaps it had been hidden. He resolved not to let his sons see his own pleasure in being back amongst the trees and valleys he knew so well.

Borte did not smile as she lowered her two youngest sons to the ground before slipping down herself. There had been few easy words between them since he had married the daughter of the Xi Xia king and he knew she would have heard of his nocturnal visits to the girl's ger. She had not mentioned it, but there was a tightness around her mouth that seemed to grow deeper every day. He could not help but compare her to Chakahai as she stood and stretched in the shade of the trees that leaned over the river, casting the water into shade. Borte was tall; wiry and strong where the Xi Xia girl was soft and pliable. He sighed to himself. Either one could stir him to lust with the right touch, but only one seemed to want to. He had spent many nights with his new wife while Borte remained alone. Perhaps because of that, he had arranged this trip away from the warriors and the families, where eyes always watched and gossip flowed like spring rain.

His gaze fell on Jochi and Chagatai as they approached the stream's edge and stared into the flowing water. No matter how things stood with their mother, he could not leave the boys to bring themselves to manhood, or allow their mother to do so. It was too easy to remember Hoelun's influence on his brother Temuge and how it had made him weak.

He strode up behind his two eldest sons and repressed a shudder at the thought of entering the freezing water. He recalled the time he had hidden from enemies in such a place, his body growing numb and useless while the life leached out of it. Yet he had survived and grown stronger as a result.

'Bring the other two close,' he called to Borte. 'I would have them listen even if they are too young to go in.' He saw Jochi and Chagatai exchange a worried glance at this confirmation of their purpose. Neither relished the idea of stepping into the icy river. Jochi stared up at Genghis with the same flat, questioning gaze he always used. Somehow, it made his father's temper prickle and he looked away as Borte brought Tolui and Ogedai to stand at the bank.

Genghis felt Borte's eyes on him and waited until she had moved off and seated herself by the ponies. She still watched, but he did not want the boys turning to her for support. They had to feel alone to test themselves and for him to see their strength, and their weaknesses. They were nervous around him, he saw, blaming himself for the time he had spent apart from them. How long had it been since he braved the disapproving glares of their mother to play with one of them? He remembered his own father with love, but how would they remember him? He pressed such thoughts from his mind, recalling Yesugei's words in the same place, a lifetime ago.

'You will have heard of the cold face,' he said to the boys. 'The warrior's face that gives nothing away to your enemies. It comes from a strength that has nothing to do with muscles, or how well you bend a bow. It is the heart of dignity that means you will face death with nothing but contempt. Its secret is that it is more than a simple mask. Learning it brings its own calm, so that you have conquered fear and your flesh.'

With a few quick jerks, he freed his sash from his deel and removed his leggings and boots, standing naked on the edge of the river. His body was marked with old scars and his chest was whiter than the dark brown of his arms and legs. He stood without embarrassment before them, then walked into the freezing torrent, feeling his scrotum tighten as the water touched it.

As he lowered himself into the water, his lungs stiffened so that each breath became a struggle. Nothing showed on his face and he watched his sons without expression as he dipped his head under the water, then lay back, half floating with his hands touching the stones of the river bed.

The four boys watched in fascination. Their father seemed completely at ease in the icy water, his face as calm as it had been before. Only his eyes were fierce and they could not hold his gaze for long.

Jochi and Chagatai exchanged a look, daring each other. Jochi shrugged and stripped without self-consciousness, striding into the water and plunging himself under the surface. Genghis saw him shiver at the cold, but the muscular boy glared back at Chagatai as if in challenge, waiting. He hardly seemed aware of his father, or the lesson he intended to teach.

Chagatai snorted in disdain, untying his own clothes. At six, Ogedai was still much smaller than the others. He too began to strip and Genghis saw their mother rise to her feet to call him away.

'Let him come in, Borte,' he said. He would watch to see his third son did not drown, though he would not give him comfort by saying it aloud. Borte winced fearfully as Ogedai stepped into the water just a pace behind Chagatai. It left just Tolui standing miserably on the bank. With great reluctance, he too began to remove his deel. Genghis chuckled, pleased with his spirit. He spoke before Borte could interfere.

'Not you, Tolui. Perhaps next year, but not this time. Stay there and listen.'

The relief was obvious on the little boy's face as he retied the cloth around his waist in a neat knot. He answered his father's smile with one of his own and Genghis winked at him, causing Tolui to grin.

Jochi had chosen a pool at the edge of the river, where the water was still. He watched his father with all but his head submerged and, in the brief exchange, he had found control of his breath. His jaw was clamped against chattering teeth and his eyes were wide and dark. As he had a thousand times before, Genghis wondered if he was the boy's father. Without that certainty, a barrier remained in his affection. At times, the barrier was strained, for Jochi was growing tall and strong, but still Genghis wondered if he saw the features of a Tartar rapist, one whose heart he had eaten in revenge. It was difficult to love such a face with those dark eyes, where his own were wolf-yellow.

Chagatai was so clearly his son it was painful. His eyes were pale with the cold as he settled himself in the water and Genghis had to take a grip on his affection before he spoiled the moment. He forced himself to take a deep, slow breath.

'In water this cold, a child can slip into sleep in six or seven hundred heartbeats. Even a grown man can become unconscious in a little longer. Your body begins to die at the hands and feet first. You will feel them grow numb and useless. Your thoughts become slow and, if you stay too long, you will not have the strength or the will to climb out.' He paused for a moment, watching them. Jochi's lips had turned blue and still he had not made a sound. Chagatai seemed to be struggling against the cold, his limbs twisting in the water. Genghis watched Ogedai closest of all as he tried to copy his older brothers. The effort was too much for him and Genghis heard his teeth clatter together. He could not keep them there much longer and he considered sending Ogedai back to the bank. No, his father had not, though little Temuge had fainted towards the end and almost drowned.

'Show me nothing of what you feel,' he said to them. 'Show me the cold face that you will show to enemies who taunt you. Remember that they too are afraid. If you have ever wondered if you were the only coward in a world of warriors, know that they feel the same, to the last man. In knowing that, you can hide your own fear and stare them down.' All three boys struggled to empty their faces of fear and pain, and on the bank, little Tolui mimicked them in earnest concentration.

'Breathe gently through the nose to slow your heart. Your flesh is a weak thing, but you do not have to listen to its cries for help. I have seen a man push a knife through his own flesh without blood falling. Let that strength come to you and breathe. Show me nothing and be empty.'

Jochi understood at once and his sipping breath became slow and long in perfect imitation of his father's. Genghis ignored him, watching Chagatai as he struggled to bring himself under control. It came at last, close to the time that Genghis knew he had to end it before they passed out in the water.

'Your body is like any other animal in your care,' he told them. 'It will clamour for food and water, warmth and relief from pain. Find the cold face and you will be able to shut out its clamouring voice.'

The three boys had grown numb and Genghis judged it was time to take them out. He expected to have to lift the limp boys to the bank and he rose to take hold of the first. Instead, Jochi stood with him, his body blooming pink with blood under the skin. The little boy's eyes never left his father as Genghis touched a hand to Chagatai's arm, not wanting to lift him after Jochi had risen on his own.

Chagatai stirred drowsily, his eyes glassy. He focused on Jochi and when he saw him standing, he clamped his mouth shut and struggled up, slipping on the soft mud below the surface. Genghis could feel the enmity between the two boys and he could not help but remember Bekter, the brother he had killed so many years ago.

Ogedai could not stand on his own and his father's strong arms placed him back on the bank to dry in the sun. Genghis strode out with water streaming from his flesh, feeling life return to his limbs with a rush of energy. Jochi and Chagatai came to stand with him, gasping as their hands and feet came back to life. They sensed their father was still watching them and each boy understood and tried to control his body once again. Their hands shook beyond any control, but they stood straight in the sunlight and watched him, not trusting their shuddering jaws for speech.

'Did it kill you?' Genghis asked them. Yesugei had asked the same thing and Khasar had said 'Almost', making the big man laugh. His own sons said nothing and he saw that he did not have the friendship with them that he had enjoyed with Yesugei. He would spend more time with them, he vowed. The Xi Xia princess was like a fire in his blood, but he would try to ignore the call more often while the boys grew.

'Your body does not rule you,' he said, as much for himself as for them. 'It is a stupid beast that knows nothing of the works of men. It is merely the cart that carries you. You control it with will and with breath through your nose, when it calls for you to pant like a dog. When you take an arrow in battle and the pain is overwhelming, you will press it away and, before you fall, you will return death to your enemies.' He glanced up the hillside, at memories of days so innocent and far away that he could hardly bear to recall them.

'Now fill your mouths with water and run to the top of this hill and back. When you return, you will spit the water to show you breathed properly. Whoever is first will eat. The others will go hungry.'

It was not a fair test. Jochi was older and, at such an age, even a year made a difference. Genghis showed no sign of his awareness as he saw the boys exchange glances, weighing the odds. Bekter too had been older, but Genghis had left his brother gasping on the hill. He hoped Chagatai would do the same.

Chagatai broke for the water without warning, charging in with a great spray and dipping his face to the surface to suck up a mouthful. Ogedai was only a little behind. Genghis remembered how the water had become warm and thick in his mouth. He could taste it with the memories.

Jochi had not moved and Genghis turned to the boy questioningly.

'Why are you not following?' he asked.

Jochi shrugged.

'I can beat them,' he said. 'I know it already.'

Genghis stared at him, seeing defiance he could not understand. None of Yesugei's sons had refused the task. The boy Genghis had been had relished the chance to humiliate Bekter. He could not understand Jochi and he felt his temper flare.

His other sons were already struggling up the hill, growing smaller in the distance.

'You are afraid,' Genghis murmured, though he was guessing.

'I am not,' Jochi replied without heat, reaching for his clothes. 'Will you love me more if I beat them?' For the first time, his voice shuddered with strong emotion. 'I do not think you will.'

Genghis looked at the little boy in astonishment. Not one of Yesugei's sons would have dared to speak to him in such a way. How would his father have responded? He winced at the memories of Yesugei's hands clipping him. His father would not have allowed it. For an instant, he considered knocking sense into the boy, but then he saw that Jochi expected it and had tensed himself for the blow. The impulse died before it was born.

'You would make me proud,' Genghis said to him.

Jochi shook, but it was not from the cold.

'Then today, I will run,' he said. His father watched without understanding as Jochi took a mouthful of the river and set off, running fast and sure over the broken ground after his brothers.

When it was quiet again, Genghis walked little Tolui back to where Borte sat by the ponies. She was stony-faced and did not meet his eyes.

'I will spend more time with them,' he told her, still trying to comprehend what had happened with Jochi.

She looked up at him and, for an instant, her face softened as she saw his confusion.

'He wants nothing more in the world than to be accepted by you as your own,' she said.

Genghis snorted.

'I do accept him. When have I not?'

Borte rose to her feet to face him.

'When have you taken him in your arms? When have you

told him how proud you are of him? Do you think he has not heard the whispers of the other boys? When have you silenced the foolish ones with some display of affection?'

'I did not want to make him soft,' he said, troubled. He had not known it had been so obvious and, for a moment, he saw how hard a life he had forced on Jochi. He shook his head to clear it. His own life had been harder and he could not force himself to love the boy. As every year passed, he saw less and less of himself in those dark eyes.

His thoughts were interrupted by Borte's laugh. It was not a pleasant sound.

'The bitterest thing of all is that he is so obviously your son, more than any of the others. Yet you cannot see it. He has the will to stand up to his own father and you are blind.' She spat into the grass. 'If Chagatai had done the same, you would be grinning and telling me the boy had his grandfather's courage.'

'Enough,' he said quietly, sick of her voice and her criticism. The day had been spoiled for him, a mockery of the joy and triumph he remembered when he had come to that place with his own father and brothers.

Borte glared at his angry expression.

'If he beats Chagatai down the hill, how will you react?' she said.

He cursed, his mood as sour as old milk. He had not considered that Jochi might still win and he knew that, if he did, he would not embrace the boy with Borte watching. His thoughts swirled without release and he did not know how he would react at all.

Temuge listened to Khasar's grunting with a furious expression. His brother had earned a great deal of goodwill among the crew with his response to the attack. In the days after those

166

terrifying moments in the dark, Chen Yi regularly included the Mongol warrior in the camaraderie of the boat. Khasar had learned many phrases in their language and shared their rations of hard spirit and balls of rice and shrimp in the evening. Ho Sa too seemed to have warmed to the boat master, but Temuge remained resolutely apart. It did not surprise him to see Khasar acting like an animal with the others. He had no understanding and Temuge wished Khasar would realise that he was nothing more than a bowman sent to protect his younger brother. Genghis, at least, knew how valuable Temuge could be to him.

On the night before they left for the river, Genghis had summoned Temuge and asked him to remember every detail of the walls of Baotou, every part of the defences. If they failed to return with the masons who had constructed the city, that knowledge might be all they had to begin a summer campaign. Genghis trusted Temuge's memory and the keen intelligence that Khasar evidently lacked. Temuge had recalled the urgency in frustration when they passed a boat with two female crew and Khasar waved silver coins at them, inviting them over.

There was no privacy in the boat and Temuge could only stare at the water rather than watch as two young women stripped off and swam across like otters, gleaming and shivering as they came on board. Chen Yi had thrown out an anchor in the deep water so the women could swim back when the crew were finished with them.

Temuge closed his eyes at the squealing sounds that came from the second of the two women. She was small-breasted and lithe, attractive in her youth, though she had not looked in his direction as she accepted Khasar's coin. The sounds she made were only interrupted when Khasar's plunging efforts knocked her hand open and the coin rolled away, causing laughter from the watching crew as she pushed him off and scrambled for it on her hands and knees. Temuge observed from the corner of his eye as Khasar took advantage of the opportunity and the girl's giggling made him swear under his breath. What would Genghis think of this delay to their planning? They had been given a task without equal in importance for the tribes. Genghis had made that clear. Without knowing how to enter the walled cities of the Chin, the Imperial soldiers would never be broken. It made Temuge furious while he waited for Khasar to finish for a second time. The day was being wasted and he knew that if he said anything, his brother would scorn him in front of the crew. Temuge burned with silent humiliation. He had not forgotten why they were there, even if Khasar had.

It was growing dark when Borte saw Jochi leading his exhausted brothers back across the river. His bare feet still bled from the run as he stood before her, his chest heaving. Borte's heart broke for the little boy as he looked in vain for his father. Something went out of him when he saw Genghis was not there. He spat out the mouthful of water and gasped loudly into the evening silence.

'Your father was called back to the camp,' Borte lied. Jochi did not believe her. She could see the pain in his face and she hid her frustration with her husband and herself for arguing with him.

'He will have gone to his new wife, the foreigner,' Jochi said suddenly. Borte bit her lip rather than reply. In that too, she had lost the man she had married. With her oldest son standing bewildered and hurt before her, it was easy to hate Genghis for his selfish blindness. She resolved to enter the ger of the Xi Xia woman if she could not find him. Perhaps he did not care for his wife any longer, but he did care for his sons and she would use that to bring him back.

Chagatai and Ogedai came stumbling along in the darkness, each boy spitting water as he had been told. Without their father to see, the victory was hollow and they seemed at a loss.

'I will tell him how you ran,' Borte said, her eyes shining with tears.

It was not enough for them and they were silent and wounded as they mounted for the ride home.

CHAPTER TWELVE

Ho Sa told the brothers that Baotou was a trek of some miles from the busy river port that kept it supplied. The city was the last trading post between the northern Chin and the Xi Xia kingdom and the river teemed with boats by the time they wound their way into the area. The journey had taken three weeks since abandoning their ponies and Temuge at least was sick of the slow hours, the damp river mists and the diet of rice and fish. Chen Yi and his crew drank from the river without ill effects and Khasar seemed to have a stomach of iron, but Temuge's bowels had grown weak for three days, leaving him in misery and his clothes foul. He had never eaten or even seen fish before and he did not trust the silver-scaled things from the river. The boat crew seemed to delight in them as they yanked them on board on thin lines, jerking and flopping madly while the men stove in their heads. Temuge had washed his garments as they moored, but his stomach continued to rumble and bring bad air from both ends.

As the Yellow River snaked between hills, more and more birds could be seen, living on scraps from the boats and traders. Temuge and Khasar were fascinated by the sheer number of men and craft bringing cargoes up and down the river, denser in this place than any other they had seen. Though Chen Yi seemed able to find a path through the press with just the sail, many of the boatmen carried long poles to fend off other boats. It was noisy and chaotic, with hundreds of shouting traders competing to sell anything from fresh fish to water-spoiled cloth that could still be used for rough clothing. The smell of strange spices hung in the air as Chen Yi manoeuvred between his competitors, looking for a space to moor for the evening.

Chen Yi was even better known in these waters and Temuge watched with narrow eyes as he was hailed by friends again and again. Despite the fact that the crew seemed to have accepted Khasar as one of their own, Temuge did not trust the little boat master. He agreed with Ho Sa that the hold was probably full of some contraband substance, but perhaps the man could earn another few coins by reporting their presence to Imperial soldiers. Remaining on board without knowing they were safe was a gnawing tension on all three men.

It was clearly no accident that they arrived at the river port as evening was coming. Chen Yi had delayed their passage around a bend in the river, not deigning to reply when Temuge pressed him to make better time. Whatever was in his hold would be unloaded in the darkness, when the tax gatherers and their soldiers would be less alert.

Temuge muttered angrily under his breath. He cared nothing for Chen Yi's problems. His task was to get to the docks as quickly as possible before making his way to the city. Ho Sa had said it was only a few hours' walk on a good road, but the alien sights and sounds all around him were making Temuge nervous and he wanted to be moving. The crew too had grown tense as they found a place where they could moor and wait their turn on the rickety dock.

The river port was not impressive to look upon, no more than a few dozen wooden buildings seeming to lean upon each other for support. It was a squalid little place, built for trade rather than comfort. Temuge did not mind that, but he could see a pair of well-armed soldiers keeping an eye on everything that was unloaded and he did not want to come to their attention.

He heard Chen Yi speak in low tones to his crew, clearly giving orders as they ducked their heads with sharp gestures. He struggled to hide his irritation at another delay. He and his companions would soon be off the river and away from this peculiar little world he did not understand. For a short time, he had wondered if he could buy illustrated manuscripts in the boat market, but there was no sign of such a trade and he had no taste for ingots of silver or carved figurines. Those items were held out in the dirty fists of boys, paddling out in reed coracles to the side of any new vessel. Temuge looked stonily past the urchins until they passed on. His mood was black by the time Chen Yi came to the stern to speak with his passengers.

'We must wait until there is a space on the docks,' he said. 'You will be on your way before midnight, or a few hours later.' To Temuge's annoyance, the little man nodded to Khasar.

'If you did not eat so much, I would take you on as crew,' he said. Khasar did not understand him, but he clapped Chen Yi on the shoulder in reply. He too was impatient to be going on and the little master sensed the mood of his passengers.

'If you wish, I can find a place on the carts to take you to the city. It will be a fair price,' he said.

Temuge saw the man was watching them closely. He had no idea whether the journey to Baotou was an easy one or not, but he suspected a merchant as he claimed to be would not turn down the offer of a ride. The idea of travelling further with Chen Yi's suspicious gaze on him made him uncomfortable, but he forced a smile and replied in the Chin tongue.

'We will say yes to you,' he said. 'Unless your unloading is long.'

Chen Yi shrugged.

'I have friends here to help. It will not take long. You are impatient for merchants, I think.' He smiled as he spoke, but his eyes remained fixed on them, taking in every detail. Temuge was thankful that Khasar could not understand. His brother was easier to read than a map.

'We will decide later,' Temuge said, turning away to make sure Chen Yi knew he was dismissed. The man might have left them alone, but Khasar pointed to the soldiers on the dock.

'Ask him about those men,' he said to Ho Sa. 'We want to get past them and I think he does as well. Ask him how he is going to unload without them noticing.'

Ho Sa hesitated, unwilling to let Chen Yi know they had guessed his cargo was illegal or untaxed. He did not know how the man would react. Before he could speak, Khasar snorted.

'Chen Yi,' he said, pointing at the soldiers again.

The master of the boat reached up and pressed Khasar's arm down before the gesture could be seen.

'I have friends on the docks,' he said. 'There will be no trouble here. Baotou is my city, where I was born, do you understand?'

Ho Sa translated and Khasar nodded.

'We should keep this one in view, brother,' he said to Temuge. 'He can't betray us while he unloads, or he would draw too much attention to whatever we've been sitting on for the last few weeks.'

'Thank you for your interest, Khasar,' Temuge replied, his voice acid. 'I have considered what to do. We will take his offer of a trip to the city and get in the walls with him. After that, we will find our men and head back.'

He spoke knowing Chen Yi could not understand, but it was still with a sense of foreboding. Finding the masons of Baotou was one part of the plan they could not predict back in the Xi Xia kingdom. No one knew how easy they would be to locate, or what dangers the city would present. Even if they were successful, Temuge was still not sure how they would bring unwilling prisoners out when a cry for help might bring soldiers running. He considered the wealth of silver Genghis had given him to ease their passage.

'Will you be returning to the river, Chen Yi?' he said. 'We may not stay long in the city.'

To his disappointment, the man shook his head.

'I am home now and there are many things I must do. I will not leave again for many months.'

Temuge remembered how much they had been charged for the passage, as if Chen Yi had been reluctant to go so far.

'So you were always coming here?' he asked, outraged.

Chen Yi grinned at him.

'Poor men do not go to Baotou,' he replied, chuckling. Temuge glared at him until he strolled back to his crew.

'I do not trust him,' Ho Sa murmured. 'He does not worry about soldiers on the docks. He is carrying something valuable enough to risk an armed attack and he is well known to every other boatman in Baotou. I do not like this at all.'

'We will be ready,' Temuge said, though the words had thrown him into a panic. The men on the docks and the river were all enemies and he hoped to pass unseen amongst them. Genghis had pinned his hopes on them, but at times it seemed he had set an impossible task.

The moon rose as a frozen sliver of white, casting only a faint sheen on the water. Temuge wondered if Chen Yi had planned their arrival with even more care than he had realised. The dark night was a hindrance at first as Chen Yi untied the ropes that held them to a river post and sent two of the crew to work a steering oar off the stern. As it swished back and forth, Chen

Yi himself used a long pole to create a path through to the docks. Sleepy men swore at him as the pole thumped into wood, the noise muffled in the dark. Temuge thought the moon had moved by the time they were in reach of the dock itself, though Chen Yi had barely broken sweat from his labours.

The docks were dark, though some of the wooden buildings still showed light in their windows and they could hear laughter somewhere within. The yellow glow from those places was all Chen Yi seemed to need to find his place on the dock and he was the first to leap out on the wooden pilings, a rope in his hand to tie up the boat. He had not ordered silence, but none of the crew talked as they dismantled the sail. Even the noise of them throwing open the hatches down to the hold was muffled.

Temuge let out a long, relieved breath to have reached land, but at the same time, he felt his pulse increase. A few shadowy figures could be seen, lounging or sleeping. Temuge squinted at them, wondering if they were beggars, whores or even informers. The soldiers he had seen would surely be ready for night landings. Temuge feared a sudden shout or a rush of armed men that would be the end of everything they had accomplished so far. They had reached the city Genghis had wanted, or at least the closest point on the river to it. Perhaps because they were so near to their goal, he became convinced it would all come to nothing and he scrambled past the others to step over the side onto the wooden planking, stumbling as he did so. It was Ho Sa who took his arm to steady him, while Khasar vanished in the dark.

Temuge wanted nothing more than to leave the boat and its crew behind, but he still worried that Chen Yi might betray them. If the master of the boat had understood the significance of Khasar carrying a Mongol bow, the information might buy him out of trouble. In a strange land, even with Ho Sa's help, they would be hard pressed to avoid a hunt, especially one that knew they were heading for Baotou.

A creaking sound came out of the darkness, making Temuge reach for his knife. He forced himself to relax as he saw two carts approaching, drawn by mules whose breath fogged the cold air. The drivers stepped down and spoke in low voices to Chen Yi, one of them chuckling as they began to unload the little boat. Temuge could not help but strain his eyes to see what was coming from it, but he could not make out details. Whatever the men carried was heavy, judging by the sounds they made as they lifted it. Temuge and Ho Sa found themselves drifting closer, drawn by curiosity. It was Khasar who spoke out of the dark, passing by with a dark mass on his shoulder.

'Silk,' he hissed at Temuge. 'I felt the end of a roll.' They heard him grunt as he heaved the weight onto the closest cart before returning to them.

'If it's all like this, we've been smuggling silk into the city,' he whispered.

Ho Sa bit his lip unseen.

'In such quantity? It must have come from Kaifeng or even Yenking itself. Such a cargo is worth more than a few sailors to defend it.'

'How much more?' Khasar asked, his voice loud enough to make Temuge wince.

'Thousands in gold,' Ho Sa replied. 'Enough to buy a hundred boats like this one and a lord's house to put it in. This Chen Yi is no small trader or thief. If he has arranged to take this by river, it can only be to divert the gaze of those who might steal it. Even then he might have lost it all if we had not been on board.' He thought for a moment before going on.

'If the hold is full, it can only be from the Imperial stock. It is not a matter of paying taxes for it. It is fiercely protected before sale. Perhaps this is just the first stage on a route to take it thousands of miles to its eventual destination.'

'What does that matter?' Khasar asked him. 'We still need to get into the city and he's the only one offering us a ride.'

Ho Sa took a deep breath to hide a spike of anger.

'If anyone is looking for the silk, we are more of a target than we would be on our own. You understand? It could be the worst thing we could do to travel into Baotou with this. If the city guards search the carts, we will be taken and tortured for everything we know.'

Temuge felt his stomach twist at the thought. He was on the point of ordering the others to walk away from the docks when Chen Yi appeared at his shoulder. He carried a shuttered lamp, but his face could be seen in the slight glow. His expression was as tense as they had ever seen it and he shone with sweat.

'Climb on, all of you,' he said. Temuge opened his mouth to make up some excuse, but the crew had abandoned their vessel. They held knives and stood ready and Temuge could find no words to offset his growing fear. It was clear enough that the passengers would not be allowed to simply walk away into the night, not after what they had seen. He cursed Khasar for helping them with the rolls of cloth. Perhaps that had raised their suspicions even further.

Chen Yi seemed to sense his discomfort and nodded to him. 'You would not wish to make your own way to the city in the dark,' he said. 'I will not allow it.'

Temuge winced, reaching up to heave himself onto one of the carts. He noticed how the crew waved Ho Sa to the second one while allowing Khasar to clamber on beside his brother. With a sinking feeling, he realised Chen Yi had split them deliberately. He wondered if he would ever see Baotou or be dumped by the road with his throat slit. At least they still had their weapons. Khasar carried his bow rewrapped in cloth and

Temuge had his little knife, though he knew he could never fight his way out.

The carts remained still when a low whistle came from the shadows of the dock buildings. Chen Yi jumped lightly down and whistled back. Temuge watched in nervous fascination as a dark form detached itself and walked towards their little group. It was one of the soldiers, or another very like him. The man spoke in low tones and Temuge strained to hear the words. He saw Chen Yi hand over a heavy leather bag and heard the soldier's grunt of pleasure at the weight.

'I know your family, Yan. I know your village, do you understand?' Chen Yi said. The man stiffened, understanding the threat. He did not respond.

'You are too old to be a dock guard,' Chen Yi told him. 'In your hands you have enough to buy retirement, a smallholding perhaps, with a wife and chickens. Perhaps it is time for you to leave the docks behind.'

The man nodded in the gloom, clutching the bag to his chest.

'If I am taken, Yan, I have friends who will find you no matter where you run.'

The man nodded again, jerkily. His fear was obvious and Temuge wondered yet again who Chen Yi was, if that was even his real name. Surely no cargo of stolen Imperial silk would be trusted to a simple boat master.

The soldier vanished back among the buildings, moving quickly with so much wealth on his person. Chen Yi climbed back on the cart and the drivers clicked in their throats to the mules, starting them off. Temuge let his fingers quest under him for the oily feel of silk, but instead met rough cloth with a heavy stitched line. The silk had been covered, but he could only hope Chen Yi had more of his bribed men waiting at Baotou. He was out of his depth, caught up in events he could not control. One good search at the city walls and he would never see the Khenti mountains again. As Kokchu had taught him, he prayed to the spirits to guide him safely through the dark waters of the days to come.

One of the crew stayed behind to take the boat back onto the river. Alone, he could hardly control it and Temuge guessed it would be sunk somewhere out of sight of questioning officials. Chen Yi was not the sort of man to make mistakes, and Temuge wished he knew whether the man was an enemy or a friend.

Ho Sa's estimate of the distance to Baotou had been correct, Temuge judged. The city had been built around eight miles from the river – some twenty-five *li*, as the Chin judged distance. The road was a good one, paved with unbroken flat stones so merchants could make good time from the river. Dawn was barely visible to the east as Temuge craned into the gloom and saw the dark shadow of the city wall coming closer. Whatever was going to happen, whether it was a search of the carts that would end in his death or a quiet entry into Baotou, it would happen soon. He felt a nervous sweat prickle on his skin and scratched at his armpits. Apart from the current danger, he had never yet entered a city of stone. He could not shake the image of an ant-hill somehow swallowing him up into a heaving mass of strangers. The thought of them pressing close made him breathe shallowly, already afraid. The families of his own people felt very far away. Temuge leaned close to the dark shadow that was his brother, almost touching his ear with his lips so that they would not be overheard.

'If we are discovered at the gate, or the silk is found, we must run and find a place to hide in the city.'

Khasar glanced to where Chen Yi sat on the front of the cart.

'Let us hope it does not come to that. We'd never find each other again and I think there is more to our friend than a simple smuggler.'

Temuge sat back on the rough sacking as Chen Yi looked round at them. In the growing light, the intelligence in the little man's gaze was disconcerting and Temuge looked past him to the city wall, feeling his nervousness increase.

They were not alone on the road any longer. The dawn light showed a line of carts assembling in front of the gates. Many more had clearly spent the night off the road, waiting to be allowed in. Chen Yi went past these as they stirred, ignoring the yawning men who had missed their place in the line. Mud-brown fields stretched into the distance, the harvest of rice plants all gone to feed the city. Baotou loomed above them all and Temuge swallowed as he looked up and up again at the grey stones.

The city gate was a massive construction of wood and iron, perhaps intended to impress travellers. At each side, towers half as high again as the gate could be seen, with a platform between them. Soldiers were visible there and Temuge knew they would have a clear view of everything that passed below. He saw they carried crossbows and felt his stomach tighten.

The gate opened and Temuge stared as more soldiers heaved it back, blocking entry with a counterweighted wooden spar. The closest carts did not move as the soldiers took their positions, ready for the day. Chen Yi's drivers pulled gently on the reins, halting their mules. They showed none of the trepidation Temuge felt and he struggled to remember the cold face he had known as a boy. It would not do for the soldiers to see him sweat on a cold morning and he rubbed his sleeves over his forehead.

Behind them, another merchant pulled up and halted, calling out a cheerful greeting to someone at the side of the road.

The line of carts moved slowly into the city and Temuge could see the soldiers were stopping one in three, exchanging curt conversation with the drivers. The wooden spar had been lifted for the first and was not brought down again. Temuge began to repeat the relaxing phrases Kokchu had taught him, taking comfort from their familiarity. The song of the wind. The land underfoot. The souls of the hills. The breaking of chains.

The sun had risen clear of the horizon by the time Chen Yi's first cart reached the gate. Temuge had been counting the pattern of searches, and he thought they might pass without interruption when the merchant in front was checked and passed on. With a growing sense of terror, he saw the soldiers look up at Chen Yi's impassive driver. One of them seemed more alert than his sleepy companions and it was that one who stepped close.

'What is your business in Baotou?' the soldier asked. He addressed the driver, who began a rambling answer. Temuge felt his heart throbbing as Chen Yi looked over the guard's head into the city. Beyond the gate was an open square and a market already bustling at the first light of dawn. Temuge saw Chen Yi nod sharply and suddenly there was a crash among the stalls that made the soldier half turn.

Running children seemed to erupt from all over the square, yelling and swerving to avoid the stallholders. To Temuge's astonishment, he saw plumes of smoke rise from more than one location and he heard the soldier swear and bark orders to his companions. Stalls went over and many more collapsed as the poles holding their awnings were kicked over. Cries of 'Thief!' went up and the chaos grew with every moment.

The guard at the gate slapped Chen Yi's cart, though whether it was an order to stay or go was not clear. With five others, he ran to control what was quickly becoming a riot. Temuge risked a glance upwards, but the crossbowmen on the bridge were hidden from his view. He hoped they too were distracted and forced himself to stare forward as Chen Yi's driver clicked in his throat and entered the city.

Fire raged in the little square as stall after stall caught and crackled over the cries of the sellers. Temuge saw glimpses of running soldiers, but the children were fast and already they were vanishing into boltholes and alleys, some carrying stolen goods.

Chen Yi did not look at the chaotic scene as his two carts turned away from the square into a quieter road. The sounds dwindled behind them and Temuge slumped on the sacking, wiping more sweat from his brow.

It could not have been coincidence, he knew. Chen Yi had given a signal. Once again, Temuge wondered about the man they had met on the river. With such a valuable cargo in his hold, perhaps he had not cared about a few extra coins at all. Perhaps he had merely wanted a few more men to defend it.

They trundled through a maze of roads, turning again and again onto smaller tracks between houses. Temuge and Khasar felt hemmed in by the press of buildings, built so close together that the rising sun could not touch the shadows between. Three times, other carts had been forced to back up into side alleys to let them pass and, as the sun rose, the streets filled with more people than Temuge or Khasar could believe. Temuge saw dozens of shops serving hot food from clay bowls. He could hardly imagine finding food whenever you were hungry, without having to slaughter or hunt for the meat. Morning workers clustered around the traders, eating with their fingers and wiping their mouths on cloths before moving back into the throng. Many of them carried holed bronze coins strung onto a cord or a wire. Although Temuge had some idea of the value of silver, he had never seen the exchange of coins for goods and he gaped at every new wonder. He saw elderly scribes writing messages for payment, squawking chickens held for sale, racks of knives and men to sharpen them on spinning stones held between their legs. He saw cloth dyers with hands stained blue or green, beggars and sellers of amulets against disease. Every street was crowded, loud and vibrant and, to his surprise, Temuge loved it.

'This is wonderful,' he said under his breath.

Khasar glanced at him.

'There are too many people and the city stinks,' he replied. Temuge looked away, irritated with his foolish brother who could not see the excitement of such a place. For a time, he almost forgot the fear that trailed him. He still half expected a shout to go up somehow, as if the gate guards would have followed them so far into the labyrinth of Baotou. It did not come and he saw Chen Yi relax as they wound their way further and further from the walls, disappearing into the teeming heart of the city.

CHAPTER THIRTEEN

The two carts rumbled on over the stone streets until they reached a pair of solid iron gates that opened as soon as they drew up. It took a matter of moments for the carts to enter and the gates to close behind them. Temuge looked back and bit his lip as he saw wooden shutters being unfolded over the bars, blocking the view of passers-by.

After the noise and press of humanity, it would have been a relief if not for the sense of being confined. The city had left him dazed and overwhelmed in its complexity. Yet even as it excited him, it pressed too close on his senses and made him long for the empty plains, just to take a breath before plunging back in once more. He shook his head to clear it, knowing he needed a sharp mind for whatever would come.

The carts creaked and jerked as the men jumped off, Chen Yi calling orders to those around him. Temuge climbed down to join Khasar, his earlier nervousness returning in full force. Chen Yi hardly seemed to notice his passengers as a crowd of men came trotting out from the buildings, each pair carrying a roll of silk on their shoulders. It did not take long for the precious cargo to vanish into the house and Temuge wondered again at the spider-web of contacts Chen Yi seemed to have in the city.

The home that enclosed the paved courtyard was surely the property of a wealthy man, Temuge thought. It was out of keeping with the shamble of housing they had passed through, though perhaps there were others as well hidden. A single storey with a red-tiled roof extended on all sides around him, though the section facing the gate rose in pointed apexes to a second level. Temuge could only blink at the labour that must have gone into so many hundreds or even thousands of tiles. He could not help but compare the building to the felt-and-wicker gers he had known all his life and felt a touch of envy. What luxury had his people ever known on the plains?

On all sides, the roof extended past the walls, held up with columns of red-painted wood to form a long cloister. Armed men stood at the corners and Temuge began to realise they were prisoners to Chen Yi's will. There was no easy escape from that place.

When the carts had been emptied, the drivers moved them away and Temuge was left standing with Ho Sa and Khasar, feeling vulnerable under the gaze of strangers. He noticed Khasar had his hand inside the roll of cloth that wrapped his bow.

'We cannot fight our way out,' he hissed at Khasar, who jumped as his thoughts were echoed.

'I don't see anyone opening the gates to let us go,' Khasar whispered back.

Chen Yi had vanished inside the house and all three men were relieved to see him return. He had put on a long-sleeved black robe as well as donning leather sandals. Temuge saw the little man wore a curved sword on his hip and seemed comfortable with the weight of it.

'This is my *jia*: my home,' Chen Yi said, to Temuge's private astonishment. 'You are welcome here. Will you eat with me?'

'We have business in the city,' Ho Sa said, gesturing towards the gate.

Chen Yi frowned. There was no trace of the affable river-boat master in his manner. He seemed to have shed the role completely and stood with his hands clasped behind his back, his face stern.

'I must insist. We have many things to discuss.' Without waiting for them to reply, he strode back into the house and they followed him. Temuge cast a lingering look over his shoulder at the gate as he walked into the shadow of the cloister. He repressed a shudder at the thought of the sheer weight of the tiles above his head. Ho Sa did not seem troubled in the least, but Temuge could imagine the massive beams crashing down, crushing them all. He repeated one of Kokchu's chants under his breath, seeking calm that would not come.

The entrance to the main house was through a wooden door layered in polished bronze, punctured many times in decorative patterns. Temuge saw the shapes of bats etched into the metal and wondered at their significance. Before he could comment, he entered a room as ornate as anything he had ever seen. Khasar dropped the cold face over his features rather than look surprised, but Temuge opened his mouth at the opulence of Chen Yi's home. For men born in gers, it was astonishing. The air smelled of some strange incense and yet was subtly stale for men who had grown up in wind and mountains. Temuge could not help but glance upwards at intervals, constantly aware of the massive weight above his head. Khasar too seemed uncomfortable and cracked his knuckles in the silence.

Couches and chairs stood against screens of ebony and

painted silk that allowed light in from other rooms beyond. At first glance, everything seemed made of rich wood in matching colours, pleasing to the eye. Columns of highly polished timber ran the length of the room, reaching up to crossbeams. The floor too was made of thousands of segments, polished so that it almost glowed. After the filth of the city streets, the room was clean and welcoming, the golden wood making it seem warm. Temuge saw that Chen Yi had exchanged his sandals for a pair of clean ones at the door. Flushing, Temuge returned to do the same. As he stepped out of his boots, a servant approached, kneeling before him to help him don a clean set in white felt.

Temuge saw lines of unbroken white smoke rising from brass dishes at a carved table on the far wall. He did not understand what could merit such a symbol of devotion, but Chen Yi bowed his head to the little altar and murmured a prayer of thanks for his safe return.

'You live with great beauty,' Temuge said carefully, striving for the right sounds.

Chen Yi inclined his head in the gesture they knew, one habit that had survived the transformation.

'You are generous,' he said. 'I think sometimes that I was happier as a young man, running goods on the Yellow River. I had nothing then, but life was simpler.'

'What are you now, to have such wealth?' Ho Sa asked.

Chen Yi nodded to him rather than reply.

'You will wish to bathe before you eat,' he said. 'The smell of the river is on us all.' He gestured for them to follow and they exchanged glances as he led them through into another courtyard beyond the first. Both Temuge and Khasar straightened a fraction as they passed out into the sunshine and left the heavy beams behind. Water could be heard there and Khasar walked up to a pool where sluggish fish stirred at his shadow.

Chen Yi had not noticed him stop, but when he looked back and saw Khasar begin to strip, he laughed delightedly.

'You will kill my fish!' he said. 'Come further, where I have baths for you.'

Khasar shrugged irritably, yanking his robe back over his shoulders. He trailed after Temuge and Ho Sa, ignoring the amusement of the Xi Xia soldier.

At the far end of the second courtyard, they saw open doors with wisps of steam spilling out into the warm air. Chen Yi gestured for them to enter.

'Do as I do,' he said. 'You will enjoy yourselves.'

He stripped quickly, revealing the scarred and wiry little frame they knew so well from the boat. Temuge saw two pools of water sunk into the floor, with steam rising lazily from one. He would have made for it, but Chen Yi shook his head and, instead, Temuge watched as two male slaves approached and Chen Yi raised his arms. To Temuge's astonishment, the men upended buckets of water over their master, then used cloths wrapped around their hands to rub him with some lathering substance until he was slick and white with it. More buckets followed and only then did he step into the pool with a grunt of pleasure.

Temuge swallowed nervously as he dropped his robe to the floor. It was as filthy as he was and he did not relish the idea of being scrubbed by strangers. He closed his eyes as the buckets were poured over his head, then kept them firmly closed as rough hands seemed to pummel his body, swaying him from side to side. The last buckets were freezing and he gasped.

Temuge stepped gingerly into the hot water. He felt the muscles in his back and thighs relax as he found a stone seat beneath the surface and he grunted in appreciation. The feeling was exquisite. This was how a man should live! Behind him, Khasar slapped away the hands of the attendants as they reached out with their cloths. They stood frozen at his action, before one of them tried again. Without warning, Khasar snapped a fist into the side of the man's head, knocking him reeling onto the hard tiles.

Chen Yi roared with laughter. He called out an order and the slaves stood back. The one who had been felled rose warily, with his head bowed as Khasar took up a cloth and wiped at his body until the rag was black. Temuge did not look as Khasar raised a leg onto a stone ledge along the wall to rub his genitals clean. He finished the process by upending a bucket over his own head, all the time glaring at the man he had struck.

Khasar handed the bucket back and murmured something that made the slave tense and set his jaw. Ho Sa endured the process with less fuss and they entered the water together, Khasar swearing in two languages as he lowered himself in.

The four men sat in silence for a time, before Chen Yi rose and plunged into the other pool. They copied him in silent frustration, tired of the routines and delays. In the second pool, Khasar hissed out a breath at the cold, plunging his head under the water and coming up roaring as new energy filled him. Neither of the Mongols had ever known hot water, but a cold dip was no worse than the rivers at home. Temuge looked longingly back at the steaming bath he had left, but did not return to it.

By the time they had settled themselves, Chen Yi was out and being dried by the towel slaves. Khasar and Temuge did not linger and climbed out after him, Khasar blowing like a beached fish. The two slaves did not approach Khasar a second time, instead handing him a large, rough piece of cloth to dry himself. He did so vigorously, his skin showing a fresh bloom. He had removed the string that held his hair and it whipped around in long black strands.

Temuge looked at the sorry pile of soiled cloth that was his robe and was reaching for it when Chen Yi clapped his hands and the attendants brought in fresh ones. There was pleasure in losing the stink of the boats, Temuge thought, running his hands over the soft material. He could only guess what Chen Yi had in mind for them as they walked back to eat.

The food was plentiful, though Khasar and Temuge looked in vain for mutton among the dishes.

'What is this?' Khasar asked, picking up a piece of white flesh in his fingers.

'Snake in ginger,' Chen Yi replied. He pointed to another bowl. 'You will know dog, I am sure.'

Khasar nodded.

'When times are hard,' he replied, dipping his fingers into a soup to search for another morsel. Showing no sign of distaste, Chen Yi took up a pair of wooden sticks and showed the Mongols how to grasp a piece of food between them. Only Ho Sa was comfortable and Chen Yi grew slightly flushed as both Khasar and Temuge dropped pieces of meat and rice on the cloth. Once more, he showed them, this time putting the pieces onto the plates in front of the Mongols so that they could pick them up with their fingers.

Khasar held his temper. He had been scrubbed, dipped and given clothes that itched. He was surrounded by strange things he did not understand and anger simmered underneath the surface. When he gave up on the strange sticks and shoved them upright into a bowl of rice, Chen Yi actually clucked under his breath, removing them with a sharp gesture.

'To leave them so is an insult,' Chen Yi said, 'though you could not have known.' Khasar found a plate of skewered crickets easier to handle, biting into the line of fried insects with evident pleasure.

'This is better,' he said, his mouth working busily.

Temuge was prepared to copy whatever Chen Yi did and dipped balls of fried dough into salt water before chewing them. When the crickets were all gone, Khasar reached for a pile of oranges, taking two. After spitting out a piece of skin, he peeled the first with his thumbs and relaxed visibly as he pulled the flesh apart and ate it. He and his brother waited for Chen Yi to speak, their impatience obvious and growing.

When they had all finished, Chen Yi eyed Khasar's efforts with the orange, then placed his chopsticks on the table and said nothing as his slaves removed all evidence of the meal. When they were alone again, he sat back on his couch. His eyes lost their hooded look and gained once more the sharpness of the river master they knew.

'Why have you come to Baotou?' he said to Temuge.

'Trade,' Temuge replied immediately. 'We are merchants.'

Chen Yi shook his head.

'Merchants do not carry a Mongol bow, nor shoot one as your brother does. You are of that people. Why would you be here in the lands of the emperor?'

Temuge swallowed painfully as he tried to think. Chen Yi had known for a long time and not given them away, but he could not bring himself to trust the man, especially after so much strangeness and confusion.

'We are of the tribes of the great khan, yes,' he said. 'But we have come to open trade between our people.'

'I am a trader. Make your offers to me,' Chen Yi replied. His face gave nothing away, but Temuge could sense the little man's fierce curiosity.

'Ho Sa asked who you were to have so much wealth,' Temuge

said slowly, choosing the words. 'You have this house and slaves, but you took the role of a smuggler on the river, bribing guards and staging a diversion at the city gate. Who are you that we should trust you?'

Chen Yi's gaze was cold as he studied them.

'I am a man who is uncomfortable at the thought of you blundering around his city. How long would it take for you to be captured by Imperial soldiers? How long after that before you told them everything you have seen?'

He waited while Temuge translated for his brother.

'Tell him if we are killed or kept as prisoners, Baotou will be burned to the ground,' Khasar said, tearing the second orange in two and sucking at a ragged half. 'Genghis will come for us next year. He knows where we are and this little man will see his precious house in flames. Tell him that.'

'You would do well to be quiet, brother, if we are to get out of here with our lives.'

'Let him speak,' Chen Yi said. 'How would my city be burned if you are killed?'

To Temuge's horror, Chen Yi spoke in the language of the tribes. His accent was rough, but it was clear enough to both of them. He froze as he considered all the conversations Chen Yi had overheard in the weeks taken to reach Baotou.

'How do you know our tongue?' he demanded, forgetting his fear for a moment.

Chen Yi laughed, a high-pitched sound that did nothing to settle the men at the table.

'Did you think you were the first to travel to Chin lands? The Uighurs have ridden the silk road. Some have stayed.' He clapped his hands and another man came into the room. He was as clean as they were and dressed in a simple Chin robe, but his face was Mongol and the breadth of his shoulders showed one

192

who had been raised with the bow. Khasar rose to greet him, clasping his hand and beating him on the back with his fist. The stranger beamed at the welcome.

'It is good to see a real face in this city,' Khasar said.

The man seemed almost overcome to hear the words.

'And for me,' he said, glancing at Chen Yi. 'How are the plains? I have not been home for many years.'

'They are the same,' Khasar replied. A thought struck him and his hand dropped to where his sword would usually lie on his hip. 'Is this man a slave?'

Chen Yi looked up without embarrassment.

'Of course. Quishan was once a merchant, but he chose to gamble with me.'

The man shrugged.

'It is true. I will not be a slave for ever. A few more years and my debt will be paid. Then I think I will return to the plains and find a wife.'

'Find me first when you do. I will give you a new start,' Khasar promised him. Chen Yi watched as Quishan bowed his head. Khasar accepted the gesture as if it was nothing new to him and Chen Yi's gaze became hard.

'Tell me again how my city will burn,' he said.

Temuge opened his mouth, but Chen Yi held up a hand.

'No, I do not trust *you*. Your brother spoke the truth when he thought I could not understand. Let him tell it all.'

Khasar shot a glance at Temuge, thoroughly enjoying his brother's frustration. He took a moment to choose his words. Perhaps Chen Yi would have them killed when he heard. He moved his hand to where he had hidden a small knife in the folds of his robe.

'We were once of the Wolves,' Khasar said, at last, 'but my brother has united the tribes. The kingdom of Xi Xia is our first vassal, though there will be more.' Ho Sa shifted uncomfortably at the words, but neither man looked at him. Khasar sat like stone as he stared into Chen Yi's eyes.

'Perhaps I will die here, tonight, but if I do, my people will come amongst the Chin and tear down your precious cities, one by one, stone from stone.'

Chen Yi's face had grown tight as he listened. His command of the language was only what he had needed for trade and he would have suggested a switch back to his own if it would not have looked like weakness.

'News travels fast on the river,' he said, refusing to respond to Khasar's deadly intensity. 'I had heard of the war in Xi Xia, though not that your people were triumphant. Is the king dead then?'

'Not when I left,' Khasar replied. 'He paid tribute and a daughter. A beautiful girl, I thought.'

'You have not answered my question, except with threats,' Chen Yi reminded him. 'Why would you come here, to my city?'

Khasar noticed the slight stress Chen Yi had put on 'my'. He did not have the subtlety to play with words, or spin a thread of lies Chen Yi would believe.

'We need masons,' Khasar said. He heard Temuge let out a sharp breath at his shoulder and ignored him. 'We need to know the secrets of your cities. The great khan himself has sent us. Baotou is just a place on a map with no great significance.'

'It is my home,' Chen Yi murmured, thinking.

'You can keep it,' Khasar said, sensing the moment was right. 'Baotou will not be touched if we bring back word of your help.'

He waited for Chen Yi to finish his thoughts, sweat dripping down his face. One shout and the room would fill with armed men, he was certain. It was true Genghis would destroy the city in revenge, but Chen Yi could not be certain of that. For all he knew, they were boasting or lying.

It was Quishan who broke the silence. He had paled at what he heard and his voice was low with awe.

'The tribes are united?' he said. 'The Uighurs among them?'

Khasar nodded, his gaze never leaving Chen Yi.

'The blue tail is part of the great khan's standard. The Chin have held us down for a long time, but that is over. We ride to war, brother.'

Chen Yi watched Quishan's face carefully, seeing how the news brought an expression of astonished hope.

'I will make a bargain with you,' he said suddenly. 'Whatever you need you will have, from my hand. You will bring the word back to your khan and tell him that there is a man here he can trust.'

'What use is a smuggler to us?' Khasar responded. Temuge almost groaned as Khasar went on, 'How can *you* bargain for the fate of a city?'

'If you fail, or if you lie, I have lost nothing. If you are telling the truth, you will need allies, will you not?' Chen Yi said. 'I have power here.'

'You would betray the Imperial court? Your own emperor?' Khasar said. He asked the question to test Chen Yi, and to his astonishment, the little man spat on the polished floor.

'This is my city. Everything that goes on here comes to my ears. I have no love for nobles who think all men can be run under their carts like animals. I have lost family and friends to their soldiers, seen loved ones hanged when they refused to give up my name. What do I care for them?'

He had risen as he spoke and Khasar stood to face him.

'My word is iron,' Khasar said. 'If I say you will have this city, it will be yours to rule when we come.'

'You can speak for the khan?' Chen Yi said.

'He is my brother. I can speak for him,' Khasar replied. Temuge and Ho Sa could only look on as the two men stared each other down.

'I knew you were a warrior on the boat,' Chen Yi said. 'You were a poor spy.'

'I knew you were a thief, but a good one,' Khasar replied. Chen Yi chuckled and they took each other's hands in a firm grip.

'I have many men who answer to me. I will give you what you need and I will see you safe back to your people,' Chen Yi said. He sat, calling for wine as Temuge began to talk. He could not understand how the little man had come to trust Khasar, but it did not matter. They had their ally in Baotou.

As evening came, Khasar, Ho Sa and Temuge accepted the offer of a few hours' sleep before a long night, retiring to rooms off the second courtyard. Chen Yi had never needed more than a few hours' rest since his days running from the soldiers in the alleyways of Baotou – lifetimes ago. He sat up with Quishan and two of his guards, and they talked in low voices as they moved counters of ivory on a mah-jongg board. Quishan was silent for a long time as he clicked the counters together in his hand. He had known Chen Yi for almost ten years and seen a ruthless desire for power come to bloom in that time. The little man had crushed three other leaders of Baotou's criminal gangs and he had not exaggerated when he had told Khasar that little went on in the city without it reaching his ears.

Quishan discarded a tile and watched as Chen Yi's hand hovered over it. The man he had come to call a friend was clearly distracted from the game, his thoughts elsewhere. Quishan wondered if he should raise the stakes and clear a little more of his debt. He decided not to, remembering other games where Chen Yi had lulled him with exactly the same approach, then won consistently.

He watched as Chen Yi took a different tile and the game went round the table, with one of the guards calling 'Pung' and making Quishan swear under his breath.

As the guard showed three matching tiles, Chen Yi put his hand down.

'No more tonight. You are getting better, Han, but your gate duty is upon us.'

Both guards rose and bowed. They had been rescued from the worst street slums, and they were strong and loyal to the man who ruled the tong. Quishan stayed, sensing Chen Yi wanted to talk.

'You are thinking of the strangers,' Quishan said as he gathered up the tiles on the table. Chen Yi nodded, staring into the darkness through the screen doors. The evening was already cold and he wondered what the hours ahead would bring.

'They are strange people, Quishan. I have said that to you before. I took them on to guard my silk, when three of my men fell ill. Perhaps my ancestors were guiding me in that.' He sighed and rubbed his eyes wearily. 'Did you see the way Khasar took note of the positions of the guards? His eyes were always moving. I thought on the boat that I had never seen him relax, but you are the same. Perhaps all your people are.'

Quishan shrugged.

'Life is struggle, master. Is that not also what the Buddhists believe? On the plains of my home, the weak die early. It has always been that way.'

'I have never seen anyone shoot a bow as well as that one. In near darkness, on a rocking boat, he killed six men without hesitation. Are all your people so skilled?'

Quishan busied his hands with the mah-jongg tiles, placing them back in their leather carrying case.

'I am not, but the Uighurs value learning and trade more than any other tribe. The Wolves are known for their ferocity.' He paused, his hands growing still. 'It is almost too much to believe that the tribes have united under one man, one khan. He must be extraordinary.'

Quishan snapped the clasp closed on the leather box, leaning back. He wanted a drink to settle his stomach, but Chen Yi never allowed alcohol when the night needed clear heads.

'Will you welcome my people when they ride to the walls?' Quishan asked softly. He felt Chen Yi's gaze on him, but he did not look up from his folded hands.

'You think I betrayed my city?' Chen Yi asked him.

Quishan raised his gaze, seeing a dark anger in the man he had grown to trust over the years.

'All this is new. Perhaps this new khan will be destroyed by the emperor's armies and those who called themselves allies will suffer the same fate. Have you considered that?'

Chen Yi snorted.

'Of course, but I have lived too long with a foot on my neck, Quishan. This house, my slaves, all those who follow me are just what the emperor's ministers have missed through sloth and corruption. We are beneath their notice, like rats in their warehouses. At times, they send a man to make an example and he hangs a few hundred. Sometimes they even catch people who are valuable to me. Or loved by me.' Chen Yi's face was like stone as he spoke and Quishan knew he was thinking of his son, no more than a boy when he had been caught in a trawl of the docks two years before. Chen Yi himself had taken the body down from where it swung in the river breeze.

'But a fire does not know who it burns,' Quishan said. 'You are inviting the flames into your home, your city. Who knows how it will end?'

Chen Yi was silent. He knew as well as Quishan that the three strangers could be made to vanish. There were always bodies in the Yellow River, naked and bloated as they floated by. The deaths would never come back to him. Yet something he had seen in Khasar had stirred a thirst for revenge Chen Yi had buried since the morning he had carried his son's limp weight.

'Let them come, these people of yours who use bows and horses. I judge them more by you than the promises of men I do not know. How long have you worked for me?'

'Nine years, master,' Quishan said.

'And you have kept honour with me to pay your debt. How many times could you have escaped and gone back to your people?'

'Three times,' Quishan admitted. 'Three when I thought I would be able to run clear before you heard.'

'I knew about them,' Chen Yi replied. 'I knew of the boat master who made the first offer. He was one of mine. You would not have gone far before he cut your throat.'

Quishan frowned at this information.

'You tested me, then.'

'Of course. I am not a fool, Quishan. I never was. Let the flames come to Baotou. I will stand alive on the ashes when they are done. Let the Imperial officers burn their plumes in them and I will know contentment. I will know joy at last.'

Chen Yi rose and stretched, his back clicking audibly in the silent rooms.

'You are a gambler, Quishan, it is why you have worked for me for so long. I have never been one. I have made this city my own, but still I must bow my head whenever I see one of the emperor's prancing favourites ride down the streets. My streets, Quishan, yet I bow and step into the filth of the gutters rather than stand in their path.'

Chen Yi looked out into the darkness, his eyes dead in his face.

'I will stand now, Quishan, and the tiles will fall as they please.'

CHAPTER FOURTEEN

As midnight came, a heavy rain began to fall on the city of Baotou. The downpour hissed on the streets and rattled on the tiles so that it sounded like distant thunder. Chen Yi seemed pleased at the turn in the weather as he handed swords to his men. Even the beggars would shrink back in their doorways while the rain came down. It was a good omen.

As they stepped out onto the dark street, Khasar and Ho Sa stared up and down its length to see if they were observed. The moon was hidden and there was only dim light when the rushing clouds drifted open in patches. Temuge had assumed the water would wash away some of the stench of the city. Instead, it seemed to bloom in the air, the taint of human filth carried on the damp so that it seeped into his lungs and made him nauseous. The gutters were already full and Temuge saw dark, wet things he could not name tumbling along, borne by the current. He shuddered, suddenly aware of the writhing press of humanity all around him. Without Chen Yi, he would not have known where to begin his search in the maze of houses and shops, piled on top of one another in all directions.

Two more of Chen Yi's men had joined them at the gate. Although there was no official curfew, ten men would be challenged by any soldiers still on the streets. Chen Yi gave one the task of scouting each crossroads, and instructed two more to hang back and see if they were followed. Temuge could not escape the feeling he was heading into a battle. As the rain poured down, he handled the wet hilt of the sword Chen Yi had pressed on him, hoping he would not have to draw it. He was shivering as they set off, moving at a light trot. The gates closed behind them with an audible clang, but no one looked back.

On some of the streets, the overhanging eaves of houses formed a strip of dry road. Chen Yi slowed to a walk as he led the group past those, unwilling to have the sound of running feet draw residents out to watch. The city was not fully dark, nor sleeping. Temuge saw occasional lights from forges and warehouses, still working into the night. Despite Chen Yi's precautions, Temuge was certain he could feel eyes on them as they passed.

In the gloom, Temuge lost track of time until it seemed he had been running for half the night. There was no pattern to the streets as they wound over and around each other, sometimes little more than dirt tracks with clotted mud that spattered them up to their knees. Temuge was winded after only a short time and more than once someone took his arm in the darkness and yanked him onwards, forcing him to keep up. He swore under his breath as one such jerk on his sleeve made him step into a gutter and something soft and cold became trapped between his toes. He hoped it was rotten fruit and nothing worse, but he did not stop.

Only once did the front runner return to guide Chen Yi down a different path. Temuge hoped the soldiers were spending the night in a warm barracks rather than being frozen and drenched as he was.

Chen Yi stopped his panting men at last in the shadow of the city wall itself. Temuge could see it as a bank of deeper darkness. On the other side lay the world he knew and he had a sense of the protection it brought to the city. Such a wall had served the Xi Xia king in Yinchuan. All the warriors Genghis had summoned could not make a breach in such a thing. It ran into the distance, looming over a wide street of houses that looked much as Chen Yi's own home. These, though, were not hidden in the slums, but rose well spaced and carried the scent of flowering gardens on the breeze. Even the pattern of streets had changed in this part of Baotou. They jogged through a grid of islands, each one separate from the city behind its gates and walls. Temuge struggled to catch his breath. He almost choked as Khasar slapped him on the shoulders, his brother standing comfortably as if he had been out for an evening stroll.

The two runners behind came up quickly, shaking their heads. They had not been followed. Chen Yi did not pause to rest, whispering orders to them to stay out of sight as he approached the closest gate. The man's gaze fell on Temuge as he stood there with his hands resting on his knees and he came close to speak into his ear.

'There will be guards. They will wake their master and I will speak to him. Make no threats in my city, Mongol. The owner will be nervous to have strangers so late in his house and I do not want weapons to be drawn.'

Chen Yi turned away, smoothing down his black robe with his hands as he neared the gate. Two of his men accompanied him and the rest of the group faded to one side where they could not be seen. Khasar took Temuge by the sleeve and dragged him with them before he could protest.

Chen Yi himself thumped on the gate and Temuge saw yellow light fall on his face as a hinged square opened in the wood.

'Tell your master he has a visitor on Imperial business,' Chen Yi said, his voice firm. 'Rouse him, if he sleeps.'

Temuge could not hear the reply, but after an age, the square opened again and Chen Yi looked into another face.

'I do not know you,' the man said clearly.

Chen Yi stood very still.

'The Blue Tong knows you, Lian. Tonight, your debts will be paid.'

The gate opened quickly, but Chen Yi did not step across the threshold.

'If you have crossbows waiting, Lian, it will be your last night. I have men with me, but the streets are dangerous. Do not be alarmed and all will be well.'

The unseen man murmured a reply, his voice shaking. Only then did Chen Yi turn his gaze on the others and gesture them to follow him in.

Temuge saw fear in the man who had been summoned from his bed. Lian was almost as wide across the shoulders as Khasar, but he trembled visibly, keeping his eyes downcast as Chen Yi strode into his home.

There was only one guard at the gate and he too kept his eyes averted from those who entered. Temuge felt his confidence grow and he looked around him with interest as soon as the gate was shut on the street. The run through the rain and darkness was behind and he enjoyed the subservient way the master mason of Baotou reacted.

Lian stood as if stunned before Chen Yi, his hair wild from sleep.

'I will have food and drink prepared,' he murmured, but Chen Yi shook his head.

'It will not be necessary. Show me to where we can talk in private.' Chen Yi looked around at the courtyard of the home. The mason had prospered under Imperial rule. As well as repairing the wall, he was responsible for the creation of three barracks and the racecourse in the heart of the Imperial district.

Yet his home was simple and elegant. Chen Yi's gaze fastened on the single guard and he saw that he stood very close to a bell hanging from a beam.

'You would not want your man to summon soldiers here, Lian. Tell him to stand away from that bell, or I will believe you doubt my word.'

The mason nodded to the soldier, who winced visibly and took up a new position near the main house. The rain grew heavier, pounding into the small courtyard. Chilled by it, the mason seemed to come to himself. He led them into the house and hid his fear in the lighting of lamps. Temuge saw his hand shake as he held the taper to wick after wick, more than they needed, as if the light could banish his fear.

Chen Yi settled himself on a hard couch as he waited for the mason to finish fussing round the room. Khasar, Ho Sa and Temuge stood together, watching the scene in silent fascination. Chen Yi's guards took positions behind their master and Temuge saw the mason's eyes flicker over them, registering the threat.

At last, he could not delay any longer. He seated himself across from Chen Yi, pressing his hands together to hide the way they shook.

'I have paid my tithe to the tong,' Lian said. 'Was it short?'

'It was not,' Chen Yi replied. He took a moment to smooth the rainwater off his face, running his hand over his hair and flicking the drops onto the wooden floor. Lian's gaze followed them. 'It is not that which brings me to you.'

Before Chen Yi could continue, Lian spoke again, unable to stop himself. 'The workers, then? I used all the men I could, but two of those you sent would not work. The others complained that they did not carry their share. I was going to dismiss them this morning, but if it is your will that they remain . . .'

Chen Yi could have been carved out of marble as he studied the master mason.

'They are the sons of friends. They will remain, but that is not why I am here.'

The mason slumped slightly in his seat.

'Then I do not understand,' he said.

'Do you have one who can take over the work of maintaining the wall?'

'My own son, lord.'

Chen Yi sat very still until the mason looked up at him.

'I am not a lord, Lian. I am a friend who must ask a favour.'

'Anything,' Lian replied, tensing for the worst.

Chen Yi nodded, pleased.

'You will summon your son and tell him he must take over the work for a year, perhaps two. I have heard good reports of him.'

'He is a fine son,' Lian agreed immediately. 'He will listen to his father.'

'That is wise, Lian. Tell him you will be gone for that time, perhaps to find a new source of marble in a quarry somewhere. Make up whatever lie you wish, but do not leave him suspicious. Remind him the debts of the father are his while you are gone and explain the tithe he must pay to the tong if he wishes to work. I do not want to have to remind him myself.'

'It is done,' Lian said. He was sweating, Temuge saw, a bright line of droplets appearing on his hairline. He saw the burly mason gather his courage to ask a question.

'I will tell my wife and children the same, but may I know the truth?'

Chen Yi shrugged, cocking his head to one side.

'Will it change anything, Lian?'

'No, lord. I am sorry . . .'

206

'It does not matter. You will accompany these friends of mine out of the city. They need your expertise, Lian. Bring your tools and, when your work is done, I will see to it that you are rewarded.'

The mason nodded miserably and Chen Yi stood abruptly.

'Speak to those you love, Lian, then come with me.'

The mason left the group alone and disappeared into the darkness of the house. Those who remained relaxed a little and Khasar wandered over to a silk hanging, using the material to dry the rain from his face and hair. Temuge heard the distant wail of a child as the man passed on what he had been told.

'I do not know what we would have done if you had not been here to help us,' Ho Sa said to Chen Yi.

The master of the tong smiled slightly.

'You would have blundered around my city until the soldiers caught you. Perhaps I would have come to watch the foreign spies impaled or hanged. The gods are fickle, but this time, they were with you.'

'Have you given thought to getting us out of the city?' Temuge asked. Before Chen Yi could respond, Lian returned. His eyes were red, but he stood tall and had lost some portion of his fear. He wore a coat of heavy waxed cloth against the rain and over one shoulder was a rolled leather pack that he clutched as if it gave him comfort.

'I have my tools,' he said to Chen Yi. 'I am ready.'

They left the house behind and, once again, Chen Yi sent a man ahead to watch for soldiers walking their patrols. The rain had lessened and Temuge saw the north star briefly through the clouds. Chen Yi had explained nothing, but they headed west along a road parallel to the wall and Temuge could only trot with them.

In the darkness ahead, they heard a voice cry out and the group halted as one.

'Keep your blades out of sight,' Chen Yi hissed. Temuge swallowed nervously, hearing footsteps on the paved road. They waited for the man ahead to come back, but instead, they heard the tramp of iron-shod sandals and Chen Yi darted his gaze around, taking in possible routes of escape.

'Stand still,' a voice snapped out of the darkness. Temuge was close enough to see Chen Yi grimace.

There were six soldiers in scaled armour, led by a man wearing a plumed helmet of hard bristles. Temuge groaned to himself at the sight of the crossbows they held. Chen Yi's men stood little chance of fighting their way through. He felt panic rise like acid in his throat and he started to back away without thinking. It was Khasar's iron grip that held him in place.

'Where is your captain?' Chen Yi demanded. 'Lujan can vouch for me.' He saw that they held his man by the scruff of his neck. The man struggled in the grip, but Chen Yi did not look at him.

The plumed officer frowned at the tone, stepping forward from his men.

'Lujan is off duty tonight. What business do you have to be running in the streets in the dark?'

'Lujan will explain,' Chen Yi said. He licked his lips nervously. 'He told me his name would let us pass.'

The officer glanced back at the hapless man being held by his neck.

'I have not been told. You will come back to the barracks and we will ask him.'

Chen Yi sighed.

'No. No, we will not do that,' he said. Chen Yi darted forward with a knife in his fist, punching it into the throat of the officer so that he fell back with a choking cry. The soldiers behind loosed their crossbows instantly, firing into the group. Someone cried out and then Chen Yi's men were among them, hacking their blades into the soldiers.

Khasar drew the sword he had been given and roared at the top of his lungs. The bark of sound made the closest soldier take a step back and Khasar knocked him down, stepping in close to hammer his forearm across the man's face. The impact took the soldier's feet out from under him and Khasar lunged past, lost in a vicious whirl where he used elbows, feet, head: anything to bring his enemies to the ground. Those who had shot their bolts could only raise the bows to defend themselves. Khasar's blade smashed one of the weapons to pieces before he hacked the edge into a soldier's neck. In the darkness, he moved through them like a breeze, kicking at an exposed knee and feeling it break. The soldiers were clumsy in their armour and Khasar was faster, whipping round as he sensed every threat before it could come close. He felt someone grasp him from behind, trapping his sword arm. He smashed his head backwards, striking with his elbows, and was rewarded with a grunt of pain as his attacker fell away.

Temuge shouted as one of the soldiers collided with him. He flailed wildly with his own sword, terror stealing his strength. Somewhere, a bell began to ring. As he registered the sound, he felt himself being lifted and he screamed, falling silent when Ho Sa slapped his face.

'Get up. It is over,' Ho Sa snapped, embarrassed for him. Temuge gripped his arm as he rose, staring at the sight of Khasar surrounded by broken bodies.

'You call these soldiers, Chen Yi?' Khasar said. 'They move like sick sheep.'

Chen Yi stood stunned as Khasar casually shoved his sword into the chest of one who still moved, finding a place under the scales of armour before leaning his full weight on it.

He could hardly believe how quickly the Mongol warrior had moved. His own guards were men picked for their skill, but Khasar had made them look like farmers. He found himself wanting to defend the soldiers of his city, much as he hated them.

'There are six city barracks, each with five hundred or more of these sick sheep,' he replied. 'It has been enough.'

Khasar prodded one of the bodies with his foot.

'My people will eat them alive,' he said. He winced then and touched his hand to his collarbone. It came away stained with blood, quickly diluted in the rain so that it ran between his fingers.

'You are cut,' Temuge said.

'I am too used to fighting in armour, brother. I let the blow through.' In irritation, Khasar kicked the officer's helmet where it lay near his feet, sending it skittering over the paving.

Two of Chen Yi's men hung limp between their fellows, blood pooling into the puddles of rainwater. Chen Yi examined them, his fingers touching the bolts that stood out in their chests. He thought quickly, his plans in disarray.

'No man can avoid the wheel,' he said. 'Let them lie here to be found. The Imperial officers will want bodies to show to the crowds tomorrow.'

The two dead men were released, sprawling on the stones. Temuge saw that others among them bore wounds and they panted like dogs in the sun. Chen Yi turned to him then, his anger becoming scorn.

'You are safe for the moment, frightened one, but they will rip the city apart looking for us. If I do not get you out tonight, you will be here until spring.'

Temuge's cheeks burned in humiliation. All the group was staring at him and Khasar looked away. Chen Yi sheathed his blade and resumed the trot that would carry them to the walls.

The runner had survived the bloody fight and he went ahead once more.

The west gate was smaller than the one they had passed through on their journey from the river. Temuge despaired when he saw light growing ahead and heard shouting. Whichever citizen had rung a warning bell, the soldiers had roused themselves from their barracks and Chen Yi was hard pressed to avoid being seen. He headed for a dark building near the gate, hammering on the door to be let in. Temuge could hear the clatter of armoured men coming closer as the door opened and they piled inside, slamming it quickly shut behind them.

'Get men to the highest windows,' Chen Yi told the one who had answered his knock. 'Have them call down what they see.' He swore under his breath then and Temuge did not dare speak to him. The sight of the ugly gash running the length of Khasar's collarbone stirred Temuge from his panic and he asked one of Chen Yi's men for a needle and cat-gut thread. His brother watched with just the occasional grunt as Temuge stitched the skin in a ragged line. The blood and rain had cleaned it and he thought it would not fester. The action helped to still his thumping heart and prevented him from dwelling on the fact that they were being hunted at that very moment.

One of the men above called down, his voice a harsh whisper as he leaned over a banister.

'The gate is shut and barricaded. I can see perhaps a hundred soldiers, though most are on the move. Thirty hold the gate.'

'Crossbows?' Chen Yi asked, looking up at the man.

'Twenty, maybe more.'

'Then we are trapped. They will search the city for us.' He turned to Temuge.

'I can no longer help you. If I am found, they will kill me

211

and the Blue Tong will have a new leader. I must leave you here.'

The mason, Lian, had not fought with the others. Unarmed, he had stepped into the gutter as soon as the fight had started. It was he who answered Chen Yi, his voice rumbling in the shocked silence.

'I know a way out,' he said. 'If you don't mind a little dirt on your hands.'

'Soldiers in the street!' the man above hissed down at them. 'They are knocking on doors, searching the houses.'

'Tell us quickly, Lian,' Chen Yi said. 'If we are caught, you will not be spared.'

The mason nodded, his face grim.

'We must go now. It is not far from here.'

Mutton-fat lamps burned and spat, casting a dim yellow light as Genghis faced a line of six kneeling men. Each of them had his hands bound behind his back. To a man, they showed the cold face, as if terror of the khan did not gnaw at them. Genghis strode up and down the line. He had been summoned from the bed of Chakahai and had risen with fury, even when he saw it was Kachiun who called his name in the darkness.

The six men were brothers, ranging from the youngest who was barely more than a boy to mature warriors with wives and children of their own.

'Each of you spoke an oath to me,' Genghis snapped. His temper flared as he spoke and, for an instant, he was tempted to take the heads of all six.

'One of you killed a boy of the Uriankhai. Let him speak and only one will die. If he does not, your lives are mine to take.' He drew his father's sword slowly, letting them hear the sound. Outside the ring of lamps, he sensed the presence of a growing crowd, called from sleep by the prospect of seeing justice. He would not disappoint them. Genghis stood over the youngest of the brothers and raised the sword as if it weighed nothing.

'I can find him, my lord,' Kokchu said softly from the edge of the darkness. The brothers looked up to see the shaman enter the dim light, his eyes terrible. 'I have only to lay my hand on each head to know the one you seek.'

The brothers were visibly trembling as Genghis nodded, sheathing his sword.

'Work your spells, shaman. The boy was torn apart. Find me who did it.'

Kokchu bowed low and stood before the brothers. They did not dare look at him, though their frozen expressions were strained and quivering.

Genghis watched in fascination as Kokchu pressed his hand lightly to the first man's head and closed his eyes. The words of the shaman's tongue erupted forth from him in a liquid roll of sound. One of the brothers jerked away and almost fell before struggling upright.

As Kokchu lifted his hand, the first brother swayed, dazed and pale. The crowd outside the light had grown and hundreds murmured in the dark. Kokchu moved to the second man and took an indrawn breath, closing his eyes.

'The boy . . .' he said. 'The boy saw . . .' He stood very still and the camp held their breath to watch him. At last, Kokchu shook himself, as if shrugging off a heavy weight. 'One of these men is a traitor, lord. I have seen it. I have seen his face. He killed the boy to stop him telling what he saw.'

With one sharp step, Kokchu stepped to the fourth man in the line, the oldest of the brothers. His hand snapped out and his fingers writhed like bones in the man's black hair.

'I did not kill the boy!' the brother shouted, struggling.

'If you lie, the spirits will steal your soul,' Kokchu hissed into the shocked silence. 'Now lie *again* and show the lord khan the fate of traitors and murderers.'

The warrior was slack-faced with terror as he cried out, 'I did not kill the boy. I swear it!' Under Kokchu's heavy hand, he convulsed suddenly and the crowd shouted in fear. They watched in horror as the man's eyes rolled up in his head and his jaw flopped open brokenly. He fell to one side, breaking the awful grip as he jerked and spasmed, his bladder releasing a great rush of steaming urine onto the frozen grass.

Kokchu stood watching until the man was still, his eyes showing white in the gleam from the lamps. The silence was immense, filling the camp. Only Genghis could break it and even he had to struggle to overcome the sense of awe and dread that gripped him.

'Cut the bonds of the other men,' he said. 'The boy's death has been answered.' Kokchu bowed to him then and Genghis dismissed the crowd to their homes to wait fearfully for the sun to return.

CHAPTER FIFTEEN

Alarm bells rang across Baotou as they hurried through the night, following Lian. Even the dark was lifting in places, as householders woke and lit lamps at every gate. They ran through pools of light where the rain showed as gold flecks, then on into blackness.

The soldiers had not seen them leave, though it had been close. Lian clearly knew the area well and darted through tiny alleys behind the houses of the rich without hesitation. Most of the Imperial guards had turned out in the area of the gates, but they were working their way inwards to the centre of the city, tightening their grip as they searched for the criminals who had killed their men.

Temuge panted weakly as he struggled on. They were heading along the wall, though at times, Lian turned away from it to avoid open courtyards and street crossings. Khasar loped at his side, watching for soldiers. After the fight, he was smiling whenever Temuge looked at him, though Temuge suspected it was the smile of an idiot who could not imagine the consequences of being caught. His own imagination was brutal enough for both of them and he cringed as he ran, imagining hot irons on his flesh.

Lian halted near a quiet section of the wall. The ant-like scurrying of soldiers had been left behind, but the warning bells had brought the people out to their doorways, peering fearfully at the running men.

Lian turned to them, breathing heavily.

'The wall is being repaired here. We can climb the ropes for the rubble baskets. You won't find another way out of Baotou tonight.'

'Show me,' Chen Yi said. Lian glanced around him at the pale faces watching from every window in sight. He swallowed nervously and nodded, leading them to where they could lay their hands on the ancient stones of the city wall.

Ropes lay coiled in the darkness and they could see the bulbous shapes of the soft baskets used to carry rubble up to the crest, where it was dumped into the core of the wall. Three of the ropes were taut and Chen Yi gripped one of them with a pleased exclamation.

'You have done well, Lian. Are there no ladders?'

'They are locked away at night,' Lian replied. 'I could break the locks easily enough, but it would delay us.'

'Then this will do. Take this one and show how it is done.'

The mason dropped his roll of tools to the ground and began climbing, grunting with the effort. It was difficult to judge the height of the wall in the dark, but it seemed huge to Temuge as he stared upwards. He clenched his fists in the darkness, desperate not to be humiliated again in front of Khasar. He would climb it. The thought of being lifted like a sack of hammers was too awful to contemplate.

Ho Sa and Khasar went up together, though Khasar looked back at Temuge before starting to climb. No doubt he thought his weak brother would slip and fall on Chen Yi like divine retribution. Temuge stared furiously at him until Khasar grinned and climbed like a rat, making it look easy despite his wound.

'The rest of you will wait here,' Chen Yi murmured to his

men. 'I will go up with these, then return to you once they are safely down. Someone will have to pull the lines back from the other side.'

He handed a thick rope to Temuge and watched as the younger man began to ascend, pulling himself up the wall with shaking arms. Chen Yi shook his head in exasperation.

'Do not fall, fearful one,' he said. A small man, Chen Yi ascended quickly, leaving Temuge climbing alone in the dark. His arms were burning and sweat poured into his eyes, but he forced himself to walk up the rough stone, hanging out over the men below. There was no light near the top and he almost let go in shock when strong hands grabbed him and dragged him onto the crest.

Temuge lay panting, ignored by the others and desperately relieved. His heart pounded wildly as they stood and looked back into the city. Below, the baskets of rubble had been cut free and they pulled the ropes up quickly, dropping them over the other side.

The wall was ten feet wide at the crest and the rope stretched over it. Lian swore under his breath as he saw the ropes would not reach right to the ground outside the city.

'We will have to jump the last part and hope no one breaks a leg,' he said.

The last rope had to be pulled up. It bumped its way to the top with the bundle of Lian's tools, Khasar's bow and three plain swords all wrapped together. Lian lowered it down the outside of the wall and paused, waiting for Chen Yi to give the order.

'Go now,' Chen Yi said. 'You will have to walk unless you can find a place to buy mules.'

'I am not riding a mule,' Khasar said immediately. 'Are there no ponies worth stealing in this land?'

'It is too much risk. Your people lie to the north, unless you

217

intend to return by way of the Xi Xia. It is not more than a few hundred *li* from here, but there will be garrisons of Imperial soldiers on every road and pass. You would do better to head west past the mountains, travelling only by night.'

'We'll see,' Khasar said. 'Goodbye, little thief. I will not forget how you have helped us.' He crouched on the far edge, then slid over to hang on his elbows before reaching for the dangling rope. Ho Sa followed with merely a nod to Chen Yi and Temuge too would have gone without a word if the little man hadn't laid a palm on his shoulder.

'Your khan has what he wanted. I will hold him to promises made in his name.'

Temuge nodded briskly. He did not care whether Genghis torched Baotou to the ground.

'Of course,' he said. 'We are an honourable people.' Chen Yi watched as he climbed down, as ungainly and feeble as before. When the leader of the Blue Tong was alone on the wall, he sighed. He did not trust Temuge, with his shifting eyes and visible cowardice. In Khasar he had sensed a fellow spirit; a ruthless man, but one he hoped would share his sense of honour and debt. He shrugged as he turned back to the city. He could not be certain. He did not enjoy the thrill of gambling and had never understood it in those who did. 'The tiles are flying,' he murmured. 'Who knows where they will fall?'

The four men were dusty and footsore by the tenth day. Unused to walking, Khasar had developed a limp and his mood was surly as they trudged on. Once out of reach of Chen Yi, Lian too had asked only a few questions before settling into a grim silence. He walked with his tools over his shoulder and though he shared the hares Khasar killed with his bow, he made no attempt to join in the conversations as the others planned their route. A biting wind made them walk with one hand on their robes, bunching the cloth tight.

Khasar had wanted to take the shortest trails north. Temuge had argued and been ignored, but Ho Sa had swayed him with descriptions of the Chin forts and the wall that guarded the empire from invaders. Though it was broken, there were still guards enough to pose a danger to four men alone. The only safe path was to head west along the banks of the Yellow River until they reached the mountains that straddled the Xi Xia kingdom and the Gobi Desert.

At the end of the tenth day, Khasar had insisted on entering a Chin village to look for ponies. He and his brother still carried a small fortune in silver and gold – enough to terrify peasants who would not have seen anything like that level of wealth. Even finding a merchant willing to change a few silvers into bronze was difficult. They left empty-handed and set off again as night fell, unwilling to remain in one place for long.

As the moon rose, the four weary men were deep in pine woods, making slow time on animal paths and trying to keep sight of the stars to guide them. For the first time in his life, Temuge had become aware of his own smell of sweat and dirt and wished for another opportunity to bathe in the Chin style. He looked back on his first experience of a city with nostalgia, remembering the cleanliness of Chen Yi's house. He cared nothing for the beggars, or the mass of people like maggots in flyblown meat. He was the son and brother of a khan and would never fall to such a low estate. To find that wealthy men could live as he had seen was a revelation and he asked questions of Lian as they walked in the darkness. The mason seemed surprised that Temuge should know so little of city life, hardly understanding how each new fact was like water to a dry soul. He told Temuge of apprenticeship and universities, where great thinkers came to exchange ideas and argue without bloodshed.

As a mason, he spoke of sewers being laid even in the poorest sections of the city, though corruption had stalled the works for more than a dozen years. Temuge drank it all in and, as he walked, he dreamed of strolling with learned men in sunlit courtyards, discussing great issues with his hands clasped behind his back. Then he would stumble on a hidden root and Khasar would laugh at him, shattering the images.

It was Khasar who stopped on the trail without warning, letting Ho Sa thump into his back. The Xi Xia soldier was too much of an old hand to break the silence. Lian stopped in confusion and Temuge raised his head from private thoughts, his breath catching in his throat. Surely they had not been tracked? They had seen a guard post on a road two days behind, giving it a wide berth. Could the word have gone out to find the fugitives? Temuge felt a stab of despair, suddenly certain that Chen Yi had given them up in exchange for his life. It was what Temuge would have done and panic overwhelmed him in the darkness, as he saw enemies in every shadow.

'What is it?' Temuge hissed to his brother's back.

Khasar turned his head this way and that, searching for sound.

'I heard voices. The wind has changed now, but they were there.'

'We should head south for a few miles to lose them,' Ho Sa whispered. 'If they are looking for us, we can use the woods to lay up for a day.'

'Soldiers don't camp in woods,' Khasar said. 'It's too easy to creep up on a man. We'll go ahead, but slowly. Have your weapons ready.'

Lian removed a long-handled hammer from his roll of tools, swinging the head onto his other shoulder. Temuge stared at Khasar in growing anger.

'What do we care who else is in these woods?' he demanded. 'Ho Sa is right, we should go around them.'

'If they have horses, it's worth the risk. I think it's going to snow and I'm tired of walking,' Khasar replied. Without another word, he padded stealthily on, forcing them to follow. Temuge cursed him in silence. Men like Khasar would not walk the avenues in the city of his imagination. They would guard the walls perhaps, while better men were given the honour and dignity they deserved.

As they walked along the narrow track, the glow of a fire could be seen through the trees and they all heard the noises Khasar's sharp ears had picked out. Laughter came clearly on the night air and Khasar beamed when he heard the whinny of a mare.

The four men crept slowly towards the light, the noise of their own movement hidden by shouts and cheering. When they were close enough, Khasar lay down on his stomach and peered into a tiny clearing where ancient roots overlaid each other in twisted patterns.

A mule was there, yanking at the leather strap that bound it to a branch. To Khasar's pleasure, three shaggy ponies were tethered on the edge of the clearing. They were small and thin, standing with their heads drooping. Khasar's gaze hardened at seeing the white lines of scars on their haunches and he unstrapped his bow, laying arrows on the briars.

There were four men around the fire, three of them taunting the fourth. He was a small figure in a robe of dark red. His shaven head shone with sweat in the firelight. The others wore no armour, but they carried knives in their belts and one had a short bow leaning against a tree. Their faces were cruel as they continued their sport, darting in and out again to strike the small man. His features were bruised and swollen, but one of the men bled freely from his nose and did not join in the laughter with the others.

As Khasar watched, the one with the bloody nose hit out with a stick, making the small man stagger. The thump of the blow could be heard across the clearing and Khasar grinned wolfishly as he strung his bow by feel. He wormed his way back to Ho Sa away from the light, his voice the barest whisper.

'We need their horses. They don't look like soldiers and I can take two with the bow if you rush the last. There is another young one with a head like an egg. He's still fighting, but he hasn't a chance against all three.'

'He may be a monk,' Ho Sa said. 'They are hard men, for all they spend their time begging and in prayer. Do not underestimate him.'

Khasar raised his eyes, amused.

'I spent my childhood learning weapons from dawn till dusk. I've yet to see one of your people who could stand against me.'

Ho Sa frowned, shaking his head.

'If he is a monk, he will be trying not to kill his attackers. I have seen them show their skills to my king.'

Khasar snorted softly.

'You are a strange people. Soldiers who cannot fight and holy men who can. Tell Lian to get his hammer ready to crack a head when I shoot.'

Khasar inched forward once more, coming slowly up to a kneeling position. To his surprise, he saw the man with the bloody nose was lying on the ground, writhing in agony. The other two had fallen into grim silence. The young monk stood straight despite the bruises he had taken and Khasar heard him speak calmly to his tormentors. One of them sneered, tossing aside his stick and pulling a wicked-looking dagger from his belt.

Khasar bent his bow and, as it creaked, the monk looked through the fire at him, suddenly light on his feet as if ready to leap away. The others hadn't noticed and one of them rushed the monk, the dagger held to punch into his chest.

Khasar let out a breath and loosed an arrow that took the bandit in the armpit, hammering him off his feet. The other swung round as Lian and Ho Sa shouted, leaping up. As they moved, the monk stepped very close to the remaining man and landed a blow to his head that knocked him into the fire. Ho Sa and Lian came roaring in then, but the monk ignored them, dragging his attacker out of the flames and patting him down where his hair had begun to smoke. The man was limp, but the weight did not seem to trouble the monk at all.

When that was done, he stood to face the newcomers, nodding to them. The one with the bloody nose now moaned in fear as well as pain. Khasar nocked another arrow as he walked, Temuge following at his heels.

The monk saw what Khasar intended and darted forward, so that Khasar's view of the writhing figure was blocked. The bald skull made him look little older than a boy.

'Step aside,' Khasar told him.

The words were received blankly, but the monk did not move and only folded his arms to stare down the arrow.

'Tell him to step away, Ho Sa,' Khasar said, gritting his teeth against the strain of holding the drawn bow. 'Tell him we need his mule, but otherwise he can go on his way once I've killed this one.'

Ho Sa spoke and Khasar saw the monk's face light up as he heard words he recognised. A blistering exchange followed and, when it showed no sign of ceasing, Khasar swore in the Chin language and eased off the strain.

'He says he did not need us and the man's life is not ours to take,' Ho Sa said at last. 'He also said he will not give up the mule, as it is not his, but only loaned to him.'

'Does he not see the bow I am holding?' Khasar demanded, jerking it in the monk's direction.

'He would not care if you had a dozen pointed at him. He is a holy man and without fear.'

'A holy boy, with a mule for Temuge,' Khasar replied. 'Unless you want to ride double with my brother?'

'I do not mind,' Ho Sa said immediately. He spoke to the monk, bowing three times in the course of the conversation. The boy nodded sharply at the end, glancing at Khasar.

'He says you may take the ponies,' Ho Sa said. 'He will remain here to tend the wounded men.'

Khasar shook his head, unable to understand.

'Did he thank me for rescuing him?'

Ho Sa looked blank.

'He did not need rescuing.'

Khasar frowned at the monk who stared calmly back.

'Genghis would love this one,' Khasar said suddenly. 'Ask him if he wants to come with us.'

Ho Sa spoke again and the boy shook his head, his eyes never leaving Khasar.

'He says the work of the Buddha may take him onto strange roads, but his place is amongst the poor.'

Khasar snorted.

'The poor are everywhere. Ask him how he knows this Buddha didn't want us to find him here.'

Ho Sa nodded and, as he talked, the monk looked increasingly interested.

'He asks if the Buddha is known among your people,' Ho Sa said.

Khasar grinned.

'Tell him we believe in a sky father above and an earth mother below. The rest is struggle and pain before death.' He chuckled as Ho Sa blinked at hearing the philosophy.

'Is that all you believe?' Ho Sa asked.

Khasar glanced at his brother.

'Some of the foolish ones believe in spirits as well, but most of us believe in a good horse and a strong right arm. We do not know this Buddha.'

When Ho Sa relayed the speech, the young monk bowed and strode to where his mule was tethered. Khasar and Temuge watched as he leaped into the saddle, causing the animal to snort and kick.

'That is an ugly beast,' Khasar said. 'Is the boy coming with us?'

Ho Sa still looked surprised as he nodded.

'He is. He says that no man can guess his path, but perhaps you are right that you were guided to him.'

'All right,' Khasar said. 'But tell him that I will not let my enemies live, that he must not interfere with me again. Tell him if he does, I will cut his little bald head right off.'

When the monk heard the words, he laughed aloud, slapping his thigh as he sat astride the mule.

Khasar frowned at him.

'I am Khasar of the Wolves, monk,' he said, pointing to himself. 'What is your name?'

'Yao Shu!' he replied, thumping a fist twice into his own chest like a salute. The action seemed to amuse the monk and he chuckled until he had to wipe his eyes. Khasar stared at him.

'Mount up, Ho Sa,' he said at last. 'The brown mare is mine. At least the walking is over.'

It did not take long for them to mount. Ho Sa and Temuge rode together once the saddle had been unstrapped and thrown down. The surviving bandits had grown quiet amidst the talk, aware that their lives hung in the balance. They watched the strangers go, only sitting up to curse when they were sure they were alone.

* * *

The pass that separated the Xi Xia kingdom from the southern edge of the desert was empty as the party of five men reached it. In the Khenti Mountains a thousand miles north, the winter would be deepening, gripping the land for many months to come. Even at the pass, a freezing gale roared through as if in pleasure at its release. There was no fort to make the pass a place of stillness any longer. Instead, the wind always blew and the air was full of sand and grit.

Khasar and Temuge dismounted as they reached the pass, remembering the first bloody efforts to take the fort that had stood there. Genghis had been efficient in having it dismantled. A few large blocks lay where they had fallen in the sand, but every other stone had been dragged away. Only a few square holes in the cliffs showed where timbers and braces had been anchored, but otherwise it was as if the fort had never existed. There was no barrier to the tribes coming south any longer and that fact alone gave Khasar a feeling of pride.

He strolled with Temuge along the pass, looking up at the high cliffs on either side. The monk and the mason watched them without understanding, neither having known the place when it boasted a fort of black stone and the Xi Xia kingdom ruled in splendid isolation.

Ho Sa looked south, turning his pony to gaze over the bare fields of his home. Dark spots in the distance showed where the rotten crops had been burned and the ashes returned to the land. There would be starvation in the villages, he was certain, perhaps even in Yinchuan. He shook his head at the thought.

He had been away for almost four months and it would be good to see his sons and wife once again. He wondered how the army had fared after the crushing defeat at the hands of the great khan. The tribes had shattered an ancient peace and he winced as he recalled the destruction. He had lost friends and colleagues in those months and the bitterness was never far from the surface. The final humiliation had been to see a royal daughter handed over to the barbarians. Ho Sa shuddered at the thought of such a woman being forced to live in their stinking tents among sheep and goats.

As Ho Sa stared into the valley, he realised with some surprise that he would miss Khasar's company. For all the man's crudity and easy violence, Ho Sa could look back on the journey with some pride. No one else from the Xi Xia could have stolen into a Chin city and returned alive with a master mason. It was true that Khasar had almost got him killed in one village where he had drunk too much rice wine. Ho Sa rubbed a scab on his side where a soldier had scraped a knife along his ribs. The man had not even been posted there and was visiting his family. Khasar could not recall the fight when he sobered up and seemed to think nothing of it. He was in some ways the most irritating man Ho Sa had ever known, but his reckless optimism had affected the Xi Xia soldier and he wondered uneasily if he would be able to return to the rigid discipline of the king's army. The annual tribute would have to be carried across the desert and Ho Sa decided then that he would volunteer to lead the guards on that trip, just to see the land that could give birth to the tribes.

Khasar walked back to his companions. He felt elation at the thought of seeing home again and bringing their quarry back to Genghis. He grinned at the others in turn, showing his pleasure. To a man, they were dust-covered and filthy, with dirt lining every crease of their faces. Yao Shu had begun to learn the speech of the tribes from Ho Sa. Lian had no ear for language, but he too had picked up a few useful words. They nodded back to Khasar uncertainly, unsure of the reason for his good mood.

Ho Sa held his gaze as Khasar approached him. He was

surprised at the tightness in his chest at the thought of leaving that strange company and struggled to find words to express it. Khasar spoke before he could think of anything.

'Take a good look, Ho Sa. You won't be seeing home again for a long time.'

'What?' Ho Sa demanded, his peaceful mood vanishing.

Khasar shrugged.

'Your king gave you to us for a year. It's been less than four months with perhaps two more before we are in the mountains. We'll need you to interpret for the mason and to teach proper speech to the monk. Did you think I would leave you here? You did!' Khasar seemed delighted at the bitter expression that flitted across Ho Sa's face.

'We're going back to the plains, Ho Sa. We'll attack a few hills with whatever the mason can teach us and when we're ready, we'll go to war. Perhaps by then, you'll be so useful to us that I'll ask your king to lend you for another year or two. I should think he'd be willing to take your price out of the tribute if we asked for you.'

'You are doing this to torture me,' Ho Sa snapped.

Khasar chuckled.

'Perhaps a little, but you are a fighting man who knows the Chin. We will need you close when we ride to them.'

Ho Sa stared furiously at Khasar. The Mongol warrior slapped him cheerfully on the leg as he turned away, calling over his shoulder.

'We'll need to collect water from the canals. After that, it's the desert and home to women and spoils. Can a man ask for more? I'll even find you a widow to keep you warm, Ho Sa. I'm doing you a favour if you only had the eyes to see it.'

Khasar mounted once more, bringing his pony up to where Temuge was being pulled into the saddle by Lian. He leaned close to his brother.

228

'The plains are calling us, brother. Can you feel it?'

'I can,' Temuge replied. In fact, he wanted to return to the tribes as much as Khasar, though only because he now had a greater understanding of what they could win for themselves. While his brother dreamed of war and plunder, Temuge saw cities in his imagination and all the beauty and the power that came with them.

PART TWO

1211 AD

Xin-Wei
(Celestial Stem of Metal. Earthly Branch of the Sheep.)
Chin Dynasty: Emperor Wei

CHAPTER SIXTEEN

Genghis stood in full armour watching the destruction of the city of Linhe. The rice fields had been churned into wet brown muck for a dozen miles in any direction as his army encircled the walls. His standard of nine horsetails hung limply without a breeze as the setting sun beat down on the army he had brought to that place.

On either side of him, bondsmen waited for orders, their horses pawing at the ground. A servant stood at his shoulder with a chestnut mare, but the khan was not yet ready to mount.

Close by the waiting column, a tent of blood-red cloth fluttered in the wind. For fifty miles around, his army had crushed resistance until only the city stood untouched, even as Yinchuan had once sheltered the Xi Xia king. Garrisons and road forts were found empty as Chin soldiers retreated before a host they could not hope to match. They carried the fear of the invasion before them and rolled back the edges of Chin control, leaving the cities naked. Even the great wall had proved no obstacle to the catapults and ladders of his people. Genghis had taken pleasure in seeing vast sections of it broken into rubble as practice for his new machines of war. His men had swept away the defenders for as far as they could reach, burning the wooden post houses with something resembling spite. The Chin could not keep them out. All they could do was run or be destroyed.

There would be a reckoning, Genghis was certain: when a general rose who could command the Chin, or when the tribes reached Yenking itself. It would not be today.

Xamba had fallen in seven days and Wuyuan had burned in only three. Genghis watched the stones from his catapults knock chips from the walls of Linhe and smiled to himself, satisfied. The mason his brothers had brought back had shown him a new way of warfare and he would never again be stopped by high walls. Over two years, his people had built catapults and learned the secrets and weaknesses of the Chin high walls. His sons had grown tall and strong and he had been there to see the eldest reach the edge of manhood. It was enough. He had returned to the enemies of his people and he had learned well.

Though he stood back from the catapult lines, he could hear the thumping strikes clearly on the still air. The Chin soldiers within would not dare march out to meet his host and, if they did, he would welcome the quick end. It would not help them now the red tent had been set. Piece by piece, the walls were hammered down, the catapult stones lofted into the air by sweating teams of his men. Lian had shown him designs for an even more fearsome weapon. Genghis pictured it in his mind, seeing again the huge counterweight Lian said would send boulders hundreds of feet with crushing force. The Chin mason had found his calling in designing the weapons for a ruler who appreciated his skill. Genghis had discovered he could grasp Lian's diagrams as if the knowledge had always been there. The written word was still a mystery to him, but force and friction, levers, blocks and ropes were all instantly clear in his mind. He would let Lian build his great machine to attack Yenking.

Yet the Chin emperor's city was no Linhe to be pounded into submission. Genghis grunted at the thought, imagining the moats and immense walls Lian had described, as thick at the base as seven men lying head to foot. Xamba's walls had collapsed into tunnels dug beneath them, but the fortress towers of Yenking were built on stone and could not be undermined. He would need more than catapults to break the emperor's own city, but there were other weapons at his disposal, and with every victory his warriors grew more skilled.

Genghis had thought at first that they would resist their new role as workers of machines. His people had never made good infantry before, but Lian had introduced the idea of engineers to them and Genghis had found many who could understand the discipline of forces and weights. He had shown his pleasure in having men to break cities and they stood proud under his gaze.

Genghis bared his teeth as a section of wall fell outwards. Tsubodai had a thousand of them working before the walls of Linhe. The main host had formed columns outside the four gates of the city, waiting to spear into it at the first sign of an opening. Genghis saw Tsubodai striding among the catapult teams, directing the blows. It was all so new and Genghis felt pride at how well his people had adapted themselves. If only his father could have lived to see it.

In the distance, Tsubodai ordered wooden barricades forward, protecting his warriors as they pulled at weakened stones with long hooked pikes. The city archers could not take a shot without risking their own lives, and even when they were successful, their arrows thumped into wood and were wasted.

As Genghis watched, a group of defenders showed their heads to tip an iron pot over the crest of the wall. Many of them fell to arrows, but there were always more to take their place. Genghis frowned as they succeeded in drenching a dozen pikemen in black liquid. The warriors ducked down behind their wooden shield, but only moments later, torches were thrown onto the oil and flames exploded, louder than the choking screams as their lungs charred.

Genghis heard men curse around him. Tsubodai's burning pikemen went stumbling into the other groups, fouling the smooth rhythms of the attack. In the confusion, Chin archers picked off anyone who stepped from his shield to fend them off or put an end to their agony.

Tsubodai roared fresh orders and the shield groups moved slowly back, leaving the writhing men until they were consumed. Genghis nodded in approval as the catapults began to whistle once more. He had heard of the oil that burned, though he had never seen it used in such a way. It took flame much faster than the mutton fat in Mongol lamps and he decided to secure a supply. Perhaps there would be some left in Linhe when it fell. His mind filled with the thousand details he needed to remember each day until his head felt swollen with plans.

Dark, smoking bodies lay under the wall and he could hear thin cheering inside the city. Genghis waited for Tsubodai to make a breach, his impatience growing. The light would not last much longer and, at sunset, Tsubodai would have to order his men to retreat for the night.

As the catapults sang again, Genghis wondered how many they had lost in the assault. It did not matter. Tsubodai commanded the least experienced of his warriors and they needed to be hardened in war. In the two years he had spent in the Khenti Mountains, another eight thousand boys had reached their adult growth and mounted to join him. Most of them rode with Tsubodai and called themselves the Young Wolves to honour Genghis. Tsubodai had almost begged to be first in the assault on Linhe, but Genghis had already planned to have those boys lead the attack. Along with their new general, they had to be blooded.

Genghis heard the cries of wounded men carry on the wind

and tapped his wrist guard unconsciously against the lacquered plates of his thigh. Two more sections of wall fell. He saw a turret of stone collapse, spilling a nest of archers almost at the feet of Tsubodai's gleeful warriors. The walls of Linhe now resembled broken teeth and Genghis knew it would not be long. Wheeled ladders were rolled up as the catapult teams stood down at last, exhausted and triumphant.

Genghis felt the excitement build around him as Tsubodai's Young Wolves swarmed over the defenders, darkening the pale grey stone with their scrambling bodies. His best archers covered the assault from below, men able to pierce an egg at a hundred paces. Chin soldiers who showed themselves on the walls were fat with quivering arrows by the time they fell back.

Genghis nodded sharply to himself and took the reins of his mare to mount. The animal snorted, sensing his mood. He looked to his left and right, seeing the patient faces of his bondsmen and the ranks and columns in a great circle around the city. He had made armies within armies, so that each of his generals commanded a tuman of ten thousand men and acted on his own. Arslan was lost to sight behind Linhe, but Genghis could see the horsetail standard of Jelme fluttering in the breeze. The sunlight cast them all in burnished gold and orange, throwing long shadows. Genghis looked for his brothers, ready to ride into the east and west gates if they opened first. Khasar and Kachiun would be keen to be first in the streets of Linhe.

At his shoulder, the huge figure of Tolui who had once been bondsman to Eeluk of the Wolves was worth only a glance, though Genghis saw the man stiffen with pride. Old friends were there, responding with nods. The front line of the column was only twenty horses wide, men approaching thirty years of age, as he was himself. It lifted Genghis' spirit to see the way they strained forward, watching the city hungrily.

Smoke spiralled into the air from a dozen points within Linhe, like the distant threads of a rainstorm on the plains. Genghis watched and waited, his hands shaking slightly with tension.

'May I bless you, great khan?' came a voice he knew, interrupting his thoughts. Genghis turned and gestured to his personal shaman, first among the men who walked the dark paths. Kokchu had thrown away the rags from his days serving the Naiman khan. He wore a robe of dark blue silk, tied with a sash of gold. His wrists were bound in leather hung with pierced Chin coins and they chimed as he raised his arms. Genghis bowed his head without expression, feeling the cool touch of sheep blood as Kokchu striped his cheeks with it. He felt a rush of calm settle on him and he kept his head lowered as Kokchu chanted a prayer to the earth mother.

'She will welcome the blood you send into her, my lord, as much as if the rains themselves ran red.'

Genghis let out a slow breath, pleasantly aware of the fear in the men around him. Every one of them was a warrior born, hardened in fire and battle from the first years, but still they closed their mouths of idle chatter when Kokchu walked amongst them. Genghis had seen the fear grow and he had used it to discipline the tribes, giving Kokchu power by his patronage.

'Shall I have the red tent taken down, my lord?' Kokchu asked. 'The sun is setting and the black cloth is ready for the frame.'

Genghis considered. It had been Kokchu himself who suggested this means to sow terror in the cities of the Chin. On the first day, a white tent was raised outside their walls, its very existence showing that there were no soldiers to save them. If they did not open their gates by sunset, the red tent went up at dawn and Genghis sent the promise that every man in the city would die. On the third day, the black tent meant that there would be only death without end, without mercy, for anyone alive within.

The lesson would be learned by cities to the east and Genghis wondered if they would surrender more easily as Kokchu said. The shaman understood how to use fear. It would be difficult not to allow the men to loot them as savagely as those which resisted, but the idea appealed to him. Speed was everything and if cities fell without a fight, he could move all the faster. He inclined his head to the shaman, giving him honour.

'The day is not yet over, Kokchu. The women will live without their husbands. Those who are too old or too plain for us will take the word further and the fear will spread.'

'Your will, my lord,' Kokchu said, his eyes gleaming. Genghis felt his own senses kindle in return. He needed clever men if he was to take the path his imagination drew for him.

'My lord khan!' an officer called. Genghis snapped his head round, seeing the north gate heaved open by Tsubodai's young warriors. The defenders were still fighting and he could see some of Tsubodai's men fall as they struggled to keep the advantage they had won. On the edge of his vision, Khasar's ten thousand kicked into a gallop and he knew the city was open in at least two places. Kachiun was still stationary on the east gate and could only watch in frustration as his brothers moved in.

'Ride!' Genghis bellowed, digging in his heels. As the air whipped past him, he recalled racing across the plains of home in distant days. He hefted a long birchwood lance in his right hand, another innovation. Only a few of the strongest men had begun to train with them, but the fashion was growing amongst the tribes. With the point held upright, Genghis thundered across the land, surrounded by his loyal warriors.

There would be other cities, he knew, but these first ones would always be sweetest in his memory. He roared with his men, the column galloping at full speed through the gates, scattering defenders like bloody leaves in their wake.

Temuge walked through pitch darkness to the ger of Kokchu. As he passed the door, he heard the muffled sound of weeping from within, but he did not stop. The moon was absent from the sky and Kokchu had told him that was when he would be strongest and most able to learn. Fires still burned in the gutted shell of Linhe in the distance, but the camp was quiet after the destruction.

Close by the shaman's ger was another, so low and squat that Temuge had to go down on his knees to enter. A single shuttered lamp cast a dim glow and the air was thick with fumes that made Temuge dizzy after just a few breaths. Kokchu sat cross-legged on a floor of wrinkled black silk. All the things inside had come from the hand of Genghis and Temuge felt envy mingling with his fear of the man.

He had been called and he had come. His place was not to question and as he sat and crossed his legs to face the shaman, he saw Kokchu's eyes were closed and that his breath was no more than a slight flutter of the chest. Temuge shuddered in the thick silence, imagining dark spirits in the smoke that filled his lungs. It came from incense burning on a pair of brass plates and he wondered which city had been looted for them. The gers of his people were host to many strange objects in these bloody days and there were few who could recognise them all.

Temuge coughed as the smoke came too thickly into his lungs. He saw Kokchu's bare chest shudder and the man's eyes opened blindly, looking for him but not seeing. As the focus returned, the shaman smiled at him, his eyes in deep shadow.

'You have not come to me for a full turn of the moon,' Kokchu said, his voice hoarse from the smoke.

240

Temuge looked away.

'I was troubled. Some of the things you told me were . . . disturbing.'

Kokchu chuckled, a dry hacking in his throat. 'As children are wary of the dark, so are men wary of power. It tempts them and yet it consumes them. It is never a game to play lightly.' He rested his gaze on Temuge until the younger man looked up and winced visibly. Kokchu's unblinking eyes were strangely bright, the pupils wider and darker than Temuge had ever seen them.

'Why have you come tonight,' Kokchu murmured, 'if not to plunge your hands into the darkness once more?'

Temuge took a deep breath. The smoke no longer seemed to irritate his lungs and he felt light-headed, almost confident.

'I heard you found a traitor while I was away in Baotou. My brother the khan spoke of it. He said it was wondrous how you picked the man out of a line of kneeling warriors.'

'Much has changed since then,' Kokchu said with a shrug. 'I could smell his guilt, my son. It is something you could learn.' Kokchu summoned his will to keep his thoughts focused. He was used to the smoke and could take a great deal more of it than his young companion, but still there were bright lights flashing at the edges of his vision.

Temuge felt all his worries dissolving as he sat there with this strange man who smelled of blood despite his new silk robes. Words tumbled out of him and he did not know he slurred them.

'Genghis said you laid your hands on the traitor and spoke words in the oldest tongue,' Temuge whispered. 'He said the man cried out and died in front of them all without a wound.'

'And you would like to do the same, Temuge? There is no one else here and there is no shame between us. Say the words. Is that what you want?'

Temuge slumped slightly, letting his hands drop to the silken floor so that he could feel it slide under his fingers with extraordinary clarity.

'It is what I want.'

Kokchu smiled wider at that, showing dark gums as his lips slid back. He did not know the identity of the traitor or even if there had been one. The hand he had pressed against the man's scalp had held two tiny fangs and a venom sac embedded in wax. It had taken him many nights of hunting the vicious little pit viper he wanted, risking being bitten himself. He began to chuckle again at the memory of the awe on the face of the khan as the victim writhed from just a touch. The dying man had gone almost black in the face before the end, the twin spots of blood hidden by his hair. Kokchu had chosen him because of the Chin girl he had taken to wife. She had roused the shaman to lust as she passed his ger to draw water and then she had refused him, as if she were one of the people and not a slave. He laughed harder as he remembered the knowledge coming into her husband's eyes before death stole it away with everything else. Since that moment, Kokchu had been feared and honoured in the camp. Not one of the other shamans of the tribes dared challenge his position, not after that display of power. He felt no guilt at the deception. His fate was to stand with the khan of the nation, triumphant over his enemies. If he had to kill a thousand to do so, he would count it worth the price.

He saw Temuge was glassy-eyed as he sat there in the stifling smoke. Kokchu clamped his jaw shut, pressing away his amusement. He needed his mind clear to bind the younger man, so close that he would never tear free.

Slowly, Kokchu reached into the small pot of thick black paste at his side, holding up a finger so that tiny seeds were visible in the gleaming muck. He reached out to Temuge and opened his mouth without resistance, smearing the paste onto his tongue.

Temuge choked at the bitter taste, but before he could spit, he felt numbness spreading quickly. He heard whispering voices behind him and he jerked his head back and forth as his eyes glazed, searching for the origin of the sound.

'Dream the darkest dreams, Temuge,' Kokchu said, satisfied. 'I will guide you. No, even better. I will give you mine.'

It was dawn before Kokchu staggered out of the ger, sour sweat staining his robe. Temuge was unconscious on the silk floor and would sleep for most of the day to come. Kokchu had not touched the paste himself, unwilling to trust the way it made him babble and not yet sure how much Temuge would remember. He had no wish to put himself in the other's power, not when the future was so bright. He took deep breaths of freezing air and felt his head clear itself of the smoke. He could smell its sweetness coming out of his pores and he giggled to himself as he crossed back to his own ger and banged open the door.

The Chin girl knelt where he had left her, on the floor by the stove. She was incredibly beautiful, pale and delicate. He felt his lust swell for her again and wondered at his own stamina. Perhaps it was the remnant of smoke in his lungs.

'How many times did you disobey me and rise?' he demanded.

'I did not,' she said, trembling visibly.

He reached out to raise her head, his hands slipping clumsily from her face and enraging him. The gesture became a blow and he knocked her sprawling.

He stood panting as she scrambled back and knelt once more. Just as he began untying the sash on his deel, she raised her head. There was blood on her mouth and he saw her lower lip was already swelling. The sight inflamed him.

'Why do you hurt me? What more do you want?' she asked, tears shining in her eyes.

'Power over you, little one,' he said, smiling. 'What does any man want but that? It is something in the blood of every one of us. We would all be a tyrant if we could.'

CHAPTER SEVENTEEN

The emperor's city of Yenking grew quiet in the hours before dawn, though it was more from a surfeit of food and drink in the Feast of Lanterns than any fear of the Mongol army. As the sun had set, Emperor Wei mounted a platform to be seen by the heaving crowds, and a thousand dancers had made a din to raise the dead with cymbals and horns. He had stood with his feet bare, showing his humility before the people as a million voices chanted, 'Ten thousand years! Ten thousand years!', the sound crashing across the city. Night was banished on the Feast of Lanterns. The city gleamed like a jewel, a myriad flames lighting squares of boiled horn or glass. Even the three great lakes were aglow, their black surfaces covered in tiny boats each carrying a flame. The water gate was open to the great canal that stretched three thousand *li* to the southern city of Hangzhou and the boats drifted out like a river of fire throughout the night, taking the light with them. The symbolism pleased the young emperor as he endured the noise and smoke from fireworks banging and echoing from the great walls. There were so many that the whole city was covered in white gunpowder smoke and the air itself was bitter on the tongue. Children would be made that night, by force or for pleasure. There would be more than a hundred murders and the lakes themselves would claim a dozen drunkards in the dark depths as they tried to swim across. It was the same every year.

The emperor had suffered through the adoring chants, buffeted by the clamour in his name that stretched from the walls and beyond. Even the beggars, slaves and whores cheered him on that night and lit their ramshackle homes with precious oil. He endured it all, though, at times, his gaze over their heads was distant and cold as he planned to crush the army that had dared to enter his lands.

The peasants knew nothing of the threat and even the sellers of news had little information. Emperor Wei had seen to it that the gossipmongers were kept quiet and, if their arrest disturbed those who looked for such signs, the festival had gone ahead with all its usual gusto, mad with drink and noise and light. Seeing the revellers, the emperor was reminded of maggots writhing on a corpse. His Imperial messengers brought grim reports as they rejoiced. Beyond the mountains, cities were aflame.

With dawn lighting the horizon, the shouting and singing in the streets died down finally, giving him peace. The last of the little wooden candle boats had vanished out to the countryside and only a few firecrackers could be heard rattling in the distance. Emperor Wei sat in his private rooms and stared out over the still, dark heart of Songhai Lake, surrounded by hundreds of great houses. The most powerful of his nobles clustered around that central mass of dark water, in sight of the man from whom they took their power. He could have named every member of the high-born families that fought and struggled like jewelled wasps to administer his northern empire.

The smoke and chaos of the festival trailed away with the morning mist on the lakes. With such a scene of ancient beauty, it was difficult to comprehend the threat from the west. Yet war was coming and he wished his father still lived. The old man had spent his life crushing the slightest hint of disobedience to the very edges of the empire and beyond. Emperor Wei had learned much at his feet, but he felt the newness of his position keenly. He had already lost cities that had been part of Chin lands since the great schism that split the empire into two halves three hundred years before. His ancestors had known a golden age and he could only dream of restoring the empire to its former glory.

He smiled wryly to himself at the thought of his father hearing of the Mongol horde on their family lands. He would have raged down the corridors of the palace, striking slaves out of his way as he summoned the army. His father had never lost a battle and his confidence would have raised them all.

Emperor Wei started from his thoughts as a throat was cleared softly behind him. He looked back from the high window to see his first minister bowing to the floor.

'Imperial Majesty, General Zhi Zhong is here as you asked.'

'Send him in and see that I am not disturbed,' the emperor replied, turning away from the dawn and seating himself. He glanced around his private rooms, seeing that nothing was out of place. His writing desk was freed of the clutter of maps and papers and there was no sign of his anger as he waited for the man who would rid him of the tribesmen. He could not help thinking of the Xi Xia king and the letter he had sent to him three years before. With shame, he recalled the spite of his words and the pleasure he had felt in sending them. Who could have known then that the Mongol threat was more than a few shouting tribesmen? His people had never feared those who could be culled whenever they grew restless. Emperor Wei bit the inside of his lip as he considered the future. If they could not be beaten quickly, he would have to bribe the Tartars to attack their ancient enemies. Chin gold could win as many battles as bows and spears. He remembered his father's words with fondness and once more wished he were there to offer his counsel.

General Zhi Zhong was a man of immense physical presence, with the build of a wrestler. His head was perfectly shaven and gleamed with oil as he bowed. Emperor Wei felt himself straighten automatically as he entered, the legacy of many hours on the training ground. It was reassuring to see that fierce glare and massive head once more, for all it had caused him to quiver as a boy.

As Zhi Zhong straightened, the emperor saw he looked murderous and once more he felt like a child. He struggled to keep his voice firm as he spoke. An emperor could not show weakness.

'They are coming here, general. I have heard the reports.'

Zhi Zhong weighed the smooth-faced young man he faced, wishing it could have been the father. The old man would already have acted, but the wheel of life had taken him and this was the boy with whom he must deal. The general clenched both fists at his sides, standing painfully straight.

'They have no more than sixty-five thousand warriors, Imperial Majesty. Their cavalry is superb and every one is an archer of extraordinary skill. In addition, they have learned the art of the siege and have weapons of great power. They have achieved a discipline I have not witnessed in my dealings with them before.'

'Do not tell me of their strengths!' the young emperor snapped. 'Tell me instead how we will crush them.'

General Zhi Zhong did not react to the tone. His silence was enough criticism and the emperor waved for him to go on, a flush staining his pale cheeks.

'To defeat the enemy, we *must* know them, my lord, Son of Heaven.' He spoke the title as an aid to control, to remind the emperor of his status at a time of crisis. General Zhi Zhong waited until the emperor had firmed his mouth and mastered his fear. At last, he went on.

'In the past we would have looked for weaknesses in their alliance. I do not believe the tactic will work here.'

'Why not?' Wei blurted out. Would the man not tell him how to defeat these tribesmen? As a boy, he had suffered through many lectures from the grizzled general and it seemed he could not escape them even with an empire at his feet.

'No Mongol force has ever come past the outer wall before, Imperial Majesty. They could only howl at it.' He shrugged. 'It is not the barrier it once was and these Mongols have not been thrown back by superior force as they might once have been. They have grown bold as a result.' He paused, but his emperor did not speak again. The general's glare lost some of its fierceness. Perhaps the boy was beginning to understand when to keep his mouth shut.

'We have tortured their scouts, Imperial Majesty. More than a dozen in the last few days. We lost men to bring them in alive, but it was worth it to know the enemy.' The general frowned in recollection.

'They are united. Whether the alliance will fall apart in time I cannot say, but for this year at least, they are strong. They have engineers, something I thought I would never see. More, they have Xi Xia wealth behind them.' The general paused, his face showing contempt for their old allies.

'I will enjoy taking the army to the Xi Xia valley, Imperial Majesty, when this is over.'

'The scouts, general,' Emperor Wei prompted, his impatience growing.

'They talk of this Genghis as beloved of their gods,' the general continued. 'I could find no hint of a disaffected group in their number, though I will not cease to search. They have been broken apart before with promises of power and wealth.'

'Tell me how you will defeat them, general,' Emperor Wei snapped, 'or I will find one who can.'

At that, Zhi Zhong's mouth became a sharp line in his face.

'With the outer wall broken, we cannot defend the cities around the Yellow River, lord,' he said. 'The land is too flat and gives them every advantage. His Imperial Majesty must reconcile himself to losing those cities as we move men back.'

Emperor Wei shook his head in frustration, but the general pressed on.

'We must not let them choose the battles. Linhe will fall as Xamba and Wuyuan have fallen. Baotou, Hohhot, Jining, Xicheng – all are in their path. We cannot save those cities, only avenge them.'

Emperor Wei rose to his feet in fury.

'Trade routes will be cut and our enemies will know we are weak! I brought you here to tell me how to save the lands I inherited, not watch them burn with me.'

'They cannot be held, Imperial Majesty,' Zhi Zhong said firmly. 'I too will grieve for the dead when this is ended. I will travel to each of the cities and spread ashes on my skin and make offerings in atonement. But they *will* fall. I have given orders to pull back our soldiers from those places. They will serve His Imperial Majesty better here.'

The young emperor was speechless, his right hand fluttering against the lining of his robe. With a vast effort of will, he steadied himself.

'Speak carefully to me, general. I need a victory and if you tell me one more time that I must give up my father's lands, I will have your head right now.'

The general held his emperor's furious gaze. There was no trace of the weakness he had seen before. For an instant, he was reminded of the boy's father and the notion pleased him. Perhaps war would bring the strong blood to the fore as nothing else could.

'I can gather almost two hundred thousand soldiers to face them, Imperial Majesty. There will be famine as supplies are diverted for the army, but the Imperial guard will keep order in Yenking. The place of battle will be of my choosing, where the Mongols cannot ride us down. I swear to the Son of Heaven by Lao Tzu himself that I will destroy them utterly. I have trained many of the officers and I tell Your Majesty they will not fail.'

The emperor raised a hand to a waiting slave and accepted a cool glass of water. He did not offer a drink to the general, nor thought of it, though the man was almost three times his age and the morning was warm. Water from the Jade Spring was for the Imperial family alone.

'This is what I wanted to hear,' he said gratefully, sipping. 'Where will the battle take place?'

'When the cities have fallen, they will move on to Yenking. They will know this city is where the emperor resides and they will come. I will stop them in the range of mountains to the west, at Yuhung Pass, the one they call the "Badger's Mouth". It is narrow enough to hamper their horses and we will kill them all. They will not reach this city. I swear it.'

'They cannot take Yenking, even if you fail,' the emperor said confidently. General Zhi Zhong looked at him, wondering if the young man had ever left the city of his birth. The general cleared his throat softly.

'The question will not arise. I will destroy them there and, when the winter has passed, I will travel to their homeland and burn the last of them from the earth. They will not grow strong again.'

The emperor felt his spirits lift at the general's words. He would not have to stand in shame before his father in the land of the silent dead. He would not have to atone for failure. For a moment, he thought again of the cities the Mongols would take, a vision of blood and flames. He forced it away from his mind, taking another sip of water. He would rebuild. When the last of the tribesmen had been cut to pieces, or nailed to every tree in the empire, he would rebuild those cities and the people would know their emperor was still powerful, still beloved of heaven.

'My father said you were a hammer to his enemies,' the emperor said, his voice gentled by his changing mood. He reached out and took hold of Zhi Zhong's armoured shoulder. 'Remember the fallen cities when you have the chance to make them suffer. In my name, exact retribution.'

'It will be as His Imperial Majesty desires,' Zhi Zhong replied, bowing deeply.

Ho Sa walked through the vast camp, lost in thought. For almost three years, his king had left him with the Mongol khan and there were times when he had to struggle to remember the Xi Xia officer he had once been. In part, it was that the Mongols accepted him without question. Khasar seemed to like him and Ho Sa had spent many evenings drinking airag in the man's ger, waited on by his pair of Chin wives. He smiled wryly as he walked. They had been good evenings. Khasar was a generous man and thought nothing of lending his wives to a friend.

Ho Sa stopped for a moment to inspect a bundle of new arrows, one of a hundred others under a rigid construction of leather and poles. They were perfect, as he had known they would be. Though the Mongols scorned the regulations he had once known, they treated their bows like another child and only the best would do for them.

He had long since realised he liked the tribes, though he could still miss the tea of his home, so different from the salty muck they drank against the cold. The cold! Ho Sa had never known such a vicious season as that first winter. He had listened to all the advice they gave him just to stay alive and, even then, he had suffered miserably. He shook his head at the memory and wondered what he would do if his king summoned him home as he surely must one day. Would he go? Genghis had promoted him to lead a hundred under Khasar and Ho Sa enjoyed the camaraderie of the officers together. Every one of them could have commanded in Xi Xia, he was certain. Genghis did not allow fools to be promoted and that was a matter of pride for Ho Sa. He rode with the greatest army in the world, as a warrior and a leader. It was no small thing for a man, being trusted.

The ger of the khan's second wife was different from every other one in that immense camp. Chin silk lined the walls and, as Ho Sa entered, he was struck once again by the scent of jasmine. He had no idea how Chakahai had managed to secure a supply, but in the years away from their home, she had not been idle. He knew that other wives of the Xi Xia and the Chin met in her ger at regular intervals. When one of the husbands had forbidden it, Chakahai had dared to bring the problem to Genghis. The khan had done nothing, but the Chin wife had been free to visit the Xi Xia princess after that. It had taken only a word in the right place.

Ho Sa smiled as he bowed to her, accepting the hands of two young Chin girls on his shoulders as they removed his outer deel. Even in that was something new. The Mongols dressed only to keep out the cold and had no thought for correctness.

'You are welcome in my home, countryman,' Chakahai said, bowing in turn. 'It is good of you to come.' She spoke in the

Chin language, though the accent was that of his home. Ho Sa sighed as he heard the tones, knowing she did it to please him.

'You are the daughter of my king, the wife of my khan,' he replied. 'I am your servant.'

'That is good, Ho Sa,' she said, 'but we are friends as well, I hope?'

Ho Sa bowed again, deeper than before. As he straightened, he accepted a bowl of dark green tea and inhaled with appreciation.

'We are, of course, but what is this? I have not smelled . . .' He took another deep breath, letting the warm scent into his lungs. He was homesick then and the force of it made him sway as he stood.

'My father sends a little in his tribute each year, Ho Sa. The tribes have let it grow stale, though this is the freshest batch.'

Ho Sa sat carefully, cradling the bowl as he sipped.

'You are too kind to have thought of me.' He did not press her, but he did not know why she had summoned him on that day. He was aware that they could not spend too much time in each other's company. As natural as it might have seemed for two of the Xi Xia to seek one another out, a man did not visit a khan's wife without a reason. Over two years, they had met barely half a dozen times.

Before she could reply, another man entered. Yao Shu pressed his hands together to bow to the lady of the ger. Ho Sa watched in amusement as the monk too was handed a bowl of real tea and breathed a sigh of delight at the scent. It was only as Yao Shu finished his greeting that Ho Sa frowned. If there was danger in meeting the wife of a khan in private, there was more in being accused of conspiracy. His concern mounted as the two slave girls bowed and left the three of them alone. Ho Sa began to rise to his feet, the tea forgotten.

Chakahai pressed a hand on his arm and he could not move

without throwing it off. He settled uncomfortably and she looked into his eyes. Her own were wide and dark against her pale skin. She was beautiful and no taint of rancid mutton fat lingered around her. He could not resist a delicate shiver running down his back at the touch of cool fingers on his skin.

'I have asked you here, Ho Sa. You are my guest. It would be an insult for you to leave now, would it not? Tell me, I do not yet understand the manners of the ger.' It was a rebuke as well as a lie. She understood the subtleties of Mongol status very well indeed. Ho Sa reminded himself that this woman had grown up as only one of many daughters to his king. Despite her beauty, she was not innocent in the affairs of the court. He sat back and forced himself to sip the tea.

'There is no one to hear us here,' she said lightly, worsening his agitation. 'You fear conspiracy, Ho Sa, where there is none. I am second wife to the khan, mother to a son and his only daughter. You are a trusted officer and Yao Shu has tutored my husband's other boys in language and martial skills. No one would dare to whisper about any one of us. If they did, I would have their tongues cut out.'

Ho Sa stared at the delicate girl who could make such a threat. He did not know if she had the power to match the words. How many friends had she cultivated in this camp with her status? How many of the Chin and Xi Xia slaves? It was possible. He forced himself to smile, though he was cold inside.

'Well then, here we are. Three friends, drinking good tea. I will finish my cup, Majesty, then I will leave.'

Chakahai sighed and her face softened. To the astonishment of both men, tears shone on the rims of her eyes.

'Must I be always alone? Must I be suspected even by you?' she whispered, clearly struggling with herself. Ho Sa would never reach out and touch a member of the Xi Xia court, but Yao Shu had no such inhibitions. The monk put an arm around her shoulder and let her rest her head on his chest.

'You are not alone,' Ho Sa said softly. 'You understand that your father has given my service to your husband. For a moment, I thought perhaps that you were conspiring against him. Why else bring us here and send your girls away?'

The princess of the Xi Xia sat up, pressing a strand of hair back into place. Ho Sa swallowed dryly at her beauty.

'You are the only man from my home in this camp,' she said. 'Yao Shu is the only man of the Chin who is not a soldier.' Her tears seemed forgotten and her voice strengthened as she spoke. 'I would not betray my husband, Ho Sa, not for you or a thousand like you. But I have children and it is the women who must look to the years ahead. Will we three sit and watch the Chin empire dragged down in flames? Will we see civilisation torn apart and say *nothing*?' She turned to Yao Shu who was listening intently. 'Where will your Buddhism be then, my friend? Will you see it crushed under the hooves of these tribes?'

Yao Shu spoke for the first time at that, looking troubled.

'If my beliefs could be burned, lady, I would not trust them, nor live by them. They will survive this war with the Chin, even if the Chin themselves do not. Men strive to be emperors and kings, but they are just names. It does not matter which man holds a name. The fields will still need to be worked. The towns will still be thick with vice and corruption.' He shrugged. 'No man knows where the future will take us. Your husband has raised no objection to having his sons trained by my hand. Perhaps the words of the Buddha will take root in one of them, but it is foolish to look so far ahead.'

'He is right, Majesty,' Ho Sa said quietly. 'You have spoken out of fear and loneliness, I see that now. I had not considered how hard this must have been for you.' He took a deep breath, knowing he played with fire, but intoxicated with her. 'You have a friend in me, as you said.'

Chakahai smiled then, her eyes bright with fresh tears. She reached out her hands and they each took one, feeling the coolness of her fingers in theirs.

'Perhaps I have been afraid,' she said. 'I have imagined my father's city being overrun and my heart goes out to the Chin emperor and his family. Can they survive this, do you think?'

'All men die,' Yao Shu replied before Ho Sa could speak. 'Our lives are no more than a bird flying through a lighted window, then out again into the darkness. What matters is that we do not cause pain. A good life will defend the weak and, by so doing, set a lamp in the darkness that will last for many lives to come.'

Ho Sa glanced at the solemn monk, seeing how his shaven head gleamed. He did not agree with the words and could almost shudder at the thought of such an earnest and joyless life. He preferred Khasar's simpler philosophy that the sky father would not have given him strength to waste. If a man could raise a sword, he should use it and there were no better opponents than the weak. They were less likely to gut you when you weren't looking. He said none of this aloud and was pleased to see Chakahai relax and nod to the monk.

'You are a good man, Yao Shu. I have sensed it. My husband's sons will learn much from you, I am certain. Perhaps one day, they will have Buddhist hearts.'

She rose suddenly then, almost making Ho Sa spill the dregs of his cold tea. He placed the bowl to one side and bowed to her once more, thankful that the strange meeting was at an end.

'We are from an old culture,' Chakahai said softly. 'I think we can influence a new one, as it grows. If we are careful, it will benefit us all.'

Ho Sa blinked at the princess of his people, before falling into the courteous routines that would take him back into the outside air, Yao Shu beside him. Both men stared at each other for a moment before taking separate paths into the camp.

CHAPTER EIGHTEEN

The usual peace and order of the Imperial barracks in Baotou was lost as the soldiers packed their equipment onto carts. The orders from Yenking had come in the night and the commander, Lujan, had wasted no time. Nothing of value was to be left for the Mongols and anything they could not take with them had to be destroyed. He had men already at work with hammers, breaking the surplus stores of arrows and spears with methodical efficiency.

Ordering the evacuation had been hard and he had not slept since receiving the command. The soldiers who guarded Baotou from bandits and criminal tongs had been in the city for almost four years. Many had families there and Lujan had looked in vain for permission to take them out with him.

The letter from General Zhi Zhong had come by Imperial messenger, the seals perfect. Lujan knew he risked demotion or worse by allowing men with wives and children to gather their families, but he could not leave them to the enemy. He saw another group of young boys take their seats on a cart and look around with frightened eyes. Baotou was all they had ever known and, in a single night, they had been told to leave everything and move quickly to the nearest barracks.

Lujan sighed to himself. With so many people involved, the secret had been impossible to keep. No doubt the wives had

259

warned their friends and the news had spread in widening ripples through the night. Perhaps that was why the orders had not included the command to evacuate the families of his men.

Outside the barracks gates, he could hear the gathering crowd. He shook his head unconsciously. He could not save them all and he would not disobey his orders. He felt shame at his own relief not to have to stay in the path of the Mongol army and tried not to hear the voices calling in confusion and terror on the streets.

The sun had risen and already he feared he had delayed too long. If he had not sent for the army families, he would have been able to slip out in the night. As it was, they would pass through a hostile crowd in full daylight. He steeled himself to be ruthless now the decision had been made. There would be bloodshed if the citizens grew angry, perhaps a running fight to the river gate, four hundred paces from the barracks. It had not seemed so far the previous day. He wished another solution had presented itself, but his path was set and soon it would be time to leave.

Two of his men ran past on some final errand. Neither acknowledged their commander and Lujan sensed their anger. No doubt they were men who kept whores or had friends in the city. They all had. There would be riots when they left, with the tongs running wild in the streets. Some of the criminals were like savage dogs, barely held in check by the threat of force. With the soldiers gone, they would glut themselves until the enemy came to burn them out.

That thought gave Lujan some satisfaction, though he still felt ashamed. He tried to clear his mind, to concentrate on the problem of getting the column of soldiers and carts out of the city. He had placed crossbowmen along the line, with orders to shoot into the crowd if they were attacked. If that failed, pikes would hold the mob at bay long enough to leave Baotou, he was almost sure. Either way, it would be vicious and he could take no pride in the planning.

Another of his soldiers came running up and Lujan recognised him as one of those he had stationed at the barracks gate. Had the rioting started already?

'Sir, there is a man wishing to speak to you. I told him to go home, but he gave me this token and said you would see him.'

Lujan looked at the little piece of blue shell marked with Chen Yi's personal chop. He winced. It was not a meeting he wanted to have, but the carts were almost ready and the men had formed ranks before the gate. Perhaps because of his guilt, he nodded.

'Have him enter through the small door and be certain not to let anyone force their way in with him.' The soldier rushed away and Lujan was left alone with his thoughts. Chen Yi would die with the rest of them and no one would ever learn of the arrangement they had formed over the years. It had profited them both, but Lujan would not regret being free of the little man's influence. He struggled against weariness as the soldier returned with the leader of the Blue Tong.

'I can do nothing for you now, Chen Yi,' Lujan began as the soldier ran back to take his place in the column. 'My orders are to withdraw from Baotou and join the army assembling before Yenking. I cannot help you.'

Chen Yi stared at him and Lujan saw he was armed with a sword on his hip. It should have been removed at the door set into the main gate, but none of the routines were in force today.

'I thought you would lie to me,' Chen Yi said, 'telling me that you were out on manoeuvres or training. I would not have believed you, of course.'

'You would have been among the first to hear last night,' Lujan said with a shrug. 'I must follow my orders.'

'You will let Baotou burn?' Chen Yi said. 'After so many years of telling us you are our protectors, you will run as soon as a real threat appears?'

Lujan felt himself flush.

'I am a soldier, Chen Yi. When my general tells me to march, I march. I am sorry.'

Chen Yi was red-faced, though whether it was from anger or the exertion of running to the barracks, Lujan could not tell. He felt the force of the man's gaze and could hardly meet it.

'I see you have allowed your men to take their wives and children to safety,' Chen Yi noted. 'Your own wife and sons will not suffer when the Mongols come.'

Lujan looked away at the column. Already there were faces turned towards him, waiting for his word to march.

'I have exceeded my authority even in that, my friend.'

Chen Yi made a snarling sound in his throat.

'Do not call a man "friend" as you leave him to be killed.' His anger was clear now and Lujan could not meet his eyes as he went on.

'The wheel will turn, Lujan. Your masters will pay for their cruelty even as you pay for this shame.'

'I must leave now,' Lujan said, staring into the distance. 'You could empty the city before the Mongols come. Many could be saved if you order it.'

'Perhaps I will, Lujan. After all, there will be no other authority in Baotou when you are gone.' Both men knew it was impossible to evacuate the population of Baotou. The Mongol army was no more than two days away. Even if they filled every boat and used the river to escape, there would not be enough places for more than a few. The people of Baotou would be slaughtered as they ran. Picturing the rice fields running red with blood, Lujan let out a long breath. He had already delayed too long.

'Good luck,' he murmured, glancing at Chen Yi's eyes. He could not understand the triumph he saw sparkling there and he almost spoke again before he thought better of it. He strode to the front of the column, where his horse was held for him. As Chen Yi watched, the barracks gates opened and those in the front rank stiffened as the crowd fell silent.

The roads were lined with people staring in. They had left the way clear for the Imperial soldiers and their carts, but the faces were cold with hatred and Lujan snapped loud orders for his crossbowmen to be ready, letting the crowd hear as he trotted out. The silence was unnerving and he expected a barrage of abuse to start at any second. His men fingered their swords and pikes nervously, trying not to see the faces of people they knew as they left the barracks behind. The same scene would be happening at the other barracks and they would meet the second and third column outside the city before moving east to Yenking and the Badger's Mouth pass. Baotou would then be defenceless, for the first time in its history.

Chen Yi watched the column of guards leave, heading towards the river gate. Lujan could not know that many of the crowd were his own men, there to keep order and prevent the more reckless citizens from showing their disgust at the withdrawal. He did not want Lujan to delay his departure, but he had not been able to resist seeing his shame before he left. Lujan had been a sympathetic voice in the garrison for many years, though they had not been friends. Chen Yi knew the orders to leave would have been hard on the man and he had enjoyed every moment of his humiliation. It had been a struggle not to show his inner satisfaction. There would be no dissenting voice when the Mongols came, no soldiers ordered to fight to the last. The emperor's betrayal had given Baotou into Chen Yi's hands in one morning.

He frowned to himself as the column of soldiers reached the river gate and Lujan passed under the shadow of the deserted archer platforms. Everything depended on the honour of the two Mongol brothers he had aided. He wished he could know for certain whether Khasar and Temuge could be trusted, or whether he would see his precious city torn apart. The crowd at the barracks watched the retreating soldiers in eerie silence and Chen Yi offered up prayers to the spirits of his ancestors. Remembering his Mongol servant, Quishan, he mouthed a final prayer to the sky father of those strange people, asking for his help in the coming days.

Leaning on the wooden bar of a goat pen, Genghis smiled at the sight of his son Chagatai, hearing the boy's whoops across the encampment. He had given the ten-year-old a set of armour that morning, specially made for his small frame. Chagatai was too young to join the warriors in battle, but he had been delighted with the armour, riding around and around the camp on a new pony to show the older men. There were many smiles as they saw him brandishing his bow and alternating between war cries and laughter.

Genghis stretched his back, running a hand along the thick cloth of the white tent he had raised before the walls of Baotou. It differed from the gers of his people, so that those in the cities would know it and beg their leaders to surrender. Twice as high as even his own great ger, it was not so solidly built and shivered in the wind, its sides snapping in and out like breath. White horsetail standards stood on tall pikes on either side of it and whipped around as if alive.

Baotou stood closed to them and Genghis wondered if his brothers were correct in their judgement of this Chen Yi. The scouts had brought news of a column of soldiers marching from the city just the day before. Some of the young warriors had ridden close enough to score distant kills with their bows before being driven off. If they had estimated the numbers correctly, the city had no soldiers to defend it and Genghis found himself in a mellow mood. One way or another, the city would fall like the others.

He had spoken to the Baotou mason and been reassured that Chen Yi would not have forgotten his agreement. Lian's family remained inside the walls he had helped to build and he had many reasons for wanting a peaceful submission. Genghis looked up at the white tent. They had until sunset to surrender, or they would see the red tent the following day. No agreement would save them then.

Genghis felt eyes on him and turned to see his oldest son, Jochi, on the opposite side of the milling goats. The boy was watching him in silence and, despite what he had promised to Borte, Genghis felt himself respond as if to a challenge. He held the boy's eyes coldly until Jochi was forced to look away. Only then did Genghis speak to him.

'It is your birthday in a month. I will have another set of armour made for you then.'

Jochi wrinkled his lip into a sneer.

'I will be twelve. It will not be long before I can ride with the warriors. There is no point in playing children's games until then.'

Genghis' temper prickled. The offer had been generous. He would have spoken again, but they were both distracted by Chagatai's return. The boy thundered up on his pony and leaped to the ground, barely stumbling as he steadied himself on the wooden pen and whipped the reins around a post in a quick knot. The goats in the pen bleated in panic and pressed away from him to the other side. Genghis could not help but smile at Chagatai's uncomplicated joy, though he felt Jochi's gaze settle on him again, always watching.

Chagatai gestured towards the silent city of Baotou, less than a mile away.

'Why are we not attacking that place, father?' he said, glancing towards Jochi.

'Because your uncles made a promise to a man inside it,' Genghis replied patiently. 'In return for the mason who helped us win all the others, this one will be allowed to stand.' He paused for a moment. 'If they surrender today.'

'And tomorrow?' Jochi said suddenly. 'Another city, and another after that?' As Genghis turned to him, Jochi straightened. 'Will we spend all our lives taking these places one by one?'

Genghis felt blood rush into his face at the boy's tone, then he recalled his promise to Borte that he would treat Jochi the same as his brothers. She did not seem to understand the way he needled him at every opportunity, but Genghis needed peace in his own ger. He took a moment to master his temper.

'It is not a game we are playing here,' he said. 'I do not choose to crush Chin cities because I enjoy the flies and the heat of this land. I am here, *you* are here because they have tormented us for a thousand generations. Chin gold has had every tribe at the throat of all the others for longer than anyone can remember. When we have peace for a generation, they set the Tartars on us like wild dogs.'

'They cannot do that now,' Jochi replied. 'The Tartars are broken and our people are one nation, as you say. We are too strong. Is it vengeance then that drives us?' The boy did not look directly at his father, only risking glances at him when Genghis turned away, yet there was genuine interest in his gaze.

His father snorted.

'For you, the history is only stories. You were not even born when the tribes were scattered. You did not know that time and perhaps you cannot understand it. Yes, this is vengeance, in part. Our enemies must learn they cannot ride us down without a storm coming after.' He drew his father's sword and turned it into the sun, so that the shining surface flashed a golden line onto Jochi's face.

'This is a good blade, made by a master. But if I buried it in the ground, how long would it keep its edge?'

'You will say the tribes are like the sword,' Jochi said, surprising him.

'Perhaps,' Genghis replied, irritated to have had his lecture interrupted. The boy was too sharp for his own good. 'Anything I have won can be lost, perhaps by a single foolish son who does not have the patience to listen to his father.' Jochi grinned at that and Genghis realised he had acknowledged him as a son even as he sought to wipe the arrogant expression off his face.

Genghis pulled open the gate to the goat pen and stepped inside, holding his sword up. The goats struggled to get away from him, climbing over each other and bleating mindlessly.

'In your cleverness, Jochi, tell me what would happen if the goats attacked me.'

'You would kill them all,' Chagatai said quickly behind him, trying to be involved in the contest of wills. Genghis did not look back as Jochi spoke.

'They would knock you down,' Jochi said. 'Are we goats then, united as a nation?' The boy seemed to find the idea amusing and Genghis lost his temper, snapping out an arm to heave Jochi over the rail and send him sprawling among the animals. They ran in bleating panic, some trying to leap the barrier.

'We are the *wolf*, boy, and the wolf does not ask about the goats it kills. It does not consider the best way to spend its time until its mouth and paws are red with blood and it has conquered all of its enemies. And if you ever mock me again, I will send you to join them.'

Jochi scrambled to his feet, the cold face dropping over his features like a mask. In Chagatai, the discipline would have earned approval, but Genghis and Jochi stood facing each other in strained silence, neither willing to be the first to turn away. Chagatai leered on the edge of Jochi's vision, enjoying his humiliation. In the end, Jochi was still a child and his eyes filled with hot tears of frustration as he broke his father's gaze and clambered back over the wooden bar.

Genghis took a deep breath, already looking for some way to smooth over the anger he had felt.

'You must not think of this war as something we do before we return to quieter lives. We are warriors, if talk of swords and wolves is too fanciful. If I spend my youth breaking the strength of the Chin emperor, I will consider every day a joy. His family has ruled for long enough and now *my* family has risen. We will not suffer their cold hands on us any longer.'

Jochi was breathing heavily, but he mastered himself to ask one more question.

'So there will be no end to it? Even when you are old and grey, you will still be looking for enemies to fight?'

'If there are any left,' Genghis replied. 'What I have begun cannot be given up. If we ever lose heart, if we ever falter, they will come for us in greater numbers than you can imagine.' He struggled to find something to say that would raise the boy's spirits. 'But by then, my sons will be old enough to ride to new lands and bring them under our rule. They will be kings. They will eat greasy food and wear jewelled swords and forget what they owe to me.'

Khasar and Temuge had walked past the edge of the camp to stare up at the walls of Baotou. The sun was low on the horizon, but the day had been hot and both men were sweating in the thick air. They never sweated in the high mountains of home, where dirt fell as dust from their dry skin. In the Chin lands, their bodies became foul and flies tormented them constantly. Temuge in particular seemed pale and sickly and his stomach roiled as he remembered the last time he had seen the city. He had spent too many evenings in the smoke-filled ger of Kokchu and some of the things he had seen distressed him still. As his throat tightened, he coughed. The action seemed to make it worse until he felt dizzy and ill.

Khasar watched him recover without a trace of sympathy.

'Your wind is broken, little brother. If you were a pony, I would cut you up to feed the tribes.'

'You understand nothing, as always,' Temuge replied weakly, wiping his mouth with the back of his hand. The flush in his cheeks was draining away and his skin looked waxy in the sunlight.

'I understand you are killing yourself to kiss the feet of that filthy shaman,' Khasar replied. 'You are even beginning to smell like him, I've noticed.'

Temuge might have ignored his brother's barb, but as he looked up, there was a wariness in Khasar's eyes that he had not seen before. He had sensed it in others who associated him with the great khan's shaman. It was not exactly fear, unless it was fear of the unknown. He had dismissed it before as the ignorance of fools, but seeing the same caution in Khasar was strangely pleasing.

'I have learned much from him, brother,' he said. 'At times, I have been frightened by the things I have seen.'

'The tribes mutter many things about him, but nothing good,' Khasar said softly. 'I heard he takes the babies whose mothers don't want them. They are not seen again.' He did not look at Temuge as he spoke, preferring to fix his gaze on the walls of Baotou. 'They say he killed a man with just a touch.'

Temuge straightened slowly from the cramp of his coughing.

'I have learned to summon death in such a way,' he lied. 'Last night, while you were sleeping. It was agony and it is why I cough today, but the flesh will recover and I will still know.'

Khasar looked sideways at his brother, trying to see if he was telling the truth.

'I'm sure it was a trick of some kind,' he said. Temuge smiled at him and the fact that his gums were stained from the black paste made the expression terrible.

'There is no need to be frightened of what I know, brother,' Temuge said softly. 'Knowledge is not dangerous. Only the man is dangerous.'

Khasar snorted.

'That's the sort of childish talk he teaches you, is it? You sound like that Buddhist monk, Yao Shu. There's one who doesn't stand in awe of Kokchu, at least. They're like spring rams on each other's territory whenever they meet.'

'The monk is a fool,' Temuge snapped. 'He should not be teaching the children of Genghis. One of them may be khan one day and this "Buddhism" will make them soft.'

'Not with the monk teaching it,' Khasar replied with a grin. 'He can split boards with his hands, which is more than Kokchu can do. I like him, though he can hardly speak a word of proper speech.'

'*He can split boards,*' Temuge said, mocking his brother's voice. 'Of course you would be impressed by such a thing. Does he keep dark spirits from entering the camp on moonless nights? No, he makes firewood.'

Despite himself, Khasar found he was growing angry. There

was something about this new assurance in Temuge that he disliked, though he could not have put it into words.

'I've never seen one of these Chin spirits Kokchu claims to banish. I do know I can use firewood.' He chuckled scornfully as Temuge flushed, his own temper rising. 'If I had to choose between them, I'd rather have a man who can fight the way he fights and I'll take my chances with the spirits of dead Chin peasants.'

Furious, Temuge raised his arm to his brother and, to his astonishment, Khasar flinched. The man who would charge into a group of soldiers without a thought took a pace back from his younger brother and dropped his hand to his sword. For an instant, Temuge almost laughed. He wanted to make Khasar see the joke, and recall that they had once been friends, but then he felt coldness steal into him and he exulted in the fear he had seen.

'Do not mock the spirits, Khasar, nor the men who control them. You have not walked the paths when the moon has gone and seen what I have seen. I would have died many times if Kokchu had not been there to guide me back to the land.'

Khasar knew his brother had seen him react to nothing more than an open palm and his heart pounded in his chest. Part of him did not believe little Temuge could know anything that he did not, but there *were* mysteries and at the feasts he had seen Kokchu push knives into his flesh without a drop of blood falling.

Khasar stared at his brother in frustration, before turning on his heel and striding back to the gers of his people, to the world he knew. Left alone, Temuge felt like howling in triumph.

As he faced Baotou, the city gates opened and warning horns sounded across the camp behind him. The warriors would be racing for their horses. Let them run, he thought, giddy with the victory over his brother. The sickness had passed and he strolled confidently towards the open gate. He wondered if Chen Yi would have archers on the walls, ready for treachery. It did not matter to him. He felt invulnerable and his feet were light on the stony ground.

CHAPTER NINETEEN

The city of Baotou was silent as Chen Yi welcomed Genghis into his home. Ho Sa accompanied the khan and Chen Yi bowed deeply to him, acknowledging that promises had been kept.

'You are welcome in my home,' Chen Yi said in the language of the tribes, bowing again as he came face to face with Genghis for the first time. Genghis towered over him, taller even than Khasar had been. The khan wore full armour and had a sword belted on his hip. Chen Yi could feel the inner force of him, as strong as anyone he had ever met. Genghis did not reply to the formal greeting, merely nodding as he strode into the open courtyard. Chen Yi had to move quickly to lead him into the main house and, in his hurry, he did not see Genghis glance at the immense roof and steel himself to enter. Ho Sa and Temuge had described it to him, but he was still curious to see how a wealthy man lived in the heart of a city.

Outside, the streets were empty even of beggars. Every house was barricaded against the tribesmen who wandered through the streets, peering through gates and looking for items worth taking. Genghis had given orders to leave the city intact, but no one thought the order could include stores of rice wine. Household images of gods were in particular demand. The tribesmen reasoned that they could not have enough protection in their own gers and collected any small statue that looked suitably potent.

An honour guard of warriors waited outside at the gate, but in truth Genghis could have walked alone anywhere in the city. The only possible danger came from men he could command with a word.

Chen Yi had to struggle not to show his nervousness as Genghis strolled around the inside of his house, examining items. The khan seemed tense and Chen Yi was unsure how to begin the conversation. His guards and servants had been sent away for the meeting and the house felt oddly empty.

'I am glad my mason could be of use to you, my lord,' Chen Yi said to break the silence. Genghis was inspecting a black lacquered pot and didn't look up as he placed it back on its stand. He seemed too large for the room, as if at any moment he could take hold of the beams and bring the whole place crashing down. Chen Yi told himself it was just his reputation that made him seem powerful, but then Genghis turned pale yellow eyes on him and his thoughts froze.

Genghis ran a finger over the pot's decoration of figures in a garden, then turned to his host.

'Do not fear me, Chen Yi. Ho Sa says you are a man who has made much of little, a man who has been given nothing but yet survived and become wealthy in this place.' Chen Yi glanced at Ho Sa on hearing the words, but the Xi Xia soldier showed him nothing. For once in his life, Chen Yi felt at a loss. Baotou had been promised to him, but he did not know if the khan would keep his word. He did know that when a great wind destroys a man's home, he can only shrug and know it was fate and could not be resisted. Meeting Genghis was like that for him. The rules he had known all his life had been thrown away. At a single command from the Mongol khan, Baotou would be razed to the ground.

'I am a wealthy man,' Chen Yi agreed. Before he could continue, he felt Genghis' eyes on him, suddenly interested. The khan picked up the lacquered pot once more and gestured with it. In his hands, it looked incredibly fragile.

'What is wealth, Chen Yi? You are a man of cities, of streets and houses. What do you value? This?'

He spoke quickly and Ho Sa bought Chen Yi time to reply by translating it. Chen Yi flashed a grateful glance at the soldier.

'That pot took a thousand hours of labour to make, lord. When I look at it, it gives me pleasure.'

Genghis turned the pot in his hands. He seemed obscurely disappointed and Chen Yi glanced at Ho Sa again. The soldier raised his eyebrows, urging more.

'But it is not wealth, lord,' Chen Yi went on. 'I have starved, so I know the value of food. I have been cold, so I know the value of warmth.'

Genghis shrugged.

'A sheep knows as much. Do you have sons?' He knew the answer, but still he wanted to understand this man who came from a world so different from his own.

'I have three daughters, lord. My son was taken from me.'

'Then what is wealth, Chen Yi?'

Under the questions, Chen Yi became very calm. He did not know what the khan wanted, so he answered honestly.

'Revenge is wealth, lord, for me. The ability to reach out and strike down my enemies. That is wealth. Having men who will kill and die for me is wealth. My daughters and my wife are my wealth.' With great gentleness, he took the pot from Genghis' hands, then dropped it on the wooden floor. It shattered into tiny pieces, exploding across the polished wood.

'Anything else is worthless, lord.'

Genghis grinned briefly. Khasar had spoken the truth when he said Chen Yi would not be cowed.

'I think if I had been born in a city, I might have led your life, Chen Yi. Though I would not have trusted my brothers, knowing them as I do.'

Chen Yi did not reply that he had trusted only Khasar, but Genghis seemed to guess his thoughts.

'Khasar speaks well of you. I will not go back on his word, given in my name. Baotou is yours. It is just a step on the path to Yenking for me.'

'I am glad, lord,' Chen Yi replied, almost shuddering with relief. 'Will you share a cup of wine?' Genghis nodded and a vast pressure left the room. Ho Sa relaxed visibly as Chen Yi looked around automatically for a servant and found none. Stiffly, he gathered the cups himself, his sandals crunching on shards of priceless pottery that had once adorned the home of an emperor. His hand shook slightly as he poured three cups and only then did Genghis sit down. Ho Sa took another seat, his armour creaking as he settled. He dipped his head a fraction to Chen Yi when their eyes met again, as if he had passed some sort of test.

Chen Yi knew the khan would not be taking the time to sit unless there was something he wanted. He watched the dark, flat face as Genghis accepted the cup from his hand. Chen Yi realised the khan too was ill at ease and searching for words.

'Baotou must seem small to you, lord,' Chen Yi ventured as Genghis sipped at the rice wine, pausing at a taste he had not known before.

'I have never been inside a city, except to burn it down,' Genghis replied. 'Seeing one so quiet is a strange thing for me.' He emptied the cup and refilled it himself, offering the bottle to Chen Yi and then Ho Sa.

'One more, but it is potent and I want a clear head,' Chen Yi replied.

'It is horse piss,' Genghis replied with a snort, 'though I like the way it warms.'

276

'I will have a hundred bottles sent to your camp, lord,' Chen Yi said quickly.

The Mongol leader watched him over the edge of his cup and nodded.

'You are generous.'

'It is not much in return for the city of my birth,' Chen Yi said.

Genghis seemed to relax at that, leaning back on the couch.

'You are a clever man, Chen Yi. Khasar told me that you ruled the city even when the soldiers were here.'

'He may have exaggerated a little, lord. My authority is strongest among the lowest castes – the dockworkers and tradesmen. The nobles live a different life and it was only rarely that I could find some way to sling reins on their power.'

Genghis grunted. He could not express the discomfort he felt sitting in such a house, surrounded by a thousand others. He could almost feel the press of humanity all around him. Khasar had been right: for one raised in the clean winds of the plains, the city smelled terrible.

'You hate them then, these nobles?' Genghis asked. It was not a casual question and Chen Yi considered his answer carefully. The language of the tribes lacked the words he needed, so he spoke in his own tongue and let Ho Sa translate.

'Most of them live lives so distant that I do not think of them, lord. Their judges make much of enforcing the emperor's laws, but they do not touch the nobles. If I steal, I can have my hands cut off or be whipped to death. If a noble steals from me, there will be no justice. Even if he takes a daughter or a son from me, I can do nothing.' He waited patiently for Ho Sa to finish speaking, knowing his feelings had become obvious as Genghis stared at him. 'Yes, I hate them,' he said.

'There were bodies hanging from the barracks gates, as I came in,' Genghis said. 'Two or three dozen. Was that your work?'

'I settled old debts, lord, before you arrived.'

Genghis nodded, refilling both cups.

'A man must always settle his debts. Are there many who feel as you do?'

Chen Yi smiled bitterly.

'More than I can count, lord. The Chin nobles are an elite who rule many times their number. Without their army they would have nothing.'

'If you have the numbers, why do you not rise up against them?' Genghis asked in genuine curiosity.

Chen Yi sighed, once more using the Chin tongue, the words pouring out at great speed.

'Bakers, masons and boatmen do not make an army, lord. The noble families are ruthless at the first sign of rebellion. There have been attempts in the past, but they have spies among the people and even a collection of weapons would have their soldiers descend upon us. If a rebellion ever took root, they would call on the emperor and his army would march. Whole towns can be put to the sword or burned. I have heard of it, in my own lifetime.' He hesitated, aware as Ho Sa spoke after him that the khan would think nothing of such acts. Chen Yi almost held up a hand to stop the Xi Xia soldier, but held still. Baotou had been spared, after all.

Genghis assessed the man he faced, fascinated. He had forced the idea of a nation on the tribes, but it was not shared by men like Chen Yi, not yet. Each city might have been ruled by the Chin emperor, but they did not look to him for leadership, or feel part of his family. It was clear that the nobles took their authority from the emperor. It was also clear that Chen Yi hated them for their arrogance, wealth and power. The knowledge could be useful.

'I have felt their gaze on my own people, Chen Yi,' he said. 'We have become a nation to resist them, no, to crush them.'

'And will you then rule as they did?' Chen Yi asked, hearing the bitterness in his tone before he could stop himself. He felt a dangerous freedom in talking to the khan, he realised. The usual curbs and cautions on his tongue were flimsy protection under that yellow gaze. To his relief, Genghis chuckled.

'I have not given thought to what comes after the battles. Perhaps I will rule. Is that not the right of a conqueror?'

Chen Yi took a deep breath before replying.

'To rule, yes, but will your lowest-ranking warrior walk like an emperor among those you have conquered? Will he sneer and take whatever he has not earned?'

Genghis stared at him.

'The nobles are the family of the emperor? If you are asking if my family will take what they want, of course they will. The strong rule, Chen Yi. Those who are not strong dream of it.' He paused, trying to understand. 'You would have me bind my people by petty rules?' he asked.

Chen Yi took another deep breath. He had spent his life with spies and falsehood, protection layered on protection against the day when the emperor's army would root him out in fire and blood from the city. That day had not come. Instead, he found himself facing one before whom he could speak without any restraint. He would never again have such an opportunity.

'I understand what you have said, but will that right be passed on to their sons and grandsons, further? When some cruel weakling kills a boy a hundred years from now, will no one dare protest because *your* blood is in him?'

Genghis remained motionless. After a long time, he shook his head.

'I do not know these Chin nobles, but my own sons will rule after me, if they have the strength. Perhaps in a hundred years, my descendants will still rule and be these nobles you despise.' He shrugged, draining his cup.

'Most men are like sheep,' he went on. 'They are not as we are.' He waved away Chen Yi's reply. 'Do you doubt it? How many in this city can match your influence, your power, even before I came? Most cannot lead – the idea terrifies them. Yet for those like you and me, there is no greater joy than knowing there is *no* help coming. The decision is ours alone.' He gestured wildly with his cup. Chen Yi broke the wax seal on another bottle and poured the wine once more.

The silence grew strained. To the surprise of both men, it was Ho Sa who broke it.

'I have sons,' he said. 'I have not seen them in three years. When they are grown, they will follow me into the army. When men hear they are mine, they will expect more from them. They will rise faster than a man with no name. I am content with that. For that, I work hard and endure anything.'

'They will never be noble, those soldier sons of yours,' Chen Yi said. 'A boy from the great houses would order them to their deaths in a fire just to save a pot like the one I broke tonight.'

Genghis frowned, troubled by the image.

'You would make all men the same?'

Chen Yi shrugged. His thoughts swirled in wine and he didn't know he spoke in the Chin tongue.

'I am not a fool. I know there is no law for the emperor, or his family. All law comes from him and the army he wields. He cannot be under it like other men. For the rest though, for the thousands of parasites who feed from his hand, why should they be allowed to murder and steal without punishment?' He emptied his cup as Ho Sa translated, nodding as if the soldier spoke in agreement.

Genghis stretched his back, wishing for the first time that Temuge were there to argue the point for him. He had intended to speak to Chen Yi and understand the strange breed that lived in cities. Instead, the little man made his head swim.

'If one of my warriors wishes to marry,' Genghis said, 'he finds an enemy and kills him, taking whatever he owns. He gives those horses and goats to the girl's father. Is that murder and theft? If I forbade that, I would make them weak.' He was light-headed from the wine, but his mood was mellow and, once more, he filled the three cups.

'Does this warrior take from his own family, his own tribe?' Chen Yi asked.

'No. He would be a criminal, beneath contempt if he did,' Genghis replied. Even before Chen Yi spoke again, he saw where the little man was going.

'Then what of your tribes now that they are bound together?' Chen Yi said, leaning forward. 'What will you do if all Chin lands are yours?'

It was a dizzying concept. It was true that Genghis had already forbidden young tribesmen to raid each other, instead providing marriage gifts from his own herd. It was not a solution he could maintain for long. What Chen Yi suggested was merely an extension of that peace, though it would encompass lands so vast it was difficult to imagine.

'I will think on it,' he said, slurring slightly. 'Such thoughts are too rich to be eaten in one sitting.' He smiled. 'Especially as the Chin emperor remains safe in his city and we have barely begun. Perhaps next year I will be scattered bones.'

'Or you will have broken the nobles in their forts and cities,' Chen Yi said, 'and have a chance to change it all. You are a man of vision. You showed that when you spared Baotou.'

Genghis shook his head blearily.

'My word is iron. When all else is lost, there is still that. But if I had not spared Baotou it would have been another city.'

'I do not understand,' Chen Yi replied.

Genghis turned his hard gaze on him again.

'The cities will not surrender if there is no benefit to them.'

He raised a clenched fist and Chen Yi's gaze was drawn to it. 'Here, I have the threat of bloodshed, worse than anything they can imagine. Once I raise the red tent, they know they will lose every man within the walls. When they see the black, they know they will all die.' He shook his head. 'If death is all I offer, they have no choice but to fight to the last man.' He dropped the fist and reached again for a fresh cup which Chen Yi filled with shaking hands.

'If I spare even one city, the word will spread that they do not *need* to fight. They can choose to surrender when the white tent goes up. That is why I spared Baotou. That is why you still live.'

Genghis recalled his other reason for seeking the meeting with Chen Yi. His mind seemed to have lost its customary sharpness and he thought perhaps he should not have drunk quite so much.

'Do you have maps in this city? Maps of the lands to the east?'

Chen Yi felt dazed at the insight he had been given. The man who faced him was a conqueror who would not be stopped by the feeble Chin nobles and their corrupt armies. He shivered suddenly, seeing a future filled with flames.

'There is a library,' he said, stammering slightly. 'It has been forbidden to me until now. I do not think the soldiers destroyed it before they left.'

'I need maps,' Genghis replied. 'Will you look over them with me? Help me plan the destruction of your emperor?'

Chen Yi had matched him drink for drink and his thoughts spun themselves to wisps in his head. He thought of his dead son, hanged by nobles who would not even look at a man of low birth. Let the world change, he thought. Let them all burn.

'He is not my emperor, lord. Everything in this city is yours. I will do what I can. If you want scribes to write new laws, I will send them to you.'

Genghis nodded drunkenly.

'Writing,' he replied, scornfully. 'It traps words.'

'It makes them real, lord. It makes them last.'

The morning after his meeting with Chen Yi, Genghis awoke with a pounding headache so bad he did not leave his ger all day except to vomit. He could not remember much after the sixth bottle had been brought out, but Chen Yi's words came back to him at intervals and he discussed them with Kachiun and Temuge. His people had only known a khan's rule, with all justice stemming from one man's judgement. Even as things stood, Genghis could have spent each day deciding arguments and punishing criminals in the tribes. It was already too much for him, yet he could not allow the small khans to resume their roles, or risk losing it all.

When Genghis gave the order to move on at last, it was strange to leave a city without seeing flames on the horizon behind them. Chen Yi had given him maps of Chin lands all the way to the eastern sea, more precious than anything they had won before. Though Chen Yi remained in Baotou, the mason Lian had agreed to accompany Genghis to Yenking. Lian seemed to regard the walls of the emperor's city as a personal challenge to his skill and he had come to Genghis to make the offer before he could be asked. His son had not beggared his business in his absence and Genghis privately thought it was a matter of going on with the invading army or settling for a quiet retirement.

The great trek continued into Chin lands, the central mass of carts and gers moving slowly, but always surrounded by tens of thousands of horsemen looking for the slightest chance to earn the praise of their commanders. Genghis had allowed messengers to travel from Baotou to other cities on their route to the mountains west of Yenking and the decision quickly bore fruit. The emperor had stripped the garrison from Hohhot and, without soldiers to bolster their nerve, the city surrendered without a single arrow being shot, then provided two thousand young men to be trained in the art of sieges and the pike. Chen Yi had shown the value of that with his own draft, choosing the best of his city to accompany the Mongols and learn the skills of battle. It was true that they had no horses, but Genghis gave them as infantry to Arslan and they accepted the new discipline without question.

Jining's garrison had refused to obey the emperor's order and the gates remained closed. It had been burned to the ground after the black tent was raised on the third day. Three other cities had surrendered after that. Those men who were young and strong were taken as prisoners, driven like sheep. There were simply too many to use as soldiers without seeing the tribes outnumbered. Genghis did not want them, but he could not leave so many at his back. His people drove half their number again over the land and, every day, there were bodies in their wake. As the nights grew colder, the Chin prisoners huddled together and whispered, a constant susurration that was eerie in the darkness.

It had been one of the hottest summers any of them had ever known. The old men said a freezing winter would follow and Genghis did not know whether he should move on the capital or leave the campaign for another year.

The mountains before Yenking were already visible and his scouts raced after mounted observers for the emperor whenever they appeared in the distance. Though their horses were swift, some of the Chin watchers were caught and each one added detail to the picture Genghis was building.

On a morning when the ground had frozen in the night, he sat on a pile of wooden saddles and stared into the weak sun.

It rose over the range of steep green crags that protected Yenking from him, shrouded in mist. Taller than the peaks between the Gobi and Xi Xia, they made even the mountains he remembered from home seem less impressive. Yet the captured observers spoke of the pass known as the Badger's Mouth and he felt he was being drawn to it. The emperor had gathered his strength there, gambling on a single massive force that dwarfed the army Genghis had brought to that place. Everything could end there and all his dreams would become ashes.

He chuckled to himself at the thought. Whatever the future held, he would meet it with his head raised and his sword drawn. He would struggle to the end and, if he fell against his enemies, it would have been a life well spent. Part of him felt a pang at the thought that his sons would not long survive his death, but he crushed the weakness. They would make their own lives as he had made his. If they were swept up in the wind of greater events, that would be their fate. He could not protect them from everything.

In the ger at his back, he heard one of Chakahai's children squalling. He could not tell if it was the son or the daughter. He brightened at the thought of the little girl who, though barely walking, toddled over to press her head affectionately against his leg whenever she saw him. He had seen a terrible jealousy in Borte when she had witnessed the simple act and he sighed at the memory. Conquering enemy cities was far less complicated than the women in his life, or the children they bore for him.

Out of the corner of his eye, he saw his brother Kachiun approach, strolling along one of the camp paths in the morning sun.

'Have you escaped out here?' Kachiun called to him. Genghis nodded, patting a place next to him on the saddles. Kachiun joined him and handed Genghis one of two hot pouches of mutton and unleavened bread, thick with warm grease. Genghis took his gratefully. He could smell snow on the air and he longed for the cold months to come.

'Where is Khasar this morning?' Genghis asked, tearing off a piece of the bread with his fingers and chewing it.

'Out with Ho Sa and the Young Wolves, teaching them how to charge against groups of the prisoners. Have you seen it? He gives the prisoners pikes! We lost three young men yesterday against them.'

'I heard,' Genghis said. Khasar used only small groups of the prisoners to train. It surprised Genghis how few were willing to take part, even with the promise of a pike or a sword. Surely it was better to die like that than in listless apathy. He shrugged to himself at the thought. The young men of the tribes had to learn to fight, as they would once have done against their own people. Khasar knew what he was doing, Genghis was almost certain.

Kachiun was watching him in silence, a wry smile on his face.

'You never ask about Temuge,' he said.

Genghis grimaced. His youngest brother made him uneasy and Khasar seemed to have fallen out with him. In truth, he could not make himself care about Temuge's latest enthusiasms. He surrounded himself with captured Chin scrolls, reading them even by lamplight in darkness.

'So why are you sitting here?' Kachiun asked to change the subject.

His brother snorted.

'Do you see the men waiting nearby?'

'I noticed one of the Woyela sons, the eldest,' Kachiun admitted. His sharp eyes missed nothing.

'I have told them not to approach me until I stand. When I do, they will come with questions and demands, as they do every morning. They will make me decide which one of them has the right to a particular colt, as one owns the mare and one the stallion. Then they will want me to commission new armour from some metalworker who just happens to be a relative. There is no end to it.'

He groaned at the thought. 'Perhaps you can delay them long enough for me to get away.'

Kachiun smiled at his brother's predicament.

'And I thought nothing could frighten you,' he said. 'Appoint another to deal with them. You must be free to plan the war with your generals.'

Genghis nodded, reluctantly.

'You have said it before, but who can I trust in such a position? At a single stroke, he would have as much power as any man in the tribes.' An answer occurred to both of them at the same time, but it was Kachiun who spoke.

'Temuge would be honoured to take on the work. You know he would.'

Genghis did not reply and Kachiun went on as if he sensed no objection.

'He is less likely to steal from you than other men, or to abuse the position. Give him a title like "Master of Trade". He will be running the camp in a few days.' Seeing that his brother was unmoved, Kachiun chose another approach.

'It might also force him to spend less time with Kokchu.'

Genghis looked up at that, seeing the waiting men take a step forward in case he was about to rise. He thought back to the conversation with Chen Yi in Baotou. Part of him wanted to make every decision himself, but it was true that he had a war to win.

'Very well,' he said reluctantly. 'Tell him the task is his for a year. I will send him three warriors who have been maimed in battle for the work. It will give them something to do and I want one of them to be your man, Kachiun, reporting only to you. Our brother will have many chances to skim the cream from whatever passes through his hands. A little will not hurt, but if he is greedy, I want to know.' He paused for a moment. 'And make sure he understands that Kokchu is to have nothing to do with his new role.' He sighed then. 'If he refuses, who else is there?'

'He will not refuse,' Kachiun said with certainty. 'He is a man of ideas, brother. This role will give him the authority he wants to run the camp.'

'The Chin have judges to pass on the laws and decide disputes,' Genghis said, looking off into the distance. 'I wonder if our people would ever accept such men among them?'

'If they were not from your own family?' Kachiun asked. 'It would be a brave man who tried to settle blood feuds, no matter what title he was given. In fact, I will send another dozen guards to Temuge to keep him safe. Our people are not beyond showing their resentment with an arrow in the back. He is not their khan, after all.'

Genghis sneered.

'No doubt he would have his dark spirits snatch it out of the air. Have you heard the stories growing around him? It's worse than with Kokchu. I sometimes wonder if my shaman knows what he has created.'

'We are from a line of khans, brother. We rule wherever we are placed.'

Genghis clapped him on the back.

'We will find out if the Chin emperor feels the same way. Perhaps he will have his army stand down when he sees us coming.'

'Will it be this year, then? In winter? I think it will snow before too long.'

'We cannot remain here without better grazing. I must make

the decision quickly, but I do not like the thought of leaving their army at this Badger's Mouth without a challenge. We can stand cold that will leave them slow and useless.'

'But they will have fortified the pass, sown spikes on the ground, dug trenches, anything they can think of,' Kachiun said. 'It will not be easy for us.'

Genghis turned his pale eyes on his brother and Kachiun looked away at the mountains they would dare to cross.

'They are so arrogant, Kachiun. They made a mistake in letting me know where they are,' Genghis said. 'They want us to ride against them where they are strongest, where they wait. Their wall did not stop me coming. Their mountains and their army will not.'

Kachiun smiled. He knew the way his brother thought.

'I saw you have all the scouts in the foothills. That is strange if we are to risk it all on a strike through the pass.'

Genghis smiled wryly.

'They think their mountains are too high to be climbed, Kachiun. Another of their walls runs across the range and only the highest peaks are left as their own protection, too high for men.' He snorted. 'For Chin soldiers, perhaps, but we are born in the snow. I remember my father turning me out of the ger naked when I was just eight years old. We can stand their winter and we can cross this inner wall.'

Kachiun too had wailed at the door of their father's ger, calling to be let back in. It was an old custom that many believed would make children strong. Kachiun wondered if Genghis had done the same with his own boys and, even as he formed the thought, he knew he had. His brother would not allow weakness, though he could break his sons in the process of making them strong.

Genghis finished his meal, sucking hardening grease from his fingers. 'The scouts will find trails around the pass. When the Chin are shivering in their tents, we will come at them from all sides. Only then, Kachiun, will I ride down the Badger's Mouth, driving their own people before me.'

'The prisoners?' Kachiun asked.

'We cannot feed them,' Genghis replied. 'They can still be useful if they soak up the arrows and bolts of our enemies.' He shrugged. 'It will be faster for them than starving to death.'

At that, Genghis rose to his feet, glancing up at the heavy clouds that would turn the Chin plain into a wilderness of snow and ice. Winter was always a time of death, when only the strongest survived. He sighed as he saw movement out of the corner of his eye. The watching men had seen him rise and they hurried closer before he could change his mind. Genghis stared sourly at them.

'Tell them to go and see Temuge,' he said, striding away.

CHAPTER TWENTY

The two scouts were starving. Even the porridge of cheese and water in their packs had frozen as they climbed high above the pass of Badger's Mouth. To the north and south, the second Chin wall ran across the mountains. It was less massive than the wall the tribes had crossed to enter Chin lands, though this one had not been allowed to crumble over the centuries. Preserved in ice, it wound its way through distant valleys, a grey snake in the whiteness. It might once have been a marvel to the Mongol scouts, though now they merely shrugged. The Chin armies had not sought to build their wall right to the peaks. They thought no one could survive the rocks and slopes of solid ice, so cold at that height that the blood would surely freeze. They were wrong. The scouts climbed past the level of the wall into a world of snow and ice, looking for a way over the mountains.

Fresh snow had come to the plains, whirling from storm clouds on the peaks that blinded them. There were moments when the gales punched a hole in the whiteness, revealing the pass and the spider legs of the inner wall stretching away. From that height, both men could see the dark smudge of the Chin army on the far side. Their own people were lost to sight on the plain, but they too were there, waiting for the scouts to return.

'There is no way through,' Taran shouted over the wind. 'Perhaps Beriakh and the others had better luck. We should go back.' Taran could feel the ice in his bones, the crystals in every joint. He was certain he was close to dying and it was hard not to show his fear. His companion, Vesak, merely grunted without looking at him. Both were part of a group of ten, one of many who had gone into the mountains to find a way to attack the rear of the Chin army. Though they had become separated from their companions in the night, Taran still trusted Vesak to smell out a route, but the cold was crippling him, too vicious to resist.

Vesak was an old man of more than thirty, while Taran had yet to see his fifteenth year. The other men in his group said Vesak knew the general of the Young Wolves, that he greeted Tsubodai like an old friend whenever they met. It could have been true. Like Tsubodai, Vesak was of the Uriankhai tribe far in the north and he did not seem to feel the cold. Taran clambered down an icy slope, almost falling. He caught himself by hammering his knife into a fissure, his hand nearly slipping from the hilt as he jerked to a stop. He felt Vesak's hand on his shoulder, then the older man was trotting again and Taran staggered on, trying to match his pace.

The Mongol boy was lost in his own world of misery and endurance when he saw Vesak stop ahead of him. They had been following an eastern ridge, so slippery and dangerous that Vesak had roped them together so one could save the other. Only the tugging at his waist kept Taran from falling asleep as he went on and he walked five paces before he even realised Vesak had fallen into a crouch. Taran lowered himself to the ground with a barely stifled groan, the ice on his deel falling away in sharp chips. He wore sheepskin gloves, but his fingers were still frozen as he packed his mouth with snow and sucked on it. Thirst was the one thing he remembered from previous attempts on the peaks. Once the water in his bottle froze, there was nothing but snow to melt. It was never enough to satisfy his parched throat.

As he crouched, he wondered how the ponies managed to survive at home, when the rivers turned to ice. He had seen them cropping at snow and it seemed enough for them. Dazed and exhausted, he opened his mouth to ask Vesak. The older scout glanced at him and gestured for silence.

Taran felt his senses sharpen, his heart beginning to lose its sluggishness. They had come close to Chin scouts before. Whoever commanded the army in the pass had sent them out in force to observe and report. With the storm making it hard to see more than a few paces ahead, the high climbs had become a deadly contest between the two forces. Taran's older brother had stumbled right into one of them, almost falling over the man. Taran remembered the ear his brother had brought back as proof and envied him. He wondered if he would get the chance to take his own trophy and stand tall with the other warriors. Fewer than a third had been blooded and it was known that Tsubodai chose his officers from among that number rather than those whose courage was unknown. Taran had no sword or bow, but his knife was sharp and he rolled his numb wrists to make them supple.

With his knees aching, he crept closer to Vesak, the howling wind hiding any sound of movement. He peered into the whiteness, looking for whatever the older man had spotted. Vesak was like a statue and Taran tried to copy his stillness, though the cold seeped into him from the ground and he shivered constantly.

There. Something had moved in the white. The Chin scouts wore pale clothing that blended with the snow, making them almost invisible. Taran recalled the stories told by the older tribesmen, that the mountains hid more than just men when the snow was whirling. He hoped they were just spinning tales to scare him, but he gripped his knife tightly. At his side, Vesak raised his arm, pointing. He too had seen the shape.

Whatever it was, it had not moved again. Vesak leaned closer to whisper and, as he did so, Taran saw the figure of a man rise jerkily from a bank of snow, a crossbow in his hands.

Vesak's instincts were good. He saw Taran's eyes widen and threw himself down, somehow spinning away as he did. Taran heard the snap of the bolt without seeing it and suddenly there was blood on the snow and Vesak was crying out in rage and pain. The cold fell away and Taran stood, ignoring the writhing figure of his friend. He had been told how to act against a crossbow and his mind went blank as he rushed forward. He had only a few heartbeats before the man heaved back the cord for another shot.

Taran slipped on the treacherous ground, the rope that held him to Vesak snaking across the snow in his wake. He had no time to cut it. He saw the Chin scout wrestling with his weapon and crashed into him, sending him sprawling. The crossbow spun away and Taran found himself locked in an embrace with a man stronger than he was.

They fought in gasping silence, alone and frozen. Taran had landed on top of the soldier and tried desperately to use the advantage. He struck out with knees and elbows, his knife hand held by both his enemy's. Taran was staring into the man's eyes when he brought his head down hard on the other's nose, feeling it break and hearing him cry out. Still his knife hand was held and he struck again and again, thumping his forehead into the bloody face under him. He managed to get his free forearm under the man's chin, heaving down at the exposed throat. The grip on his wrist fell away then and fingers clawed at his eyes, trying to blind him. Taran screwed up his face, smashing his head down without looking.

It ended as quickly as it had begun. Taran opened his eyes to see the Chin soldier staring blindly upwards. His knife had gone in without him even feeling it and still stuck out from the man's fur-lined robe. Taran lay gasping in the thin air, unable to take a proper breath. He heard Vesak call and realised the sound had been going on for some time. He struggled then for the cold face, summoning his discipline. He would not be shamed in front of the older warrior.

With a jerk, Taran freed his knife and heaved himself off the body. The rope had tangled itself around his feet in the struggle and he stepped out of the coils, kicking them away. Vesak called again, the sound weaker than before. Taran could not tear his eyes from the man he had killed, but he did not stop to think. It was the work of moments to yank the heavy robe from the soldier, wrapping it around himself. The body seemed smaller without it and Taran stood staring down at the spattered blood on the snow, a ring of droplets forming the shape where the head had been. He could feel blood stiffening on his skin and he rubbed his face roughly, suddenly sickened. When he looked again at Vesak, his companion had dragged himself to a sitting position and was watching him. Taran nodded at the older man, then reached down to saw off an ear from his first kill.

Tucking the grisly scrap into a pouch, he staggered back to Vesak, still dazed. The cold had vanished in the struggle, but it returned in force and he found himself shivering, his teeth clicking whenever he unclenched his jaw.

Vesak was panting, his face tight with pain. The bolt had struck him in the side below the ribs. Taran could see the black end of the shaft protruding, the blood already beginning to freeze like red wax. He reached out an arm to help Vesak to his feet, but the older man shook his head wearily.

'I cannot stand,' Vesak murmured. 'Let me sit here while you go further on.'

Taran shook his head, refusing to accept it. He heaved Vesak up, though the weight was too much for him. Vesak groaned and Taran fell with him, ending up on his knees in the snow.

'I cannot go with you,' Vesak said, gasping. 'Let me die. Scout the man's back trail as best you can. He came from further up. Do you understand? There must be a way through.'

'I could drag you on the soldier's robe, like a sled,' Taran said. He could not believe his friend was giving up and he started laying out the fur on the snow. His legs almost buckled as he did so and he steadied himself on a rock, waiting for his strength to return.

'You must find the back trail, boy,' Vesak whispered. 'He did not come from our side of the mountain.' His breath was coming at longer intervals and he sat with his eyes closed. Taran looked past him to where the soldier lay in blood. The sudden memory of it made his stomach clench and he leaned over and heaved. There was nothing solid to come out, though a spool of thick yellow liquid spilled from his lips and drew lines in the snow. He wiped his mouth, furious with himself. Vesak had not seen. He glanced at his companion, at the flakes settling on his face. Taran shook him, but there was no response. He was alone and the wind howled for him.

After a time, Taran staggered up and returned to where the Chin soldier had lain in wait. For the first time, Taran looked beyond the body and his strength returned in a rush. He cut the rope with his knife, then staggered on, climbing recklessly and slipping more than once. There was no trail, but the ground seemed solid as he punched grips into the snow and clambered up a slope. He was sobbing each breath in the thin air when the wind died and he found himself in the lee of a great rock of granite. The peak was still far above, but he did not need to reach it. Ahead, he saw a single rope where the soldier had climbed to that point. Vesak had been right. There was a route to the other side and the precious inner wall of the Chin had proved no better a defence than the other.

Taran stood numbly in the cold, his thoughts sluggish. At last, he nodded to himself, then began to walk back past the two dead men. He would not fail. Tsubodai was waiting for news.

Behind him, the snow fell thickly, covering the dead and erasing all the signs of the bloody struggle until it was frozen and perfect once more.

The encampment was not silent in the snow. The generals of Genghis had their men riding across it, practising manoeuvres and archery, hardening themselves. The warriors covered their hands and faces in thick mutton grease and they worked for hours firing arrows at full gallop into straw dummies, ten paces apart. The straw men jerked again and again and boys ran to yank the arrows out, judging their chance before the next rider came down the line.

The prisoners they had taken from the cities still numbered in their thousands, despite the war games Khasar had made them play. They sat or stood in a mass outside the gers. Only a few herdsmen watched over the starved men, but they did not run. In the early days, some had escaped, but every warrior of the tribes could track a lost sheep and they brought back only heads, casting them high into the crowd of prisoners as a warning to the others.

Smoke hung over every ger as the stoves worked, the women cooking the slaughtered animals and distilling black airag to warm their men. When the warriors were training, they ate and drank more than usual, trying to add a layer of fat against the cold. It was hard to build it with twelve hours in the saddle each day, but Genghis had given the order and almost a third of the flocks had been killed to satisfy their hunger.

Tsubodai brought Taran to the great ger as soon as the young scout reported. Genghis was there with his brothers Khasar and Kachiun and he came out as he heard Tsubodai approach. The khan saw that the boy with Tsubodai was exhausted, swaying slightly in the cold. Black circles lay under his eyes and he looked as if he had not eaten for days.

'Come with me to my wife's ger,' Genghis said. 'She will put hot meat in your stomach and we can talk.' Tsubodai bowed his head and Taran tried to do the same, awed at speaking to the khan himself. He trotted behind the two men as Tsubodai told of the pass he and Vesak had found. As they spoke, the boy glanced at the mountains, knowing that Vesak's frozen body was up there somewhere. Perhaps the spring thaw would reveal him once again. Taran was too cold and tired to think and, when he was out of the wind, he took a bowl of greasy stew in numb hands, shovelling it into his mouth without expression.

Genghis watched the young boy, amused at his ravenous appetite and the way he cast envious glances at the khan's eagle on its perch. The red bird was hooded, but it turned towards the young newcomer and seemed to watch him in turn.

Borte fussed around the scout, refilling his bowl as soon as it was empty. She gave him a skin of black airag as well, making him cough and splutter, then nodded as a bloom appeared once more on his frozen cheeks.

'You found a way through?' Genghis asked him, when Taran's eyes had lost their glassy look.

'Vesak did, lord.' A thought seemed to strike him and he fumbled with stiff fingers in his pouch, producing something that was clearly an ear. He held it up with pride.

'I killed a soldier there, waiting for us.'

Genghis took the ear from him, examining it before handing it back.

'You have done well,' he said patiently. 'Can you find the way again?'

Taran nodded, gripping the ear like a talisman. Too much had happened in a short time and he was overwhelmed, once again aware that he was speaking to the man who had formed a nation from the tribes. His friends would never believe he had met the khan himself, with Tsubodai watching like a proud father.

'I can, lord.'

Genghis smiled, his gaze far away. He nodded to Tsubodai, seeing his own triumph reflected there.

'Go and sleep then, boy. Rest and eat until you are full, then sleep again. You will need to be strong to lead my brothers.' He clapped Taran on his shoulder, staggering him.

'Vesak was a good man, lord,' Tsubodai said. 'I knew him well.'

Genghis glanced at the young warrior he had promoted to lead ten thousand of the people. He saw a depth of grief in his eyes and understood that Vesak was of the same tribe. Though he had forbidden talk of the old families, some bonds went deep.

'If his body can be found, I will have it brought down and honoured,' he said. 'Did he have a wife, children?'

'He did, lord,' Tsubodai replied.

'I will see they are looked after,' Genghis replied. 'No one will take their flock, or force his wife into another man's ger.'

Tsubodai's relief was obvious.

'Thank you, lord,' he said. He left Genghis to eat with his wife and took Taran out into the wind once more, gripping him around the back of the neck to show his pride.

The storm still raged two days later when Khasar and Kachiun gathered their men. Each of them had supplied five thousand warriors and Taran would lead them over the peaks in single file. Their horses were left behind and Genghis had not wasted those two days. The archery dummies had been copied by the thousand, placing men of straw, wood and cloth on every spare horse. If Chin scouts were able to see the plain at all in the snow, they would not notice the smaller number of men.

Khasar stood with his brother, rubbing grease into each other's faces in preparation for the hard climb to follow. Unlike the scouts, their men were burdened with bows and swords as well as a hundred arrows in two heavy quivers strapped to their backs. Between them, the ten thousand men carried a million shafts – two years of labour in the making and more valuable than anything else they owned. Without birch forests, they could not be replenished.

Everything they carried had to be wrapped in oiled cloth against the wet and they moved stiffly under the extra layers, stamping their feet and clapping their gloved hands together against the wind.

Taran was stiff-backed with pride at leading the khan's brothers, so filled with excitement that it was all he could do to stand still. When they were ready, Khasar and Kachiun nodded to the boy, looking back at the column of men who would cross the mountains on foot. The ascent would be fast and hard, a cruel trial even for the fittest. If they were spotted by Chin scouts, the men knew they had to reach the high pass before their movements were reported. Anyone who fell would be left behind.

The wind tore through the ranks as Taran started off, looking back as he felt their eyes on him. Khasar saw his nervousness and grinned, sharing the moment of excitement with his brother Kachiun. It was the coldest day yet, but the mood was light amongst the men. They wanted to smash the army that waited for them on the other side of the pass. Even more, they revelled in the thought of coming up behind them and shattering their clever defences. Genghis himself had come out to see them off.

'You have until dawn on the third day, Kachiun,' Genghis had told his brother. 'Then I will come through the pass.'

CHAPTER TWENTY-ONE

It took until the morning of the second day to reach the spot high in the peaks where Vesak had died. Taran dug his friend's body out of a snowdrift, wiping snow from the grey features in awed silence.

'We could leave a flag in his hand to mark the path,' Khasar murmured to Kachiun, making him smile. The line of warriors stretched down the mountain and the storm seemed to be easing, but they did not hurry the young scout as he took a strip of blue cloth and draped it around Vesak's corpse, dedicating him to the sky father.

Taran stood and bowed his head for a moment before hurrying up the final stretch of icy ground that led to the downward slope. The column moved past the frozen figure, each man glancing at the dead face and murmuring a few words in greeting or a prayer.

With the high pass behind them, Taran was on new ground and the pace slowed frustratingly. The sun's light was diffused into a glare from all directions, making it difficult to keep going east. When the wind revealed the mountains on either side, Khasar and Kachiun peered into the distance, marking details of the terrain. By noon, they judged they were halfway down the descent, the twin forts of the pass far below them.

A sheer drop of more than fifty feet slowed them again,

though old ropes showed where the Chin scout had climbed. After days in the cold, the braided cords were brittle and they tied new ones, climbing down with elaborate care. Those who had gloves tucked them into their deels for the descent and then found that their fingers grew pale and stiff with alarming speed. Frostbite was more than a worry to men who expected to use their bows. As they jogged along the broken slopes, every warrior clenched and unclenched his hands, or kept them tucked into his armpits so that the deel sleeves swung freely.

Many slipped on the icy ground and those who had hidden their hands fell hardest. They rose stiffly, their faces screwed tight against the wind as other men trotted past without looking at them. Each of them was alone and struggled to his feet rather than be left behind.

It was Taran who called out a warning when the trail split. Under such a blanket of snow, it was barely more than a crease in the white surface, but it snaked in another direction and he did not know which one would take them down.

Khasar came up to him, halting those behind with a raised fist. The line of men stretched almost back to Vesak's body. They could not delay and a single mistake at that point could mean a lingering death, trapped and exhausted in a dead end.

Khasar gnawed a piece of broken skin on his lips, looking to Kachiun for inspiration. His brother shrugged.

'We should keep going east,' Kachiun said wearily. 'The side path leads back towards the forts.'

'It could be another chance to surprise them from behind,' Khasar replied, staring into the distance. The path was lost to sight in no more than twenty paces as the wind and snow swirled.

'Genghis wants us behind the Chin as fast as possible,' Kachiun reminded him. Taran watched the exchange in fascination, but they both ignored the boy.

'He didn't know there could be another path right up behind the forts,' Khasar said. 'It's worth a look, at least.'

Kachiun shook his head, irritated.

'We have one more night in this dead place, then he moves at dawn. If you get lost, you could freeze to death.'

Khasar looked at his brother's worried face and grinned.

'I notice how you are certain it would be me. I could order you to take the path.'

Kachiun sighed. Genghis had not put either one of them in charge and he considered that an error when dealing with Khasar.

'You could not,' he said patiently. 'I am going on, with or without you. I will not stop you if you want to try the other way.'

Khasar nodded thoughtfully. For all his light tone, he knew the risks.

'I'll wait here and take the last thousand. If it leads nowhere, I'll double back and join you in the night.' They clasped hands briefly, then Kachiun and Taran moved off again, leaving Khasar there to hurry the others along.

Counting nine thousand slow-moving men took a lot longer than he had thought it would. When the last thousand came into sight, it was already growing dark. Khasar approached a stumbling warrior and took him by the shoulder, shouting over the wind.

'Come with me,' he said. Without waiting for a reply, he stepped onto the other path, sinking almost to his hips in fresh snow. The weary men behind him did not question the order, each one numb from misery and cold.

Without his brother to talk to, Kachiun spent many of the remaining hours of daylight in silence. Taran still led them, though he knew the path no better than any of the others.

The way down was a little clearer on the far side of the mountains and, after a long time, the air seemed less thin. Kachiun realised he was not gasping quite so fiercely to fill his lungs and, though he was exhausted, he felt stronger and more alert. The storm died out in the darkness and they could see the stars for the first time in several days, bright and perfect through the drifting clouds.

The cold seemed to intensify as the night wore on, but they did not stop, eating dried meat from their pouches to give them strength. They had slept the first night on the slopes, each man digging a hole for himself as wolves did. Kachiun had managed to snatch only a few hours then and he was desperately tired. Without knowing how close they were to the Chin army, he did not dare allow them to rest again.

The slope began to ease after a time. Pale birches mingled with black pines, growing so thick in places that they walked on dead leaves rather than snow. Kachiun found the sight of them comforting, proof that they were close to the end of their journey. Yet he did not know if they had made their way past the Chin soldiers, or still walked parallel to the Badger's Mouth.

Taran too was suffering and Kachiun saw him windmill his arms at intervals. It was an old scout trick to force blood back into the fingertips so that they would not freeze and go black. Kachiun copied him and sent the word back down the line to do the same. The thought of the line of grim soldiers flapping like birds made him chuckle, despite the pain in every muscle.

The moon rose full and bright above the mountains, illuminating the tired column as they trudged onwards. The peak they had climbed was high above them, another world. Kachiun wondered how many of his men had fallen on the high passes, to be left behind like Vesak. He hoped the others had had the sense to take their quivers of arrows before the snow covered them. He should have remembered to give the order and muttered irritably to himself as he walked. Dawn was a long way off and he could only hope he would find his way to the Chin army before Genghis attacked. His thoughts drifted as he strode through the snow, fastening on Khasar for a moment, then on his children back in the encampment. At times, he dreamed just as if he were in a warm ger and it was with a start that he surfaced to find himself still walking. Once, he fell and it was Taran who hurried back to help him up. They would not let the khan's brother die on the side of the path, his quivers of arrows taken for the others. For that at least, Kachiun was grateful.

He felt as if he had been walking for ever when they passed out of the tree line and Taran fell into a crouch ahead. Kachiun copied the boy before creeping forward on protesting knees. Behind him, he heard muffled curses as his men bumped into each other in the moonlight, woken from their drifting trances by the sudden halt. Kachiun looked around him as he wormed his way forward. They were on a gentle slope, a valley of perfect whiteness that seemed to go on for ever. On the far side, the mountains rose again in cliffs so sheer he doubted anyone would ever climb them. To his left, the pass of the Badger's Mouth ended in a great flat area no more than a mile away. Kachiun's vision seemed sharper than usual in the moonlight and he could see right across the emptiness, beautiful and deadly. A sea of tents and banners lay across the end of the pass. Smoke rose above them to join the mist from the peaks and, as Kachiun's senses came alive, he could smell wood smoke on the air.

He groaned to himself. The Chin had assembled an army so vast he could not see the end of them. The Badger's Mouth gave way to flats of ice and snow, almost the bottom of a bowl of high peaks before the road that led to the emperor's city. Yet the Chin soldiers filled it and spilled further and further back onto the plain beyond. The white mountains hid the full extent of them, but even so, they had more men than Kachiun had ever seen before. Genghis did not know how many and he would be riding slowly down the pass in just a few short hours.

With a sudden stab of fear, Kachiun wondered if his men could be seen from the camp. Chin scouts had to be patrolling the area. They would be fools not to, and there he was, with a line of warriors stretching back into the white fastness of the hills. They needed surprise and he had almost thrown it away. He clapped Taran on the back in thanks for the warning and the boy smiled in pleasure.

Kachiun made his plans, passing word down the line. The men behind would retreat far enough for dawn not to reveal them to sharp-eyed enemies. Kachiun looked up at the clear sky and wished for more snow to cover their tracks. Dawn was close and he hoped Khasar had made it to safety. Slowly, painfully, the line of warriors began moving back up the slope to the trees they had left behind. A memory came to Kachiun of his childhood as he climbed. He had hidden with his family in a cleft in the hills of home, with death and starvation always close. Once more, he would hide, but this time he would come roaring out and Genghis would ride with him.

In silence, he sent up a prayer to the sky father that Khasar too had survived and was not freezing to death on the high slopes, lost and alone. Kachiun grinned at the thought. His brother was not easy to stop. If anyone could make it out, it would be him.

Khasar whipped a hand back and forth over his throat, signalling for silence from the men behind him. The storm had died at last and he could see stars overhead, revealed through drifting clouds. The moon lit the sterile slopes and he found himself on a sharp edge over a sheer drop. His breath caught in his throat as he saw the black tower of one of the Chin forts below him, almost under his feet, but separated by a plunge into blackness over rocks so sharp that only a little snow had settled on them. Great drifts humped themselves around the fort where they had slid from the crags and Khasar wondered if his men could make the final descent. The fort itself had been built on a ridge overlooking the pass, no doubt filled with weapons that would smash anyone coming through. They would not expect an attack from the cliffs at their back.

At least there was moonlight. He went back to where his men had begun to cluster. The wind had dropped to no more than a gentle moan and he was able to whisper his order, beginning with a command for them to eat and rest while they passed their ropes forward. This last thousand had come from the tuman of Kachiun and Khasar did not know them, but the officers came forward and only nodded as they heard his orders. The word spread quickly and the first group of ten began tying ropes together, coiling them near the edge. They were cold and their hands were clumsy with the knots, making Khasar wonder if he was sending them all to their deaths.

'If you fall, remain silent,' he whispered to the first group. 'Or your shout will wake the fort below us. You might even survive if you hit the deep snow.' One or two of them grinned at that, looking over the edge and shaking their heads.

'I will go first,' Khasar said. He removed his fur gloves, wincing at the cold as he took hold of the thick rope. He had climbed worse cliffs, he told himself, though never when he was this tired or cold. He forced a confident expression onto his face as he jerked on the line. The officers had tied it to the trunk of a fallen birch and it seemed solid. Khasar backed to the edge and tried not to think of the drop behind him. No one could survive it, he was certain.

'No more than three men on a rope,' he said as he went over. He hung out as far as he could, beginning to walk down the icy rock. 'Tie some more together or it will take all night to get down.' He was giving orders to conceal his own nervousness, forcing the cold face to hide his fear. They gathered around the edge to watch him until, finally, he was past the edge and clambering down. The closest men began tying more ropes together to allow a second descent and one of them nodded to his friends and lay on his stomach to take hold of the quivering rope that held Khasar. He too vanished over the edge.

Genghis waited impatiently for dawn. He had sent scouts down the pass as far as they could go, so that some of them returned with crossbow bolts buried in their armour. The last of them had come back to the camp as the sun set, two bolts sticking out of his back. One had penetrated the overlapping iron and left a streak of blood that smeared his leg and his pony's heaving flanks. Genghis heard his report before the man could have his wounds tended, needing the information.

The Chin general had left the pass open. Before the scout was driven back by a storm of bolts, he had seen two great forts looming over the strip of land below. Genghis did not doubt the soldiers in them were ready to pour death on anyone trying to force their way through. The fact that the pass had not been blocked worried him. It suggested the general wanted him to try a frontal assault and was confident the Mongol army could be funnelled into his men and smashed where they were weakest.

At its opening, the pass was almost a mile wide, but under the forts, the rock walls narrowed to a pinch of no more than a few dozen paces. Even the thought of being hemmed in and unable to charge brought a sick feeling to Genghis' stomach that he crushed as soon as he recognised it. He had done every-thing he could and his brothers would attack as soon as they could see well enough to aim. He could not call them back, even if he found a better plan in the last moments. They were lost to him, hidden by the mountains and the snow.

At least the storm had eased. Genghis looked up at the stars, revealing the huddled mass of prisoners he had herded to the mouth of the pass. They would go ahead of his army, soaking up the bolts and arrows of the Chin. If the forts poured fire oil, the prisoners would take the brunt of it.

The air was frozen in the night, but he could not sleep and took deep breaths, feeling the chill reach into his lungs. Dawn was not far away. He thought through his plans once more, but there was nothing else to do. His men were well fed, better than they had been in months. Those he would lead into the pass were veteran warriors in good armour. He had formed the first ranks of men with lances, in part to aid them in herding the prisoners forward. Tsubodai's Young Wolves would come behind him, then the warriors of Arslan and Jelme, twenty thousand who would not run, no matter how vicious the fighting.

Genghis drew his father's sword, seeing the wolf's-head hilt shine in the starlight. He lunged with it, grunting as he did so. The camp was silent around him, though there were always eyes watching. He put his body through a routine Arslan had taught him that stretched his muscles as well as strengthening them. The monk Yao Shu was teaching a similar discipline to his sons, hardening their bodies like any other tool. Genghis sweated as he whipped his sword through the sequences. He was not as lightning quick as he had once been, but he had grown in strength and sheer power and he was still supple, despite the scarring of so many old wounds.

He did not want to wait for dawn. He considered finding a

woman, knowing it would help to burn off a little of his nervous energy. His first wife Borte would be sleeping in the ger, surrounded by his sons. His second wife was still nursing their baby daughter. He brightened at that thought, imagining her pale breasts heavy with milk.

He sheathed his sword as he strode through the camp to Chakahai's ger, already aroused at the prospect. He chuckled to himself as he walked. A warm woman and a battle to come. To be alive on such a night was a wondrous thing.

In his tent, General Zhi Zhong sipped a cup of hot rice wine, unable to sleep. The winter had closed over the mountains and he thought he could well spend the coldest months in the field with his army. It was not such an unpleasant thought. He had eleven children with three wives in Yenking and, when he was at home, there was always something to distract him. He found the routines of camp life restful in comparison, perhaps because he had known them all his life. Even there in the darkness, he could hear the murmured passwords as the guards changed and he knew a sense of peace. Sleep had always come slowly for him and he knew it was part of his legend amongst the men that he sat up night after night, the lamps showing through the heavy cloth of the command tent. Sometimes he slept with the lamps still burning, so that the guards thought he needed no rest as they did. It did not hurt to encourage their awe, he believed. Men needed to be led by one who showed none of their weaknesses.

He thought of the vast army around him and the preparations he had made. His sword regiments and pikemen alone outnumbered the Mongol warriors. Simply feeding so many had stripped the storehouses of Yenking. The merchants could only wail in disbelief as he showed them the documents the emperor had signed. The memory made him smile. Those fat grain sellers thought they were the heart of the city. It had amused Zhi Zhong to remind them where true power lay. Without the army, their fine houses were worth nothing.

To keep two hundred thousand men fed all winter would beggar the farmers for a thousand miles east and south. Zhi Zhong shook his head at the thought, his mind too busy to consider trying for sleep. What choice did he have? No one fought in winter, but he could not leave the pass unguarded. Even the young emperor understood it could be months before battle was joined. When the Mongols came in spring, he would still be there. Zhi Zhong wondered idly if their khan had the same supply problems he had. He doubted it. The tribesmen probably ate each other and considered it a delicacy.

He shivered as the cold night seeped into his tent, pulling his blankets close around his massive shoulders. Nothing had been the same since the old emperor died. Zhi Zhong had given his loyalty utterly to the man, revering him. Truly, the world had been shaken when he died at last, taken in his sleep after a long illness. He shook his head, sadly. The son was not the father. For the general's generation, there could only ever be one emperor. Seeing a young, untried boy on the throne of the empire ate at the foundations of his entire life. It was the end of an era and perhaps he should have retired with the old man's death. That would have been a fitting and dignified response. Instead, he had hung on to see the new emperor established and then the Mongols had come. Retirement would not come for another year, at least.

Zhi Zhong grimaced as the cold worked its way into his bones. The Mongols did not feel cold, he recalled. They seemed able to stand it as a wild fox can, with nothing more than a single layer of fur over bare skin. They disgusted him. They built nothing, achieved nothing in their short lives. The old

312

emperor had kept them in their place, but the world had moved on and now they dared to threaten the gates of the great city. He would not show mercy when the battle was over. If he let his men run wild in their camps, the blood of the tribes would survive in a thousand ill-born children. He would not let them breed like lice to threaten Yenking again. He would not rest until the last of them lay dead and the land was empty. He would burn them out and, in the future, if another race dared to rise against the Chin, perhaps they would remember the Mongols and slink away from their plots and ambitions. That was the only response they deserved. Perhaps that could be the legacy he left as he retired, a vengeance so bloody and final that it would echo through the centuries ahead. He would be the death of an entire nation. It would be immortality of a sort and the idea pleased him. His thoughts whirled as the camp slept. He decided to leave the lamps burning and wondered if he would get any sleep at all.

As the first light of dawn appeared behind the mountains, Genghis looked up at the clouds that wreathed the high peaks. The plains below were still in darkness and he felt his heart lift at the sight. The army of prisoners he would drive through the pass had fallen silent. His people had formed up behind his bondsmen, hands tapping on lances and bows as they waited for his order. Only a thousand would remain behind to protect the women and children in the camp. There was no danger. Any threat on the plains had already been met and crushed.

Genghis clenched his hands tight on the reins of a dark brown mare. At the first sign of dawn, the drummer boys had begun to beat out a rhythm that was the sound of war to his ears. A thousand of them waited in the ranks with the drums strapped to their chests. The noise they made echoed back from the mountains and made his pulse thump faster. His brothers were somewhere ahead, half frozen after their trek across the high trails. Beyond them lay the city that had spilled Chin seed among his people for a thousand years, bribing them and slaughtering them like a pack of dogs when they saw the need. He smiled to himself at the image, wondering what his son Jochi would make of it.

The sun was hidden as it rose above him, then, in an instant, the plains were lit in gold and Genghis felt warmth touch his face. His gaze came up from the ground. It was time.

CHAPTER TWENTY-TWO

Kachiun waited as the dawn drew fingers of shadow from the trees. Genghis would move through the pass as fast as possible, but it would still take time for him to reach the main Chin army. All around him, Kachiun's men readied their bows and loosened the tightly packed arrows in their quivers. Twelve men had died in the high passes, their hearts bursting in their chests as they gasped in the thin air. Another thousand had gone with Khasar. Even without those, almost nine hundred thousand shafts could still be loosed upon their enemy when the time came.

Kachiun had searched in vain for a place to form ranks that would not be seen by the Chin, but there was none. His men would be exposed in the valley, with only volleys of arrows to hold off a charge. Kachiun grinned at the thought.

The Chin camp was barely stirring in the dawn cold. Snow had erased the marks of their time there, so that the pale tents looked beautiful and frozen, a place of calm that hardly hinted at the number of fighting men within. Kachiun prided himself on his sharp vision, but there was no sign that they knew Genghis was on the move at last. The guards changed at dawn, hundreds of them heading back for a meal and sleep while others took their places. There was no panic in them yet.

Kachiun had formed a grudging respect for the general who organised the camp in the distance. Just before dawn, horsemen had been sent to scout the valley, riding its length to the south before returning. It was clear they were not expecting an enemy to be so close and Kachiun had heard them calling lightly to one another as they rode, hardly looking up at the peaks and foothills. No doubt they thought it was an easy duty to spend a winter warm and safe, surrounded by so many other swords.

Kachiun started when one of the officers tapped his shoulder and pressed a package of meat and bread into his hand. It was warm and damp from where it had been pressed against someone's skin, but Kachiun was ravenous and only nodded in thanks as he sank his teeth into it. He would need all his strength. Even for men who had been born to the bow, drawing a hundred shafts at full speed would leave their shoulders and arms in agony. He whispered an order for the men to form pairs as they waited, using each other's weight to loosen muscles and keep the cold at bay. The warriors all knew the benefit of such work. None of them wanted to fail when the moment came.

Still the Chin camp was quiet. Kachiun swallowed the last of the bread nervously, packing his mouth with snow until he had enough moisture to let it slide down his throat. He had to time his attack perfectly. If he went before Genghis was in sight, the Chin general would be able to divert some part of his vast army to run Kachiun's archers down. If he left it late, Genghis would lose the advantage of a second attack and perhaps be killed.

Kachiun's eyes began to ache with the strain of staring into the distance. He dared not look away.

*   *   *

The prisoners began to moan as they moved into the pass, sensing what lay ahead. The front ranks of the Mongol riders blocked the retreat so that they had no choice but to keep trotting further in. Genghis saw a few of the younger men make a dart between two of his warriors. Thousands of eyes watched the attempt to escape with feverish interest, then turned away in despair as the men were beheaded with quick blows.

The noise of drums, horses and men echoed back from the high walls of the pass as they entered its embrace. Far ahead, Chin scouts were racing back with the news for their general. The enemy would know he was coming, but he was not depending on surprise.

The horde of prisoners trudged forward on the rocky ground, looking fearfully for the first sign of Chin archers. Progress was slow with more than thirty thousand men walking ahead of the Mongol riders and there were some that fell, lying exhausted on the ground as the horsemen reached them. They too were impaled on lances, whether they were feigning or not. The others were urged on with sharp cries from the tribesmen, just as they would have hooted and yipped to goats at home. The familiar sound was strange in such a place. Genghis took a last look at his ranks, noting the positions of his trusted generals before he stared hungrily ahead. The pass was two miles long and he would not turn back.

Kachiun saw frantic movement in the Chin camp at last. Genghis was moving and word had reached the man in command. Cavalry cantered through the tents, a better quality of animal than Kachiun had seen them use before. Perhaps the emperor kept the best blood lines for his Imperial army. The animals were larger than the ponies he knew and they shone in the dawn sun as their riders formed up, facing the Badger's Mouth.

Kachiun could see regiments of crossbow- and pikemen hurrying to the front ranks and he winced at the sheer number of them. His brother could be engulfed in a charge against so many. His favourite tactic of encircling a foe was impossible in the narrow space.

Kachiun turned to the men behind him and found them staring in his direction, waiting for the word.

'When I give the order, come out at the run. We'll form three ranks across the valley, as close to them as we can get. You will not be able to hear me over the sound of bows, so pass the word to loose twenty shafts and then wait. I will raise and drop my arm for twenty more.'

'Their cavalry are armoured. They will run us down,' a man said at his shoulder, staring past Kachiun. All of them were horsemen. The idea of standing alone against a charge went against everything they knew.

'No,' Kachiun said. 'Nothing in the world can stand against my people armed with bows. The first twenty shafts will cause panic. Then we will advance. If they charge, and they will, we will put a long shaft through the throat of every man.'

He gazed back down the valley at the Chin camp. It looked now as if someone had kicked a nest of ants. Genghis was coming.

'Pass the word to be ready,' Kachiun muttered. Sweat broke out on his forehead. His judgement had to be perfect. 'Just a little longer. When we go, we go fast.'

Almost halfway along the pass, the prisoners came abreast of the first nests of crossbowmen. Chin soldiers had taken positions on shelves of rock fifty feet above the ground. The prisoners saw them first and swung away from the sides, slowing them all as they compressed the centre. The Chin soldiers could hardly miss and they sent bolts whirring into the press. As the screams echoed, the front three ranks with Genghis raised their bows. Every one of them could hit a bird on the wing, or three men in a line at full gallop. As they came into range, their shafts tore through the air. The soldiers fell onto the heads of those passing below. The bloody crevices were left behind as the warriors went on, forcing the wailing prisoners into a stumbling trot.

The first pinch between two great shelves of rock came just a little further down the pass. The prisoners funnelled towards it, staggering into a run as the Mongols yelled and prodded them with their lances. All of them could see the two great forts that hung over the only path through. That was as far as any scout had managed to see before they had ridden back. After that, they were on new ground and no one knew what lay ahead.

Khasar was sweating. It had taken a long time to get a thousand men down only three ropes and, as more and more made it safely to flat ground, he had been tempted to leave the others. The snow was deep enough for men to sink to the waist as they moved around and he no longer believed the trail had been a hunting track for men at the fort, unless he had missed steps cut into the rock further along. His men had found their way to the rear of the fort, but in the darkness, he could not see a way in. Like its partner on the other side of the pass, the fort had been designed to be impregnable to anyone passing through the Badger's Mouth. For all he knew, those who manned it were hauled up on ropes.

Three of his men had fallen on the descent and, against all expectations, one of them had survived, landing in a drift so deep that the stunned warrior had to be dug out by his companions. The other two were not so lucky and struck exposed rocks. Neither had called out and the only sound was the hooting of night owls returning to their nests.

When dawn came, Khasar had moved the men on through the heavy snow, the first ones making slow progress as they tramped it down. The fort loomed blackly above their heads and Khasar could only swear in frustration, convinced that he had taken a tenth of Kachiun's force for no good reason.

When he reached a path across their route, he felt a rush of excitement. Nearby, they found a vast pile of firewood, hidden from the pass below. It made sense that the Chin warriors took their wood from the cliffs at their back, piling it up for a long winter. One of Khasar's men found a long-handled axe buried in a log. The blade was oiled and showed only specks of rust. He grinned at the sight of it, knowing there had to be a way in.

Khasar froze as he heard the tramp of feet and the wailing voices of the prisoners in the distance. Genghis was coming and he was still in no position to help his brothers.

'No more caution,' he said to the men around him. 'We need to be in that fort. Get forward and find whatever door they use to bring in the wood.'

He broke into a run then and they followed him, readying swords and bows as they went.

General Zhi Zhong was at the centre of a swirl of running messengers, giving orders as quickly as he received news. He had not slept, but his mind sparked with energy and indignation. Though the storm had passed, the air was still frozen and ice lay on the ground of the pass and layered the cliffs all around them. Frozen hands would slip on swords. Horses would fall and every man there would feel his strength stolen away by the cold. The general looked wistfully to where a cooking fire had been set but not lit. He could have ordered hot food brought, but the alarm had come before his army had eaten and now he did not have time. No one went to war in winter, he told himself, mocking the certainty he had felt in the night.

He had held the end of the pass for months while the Mongol army ravaged the lands beyond. His men were ready. When the Mongols came in range, they would be met with a thousand crossbow bolts every ten heartbeats and that was just the beginning. Zhi Zhong shivered as the wind built, roaring through the camp. He had brought them to the only place where they could not use the tactics of plains warfare. The Badger's Mouth would guard his flanks better than any force of men. Let them come, he thought.

Genghis squinted ahead as the prisoners streamed under the forts. The pass was crammed with men so far ahead of his own people that he could barely see what was happening. In the distance, he heard screams come back on the frozen air and saw a sudden bloom of flame. The prisoners at the rear had seen it too and they faltered in the mad rush before his riders, terrified. Without an order from him, lances came down and forced them onward into the maw between the forts. No matter what weapons the Chin had, thirty thousand prisoners were hard to stop. Already some of them were past the pinch and streaming out beyond it. Genghis rode on and could only hope that by the time he came under the forts, they would have exhausted their oil and shafts. Bodies lay still on the ground, more and more of them as he closed on the narrow place.

Above his head, Genghis saw archers on the forts, but to his astonishment, they seemed to be aiming across the pass itself, loosing shaft after shaft at their own men. He could not understand it and a spike of worry came into his thoughts at the development. Though it seemed a gift, he did not like to be surprised when he was hemmed into such a place. He felt the walls of rock pressing on him, forcing him on.

Closer to the forts he could hear the thump of catapults, now a sound he knew well and understood. He saw a smoke trail crease the air above the pass and a wash of fire spread over the walls of the fort on his left hand. Archers fell burning from their platforms and a cheer went up from the other side. Genghis felt his heart leap. There could only be one explanation and he roared orders to thin the column so that it passed on the right side of the Badger's Mouth, as far from the left as they could manage.

Kachiun or Khasar had taken the fort. Whoever it was up there, Genghis would honour him when the battle was over, if they both still lived.

More and more corpses lay sprawled on the floor of the pass, so that his horse had to step on them, whinnying in distress. Genghis felt his heart hammer in fear as a bar of shadow crossed his face. He was almost under the forts, in the heart of a killing ground designed by long-dead Chin nobles. Thousands of his prisoners had died and there were places he could hardly see the ground for bodies. Yet his ragged vanguard had pushed through, running now in wild terror. The Mongol tribes themselves had hardly lost a man and Genghis exulted. He passed under the right-hand fort, shouting loudly to those of his people above who had smashed their way in. They could not hear him. He could hardly hear himself.

He leaned forward in the saddle, needing to gallop. It was difficult to hold his mount to a trot with arrows in the air, yet he controlled himself, holding up a flat palm to keep the men steady. One of the forts was burning inside, the flames licking out of the killing holes. Even as Genghis glanced up, a wooden platform collapsed in fire, tumbling to the ground below. Horses screamed in distress and some of them bolted, racing after the prisoners.

Genghis stood in the saddle to look down the pass. He swallowed nervously as he saw a dark line across its end. There the pass was as narrow as the pinch between the forts, a perfect natural defence. There was no way through but over the army of the Chin emperor. Already the prisoners were reaching it and now Genghis heard the snap of crossbow volleys like thunder, so loud in the confined space that it hurt his ears with every strike.

The prisoners went berserk in their panic, bolts hammering them from their feet as each man was struck over and over, spinning and torn as he fell. They ran into a hailstorm of iron and Genghis bared his teeth, knowing his turn would come.

The general's messenger was pale with fear, still shaking at what he had seen. Nothing in his career to that point had prepared him for the carnage of the pass.

'They have taken one of the forts, general,' he said, 'and turned the catapults on the other.'

General Zhi Zhong looked calmly at the man, irritated by his show of fear.

'The forts could only have thinned so many,' he reminded the man. 'We will stop them *here.*' The messenger seemed to take confidence from the general's composed manner and let out a long breath.

Zhi Zhong waited for the messenger to control himself, then gestured to one of the soldiers nearby.

'Take this one out and whip the skin from his back,' he said. The messenger gaped at hearing the order. 'When he has learned courage, you may cease the instruction, or at sixty strokes of the cane, whichever comes first.'

The messenger bowed his head in shame as he was led away and, for the first time that morning, Zhi Zhong was left alone. He swore under his breath for a moment before striding outside his tent, hungry for information. He knew by then that the Mongols were driving Chin prisoners before them, soaking up the defences with his own people. Zhi Zhong could silently applaud the tactic, even as he sought ways to counter it. Tens of thousands of unarmed men could be as dangerous as an army if they reached his lines. They would foul the crossbow regiments he had spread across the pass. He ordered a waiting soldier to send fresh carts of bolts to the front and watched as they trundled away.

The khan had been clever, but the prisoners would only be a shield until they were dead and Zhi Zhong was still confident. The Mongols would have to fight for every foot. Without space to manoeuvre, they would be drawn in and slaughtered.

He waited, wondering if he should move closer to the front line. From his viewpoint further back, he could see black smoke rising from the captured fort and cursed again. It was a humiliating loss, but the emperor would not care once the last of the tribesmen was dead.

Zhi Zhong had hoped to kill many of them before opening a path into his army, compressing them further. They would race forward into the gap and find themselves attacked on all sides, the spearhead lost in a mass of veteran soldiers. It was a good tactic. The alternative was to block the pass completely. He had planned for both and he weighed one against the other.

He calmed his racing heart, showing a confident expression to the men around him. With a steady hand, he took a jug of water and poured it into a cup, sipping as he stared down the pass.

Out of the corner of his eye, he saw movement in the snow-covered valley. He glanced over and froze for a moment. Dark lines of men were spilling out of the tree line, forming ranks as he watched.

Zhi Zhong threw the cup down as messengers raced through the camp to tell him of the development. The peaks could not be climbed. It was impossible. Even in his shock, he did not hesitate, snapping orders before the messengers could reach him.

'Cavalry regiments one to twenty, form up!' he roared. 'Hold the left flank and sweep those lines away.' Horsemen raced to pass on the orders and half his cavalry force began to peel off from the main army. He watched the Mongol lines form, striding through the snow towards him. He did not allow himself to panic. They had climbed the peaks on foot and they would be exhausted. His men would ride them down.

It seemed to take an age for twenty thousand Imperial riders to form in blocks on the left flank and, by that point, the Mongol lines had halted. Zhi Zhong clenched his fists as orders sounded up and down the line and his horsemen began to trot towards the enemy, standing in the snow. He could see no more than ten thousand of them, at most. Infantry could not stand against a disciplined charge. They would be destroyed.

As the general watched, his cavalry accelerated, swords raised to take heads. He forced himself to look back at the pass, his mouth dry. They had driven prisoners before them, taken one of his forts and flanked him over the peaks. If that was all they had, he could still break them. For an instant, his certainty wavered and he considered ordering the pass blocked. No, it had not yet come to that. His respect for the Mongol khan had increased sharply, but the general remained confident as his cavalry thundered down the valley.

CHAPTER TWENTY-THREE

At nine hundred paces away, the Chin cavalry hit full gallop. It was too early, Kachiun thought. He stood calmly watching with his nine thousand. At least the valley wasn't so wide that he would automatically be flanked. He could feel the nervousness in the men around him. None of them had ever faced a charge on foot and they realised how their own enemies must feel. The sun shone on Chin armour and the swords the horsemen raised, ready to crash through the line.

'Remember this!' Kachiun shouted. 'These men have not met us in war. They do not know what we can do. One shaft to knock them down, then one more to kill them. Choose your men and on my signal, loose twenty!'

He drew his bow back to his ear, feeling the power of his right arm. This was why he had trained for years, building muscles until they were like iron. His left arm was nowhere near as strong as his right and the hump of muscle on his shoulder gave him a lopsided look when he was bare-chested. He could feel the ground shake as the mass of riders came on. At six hundred paces, he glanced up and down his ranks, risking a look at the men behind. They had their bows bent, ready to send death to the enemy.

The Chin soldiers yelled as they came, the sound filling the valley and crashing over the silent Mongol lines. They were well armoured and carried shields that would protect them from many of the shafts. Kachiun noted every detail as they closed at frightening speed. The furthest killing range was four hundred yards and he let them come through that untouched. At three hundred yards, he could see his men glancing at him out of the corner of his eye, watching for him to release his shaft.

At two hundred, the line of horses was like a wall. Kachiun felt fear gnaw at him as he gave his order.

'Take them!' he bellowed, snarling as he let go. Nine thousand shafts followed on the instant, snapping across the space.

The charge faltered as if it had hit a trench. Men spun out of the saddles and horses fell. Those behind smashed into them at full gallop and, by then, Kachiun had the second shaft on the string and was drawing back. Another volley slammed into the charge.

The Chin horsemen could not have stopped, even if they had understood what was happening. The front ranks collapsed and those who kicked their horses over them were met with another wave of arrows, each man punched by three or four shafts moving too fast to see. Reins were torn out of fingers and, even when the armour or shields saved them, sheer force of impact flung them to the ground.

Kachiun counted aloud as he shot, aiming for the bare faces of the Chin soldiers as they staggered up. If he could not see a face, he aimed for the chest and depended on the heavy arrow tip to punch through the scales. He felt his shoulders begin to burn as he reached his fifteenth arrow. The charging horsemen had run full speed into a hammer and they had not come closer. Kachiun reached down and found he had used his twenty.

'Thirty paces forward, with me!' he shouted, breaking into a slow run. His men came with him, yanking fresh bundles of arrows from their quivers. The Chin soldiers saw them move and there were still thousands struggling through the lines of dead. Many had fallen without a wound, their horses going down in the press of dying men and animals. The officers barked orders to remount and the soldiers cried out as they saw the Mongols padding forward.

Kachiun held up his right fist and the line stopped. He saw one of his own officers cuff a younger man hard enough to send him staggering.

'If I see you hit another horse, I will kill you myself!' the officer snapped. Kachiun chuckled.

'Twenty more! Aim for the men!' he shouted, the order repeated up and down the line. The Chin cavalry had recovered from their first collapse and he could see plumed officers urging them onwards. Kachiun took aim at one of them as the man pirouetted on his mount, waving a sword in the air.

Another nine thousand arrows followed Kachiun's shaft as it took his man through the neck. At this range, they could pick their shots and the volley was devastating. A ragged second charge disintegrated against the whirring arrows and the Chin soldiers began to panic. A few men galloped unscathed out of the chaos, their shields bristling with arrows. Though it hurt to give the order, Kachiun roared, 'Horses!' to the men around him and the animals went down in a crackle of snapping bones.

Ten shafts came in every sixty heartbeats and there was no respite. The bravest of them died quickly and left only the weak and frightened, trying to turn their mounts back into their own men. The lines behind were fouled by bolting horses, their riders lolling in the saddles with arrows through their chests.

Kachiun's shoulder was aching as he shot his fortieth arrow and waited as the men around him finished their strike. The valley ahead was churned with blood and dead men, a red stain of kicking hooves and flailing soldiers in the snow. There was no way for them to charge now and though the Chin officers still yelled for them to force a way through, they could not build momentum once more.

Kachiun ran forward without giving an order and his men came with him. He counted twenty paces, then let his excitement override his better judgement, jogging another twenty so that he was dangerously close to the mass of broken men and horses. Only a hundred yards separated the two forces as Kachiun plunged another twenty arrows into pristine snow and cut the knot that bound them. Chin soldiers wailed in terror as they saw the action and the bows bent again. Panic was spreading through their ranks and as yet more arrows ripped into them, they broke.

At first, the rout was slow and as many men died trying to get away as pressed forward from behind. The Mongols shot methodically at anything they could see. The officers went down quickly and Kachiun shouted wildly as he saw the rout spread. Those who had not come near the front ranks were knocked aside and infected by fear and blood.

'Slow down!' Kachiun shouted to his men. He loosed his fiftieth arrow as he called to them and considered striding even closer to the soldiers to complete the rout. He cautioned himself then, though he wanted to race after the fleeing soldiers. There was time, he told himself. The rate slowed as he had ordered and the accuracy increased even more, so that hundreds of men fell with more than one arrow in them. Sixty, and now the quivers were light on their backs.

Kachiun paused. The cavalry had been shattered and many were racing back with loose reins. They could still reform and, though he did not fear another charge, he saw a chance to rout them right into their own lines. Moving closer was dangerous, he knew. If the Chin soldiers ever reached his men, the day could still turn in their favour. Kachiun looked around at the grinning faces near him and responded with a laugh.

'Will you walk with me?' he said. They cheered and he strode forward, drawing another arrow from his quiver. This time, he held it on the string as they stalked right up to the first lines of the dead. Many of them still lived and some of the Mongols picked up their valuable swords, taking precious moments to slide them under the sash of their deels. Kachiun was almost knocked down by a loose horse racing across the line. He reached out a hand for the reins and missed, though it was stopped by two of his men further down. There were hundreds of riderless animals and he grabbed for another as it ran, snorting and shying at the solid line of archers. Kachiun quieted the beast, rubbing its nose as he watched the Chin riders begin to reform. He had shown them what his people could do with bows. Perhaps it was time to show what they could do from the back of a horse.

'Take swords and mount!' he shouted. Once more, the order was repeated and he saw his men dash joyfully over the dead to leap into the saddles of Chin horses. There were more than enough, though some of the mounts were still wide-eyed with terror and spattered with the blood of their last rider. Kachiun sprang into the saddle then, standing in the stirrups to see what the enemy was doing. He wished Khasar was there to see this. His brother would have loved the chance to charge the Chin army with their own horses. He bellowed a challenge and dug in his heels, leaning low over the saddle as his mount hit its stride and leaped forward.

The end of the pass was in chaos as Genghis rode over the dead. The crossbows of the Chin soldiers had killed almost all of his prisoners, with half a million iron bolts lying in shifting piles underfoot. Yet some of them had run on to the Chin ranks, berserk in their terror. Genghis had seen them grabbing weapons and barricades with bloody hands.

The organised volley fire became sporadic as the last of them tore at the lines. Hundreds forced their way past the first rank, clawing and kicking in desperation. When they found a weapon, they used it to strike wildly around them until they were cut down.

As Genghis pressed forward, he felt bolts zipping by him and ducked in his saddle as one came too close. The vast Chin army was ahead and he had done everything he could. The gap opened as he rode at it and he realised only one side was a wall of rock. From far back, he had thought of the gap as a great gate, but close to, he saw the Chin had raised a huge tree trunk upright on one side. Ropes stretched from the top and Genghis realised it could be dropped across the pass itself, cutting his army in half. If it fell, he was finished. As panic swept through him, his advance staggered to a halt against a hill of dead bodies. Genghis cried out in frustration, waiting to be struck or see the tree fall. He called men ahead of him by name, ordering them forward on foot and pointing to the great bole that would crash down on all his hopes. They struggled to reach the ropes and cut them.

Beyond the gap, Genghis could see the Chin lines swirl. Something was wrong and he risked standing in his stirrups to see what it was. The last of the prisoners were heaving at the wicker barricades that protected the Chin soldiers while they reloaded. Genghis held his breath as his warriors joined the exhausted prisoners, their swords bright lines in the sun. The crossbows had fallen silent at last and Genghis could see gesturing arms calling for more.

They had run out of bolts at last, as he had hoped. The ground was black with the ugly little spikes of iron and every sprawled body was fat with them. Let the tree stand and he would have his breach yet in the Chin ranks. Genghis drew his father's sword, feeling the pressure give suddenly like a breaking dam. Behind him, the Mongols lifted lances or long blades and jammed in their heels, forcing their mounts to leap up piles of dead men. The remaining barricades were kicked aside. Genghis passed under the shadow of the huge tree and could not stop as he was carried into the army of the Chin emperor.

The line of horsemen speared into the Chin soldiers, cutting deeply into their ranks. The risk increased with every length they travelled, as they were faced with men not only at the front, but at the sides. Genghis hacked at anything that moved, a butcher's style he could keep up for hours. Ahead, he saw a line of panicking cavalry smash into their own lines, breaking them apart. He could not take a moment to look back at the tree with so many blades whirling around him. Only when another line hit the cavalry at full gallop did he glance up, recognising his own people on the back of the Chin mounts. He yelled hoarsely then, sensing the swelling panic and confusion in his enemies. Behind him, the impotent crossbow regiments were being gutted by his men as they cut a path deeper and deeper into the massed ranks. It would not have been enough without the flanking charge, but Genghis saw the riders wreak havoc in the Chin lines, the best horsemen in the world running wild amidst their enemies.

A blade caught his mount in the throat, opening up a great gash that pumped blood onto the faces of struggling soldiers. Genghis felt the animal falter and jumped free, knocking two men down as he hit them with his full weight.

His feel for the battle was lost in that instant and he could only continue the fight on foot, hoping they had done enough. More and more of his warriors were surging out of the pass, crashing into the centre . . . The Mongol army came through like an armoured fist, sending the Chin ranks reeling.

General Zhi Zhong could only watch open-mouthed as the Mongols gutted his front lines. He had seen his cavalry routed and then driven back into the main army, spreading panic through the ranks. He could have held them steady, he was certain, but then the cursed Mongols followed them in on stolen horses. They rode with astonishing skill, balancing perfectly as they shot volleys of arrows at the gallop, opening a hole. He saw a sword regiment collapse and then the front ranks at the pass crumpled back and a new wave of them sprang through his soldiers as if they were children with swords.

The general gaped, his mind blank. His officers were looking to him for orders, but too much was happening too quickly and he froze. No, he could still recover. More than half his army had yet to meet the enemy and another twenty cavalry regiments waited further down the line. He called for his horse and mounted.

'Block the pass!' he shouted, his messengers racing through the line to the front. He had men ready for the order, if they still lived. If he could cut off the Mongols coming through the pass, he could surround and destroy those who rode so recklessly through his own lines. He had raised the tree as a last resort, but it had become the only thing that would buy him time enough to regroup.

Tsubodai saw Genghis crash through the end of the pass, his horse wild. He felt the terrible pressure begin to give around him as more and more men followed their khan through the gap. Tsubodai's Young Wolves bayed in excitement. Many of them were still so hemmed in by men and horses that they could not move. Some had even been turned around in the heaving mass and were struggling to get back to the fighting ahead.

Tsubodai had lost sight of Genghis when he saw one of the ropes above his head grow taut as men heaved on it. He looked up, understanding in an instant that the shuddering tree could be dropped and cut him off from those who had gone through.

His men did not see the danger and kicked and urged their mounts forward, whooping like the young men they were. Tsubodai swore as another rope lost its slackness. The tree was enormous, but it would not take much to pull it down.

'Targets there!' he roared to his men, giving them the direction as he drew and loosed as fast as he ever had before. His first shaft took one of the struggling Chin in the throat and he fell away from a rope, sending two companions sprawling. It went slack, but more ran to complete Zhi Zhong's order and the tree began to tip. Tsubodai's Young Wolves answered with a swarm of arrows, dropping dozens of men. It was too late. The last of the Chin soldiers pulled the massive trunk right on top of them, with a crash that slammed up and down the pass. Tsubodai was no more than twenty paces from the plain beyond when it fell. His horse reared in panic and he had to heave to bring it back under control.

Even the surviving prisoners were jolted from their bloody frenzy by the sound. As Tsubodai stared in stunned horror, silence fell across the packed lines for a moment before a single terrible cry came from a warrior whose legs had been crushed. The side of the tree blocked the pass to the height of a man. No horse could leap it. Tsubodai felt thousands of eyes turn automatically to him, but he did not know what to do.

His stomach twisted as he saw lines of Chin pikemen appear behind the barrier. Those who dared to show their faces were hammered back with arrows, but their weapons remained, a line of heavy iron that showed like teeth along the length of the trunk. Tsubodai swallowed against a dry throat.

'Axes!' Tsubodai bellowed. 'Axes here!' He did not know how long it would take to cut through such a massive trunk. Until they did, his khan was trapped on the other side.

CHAPTER TWENTY-FOUR

Genghis saw the tree fall and howled in anger, cutting a man's head from his shoulders with a single massive blow. He was in a sea of red and gold banners, fluttering with a noise like birds' wings. He fought alone, desperately. They had not yet realised who he was. Only those close to him tried to crush the dervish of a warrior who fought and snarled into their faces. He spun and darted between them, using every piece of armour as a weapon; anything that would keep him alive. He left a trail of pain in his wake and he never stopped moving. To stop was to die in such a host of flags.

The Chin sensed the sudden uncertainty in their enemies and roared a challenge, their confidence returning. Genghis could see a vast force of fresh cavalry thundering along the flank and he had lost sight of his brother Kachiun. He was unhorsed among the enemy. Dust was everywhere and he knew death was just a whisper away.

As he despaired, a horseman smashed soldiers out of the way and heaved the khan behind him by sheer strength. It was the wrestler, Tolui. Genghis gasped thanks to the massive warrior as they brought their blades down on those who screamed at them. Crossbow bolts rattled off their armour and Tolui grunted as the finger-width plates were snapped by the impacts, many of them falling away.

'To me! Defend the khan!' Tolui bellowed across the heads of the swarming Chin. He saw a riderless horse and aimed his mount at it. As Genghis lunged for the empty saddle, he took a cut on the thigh and shouted in pain. He kicked out wildly, his foot breaking a man's jaw. The sting brought his senses back from despair and he looked around between blows, taking in an impression of the battlefield.

It was chaos. The Chin seemed to have no formations, as if sheer numbers could be enough. Yet to the east, their general was restoring order. The cavalry along the flank would reach Genghis' men even as they fought in the boiling mass of soldiers. Genghis shook his head to clear his eyes of blood. He did not remember taking the wound, but his scalp was raw and his helmet had been knocked away. He could taste blood and spat downwards as he slashed another soldier across the neck.

'The khan!' Tolui shouted, his voice carrying far. Kachiun heard him and answered, his sword swinging. He could not reach his brother and many of his men were already dead, crushed underfoot. He had perhaps five thousand of his original nine. Their quivers were all empty and they were too far from the Badger's Mouth and the khan.

Kachiun swung his sword and drew a great gash along his own horse's flank. Blood poured as the animal screamed and bolted over men, knocking them flying. Kachiun echoed the sound with a desperate call for his men to follow him as he hung on, barely able to guide the stricken animal. He careered through the Chin soldiers, swinging at anything he could reach. The horse was running mad and Kachiun heard its breastbone break as it hit some obstacle. He went flying over its head, hitting another man with his armour. Another of his warriors yelled behind him and Kachiun gripped a lowered arm, dazed and in pain as he swung up behind him.

The five thousand fought as if they had lost their minds, with no thought for their own safety. Those who were hemmed in cut their own mounts as Kachiun had, sending them kicking and snorting for the open plain between the mountains. They had to reach Genghis before he was killed.

Kachiun felt the second mount stumble and nearly fell once more. Somehow it righted itself and he broke through the lines onto open ground, the horse wide-eyed in terror. Riderless horses were everywhere and Kachiun leaped for one without thinking, almost tearing his right arm from the socket as he caught the reins. He looped out from the battle then as he fought the horse's panic and brought it back in. His men had come with him, though there could not have been more than three thousand after that wild charge through the heart of the Chin army.

'Ride!' Kachiun shouted, shaking his head to clear it. He could barely see and his head throbbed from the first impact with the ground. He could feel his entire face swelling as he galloped along the army's edge back to his brother. Half a mile ahead, the rear of Zhi Zhong's cavalry were riding to seal the pass, twenty thousand fresh horses and men. Kachiun knew it was too many, but he did not slow. He raised his sword as he rode, putting aside the pain and showing red teeth to the wind.

No more than a thousand had come through the pass before the tree fell. Half of those were already dead and the rest clustered around their khan, prepared to defend him to the last man. The Chin soldiers swirled around them like a wasps' nest, but they fought like men possessed and, all the time, Genghis was darting glances back at the trunk that blocked the pass. His men were born to war, each one of them more skilled than the Chin soldiers who struggled at their stirrups and died. Their quivers were all empty, but many of the men manoeuvred their mounts as if they were one creature. The ponies knew when to step back from a swinging blade and when to kick and cave in the chest of anyone daring to come too close. Like an island in a raging sea, the Mongol horsemen moved across the face of the Chin army and no one could bring them down. Crossbow bolts rattled their armour, but the regiments were too hemmed in for volley fire. No one wanted to come near those red blades and grim warriors. Those who rode with Genghis were slippery with blood, their hands gummed onto their swords with it. They were men who were hard to kill. They knew their khan was with them and that they only had to hold on until the barrier was cut through. Even then, their number began to dwindle, though they took ten or twenty for every man that fell. More and more began to look back at the pass, their eyes grim and growing in desperation as they fought on.

Jelme and Arslan arrived together at the blocked pass, seeing Tsubodai pale. The young general nodded to the senior men.

'We need more axemen,' Jelme snapped. 'At this rate it will take hours.'

Tsubodai glared coldly at him.

'The command is yours, general. I was merely waiting for you to come to the front.' He turned his horse away from them without another word, taking a deep breath to shout over the heads of his men.

'Wolves dismount!' he snapped. 'Bows and swords! On foot! With me!'

As the senior men took charge of the axe teams, Tsubodai climbed onto the trunk with his sword drawn, looking down at the Chin pikemen before he kicked one weapon aside and leaped into them. His men followed in a great scrambling rush that knocked their own axe teams sprawling. They would not let their young general go alone to save the khan and they were fresh and furious at the tricks of the Chin.

Genghis looked up as the Young Wolves joined the battle. They cut down the surprised Chin from behind, opening up a great rift in their ranks. Those who took wounds seemed not to feel them as they kept their eyes locked on Tsubodai as he raced on. He had seen the khan and his arm was untried that day. He hit the Chin with a rank no more than a dozen wide, young warriors who moved at such a speed that they could not be stopped. They cut a path through to Genghis over a trail of dead.

'I have been waiting for you!' Genghis called to Tsubodai. 'What do you want from me this time?'

The young general laughed to see him alive, even as he ducked under a sweeping sword and gutted the man who held it. He pulled the blade out with a great heave and stamped down on a dead body as he stepped past. The Chin were reeling, but they still swarmed in such numbers that even Tsubodai's ten thousand could be engulfed. On the flank of the great army of the Chin, cavalry horns sounded and Genghis turned in the saddle as the Chin ranks fell back in order, opening a path for the charge. The Mongol warriors looked at each other as the Chin cavalry broke into a gallop through their own ranks. Genghis grinned, panting as his men formed up around him.

'Those are good horses,' he said. 'I will have the first choice of them when we are done.' Those who heard him laughed, then, as one, they kicked their weary mounts into a canter, leaning low over the saddles. They left Tsubodai alone to hold the ground around the pass and slid into a gallop on their ponies just before the two forces crashed together.

The Chin cavalry commander died in the first instant of meeting the Mongol horsemen. Over the thunder of hooves, his men were cut from their saddles. Those who could strike back swung on empty air as the Mongols ducked or swayed aside. They had practised for this all their lives. Genghis galloped on, deeper and deeper into the ranks of horsemen, his sword arm burning. There was no end to them and he took a fresh cut above his hip where the armour had broken away. Another impact knocked him back so that he saw the pale sky swinging above before he could recover. He did not fall; he could not. He heard screams as Kachiun's mounts hit the Chin riders from behind and wondered if he would meet his brother in the middle or die first. There were just so *many* enemies. He no longer expected to survive and that brought a lightness to his mood that made the gallop through his enemies a moment of pure joy. It was easy to imagine his father riding with him. Perhaps the old man would be proud at last. His sons could not have chosen a better end.

Behind him, the tree was finally rolled back in three pieces. The Mongol army rode slowly out onto the icy flats, grim and poised to avenge their khan. Jelme and Arslan rode at the head and both father and son were ready. They looked out at the Chin flags and banners that swirled into the distance.

'I would not change my life, Jelme, if I could go back,' Arslan called to his son. 'I would still be here.'

'Where else would you be, old man?' Jelme replied with a smile. He set an arrow on the bowstring and took a deep breath before loosing the first shaft into the enemy ranks.

* * *

Zhi Zhong watched in frustration as the pass opened and twenty thousand warriors came storming out, ready to fight. The gods had not given the khan into his hands. Zhi Zhong's own cavalry was engaging the khan's small force, while another group cut into the Chin like a tiger ripping at the belly of a running deer. The Mongols did not seem to communicate, yet they worked together across the battlefield, while his was the only centre of command. Zhi Zhong rubbed his eyes, staring into the dust clouds as they fought.

His pikemen were in chaos and some had left the plain, the figures already distant specks among the hills. Could he yet save the battle? All the tricks were finished. It came down to a fight on a flat plain and he still had the numbers.

He gave fresh orders to his messengers and watched as they galloped across the battlefield. The Mongols from the pass were hammering his men with shaft after shaft, cutting a trench right through the centre of the army that waited for them. The relentless accuracy was forcing his ranks back on themselves, making them bunch up where they should have stayed apart. Zhi Zhong wiped sweat from his brow as he saw riders ripping through his pikemen as if they were unarmed. He could only watch frozen as they split into groups of a hundred, attacking from all angles with their shafts, cutting his army to pieces.

It seemed only a moment before one of the marauding groups spotted him standing there, directing the battle. Zhi Zhong saw their faces light up as they saw the massive war banners around his command tent. As he stared, he saw a dozen bows bent in his direction and others yanking at reins to turn their mounts. Surely the range was too great? Hundreds of his personal guard lay in their path, but they could not stop the arrows and the general was suddenly terrified. They were demonic, these men from the plains. He had tried everything and still they came. Many of them had been cut in the fighting, but they seemed to feel no pain as they drew their bows with bloody hands and kicked their horses at him.

A half-spent arrow thumped into his chest, sticking out of his armour and making him cry out. As if the sound released his fear, his nerve failed completely and he yelled for his guard, pulling his horse around by brute strength and hunching low in the saddle. Other shafts whistled over his head, killing men around him. General Zhi Zhong was mindless in the face of his own death, his confidence shattering. He dug in his heels and his horse bolted, galloping through the ranks to leave his guard behind.

He did not look down at the wide-eyed faces of his soldiers as they saw him desert them. Many threw down their weapons and simply ran, following his example. Some were knocked aside by his horse as they moved too slowly. His eyes blurred in the frozen wind and he knew nothing except the need to escape the cruel-faced Mongols at his back. Behind him, his army crumbled in complete rout and the slaughter went on. The army of Genghis rolled over the Imperial soldiers, killing until their arms were exhausted and the mouths of their horses were white with frothy spit.

Senior officers tried three times to rally their men, each attempt failing as Genghis was able to use the wider ground to send charges in to smash them. When the last of Jelme's arrows were gone, the lances worked well at full speed, taking men off their feet with the impact. Genghis had seen the Chin general run and no longer felt the terrible wounds he had taken. The sun rose higher on the killing and, by noon, the forces of the emperor lay in bloody mountains of the dead, the remainder scattered in every direction and still pursued.

* * *

As Zhi Zhong rode, his mind lost the numbness that had unmanned him. The sounds of battle faded into the distance as he galloped along the road to Yenking. He looked back only once at the great roiling mass of fighting men, and shame and rage were bitter in his throat. Some of his personal guard had taken horses to follow their general, loyal despite his failure. Without a word, they formed up around him, so that a grim phalanx of almost a hundred riders approached the gates of the emperor's city.

Zhi Zhong recognised one man riding abreast, a senior officer from Baotou. At first he could not recall his name and he could only wonder at his spinning thoughts. The city grew quickly before them and it took a huge effort of will to steady himself and calm his thumping heart. Lujan. The man's name was Lujan, he remembered at last.

The general sweated in his armour as he looked at the high walls and the moat surrounding the city. After the chaos and bloodshed, it looked sleepily peaceful, waking slowly for the new day. Zhi Zhong had outraced any messengers and the emperor remained unaware of the catastrophe only twenty miles away.

'Do you want to be executed, Lujan?' he said to the man at his side.

'I have a family, general,' the man replied. He was pale, understanding what they faced.

'Then listen to me and follow my orders,' Zhi Zhong replied.

The general was recognised at a distance and the outer gate was lowered over the expanse of water. Zhi Zhong turned in the saddle to shout orders to the men with him.

'The emperor must be told,' he snapped. 'We can counterattack with the city guard.' He saw the words have an effect on the defeated men, straightening them in their saddles. They still trusted their general to salvage something from the disaster. Zhi Zhong made his face a mask as he passed into the city, the sound of hooves on paved streets loud in his ears. He had lost. Worse, he had run.

The Imperial palace was a huge construction inside the city, surrounded by gardens of great beauty. Zhi Zhong headed for the closest gate that would take him to an audience room. He wondered if the young emperor was even awake at that hour. He would be alert soon enough, when he received the news.

The guards were forced to dismount at the outer gate, striding inward along a wide road of lime trees. They were met by servants, then passed through a chain of halls. Before they could come into the emperor's presence, soldiers from the emperor's own guards blocked their way.

Zhi Zhong showed nothing as he handed over his sword and waited for them to step aside. His soldiers would remain in the outer halls while he went in. He imagined Emperor Wei being woken at that very moment, his slaves fussing around him with the news that the general had returned. The palace would be awash with rumour, but they knew nothing yet. The full scope of the tragedy would come later, but the emperor had to know first.

It was a long time before Zhi Zhong saw the doors of the audience chamber open before him and strode across the wooden floor to the figure seated at the far end. As he had thought, the emperor's face was puffy from sleep, his hair braided hurriedly so that wisps of it were out of place.

'What news is so important?' Emperor Wei said, his voice strained.

The general felt calm at last and took a deep breath as he knelt.

'His Imperial Majesty does me honour,' he said. He raised his head then and the eyes that looked out from the heavy brows made the young emperor clutch at the front of his robe in fear. There was madness there.

Zhi Zhong stood slowly, glancing around the hall. The emperor had dismissed his ministers to hear the private communication from his general. Six slaves stood around the room, but Zhi Zhong cared nothing for them. They would carry the news to the city as they always did. He let out a long breath. His mind had been confused for a time, but at last it was clear.

'The Mongols have come through the pass,' he said, at last. 'I could not hold them.' He saw the emperor pale, his skin turning waxy in the light coming through the high windows.

'The army? Have we been forced to retreat?' Emperor Wei demanded, rising to stand before him.

'It has been broken, Imperial Majesty.'

The general's eyes bored into the young man who faced him and this time they did not look away.

'I served your father well, Imperial Majesty. With him, I would have won. With you, a lesser man, I have failed.'

Emperor Wei opened his mouth in amazement.

'You come to me with this and dare to insult me in my own palace?'

The general sighed. He had no sword, but he drew a long knife from where it had been hidden under his armour. The young emperor gaped at the sight of it, suddenly frightened.

'Your father would not have let me come to him, Imperial Majesty. He would have known not to trust a general who returns from a defeat.' Zhi Zhong shrugged. 'In failing you, I earned my death. What choice is there for me, but this?'

The emperor took a deep breath to scream for his guards. Zhi Zhong lunged at him and clamped a hand around his throat, stifling the cry. He felt hands batter at his armour and his face, but the boy was weak and his grip only tightened.

He could have strangled him then, but it would have been a dishonour to the son of a great man. Instead, he found a place in the emperor's chest as it writhed and twitched, pressing the blade into the heart.

The hands fell away and only then did he feel the sting of the scratches on his cheeks. Blood stained the robe around the blade and the general lifted him up to place him back in his seat.

The slaves were screaming and Zhi Zhong ignored them, standing before the body of the young emperor. There had been no choice, he told himself.

The outer door swung open as the emperor's guards burst in. They raised their weapons and Zhi Zhong stood to face them, seeing the figures of his men fill the corridor behind. Lujan had followed the orders he had been given and he was already bloody. It did not take long to finish the last of them.

Lujan stood with his chest heaving, staring in wonder at the white face of a dead emperor.

'You have killed him,' he said, awed. 'What do we do now?'

The general looked at the exhausted, bloody men who brought the stink of the battlefield into such a place. Perhaps later he would weep for everything he had lost, everything he had done, but now was not the time.

'We tell the people the emperor is dead and that the city must be closed and fortified. The Mongols are coming here and we can do nothing else.'

'But who will be emperor now? One of his children?' Lujan said. He had gone very pale and he did not look again at the sprawled figure on the throne.

'The eldest boy is only six,' Zhi Zhong replied. 'When the funeral has been held, have him brought to me. I will rule as his regent.'

Lujan stared at his general.

'Hail the new emperor,' he whispered, the words repeated by those around him. Almost in a trance, Lujan lowered himself until his forehead touched the wooden floor. The other soldiers followed suit and General Zhi Zhong smiled.

'Ten thousand years,' he said softly. 'Ten thousand years.'

CHAPTER TWENTY-FIVE

The sky burned black over the mountains, the oily smoke reaching for miles. Many of the Chin had surrendered at the end, but the tribes had lost too many of their own to consider mercy. The killing had gone on for days around the pass, those who still wanted to seeking out every last one of the fleeing soldiers and slaughtering them like the marmots of home.

Great bonfires had been built of the pike poles and flags, leaving only food and the dead. The families had come slowly through the pass behind the warriors, bringing carts and forges to melt down the pike heads for their steel. The Chin supplies were dragged into snowbanks where they would remain fresh.

There was no tally of the Chin corpses, nor need for one. No one who saw the mountains of broken flesh would ever forget it. The children and women helped to strip the bodies of their armour and anything else of value. The stench was awful after only a day and the air was rich with flies that crackled and burned in the swirling smoke of the bonfires.

On the edge of it, Genghis waited for his generals. He wanted to see the city that had sent such an army against him. Kachiun and Khasar rode out to join him, staring back in awe across the field of blood and fire that stretched into the distance. The bonfires threw flickering shadows on the mountains of the valley and even the tribes were subdued as they sang in low voices for the dead.

The three brothers waited in silence as the men Genghis had summoned trotted up, their backs stiff. Tsubodai came first, pale and proud with ugly black stitches running the length of his left arm. Jelme and Arslan rode together, dark against the fires. Ho Sa and Lian the mason came last of all. Only Temuge remained behind to move the camp to a river ten miles north. The flames would burn for days yet, even without the tribes to feed them. The flies were getting worse and Temuge was sickened by the constant buzzing and the rotting dead.

Genghis could hardly drag his gaze away from the plain. It was the death of an empire he was seeing, he was certain of it. He had never come so close to defeat and destruction as in the battle through the pass. It had left its mark on him and he knew he would always be able to close his eyes and summon the memories. Eight thousand of his own men had been wrapped in white cloth and taken up to the mountains. He glanced to where they lay like fingers of bone in the snow, far away. Already, hawks and wolves tore at their flesh. He had stayed only to see them sky-buried, to honour them and give their families honour.

'Temuge has the camp,' he told his generals. 'Let us see this Yenking and this emperor.' He dug in his heels and his horse jerked into a run. The others followed him, as they always had.

Built on a great plain, Yenking was by far the largest construction any of them had ever seen. As it grew before him, Genghis recalled the words of Wen Chao, the Chin diplomat he had met years before. He had said that men could build cities like mountains. Yenking was such a place.

It rose in dark grey stone that was at least fifty feet from bedrock to the crest. Genghis sent Lian and Ho Sa around the city to count the wooden towers that rose even further. When they returned, they had travelled more than five miles around and reported almost a thousand towers, like thorns along the walls. Even worse were the descriptions of huge bow weapons on the battlements, manned by silent, watching soldiers.

Genghis studied Lian for some sign that the mason was not intimidated, but the man visibly drooped in the saddle. Like the Mongols, he had never visited the capital and could not think of a way to break walls of that size.

On the corners of the immense rectangle, four forts stood apart from the main walls. A wide moat ran between the forts and the walls and yet another girdled them on the outside. A huge canal was the only breach in the walls themselves, running through an immense water gate of iron that was in turn protected by platforms for archers and catapults. The waterway stretched into the south, as far as any of them could see. Everything about Yenking was on a scale too great for the imagination. Genghis could not begin to think of a way to force the gates.

At first, Genghis and his generals kept as close as they had to Yinchuan, or some of the other Chin cities to the west. Then a hammer blow sounded on the evening air and a dark blur shot past them, staggering Kachiun's horse with the power of its wake. Genghis almost lost his seat as his own mount reared and could only gaze in amazement at a shaft half sunk in the soft ground, more like a smooth tree trunk than an arrow.

Without a word, his generals retreated past the range of the fearsome weapon, their spirits sinking even lower as they understood another part of the defences. To come closer than five hundred paces was to invite more of the great poles with their iron tips. Just the thought of one of them striking a mass of his riders was appalling.

Genghis turned in the saddle to the man who had broken lesser walls.

'Can we take this place, Lian?' he demanded. The mason would not meet his stare and looked over the city. At last, he shook his head.

'No other city has a wall so wide at the top,' he said. 'From that height, they will always have more range than anything I can make. If we built stone ramparts, I might be able to protect the counterweighted catapults, but if I can reach them, they can certainly reach me to smash them to firewood.'

Genghis glared in frustration at Yenking. To have come so far and yet be baulked at the final obstacle was infuriating. Only the day before, he had been congratulating Khasar on taking the fort in the pass and Kachiun for his inspired charge. He had believed then that his people were unstoppable, that conquest would always come easily. His army certainly believed it. They whispered that the world was his to take. Facing Yenking, he could almost feel the emperor's scorn at such ambition.

Genghis kept the cold face as he turned to his brothers.

'The families will find good land here for grazing. There will be time to plan an attack on this place.'

Khasar and Kachiun nodded uncertainly. They too could see the great sweeping conquest halted at the foot of Yenking. Like Genghis himself, they had become used to the fast and exciting pace of taking cities. The carts of their people were now so laden with gold and wealth that they broke axles on any long trip.

'How long will it take to starve such a city?' Genghis demanded suddenly.

Lian had no better idea than any of them, but did not want to admit his ignorance.

'I have heard more than a million of the emperor's subjects live in Yenking. To feed so many is difficult to imagine, but they will have vast granaries and stores. They have known we were coming for months, after all.' He saw Genghis frown and hurried on. 'It could be as long as three years, even four, lord.'

Khasar groaned aloud at the estimate, but the youngest of them, Tsubodai, brightened.

'They have no army left to break a siege, lord. You will not need to keep us all here. If we cannot bring the walls down, perhaps you will allow us to raid in this new land. As things stand, we don't even have maps beyond Yenking.'

Genghis glanced at his general, seeing the hunger in his eyes. He felt his own mood lift.

'That is true. If I have to wait until this emperor is skin and bone before he submits, at least my generals will not be idle.' He swept an arm across the landscape that blurred into distance too great for any of them to imagine.

'When the families are settled, come to me with a direction and it will be yours. We will not waste the time here and grow fat and sleepy.'

Tsubodai grinned, his enthusiasm kindling that of the others to replace the dark mood of moments earlier.

'Your will, my lord,' he replied.

In shining, black-lacquered armour, General Zhi Zhong paced angrily as he waited for the emperor's ministers to join him in the coronation hall. The morning was peaceful and he could hear the creaking squawks of magpies outside. No doubt the omen takers would read something into the quarrelsome birds, if they saw them.

The funeral of Emperor Wei had taken almost ten days, with half the city tearing their clothes and rubbing ash into their skin before the body was cremated. Zhi Zhong had suffered through endless orations by the noble families. Not one of them had mentioned the manner of the emperor's death, not with

Zhi Zhong glowering at them and his guards standing with their hands on their sword hilts. He had taken the head from the Imperial rose, nipping it off with a single blow so that everything else remained.

The first few days had been chaotic, but after three ministers had been executed for speaking out, any further resistance collapsed and the great funeral went ahead just as if the young emperor had died in his sleep.

It had been useful to find that the governing nobles had made plans for the event long before it was needed. The Chin empire had survived upheaval and even regicide before. After the initial spasm of outrage, they had fallen into the routines almost with relief. The peasants in the city knew nothing except that the Son of Heaven had left his mortal flesh. They wailed ignorantly in the streets of the city, mindless in hysteria and grief.

The emperor's young son had not wept when he heard of his father's demise. In that at least, Emperor Wei had prepared his family well. The boy's mother had enough sense to know that any protest would mean her own death, so she had remained silent through the funeral, pale and beautiful as she watched her husband's body burned to ash. As the funeral pyre collapsed with a cough of flame, Zhi Zhong thought he had felt her gaze on him, but when he looked up, she had her head bowed in supplication to the will of the gods. His will, he thought, though the result was much the same.

The general ground his teeth in irritation as he paced. First the funeral had taken longer than he would have believed possible and then he had been told the coronation would take another five days. It was infuriating. The city mourned and none of the peasants actually worked while great events played themselves out. He had borne the endless fittings for new robes to mark his position as regent. He had even remained still while the ministers lectured him nervously on his new responsibilities.

All the while, the Mongol khan prowled like a wolf at the door, watching the city.

In his free hours, Zhi Zhong had climbed the steps to a dozen places on the wall to watch the filthy tribes settle themselves on Imperial land. He thought sometimes that he could smell their rancid mutton and goats' milk on the breeze. It was galling to have been beaten by sheep herders, but they would not take Yenking. The emperors who had built the city had intended it to demonstrate their power. It would not fall easily, Zhi Zhong told himself.

He still woke at night from nightmares of being chased, the humming of arrow shafts like mosquitoes whining in his ears. What else could he have done? No one thought the Mongols could climb the highest peaks to flank him. Zhi Zhong felt no more shame at the defeat. The gods had been against him and yet they had given the city into his hands as regent. He would watch the Mongols shatter their army against the walls and, when they were bloody, he would take the head of their khan in his hands and bury it in the deepest shit hole in the city.

The thought lightened his mood as he waited for the boy emperor to make his appearance. Somewhere in the distance, he could hear gongs booming, announcing the presence of a new Son of Heaven to the people.

The doors to the coronation chamber opened to reveal the sweating face of Ruin Chu, the first minister.

'My Lord Regent!' he said on seeing Zhi Zhong. 'You are not wearing your robes! His Imperial Majesty will be here at any moment.' He seemed about to collapse, after days of organising the funeral and the coronation. Zhi Zhong found the fat little man irritating and took pleasure from the impact his words would have.

'I have left them in my rooms, minister. I will not need them today.'

'Every moment of the ceremony has been planned, Lord Regent. You must . . .'

'Do not tell me "must",' Zhi Zhong snapped. 'Get the boy in here and place a crown on him. Chant, sing, light tapers of incense, whatever you want, but say one more word to me about what I *must* do and I will have your head.'

The minister gaped at him, then lowered his eyes, shuddering visibly. He knew that the man he faced had murdered the emperor. The general was a brutal traitor and Ruin Chu did not doubt he would even shed blood on the day of a coronation. He bowed as he walked backwards, opening the doors. Zhi Zhong heard the slow pace of the procession and waited in silence as the minister reached it. He chuckled as he heard the pace increase.

When the doors opened again, there was a definite look of fear in the entourage around the six-year-old boy who would become emperor. Zhi Zhong saw he was bearing up well, despite having little sleep over the previous days.

The procession slowed again as it passed Zhi Zhong, heading towards the golden throne. Buddhist monks waved censers, filling the air with white smoke. They too were nervous to find the general in his armour, the only man with a sword in the room. He stalked behind them as Emperor Wei's son took his place on the throne. It was only the beginning of the final stage. Reciting the titles alone would take until noon.

Zhi Zhong watched sourly as the ministers settled themselves comfortably, sitting like peacocks around the centre of the ceremony. The incense made him drowsy and he could not help but think of the Mongols on the plain outside the city. At first, he had seen the need for the rituals, a way of keeping order after he had killed the emperor. The city could have erupted without a strong hand to rule it and it had been necessary to allow the nobles the comfort of their traditions. Now he was tired of it. The city was calm in its grief and the Mongols had begun building great trebuchets, raising walls of stone to protect the weapons.

With an exclamation of impatience, Zhi Zhong strode forward, interrupting the droning voice of a priest. The little boy froze as he looked up at the dark-armoured figure. Zhi Zhong took the Imperial crown from where it lay on a gold silk cushion. It was surprisingly heavy and, for an instant, he was touched with awe at the thought of handling it. He had killed the man who wore it last.

He placed it firmly on the new emperor's head.

'Xuan, you are Emperor, the Son of Heaven,' he said. 'May you rule wisely.' He ignored the shock in the faces of the men around him. 'I am your regent, your right hand. Until you are twenty years of age, you will obey me in everything, without question. Do you understand?'

The little boy's eyes filled with tears. He could hardly comprehend what was happening, but he stammered a response.

'I . . . I understand.'

'Then it is done. Let the people rejoice. I am going to the wall.'

Zhi Zhong left the stupefied ministers behind with their charge as he flung open the doors and strode out of the palace. Built high on the edge of Songhai Lake, which fed the great canal, the view at the top of the steps allowed him to look out on the city as the subjects waited for news. Every bell would sound and the peasants would be drunk for days. He took a deep, shuddering breath as he stood there, looking out at the dark walls. Beyond those, his enemies looked for a weakness. They would not get in.

Temuge sat staring dreamily at three men who had once been khans amongst the people. He could see their arrogance in every action, their disdain for him held barely in check. When would they understand they had no power in the new order his brother had created? There was only one *gur*khan, one man superior to them all. His own brother sat before them, yet they dared to speak to Temuge as if they were his equal.

As the tribes erected their gers on the plain in front of Yenking, it had pleased Temuge to keep the men waiting on his pleasure. Genghis had shown his trust in him with the title of Master of Trade though Temuge himself had defined the role against surly opposition. He delighted in the power he exercised and still smiled when he thought of how long he had kept Kokchu waiting to see him the previous day. The shaman had been pale with fury by the time Temuge finally allowed him into the khan's ger. In allowing him to use it for his work, Genghis showed his approval, a gesture not wasted on the supplicants. There was no point appealing to Genghis if they disliked a ruling made in his name. Temuge had made sure they understood. If Kokchu wanted to gather men to explore an ancient temple a hundred miles away, the request had to be granted and the spoils looked over by Temuge himself.

Temuge laced his hands in front of him, barely listening to the men who had been khans. The father of the Woyela was supported by two of his sons, unable to stand on his own. It would have been a courtesy to offer him a chair, but Temuge was not one to let old wounds be forgotten. They stood and droned on about grazing and timber, while he looked into the distance.

'If you will not allow the herds to move to new grazing without one of your little tokens,' the Woyela was saying, 'we will be slaughtering healthy animals as they starve.' He had increased in bulk since Genghis had cut the tendons in his legs. Temuge enjoyed seeing the man grow red in the face with anger and only glanced lazily at him without a reply. Not one of them could read or write, he reminded himself with satisfaction. The tokens had been a fine idea, carrying the symbol of a wolf burned into the squares of pine wood. He had men in the camp who would demand to see such a token if they saw warriors cutting trees, or bartering looted wealth, or any one of a thousand things. The system was not yet perfect, but Genghis had supported him in sending back the ones who complained, their faces pale with fear.

When the men had finished their tirade, Temuge spoke to them as gently as if they discussed the weather. He had found the soft tone served to heighten their anger and it amused him to prick them in that way.

'In all our history, we have never gathered so many in one place,' he said, shaking his head in gentle reproof. 'We must be organised, if we are to thrive. If I let trees be cut as they are needed, there will be none left for next winter. Do you understand? As I have it now, we take timber only from woodland that is more than three days' ride away, dragging it back. It takes time and effort, but you will see the benefit next year.'

As much as his soft speech galled them, the delicious part was that they could not fault his logic. They were men of the bow and sword and he had found he could think circles around them now that they were forced to listen.

'The grazing though?' the crippled Woyela khan demanded. 'We cannot move a *goat* without one of your maimed men demanding a token to show your approval. The tribes are growing restless under a controlling hand they have never known.'

Temuge smiled at the furious man, seeing how his weight was becoming a strain on his sons at each shoulder.

'Ah, but there are no tribes any longer, Woyela. Is that not a lesson you have learned? I would have thought you remembered it every day.' He made a gesture and a cup of airag was placed in his hand by a Chin servant. Temuge had found his staff among those Genghis had recruited from the cities. Some of them had been servants to noble families and they knew how to treat a man of his position. He began each day with a hot bath in an iron tub built specially for the purpose. He was the only man in the camp who did and, for the first time in his life, he could smell his own people. He wrinkled his nose at the thought. This was how a man should live, he told himself, sipping as they waited.

'These are new days, gentlemen. We cannot move from here until the city falls, which means grazing must be carefully managed. If I do not exercise *some* control, the ground will be bare of grass come the summer and where will we be then? Will you have my brother separated from his herds by a thousand miles? I do not think you would.' He shrugged. 'We may be a little hungry by the end of summer. Perhaps some of the herds will have to be slaughtered, if the land cannot support so many. Have I not sent men to look for salt to cure the meat? The emperor will starve before we do.'

The men stared at him in silent frustration. They could voice examples of how his control had spread through the vast encampment. He had an answer for each one. What they could not express was their irritation at being called to heel at every turn by some new rule from Temuge. Latrine pits must not be dug too close to running water. Ponies could be mated only according to a list of blood lines that Temuge had made himself, without consulting anyone. A man with a fine mare and stallion could no longer put them together without begging for permission. It irked them all and it was true that discontent was spreading through the camp.

They did not dare complain openly, not while Genghis supported his brother. If he had listened to their complaints, he would have undermined Temuge and made a mockery of the new position. Temuge understood that, knowing his brother far better than they did. Once Genghis had given him the role, he would do nothing to interfere. Temuge revelled in the chance to show what an intelligent man could achieve when he was not restrained.

'If that is all, I have many others I must see this morning,' Temuge said. 'Perhaps now you understand why it is difficult to see me. I find there are always some who will talk the day away before they understand what we *must* do here; what we must become.'

He had given them nothing and their enraged frustration was like cool wine to him. He could not resist driving in the barbs a little deeper.

'If there is anything else, I am busy, but I will find time to listen, of course.'

'You listen, but you do not hear,' the crippled khan said wearily.

Temuge spread his hands in regret.

'I find that not everyone who comes before me can fully understand the problems they raise. There are even times when trade goes on in the camp without the khan's tithe being removed and sent to me.'

He stared at the old khan hanging in the arms of his sons as he spoke and the man's feverish gaze faltered. How much did Temuge know? There were rumours that he paid spies to report every transaction to him, every bargain and exchange of wealth. No one knew the full extent of his influence.

Temuge sighed and shook his head as if disappointed.

'I had hoped you would bring it up without my prompting, Woyela. Did you not sell a dozen mares to one of our Chin recruits?' He smiled encouragingly. 'I have heard that the price was a fine one, though the mares were not the best quality. I have not yet received the tithe of two horses that you owe my brother, though I assume they will be here by sunset. Is that a reasonable thing to assume, do you think?'

The khan of the Woyela wondered who had betrayed him. After a time, he nodded and Temuge beamed.

'Excellent. I must thank you for taking time away from those who still look to you for authority. Remember that I am always here should anything else need my attention.'

He did not stand as they turned to leave the khan's ger. One of those who had not spoken looked back in naked anger and Temuge decided to have him watched. They feared him, both for his role as a shaman and as his brother's shadow. Kokchu had spoken the truth in that. Seeing fear in another man's eyes was perhaps the most wonderful feeling of all. It brought a sense of strength and lightness that came otherwise only from the black paste Kokchu supplied.

There were other men waiting to see him, some of whom he had summoned himself. He considered a dull afternoon spent in their company and, on a whim, decided against it. He turned his head to the servant.

'Prepare a cup of hot airag laced with a spoonful of my medicine,' he said. The black paste would bring colourful visions and then he would sleep through the afternoon, letting them all wait. He stretched his back at the thought, pleased with the day's work.

CHAPTER TWENTY-SIX

It took two months to build ramparts of stone and wood to protect the great engines of war. The trebuchets Lian had designed had been constructed in the forests to the east. With their great beams still sticky with sap, they sat like brooding monsters a full mile away from the walls of the city. When the ramps were built, they would be rolled up into their protective shadow. It was slow and tiring work, but in some ways, the confidence of the Mongol host had grown in the time. No army sallied out to attack them, there was a freshwater lake to the north of the city and the shores teemed with birds they could trap during the winter months. They were the lords of the Chin plain. Yet there was nothing to do but live and they were used to fast conquest and victory, with new lands discovered each day. Coming to a sudden halt began to sour the camaraderie between the tribes. Already there had been knife fights stemming from ancient grudges. Two men and a woman had been found dead on the shore of the lake, their murderers unknown.

The army waited restlessly for the city to starve. Genghis had not known whether the stone ramps could protect the heavy catapults, but he needed something to keep his people from idleness. At least working them to exhaustion kept them fit and too tired to bicker. The scouts had found a hill of slate, less than a day's ride from Yenking. The warriors quarried the stone with the enthusiasm they brought to every task, breaking it with wedges and hammers, then heaving the blocks onto carts. Lian's expertise was vital there and he hardly left the quarry site in those weeks. He showed them how to bind the stones with a paste of burned limestone and the ramps grew daily. Genghis had lost count of how many thousands of carts had trundled past his ger, though Temuge kept a careful record on their dwindling supply of looted parchment.

The counterweights Lian had designed were rope nets of larger stones, hanging from the levers of the machines. Two men had crushed their hands in the construction, suffering agonies as Kokchu cut the mangled limbs from them. The shaman had rubbed a thick, gritty paste into their gums to dull the pain, but they had still screamed. The work went on, watched always from the walls of Yenking. Genghis had been helpless to prevent the massive war bows being moved along the crest to face his own weapons. Sweating teams of Imperial guards built new cradles for them, working as many hours as the Mongol warriors below.

It took hundreds of strong men to roll the trebuchets up to the ramps in front of Yenking. With fresh snow falling on the plain, Genghis stood in frustration as the Chin engineers wound back seven great bows, sending iron-tipped poles crashing against the ramparts. The trebuchets answered with two boulders that cracked against the walls, sending splinters flying. The Chin weapons were untouched.

It took an age to reset Lian's great levers. In that time, the wall bows hammered the ramps over and over. Before the trebuchets were ready for a second shot at the city, cracks appeared in the ramps the tribes had built. After that, destruction came quickly. Stones exploded into the air with each strike, showering Lian and his men with splinters. Many of them fell clutching at their hands and faces, staggering back as the barrage continued. Lian himself was untouched and he stood watching in grim silence as his ramparts were torn apart and his machines exposed.

For a time, it seemed that the trebuchets themselves might survive, but then a direct hit cracked across the plain, followed almost instantly by three more. As the wall teams tired, the rate had slowed, but each blow carried terrific force. Warriors died trying to drag the machines out of range. One moment, they were there, sweating and shouting. The next, they were bloody smears on the wood and the air around them was filled with snow and dust.

Nothing could be salvaged. Genghis growled softly in his throat as he looked over the broken men and timbers. He was close enough to the city to hear cheering inside and it galled him that Lian had been right. Without protection, they could not match the range of the wall weapons and whatever they built would be hammered down. Genghis had discussed making high towers to wheel towards the city, perhaps even sheathed in iron, but the heavy bolts would punch straight through them, just as his own arrows pierced sheet armour. If his metalworkers made the towers strong enough to withstand the blows, they would be too heavy to move. It was maddening.

Genghis paced up and down as Tsubodai sent brave warriors in to collect the wounded and take them out of range. His men believed he could take Yenking as he had taken other cities. Seeing Lian's extraordinary constructions smashed to kindling would not help morale in the camp.

As Genghis watched the Young Wolves risk their lives, Kachiun approached and dismounted. His brother's expression was inscrutable, though Genghis thought he could detect the same deep irritation at the failure.

'Whoever built this city gave thought to its defence,' Kachiun said. 'We won't take it by force.'

'Then they will starve,' Genghis snapped. 'I have raised the black tent before Yenking. There will be no mercy.'

Kachiun nodded, watching his older brother closely. Genghis was never at his best when forced into inaction. Those were the times when the generals walked with care around him. Over the previous days, Kachiun had seen Genghis lose his dark moods as the ramps rose, wondrously strong. They had all been confident, but it was clear now that the Chin commander had only waited for them to drag the new weapons into range. Whoever he was, the man was patient, and patient enemies were the most dangerous.

Kachiun knew Genghis was capable of being stung into rash decisions. As things stood, he still listened to his generals, but as the winter wore on, Genghis would be tempted to try almost anything and the tribes could suffer as a result.

'What do you think of sending men to climb the walls at night?' Genghis asked, echoing Kachiun's thoughts. 'Fifty or a hundred of them, to light fires in the city.'

'The walls can be climbed,' Kachiun replied carefully. 'But the Chin patrols at the top are as thick as flies. You said it would be a waste of men, before.'

Genghis shrugged irritably.

'We had catapults then. It might still be worth trying.'

Genghis turned his pale eyes on his brother. Kachiun held his gaze, knowing his brother would want the truth.

'Lian said they had more than a million in the city,' Kachiun said. 'Whoever we sent would be hunted down like wild dogs and become sport for their soldiers.' Genghis grunted in response, grim and despairing. Kachiun searched for a way to lighten his mood.

'Perhaps it is now time to send the generals out to raid, as

367

you said you would. There will be no quick victory here and there are other cities in this land. Let your sons go with them, that they can learn our trade.'

Kachiun saw doubt cross his brother's face and thought he understood. The generals were men Genghis trusted to act without his supervision. They were loyal by any test that mattered, but the war up to that point had been fought with Genghis watching. To send them out, perhaps for thousands of miles, was not an order Genghis would give lightly. He had agreed to it more than once, and yet somehow, the final command had not come.

'Is it betrayal you fear, brother?' Kachiun asked softly. 'Where would it come? From Arslan and his son Jelme who have been with us from the beginning? From Khasar, or Tsubodai who worships you? From me?'

Genghis smiled tightly at the idea. He looked up at the walls of Yenking, still untouched before him. With a sigh, he realised he could not keep so many active men on that plain for as long as three years. They would be at each other's throats long before that, doing the work of the Chin emperor for him.

'Shall I send the entire army? Perhaps I will stay here on my own and dare the Chin to come out.'

Kachiun chuckled at the image.

'In truth, they would probably think it was a trap and leave you there,' he replied. 'Yet if I were the emperor, I would be training every able man as a warrior, building an army from within. You cannot leave too few to guard Yenking, or they could see a chance to attack.'

Genghis snorted.

'You do not make a warrior in a few months. Let them train, these bakers and merchants. I would welcome the chance to show them what it means to be a warrior born.'

'With a voice of thunder, no doubt, and perhaps a penis of

lightning,' Kachiun said with a straight face. After a moment of silence, both of them broke into laughter.

Genghis had lost the black mood that had settled on him with the destruction of the catapults. Kachiun could almost see the energy rise in him as he thought about the future.

'I have said I will send them out, Kachiun, though it is early yet. We do not know if other cities will try to relieve Yenking and we may need every man here.' He shrugged. 'If the city hasn't fallen by spring, I will set the generals free to hunt.'

Zhi Zhong was in a pensive mood as he stood before the high window in the audience chamber of the summer palace. He had hardly spoken to the boy emperor since the day he had crowned him. Xuan was somewhere in the labyrinth of corridors and rooms that had formed his father's official residence and Zhi Zhong rarely thought of him.

The soldiers had cheered their general as the Mongol trebuchets were destroyed that morning. They had looked to Zhi Zhong for approval and he had shown it in a brief nod to their officer before striding down the steps into the city. Only in private had he clenched a fist in silent triumph. It was not enough to expunge the memory of the Badger's Mouth, but it was a victory of sorts and the frightened citizens needed something to raise them from their despair. Zhi Zhong sneered to himself as he recalled the reports of suicides. Four high-born daughters had been found dead in their rooms as soon as the news of the army's defeat had filtered through Yenking. All four had known each other and it seemed they preferred a dignified end to the rape and destruction they saw as inevitable. Eleven more had taken the same path in the weeks that followed and Zhi Zhong had worried the new fashion for death might spread right across the city. He clasped his hands behind his

369

back, peering out across the lake at the noble houses. They would have better news today. Perhaps they would hesitate with their knives of ivory and their scorn for his skill. Yenking could still resist the invaders.

The lord regent realised he was tired and hungry. He had not eaten since the morning and the day had been spent in too many meetings to recall. Every man in authority in Yenking seemed to need his approval and his advice. As if he knew any better than they what to expect over the coming months. He frowned at the thought of the food supplies, glancing to a side table where scrolls lay in a pyramid. The citizens of Yenking were eating themselves into defeat. That one thing could make a mockery of his defences, but Zhi Zhong himself had stripped the city stores to feed the army. It galled him to think of the Mongols eating the supplies he had gathered for a year at the pass, but there was no point looking back at bad decisions. After all, he and the emperor had believed the Mongols would be stopped before they ever came in sight of the Imperial city.

Zhi Zhong pursed his mouth. The Yenking merchants were not fools. Rationing was already in force across the city. Even the black market had collapsed as they realised the siege might not be broken quickly. Only a few were still selling food for huge profits. The rest were hoarding supplies for their own families. Like all their class, they would try to wait out the storm and then grow fat and rich again in the aftermath.

Zhi Zhong made a mental note to have the wealthiest merchants brought before him. He knew how to apply the sort of pressure that would reveal their secret stores. Without them, the peasants would be eating cats and dogs inside a month and after that . . . ? He cracked his neck wearily. After that, he would be trapped in a place with a million starving people. It would be hell on earth.

The one hope was that the Mongols would not wait outside the walls for ever. He told himself they would tire of the siege and ride to other cities less well defended. Zhi Zhong rubbed his eyes, glad there was no one but slaves to see his weakness. In truth, he had never worked as hard in his life as in this new role. He hardly slept and when he did find rest, his dreams were filled with plans and stratagems. He had gone without any sleep at all the night before as he stood with the bow teams.

He smiled tightly as he remembered again the destruction of the Mongol machines. If only he could have seen the khan's face at that moment. He was tempted to summon the ministers for a final meeting before he bathed and slept. No, not while they looked at him with something more than defeat in their eyes. He would let them have this day complete, one where he had cracked the image of invincibility around the Mongol khan.

Zhi Zhong turned away from the window and took a path through dark corridors to where Emperor Wei had bathed each evening. He sighed in anticipated pleasure as he reached the door and entered a room centred around a sunken pool. The slaves had heated the water ready for his ritual and he cracked his neck as he prepared to have the cares of the day soothed from him.

Slaves undressed Zhi Zhong with casual efficiency as he gazed at the two girls waiting to rub his skin with oils in the pool. Silently, he congratulated Emperor Wei on his taste. The slave women of the Imperial household would be wasted on his son, at least for a few more years.

Naked, Zhi Zhong lowered himself into the water, enjoying the sense of space in the high-ceilinged room. Water dripped and echoed and he began to relax as the girls soaped his skin with soft brushes. Their touch revived him. After a time, he drew one of them out of the pool, laying her on her back on the cold tiles. Her nipples stiffened in the sudden chill. Only her lower legs remained in the hot water as he took her in silence. She was well trained and her hands writhed across his back as she gasped under the man who ruled the city. Her companion observed the rutting pair with dispassionate interest for a few moments, then resumed soaping his back, pressing her breasts into him so that he groaned in pleasure. Without opening his eyes, Zhi Zhong reached for her hand, guiding it down to where the bodies met so that she could feel him enter her companion. She clung to him with professional skill and he smiled, his mind growing calm even as his body tensed and jerked. There were compensations in ruling Yenking.

Three nights after the destruction of the Mongol catapults, two men slipped unseen down the walls of Yenking, dropping the last few feet without a sound. The ropes disappeared above their heads, pulled up by the lord regent's guards.

In the darkness, one of the men glanced at the other, controlling his nervousness. He did not like the company of the assassin and would be pleased when their paths diverged. His own mission was one he had undertaken before for Emperor Wei and he relished the prospect of stealing among the Chin recruits who laboured so tirelessly for the Mongol khan. To a man, the traitors deserved death, but he would smile at them and work just as hard as they while he gathered information. In his own way, he knew his contribution would be as valuable as that of any of the soldiers on the walls. The lord regent needed every scrap of information about the tribes and the spy did not underestimate his own importance.

He had not learned the name of the assassin, perhaps as well protected as his own. Though they had stood together inside the wall, the dark-clothed man had not spoken a word. The spy had not been able to resist watching as the man checked his weapons, tying and securing the small blades of his trade as they waited. No doubt Zhi Zhong had paid a fortune in gold for the service, one that would almost certainly mean death for the assassin himself.

It was strange to crouch next to a man who expected to die that night, yet showed no sign of fear. The spy shuddered delicately. He would not want to exchange places and could hardly understand the way such a man must think. What devotion could inspire such fanatical loyalty? As dangerous as his own missions had been in the past, he had always hoped to make it back to his masters, to his home.

In his dark cloth, the assassin was little more than a shadow. His companion knew that he would not reply even if he dared to whisper a question to him. The man was focused, his life bought. He would not allow distraction. In utter silence, they stepped into a small wooden boat and used a pole to cross the black moat. A rope trailed from it to the other side for it to be pulled back and hidden, or sunk. There would be no trace of the men to cause suspicion in daylight.

On the far side, both men crouched as they heard a jingle of harness. The Mongol scouts were efficient, but they could not see into every pool of darkness and they watched for a show of force, not two men waiting to walk stealthily into their camp. The spy knew where the Chin recruits had pitched their gers, mimicking the homes of their new masters without shame. There was a chance that they would discover him and then he too would be killed, but that was a risk weighed against his skill and he did not let the thought disturb him. He glanced again at the assassin and, this time, he saw the man's head turn towards him. He looked away, embarrassed. All his life, he had heard of the cult, men who trained every waking hour to bring death. They had no honour as soldiers understood honour. The spy had played the part of a soldier enough times to know the creed and he felt a twinge of disgust at the thought of a man who lived only to kill. He had seen the vials of poison the man tucked away and the wire garrotte he had looped expertly about his wrist.

It was said the assassins' victims were their sacrifice to dark gods. Their own death was the ultimate proof of faith and guaranteed them a high place on the wheel of life. The spy shuddered again, disturbed that his work should have brought him into contact with such a destroyer.

The sounds of Mongol scouts died away and the spy jerked in surprise as he felt a light touch on his arm. The assassin pressed a sticky jar into his hand. It stank of rancid mutton fat and the spy could only look at it in confusion.

'Rub it onto your skin,' the assassin murmured. 'For the dogs.'

As the spy understood, he looked up, but the black figure was already padding away on noiseless feet, vanishing in the darkness. The spy thanked his ancestors for the gift as he rubbed the muck over his skin. He thought at first that it had been kindness, though it was more likely the assassin did not want the camp roused while he set about his own work. His face flushed in humiliation at the thought. Let there be no other surprises that night.

When he had composed himself, he stood and trotted through the darkness, heading to a destination he had marked while there was still light. Without his grim companion, he felt his confidence begin to return. In a little while, he would be among the Chin recruits, chatting and talking as if he had known them for years. He had done it before, when the emperor suspected the loyalty of a provincial governor. He put aside the thought, realising that he must be in place before the assassin struck or he could be caught and questioned. He strolled into the sleeping camp, calling a greeting to a Mongol warrior as the man came out to urinate in the night. The man responded sleepily in his own grunting language without expecting to be understood. A dog raised its head as he passed, but only growled softly as it caught his scent. The spy smiled, unseen in the darkness. He was in.

The assassin approached the great ger of the khan, moving through the dark camp like a wraith. The Mongol leader was a fool to reveal his location to everyone on the walls of Yenking. It was the sort of mistake a man made only once, when he knew nothing of the Black Tong. The assassin did not know if the Mongols would go back to their mountains and plains when the khan died. He did not care. He had been given a scroll tied in black silk ribbon in a formal ceremony by his master, pledging his life in a blood bond. No matter what happened, he would not return to his brothers. If he failed, he would take his own life rather than be captured and perhaps reveal the secrets of his order. The corners of his mouth tightened in dark amusement. He would not fail. The Mongols were sheep herders: good with a bow, but like children against a man of his training. There was little honour in being chosen to kill even a khan of these stinking tribesmen, but he gave no thought to that. His honour came from obedience and a perfect death.

He was not seen as he reached the great ger on its cart, shining whitely in the darkness. It loomed above him as he crept around it, looking for guards. There were two men nearby. He could hear them breathe as they stood in bored stillness, waiting for others to relieve them. From the walls of Yenking, it had been impossible to discern details and he did not know how often they were replaced in the night. He would have to act quickly once he had brought death to that place.

Standing in perfect stillness, the assassin watched as one of the men moved away and took a tour around the khan's ger. The warrior was not alert and, by the time he sensed someone standing in the shadows, it was too late. The guard felt something whip round his neck and slice into his throat, cutting off his cry. A sigh of bloody air came from his lungs and the other guard called a whispered question, not yet alarmed. The assassin lowered the first and edged to the corner of the cart, taking the second quickly as he came around. He too died without a sound and the assassin left him where he fell, crossing quickly to the steps that led upwards. He was a small man and they barely creaked under his weight.

In the blackness within, he could hear the slow breaths of a man deep in sleep. The assassin crept lightly across the floor. In perfect balance, he reached the sleeping figure and crouched by the low bed. They were alone. He drew a sharp blade, its metal blackened with oily soot so that it would not shine.

He pressed one hand down on the source of the breath, finding the mouth. As the sleeper jerked, he brought the knife quickly across the throat. A moan was cut off as quickly as it had begun and the spasming body fell still. The assassin waited until silence had returned, breathing shallowly against the stench of opening bowels. In the blackness, he could not see the face of the one he had killed and he used his fingers to trace the features, a frown creasing his brow. The man did not smell like the warriors outside. His hands quivered slightly as they explored the open mouth and the eyes, moving up to the hair.

The assassin cursed to himself as he fingered the oiled

braid of one of his own people. It could only have been a servant, one who deserved death by the rope for aiding the Mongols with his service. The assassin sat back on his heels as he considered what to do. The khan would surely be close, he thought. There were a number of gers clustered around the largest. One of them would contain the man he sought. The assassin composed himself, reciting a mantra from his training that brought instant calm. He had not yet earned the right to die.

CHAPTER TWENTY-SEVEN

The assassin could hear breathing as he entered another ger. The darkness was absolute, but he shut his eyes and concentrated on the sounds. There were five sleepers in that small space, all unaware of the man standing over them. Four breathed shallowly and he grimaced to himself. Children. The other sleeper was probably their mother, though he could not be certain without a light. A single spark from a flint and steel would be enough, but it was a risk. If they woke, he would not be able to kill them all before they cried out. He made the decision swiftly.

One quick strike brought a flash of light in the ger, enough to show five sleeping bodies. None of them was large enough to be a grown man. Where *was* the khan?

The assassin turned to leave, aware of time running out. It could not be much longer before the dead guards were discovered. When they were found, the peaceful night would be shattered.

One of the sleeping children snorted in his sleep, the rhythms changing. The assassin froze. He waited an age until the long breaths resumed, then stepped lightly to the ger door. He had greased the hinges and it opened without a sound.

He straightened as he pulled the door closed behind him, turning his head slowly to choose the next ger. With the exception of the impudent black tent facing the city and the one on the cart, all the others looked exactly the same.

The assassin heard a sound behind him and his eyes widened as he realised it was an indrawn breath, the sort that went before a shout or scream. He was moving even as the sound began, darting away into the deep shadows. He could not understand the words that echoed through the night, but the response was almost immediate. Warriors came stumbling out of every ger in sight, bows and swords ready in their hands.

It was Jochi who had shouted and whose sleep had been interrupted by the silent presence of the man in his home. His three brothers were jerked awake by his yell and as one they began calling questions into the darkness.

'What is it?' Borte demanded over the noise, throwing back the blankets.

Jochi was already standing in the darkness.

'There was someone in here,' he said. 'Guards!'

'You will wake the entire camp!' Borte snapped. 'It was just a bad dream.'

She could not see his face as he replied.

'No. I saw him.'

Chagatai rose to stand beside his brother. Alarm horns sounded in the distance and Borte cursed under her breath.

'Pray you are right, Jochi, or your father will have the skin off your back.'

Jochi threw open the door and stepped out without bothering to reply. Warriors were swarming around the gers, searching for an intruder before they even knew there was one. He swallowed painfully, hoping he had not dreamed the figure.

Chagatai came out with him, bare-chested and with only leggings to keep out the cold. There was a little starlight outside, but all was confusion and twice men grabbed them only to loosen a fierce grip when they were recognised.

Jochi saw his father come striding through the gers, his sword drawn, but held loosely in one hand.

'What is happening?' he said. His gaze fastened on Jochi, seeing his nervousness. The boy quailed under the flat stare, suddenly convinced that he had roused them all for nothing. Nonetheless, he brazened it out, refusing to be shamed in front of his father.

'There was a man in the ger. I woke and saw him as he opened the door to leave.'

Genghis snorted, but before he could reply, fresh voices called through the night.

'Dead men here!'

Genghis lost interest in his sons, snarling aloud at the thought of an enemy loose in the camp.

'Find him!' he bellowed. He saw Kachiun coming at a run, a long blade in his hands. Khasar was not far behind and the three brothers stood together as they tried to make sense of the chaos.

'Tell me,' Kachiun said as he came to a halt, his face still puffy from sleep.

Genghis shrugged, tense as a bowstring himself.

'Jochi saw a man in his ger and there are dead guards. Someone is among us and I want him found.'

'Genghis!'

He heard Borte call his name and turned to her. Out of the corner of his eye, he saw a dark shadow jerk into movement at the name.

Genghis spun and had a glimpse of the assassin leaping at him. He swung his sword and the man twisted aside, coming up from a tumbler's roll with knives in his hands. Genghis saw he would throw them before he could strike again and he jumped at the dark figure, hammering him off his feet. A spark of pain touched his throat and then his brothers were stabbing at the assassin, jamming their blades in with such force that they sank into the ground beneath. The man did not cry out.

Genghis tried to scramble up, but the world swam lazily and his vision was strangely blurred.

'I'm cut . . .' he said dazedly, falling to his knees. He could hear the assassin's feet drumming on the ground as his brothers dropped their knees onto his chest, smashing his ribs. Genghis raised a hand to his neck and blinked at bloody fingers. The hand was terribly heavy and he slumped backwards onto the dry earth, still confused.

He saw the face of Jelme loom above him, moving slowly. Genghis stared upwards, unable to hear what he was saying. He saw Jelme reach down and yank cloth away from the wound in his neck. When he spoke again, the voice seemed to boom in Genghis' ears, almost drowning out the rushing whispers that deafened him. Jelme picked up the assassin's knife and cursed at the dark stain along the edge.

'The blade is poisoned,' Jelme said, his own fear reflected in Kachiun and Khasar as they stood dumbstruck over their brother. The general did not speak again, instead lowering his mouth to Genghis' neck and sucking on the flow of blood. It was hot and bitter, making him gag as he spat it to one side. He did not stop, though Genghis' hands slapped weakly at his face whenever he pulled away, all strength gone.

Jelme could hear the younger sons of the khan wailing in distress as they saw their father lying close to death. Only Jochi and Chagatai were silent, watching as Jelme spat mouthfuls of blood until the front of his deel was covered in a dark slick.

Kokchu pressed through the crowd, pausing in shock as he saw his khan on the ground. He knelt at Jelme's side and ran his hands over Genghis' chest to feel the heart. It was racing at incredible speed and, for a time, Kokchu could not feel individual beats. Sweat had broken out all over the khan's body and his skin was flushed and hot to the touch.

Jelme sucked and spat and the blood flowed. The general could feel his own lips growing numb and he wondered if the poison would enter him. It did not matter. He thought of it as if he watched someone else. Blood dribbled from his lips as he gasped between each attempt.

'You must not take too much blood,' Kokchu warned him, still with his bony hands on the chest. 'Or he will be too weak to resist whatever poison remains.' Jelme looked at him with glassy eyes before nodding and dipping his face to the searing skin once more. His own cheeks were flushed from contact with such heat and he went on because to stop was to watch his khan die.

Kokchu felt the racing heart jolt and he feared it might stop under his hands. He needed the man who had won him such respect among the tribes, especially now that Temuge had abandoned him. Kokchu began to pray aloud, summoning the spirits by their ancient names. He called on the line of Genghis himself in a torrent of sound. Yesugei he called, even Bekter, the brother Genghis had killed. He needed them all to keep the khan from their realm. Kokchu could feel them gather as he chanted their names, pressing in on him so that his ears filled with whispers.

The heart jolted again and Genghis gasped aloud, his open eyes staring blindly. Kokchu felt the fluttering pulse settle, suddenly slowing as if a door had shut inside. He shivered in the cold, thinking that, for a few moments, he had held the future of the tribes in his hands.

'Enough now, his heart is stronger,' he said hoarsely. Jelme sat back. As he would have done with a gashed horse, the general made a paste of dust and spit and pressed it over the wound. Kokchu leaned over to observe the process, relieved to see the blood slow to a trickle. None of the major veins had been cut and he began to rejoice at the thought that Genghis might still live.

Once more, Kokchu began to pray aloud, forcing the spirits of the dead to attend the man who had formed a nation. They would not want such a man with them while he took their people onwards. He knew it with a certainty that frightened him. The tribesmen watched in awe as Kokchu ran his hands over the supine form, gathering invisible strands as if his trailing fingers wrapped the khan in a web of spirits and faith.

Kokchu looked up at Borte as she stood red-eyed and swaying in shock. Hoelun too was there, desperately pale as she recalled the death of another khan many years before. Kokchu gestured for them to come closer.

'The spirits hold him here, for now,' he told them, his eyes shining. 'Yesugei is here, with his father Bartan. Bekter is here to hold the khan, his own brother.' He shuddered in the cold, his eyes glazing for a moment. 'Jelme has sucked out a great deal of poison, but the heart is fluttering; sometimes strong, sometimes weak. He needs rest. If he will eat, give him blood and milk for strength.' Kokchu could no longer feel the deep coldness of the spirits clustering around him, but they had done their work. Genghis still lived. He called the man's brothers forward to carry him into the ger. Kachiun broke from his trance to order the camp searched for any other enemy still hiding. After that, he shouldered his brother's limp weight with Khasar and carried Genghis into Borte's ger.

Jelme was left kneeling, shaking his head in distress. His father Arslan reached him just as the young general vomited over the bloody ground.

'Help me with him,' Arslan ordered, heaving his son to his feet. Jelme's face was slack and his full weight fell on his father before two warriors stepped in and draped his arms over their shoulders.

'What is wrong with him?' Arslan demanded of Kokchu. The shaman broke his gaze from the ger of Genghis. He used his fingers to open Jelme's eyes to their widest, staring into them. The pupils were large and dark and Kokchu swore softly.

'He may have swallowed the blood. Some of the poison has entered him also.' Kokchu shoved a hand under Jelme's wet tunic, feeling his chest.

'It cannot be much and he is strong. Keep him awake if you can. Walk him. I will bring a draught of charcoal for him to drink.'

Arslan nodded. He motioned to one of the warriors supporting Jelme and took his place, pulling his son's arm around his neck like an embrace. With the other man, he began walking Jelme between the gers, talking to him as he went.

The growing crowd of warriors, women and children did not move. They would not go back to sleep until they were certain their khan would live. Kokchu turned from them, filled with the need to make a paste of charcoal that could soak up whatever poison Jelme had taken in. It would be little use to Genghis, but he would bring a second bowl for him as well. As he approached the ring of staring faces, they gave way before him and it was then that he saw Temuge pushing his way through to the front. Malice sparkled in Kokchu's eyes.

'You are too late to help the khan,' Kokchu said softly as Temuge came close. 'His brothers killed the assassin and Jelme and I kept him alive.'

'Assassin?' Temuge exclaimed, staring around at the misery and fear on so many faces. His gaze passed over the dark-clad figure lying sprawled on the ground and he swallowed in horror.

'Some things must be handled in the old ways,' Kokchu told him. 'They cannot be counted or put into one of your lists.'

Temuge reacted to the shaman's scorn as if he had been struck.

'You dare to speak so to me?' he said. Kokchu shrugged and strode away. He had not been able to resist the barb, though he knew he would regret it. That night, death had walked the camp and Kokchu was in his element.

The crowd became thicker as late arrivals pressed forward, desperate for news. Torches were lit across the camp as they waited for dawn. The body of the assassin lay crushed and broken on the ground and they stared at it in simple dread, unwilling to come too close.

When Kokchu returned with two bowls of thick black liquid, he thought they resembled a herd of yaks on a day of slaughter, miserable and dark-eyed but unable to understand. Arslan held his son's jaw and tilted his head as Kokchu forced the bitter liquid into him. Jelme choked and coughed, spattering black drops onto his father's face. He had regained some awareness in the time it had taken to grind the charcoal and Kokchu did not linger with him. He pressed the half-empty bowl into Arslan's free hand and went on with the other. Genghis could not die, not in the shadow of Yenking. Kokchu was filled with a cold dread as he considered the future. He crushed his own fear as he entered the tiny ger, dipping his head to pass under the lintel. Confidence was part of his trade and he would not let them see him so shaken.

* * *

As dawn approached, Khasar and Kachiun came out, blind to the thousands of eyes that fastened on them. Khasar retrieved his sword from where it had stuck in the dead man's chest and kicked the lolling head before sheathing the blade.

'Does the khan live?' someone called.

Khasar cast a weary gaze over them, not knowing who had spoken.

'He lives,' he said. His words were repeated as a whisper until they all knew.

Kachiun picked up his own blade from where it had fallen and raised his head at the sound. He was helpless to aid his brother in the ger and perhaps that was why his temper kindled at the sight of them.

'Will our enemies sleep while we are gathered here?' Kachiun snapped. 'They will not. Go home to your gers and wait for news.' Under his fierce gaze, the warriors turned away first, pressing through the throng of women and children. They too began to drift away, staring backwards as they went.

Kachiun stood with Khasar as if they guarded the ger where Genghis lay. The khan's second wife Chakahai had come, her face a mask of pale fear. All the men had looked to Borte to see how she would react, but she had only nodded to the Xi Xia woman, accepting her presence. In the silence, Kachiun could hear the drone of Kokchu's chanting in the ger. For a moment, he did not want to return to the foetid interior, packed with those who loved his brother. His own grief felt undermined somehow by the presence of the others. He breathed deeply in the cold air, clearing his head.

'There is nothing more we can do,' he said. 'Dawn is not far off and there are things we must discuss. Walk with me, Khasar, for a little while.'

Khasar followed him to where they would not be heard. It

was a long time before they were clear of the camp, their footsteps crunching on frozen grass.

'What is it? What do you want?' Khasar said at last, stopping his brother with a hand on his arm.

Kachiun turned to him, his face darkly furious.

'We failed tonight. We failed to keep the camp safe. I should have considered that the emperor would send assassins. I should have had more guards watching the walls.'

Khasar was too tired to debate the point.

'You cannot change it now,' he said. 'If I know you, it will not happen again.'

'One time could be enough,' Kachiun snapped. 'If Genghis dies, what then?'

Khasar shook his head. He did not want to think of that. As he hesitated, Kachiun gripped him by the shoulders, almost shaking him.

'I don't know!' Khasar replied. 'If he dies, we will return home to the Khenti Mountains and lay him out for the hawks and vultures. He is a khan; what would you expect me to say?'

Kachiun let his hands fall.

'If we do that, the emperor will claim a great victory against us.' He seemed almost to be speaking to himself and Khasar did not interrupt. He could not begin to imagine the future if Genghis were not there.

'The emperor would see our army retreat,' Kachiun went on grimly. 'In a year, every Chin city would know we had been turned back.'

Khasar still said nothing.

'Can't you see, brother?' Kachiun said. 'We would lose everything.'

'We could return,' Khasar replied, yawning. Had he slept at all? He wasn't sure.

Kachiun snorted.

'Within two years, they would be attacking *us*. The emperor has seen what we can do and he will not make the same mistakes again. One chance we have made for ourselves, Khasar. You cannot wound a bear and run. It will chase you down.'

'Genghis will live,' Khasar said stubbornly. 'He is too strong to fall.'

'Open your eyes, brother!' Kachiun replied. 'Genghis can die like any other man. If he does, who will lead the tribes, or will we see them splinter apart? How easy would it be then for the Chin army when they come hunting?'

Khasar saw the first pink light of dawn behind Yenking in the distance. He welcomed it in a night he'd thought would never end. Kachiun was right. If Genghis died, the new nation would break apart. The old khans would assert their authority over the quarrelling tribes. He shook his head to clear it.

'I understand what you are saying,' he told Kachiun. 'I am not a fool. You want me to accept you as khan.'

Kachiun stood very still at that. There was no other way, but if Khasar could not see it, the new day would begin with bloodshed as the tribes fought to leave or remained loyal. Genghis had bound them together. At the first hint of weakness, the khans would taste freedom and fight to keep it.

Kachiun took a deep breath, his voice calm.

'Yes, brother. If Genghis dies today, the tribes will need to feel a strong hand on their necks.'

'I am older than you,' Khasar said softly. 'I command as many warriors.'

'You are not the man to lead the nation. You know it.' Kachiun's heart was racing with the strain of making Khasar understand. 'If you think you *are*, I will take an oath to you. The generals will follow my lead and carry the khans with them. I will not fight you for this, Khasar, not with so much at stake.'

388

Khasar knuckled the tiredness out of his eyes as he thought it through. He knew what it must have cost Kachiun to make the offer. The thought of leading the tribes was intoxicating, something he had not dreamed of before. It tempted him. Yet he was not the one who had seen the dangers to the fragile nation. That remained like a thorn in his flesh to worry him. The generals would come to him expecting him to solve their problems, to see a way through difficulties that they could not. He would even have to plan battles, with triumph or failure resting on his word.

Khasar's pride warred with the knowledge that his brother was better able to lead. He did not doubt that Kachiun would give him complete support if he became khan. He would rule his people and no one would ever know this conversation had taken place. As Genghis had been, he would be father to all their people. He would be responsible for keeping them all alive against an ancient empire bent on their destruction.

He closed his eyes, letting the glowing visions drain from his mind.

'If Genghis dies, I will take an oath to you, little brother. You will be khan.'

Kachiun sighed in exhausted relief. The future of his people had hung on Khasar's trust in him.

'If he does, I will see every Chin city destroyed in fire, beginning with Yenking,' Kachiun said. Both men glanced at the looming walls of the city, united in their desire for vengeance.

Zhi Zhong stood on an archery platform, high above the plain and the Mongol camp. A cold breeze was blowing and his hands were numb on the wooden railing. He had been standing there for hours, watching the tribes for some sign that the assassin had been successful.

Just a little while before, his vigil had been rewarded. Points of light sprang up among the gers and Zhi Zhong had gripped the railing tighter, his knuckles whitening as he squinted into the distance. Dark shadows raced through the flickering pools of light and Zhi Zhong's hopes rose, imagining the spreading panic.

'Be *dead*,' he whispered, alone in the watchtower.

CHAPTER TWENTY-EIGHT

Genghis opened bloodshot eyes, finding both of his wives and his mother at his side. He felt appallingly weak and his neck throbbed. He raised a hand to it and Chakahai caught his wrist before he could disturb the bandage. His thoughts moved sluggishly and he stared at her, trying to remember what had happened. He recalled standing outside the ger, with warriors rushing around him. It had been night and it was still dark in the ger, with only a small lamp to banish the gloom. How much time had passed? He blinked slowly, lost. Borte's face was pale and worried, with dark circles under her eyes. He saw her smile at him.

'Why . . . am I lying here?' he asked. His voice was feeble and he had to force the words out.

'You were poisoned,' Hoelun said. 'A Chin assassin cut you and Jelme sucked out the filth. He saved your life.' She did not mention Kokchu's part. She had endured his chanting, but not allowed him to stay, nor anyone else to enter. Those who did would always remember her son this way and it would undermine him. As wife and mother to a khan, Hoelun knew enough of the minds of men to know the importance of that.

With a vast effort, Genghis struggled up onto his elbows. As if it had waited for exactly that moment, a headache slammed into his skull.

'Bucket,' he groaned, leaning over. Hoelun was just fast enough to shove a leather pail under his head as he emptied black liquid from his stomach in a series of painful spasms. The action made his headache almost unbearable, but he could not stop, even when there was nothing more to come out. At last, he slumped back on the bed, pressing a hand over his eyes to shut out the dim light that pierced him.

'Drink this, my son,' Hoelun said. 'You are still weak from the wound.'

Genghis glanced at the bowl she held to his lips. The mixture of blood and milk was sour on his tongue as he swallowed twice then pushed it away. His eyes felt gritty and his heart thumped in his chest, but his thoughts were clearing at last.

'Help me to rise and dress. I cannot lie here, knowing nothing.'

To his irritation, Borte pressed him back onto the bed as he tried to rise. He lacked the strength to push her away and considered calling for one of his brothers. It was unpleasant to be so helpless and Kachiun would not ignore his commands.

'I have no memory,' he said hoarsely. 'Did we catch the man who did this to me?'

The three women exchanged glances. It was his mother who replied.

'He is dead. It has been two days, my son. You were close to death for all that time.' Her eyes filled with fresh tears as she spoke and he could only stare at her in bewilderment. Anger surfaced without warning in his mind. He had been fit and well, then suddenly awoke to find himself in this state. Someone had hurt him: this assassin that they mentioned. Fury seeped into him like smoke as he tried again to rise.

'Kachiun!' he called, but it was just a breath in his throat.

The women fussed around him, laying a cool wet cloth on his brow as he lowered his head onto the blankets, still glaring. He could not remember both of his wives being in the same ger before. He found the idea uncomfortable, as if they would discuss him. He needed . . .

Sleep came again without warning and the three women relaxed. It was the third time he had woken in two days and, each time, he asked the same questions. They were thankful he did not remember them helping him to urinate into the bucket, or changing the blankets when his bowels emptied in a black slick, carrying the poison out of his body. Perhaps it was the charcoal Kokchu had brought, but even his urine was darker than any of the women had seen before. There had been tension in the ger as the bucket filled. Neither Borte nor Chakahai had moved to empty it, though they glanced in its direction and challenged each other with their eyes. One was the daughter of a king and the other was first wife to Genghis himself. Neither gave way. In the end, it was Hoelun who had carried it out with bad grace, glaring at both of them.

'He seemed a little stronger that time,' Chakahai said. 'His eyes were clear.'

Hoelun nodded, wiping a hand across her face. They were all exhausted, but they left the ger only to take away waste, or to bring fresh bowls of blood and milk.

'He will survive. And those who attacked us will regret it. My son can be merciful, but he will not forgive them for this. Better for them that he died.'

The spy moved quickly through the darkness. The moon had passed behind clouds and he had only a little time. He had found his place among thousands of Chin recruits. As he had hoped, no one knew if a man was from Baotou, or Linhe or any of the other cities. He could have passed as a resident of any of them. There were only a few Mongol officers to train the city men as warriors and they saw no great honour in the task. It had been easy enough for him to wander up to a group and report for work. The Mongol officer had barely looked at him as he handed him a bow and sent him to join a dozen other archers.

When he had seen the wooden tokens changing hands in the camp, he had worried that they were proof of some controlling bureaucracy. It would not have been possible to join a Chin regiment in such a way, or even to approach without being challenged many times. Chin soldiers understood the danger of spies in their midst and had evolved techniques to baulk them.

The spy grinned to himself at the thought. There were no passwords or codes here. His only difficulty was in forcing himself to show as much ignorance as the others. He had made a mistake on the very first day when he shot an arrow straight into the centre of the target. At that time, he had no idea of the useless Chin farmers he was working with, and as they loosed after him, not one did as well. The spy had hidden his fear as the Mongol officer strolled over to him, asking in mime for him to shoot another arrow. He had been careful to shoot poorly after that and the warrior had lost interest, his face barely hiding his disgust at their skills.

Though all the guards grumbled about taking a watch in the middle of the night, the failed assassination had rippled an effect through the entire camp. The Mongol officers insisted on maintaining a perimeter against another attempt, even in the section of the camp that housed the Chin recruits. The spy had volunteered for a late watch, from midnight to dawn. It put him out on the edge of the camp and alone. Even then, leaving his position was a risk, but he had to check in with his master, or all his efforts would be wasted. He had been told to gather information, to learn anything. It was up to them what they did with what he discovered.

He ran on bare feet in the darkness, pressing away the thought of an officer checking his guards were awake. He could not control his fate and would surely hear the alarm if they found him gone. He did have a password he could call up to the wall and it would be only moments before his people threw down a rope and he was safe once more.

Something moved to his right and he collapsed to the ground, controlling his breath and lying absolutely still as he strained his senses. Since the attack on the khan, the scouts rode all night, in shifts, more alert than they had ever been before. It was a hopeless task for them to patrol the dark city, but they were fast and silent, deadly if they caught him. As he lay there, the spy wondered if there would be other assassins coming for the khan if he survived the first.

Whoever the rider was, he saw nothing. The spy heard the man clucking softly to his pony, but the sounds faded away and then he was off again like a hare. Everything depended on speed.

The city walls were black under the clouds and he depended on his memory for the right place. He counted ten watchtowers from the southern corner and ran right up to the moat. He went down on his belly to feel along the edge, smiling as he felt the roughness of the reed coracle they had tied for him. He dared not get wet and he was careful in the dark as he knelt in it, crossing the water with a few strokes. In the darkness, he did everything by feel, stepping out of the coracle and whipping the wet rope around a stone. It would not do to have the tiny boat float away.

The moat did not reach the walls that loomed over him. A wide stone walkway ran all round the city, damp and slippery with mould. On summer days, he had seen the nobles race horses along it, wagering huge sums on the first man back to the beginning. He crossed it quickly and touched the city of his birth, a brief press of a hand on the wall that meant safety and home.

Above his head, perhaps a dozen men crouched beneath the crest in silence. Though they would not speak, they understood him and, for those few moments, the tension he lived with dwindled to nothing, unnoticed except in its absence.

His hands ran quickly along the ground, searching for a pebble. Far above his head, the clouds were blown quickly across the sky. He judged the position of the moon with care. There would be a gap in the cover in only a short while and he had to be away from the walls by then. He tapped the stone on the wall, the sound loud in the night silence. He heard the slithering rope before he saw it. He began to climb its length and, at the same time, they dragged it back so that he rose at great speed.

After only moments, the spy was standing on the top of Yenking's walls. A bow team were coiling the rope, ready to drop it back. One other man stood there and the spy bowed before him.

'Speak,' the man said, gazing out over the Mongol camp.

'The khan was wounded. I could not get too close, but he still lives. The camp is full of rumours and no one knows who will take control if he dies.'

'One of his brothers,' the man replied softly and the spy checked, wondering how many others reported to this one.

'Perhaps, or the tribes will break apart under the old khans. This is a time to attack.'

His master hissed under his breath in irritation.

'I do not want to hear your conclusions, just what you have learned. If we had an army, do you think the lord regent would be content to sit inside the walls?'

'I am sorry,' the spy replied. 'They have supplies enough for years, with what they salvaged from the army's stores at Badger's

Mouth. I have found a faction who wish to try again with more catapults against the walls, but they are only a few and none of them have influence.'

'What else? Give me something to report to the lord regent,' his master said, gripping his shoulder tightly.

'If the khan dies, they will return to their mountains. All the men say that. If he lives, they could remain here for years.'

His master swore under his breath, cursing him. The spy endured it, dropping his gaze to his feet. He had not failed, he knew. His task was to report truthfully and he had done that.

'Find me one we can reach. With gold, with fear, anything. Find me someone in this camp who can make the khan take down the black tent. While it stands, we can do nothing.'

'Yes, master,' the spy replied. The man turned away from him and he was dismissed, the rope already snaking down the wall. He climbed down almost as fast as he had gone up and moments later he was tying the coracle on the far side and running lightly across the grass to his post. Someone else would take it in and the Mongols would know nothing.

It was hard to watch the clouds at the same time as remaining aware of the land around him. The spy was good at his work, or he would never have been chosen. He ran on and as the moon broke through and lit the plain, he was already down, hidden by scrub bushes and still outside the main camp. In the silver light, he thought of the men around the khan. Not Khasar, or Kachiun. Not any one of the generals. They wanted nothing more than to see Yenking broken, stone by stone. He considered Temuge for a moment. He at least was not a warrior. The spy knew very little about the Master of Trade. Clouds darkened the land once more and he darted to the outer ring of sentries. He resumed his place as if he had never left, taking up his bow and knife and stepping into a pair of rope sandals. He stiffened suddenly as he heard someone approach, standing straight like any other guard.

'Anything to report, Ma Tsin?' Tsubodai called from the darkness in the Chin language.

It took a huge effort to control his breath enough to reply. 'Nothing, general. It is a quiet night.' The spy breathed through his nose in silence then, waiting for some sign that his absence had been discovered.

Tsubodai grunted a response and strode away to check on the next man in the line. Left alone, fresh sweat broke out on the spy's skin. The Mongol had used the name he had given. Was he suspected? He thought not. No doubt the young general had checked with his officer before beginning his rounds. The other guards would be in awe of such a feat of memory, but the spy only smiled in the darkness. He knew armies too well to be impressed by the tricks of officers.

As he stood his watch and allowed his pounding heart to settle, he considered the reasoning behind the order. It could only be surrender. Why else could the lord regent want the black tent removed if not to offer tribute for Yenking? Yet if the khan heard, he would know they were close to breaking and rejoice that the siege was nearing its end. The spy shook his head in numb fear as he thought it through. The army had taken the city's stores and lost them all to the enemy at the pass. Yenking had been hungry almost from the beginning and Zhi Zhong was more desperate than anyone knew.

His pride surfaced then. He had been chosen for the task because he was as skilful as any assassin or soldier, more useful than any of them. He had time to find a man who valued gold more than his khan. There was always one. In just a few days, the spy had learned of disaffected khans whose power had been stripped from them. Perhaps one of them could be made to see the value in tribute over destruction. He considered Temuge once again, wondering why his instincts returned to the man. He nodded to himself in the dark, relishing the challenge to his skill, for the highest stakes.

When Genghis woke again on the third day, Hoelun was outside fetching food. He asked the same questions, but this time he would not lie back down. His bladder was full to the point of pain and he swung his legs out of the blankets, placing his feet firmly before trying to stand. Chakahai and Borte helped him to the central pole of the ger, wrapping his fingers around it until they were certain he would not fall. They placed the bucket where his arc of urine would reach and stood back.

He blinked at his wives and the strangeness of seeing them together.

'Are you two going to watch?' he said. For some reason he could not understand, both women smiled. 'Out,' he told them, barely holding on until they had left the ger and he could empty his bladder. He wrinkled his nose at the foul smell of the urine, far from a healthy colour.

'Kachiun!' he called suddenly. 'Come to me!' He heard an answering shout of joy and he grinned. No doubt the khans had been watching to see if he died. He gripped the wooden pole tightly as he considered how best to take a hold on the camp once more. There was so much to do.

The door slammed back on its hinges as Kachiun entered the ger over the protests of his brother's wives.

'I heard him call me,' Kachiun was saying, pushing through them as gently as he could. He fell silent as he saw his brother standing at last. Genghis wore only grubby leggings and was paler and thinner than he had ever seen him.

'Will you help me dress, Kachiun?' Genghis asked. 'My hands are too weak to do it on my own.'

Kachiun's eyes brimmed with tears and Genghis blinked at him.

'You're not weeping?' he asked in astonishment. 'By the spirits, I am surrounded by women.'

Kachiun laughed, wiping his eyes before Chakahai or Borte could see.

'It is good to see you standing, brother. I'd almost given up on you.'

Genghis snorted. He was still weak and he did not let go of the pole in case he humiliated himself and fell.

'Send someone for my armour and food. My wives have half starved me with their neglect.'

Outside, they could all hear the news passing round the camp, shouted louder and louder. He was awake. He lived. It built into a roar of sound that carried even to the walls of Yenking and interrupted Zhi Zhong in council with the ministers.

The general froze in the middle of a discussion as he heard the sound and felt a cold lump settle in his stomach.

When Genghis emerged at last from his sick-tent, the tribes gathered to cheer him, beating their bows on their armour. Kachiun stayed at his shoulder in case he stumbled, but Genghis walked stiffly to the great ger on its cart, climbing the steps without a sign of weakness.

As soon as he passed inside, he almost fell as he released the grip of his will on his weakened body. Kachiun summoned the generals, leaving his brother sitting painfully straight and alone.

As they took their places, Kachiun saw Genghis was still unnaturally pale, with sweat beading his forehead despite the cold. Genghis' neck was wrapped in fresh bandages, like a collar. Though his face was thin enough to see the shape of his skull, his eyes shone with feverish brightness as he welcomed each man.

Khasar grinned to see the hawk-like expression as he took his place by Arslan and Tsubodai. Jelme came last and Genghis gestured for him to approach. He did not think his legs would hold him if he rose, but Jelme dropped to one knee in front of him and Genghis gripped him by the shoulder.

'Kachiun said you suffered with the poison you took from me,' Genghis said.

Jelme shook his head.

'It was a small thing,' he said.

Genghis did not smile at that, though Khasar did.

'We have shared blood, you and I,' he said. 'It makes you my brother, as much as Khasar or Kachiun or Temuge.'

Jelme did not respond. The hand on his shoulder trembled and he could see how the eyes of his khan burned, sunk in the skull. Still, he lived.

'You will take a fifth of my herds, a hundred bolts of silk and a dozen fine bows and swords. I will honour you in the tribes, Jelme, for what you have done.'

Jelme bowed his head, feeling Arslan's proud gaze on him. Genghis took back his hand and looked around at the men who had gathered in his name.

'If I had died, which of you would have led the tribes?' Eyes turned to Kachiun and his brother nodded to him. Genghis smiled, wondering how many conversations he had missed while he slept like the dead. He had thought it might be Khasar, but there was no humiliation in his clear gaze. Kachiun had handled him well.

'We have been foolish not to plan for such a thing,' Genghis told them. 'Take this as a warning. Any one of us can fall and, if we do, the Chin will sense our weakness and strike. Each of you is to name a man you trust to take your place. And another to take his. You will establish a line of command down to the lowest soldier so that every man knows he is led, no matter how many die around him. We will not be caught by this again.'

He paused to let a wave of weakness wash through him. The meeting would have to be short.

'For me, I will accept your will and name Kachiun as my successor, until my sons are grown. Khasar will follow him. If we fall, Jelme will rule the tribes and strike back in our name.'

One by one, the men he mentioned bowed their heads, accepting the new order and taking comfort from it. Genghis could not know how close they had come to chaos while he lay injured. Every one of the old khans had gathered his men around him, an older loyalty taking precedence over the tumans and their generals. In a single stroke, the assassin had sent them back to the old ties of blood.

Though his body had been hurt, Genghis had not lost his understanding of the tribes. He could have named fifty men who would have welcomed freedom from his rule if he died. No one spoke as he considered the future, knowing he had to re-establish the structures of the army that had won them the Chin cities. Anything else would see them splintered and eventually destroyed.

'Kachiun and I have discussed sending you out many times. I have been reluctant before, but we need to separate the tribes now. Some of them will have forgotten the oath they gave to me and to their generals. They must be reminded.' He looked around at the faces of his generals. Not one of them was weak, but still they needed him to lead, to give them their authority. Perhaps Kachiun would have kept them together if he had died, but he could not be sure.

'When you leave here, form the tumans on the plain, in sight of the walls. Let them see our strength and then our contempt for them when you leave. Let them fear what so many will achieve when you take other cities.' He turned to Tsubodai, seeing bright excitement in his gaze.

'You will take Jochi, Tsubodai. He respects you.' Genghis thought for a moment. 'I do not want him treated like a prince. He is a prickly, arrogant boy and that must be hammered out of him. Do not fear to discipline him in my name.'

'Your will, lord,' Tsubodai replied.

'Where will you go?' Genghis asked, curious.

Tsubodai did not hesitate. He had thought of his answer many times since the battle of the Badger's Mouth.

'North, lord. Past the hunting grounds of my old tribe, the Uriankhai, and still further.'

'Very well. Kachiun?'

'I will stay here, brother. I will see this city fall,' Kachiun replied.

Genghis smiled at the grim expression on his brother's face.

'Your company is welcome. Jelme?'

'East, lord,' Jelme replied. 'I have never seen the ocean and we know nothing of those lands.'

Genghis sighed at the thought. He too had been born to the sea of grass and the idea was tempting. Yet he would see Yenking brought down first.

'Take my son, Chagatai, Jelme. He is a fine boy who may yet be khan when he has his growth.' His general nodded solemnly, still overwhelmed by the honour Genghis had paid him. Only the day before, they had all been nervous, waiting to see what would happen in the tribes when the news came that Genghis had died. Hearing him give his orders restored their confidence. As the tribes whispered, Genghis was clearly beloved of the spirits. Jelme felt his pride swell and his attempt to keep the cold face was lost in a grin.

'I want you here with me, Arslan, for when the city is starved into surrender,' Genghis continued. 'Perhaps then we will take a slow road home and enjoy a few years of riding the plains in peace.'

Khasar tutted under his breath.

'That is a sick man talking, brother. When you are well you will want to follow me south and take the Chin cities like ripe fruit, one by one. You remember the ambassador Wen Chao? I am for Kaifeng and the south. I would like to see his face when he sees me again.'

'South it is, Khasar. My son Ogedai is barely ten years old, but he will learn more with you than staying here to stare at walls. I will keep only little Tolui. He adores the Buddhist monk you brought back with Ho Sa and Temuge.'

'I will take Ho Sa as well, then,' Khasar replied. 'In fact, I could take Temuge away where he won't cause any other problems.'

Genghis considered the idea. He was not as deaf as he pretended to the complaints about his youngest brother.

'No. He is useful enough. He stands between me and a thousand questions from fools and that is worth something.' Khasar snorted at that, making his feelings clear. Genghis continued thoughtfully, tasting new ideas as if his illness had freed his mind.

'Temuge has been wanting to send out small groups to learn of other lands. Perhaps he is right that the information they bring will be useful. Waiting for them to return will at least ease the tedium of this cursed place.' He nodded to himself. 'I will choose the men and they too will leave when you ride. We will spring out in *all* directions.' He felt his energy leaving him then, as suddenly as it had come and closed his eyes against a wave of dizziness.

'Leave me now, except for Kachiun. Form your tumans and say goodbye to your wives and mistresses. They will be safe with me, unless they are very attractive.'

He smiled weakly as they rose, pleased to see them visibly more confident than when they had arrived. When Kachiun stood alone in the great ger, Genghis let the animation fall from him, looking suddenly older.

'I must rest, Kachiun, though I do not want to return to that ger that smells of sickness. Will you post a guard on the door so that I can sleep and eat in here? I do not want to be seen.'

'I will, brother. May I send Borte in to undress and feed you? She has seen the worst already.'

Genghis shrugged, his voice weak.

'You had better send both my wives. Whatever peace they have found will not last long if I favour one over the other.' Already his eyes were glazed. The effort of the single meeting had brought him to the brink of exhaustion and his hands shook as they lay loose in his lap. Kachiun turned to leave.

'How did you make Khasar accept you to succeed me?' Genghis murmured to his back.

'I told him he could be khan,' Kachiun replied. 'I think it terrified him.'

CHAPTER TWENTY-NINE

It took another six days for the generals to gather their men in squares of ten thousand, ready to ride. In essence, each tuman was a raiding party on a vast scale, something they all knew well. Yet that scale required organisation and Temuge and his cadre of maimed men were busy with supplies, remounts, weapons and their lists. For once, the officers didn't grumble at the interference. Ahead of them lay lands that no one among their people had ever seen. The wanderlust was strong in the men as they stared in the direction their generals had chosen.

Those who remained behind were less cheerful and Genghis depended upon Kachiun to keep discipline while he recovered. The tactic had proved surprisingly successful as his brother only had to glance at the khan's great ger for the arguing men to fall silent. No one wanted to disturb Genghis while he regained his strength. The simple fact of his being alive had stolen away the growing power of the old khans in the camp. Even so, the father of the Woyela was one who had demanded to see Genghis, heedless of consequences. Kachiun had visited the man in his own ger and, after that, the Woyela khan did not speak another word to anyone. His sons would ride south with Khasar and he would be left alone with only servants to lift him upright each day.

Snow had fallen the night before, but the morning was

bright and the sky an aching blue over Yenking. In vast squares on the frozen plain, warriors waited for orders, standing ready to mount while their ponies cropped the snow. Their officers were busy checking the lines and equipment though there were few there careless enough to leave something behind, not when their lives depended on it. Many of the men laughed and joked with each other. They had moved across the face of the land all their lives and the forced halt at Yenking was unnatural to them. There would be less formidable cities on their journey and each tuman travelled with catapults in a dozen carts and men trained to use them. The carts would slow them down, of course, but every man there remembered Yinchuan in the Xi Xia kingdom. They would not have to howl outside distant walls. Instead, they would break city gates and throw small kings from the heights. It was a cheerful prospect and the mood was like that of a summer feast day.

The final items that Temuge produced were tents of white, red and black for each general to use. The warriors took heart from seeing those rolled and loaded, tied down with long ropes. As nothing else, the presence of the tents showed their intention to conquer all those who stood against them. Their strength gave them the right.

In addition to the tumans, Genghis had assembled ten groups of twenty warriors to scout new lands. At first, he thought of them as raiding parties, but Temuge had persuaded him to give them cartloads of gold and looted gifts. Temuge had spoken to the officer of each group, making sure the man understood his task was to observe and learn, even to bribe. Temuge had called them diplomats, a term he had learned from Wen Chao, many years before. In that, as in so much else, Temuge had created a new thing for the tribes. He could see their value even though they themselves could not. Those men were far less cheerful than the ones who knew they would carry cities before them.

Genghis had removed the bandages on his neck, showing a thick scab over yellow and black bruising. He breathed deeply in the cold air, coughing into his hand over a wave of weakness. He was nowhere near fit, but he too wished he was riding with the others, even those who expected to talk and spy rather than raid. He shot an irritable glance at Yenking at the thought, the city squatting like a toad on the plain. No doubt the Chin emperor was on the walls at that very moment, watching this strange movement of men and horses. Genghis spat on the ground in the direction of the city. They had hidden behind soldiers at the Badger's Mouth and now they hid behind walls. He wondered how many more seasons they would hold out and his mood was bitter.

'The men are ready,' Kachiun said, riding up and dismounting. 'Temuge cannot think of another thing to irritate them, thank the spirits. Will you blow the horn yourself?'

Genghis looked at the polished scout horn hanging around his brother's neck. He shook his head.

'I will say goodbye to my sons first,' he said. 'Bring them to me.' He gestured to a large blanket on the ground, with a bottle of black airag and four cups on the cloth.

Kachiun bowed his head and leaped back into the saddle, kicking the animal into a gallop through the squares of waiting men. It was a long way to ride to reach his nephews. Every warrior there had two other horses with him in a vast herd and the morning was loud with their snorts and whinnying.

Genghis waited patiently until Kachiun returned with Jochi, Chagatai and Ogedai, his brother standing aside to let the sons approach. Kachiun watched from the corner of his eye as Genghis sat cross-legged and the three boys faced him on the rough blanket. In silence, he poured each a cup of fiery spirit and they took them formally in their right hands, cupping the elbow with their left to show that they held no weapon.

Genghis could find nothing to criticise in their bearing as he looked them over. Jochi wore new armour, a little large on his frame. Chagatai still had the set he had been given. Only Ogedai wore the traditional padded deel robe, too small at ten to warrant a man's armour, even with the amount they had captured at the Badger's Mouth. The little boy regarded the cup of airag with some misgiving, but sipped it with the others, showing no expression.

'My little wolves,' Genghis said with a smile. 'You will all be men by the time I see you again. Have you spoken to your mother?'

'We have,' Jochi replied. Genghis glanced at him and wondered at the depth of hostility in the boy's eyes. What had he ever done to deserve it?

Returning Jochi's dark gaze, Genghis spoke to them all.

'You will not be princes away from this camp. I have made that clear to your generals. There will be no special treatment for my sons. You will travel as any other warrior of the people and when you are called to fight, there will be no one to save you because of who you are. Do you understand?'

His words seemed to suck the excitement out of them, their smiles fading. One by one, they nodded. Jochi drained his cup and put it down on the blanket.

'If you are raised to be officers,' Genghis continued, 'it will only be because you have shown yourselves to be quick-thinking, skilled and brave *beyond* the men around you. No one wants to be led by a fool, even a fool who is my son.'

He paused, letting this sink in as his gaze fell on Chagatai.

'However, you *are* my sons and I expect to see the blood run true in each of you. The other warriors will be thinking of the next battle, or the last. You will be thinking of the nation you could lead. I expect you to find men you can trust and bind them to you. I expect you to push yourselves harder and more ruthlessly than anyone else ever could. When you are frightened, hide it. No one else will know and whatever causes it will pass. How you held yourself will be remembered.'

There was so much to tell them. It was gratifying to have even Jochi hang on every word, but who else could tell them how to rule if not their own father? This was his last duty to the boys before they became men.

'When you are tired, never speak of it and others will think you are made of iron. Do not allow another warrior to mock you, even in jest. It is something men do to see who has the strength to stand against them. Show them you will not be cowed and if it means you must fight, well, that is what you must do.'

'What if it is an officer who mocks us?' Jochi said softly.

Genghis looked sharply at him.

'I have seen men try to deflect such things with a smile, or dipping their head, or even capering to make the others laugh all the harder. If you do that, you will never command. Take the orders you are given, but keep your dignity.' He thought for a moment.

'From this day, you are no longer children. You too, Ogedai. If you have to fight, even if it is a friend, put him down as fast and hard as you possibly can. Kill if you have to, or spare him – but beware putting any man in your debt. Of all things, that causes resentment. Any warrior who raises his fist to you must know he is gambling with his life and that he *will* lose. If you cannot win at first, take revenge if it is the last thing you do. You are travelling with men who respect only strength greater than theirs, men harder than themselves. Above everything else, they respect success. Remember it.'

His hard gaze swept across them and Ogedai shivered, feeling the cold of the words. Genghis did not smile to see it as he went on.

'Never allow yourself to become soft, or one day there will be a man who will take everything away from you. Listen to those who know more than you and be the last in every conversation to speak, until they wait on you to show them the way. And beware of weak men who come to you because of your name. Choose those who follow you as carefully as wives. If I have only one skill that has brought me to rule our people, it is that. I can see the difference between a blustering warrior and a man like Tsubodai, or Jelme, or Khasar.'

The ghost of a sneer touched Jochi's mouth before he looked away and Genghis refused to allow his irritation to show.

'One more thing before you go. Be wary of spilling your seed.' Jochi flushed then and Chagatai's mouth dropped open. Only Ogedai looked confused. Genghis went on.

'Boys who spend each night playing with their parts become weak, obsessed with the needs of their body. Keep your hands away and treat desire as any other weakness. Abstinence will make you strong. You will have wives and mistresses in time.'

As the three boys sat there in embarrassed silence, he untied his sword and scabbard. He had not planned it, but it seemed right and he wanted to do something they would remember.

'Take it, Chagatai,' he said. He slapped the scabbard into his son's hands. Chagatai almost fumbled it in amazed pleasure. Genghis watched as the boy held the wolf's-head hilt up to catch the sun, then slowly drew the blade his father had carried for all his young life. The eyes of the others were on the shining metal, bright with envy.

'My father Yesugei wore it on the day he died,' Genghis said softly. '*His* father had it made at a time when the Wolves were the enemy of every other tribe. It has taken lives and seen the birth of a nation. Be sure you do not dishonour it.'

Chagatai bowed where he sat, overcome.

'I will not, lord,' he replied.

Genghis did not look at Jochi's white face.

'Now go. When you return to your generals, I will sound the horn. We will see each other again when you are men and we can meet as equals.'

'I look forward to that day, father,' Jochi said suddenly. Genghis raised his pale gaze to him, but said nothing. The boys did not speak to each other as they galloped away on the hard ground and they did not look back.

When Genghis was once again alone with Kachiun, he felt his brother's stare.

'Why did you not give the blade to Jochi?' Kachiun asked.

'To a Tartar bastard?' Genghis snapped. 'I see his father looking back at me whenever we meet.'

Kachiun shook his head, saddened that Genghis could be so blind in this one thing and see so far in all the rest.

'We are a strange family, brother,' he said. 'If you leave us alone, we grow weak and soft. If you challenge us, make us hate, we grow strong enough to strike back.' Genghis looked at him questioningly and Kachiun sighed.

'If you truly wanted to weaken Jochi, you should have given *him* the sword,' Kachiun said. 'Now he will think of you as an enemy and he *will* make himself iron, just as you did. Is that what you intended?'

Genghis blinked, astonished at the idea. Kachiun saw things with painful clarity and he could not find a response.

Kachiun cleared his throat.

'It was interesting advice, brother,' he said, 'especially the bit about spilling their seed.' Genghis ignored him, watching the distant figures rejoin the squares of warriors.

'It didn't seem to do Khasar any harm,' Kachiun said. Genghis chuckled, holding out his hand for Kachiun's horn. He rose to his feet then and blew a long deep note across the plain. Before it had died away, the tumans rumbled into movement, his people riding to conquer. He ached to be with them, but he would yet see Yenking fall.

Temuge groaned as his servant massaged the cares of the day from his shoulders. The Chin people seemed to have an idea of civilisation that no one among the tribes could match. He smiled sleepily at the thought of a warrior being asked to work the muscles of his calves with oil. The man would either take it as an insult, or pound them like a woollen fleece.

At first, he had regretted the loss of his first servant. The man had rarely spoken and indeed knew nothing of the Mongol tongue. Yet he had introduced Temuge to a structured day, so that events seemed to flow around him without tension. Temuge had become accustomed to waking after dawn and bathing. His servant would then dress him and prepare a light break-fast. He would read the reports of his men until late morning, then begin the proper business of the day. Losing such a man to an assassin's blade had seemed a tragedy at first.

Temuge sighed in pleasure as the new servant worked at a muscle, his thumbs digging deeply. Perhaps it was not such a loss, after all. Old Sen had known nothing of oils and massage and, though his presence had been relaxing, the new man talked whenever Temuge allowed him to speak, explaining any aspect of Chin society that caught Temuge's attention.

'That is very good, Ma Tsin,' he murmured. 'The tenderness is almost gone.'

'My master is welcome,' the spy replied. He did not enjoy rubbing the man's back, but he had once spent almost a year as a brothel guard and he knew how the girls relaxed their customers.

'I saw the armies move away this morning, master,' he said lightly. 'I have never seen so many horses and men in one place.'

Temuge grunted.

'It makes my life simpler to have them far away. I have had enough of their complaints and bickering. I think my brother has as well.'

'They will bring back gold for the khan, I do not doubt it,' the spy went on. He began to pummel the heavy muscles of Temuge's back, before finding another knot to work with stiff fingers.

'We do not need more of it,' Temuge muttered. 'There are already carts of coins and only the Chin recruits seem interested.'

The spy paused for a moment. This was one aspect of the Mongol mind that confused him. Temuge was already relaxed, but he continued to work, trying to understand.

'It is true then that you do not seek wealth?' he asked. 'I have heard it said.'

'What would we do with it? My brother has collected gold and silver because there are some who look greedily on such hoards. But what use is it? Real wealth is not found in soft metals.'

'You could buy horses with it though, weapons, even land,' the spy persisted. Under his hands, he felt Temuge shrug.

'From whom? If a pile of coins will make another man give us his horses, we take them from him. If he has land, it is ours anyway, to ride as we please.'

The spy blinked in irritation. Temuge had no reason to lie to him, but bribery was not going to be easy if he spoke the truth. He tried again, suspecting it was hopeless.

'In Chin cities, gold can buy huge houses by a lake, delicate foods, even thousands of servants.' He struggled for more examples. For one who had been born into a society that used coins, it was difficult to explain something so obvious. 'It can even buy influence and favours from powerful men, lord. Rare pieces of art, perhaps as gifts for your wives. It makes all things possible.'

'I understand,' Temuge replied irritably. 'Now be silent.'

The spy almost gave up. The khan's brother could not grasp the concept. In truth, it made him realise the artificial nature of his own world. Gold *was* too soft for any real use. How had it ever been seen as valuable?

'What if you wanted a man's horse in the tribes, master? Let us say it is a horse better than all the others.'

'If you value your hands, you will not speak again,' Temuge snapped. The spy worked in silence for a time and Temuge sighed. 'I would give him five horses of lesser breed, or two captured slaves, or six bows, or a sword made by a skilled man, whatever he wanted depending on my need.' Temuge chuckled, drifting towards sleep. 'If I told him I had a bag of valuable metal that would buy him *another* horse, he would tell me to try it on some other fool.'

Temuge sat up then. The evening sky was clear and he yawned. It had been a busy day, arranging the departure of so many.

'I think I will take a few drops of my medicine tonight, Ma Tsin, to help me sleep.'

The spy helped Temuge into a silk robe. The man's pretensions amused him, but he could not escape the frustration he felt. The power of the small khans had been strangled when Genghis gave the order for the tumans to form. It was no loss. None of them had real influence in the camp. The spy had cut his losses and worked quickly to replace the servant killed by the assassin. Moving at such a speed brought many dangers and he felt the strain grow daily. He still thought Temuge a vain and shallow man, but he had not found a lever that might tempt him into a betrayal, nor any better candidate. The black tent had to come down, but Genghis could not know the agony of Yenking. The spy considered the lord regent had set him a near impossible task.

Lost in his own thoughts, the spy prepared the draught of hot airag and added a spoonful of the shaman's black paste, scraping it out of a pot. When Temuge wasn't looking, he sniffed at it, wondering if it was an opiate. The nobles smoked opium in the cities and seemed attached to their pipes, much as Temuge was to the drink.

'We are almost at the end of the supply, master,' he said.

Temuge sighed.

'Then I will have to ask for more from the shaman.'

'I will go to him, master. You should not be troubled with small things.'

'That is true,' Temuge replied, pleased. He accepted the cup and sipped at it, closing his eyes in pleasure. 'Go to him, but tell him nothing of what you do for me. Kokchu is not a pleasant man. Make sure you do not tell him anything you have seen and heard in this ger.'

'It would be easier if you could buy the paste from him with gold coins, master,' the spy said.

Temuge replied without opening his eyes.

'Kokchu does not want your gold. I think he cares only for power.' He drained the cup, grimacing at the bitter dregs, but still tipping it back to catch every drop. The thought of the empty pot troubled him strangely. He would need it again in the morning.

'See him tonight, Ma Tsin. If you can, try to discover how he makes the paste, so that you can prepare it yourself. I have asked him before, but he hides it from me. I think he enjoys the fact that he has some hold on me still. If you can find the secret, I will not forget.'

'Your will, master,' the spy replied. He was due back at the wall that night, to report. There was time to see the shaman before he went. Anything and everything could be useful and, as things stood, he had achieved little in the camp, while Yenking starved.

CHAPTER THIRTY

That summer was the most peaceful Genghis could remember. If it had not been for the looming presence of the city that filled the eye every day, it would have been a restful time. The khan's attempts to rebuild his fitness were hampered by a persistent cough that left him gasping and only worsened as the year turned cold. Kokchu had become a regular visitor to his ger, bringing syrups of honey and herbs so bitter that Genghis could barely swallow them. They brought only temporary relief and Genghis lost weight alarmingly, so that his bones showed white under skin that looked sallow and ill.

Throughout the cold months, Yenking sat on the edge of his vision, unchanged and solid, mocking his presence in that land. It was almost a year since he had won the battle at the Badger's Mouth. There were times when he would have given anything to be able to travel home and regain his strength in the clean hills and streams.

In the grip of the lethargy that affected them all, Genghis barely looked up when Kachiun darkened the door of the great ger. When he saw his brother's expression, he forced himself upright.

'You're bursting with news, Kachiun. Tell me it's something that matters.'

'I think so,' Kachiun replied. 'The scouts from the south say there is a relief column heading this way. As many as fifty thousand soldiers and a huge herd of prime cattle.'

'Khasar missed them then,' Genghis replied, his mood lifting. 'Or they came from somewhere off his path.' Both men knew armies could pass each other only a valley apart. The land was vast beyond imagining, colouring the dreams of men forced to stay in one place for longer than they ever had before.

Kachiun was relieved to see a spark of the old pleasure in Genghis. His older brother had been weakened by the poison running in his blood, anyone could see that. Even as he tried to reply, his wind was stolen by a fit of coughing that left him red-faced and clinging to the central spar of the ger.

'The city will be desperate for them to get through,' Kachiun said over the hacking sound. 'I wonder if we will regret sending half our men away?'

Genghis shook his head mutely before pulling in a clean breath at last. He strode past Kachiun to the door and spat a wad of phlegm on the ground, wincing as he tried to clear his throat.

'See this,' he said hoarsely, picking up a Chin crossbow they had captured at the Badger's Mouth. Kachiun followed his brother's gaze to a straw target three hundred yards away along a path. Genghis loosed arrows for hours every day to restore his strength and he had been fascinated by the mechanisms of the Chin weapons. As Kachiun watched, he took careful aim and pulled the carved trigger, sending a black bolt whipping through the air. It fell short and Kachiun smiled, understanding immediately. Without a word, he picked up one of his brother's bows and selected an arrow from a quiver, drawing it back to his ear before sending it unerringly into the centre of the straw shield.

The blood had faded from Genghis' cheeks and he nodded to his brother.

'They will be slow with supplies for the city. Take your men and ride up and down the lines, never close enough for them to reach you. Thin them a little and I will do the rest when they arrive.'

As Kachiun galloped through the camp, word from the scouts travelled even faster. Every warrior there was ready in just the few moments it took to race to his pony and grab his weapons from the walls of the gers.

Kachiun shouted orders to his senior officers and they spread the word, halting many men in their tracks. The new form of warfare was still only a veneer over the raiding bands, but the command structure was solid enough for groups of ten to gather and receive their instructions. Many had to return to their gers for another quiver of fifty arrows on Kachiun's order before racing to form up in the great square of ten thousand. Kachiun himself marked the furthest line by riding his pony up and down, a long war banner of gold silk streaming out behind him.

He conferred once more with the scouts who had sighted the relief column and passed the fluttering standard to a messenger in the front rank, a boy of no more than twelve. Kachiun looked along the ranks as they formed and was satisfied. Each man carried two heavy quivers looped over his shoulders. They needed no supplies for a lightning raid and only bows and swords slapped on their thighs and saddles.

'If we let them through to the city,' he bellowed, turning his horse in place, 'it will take another year to see it fall. Stop them and their mounts and weapons are yours, after the khan's tithe.'

Those who could hear roared their appreciation of this and Kachiun raised his right arm and dropped it, signalling the advance. The lines moved forward in perfect formation, the product of months of training on the plain in front of the city when there were no enemies to fight. Officers shouted orders out of habit but, in fact, there were no flaws in the lines. They had at last thrown reins on their enthusiasm for war, even after so long a wait.

The column had been forty miles south of Yenking when the scouts crossed its path. In the time it had taken Kachiun to return, the slow-moving mass of men and animals had shortened the distance to only twelve. Knowing they had been seen, they had pushed the herds as fast as possible, but there was only so much they could do before they saw the dust cloud of approaching warriors.

The senior officer, Sung Li Sen, hissed under his breath as he saw the enemy for the first time. He had brought almost fifty thousand warriors north and east from Kaifeng to relieve the emperor's city. The column was a massive, ponderous thing, with carts and bullocks stretching back along the road. He squinted at the squares of cavalry guarding his flanks and nodded to their commander over the heads of the men. This was a battle long in coming.

'First position!' he snapped, his command repeated up and down the trudging lines. The orders he had been given were perfectly clear. He would not stop until he reached Yenking. If the enemy engaged him, he was to fight a running battle all the way to the city and avoid being bogged down in skirmishes. He frowned at the thought. He would have preferred a blanket order to crush the tribesmen and worry about resupplying Yenking when they were bones.

All along the vast snake of men, the soldiers raised long pikes like bristles. Crossbows were cocked by the thousand and Sung Li Sen nodded to himself. He saw the lines of Mongol riders

421

more clearly now and he braced himself in the saddle, aware that his men looked to him for an example of courage. Few of them had ever travelled this far north and all they knew of these wild tribesmen lay in the emperor's demand for support from his southern cities. Sung Li Sen felt his curiosity swell as the riders split along an invisible line, as if his own column was a spearhead they did not dare approach. He saw that they would pass on either side of him and smiled tightly. It suited his orders that they do so. The road lay open to Yenking and he would not stop.

Kachiun held back the gallop to the last possible moment before leaning into the wind and yelling for his mount to stretch its gait. He loved the thunder that sounded around him as he stood in the stirrups. Over such a distance, they seemed to close slowly, then everything was rushing towards him. His heart pounded as he reached the Chin column and sent his first arrow snapping through the air. He saw the Chin bolts streak out, falling uselessly into the grass. To ride along that endless line was to be untouchable and Kachiun laughed aloud at the joy of it, sending shaft after shaft. He hardly had to aim with five thousand men on either side of the column, pinching it between them in whipping strikes.

The Chin cavalry hardly managed to reach full gallop before they were annihilated to a man, smashed from their mounts. Kachiun grinned when he saw not one of the enemy horses had been killed. His men were being careful, especially now they had seen how few riders the Chin had brought to the field.

When the cavalry were broken, Kachiun chose his targets with precision, aiming at any officer he could see. Within sixty heartbeats, his tuman loosed a hundred thousand shafts at the column. Despite the lacquered Chin armour, thousands fell in their tracks, with those behind stumbling over them.

Kachiun could hear the cattle lowing in distress and panic and, to his pleasure, he saw the herd stampede, crushing more than a hundred of the Chin soldiers and breaking a hole in the column before they lumbered off into the distance. He had reached the end of the tail and swung in a little further, ready to double back. Crossbow bolts rattled off his chest, near spent. After the months of tedious training, it was simply wonderful to be riding against an enemy and, better, one who could not touch them but only die. He wished he'd known to bring more quivers. His grasping fingers found the first one empty and began his last fifty shafts, taking a Chin bannerman off his feet with the first.

Kachiun blinked wind-tears out of his eyes. He had thinned the column enough to see through it to the second five thousand on the eastern flank. They too were riding with impunity, striking at will. Another sixty heartbeats and a hundred thousand arrows followed the rest. The Chin soldiers could not hide and the neat column began to disintegrate. Men who trudged near carts threw themselves under them for protection while their colleagues died around them. A great wail of fear went up from the pikemen and there were no officers left alive to rally them or keep them on the road to Yenking.

Kachiun began his second run, this time too far from the column to waste a shot. The lines reversed with the ease that comes of ceaseless hours of drill and fresh quivers were emptied quickly. Kachiun galloped flat out along the lines, glancing back at the trail of dead they left behind as the column pushed onwards through the storm. The soldiers had kept their discipline, though the pace was slowing. Other men bawled orders in the place of dead officers, knowing that to panic was to invite complete destruction.

423

Kachiun grunted to himself in grudging admiration. He had seen many forces who would have broken before this. He reached the head of the column and swung back to the inside line once more, feeling his shoulders burn as he bent the bow again at full speed. He imagined his brother's face when the straggling remnants reached the welcome they had prepared at Yenking. Kachiun barked a laugh at the thought, his fingers growing sore as he scrabbled in the fast-emptying quiver. Ten more at most, but the column seemed to shudder as panic spread again through the ranks. The crossbow bolts had not stopped and Kachiun had to make a decision. He could feel his men looking to him for the order that would have them draw swords and carve the column to pieces. They were all running low on shafts and when the last massed volley was shot, their work was over. They knew the orders as well as he did, but still they watched him, hoping.

Kachiun tensed his jaw. Yenking was far away and Genghis would surely forgive him if he finished the column on his own. He could feel how close they were to breaking. Everything he had learned over the years of war made it something he could almost taste.

He grimaced, chewing his own cheek as the moment swelled around him. At last, he shook his head and drew a wide circle in the air with his fist. Every officer in sight repeated the gesture and the lines fell back from the shattered remnants of the column.

Kachiun watched his men form up in panting lines, exhilarated. Those who still had arrows loosed them with enormous care, taking men as they pleased. Kachiun could see their frustration as they reined in behind the column and watched it move away from them. Many of them patted the necks of their mounts and stared at their officers, furious at being called back from the killing. It made no sense and Kachiun had to be deaf to the shouts of complaint from all quarters.

As the column put distance between them, many of the soldiers looked back in terror, convinced they were going to be attacked from behind. Kachiun let a gap open, then walked his pony forward. He ordered the right and left wings to move up, so that they cupped the rear of the column and herded it onwards to Yenking.

Behind them, they left a trail of dead men over more than a mile, with fluttering pennants and pikes in piles. Kachiun sent a hundred warriors to loot the bodies and dispatch wounded men, but his gaze didn't leave the column as it made its way to his waiting brother.

It took until late afternoon for the battered column to sight the city it had come to relieve. By that point, the Chin soldiers who had survived the slaughter walked with their heads down, their spirits broken after so long with death at their backs. When they saw another ten thousand barring their way, fresh men with lances and bows, they sent up a moan of utter misery. The column shuddered again as they hesitated, knowing they could not fight their way through. Without a signal, they halted at last and Kachiun raised a fist to stop his men riding too close. In the gathering gloom, he waited for his brother to approach. He was pleased he had not denied Genghis this moment when he saw him ride apart from the tuman of warriors and come cantering across the grass.

The dull-eyed Chin soldiers watched him, panting and exhausted at the pace they had been forced to set. The carts of goods had drifted back through the hurrying ranks, left behind while Kachiun peeled men off to investigate the contents.

In a deliberate show, Genghis judged the mood of the column and rode right along the edge of it. Kachiun heard his men murmur in pleasure at the khan's display of courage. Perhaps there was still a risk that crossbows might take him from the saddle, but Genghis did not look at the Chin soldiers as he passed, seemingly unaware of the thousands of men turning to watch him from under lowered brows.

'You have not left me with many, brother,' Genghis said. Kachiun could see he was pale and sweating from the ride. On impulse, Kachiun dismounted and touched his head to his brother's foot.

'I wish you could have been there to see the faces of their officers,' Kachiun replied. 'We are truly wolves in a world of sheep, brother.'

Genghis nodded, his weariness preventing him from sharing Kachiun's light spirits.

'I see no supplies here,' he said.

'They have left them all behind, including as fine a herd of oxen as you will ever see.'

Genghis perked up at that.

'I have not eaten beef in a long time. We will roast them before Yenking and waft the smell of the meat over the walls. You have done well, brother. Shall we finish them?' Both men looked over the grim column of soldiers, now no more than half the original size.

Kachiun shrugged. 'They are too many mouths to feed, unless you will give them the supplies they brought to this place. Let me try to disarm them first, or they could still fight.'

'You think they will surrender?' Genghis asked. His eyes sparkled at his brother's suggestion, touched by Kachiun's evident pride. Of all things, the tribes revered a general who could win with wits rather than force.

Kachiun shrugged.

'Let us see.'

He summoned a dozen men who could speak the Chin language and sent them out to ride along the column as close as Genghis had himself, offering peace terms if they gave up their weapons. No doubt it helped that the men were near exhaustion after a day of being chased by an enemy who struck with shocking power while remaining untouched. Their morale had been left on the march and Genghis smiled as he heard the crash of weapons being thrown down.

It was almost dark before the pikes, crossbows and swords had been removed from the silent ranks. Genghis had sent fresh quivers by the thousand back to Kachiun and the Mongols waited in calm anticipation as the sun made the plains gold.

Before the last light faded, a horn rang across the plain and twenty thousand bows bent. The Chin soldiers screeched in horror at the betrayal, the sound choked off as the volleys struck and struck and struck until it was too dark to see.

As the moon rose, hundreds of oxen were killed and roasted on the plain and, on the walls of the city, Zhi Zhong tasted his own bitter saliva, filled with a grinding despair. In Yenking, they were eating the dead.

When the feast was at its height, the spy saw the shaman rise and stagger drunkenly through the gers. He rose like a shadow to follow him, leaving Temuge to sleep off the haunch of bloody beef he had devoured. The warriors were chanting and dancing around the fires and the drummer boys pounded out a fierce rhythm that hid the small noise of his steps. The spy kept the older man in sight as Kokchu paused to urinate on the path, fumbling blearily at himself and cursing in the darkness as he splashed his feet. The spy lost sight of his quarry as the man slipped into deep darkness between two carts. He did not hurry, guessing the man was going back to the Chin girl he kept as a slave in his home. As he walked, he thought what he might say to the shaman. On his last trip to the walls, he heard the lord regent had begun a death lottery in the city, where a member of each peasant family was forced to reach into a clay pot as deep as his arm. Those who pulled out a white tile were butchered to feed the rest. Every day brought scenes of unimaginable pain and grief.

Lost in thought, he saw a shadow twitch as he came round the edge of a ger and let out a cry of shock and pain as he was knocked back into the side of it. The wicker braces creaked against his back and he could feel a cold blade at his throat, stopping his breath.

When Kokchu spoke, his voice was low and firm, with no sign of the extravagant drunkenness the spy had witnessed before.

'You have been watching me all night, slave. And now you follow me home. Hsst!' Kokchu made the sound as the spy raised his hands automatically in fear.

'If you move, I will cut your throat,' Kokchu whispered into his ear. 'Be like a statue, slave, while I search you.' The spy did as he was told, enduring the bony hands as they ran over his body. The shaman could not reach right down to his ankles and still hold the blade to his neck. He did find a small blade and threw it away into the darkness without looking. The one in the boot went undetected and the spy let out a slow breath of relief.

They stood in complete darkness between the gers, hidden from the moon and the feasting warriors.

'Why would a slave follow me, I wonder? You come to me for your master's paste and your little darting eyes are everywhere, your questions so innocent. Are you a spy for Temuge, or another assassin? If you are, you are a poor choice.'

The spy did not reply, though he set his jaw at the sting to his pride. He knew he had barely glanced at the shaman all evening and he could only wonder what sort of mind produced such constant suspicion. He felt the knife press more firmly into his neck and blurted out the first words that came to his lips.

'If you kill me, you will learn nothing,' he said.

Kokchu remained silent for an age, digesting this. The spy swivelled his eyes in his head to see the man's expression and found curiosity mingling with spite.

'What could there be to learn, slave?' Kokchu asked.

'Nothing you would want overheard,' the spy replied. He ignored his usual caution, knowing his life hung in the moment. Kokchu was quite capable of killing him just to deprive Temuge of a supporter. 'Let me speak and you will not regret it.'

He felt a shove and stumbled forward. Even in the dark, he sensed Kokchu behind him. The spy considered ways of disarming the man without killing him, but forced himself to relax. He put his hands on his head and let Kokchu walk him forward to his ger.

It took courage to duck low at the doorway with the shaman holding a blade at his back, but the spy had gone too far to pass off his words as a bad joke even then. He knew the offer he had to make. The lord regent himself had met him on the wall on his last report. He took a deep breath and pushed the small door open.

A girl of great beauty knelt on the floor by the open door. A lamp lit her features as she looked up at him and the spy felt his chest tighten that such a delicate girl should be made to wait on the shaman like a dog. He hid his anger as Kokchu motioned for her to leave them alone. She exchanged one final glance with her countryman as she turned in the door and Kokchu chuckled.

'I think she likes you, slave. I am growing tired of her. Perhaps I will give her to your Chin officers. You could have a turn when they are finished teaching her humility.' The spy ignored the words, taking a seat on a low bed, so that his hands dropped naturally near his ankles. If the meeting went sour, he could still kill the shaman and be back at the walls before anyone else found out. That thought gave him a confidence that Kokchu sensed, frowning.

'We are alone, slave. I do not need you, or anything you have to say to me. Speak quickly, or I will give you to the dogs tomorrow morning.'

The spy took a long, slow breath, preparing words that could mean death by torture before the sun rose. He had not chosen the moment. The bodies in Yenking had done that. Now, he was either right about the shaman, or dead.

He straightened his back and rested one hand on his knee, looking sternly up at Kokchu with a faint expression of disapproval. The shaman glowered at the change in the man, going from frightened slave to a dignified warrior in just a moment.

'I am a man of Yenking,' the spy said softly. 'A man of the emperor.'

Kokchu's eyes widened. The spy nodded to him.

'Now my life is truly in your hands.' A sudden instinct made him take the dagger from his boot and place it on the floor at his feet. Kokchu nodded at the act of faith, but did not lower his own blade.

'The emperor must be desperate, or mad with hunger,' Kokchu said softly.

'The emperor is a seven-year-old boy. The general your khan defeated now runs the city.'

'He sent you here? Why?' Kokchu asked him, genuinely curious. Before the man could speak, Kokchu answered his own question. 'Because the assassin failed. Because he wants the tribes to leave before the people starve to death, or burn the city down in riots.'

'It is as you say,' the spy confirmed. 'Even if the general wanted to pay tribute for the city, the black tent is up before the walls. What choice does he have but to hold out for another two years, or even longer?' No trace of the desperate lie showed on the spy's face. Yenking would fall in another month, three at the most.

At last, Kokchu put away his knife. The spy did not know how to read the action. The lord regent had thrown him to the wolves to make the offer. All he had was an instinct that Kokchu was in the tribes but not of them, a man apart. Such men were ripe for picking, but he knew his life could still be measured in heartbeats. A single spasm of loyalty from the shaman, a single shout could end it all. Genghis would know he had broken Yenking and the jewel of the empire would be lost for ever. The spy felt sweat break out on his skin despite the frozen air. He went on before Kokchu could reply.

'If they have the white tent raised once more, my emperor will pay a tribute to make a hundred kings weep. Silk enough to line the roads back to your homeland, gems, slaves, written works of great magic, science and medicine, ivory, iron, timber . . .' He had seen Kokchu's eyes flicker at the mention of magic, but did not falter in his list. '. . . paper, jade, thousands upon thousands of carts laden with wealth. Enough to found an empire if the khan desires it. Enough to build cities of his own.'

'All of which he would have anyway when the city falls,' Kokchu murmured.

The spy shook his head firmly.

'At the last, when defeat is inevitable, the city will be fired from within. Know that I speak truth when I say your khan will have only ashes and two more years of waiting on this plain.' He paused, trying and failing to see how his words were being received. Kokchu stood like a statue, barely breathing as he listened.

'Why have you not made this offer to the khan himself?' Kokchu asked.

Ma Tsin shook his head, suddenly weary.

'We are not children, shaman, you and I. Let me speak plainly. Genghis has raised his black tent and all his men know that it means death. It would cost him pride to accept the emperor's tribute and, from what I have seen, he would let Yenking burn first. But if another man, one he trusted, could take the news to him in private? He could suggest a show of mercy, perhaps, for those innocents in the city who suffer.'

To his astonishment, Kokchu barked laughter at the idea.

'Mercy? Genghis would see it as weakness. You will never meet a man who understands fear in war as well as the khan I follow. You could not tempt him with such a thing.'

Despite himself, the spy felt anger surface at the shaman's mocking tone. 'Then tell me how he can be turned from Yenking, or kill me here for your dogs. I have told you all I know.'

'I *could* turn him,' Kokchu said softly. 'I have shown him what I can do.'

'You are feared in the camp,' the spy replied quickly, grabbing his bony arm. 'Are you the one I need?'

'I am,' Kokchu replied. His face twisted at the other man's relief. 'All that remains is for you to name the price for my help in this small thing. I wonder, how much is your city worth to your emperor? What price should I put on his life?'

'Anything you want will be part of the tribute paid to the khan,' the spy replied. He dared not believe the man was toying with him. What choice did he have but to follow where the shaman led?

Kokchu was silent for a time then, weighing up the man who sat so stiffly erect on the bed.

'There is real magic in the world, slave. I have felt it and used it. If your people know anything of the art, your boy emperor will have it in his precious city,' he said at last. 'A man cannot learn enough in a hundred lifetimes. I want to know every secret your people have found.'

432

'There are many secrets, shaman: from making paper and silk to the powder that burns, the compass, oil that will not go out. What do you wish to know?'

Kokchu snorted.

'Do not bargain with me. I want them all. Do you have men who work these arts in the cities?'

The spy nodded.

'Priests and doctors of many orders.'

'Have them bind their secrets for me, as a gift between colleagues. Tell them to leave nothing out or I will tell my khan a bloody vision and he will come back to burn your lands all the way to the sea. Do you understand?'

The spy freed his tongue and answered, weak with relief. He could hear raised voices somewhere nearby and he rushed along, desperate to finish.

'I will make it so,' he whispered. 'When the white tent is raised, the emperor will surrender.' He thought for a moment, then spoke again. The voices outside were louder.

'If there is betrayal, shaman, everything you want to know will go up in flames. There is enough of the powder that burns in the city to tear the stones to dust.'

'A brave threat,' Kokchu replied, sneering. 'I wonder if your people would truly have the will to do such a thing. I have heard you, slave. You have done your work. Now, go back to your city and wait for the white tent with your emperor. It will come in time.'

The spy wanted to urge the shaman on, to make him understand that he should move quickly. Caution stopped his mouth with the thought that it would only weaken his position. The shaman simply did not care that the people of the city were dying every day.

'What *is* happening out there?' Kokchu snapped, disturbed by the shouts and calls outside the ger. He gestured for the spy to leave and followed him out into the moonlight. Everyone around them was staring at the city and both men turned to gaze at the walls.

The young women walked slowly up the stone steps, wearing white, the colour of death. They were skeletally thin and barefoot, but they did not shiver. The cold did not seem to touch them at all. The soldiers on the walls fell back in superstitious dread and no one barred their path. By the thousand, they gathered above the city. By the ten thousand. Even the wind fell to a whisper across Yenking and the silence was perfect.

The walkway around the city was frozen white and hard, fifty feet below where they stood. Almost as one, the young women of Yenking stepped to the very edge. Some held hands, others stood alone, gazing out into the darkness. For all the miles of wall, they stood there, looking down into the moonlight.

The spy caught his breath, whispering a prayer he had not remembered for years, from before he had forgotten his true name. His heart broke for his people and his city.

All along the walls, figures in white had climbed like a line of ghosts. The Mongol warriors saw they were women and called out to them raucously, laughing and jeering at the distant figures. The spy shook his head to shut out the coarse sounds, tears sparkling in his eyes. Many of the girls held hands as they stared down at the enemy who had ridden right to the gates of the emperor's city.

As the spy watched in frozen grief, they stepped off. The watching warriors fell silent in awe. From a distance, they dropped like white petals and even Kokchu shook his head, astonished. Thousands more took their place on the wall and stepped to their deaths without a cry, their bodies breaking on the hard stones below.

'If there is betrayal, the city and everything in it will be destroyed in fire,' the spy whispered to the shaman, his voice thick with sorrow.

Kokchu no longer doubted it.

CHAPTER THIRTY-ONE

As the winter deepened, children were born in the gers, many of them fathered by men away with the generals or one of the diplomatic groups Temuge had sent out. Fresh food was plentiful after the capture of the supply column and the vast camp enjoyed a period of peace and prosperity they had never known before. Kachiun kept the warriors fit with constant training on the plain around Yenking, but it was a false peace and there were few men there who did not turn their eyes to the city many times each day, waiting.

Genghis suffered in the cold for the first time in his life. He had little appetite, but he had gained a layer of fat by forcing himself to eat beef and rice. Though he lost some of his gauntness, his cough remained, stealing his wind and infuriating him. For a man who had never known sickness, it was immensely frustrating to have his own body betray him. Of all the men in the camp, he stared most often at the city, willing it to fall.

It was in the middle of a night filled with swirling snow that Kokchu came to him. For some reason, the coughing was worse at night and Genghis had become used to the shaman visiting him before dawn with a hot drink. With the gers as close as they were, his hacking grunts could be heard by all those around him.

Genghis sat up when he heard Kokchu challenged by his guards. There would be no repeat of the assassination attempt, with six good men around the great ger in shifts each night. He stared into the gloom as Kokchu entered and lit a lamp swinging from the roof. Genghis could not speak to him for a moment. Spasms racked his chest until he was red in the face. It passed, as always, leaving him gasping for breath.

'You are welcome in my home, Kokchu,' he whispered hoarsely. 'What new herbs will you try tonight?'

It may have been his imagination, but the shaman seemed strangely nervous. Kokchu's forehead glistened with sweat and Genghis wondered if he too was falling ill.

'Nothing I have will make you better, lord. I have tried everything I know,' he said. 'I have wondered if there is something else that prevents you from becoming well again.'

'Something else?' Genghis asked. His throat tickled infuriatingly and he swallowed hard against it, the action now part of his usual manner, so that he gulped constantly.

'The emperor has sent assassins, lord. Perhaps he has other ways to attack you, ways that cannot be seen and killed.'

Genghis considered this, interested.

'You think he has magic workers in his city? If the best they can do is a cough, I will not fear them.'

Kokchu shook his head.

'A curse can kill you, lord. I should have considered it before this.'

Genghis sat back on his bed wearily.

'What do you have in mind?'

Kokchu gestured for his khan to stand and looked away rather than see Genghis struggle up.

'If you will come to my ger, lord, I will summon the spirits and see if you are marked by some dark work of the city.'

Genghis narrowed his eyes, but he nodded.

437

'Very well. Send one of my guards for Temuge to join us.'

'That is not necessary, lord. Your brother is not as accomplished in these matters . . .'

Genghis coughed, a sound which he turned into a furious growl of anger at his failing body.

'Do as I tell you, shaman, or get out,' he said. Kokchu tightened his mouth and bowed briefly.

Genghis followed Kokchu to the tiny ger, waiting in the snow and wind as Kokchu ducked inside. Temuge was not long in coming, accompanied by the warrior who had fetched him from his sleep. Genghis drew his brother aside where Kokchu could not hear.

'It seems I must endure his smoke and rituals, Temuge. Do you trust the man?'

'No,' Temuge snapped, still irritable at being woken.

Genghis grinned at his brother's waspish expression in the moonlight.

'I thought you might not, which is why you are here. You will accompany me, brother, and watch him all the while I am in his ger.' He gestured to the warrior standing nearby and the man came quickly.

'You will guard this ger, Kuyuk, against anyone who might disturb us.'

'Your will, lord,' the warrior replied, bowing his head.

'And if Temuge or I do not walk out, your task is to kill the shaman,' Genghis said. He felt Temuge's gaze on him and he shrugged.

'I am not a trusting man, brother.'

Taking a deep breath of the freezing air, Genghis stifled his twitching throat and entered the ger of the shaman, Temuge behind him. There was barely room for three in that tiny space, but they sat on the silk floor with their knees touching, waiting to see what Kokchu could do.

Kokchu lit cones of powder in gold dishes on the floor. They sparked and spat, producing a thick cloud of narcotic smoke. As the first wisps reached Genghis, he doubled over in a fit of coughing. Every gasp made it worse and Kokchu grew visibly nervous that the khan would collapse. At last, Genghis took a clean breath and felt coolness in his tortured throat, like stream water on a hot day. He took another breath and another, rejoicing at the numbness that flowed in him.

'That is better,' he admitted, staring at the shaman with bloodshot eyes.

Kokchu was in his element, despite Temuge's hard gaze on him. He produced a pot of the black paste and reached out to Genghis' mouth. He jerked as a hand snapped around his wrist.

'What is that?' Genghis said, suspiciously.

Kokchu swallowed. He had not seen him move.

'It will help you to break the bonds of flesh, lord. Without it, I cannot bring you onto the paths.'

'I have had it,' Temuge said suddenly, his eyes brighter than before. 'It does no harm.'

'You will not, tonight,' Genghis replied, ignoring his brother's disappointment. 'I want you to observe, Temuge, that is all.'

Genghis opened his mouth and endured the shaman's black-nailed fingers rubbing the paste into his gums. At first, there was no effect, but as Genghis began to mention this, he noticed the dim light of the shaman's lamp had become brighter. He stared at it in wonderment and the light swelled to fill the little ger, bathing them all in gold.

'Take my hand,' Kokchu whispered, 'and walk with me.'

Temuge watched mistrustfully as his brother's eyes rolled up in his head and he slumped. Kokchu had closed his own so that Temuge felt oddly alone. He winced as Genghis' mouth flopped open, made black by the paste. The silence stretched and Temuge lost some of his tension as he remembered his own visions in that small ger. His gaze drifted to the pot of black paste and, with the two men deep in a trance, he replaced the lid and made it disappear inside his deel. His servant Ma Tsin had secured a regular supply for a time before the man vanished. Temuge had long ceased to wonder where he had gone, though he suspected Kokchu had some hand in it. There were other servants to be found among the Chin soldiers Genghis had taken in, though none were as adept.

Temuge had no way to judge the passage of time. He sat for an age in perfect stillness, then was jerked out of his reverie by Kokchu's voice, hoarse and distant. The words filled the ger and Temuge inched back from the rush of nonsense syllables. Genghis too stirred at the sound, opening glassy eyes as Kokchu began to talk louder and faster.

Without warning, the shaman collapsed, breaking his hold on Genghis' hand. Genghis felt the fingers slip away and blinked slowly, still deep in the grip of the opiate.

Kokchu lay on his side, spittle dribbling from his mouth. Temuge stared at him in distaste. Without warning, the babble of alien sounds ceased and Kokchu spoke without opening his eyes in a firm, low voice.

'I see a white tent raised before the walls. I see the emperor talking to his soldiers. Men pointing and pleading with him. He is a little boy and there are tears on his face.'

The shaman fell silent and Temuge leaned close to him, worried that his stillness meant the man's heart had given way. He touched the shaman's shoulder lightly and, as he did so, Kokchu jerked, writhing, producing sounds that had no meaning. Once more he fell silent and the low voice spoke again.

'I see treasures, a tribute. *Thousands* of carts and slaves. Silk, weapons, ivory. Jade in mountains, enough to fill the sky. Enough to build an empire. It gleams so!'

Temuge waited for more, but no more came. His brother had slumped against the wicker-braced wall of the ger and was snoring softly. Kokchu's breathing relaxed and his clenched fists fell loose as he too slept. Once more, Temuge was alone and in awe of what he had heard. Would either of the men remember the words? His own recollection of visions was patchy at best, but he recalled that Kokchu had not taken the black paste into his own mouth. No doubt he would tell the khan everything he had seen.

Temuge knew he could not shake his brother awake. He would sleep for many hours, long after the camp had risen around him. Temuge shook his head wearily. Genghis was sick of the siege as the end of the second year approached. He might well grasp at any chance. Temuge grimaced to himself. If Kokchu's vision was true, Genghis would turn to him in future, in all things.

Temuge considered cutting Kokchu's throat as he lay in sleep. For a man who dabbled in dark magics, it would not be too hard to explain away. Temuge imagined telling Genghis how a red line appeared on Kokchu's throat while he watched in horror. It would be Temuge who told Genghis what the shaman had seen.

Temuge drew his knife slowly, making no sound. His hand shook slightly, even as he told himself to act. He leaned over the shaman and, at that moment, Kokchu's eyes snapped open, warned by some sense. He jerked his arm to knock the blade aside, trapping it in the folds of his robe.

Temuge spoke quickly.

'You live then, Kokchu? I thought for a moment that you had been possessed. I was ready to kill whatever spirit had taken you from your body.'

Kokchu sat up, his eyes sharp and alert. A sneer touched his face.

'You fear too much, Temuge. There is no spirit that can harm me.' Both men knew the truth of the moment, but for their own reasons, neither was willing to force it into the open. They stared at each other as enemies and, at last, Temuge nodded.

'I will have the guard carry my brother back to his ger,' he said. 'Will his cough ease, do you think?'

Kokchu shook his head.

'There is no curse that I could find. Take him, as you wish. I must think about what the spirits revealed to me.'

Temuge wanted to prick the man's vanity with a barbed comment, but he couldn't think of one and crawled out of the door to fetch the guard for his brother. Snow whirled around him as the burly warrior hefted Genghis onto his shoulders and Temuge's expression was bitter. No good could come of Kokchu's rise, he was certain.

Zhi Zhong woke abruptly at the clatter of sandals on a hard floor. He shook his head to clear it of sleep and ignored the spasm of hunger that remained with him at all hours. Even the emperor's court was suffering in the famine. The day before, Zhi Zhong had eaten only a single, watery bowl of soup. He had told himself the floating slivers of flesh were the last of the emperor's horses, slaughtered months before. He hoped it was true. As a soldier he had learned never to refuse a meal, even if the meat was rotten.

He stood, throwing aside his blankets and reaching for his sword as a servant entered.

'Who are you to disturb me at this hour?' Zhi Zhong demanded. It was still dark outside and he was drugged with exhausted sleep. He lowered his blade as the servant threw himself down, touching his head to the stones.

'My Lord Regent, you are summoned to the presence of the

Son of Heaven,' the man said without looking up. Zhi Zhong frowned in surprise. The boy emperor, Xuan, had never dared to summon him before. He repressed the twitch of anger he felt until he knew more, calling for his slaves to dress and bathe him.

The servant quivered visibly as he heard the call.

'My lord, the emperor said to come at once.'

'Xuan will wait on my pleasure!' Zhi Zhong snapped, terrifying the man further. 'Wait outside for me.' The servant scrambled to his feet and Zhi Zhong considered starting him on his way with a kick.

His own slaves entered and, despite his response, Zhi Zhong had them hurry. He chose not to bathe and merely had his long hair tied behind with a bronze clasp so that it hung down his back over his armour. He could smell his own sweat and his mood soured even further as he wondered if the emperor's ministers were behind this summons.

When he left his rooms, with the servant trotting ahead of him, he could see the greyness of dawn from every open window. It was his favourite time of day, though again, his stomach clenched.

He found the emperor in the audience chamber where Zhi Zhong had killed his father. As the lord regent passed through the guards, he wondered if anyone had told the boy he sat on the same chair.

The ministers were in attendance like a flock of brightly coloured birds. Ruin Chu, first among them, was standing at Xuan's right hand while the boy sat on the throne, which dwarfed his tiny frame. The first minister looked nervous and defiant at the same time and Zhi Zhong was curious as he approached and went down on one knee.

'The Son of Heaven summoned me and I have come,' he said clearly into the silence. He saw Xuan's eyes fasten on the sword at his hip and he guessed the boy knew very well what had happened to his father. If so, it made the choice of room a statement and Zhi Zhong mastered his impatience until he knew what had given the emperor's birds their new confidence.

To his surprise, it was Xuan himself who spoke.

'My city is starving, Lord Regent,' he said. His voice trembled slightly, but firmed as he went on. 'With the lottery, perhaps as many as a fifth have died, including those who threw themselves from the walls.'

Zhi almost snapped an answer at the reminder of that shameful incident, but he knew there had to be more for Xuan to have dared to call him to his presence.

'The dead are not buried, with so many mouths to feed,' the emperor continued. 'Instead we must endure the shame of eating our own, or joining them.'

'Why have I been summoned here?' Zhi Zhong said suddenly, tired of the boy's airs. Ruin Chu gasped at his effrontery in interrupting the emperor. Zhi Zhong cast a lazy glance in the man's direction, hardly caring.

The boy on the throne leaned forward, summoning his courage.

'The Mongol khan has raised a white tent once more on the plain. The spy you sent was successful and we can pay a tribute at last.'

Zhi Zhong clenched his right fist, overwhelmed. It was not the victory he had wanted, but the city would soon be a tomb for all of them. Still, it took an immense effort of will to force a smile onto his face.

'Then His Majesty will survive. I will go to the walls and see this white tent, then send word to the khan. We will talk again.'

He saw scorn on the faces of the ministers and hated them for it. To a man, they saw him as the architect of the disaster that had befallen Yenking. The shame of surrendering would ripple through the city along with the relief. From the high court to the lowest fisherman, they would know the emperor had been forced to pay a tribute. Still, they would live and escape the rat trap that Yenking had become. Once the Mongols had been paid their blood money, the court could travel south and gather strength and allies in the southern cities. Perhaps they would even find support from the Sung empire of the far south, calling on blood to smash the invader. There would be other battles with the Mongol horde, but they would never again allow the emperor to be trapped. Either way, they would live.

The audience room was cold and Zhi Zhong shivered, realising he had been standing in silence while the emperor and his ministers watched. He had no words that could ease the bitter pain of what he must do and he tried to shrug off the enormity of it. There was no point in seeing the entire city starve to death, so that the Mongols could climb the walls and find only dead men. In time, the Chin would be strong again. The thought of reaching the soft luxury of the south raised his spirits a little. There would be food and an army there.

'It is the right decision, Son of Heaven,' he said, bowing deeply before he left the room.

When he had gone, one of the slaves standing against the wall stood forward. The boy emperor's eyes flickered to him and now there was malice and anger showing where there had been only nervousness before.

The slave straightened subtly, altering the way he held himself. His head was completely hairless, even to bare brows and eyelids and it shone with some rich unguent. The man stared after the lord regent as if he could see through the great doors to the chamber.

'Let him live until the tribute has been paid,' Xuan said. 'After that, he is to die as painfully as possible. For his failure and for my father.'

The master of the Black Tong of assassins bowed respectfully to the boy who ruled the empire.

'It will be so, Imperial Majesty.'

CHAPTER THIRTY-TWO

It was a strange thing to see the gates of Yenking open at last. Genghis stiffened in the saddle as he watched the first heavily laden cart come trundling through. The fact that it was pulled by men and not draught animals showed the state of the city within. It was hard not to dig in his heels and attack, after so many months dreaming of this moment. He told himself that he had made the right decision, glancing at Kokchu on his right hand, sitting a pony from the best blood line in the tribes.

Kokchu could not hold back a smile as his prophecy was confirmed. When he had told Genghis the details of his vision, when the black tent still sat before the city, Genghis had promised him the pick of the tribute if it ever came. Not only had he risen in power and influence in the tribes, he would be wealthier than he had ever dreamed. His conscience was quiet as he watched the treasure of an empire coming out. He had lied to his khan and perhaps deprived him of a bloody victory, but Yenking *had* fallen and Kokchu was the architect of the Mongol triumph. Thirty thousand warriors cheered the approach of the carts until they were hoarse. They knew they would be wearing green silk before the day was over and, for men who lived for plunder, it was a sight they would tell their grandchildren. An emperor had been brought to heel for them and the impregnable city could only vomit forth its riches in defeat.

With the gates open, the waiting generals could catch a glimpse of the inner city for the first time, a road that vanished into the distance. Genghis coughed into his fist as the tribute came out like a tongue, with men buzzing around the column in what was almost a military operation. Many were almost skeletal from starvation. They staggered as they worked and, when they tried to rest, Chin officers whipped them savagely until they moved or died.

Hundreds of carts had been brought out to the plain, placed in neat lines while their sweating teams walked back to the city for more. Temuge had warriors making a tally of the total, but it was already chaos and Genghis chuckled to see him trotting around red-faced, calling orders as he walked down new streets of wealth, sprung from nothing on the plain.

'What will you do with the tribute?' Kachiun asked at his side.

Genghis looked up from his thoughts. He shrugged.

'How much can a man carry without being too slow to fight?'

Kachiun laughed.

'Temuge wants us to build our own capital, did he tell you? He is drawing up plans for a place that has more than a little resemblance to a Chin city.'

Genghis snorted at that, then bent over his saddle in a fit of coughing that left him gasping for air. Kachiun spoke again as if he had not seen the weakness.

'We cannot just bury the gold, brother. We should do something with it.'

When Genghis was able to respond, he had lost the sharp reply he would have made.

'You and I have walked down streets of Chin houses, Kachiun.

Do you remember the smell? When I think of home, I think of clean streams and valleys soft with sweet grass, not a chance to pretend we are Chin nobles behind walls. Have we not shown that walls make you weak?' He gestured to the train of carts still coming out of Yenking to make his point. More than a thousand had left the city and still he could see the line stretching back along the gate road inside.

'Then we will have no walls,' Kachiun said. 'Our walls will be the warriors you see around you, stronger than any construction of stone and lime paste.'

Genghis looked at him quizzically.

'I see Temuge has been persuasive,' he said.

Kachiun looked away, embarrassed.

'I do not care for his visions of market squares and bathhouses. He talks of places of learning, of medicine men trained to heal the wounds of the warriors. He looks to a time when we are *not* at war. We have never had such things, but that does not mean we never should.'

Both men stared at the lines of carts for a time. With every spare horse from the tumans, they would be hard pressed even to move such a hoard. It was natural to dream of the possibilities.

'I can barely imagine peace,' Genghis said. 'I have never known it. All I want is to return home and recover from this illness that plagues me. To ride all day and grow strong again. Would you have me building cities on my plains?'

Kachiun shook his head.

'Not cities. We are horsemen, brother. It will always be so. But perhaps a capital, one single city for the nation we have made. The way Temuge told it, I can imagine great training grounds for our men, a place for our children to live and never know the fear we knew.'

'They would grow soft,' Genghis said. 'They would become

as weak and useless as the Chin themselves and, one day, someone else will come riding, hard and lean and dangerous. Then where will our people be?'

Kachiun looked over the tens of thousands of warriors who walked or rode through the vast camp. He smiled and shook his head.

'We are wolves, brother, but even wolves need a place to sleep. I do not want Temuge's stone streets, but perhaps we can make a city of gers, one that we can move whenever the grazing has gone.'

Genghis listened with more interest.

'That is better. I will think about it, Kachiun. There will be time enough on the journey home and, as you say, we can hardly bury all this gold.'

Thousands of slaves had come out with the carts by then, standing miserably in lines. Many were young boys and girls, given as property by the young emperor to the conquering khan.

'They could build it for us,' Kachiun said, indicating them with a jerk of his hand. 'And when you and I are old, we would have a quiet place to die.'

'I have said I will think about it, brother. Who knows what lands Tsubodai, Jelme and Khasar have found to conquer? Perhaps we will ride with them and never need a place to sleep that is not on a horse.'

Kachiun smiled at his brother's words, knowing not to push him any further.

'Look at all this,' he said. 'Do you remember when it was just us?' He did not need to add details. There had been a time for both of them when death was just a breath away and every man was an enemy.

'I remember,' Genghis said. Against the images of their childhood, the plain with its carts and swarming warriors was awe-inspiring. As he gazed across the scene, Genghis saw the figure of the emperor's first minister trotting towards him. He sighed to himself at the thought of another strained conversation with the man. The emperor's representative pretended goodwill, but his distaste for the tribes was evident in every shuddering glance. He was also nervous around horses and made them nervous in turn.

As Genghis watched, the Chin minister bowed deeply to him before unrolling a scroll.

'What is that?' Genghis asked in the Chin language before Ruin Chu could speak. Chakahai had taught him, rewarding his progress in inventive ways.

The minister seemed flustered, but he recovered quickly.

'It is the tally of the tribute, my lord khan.'

'Give it to my brother, Temuge. He will know what to do with it.'

The minister flushed and began to roll the scroll into a tight tube.

'I thought you would want to check the tribute is accurate, my lord,' he said.

Genghis frowned at him.

'I had not considered that anyone would be foolish enough to hold back what was promised, Ruin Chu. Are you saying your people have no honour?'

'*No*, my lord . . .' Ruin Chu stammered.

Genghis waved a hand to silence him.

'Then my brother will look it over.' He thought for a moment, staring over the minister's head to the line of laden carts.

'I have not yet seen your master to offer formal surrender, Ruin Chu. Where is he?'

Ruin Chu grew even redder in the face as he considered how to answer. General Zhi Zhong had not survived the night and the portly minister had been called to his apartments at dawn.

He shuddered at the memory of the body's stripes and marks. It had not been an easy death.

'General Zhi Zhong has not survived these difficult times, my lord,' he said at last.

Genghis looked blankly at him.

'What do I care for another of your soldiers? I have not seen your emperor. Does he think I will take his gold and ride away without ever laying eyes on him?'

Ruin Chu's mouth worked, though no sound came out.

Genghis stepped closer to him.

'Go back to Yenking, minister, and bring him out. If he is not here by noon, all the riches in the world will not save your city.'

Ruin Chu swallowed, visibly afraid. He had hoped that the Mongol khan would not ask to see a seven-year-old boy. Would little Xuan survive the meeting? Ruin Chu could not be sure. The Mongols were cruel and nothing was beneath them. Yet there was no choice and he bowed even deeper than before.

'Your will, my lord.'

As the sun rose in the sky, the great train of treasures was halted to allow the emperor's litter out onto the plain. With him came a hundred men in armour, walking at the side of the box borne by matching slaves. They came in grim silence and the Mongols too fell quiet at the sight, beginning to drift in after the group as they made their way to where Genghis waited with his generals. No special tent had been raised for the emperor, yet Genghis could not help a twinge of awe as the ranks marched towards him. It was true that the boy had played no part in the history of the tribes. Yet he was the single symbol of everything they had come together to resist. Genghis dropped his hand to the hilt of one of Arslan's swords at his waist. When it had been forged, he had been khan of less than fifty men in a camp of snow and ice. He would hardly have dared dream then that the emperor of the Chin would one day come at his command.

The litter shone in the sun as it was lowered with incredible gentleness. The slaves straightened from the poles, staring straight ahead. Genghis watched in fascination as small curtains were lifted aside by Ruin Chu and a small boy stepped onto the grass. He wore a long, jewelled green jacket over leggings of black. A high collar made the boy hold his head up. His eyes were not afraid as they met those of the khan and Genghis felt a touch of admiration for the child's courage.

Genghis took a step forward and sensed the hard gaze of the soldiers on him.

'Have these men stand back, Ruin Chu,' he said softly. The minister bowed his head and gave the order. Genghis stood stiffly as the officers glared at him before retreating a grudging distance. The idea that they could protect the little boy in the heart of the Mongol camp was ludicrous, but Genghis could feel the fierce loyalty in them. He did not want them startled into an attack. Once they had moved, he thought no more of their presence and approached the emperor.

'You are welcome in my camp,' he said in the Chin tongue. The little boy stared up at him without a reply and Genghis saw his hands were shaking.

'You have everything you wanted,' Xuan said suddenly, his voice high and brittle.

'I wanted an end to the siege,' Genghis replied. 'This is one end.'

The boy raised his head even further, standing like a gleaming mannequin in the sun.

'Will you attack us now?'

Genghis shook his head.

'I have said my word is iron, little man. I think perhaps if your father stood before me now, I would consider it. There are many among my people who would applaud me for the strategy.' He paused to swallow against his itching throat and could not stop a hacking cough working its way loose. To his irritation, an audible wheeze remained as he continued.

'I have killed wolves. I will not hunt rabbits.'

'I will not always be so young, my lord khan,' the little boy replied. 'You may regret leaving me alive.'

Genghis smiled at the show of precocious defiance, even as Ruin Chu winced. With a smooth movement, Genghis drew his sword and rested the tip on the boy's shoulder, touching his collar.

'All great men have enemies, emperor. Yours will hear that you stood with my sword at your neck and not all the armies and cities of the Chin could remove the blade. In time, you will understand why that gives me more satisfaction than killing you ever could.' Another cough made his throat clench and he wiped his mouth with his free hand.

'I have offered you peace, boy. I cannot say I will not be back, or that my sons and their generals will not stand here in years to come. You have bought peace for a year, perhaps two or three. That is more than your people have ever given mine.' With a sigh, he sheathed the blade.

'There is one last thing, boy, before I go home to the lands of my childhood.'

'What more do you want?' Xuan replied. He had gone a sickly white now that the blade had been removed from his neck, but his eyes were cold.

'Kneel to me, emperor, and I will leave,' Genghis said. To his surprise, the boy's eyes filled with furious tears.

'I will not!'

Ruin Chu came closer, hovering nervously at the emperor's shoulder.

'Son of Heaven, you must,' he whispered. Genghis did not speak again and, at last, the boy's shoulders slumped in defeat. He stared blindly as he knelt before the khan.

Genghis stood in the breeze and enjoyed a long moment of silence before he motioned to Ruin Chu to help the boy to his feet.

'Do not forget this day, emperor, when you are grown,' Genghis said, softly. The boy did not reply as Ruin Chu guided his steps back to the litter and saw him safely inside. The column formed up around it and began the march back to the city.

Genghis watched them go. The tribute was paid and his army waited for his order to move. Nothing more held him to the cursed plain that had brought weakness and frustration from the moment he set foot on it.

'Let us go home,' he said to Kachiun. Horns sounded across the plain and the vast host of his people began to move.

The sickness in Genghis' chest worsened in the first weeks of travel. His skin was hot to the touch and he sweated constantly, suffering from rashes at his groin and armpits, wherever there was hair to grow foul. His breath came painfully, so that he wheezed every night and could never clear his throat. He longed for the cool, clean winds of the mountains of home and, against reason, he spent every day in the saddle, looking to the horizon.

A month out from Yenking, the outskirts of the desert realm were in sight and the tribes halted by a river to take on water for the trip. It was there that the last of the scouts Genghis had left behind came riding into camp. Two of them did not join their friends around the campfires and, instead, rode straight to the khan's ger on its cart.

Kachiun and Arslan were there with Genghis and all three men came out to hear the final report. They watched as the two scouts dismounted stiffly. Both were caked in dust and dirt and Genghis exchanged a glance with his brother, swallowing against a twitch of his tortured throat.

'My lord khan,' one of the scouts began. He swayed as he stood and Genghis wondered what could have made the man ride himself to exhaustion.

'The emperor has left Yenking, lord, heading south. More than a thousand went with him.'

'He ran?' Genghis demanded in disbelief.

'South, lord. The city was left open, abandoned behind him. I did not stay to see how many people survived inside. The emperor took many more carts and slaves, every one of his ministers.'

No one else spoke as they waited for Genghis to cough into a closed fist, straining for air.

'I gave him peace,' Genghis said at last. 'Yet he shouts to the world that my word means nothing to him.'

'What does it matter, brother?' Kachiun began. 'Khasar is in the south. No city would dare give sanctuary . . .'

Genghis silenced him with a furious gesture.

'I will not go back to that place, Kachiun. But there is a price for all things. He has broken the peace I offered him to run to his armies in the south. Now you will show him the result.'

'Brother?' Kachiun asked.

'No, Kachiun! I have had enough of games. Take your men back to that plain and burn Yenking to the ground. That is the price I will have from him.'

Under his brother's fury, Kachiun could only bow his head.

'Your will, my lord,' he said.

HISTORICAL NOTE

'Nature has left this tincture in the blood,
That all men would be tyrants if they could.'
– Daniel Defoe

The birth date of Genghis can only ever be estimated. Given the nomadic nature of the Mongol tribes, the year and location of his birth were never marked. In addition, small tribes would record the years in terms of local events, making it hard to match to calendars of the day. It is only when Genghis comes into contact with the larger world that the dates are known with any certainty. He invaded the Xi Xia region south of the Gobi in 1206 AD and was proclaimed khan of all the tribes in the same year. In the Chinese calendars, that was the year of Fire and of the Tiger, at the end of the Taihe era. He may have been as young as twenty-five, or as old as thirty-eight when he united his people. I have not dwelled on the years of war and alliances as he slowly brought the great tribes together under his command. Interesting as that was, his story always had a wider scope. I recommend *The Secret History of the Mongols*, translated by Arthur Waley, for anyone wishing to know more of that period.

*   *   *

The Naiman alliance was the last major coalition to resist being swept up into the new nation. The khan of the Naimans did climb Mount Nakhu, moving further and further up the slopes as the army of Genghis advanced. Genghis offered to spare his bondsmen, but they refused and he had them killed to the last man. The rest of the warriors and families were absorbed into his own forces.

Kokchu was a powerful shaman, also known as Teb-Tenggeri. Little is known of exactly how he became influential. Both Hoelun and Borte complained to Genghis about him at various points. His ability to influence Genghis became a great source of concern for those around the khan. Genghis himself believed in a single sky father: deism supported by the spirit world of shamanism. Kokchu remains something of an enigma. One law of the tribes was that it was forbidden to shed royal blood or that of holy men. I have not yet finished telling his story.

As the tribes gathered to Genghis' call, the khan of the Uighurs wrote a declaration of loyalty almost exactly as I have it here. However, the incident of Khasar being beaten and Temuge forced to kneel involved sons of the Khongkhotan clan rather than the Woyela.

Genghis did flood the plain of the Xi Xia and was forced to retreat before the rising waters. Although it must have been embarrassing, the destruction of the crops brought the king to the negotiating table and eventually won a vassal for the Mongol people. It would not have been Genghis' first encounter with the idea of paying tribute. Mongol tribes were known to negotiate in this way, though never on this scale. It is interesting to consider what Genghis must have made of the riches of the Xi Xia and, later, the emperor's own city. He had no use for personal possessions beyond those he could carry on his horse. Tribute would have impressed the tribes and signalled his dominance, but otherwise had very little practical use.

The outcome for the Xi Xia might have been different if Prince Wei of the Chin empire had answered the call for aid. His message (in translation) was: 'It is to our advantage when our enemies attack one another. Wherein lies the danger to us?'

When Genghis went round the Great Wall of China, he did so only by accident. His path to Yenking through Xi Xia lands neatly circumvented the wall. However, it is important to understand that the wall was a solid obstacle only in the mountains around Yenking – later known as Peking, then Beijing today. In other places, the wall was broken, or no more than a rampart of earth with an occasional guard post. In later centuries, the wall was joined into one continuous barrier to invasion.

It is worth noting that the western pronunciation of Chinese place names is always an approximation, using an alien alphabet to create the same sound. Thus, Xi Xia is sometimes rendered as Tsi-Tsia, or Hsi-Hsia, and the Chin are sometimes written as the Jin or even the Kin. Sung is written as Song in some texts. I have managed to find twenty-one spellings of Genghis, from the exotic Gentchiscan and Tchen-Kis to the more prosaic Jingis, Chinggis, Jengiz and Gengis. The Mongolian word 'Ordo' or 'Ordu' means camp or general headquarters. From this we derive the word 'Horde'. Some dictionaries give 'Shaman' as a word of Mongolian origin, and the Gurkhas of Nepal could well derive their name from 'Gurkhan' or khan of khans.

Genghis had four legitimate sons. As with all Mongol names, there are differences in spelling, much as the word Shakespeare is occasionally written as Shaksper, or Boadicea as Boudicca. Jochi is sometimes seen as Juji, Chagatai as Jagatai, Ogedai as Ogdai. His last son was Tolui, sometimes written as Tule.

As well as the Xi Xia princess, Genghis often accepted wives from his beaten enemies. One of his later decrees made all children legitimate, though the ruling did not seem to affect the right to inherit among his own sons.

Walled cities were always a problem for Genghis. At the time of his attack on Yenking, that city was surrounded by fortress villages containing granaries and an arsenal. There were moats around the city walls and the walls themselves were almost fifty feet thick at the base, rising as high. The city had thirteen well-constructed gates and what is still the longest canal in the world, stretching more than a thousand miles south and east to Hangzhou. Most of the world's capital cities have their beginnings on the shores of a great river. Beijing was built around three great lakes – Beihei to the north, Zhonghai (or Songhai) in the centre and Nanhai to the south. It may well be the oldest continuously occupied human settlement, as evidence of inhabitants has been found from half a million years ago – Peking man, as he is sometimes known.

At the time of Genghis' attack through the pass of the Badger's Mouth, Yenking had undergone a period of growth that resulted in walls five miles in circumference and a population of a quarter of a million households, or approximately a million people. It is possible to imagine as many as half a million more who would not show up on any official count.

Even then, the famous Forbidden City within the walls and the emperor's Summer Palace (destroyed by British and French soldiers in 1860) had not yet been built. Today, the city has a population of approximately *fifteen* million people and it is possible to drive through the pass that was once host to one of the bloodiest battles in history. That too is a known date: 1211 AD. Genghis had been leader of his people for five years at that point. He was in the prime of his physical strength and fought with his men. It is unlikely that he was much older than forty, but he may have been as young as thirty, as I have written here.

The battle of Badger's Mouth pass is regarded as one of Genghis' greatest victories. Vastly outnumbered and unable to manoeuvre, he sent men to flank the enemy, climbing mountains the Chin thought were impassable. The Chin cavalry were routed back into their own lines by the Mongol horse and, even ten years later, skeletons littered the ground around that place for *thirty miles*. With the usual problems of anglicised pronunciation, the pass is known in earlier works as Yuhung, which roughly translates as Badger.

Having lost the battle, General Zhi Zhong did indeed return and slay the young emperor, appointing another while he ruled as regent.

The city of Yenking was made to be impregnable and there were almost a thousand guard towers on the walls. Each one was defended by enormous crossbows that could fire huge arrows two thirds of a mile. In addition, they had trebuchet catapults capable of firing heavy loads for hundreds of yards over the walls. They had gunpowder and were just beginning to use it in war, though at this time it would have formed part of the defences. Their catapults could have launched clay pots filled with distilled oil – petrol. Assaulting such a city fortress would have broken the back of the Mongol army, so they chose to devastate the country around it and starve Yenking to surrender.

It took four years and the inhabitants of Yenking were reduced to eating their own dead by the time they opened the gates and surrendered in 1215. Genghis accepted the surrender along with tribute of unimaginable value. He then travelled back to the grasslands of his youth, as he did throughout his life. With the siege ended, the emperor fled south. Though he did not turn back himself, Genghis sent an army to the city to take vengeance. Parts of Yenking burned for a month.

Despite his hatred of the Chin, Genghis would not be the one who would see them occupied and subdued at last. That would fall to his sons and grandson Kubla. At the peak of his success, he left China and went west. It is true that the Islamic rulers refused to recognise his authority, but Genghis was too much of a visionary to react without thought. It is an odd fact, usually glossed over in the histories, that he left China when it was ready to fall at his feet. Perhaps it is simply because he was distracted from his hatred by the challenge of the Shah of Khwarazm, Ala-ud-Din Mohammed. Genghis was not a man to let any challenge go unanswered. In fact, he seemed to revel in them.

He understood the idea of nations and laws, slowly developing his own code, called the Yasa.

'If the great, the military leaders and the leaders of the many descendants of the ruler who will be born in the future, should not adhere strictly to the Yasa, then the

462

power of the state will be shattered and come to an end. No matter how they seek Genghis Khan, they will not find him.' – Genghis Khan

In this, we see the visionary who could dream nations out of scattered tribes and understand what it entailed to rule across such a vast land.

The system of white tent, red tent, black tent, was used by Genghis as I have described. It was propaganda of a sort, designed to have cities fall quickly from fear. With grazing always an issue for the Mongol herds, prolonged sieges were to be avoided if possible. It suited neither their temperaments nor Genghis' style of warfare, where speed and mobility were central factors. In a similar way, driving enemies towards a city to strain their resources is ruthless common sense. In some ways, Genghis was the ultimate pragmatist, but one feature of Mongol warfare is worth mentioning: revenge. The line 'We have lost many good men' was often used to justify an all-out attack after a setback.

He was also willing to try new techniques and weapons, such as the long lance. The bow would always be the weapon of choice for Mongol cavalry, but they used the lance in exactly the same way as medieval knights, as an immensely successful heavy charge weapon against infantry and other horsemen.

Deception is another key to understanding many of the Mongol victories. Genghis and the men who served under him regarded a straight fight almost as discreditable. Victories won by cunning brought far more honour and they always looked for a way to fool the enemy they faced, whether it was a false withdrawal, hidden reserves or even straw dummies on spare horses to give the illusion of reserves they didn't actually have. It may interest some to consider that Baden-Powell took exactly the same approach in his defence of Mafeking seven centuries later, with dummy minefields, sending the men to lay invisible barbed wire and all manner of tricks and ruses. Some things don't change.

The incident where Jelme sucked blood from Genghis' neck is an interesting one. No mention of poison survives, but how else can the action be explained? It is not necessary to suck clotted blood from a neck wound. It does not aid healing and, in fact, the act could burst artery walls already weak from the cut. The historical incident took place earlier than I have it here, but it was so extraordinary that I could not leave it out. It is the sort of incident that tends to be rewritten in history, if perhaps a partially successful assassination attempt was seen as dishonourable.

One event from the histories that I did not use was when a banished and starving tribesman took hold of Genghis' youngest son Tolui and drew a knife. We cannot know what he intended as he was killed quickly by Jelme and others. Such events might help to explain why, when the Mongols later came into contact with the original Arab Assassins, they stopped at nothing to destroy them.

Genghis was far from invincible and was wounded many times in his battles. Yet luck was always with him and he survived again and again – perhaps deserving the belief his men had in him, that he was blessed and destined to conquer.

A note on distances travelled: One of the chief advantages of the Mongol army was that it could turn up just about anywhere in a surprise attack. There are well-attested records of covering six hundred miles in nine days, at seventy miles a day, or more extreme rides of 140 miles in a day with the rider still able to continue. The greatest rides involved changes of ponies, but Marco Polo records Mongol messengers covering 250 miles between sunrise and dark. In winter, the incredibly hardy ponies are turned loose. They eat enough snow to satisfy their thirst and are adept at digging through it to find sustenance beneath. When the Franciscan monk, John de Plano Carpini, crossed the plains to visit Kubla Khan, then at Karakorum, the Mongols advised him to change his horses for Mongol ponies, or see them starve to death. They had no such worry for the ponies. Western horses have been bred for brute strength in breeds like the Suffolk Punch shire horse, or for racing speed. They have never been bred for endurance.

The incident of falling petals is true. Up to sixty thousand young girls threw themselves from the walls of Yenking rather than see it fall to the invader.

Conn Iggulden

WOLF OF THE PLAINS

The epic story of the great conqueror continues

One man would become a legend.

The young boy abandoned with his siblings on the harsh Mongolian plains faced almost certain death. But his remarkable survival skills helped him fight off starvation and hostile attacks. Hunted and alone, he dreamed of uniting the great tribes into one nation. He would become a great warrior. He would become father to his people. He would be Genghis Khan.

'I felt as if a blockbuster movie was unfolding before me. Read the book before Hollywood takes it over.'
Daily Express

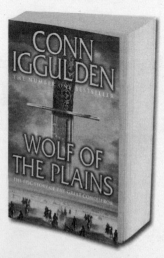

BONES OF THE HILLS

The epic story of the great conqueror continues

One man would become a legend.

Genghis Khan has fulfilled his dream of uniting the many warring tribes of his lands into one great nation. He has taken his armies against the mighty cities of their oldest enemies. Now he finds trouble rising west of the Mongolian plains. He decides to divide his armies to conquer, using his sons as generals and sending them out simultaneously in many directions.

As well as discovering new territories and laying waste to the cities which resist, Genghis knows that the actions of his generals will help him decide who, from his rival sons and heirs, should succeed him as khan.

'Iggulden is in a class of his own when it comes to epic historical fiction'
Daily Mirror

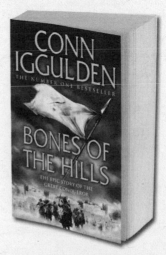

EMPIRE OF SILVER

The epic story of the Khan dynasty continues

Genghis Khan is dead, but his legend and his legacy live on.

His son Ogedai has built a white city on a great plain and made a capital for the new nation. Now the armies have gathered to see which of Genghis' sons has the strength to be khan. The Mongol empire has been at peace for two years, but whoever survives will face the formidable might of their ancient enemy, China's Song dynasty.

The great leader Tsubodai sweeps into the west: through Russia, over the Carpathian mountains and into Hungary. The Templar knights have been broken and there is no king or army to stop him reaching France. But at the moment of Tsubodai's greatest triumph, as his furthest scouts reach the northern mountains of Italy, he must make a decision that will change the course of history forever.

'Iggulden is in a class of his own when it comes to epic historical fiction'
Daily Mirror

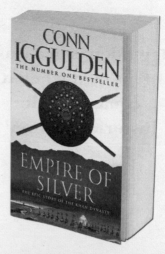